Frommer's®

National Parks with Kids

2nd Edition

by Kurt Repanshek

Here's what the critics say about Frommer's:

"Amazingly easy to use. Very portable, very complete."
—*Booklist*

"Detailed, accurate, and easy-to-read information for all price ranges."
—*Glamour Magazine*

"Hotel information is close to encyclopedic."
—*Des Moines Sunday Register*

"Frommer's Guides have a way of giving you a real feel for a place."
—*Knight Ridder Newspapers*

WILEY

Wiley Publishing, Inc.

About the Author

Kurt Repanshek lives in Park City, Utah. His work has appeared in *Smithsonian, Audubon, Hemispheres, National Geographic Traveler, National Wildlife,* the *Atlanta Journal-Constitution, Denver Post, Miami Herald, New Orleans Times-Picayune, Pittsburgh Post-Gazette,* and many other periodicals. His other books published by Wiley include *America's National Parks For Dummies* and *National Parks of the West For Dummies.* With his wife, Marcelle, Repanshek spends much of his time outdoors, paddling, hiking, and camping in national forests and parks in the summer and cross-country skiing and snowshoeing through them in the winter. He's also the creator of www.nationalparkstraveler.com, a blog dedicated to "Commentary, News, and Life in America's National Parks."

Published by:

Wiley Publishing, Inc.

111 River St.
Hoboken, NJ 07030-5774

ISBN 978-0-470-18406-6
Editor: Christina Summers and William Travis
Production Editor: Heather Wilcox
Cartographer: Elizabeth Puhl
Photo Editor: Richard Fox
Production by Wiley Indianapolis Composition Services

Front/Back Cover Panoramic Shot: Olympic National Park: Sol Duc Falls
Front Cover: Grand Canyon: A young hiker jumps across rocks

For information on our other products and services or to obtain technical support, please contact our Customer Care Department within the U.S. at 800/762-2974, outside the U.S. at 317/572-3993 or fax 317/572-4002.

Wiley also publishes its books in a variety of electronic formats. Some content that appears in print may not be available in electronic formats.

Manufactured in the United States of America

Contents

11 Yellowstone National Park 271

12 Grand Teton National Park 310

13 Rocky Mountain National Park 339

List of Maps

Acknowledgments

This book is dedicated to the women and men of the National Park Service who make the parks such a wonderful escape from the rigors of everyday life. My deepest thanks go out to Charles Wohlforth, who conceived and originally authored this guidebook and who poured his heart and soul into its pages. I merely followed his lead. As a book moves through editions, many hands are involved in cobbling its pages together. Countless behind-the-scenes individuals helped as I worked to update this edition. Rather than risk leaving someone out, I won't name them individually but rather thank them all collectively. Finally, thanks to my editors, Christina Summers and William Travis, who prodded me when necessary and made sure the book read like, well, a book.

An Invitation to the Reader

In researching this book, we discovered many wonderful places—hotels, restaurants, shops, and more. We're sure you'll find others. Please tell us about them, so we can share the information with your fellow travelers in upcoming editions. If you were disappointed with a recommendation, we'd love to know that, too. Please write to:

Frommer's National Parks with Kids, 2nd Edition
Wiley Publishing, Inc. • 111 River St. • Hoboken, NJ 07030-5774

An Additional Note

Please be advised that travel information is subject to change at any time—and this is especially true of prices. We therefore suggest that you write or call ahead for confirmation when making your travel plans. The authors, editors, and publisher cannot be held responsible for the experiences of readers while traveling. Your safety is important to us, however, so we encourage you to stay alert and be aware of your surroundings. Keep a close eye on cameras, purses, and wallets, all favorite targets of thieves and pickpockets.

Other Great Guides for Your Trip:

Frommer's National Parks of the American West
National Parks of the American West For Dummies
Frommer's Grand Canyon National Park
Frommer's Rocky Mountain National Park
Frommer's Yellowstone & Grand Teton National Parks
Frommer's Yosemite and Sequoia & King's Canyon National Parks
Frommer's Zion & Bryce Canyon National Parks

Frommer's Star Ratings, Icons & Abbreviations

Every hotel, restaurant, and attraction listing in this guide has been ranked for quality, value, service, amenities, and special features using a **star-rating system.** In country, state, and regional guides, we also rate towns and regions to help you narrow down your choices and budget your time accordingly. Hotels and restaurants are rated on a scale of zero (recommended) to three stars (exceptional). Attractions, shopping, nightlife, towns, and regions are rated according to the following scale: zero stars (recommended), one star (highly recommended), two stars (very highly recommended), and three stars (must-see).

In addition to the star-rating system, we also use **six feature icons** that point you to the great deals, in-the-know advice, and unique experiences that separate travelers from tourists. Throughout the book, look for:

Finds	Special finds—those places only insiders know about
Fun Fact	Fun facts—details that make travelers more informed and their trips more fun
Moments	Special moments—those experiences that memories are made of
Overrated	Places or experiences not worth your time or money
Tips	Insider tips—great ways to save time and money
Value	Great values—where to get the best deals

The following **abbreviations** are used for credit cards:

AE	American Express	DISC	Discover	V	Visa
DC	Diners Club	MC	MasterCard		

Frommers.com

Now that you have this guidebook to help you plan a great trip, visit our website at **www.frommers.com** for additional travel information on more than 3,600 destinations. We update features regularly to give you instant access to the most current trip-planning information available. At Frommers.com, you'll find scoops on the best airfares, lodging rates, and car rental bargains. You can even book your travel online through our reliable travel booking partners. Other popular features include:

- Online updates of our most popular guidebooks
- Vacation sweepstakes and contest giveaways
- Newsletters highlighting the hottest travel trends
- Online travel message boards with featured travel discussions

Becoming a National Parks Family

There's something special about the awe in a 5-year-old's eyes when he sees for the first time the Old Faithful Geyser in full eruption, spitting thousands of gallons of steaming hot water into a robin's-egg-blue sky, all the while thundering like a rocket engine at liftoff. Too, the sense of accomplishment that a 14-year-old basks in atop a 13,770-foot outcrop of granite called the Grand Teton is something that can't be duplicated in the classroom. And when you're standing beside them as they enjoy these experiences, well, it's something *you'll* never forget.

Collectively, our national parks are a vast, and at times seemingly boundless, touchstone that cradles our nation's conservation ethic, our connection to the North American continent's wild side, and even our own self-inspection. Through parks like Yellowstone, Grand Teton, Yosemite, and Sequoia we can walk off into the forest, or to the top of a mountain, and discover things about ourselves we never truly realized before: how self-reliant we are or are not, how we can see beauty in something as simple as a lily pad in bloom, how fit we truly are, or how little we really know about the world around us. In the parks, we can find enjoyment in nature without need for electronic stimulation from a video game or stereo, and come to understand how fragile earth is.

For nearly a quarter-century I've traveled to national parks from coast to coast specifically to relate to others the experiences that can be found, enjoyed, and profited from (educationally, that is) in this incredible slice of our natural, cultural, and historical heritage. And every visit to a park, whether it's one I've been to many times before or one I've never been to, rewards me with an experience that can't be matched.

There's really no perfect age for a trip to a national park. That's one of the beauties of our national park system. Young and old alike can enjoy, and learn from, our parks side by side. That's just what Gail and Wayne Lundeen were hoping for when they took 9-year-old Sienna and 7-year-old Evan to Acadia National Park off the coast of Maine. The Lundeens had left their home in St. Paul, Minnesota, on a 3-week journey to explore New England on their summer vacation. They were looking for a national park that would fit the couple's desires for an outdoorsy experience, yet not overpower their youngsters. After reading and Internet browsing, they settled on Acadia.

"Acadia is one of the most kid-friendly parks," Wayne told me as my wife and I joined his young family atop the Beehive, a rocky hummock that juts out above the Gulf of Maine along Acadia's eastern boundary. "It's intermingled with services nearby in case you need them."

Plus, Gail pointed out, there are great hikes that don't take all day to complete, and broad bike trails that wind through dense forests without the threat of automobile traffic. And, she added, there's the educational aspect.

"The ranger program we went to was on tide pools, and it was really interesting and fun," she said.

For Evan, though, looking down on the park's landscape was perhaps the best part of the visit.

"I liked climbing the mountains," he said, a broad smile wrapping his face.

Don't misunderstand. Choosing a national park vacation for your family won't magically make all frets, concerns, and anxieties vanish. But it's a good start. For more information on figuring out which park to visit, see chapter 2, "Planning a Family Trip to a National Park."

GETTING THE MOST OUT OF THIS BOOK

This book is intended to help you make the best out of your national park vacation, to find the most enjoyable and rewarding locations, activities, and experiences for you and your family. While there's an inkling of each individual park's history, I don't toss a lot of that information in because, well, this isn't a history book. It's nice to know a little bit about each park's background, but it's even better to know what sort of experiences you can bring away from your visit.

A beauty of our national park system is that every park is unique. While there are nearly 400 units in the system, I wouldn't even consider attempting to capture each and every one between this book's front and back cover. I couldn't do justice to them. Instead, I've focused on 15 parks I believe offer a wonderful cross section of our national park system. I've tossed in Cape Hatteras and Cape Cod national seashores to provide some beach time; the Rocky Mountain jewels of Glacier, Grand Teton, Rocky Mountain, and Yellowstone because they're so visually stunning; the deep chasm known as the Grand Canyon because it is so grand; and seven other parks that round out this wonderful smorgasbord with deep forests, enticing islands, tall trees, hoodoos and goblins, and towering canyon walls.

With that introduction out of the way, let me toss in a cheat sheet of superlatives that I hope will help you chart your path through some of the national parks.

1 The Best National Park Experiences

- **Oh Say Can You See:** Whenever I visit a park, I seem to gravitate to high spots, and there are some great high spots to take in the surrounding landscape. Perhaps the most notable is the one I mentioned above, climbing to the top of the **Grand Teton** in Grand Teton National Park (p. 335). Lesser in elevation, but not significance, are the views from the **North and South rims** of the Grand Canyon (see chapter 7), from **Moro Rock** in Sequoia National Park with its view into the rugged canyon cut by the Middle Fork of the Kaweah River (p. 427), from **Cadillac Mountain** rising over Acadia (p. 61), and from **Hurricane Ridge** in Olympic National Park (see chapter 16).

- **Lions and Tigers and Bears:** Although wildlife are residents of our national parks, don't mistake the parks for open-air zoos. These animals aren't restrained by cages or fences, come and go as they please and, from time to time, prey on each other. **Yellowstone** (see chapter 11) arguably offers the best views of the most complete wildlife ecosystem in the Lower 48. Pan your binoculars across the Lamar Valley in late spring and you're bound to see wolves, grizzlies, elk, bison, mule deer, ravens, coyotes, and maybe even bighorn sheep. At **Cape Cod National Seashore** (p. 99) and **Acadia** (p. 70), sign on for whale-watch cruises that take you out into the Atlantic to view **humpbacks** and **right whales** up close. Or simply gaze into the waters off Olympic's shores and see if you can't spot some **seals.** At **Glacier,** walk the trail to Hidden Lake (p. 264) and you're bound to encounter **mountain goats** practically face-to-face.

- **Up a Creek, or in a Lake:** I'm always looking for a park where I can paddle away from shore. Fortunately, there are plenty of places in the national park system to do just that. If you like **canoeing,** Yellowstone's Lewis, Shoshone, and Yellowstone lakes (p. 304) offer incredible backcountry adventures. Visit Shoshone Lake and you can paddle up to a geyser basin. At Acadia, Cape Cod, Cape Hatteras, and Olympic (p. 69, 97, 133, and 461, respectively) you can push off from shore in a **sea kayak.** And in the Grand Canyon (p. 189), as well as near Glacier (p. 269) and Olympic (p. 461), you can buck the white water from the relative comfort of a **rubber raft.**

- **What a View!:** Jaw-dropping views? Parks seem to claim a monopoly on those. Just look down into the **amphitheaters** at **Bryce Canyon National Park** (p. 229), take in the sweep of horizon from atop **Glacier Point** in **Yosemite National Park** (p. 395), or look *up* 2,000 feet into the belly of **Zion Canyon Narrows** in Zion National Park (p. 208). Of course, at times you can't see the forest for the trees in Sequoia National Park, where those **giant Sequoias** require a wide-angle lens (p. 427). Another of my favorites is simply gazing up at the star-crowded skies that seem to hover over our national parks, which harbor some of the darkest night skies in the country.

- **Surf's Up:** If, during your visit to **Cape Cod National Seashore** or **Cape Hatteras National Seashore** (chapters 4 and 5), a storm roils up over the Atlantic, a stroll along the beach unveils nature's fury at work, as wave after monstrous wave comes crashing ashore, flinging spray in all directions and even redesigning the beach at times. Cross the continent to **Olympic National Park** (chapter 16) during the stormy season and you'll find that watching the waves explode as they smack into the sea stacks just off the coastline is an incredible pastime.

2 The Best Day Hikes

- **Lone Star Geyser, Yellowstone National Park:** This is a pleaser for families with youngsters. The bulk of this 5-mile round-trip hike (p. 305) down to the geyser is along an asphalt trail that parallels the Firehole River, making for firm footing summer and winter, when you can travel via cross-country skis or snowshoes. And once you get there, you're confronted by a

thick, 12-foot-tall geyserite cone that blows its top about every 3 hours. Bicycles are allowed on this nearly level trail, which makes it even easier in summer.

- **Mist Trail, Yosemite National Park:** This steep but decidedly kid-friendly trail (p. 394) is one of the Yosemite Valley's classics. Why? Follow it to the top, a 7-mile round-trip, and you not only pass two frothing waterfalls (Vernal and Nevada) but get great views of the Yosemite Valley as well as find yourself at the very spot where the Merced River tumbles out of the Little Yosemite Valley and down into its big brother. Plus, on hot, sultry summer days you get a wonderfully cool drenching from the falls' spray. From the top you can either backtrack to the bottom, or take the John Muir Trail, which is not quite as steep.

- **South Ridge of Cadillac Mountain, Acadia National Park:** "Barbara," a 67-year-old Marylander who has summered in Mount Desert Island's Northeast Harbor every year since she was 4, makes at least 20 treks up the South Ridge of Cadillac Mountain (p. 61) during her stays. Armed with a hiking pole, she doesn't dawdle on her way up to a rock outcrop that overlooks a pond cupped by the mountainside. "I hike it a lot because if I died, somebody will find me because so many people hike it," she jokes as we share the sprawling blue view of Frenchman Bay, the Atlantic Ocean, and the Gulf of Maine from Cadillac's granite shoulder. "I think it has absolutely wonderful views. It's gradual going up, and just gorgeous views going down." That sums it all up.

- **Hall of Mosses Nature Trail, Olympic National Park:** Only got time for one hike in the Hoh Rain Forest? Then this would be it. It takes just about 40 minutes to navigate this .75-mile loop trail (p. 458) as it winds through a green kingdom of lush vegetation. It's not steamy, like a tropical rainforest, but you can feel the humidity. Along the trail, *epiphytes*—plants that grow on other plants—in the form of spongy club mosses, lichens, liverworts, and licorice ferns scramble across tree

trunks and limbs and up into the leafy canopy where they manage to block most of the sun's rays. Scattered here and there on the ground are toppled trees and rotting stumps that serve as nurseries for the next generation of trees. And for kids who like creepy-crawly things, there are the slimy, 8-inch-long banana slugs that seemingly have misplaced their shells.

- **Tharp's Log, Sequoia National Forest:** What makes this one of Sequoia's best trails? Kids love visiting Tharp's Log, which, in truth, is a real log cabin. You see, Hale Tharp lived in this hollowed-out Sequoia during summers from 1861 to 1890 when he would bring his cows up to graze in Huckleberry, Crescent, and Log meadows. Judging from the wooden bunk inside, I don't think his nights were entirely comfy, but he was no doubt dry when the rains came. You can find this mile-long trail at the Crescent Meadow parking lot, which is located 1.25 miles beyond Tunnel Log and marks the western terminus of the High Sierra Trail. See Giant Forest on p. 427.

- **Queen's Garden Trail, Bryce Canyon National Park:** Looking down into the fairylands of Bryce's amphitheaters is one thing. Walking down into them is quite another. Along red-dirt paths you wind back and forth through the hoodoos that make Bryce such a wonder. The Queen's Garden Trail is not even 2 miles in length, making it doable for all but the youngest of toddlers, and the climb down and back up isn't too terrible, either. Link Queen's Garden with the Navajo Loop Trail and you'll have a nearly 3-mile-long hike that is a perfect way to whet your appetite for dinner, or burn off any of your children's leftover energy before bedtime. See p. 229.

- **Angel's Landing, Zion National Park:** Perhaps my favorite trail in Zion, this also happens to be one of the park's most challenging hikes, and not one to be taken lightly for it tests your fear of heights. Definitely not a hike for preteens, this is a good 5-mile challenge for teens who like to push themselves. The trail (p. 214) climbs 1,488 feet—at one point traversing 21 short switchbacks known as "Walter's Wiggles"—to a summit with incredible views of Zion Canyon. But be prepared: The final .5-mile to the top crawls along a narrow, knife-edge trail where footing can be dicey under even the best of conditions. To help you along this section, the park has mercifully installed stout chains that you can cling to. The view from the top is definitely worth the work. You can gaze in all directions, taking in the Virgin River sweeping through the bottom of the canyon, the Great White Throne, Red Arch Mountain to the southeast, and the entrance to Zion Canyon Narrows beyond the Temple of Sinawava.

- **Ramsey Cascade Trail, Great Smoky Mountains National Park:** If you're like me, the taller the waterfall, the better the hike. If that's the case, this hike is the best in the park because Ramsey Cascades, which falls 100 feet, is the park's tallest waterfall. This 8-mile round-trip hike gains more than 2,000 feet in elevation, so it's not for everyone. But the trail winds through stands of old-growth hardwood forest, so you enjoy the trees along the way. Just don't think of climbing to the top of the falls—over the years a few folks have tried and have met unpleasant deaths. See p. 155.

- **Hidden Lake, Glacier National Park:** This is a great hike along the "Crown of the Continent," one that brings you in close contact with wildlife as you traverse wildflower-studded alpine meadows, with breathtaking views in all directions. True, it's one of the most popular hikes in Glacier, and so one of the most crowded. But it offers immediate payoffs. I encountered shaggy mountain goats within 10 minutes of leaving the Logan Pass parking lot. During the entire hike I could easily gaze up at snowcapped peaks, or down below to U-shaped valleys cut long ago by glaciers. The moderate grade and short distance, 3 miles round-trip, make this is a good hike for youngsters. See p. 264.

- **Jenny Lake Loop, Grand Teton National Park:** This mostly level trail winds around the lake close to the shoreline, a fact that makes it a nice hike for families. The setting is great, with the lake wrapped by a thick forest and the Tetons towering over the western shore. The downside is that this is one of the more popular trails in the park. If you have really young children and prefer a shorter hike, you can take a shuttle boat across the lake to the West Shore Boat Dock and then walk back to the east shore. This trail also connects with hikes up into Cascade Canyon (an even more popular hiking destination, but one with great scenic payoffs) and to String and Leigh lakes to the north. See p. 330.

- **Alberta Falls, Rocky Mountain National Park:** This isn't a long, full-day hike, but for families with youngsters, this is a great jaunt. Located near Bear Lake, this trail runs only 1.2 miles round-trip but it leads you into the woods to one of the park's most revered waterfalls as its comes crashing down Glacier Creek (p. 357). The easy grade is a good place to start young hikers, and the prospect of seeing a waterfall keeps them interested.

3 The Best Little-Known Park Spots

• **Cataloochee Valley, Great Smoky Mountains National Park:** What does Cades Cove look like without the crowds? Cataloochee (p. 147). Here you don't have to jockey with crowds to enjoy the views or the historic buildings. When I visited one mid-June day I practically had the place to myself. But like Cades Cove, Cataloochee features preserved 19th-century buildings and rolling orchards alive with wildlife. Along with the historic buildings, the Cataloochee Valley is where park biologists in 2001 launched an experimental program to return elk to the Smokies. Visit early in the day or just as evening falls and you might spy some.

• **Kolob Canyons, Zion National Park:** Most tourists confine their visit to the highlights of Zion Canyon, but those with a bit more ambition also venture 45 miles to the park's northwest corner to see Kolob Arch, one of the world's longest free-standing arches, with a span of 310 feet. You can hike to the arch and back in 1 long day on the La Verkin Creek Trail, a 14-mile round-trip hike from Lee Pass along the Kolob Canyons Road, although I wouldn't recommend it for inexperienced hikers or families with youngsters. A shorter, but equally worthwhile, hike in this area leads to Double Arch Alcove, an arched alcove topped overhead by an arch in the cliff. You reach the formation on the Taylor Creek Trail, a 5.4-mile round-trip hike that crosses the Middle Fork of Taylor Creek and passes two log cabins before arriving at a viewpoint of the arch. You access the trail head from Kolob Canyons Road. See p. 212.

• **Tuolumne Meadows, Yosemite National Park:** Unofficially, I'd venture that 90% to 95% of the folks who trek to Yosemite go into and out of Yosemite Valley without visiting any other portion of the park. And that's a shame, because places like Tuolumne Meadows are breathtaking and provide a view of the High Sierra that you can't get from the Yosemite Valley. To reach this area you need to drive almost the entire length of the Tioga Road, but if you make the trip you uncover sprawling meadows capped by bulbous mounds of granite that make for great playgrounds for kids who like to scamper on rocks, gorgeous lakes for skipping stones, and great hikes, like the 7-mile round-trip down to Cathedral Lakes. See p. 385.

• **Cape Alava, Olympic National Park:** Located along the coast in the northwest corner of Washington State's Olympic Peninsula, this is a good place to retreat if you shun crowds and want to view images left behind by an earlier culture. The Cape Alava–Sand Point Loop is a three-legged loop trail that offers ocean views, beach camping, and petroglyphs; it's an easy round-trip back to your car. The hike covers 9.3 miles and takes you to Cape Alava, the westernmost point in the Lower 48. Your trek begins on a 3-mile-long stretch that begins on a cedar-plank boardwalk that winds through a lush, and dense, forest. Once you reach the beach, you swing south and make your way 3 miles along the coast. During this stretch be sure to look for the petroglyphs on the rocks along the shore next to the high-tide mark. The final leg follows the Sand Point Trail for 3 miles back to your starting point. See p. 462.

• **Mineral King, Sequoia National Park:** Unfortunately, because it's time-consuming, or fortunately, because not many people do it, you have to temporarily leave Sequoia National Park to reach Mineral King. This primitive area once was eyed by ski resort developers. Today its scenery is dotted not by chairlifts but by lakes and laced by trails heading into the high country. The valley is breathtaking, with thick stands of conifers and outcrops of red and orange shale offset by white marble and black metamorphic shale and granite. Towering over the basin is Sawtooth Peak, which stands 12,343 feet tall and holds snowfields year-round. See p. 420.

4 The Best Campgrounds

- **Rising Sun, Glacier National Park:** Though Glacier has 13 campgrounds to choose from, this one struck me as one of the best places to spend a night or two under the stars. Why? The individual sites are well spaced, there are plenty of trees for shade, and the Rising Sun Lodge is nearby in case you feel the urge for a hot shower or for someone else's cooking. Plus, you've got St. Mary Lake right across the road for boating or swimming (if it's a really, really hot day), and the east side of Glacier is just as interesting, and less crowded, than the west side. See p. 250.

- **Jenny Lake, Grand Teton National Park:** This campground (p. 322) just might be the most picturesque campground with a paved road leading to it that you'll ever find. The 51 tent-only sites are carefully sprinkled amid evergreens and boulders left behind by retreating glaciers, and the crags we call the Tetons tower overhead. And there's even a lake.

- **Nickerson State Park, Cape Cod National Seashore:** True, this state park isn't inside the national seashore's borders, but let's not split hairs. It's a great place to call home during your visit. At 1,900 acres, this is the largest state park on the Cape and the nicest one because of the many "ponds" (I call them small lakes) scattered within its borders. The park's 418 campsites are nestled among towering white pines and clumped in seven groups scattered about the ponds, so you don't get claustrophobic. Not only can you swim and sail in the ponds, but the Cape Cod Rail Trail runs through the park so you can peddle from the state park to the national seashore. See p. 83.

- **Ozette Lake, Olympic National Park:** This is a great campground for families with teens who like to backpack, or who want an introduction to backpacking. You can opt for one of the 15 drive-up campsites on the lake, or reserve one of the backcountry campsites and hike in. Located in the northwest corner of the Olympic Peninsula, away from the heart of the national park, this location takes a little extra driving, but the solitude and scenery are worth it. See p. 450.

- **Slough Creek, Yellowstone National Park:** Like Ozette Lake in Olympic National Park, this campground is removed from the heart of the park. Located in the northeastern corner of Yellowstone, just off the Lamar Valley Road, Slough Creek (p. 289) is the park's smallest campground with just 29 sites. And there are no flush toilets or showers. Its beauty, though, is its location in one of the busiest wildlife corridors in the park. If luck strikes, you'll find yourself falling to sleep to a wolf serenade.

- **Cape Point, Cape Hatteras National Seashore:** Perhaps the best Cape Hatteras National Seashore camping experience comes from a stay at this campground. Located on a large sprawl of grass, the 202-site campground is the park's closest to a beach with lifeguards. And from the campground, it's just a 1.5-mile walk to the end of the point itself. True, the showers spew only cold water, but on a hot, muggy beach day, that's a treat. See p. 117.

5 The Best Hotel Bets

- **Colter Bay Village, Grand Teton National Park:** What makes Colter Bay (p. 325) tops in Grand Teton when it comes to families? It's reasonably priced for family vacations and surrounded by a small village with restaurants, showers, laundry facilities, camp stores, and activities. And it's charming, as well. Some of my best boyhood vacation memories flow from the cabins we stayed in, no matter how rustic they were. Kids, I think, just seem to have an affinity for wood and rock. And these cabins, while appearing rustic, are very comfortable.

- **Wuksachi Lodge, Sequoia National Park:** Key to finding lodging in a national park is finding lodging that's ideally located, and the Wuksachi Lodge (p. 423) is that. This lodge with its glorious setting, comfortable rooms, and nice dining room is not far from the park's Giant Forest with its towering trees, not far from hiking trails, and not far from the entrance to Kings Canyon National Park.

- **Old Faithful Inn, Yellowstone National Park:** There's something about sleeping in what just very may well be the largest log cabin on earth (p. 294) that makes this place very, very special. Of course, having the Old Faithful Geyser spouting off every 90 minutes or so right outside the front door says something, too. But when you walk through the front doors, and your head drops back as you measure the height of the fireplace's chimney, or when you run your hands along the log banisters

that have been worn smooth over the past century by who knows how many other hands, or when you sit on one of the upper balconies with a favorite book or while playing checkers or cards with your children, you cache away memories you'll hold for the rest of your life.

- **Many Glacier Hotel, Glacier National Park:** From a setting I truly believe is one of the most awe-inspiring in the national park system, to the abundant activities for those who enjoy boating, hiking, horseback riding, or simply staring at glacially sculpted peaks, this lodge has few counterparts that can measure up. True, the rooms aren't the best you'll find in the park system. But you're here for the scenery, right? See p. 254.

- **Kalaloch Lodge, Olympic National Park:** My youngest son loved the time we spent in one of Kalaloch's seaside cabins (p. 452). True, the woodburning stove was a draw. But so, too, was the ocean just a few short steps away from our front door. And falling asleep at night to the crash of the surf is something neither of us will ever forget. With the kitchen in the cabin, and the restaurant in the main lodge building, we had the best of both worlds when it came to mealtime.

- **Grand Canyon Lodge, Grand Canyon National Park:** Far from the sometimes maddening crush of the South Rim, this lodge (p. 183) on the canyon's North Rim reflects one of the classic styles of park architecture. And the setting can't be beat, either.

Plus, what kid doesn't like to spend a night or two in a log cabin? It's all right here on the North Rim, surrounded by virtual wilderness, hiking, and stellar views into one of the grandest canyons on earth.

- **LeConte Lodge, Great Smoky Mountains National Park:** Okay, I cheated with this choice, since it's the *only* lodge inside the park's boundaries. It's a throwback, at that, a lodge you have to hike, not drive, up to for a room. The setting is breathtaking, you get exercise coming and going, and you and your family have an opportunity to make new friends in a setting you all value. See p. 151.

6 The Best Museums in the National Parks

- **Giant Forest Museum, Sequoia National Park:** The life and times of Sequoia trees are best explained in this neat museum in the park's Giant Forest section. A visit here will teach you and your kids how Sequoias naturally ward off fire and insects, how many seeds are stored in one of the tree's pine cones, and what sort of climate the trees thrive in. See p. 430.

- **Albright Visitor Center, Yellowstone National Park:** At Mammoth Hot Springs, the museum offers exhibits depicting park history from prehistory through the creation of the National Park Service and features a wildlife display. My favorite aspect of this museum, though, is the exhibit on landscape painter Thomas Moran, whose works helped convince Congress to turn to Yellowstone to kickstart the world's national parks movement. See p. 278.

- **Yosemite Museum and Indian Village of Ahwahnee, Yosemite National Park:** Yosemite's cultural history is tracked here. The Indian Cultural Exhibit explains the lives of the Ahwahneeche, Miwok, and Paiute tribes that once lived in the area. You occasionally find Native Americans speaking here or giving demonstrations of long-forgotten arts, such as basket weaving. A replica of an Ahwahneeche village is behind the museum. Its exhibits guide you through the tribe's transformation in the years after whites discovered the valley. A ceremonial roundhouse, which is still used, is also on-site. See p. 397.

- **Olympic National Park Visitor Center:** Inside this building you'll find a nice little museum that tracks the Native Americans who once lived across the Olympic Peninsula and examines the wildlife that calls it home. Too, younger kids enjoy the Discovery Room, where they can play in a miniature log ranger station, learn about ecology, and build a totem pole with felt stick-on pieces. In the main visitor center, older kids can keep busy with a virtual scavenger hunt that requires them to study the exhibits in order to answer questions about the park. See p. 442.

7 The Best Bargains in the National Parks

- **America the Beautiful Pass:** Eighty bucks. That's what this pass (p. 18) will set you back. And in return, it will provide you and everyone in your car with access into nearly 400 units of the national park system, as well as public lands managed by the U.S. Forest Service, the U.S. Bureau of Land Management, the U.S. Fish and Wildlife Service, and even the U.S. Bureau of Reclamation. Name me a theme park that offers you such a return on investment. And once you leave a park, if you hold this pass you don't have to pay to get back in. (*Note:* There was scuttlebutt in 2007 that some members of Congress might try to restore the National Parks Pass, so be sure to check at www.nps.gov before you buy your next annual pass.)

- **Free Entertainment:** Travel to Yellowstone and you can spend hours, or days, watching Old Faithful and its fellow geysers spit and fume and boil and hiss. You also can keep count of all the elk, moose, wolves, bison, bears, and other wildlife that you see. Spend a few days at Cape Hatteras National Seashore and you can mesmerize yourself watching the waves roll in to shore, count the seabirds, or simply walk the dunes. Go to Yosemite and you can watch some of the world's tallest waterfalls plummet wispily into Yosemite Valley. Travel a bit south to Sequoia and you can see some of the tallest trees on earth. Go to the northwest and into Olympic and you can marvel at basically three parks in one, what with the Pacific beaches, temperate rainforests, and high, glacial-covered alpine reaches. And the charge for these activities? Nothing once you get in the gate. True, more and more ranger-led interpretive programs are carrying fees, but there still are many that do not.

- **Fresh Air and Exercise:** These two amenities are getting tougher and tougher to find these days. Fortunately, travel to a national park and you're likely to find some of the freshest air in the country and plenty of exercise to go along with it, exercise that you don't always appreciate you're racking up because you're so busy enjoying your visit.

- **Getting Back to Basics:** Okay, this is one of those touchy-feely, amorphous kinds of rewards of a national park

vacation. Pack your kids into the car, tell them they have to leave the video games and iPods behind, and once you reach the park of your choice you can get to know one another better by actually communicating face-to-face while enjoying a hike, paddle, or quiet dinner. National park vacations are perfect for bonding with your teens, particularly if you share your experience mountain climbing or backpacking or sea kayaking.

- **No Closing Time:** Parks are open 24/7 every day of the year. There's no closing time. You don't have to go to bed when the sun goes down. In fact, sometimes it's more enjoyable to stay up, watch for shooting stars, or listen for owls.

- **Go at *Your* Pace:** You can be as organized, or as laid-back, as you wish on a park vacation. You can rise with the sun to get out on the trails before anyone else, or sleep in and enjoy a leisurely breakfast while others are out beating the trails. You can sign up for a naturalist-led course in sketching or wildflower identification, or sit back in a tour bus and let someone else drive while the guide tells you what you're seeing.

- **Learning without Realizing It:** It surely must be a scientifically proven fact: Kids learn more when they're having fun. That's part of the beauty of ranger-led hikes and programs where kids have someone other than their parents to bounce questions up against. And where those rangers fire back with their own set of questions that force kids to learn all the while that they're having a great time. Check out any park's supporting nonprofit foundation and you'll find a slew of programs that range from a few hours to a week or more of family-oriented activities that will help you bond with your kids while you all learn something.

2

Planning a Family Trip to a National Park

Approaching a cross-country, or even regional, family vacation to a national park can be daunting if your family includes finicky toddlers, demanding "tweens," or seemingly disinterested teens. If your family includes a mix of those age groups, well, then you might decide to abandon your trip even before you decide where to go. After all, there are plenty of horror stories out there that revolve around miserable flights and restaurant meals with toddlers. What to do with the kids? You could leave them at home with family or friends, or even put off your national park vacation until the kids are older. But that approach would deprive both you and your kids of a wonderful experience.

I'll never forget my first trip to Yellowstone with my oldest son, who was a somewhat precocious 3-year-old at the time. As we rounded Dunraven Pass and started down toward Canyon Village he began a singsong chorus of "Yogi, where are you!" Since that first trip, both my boys have bonded with each other during park visits and developed an appreciation, if not a love, for parks. Granted, the prospect of a park vacation might not initially thrill them as much as a new video game, but they've gamely hiked to the top of Angel's Landing in Zion National Park, paddled the Snake River through Grand Teton National Park, hiked through a snowstorm to Yellowstone's Lone Star Geyser, explored Olympic National Park's Hoh Rain Forest and Hurricane Ridge, and studied the precarious formations in Arches National Park. And enjoyed every minute of it. Times like these, away from the television, in a beautiful setting with the entire family, provide wonderful opportunities not just for exploration but, perhaps more important, communication. With no distractions.

To be sure, traveling with children means extra planning and requires narrower limits than traveling alone. Certain sacrifices go hand-in-hand with the reward of living your life deeply with your children. Yet, you can minimize those sacrifices with a little forethought, some realistic expectations, and careful planning. Reserve campsites or hotel rooms months in advance and you won't find yourself praying that a last-minute cancellation will open up a room at the lodge you really wanted to stay in. Be realistic with how far you can drive in 1 day before your kids melt down in the back seat. Appreciate that a sunset over the Grand Canyon, or a sunrise over Acadia National Park, is a true plein-air masterpiece the whole family can share and enjoy.

Don't go to the national parks because you think you are supposed to see certain places before you grow up. Be concerned, instead, to make the most of a time when you may be closer to your children, and come to know them better, than at any other time in your lives. These natural places make children and adults equals in their wonder. You don't need to know how to read to understand the splendor; in fact, it may be an impediment. Parents can teach their children about natural history; children can teach their parents to see the beauty around them.

The parks can challenge every member of the family, both physically and mentally. You can come home with real accomplishments to think back on. And the towns around the parks are accustomed to serving families. You don't have to worry about fitting in, and you'll likely meet other families with children. Many park areas even have educational programs and camps that allow children and parents to spend time apart, learning on their own.

1 Choosing the Perfect Park

This book's philosophy can be summed up in five words: Get out of the car. You will find no tips on the best highlights for a 1-day visit, because a 1-day visit to a place like Yellowstone or Cape Cod is simply a waste. You will find, however, suggestions as to how long to stay in a certain area.

For the parks included in this book there are details that help make your visit as easy and pleasant as possible. You can get away from crowds, but often the only way is by possessing information the rest of the crowd doesn't have: certain places they don't know about, tricks of the reservation systems for scarce campsites and backcountry permits, and times when the trails are clear. Along with providing thorough details on campgrounds not only within the national parks but also in nearby national forests, state parks, and towns, the chapters also have hotel reviews and price ranges for almost everything. The restaurant reviews cover places where you can relax with children and those where the kids are welcome but need to be on their best behavior.

Some material, such as the travel-planning information, is written for adults. The educational and fun stuff and descriptions of places are written to be read aloud to kids or to be read by older children. Rather than reading aloud in the car, consider reading the chapters to yourself before you go, then explaining what you see in the park when the topic comes up.

THE PARKS

Acadia National Park preserves a section of the rocky Maine shoreline, mostly on the east side of Mount Desert Island, a former resort for the very rich. Lovely, genteel carriage roads pass through the woods around the small, rounded granite mountains. Offshore, the park is a center for sailing, sea kayaking, and whale-watching. The area has lots of attractive campgrounds, both commercial and within the park, plenty of family-oriented motels and cottages, and several quaint towns.

Cape Cod National Seashore takes in the eastern beaches and sand dunes of Massachusetts's arm-shaped cape—the outer side from the elbow to the fist. Though the Cape offers more than 400 years of human history, the dunes and beaches remain wild and inspiring. There are museums, nature education facilities, and organizations offering summer day camps. The seashore has no campgrounds, but plenty of attractive campgrounds are nearby, as are good motels, cottages, and historic inns.

Cape Hatteras National Seashore protects 75 miles of the Outer Banks, a thin strand of sand islands draped along North Carolina's eastern coast 10 to 40 miles off the mainland. The ocean swimming and watersports are supreme, and miles of beach invite exploration and ecological interpretation. Nearby historic sites, including the Wright Brothers National Memorial and the site of England's first American settlement, fascinate most children and adults. The National Park Service has several sandy seaside campgrounds, and there are plenty of hotel rooms and houses for rent.

Great Smoky Mountains National Park in North Carolina is a place of trails over wooded mountains and through great hardwood forests full of historical interest as well as natural beauty. Families go for fun, hiking, horseback riding, inner-tubing, and backpacking.

Grand Canyon National Park protects one of the world's most famous and admired natural wonders, the incredible canyon through northern Arizona gouged by the Colorado River. Most visitors come to the edge and look in, arriving by car at the visitor village on the South Rim or the higher, less-visited North Rim. Hikers can get down into the canyon and see much more; how far you can go depends on your group's physical abilities.

Zion National Park contrasts the rugged immensity of the Grand Canyon with smooth, soaring shapes. Ancient sand dunes have been hardened by time into the park's gracefully waving Navajo sandstone. Among the billowing rocks, the river, trees, and plants add to the serenity. Strong hikers also can follow paths up canyon walls that stand 2,000 feet high.

Bryce Canyon National Park surrounds some of the oddest and most strangely beautiful landforms at any of the parks. Northeast of Zion in Utah, high in the pines at the top of the Grand Staircase, erosion has carved soft, red rock into amazing towers and channels you can walk among. The park offers a more intimate experience than the vast cliffs and canyons. Most hikes are easy, and there are other activities for families at the park and just outside.

Glacier National Park, which shares the U.S.-Canadian border with Waterton Lakes National Park, features ice-covered peaks, thick forests, and alpine meadows reflected in numerous lakes that ripple across the park's lower elevations. Backcountry escapes lure many visitors to this northern Montana park, although many others are content simply to gaze at the jagged mountains, float along the lakes, or take short hikes into the wild.

Yellowstone National Park, the world's first national park, never fails to amaze. It has geysers, the Grand Canyon of the Yellowstone River, bison and elk that walk close to roads, glorious alpine meadows, and Yellowstone Lake. You can drive through in a few days, ogling these places, but then you'd miss an incredible network of trails and campgrounds. Yellowstone lies in the northwest corner of Wyoming and on strips of Montana and Idaho.

Grand Teton National Park nearly touches Yellowstone on the south side. It has a single great show rather than many sideshows, but it's an unforgettable one. The ferocious daggers of the Teton Range rise straight up from the flat stage of a valley and a string of lakes. The overwhelming view meets you almost everywhere, but the best of the park for families is down below, on lakes and hiking trails rich in wildlife. Just south of the park, the fun town of Jackson, Wyoming, offers downhill skiing and a pleasant dose of civilization.

Rocky Mountain National Park, just north of Denver, takes in one of the highest parts of the nation's greatest mountain range. It's unique in permitting easy access to broad areas of alpine terrain, much of it over 10,000 feet in elevation. The camping and hiking are supreme and include opportunities for walking without trails on the tundra above the tree line. Small towns on either side of the park offer cute and friendly places to stay, eat, and shop.

Yosemite National Park lies east of San Francisco roughly in the middle of

The National Parks

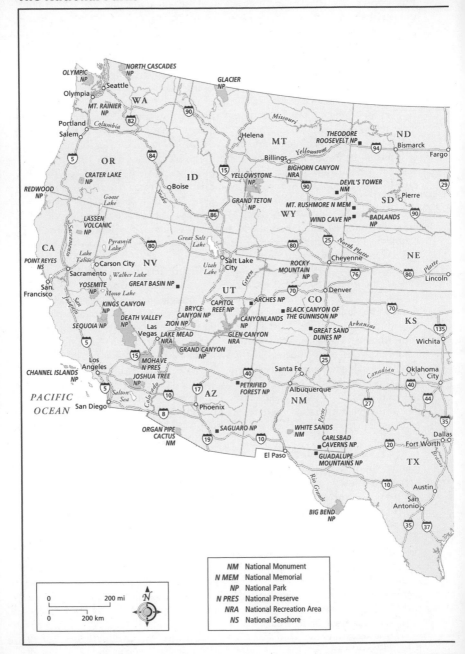

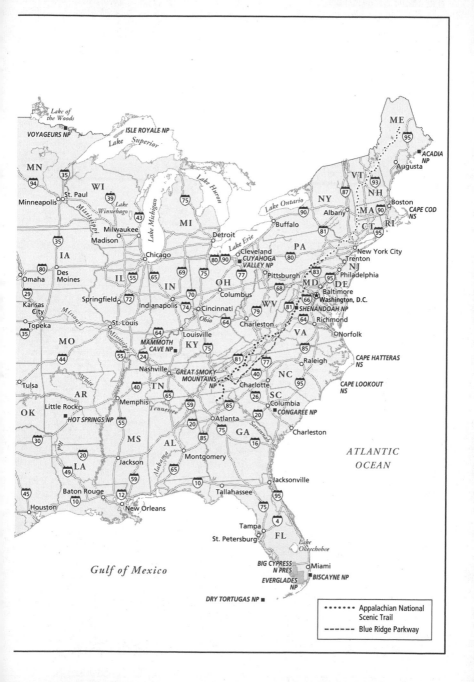

Appalachian National Scenic Trail

Blue Ridge Parkway

Choosing a Park & a Season

	Best Activities	Spring Break
Acadia Bar Harbor, ME *Chapter 3*	Bicycling, canoeing, day hiking, tide pooling, sea kayaking, whale-watching.	Cool, foggy, not much open until May.
Bryce Canyon Southern UT *Chapter 9*	Day hiking, backpacking, horseback riding, cross-country skiing; mountain biking nearby.	Cold at night, with some snow left, but quiet and especially beautiful.
Cape Cod Eastham, MA *Chapter 4*	Swimming, beach and nature walks, boating, birding, whale-watching, historic sites.	Cool, quiet; water too cold for swimming. Not much open.
Cape Hatteras Manteo, NC *Chapter 5*	Swimming, beach and nature walks, boating, fishing, historic sites.	Comfortable weather, quiet, with off-season prices. Water cold for swimming.
Glacier West Glacier, MT *Chapter 10*	Day hiking, backpacking, boating, horse rides.	Cold, snowy, gray. Going-to-the-Sun Road doesn't fully open until late May.
Grand Canyon Northern AZ *Chapter 7*	Sightseeing, hiking, backpacking.	Snow possible in early spring, comfortable in canyon. Best time for hiking and backpacking. Crowds.
Grand Teton Jackson, WY *Chapter 12*	Hiking, backpacking, horseback riding, mountain biking, canoeing, river rafting, fishing.	Cold and snowy.
Great Smoky Mountains Gatlinburg, TN *Chapter 6*	Hiking, backpacking, historic sites, horseback riding, inner-tubing, swimming; river rafting, mountain biking near park.	Comfortable daytime temperatures, cool evenings, weather changeable in March, few crowds. Best flowers.
Olympic Port Angeles, WA *Chapter 16*	Hiking, backpacking, wildlife-watching, tide pooling, sea kayaking, river rafting, skiing.	Cool and damp; whale-watching, no crowds, skiing through March.
Rocky Mountain Estes Park, CO *Chapter 13*	Hiking, backpacking, wildlife-watching, climbing, snowshoeing.	Snow still on ground, major routes not open.
Sequoia/Kings Canyon Three Rivers, CA *Chapter 15*	Hiking, backpacking, horseback riding, river swimming, giant trees, cross-country skiing.	Snow still in campgrounds, some routes closed. Foothills area comfortable.
Yellowstone Northwest WY *Chapter 11*	Hiking, backpacking, sightseeing, horseback riding, boating, fishing, cross-country skiing.	Roads still closed by snow, sometimes bike season in April.
Yosemite El Portal, CA *Chapter 14*	Hiking, backpacking, sightseeing, climbing, rafting, horseback riding, river swimming, skiing.	Still snowy in high country, Yosemite Valley open, cold in March, cool in April.
Zion Springdale, UT *Chapter 8*	Hiking, backpacking, sightseeing; nearby mountain biking and inner-tubing.	Comfortable temperatures in canyon, still snowy or muddy above the rim. Manageable crowds.

Summer Vacation	Fall	Winter
Peak season. June has bugs, but fewer crowds than July and August. Whale season ends mid-August.	Cool and quiet. Things start closing in September.	Not practical. Some skiing, but snow not reliable. Most tourist facilities closed.
Peak season. Comfortable temperatures, lots of people.	Cool and quiet. Wintry weather starts in October.	Cross-country skiing and snowshoeing. Park hotel closed.
Peak season. Quieter in June, but water still cold. July and August warm and busy.	Quiet, with good weather into October. Whales gone.	Cold and deserted.
Peak season. Hot in July and August with warm water, cooler in June with ocean water still cool.	Temperatures and swimming perfect into October. Hurricane season peaks mid-August through October.	Cold and deserted.
July and August are peak season. Sunny, warm days, cool nights, visible wildlife, reservations mandatory.	Cool and quiet. September can be wonderful, with mild days and gorgeous fall colors, but it can also bring an early season snowstorm.	Cold and snowy. Most park facilities closed, Going-to-the-Sun Road closed past Lake McDonald Lodge, St. Mary's shuttered. Good snowshoeing and cross-country skiing between Apgar Village and the Lake McDonald complex.
Busiest season, with heavy crowding. Temperatures comfortable on rim, too hot in canyon for much hiking.	Comfortable temperature on rim and in canyon, fewer crowds.	Snowy on the rim, comfortable in the canyon. unpredictable weather, few visitors.
Busiest season and best weather in July and August, with June also good at lower elevations.	September good, quiet. Everything shuts down mid-October.	Skiing at Jackson, but park largely snowed in.
Warm and humid at lower elevations, comfortable in mountains. Popular areas crowded, especially on weekends.	October foliage season brings peak crowding on roads and high prices. Weather comfortable, drier than rest of year.	Snow in the mountains, rain below. Cool weather, few visitors.
Peak season. Drier weather July and August, marine-mammal watching, room reservations needed.	Cool and damp. Few visitors.	Heavy snow at higher elevations, extremely wet at lower elevations.
Peak season July and August. Snow still in high country in June. Warm, thunderstorms. Crowded weekends.	September weather excellent, few crowds. Snow closes high country in later fall.	Best winter sports January and February.
Peak season. Comfortable temperatures in most of park, crowding on weekends.	Perfect weather with few visitors; snow in late fall.	Cross-country skiing. Much of park snowed in.
Peak season. Comfortable temperatures, thunderstorms, heavy crowding, reservations essential.	September days comfortable, cool at night, no crowds, most facilities close in October.	Excellent cross-country skiing and snowmobiling late December to early March; deep snow.
Comfortable temperatures. Extreme crowds in Yosemite Valley. High country opens late June.	Comfortable, growing cooler and damper in October, crowds into September.	Heavy snow above, with down-hill and cross-country skiing; snow spotty in Yosemite Valley.
Hot in canyon, comfortable on high-country trails. Heavy crowds in canyon. Thunderstorms.	Best time. Warm temperatures, few crowds, foliage peaks in October in canyon.	Snowy above, cool and changeable in the canyon.

the Sierra and is best known for Yosemite Valley, an amazing canyon where waterfalls drop thousands of feet from granite walls. The valley is a small part of the park, however, and is overrun with people. You'll want to spend most of your time hiking in the spectacular high-country areas and in the mountainside forests that aren't nearly as crowded.

Sequoia & Kings Canyon National Parks are connected and jointly managed parks in the southern Sierra. They are not as crowded as Yosemite, but otherwise they have much in common with it. Sequoia is famous for its huge groves of the big trees, and has wonderful hiking and camping areas, swimming, high-country trails, cave exploring, and other qualities that have nothing to do with giant Sequoias. Kings Canyon centers on the magnificent canyon of the Kings River. Its granite walls tower over the desertlike floor of the canyon like the cliffs of Yosemite Valley, but few people visit. Explore beyond the canyon and you'll find spectacular backpacking options.

Olympic National Park is a diverse area residing on Washington state's Olympic Peninsula, west of Puget Sound and Seattle. The park is a collection of exceptional places: along the coast, a strip of wild shoreline; on the west side of the Olympic Mountains, rainforest valleys of huge trees; up in the mountains, snowy alpine terrain and a glacier; in various places, lovely lakes, backpacking trails, and hot springs. There's plenty to do and more than you can see in a typical vacation. The weather, though often wet, is mild over a long season.

2 Visitor Information

One of the busiest Internet portals in the federal government is the one that opens the door to the National Park Service, **www.nps.gov**. From here you can jump to the park of your choice, find out how to purchase an America the Beautiful Pass, or research any aspect of the national park system.

ENTRANCE FEES

To help make up for funding shortfalls, Congress lets national parks charge higher fees and keep most of the money for improvements. While that's not the solution to the parks' funding woes, the program is making a visible difference in the parks, and the fees still amount to an insignificant percentage of the cost of a vacation, topping out at $25 per car for 7 days at some of the most popular parks, with most others charging $10 or less. The relevant chapters list the fee at each park. Technically, the entrance fee only covers four adults per car, with kids under 16 admitted free, but I've heard that limit is loosely enforced.

PASSES

You may be able to save on park fees by getting one of the various editions of the America the Beautiful Pass. With a pass, people over 62 or with a disability get in for almost nothing, along with anyone else in the car (again, technically not to exceed four adults). If you are over 62, get a **Senior Pass,** which costs only $10 and never has to be renewed. The **Access Pass** is free to anyone with medical proof of blindness or disability and eligibility for federal benefits, and is also good for a lifetime. Either one also gives 50% off on campsites and some other park fees. Since these passes are good at all federal recreation areas that charge fees, you can purchase them at offices run by the National Park Service, U.S. Forest Service, U.S. Fish and Wildlife Service, and U.S. Bureau of Reclamation. Some retail outlets also exist, such as at REI stores. Be prepared with proof of age or medical disability when you request one. For everyone else, the basic **America the Beautiful Pass** costs $80 and is good for 1 year; it covers park entrance fees only. In addition to buying it at the above locations, you also can purchase this pass at www.recreation.gov. If you plan to visit many parks—on a Southwest tour, perhaps—the pass may be worth the price; we've saved a little with ours on our extensive travels. (If you visit only one park many times in a year, you can buy an annual pass for that specific park for $50 or less.) The national pass also makes it a wee bit quicker to get through the gate. To order one of these new passes, visit www.recreation.gov. If you have questions, call © **888/ASK-USGS** and press 1.

3 When to Go

Besides your interests, two factors should lead your considerations in narrowing your choices: when you can travel and what your kids can handle.

TIMING

For most of us, work and school requirements determine vacation dates. With this settled, check in the individual park chapters to learn whether the park you want to visit has restrictions on making reservations. Some places require you send in campground deposits 4 months in advance. Others have lottery systems. And some deposits must be paid in October for the following summer. Yet, even at some of the most popular parks, you can get by with only a couple of weeks' planning with our tips.

CROWDING

Most families can go on vacation only when school is out: during summer vacation, spring break, or the winter holidays. For that reason, these are the busiest times at the national parks. Within these times, however, are considerable variations. For some parks, avoiding weekends gets you away from crowds, although that is less true away from major cities. In other parks, earlier in the summer is better than later. Spring break is almost always less crowded than summer, and can be the best time to visit the hot Southwest parks. (You'll find details under the "When to Go" section of each park chapter.)

At any time of year, crowding is only as bad as you let it be. Crowds are enough to spoil the experience only at the truly busy times at famous places. If you feel you have to see all the famous places, expect to be crowded. But you can get away from people at every park—it's just a question of how hard you try. The best way to do it is to use your feet, a horse, or a canoe to get off the road and into the landscape. Planning well ahead and using the reservation systems to your advantage also help you experience the best the parks have to offer even at the busiest times. Most park campgrounds don't feel crowded even when they're full—but you have to have a reservation months ahead. See p. 29 for info on the national reservation system and under "Campgrounds" in each park.

If you don't have to go during school breaks, or if your breaks are different from most, crowds won't be a major consideration. I've often found parks deserted during the shoulder seasons, which are the months adjacent to the most popular visiting periods at the park. (For example, if the high season at a park is June–Sept, then the shoulder-season months are May and Oct.) On some of our shoulder-season trips, prices were lower and the weather was as good as or better than in the high season. September is the best month at many mountain parks and national seashores. The dead off-season months offer lots of open country and very low prices, but facilities often operate shorter hours or close altogether, and the weather can shut down activities.

Packing 101: Clothing

- **Synthetic thermal underwear is like magic.** It keeps you warm even when you're wet. And, for the amount of warmth it provides, it is far more compact and less expensive than equivalent outer layers. You can sleep in it, too. We take it along whenever cool, damp weather is possible. *Tip:* Avoid cotton and denim if you think you might get wet.
- **Cover your butt.** If you don't bring rain pants, bring a raincoat that will keep you dry when you sit down.

CLIMATE

Summer weather is the best at most of the parks, and for most families with children in school summer is the only practical time to visit the mountain parks and national seashores. Aiming for the best weather within the summer probably won't be a productive effort: The variations are too small to give you more than a small chance of better weather in, say, July rather than August. On the other hand, it may be worth a few more bugs or colder ocean water to go in less-crowded June. Summertime generally is too hot for hiking in the Southwest, except at high elevations.

Spring break is a good time to visit some parks, especially in the Southwest, even if the weather isn't the best—often you don't need the very best weather to enjoy a park, anyway. Winter-break trips mostly are for skiing, snowshoeing, or sightseeing. Snowy parks are an entirely different experience, but a rewarding one. On the other hand, some parks are simply impossible at off-season times. I've included weather statistics and seasonal climate descriptions in each park chapter. The "Choosing a Park & a Season" chart earlier in this chapter summarizes the best seasons for each park in terms of crowding, weather, and key activities.

THE RIGHT AGE?

The ages and capabilities of your children should guide your trip planning. Here are some considerations.

KINDS OF PARKS

We have never found a park that we and our children did not enjoy, but you must make some age-related choices. The national seashores and Acadia National Park lack long hiking trails, but they have lots of recreation opportunities for children under 10, at the beach, in the marsh, biking, swimming, and boating. Families with strong hikers may prefer to challenge themselves with overnights and long day hikes in the big wilderness parks, such as Glacier, Grand Canyon, Grand Teton, Great Smoky, Olympic, Rocky Mountain, Sequoia/Kings Canyon, Yellowstone, and Yosemite. Of these, all except Grand Canyon are also great for younger children. Nonhikers should plan to visit the Grand Canyon on a tour that also includes Zion and Bryce Canyon because that makes sure there are things to do for younger children.

TRAVEL DISTANCES

How far can you haul your kids? Long drives and flights with small children can be torture. (For tips on how to keep them busy, see p. 22.) Also, we've observed a strange physical principle, the law of the inverse relation of child size and luggage quantity. It states that the younger the child, the more luggage involved. If you've ever traveled with an infant, you know what I mean: diaper bag, bottle paraphernalia, portable crib, stroller, special bedding, and so on. Add your camping gear to the pile, and you feel as if you need a caravan of camels to move around. (I've included some tips on how to reduce the load on p. 34.)

Thought and planning overcome many of the drawbacks of going a long way with children. If a drive would be too hard, for instance, take a plane or a train and rent a car when you get there. If you've whittled down your luggage and you still can't manage it, buy or rent gear when you get there. You can use the post office to send back extra gear or things you pick up on the way. Renting an RV can make it all easier, too (that's covered under "Practicalities: The RV Advantage," on p. 24).

APPROPRIATE CHALLENGES

Know what your children are capable of and plan a trip that's within those limits. Adults can challenge themselves physically, but if you try that with kids, you make everyone unhappy and teach your children to hate the outdoors. That goes for both young children and teens—any physical test has to be self-inflicted.

How much is too much? Many books give guidelines on how old children should be for certain activities or how far they can hike at certain ages. The guidelines aren't accurate or helpful, because every child is dramatically different in physical ability and attitude. The only good solution is to know your child's personal best, and then plan trips that stay within or just barely push that limit.

An important part of this philosophy is not to get hung up on destinations. Having your mind set on climbing a certain peak or focusing on a certain activity the kids haven't done before can lead to trouble and disappointment. Don't make extended time on horseback or in a sea kayak a major part of your vacation unless you already know that your kids enjoy doing those things and are ready for the challenge. (The parks *are* a great place to try these activities for the first time on short outings.)

The families who have the most fun outdoors, and who grow the toughest, most enthusiastic children, are those who spend a lot of relaxed time together doing things that they all enjoy. The adults I know who hate the outdoors had parents who made them go on long hikes with the drill-sergeant attitude that they had to toughen up and learn to enjoy it. They learned the opposite.

4 Getting There

Choosing how you travel depends on how you value your time, money, and comfort, and how much luggage you need.

How far can you go without ruining the day for everyone? Depending on age and personality, children have different levels of travel tolerance, but that's true of all of us. Anyone can stand to be strapped in for only so long before turning into a monster. My experience tells me that tolerance levels are shortest on airplanes, followed by cars, trains, and boats.

Of course, planes get the misery over fast. You may be able to put up with 1 bad day traveling, but not with the pain of spending a large percentage of your vacation driving with kids saying, "Are we there yet?" hour after hour. On the other hand, flying and renting a car is expensive and creates problems with moving your stuff around.

BY CAR

Going by car is the classic and most popular way to visit the national parks, and that's the approach I've covered in greatest depth. At most parks, having a family car is a virtual necessity. The question is, should you bring your own from home or rent one there? Driving your own car offers simplicity, familiarity, and low cost. There's almost no limit to how much **luggage**

Practicalities: Our Favorite Car Entertainment

Every family has its favorite games and entertainment to get through car trips and plane rides. They're fun to trade with other families. Here are some popular games and activities:

- **Supplies:** Bring crayons, pencils, pads of paper, stickers, pipe cleaners, cards, magnetic checkers, picture books, coloring books, activity books, and a road atlas (kids' editions are fun). Also, bring little prizes to make car games more exciting.
- **MP3 Players:** See that your child's MP3 player or CD player has recordings of music or stories. Kids enjoy listening to something no one else can hear. Buy some new story CDs to break out on the way when the going gets rough.
- **Easy guessing games:** Follow the rules of 20 questions (yes-or-no questions only), but narrow the possibilities to help younger players. For a 7-year-old, you could play with only animals as the thing you try to guess. With a 4-year-old, guess family members, toys, or characters from a favorite movie.
- **Monster Math/Fact Quiz:** Make up simple math problems about silly subjects for the children to solve in their heads. In another version, they answer factual questions about geography, science, or whatever we think of. Each kid is the center of attention during his or her own question; that's less competitive and allows you to tailor the question to the child's ability level. You can give treats for correct answers. Let them quiz you, too.
- **"My Grandmother Went To . . .":** The first player says, for example, "My grandmother went to Alaska, and in her trunk she packed an anvil." The next player repeats the sentence, then adds another place and item beginning with B. The process continues in alphabetical order with players repeating an ever-longer list, adding their usually silly items in turn. In the competitive version, a player who forgets an item is knocked out.

you can take if you put on a roof rack, bike rack, or trailer. That means you don't have to rent gear at the park, and can take along bulky extras—even your canoe or kayak.

On the other hand, if you look no further than the parks you can drive to from home, you will be missing out on a lot of wonderful places. And driving all the way across the country is expensive as well as tiring. The driving time from New York to San Francisco is about 60 hours without stops. Counting the cost of food, rooms, and gas, the round-trip cost for a

family of four is roughly the same to fly or drive, and that's driving 10 hours a day. As the distances get shorter, the savings of driving increase, but don't forget to count the cost of your time sitting in the car rather than having fun.

BY AIR
COPING

Short flights can be easy and fun, a wise alternative to a day or two of driving. But an airplane's advantage of novelty and excitement wears off long before the end of a long flight, and soon the kid realizes

- **License Plate Collecting:** This game is hard to resist at the big western parks, where you can get almost all the state license plates very quickly. To make it challenging, also look for the Canadian provinces and the different plate designs from each state. Keep your list on a piece of paper. Sightings of rare plates are good conversation starters with other families, since everyone does it.
- **Postcard Collection:** Make a journal of your trip by buying postcards everywhere you go (even gas stations) for your child to put in a cheap photo album or otherwise make into a book. He or she can write or draw pictures on the back of the postcards and put them in the album. Rearranging, editing, and showing off the book will use up a lot of time. And when you get home, it's a good souvenir.
- **Joint Storytelling or Drawing:** In the verbal version, each person adds a sentence to a story in turn, which usually gets silly fast. In the visual version, kids take turns adding to a picture—preferably one of actions or mishaps, like a Richard Scarry illustration.
- **Interpreting the Landscape:** Talk about how the land you are driving through might have come to look the way it does. Why are the hills or fields shaped as they are? Why do certain plants grow there? What do the people do to make a living, and how has that affected the way things look? What might it have looked like before people arrived?
- **Scavenger Hunt:** A grown-up calls for an item—a boat trailer, a sign with a certain word, a truck carrying food—and the kids holler out and get a reward when they see it. Try a couple of things at once.
- **Exercise Breaks:** Stop for a spontaneous break for footraces, a game of tag, or just romping around.
- **Real Conversation:** The time in the car is a perfect opportunity to find out more about your kids. The best way to keep a conversation going is to ask questions. Make a game of it by taking turns asking one another questions.

he or she is strapped into a seat in a noisy metal tube. That's when life gets difficult. The solution is to plan the trip the way a circus ringmaster prepares a show, with new sources of entertainment always readily available. Regardless of your preparations, however, toddlers can't stand long flights, and will administer a unique and humiliating form of torture for the last couple of hours. Don't forget a full medicine kit in case of stomachaches, earaches, airsickness, diarrhea (the stories I could tell), and general misery.

If your kid falls asleep on an airplane, you feel like you've won the lottery. Can you bring this about intentionally? You can fly at night, with a cranky, tired child who will probably sleep, or fly during the day, with a cheerful child who will probably stay awake. The night flight is only for gamblers. If the kid sleeps, great, but if he or she doesn't, you're in for a night with a tired, unhappy kid strapped into a seat with 300 trying-to-sleep strangers—a nightmare for you and everyone else.

Practicalities: The RV Advantage

As a tent camper, at times I've been puzzled and annoyed by big motor homes. Bringing along a home on wheels, with air-conditioning, beds, a kitchen, and other comforts, seemed to defeat the purpose of camping, which is to experience the outdoors. But in the Southwest, much more than in other parts of the U.S., RVs are everywhere, and after trying one for a couple of weeks, I understand why. RV camping in this part of the country is fun and makes a lot of practical sense.

If an RV insulates you from the outdoors somewhat, that's often a good thing in this land of extremes. In many ways, spring break is the best time to visit the Southwest—that's when we went for our first research trip, and we found no crowds and comfortable daytime temperatures. But higher elevations were too cold for tent camping at that time of year. Most people visit in the summer, when the weather is too hot during the day. Because of the way climate varies with elevation, you can run into both extremes on a single trip. Our coldest night was in the 20s (below zero Celsius) and our hottest day nearly 100°F (38°C). We were glad to have air-conditioning and a heater. We spent as much time outside as we liked, but we didn't have to worry about the elements because home was always close by. We also got used to having a sink to do the dishes in and a bathroom onboard.

An RV has major advantages over staying in hotels, too. You have your own cooking facilities and dining table, so you don't have to spend time and money eating stressful meals with kids in forgettable restaurants. If you want to eat out, you still have the opportunity. You also have greater flexibility and don't have to worry so much about reservations. During busy seasons, park accommodations in the region are booked up many months in advance; your itinerary has to be locked in long before you know how you'll feel about different areas. Campgrounds often require reservations, too, but not as far ahead; if you change your mind, you're out a lot less money than if you cancel a guaranteed hotel reservation. Finally, camping gives kids more freedom to be themselves than a hotel room can. Your campsite is a built-in playground.

Of course, there are disadvantages, too. One is cost. Renting an RV is expensive and can cost as much as or more than staying in a hotel, renting a car, and eating all your meals out. RVs also use prodigious amounts of gasoline, with a gallon typically taking you less than 10 miles. Another disadvantage is reduced mobility. Ungainly RVs are justifiably outlawed from many crowded park areas. In some parks, RV-rental drivers and the accidents they cause have become notorious (I don't know how many times I've heard stories of people bashed in the head by passing RV side mirrors). It's often best to set up camp and then find some other way to get around—on a park shuttle or bicycles, for example.

Also, someone has to drive the thing and drain the sewage tanks. Even smaller RVs take a lot of concentration and awareness to drive, because the vehicle fills the lane, you don't have much power, and you have huge blind spots. Now that I've driven one, I steer well clear of them on the highway. And draining the tanks can be revolting. We made it a rule to use campground toilets whenever possible, but just dishwashing water forces you to drain the tanks every few days. There's a lot of gadgetry to learn, too. Go slowly through your rental briefing and take notes. Finally, kids who get carsick might easily find that the configuration of seats and windows in an RV sets them off.

On balance, we found that the advantages outweigh the annoyances. If you decide to do it, here are some tips we learned:

- Shop on the phone by gateway city as well as by agency. Prices may vary widely in the region's major cities—Las Vegas, Salt Lake City, and Phoenix. Often you'll pay a mileage charge if you go over a certain limit (1,000 miles a week, for example), so you should plan your departure point with that in mind. You'll probably have to research this by calling around yourself, because travel agents don't have a simple way of comparison shopping.

- Off-season rentals are a great bargain. In the slower seasons, you can shop and even dicker for a deal. In the early spring, the agencies have RVs sitting idle. If you're daring, you can show up without a reservation and shop around town for a really low price.

- Rent the smallest vehicle you can be comfortable in. A bigger RV will cost more, use more gas, and make it more difficult for you to navigate and fit into campsites.

- Reserve early for the high season, and get all the details before you commit. What is provided and what do you need to bring? What are the security deposit arrangements? Are there any restrictions on where you can go? How old is the vehicle? What will the agency do if the vehicle breaks down? What are the insurance conditions and deductibles? Are there any extra costs for full coverage? What tax rate will you pay? Will the agency pick you up at the airport? How far is it from the rental office to a grocery store and an attractive campground?

- Reserve popular campgrounds well ahead. If you decide to change your plans, it doesn't matter much—campsites are relatively cheap.

- Do as much grocery shopping at one time as possible. You'll want to avoid taking the RV on unnecessary shopping trips. Plan meals and make a shopping list before you leave home.

- Ask the rental agency for boards to put under the wheels in campsites. Most RVs have propane refrigerators that work best when the vehicle is level.

Listed below are some major agencies in the region.

- Cruise America. Las Vegas, Salt Lake City, Phoenix, Flagstaff, Albuquerque, other locations nationally. ℂ 800/671-8042; www.cruiseamerica.com.
- Bates Motorhome Rental Network. ℂ 800/732-2283 in Las Vegas and Phoenix; or check the website, www.batesintl.com.
- Access RV Rental Group. Salt Lake City and Jackson, Wyoming. ℂ 800/327-6910; www.accessrvrental.com.

TICKET PRICES

Flying with a family is expensive, and time spent shopping for a good deal is well worth the effort. Start well ahead, watching for fare sales, which crop up at certain times of year for different destinations. A good travel agent can help you here, more than earning any added commission you have to pay. He or she will know what a good deal is, and will know how to find children's companion fares, which vary by airline and route and can save as much as 50%; that's tough to do shopping on the Internet. If you want to go it alone, sign up for e-mail notification of fare sales at any of many websites, including **Travelocity's Fare Watcher,** at www.travelocity.com. The more complicated your itinerary, the harder it becomes to get a good deal on the Internet. The cheapest tickets, however you book them, are usually simple round-trips between two large cities; avoid flying in triangles or using small commuter airports (see "Gateways," below). You can carry infants on your lap, saving the cost of a ticket, if you think you can stand it.

LUGGAGE & THE RENTAL CAR

Flying makes moving your luggage more complicated. The problem arises in the rental car itself, not the plane or transfers. After all, each passenger is allowed two bags, which can be huge duffel bags: You can fit an awful lot of stuff in these things. Check the airline website or call to get excess-baggage limits and charges, and weigh your bag before you leave home. When you arrive you can rent a cart or hire a skycap to get the luggage to the car. If you have to take a van to the car, bring the car back to the ramp to get the luggage.

Trouble begins when you try to fit the stuff into the car. Even a so-called full-size car (a Taurus, Impala, or Intrepid) may not have enough cargo space for all the stuff a family needs for a camping vacation. It's difficult to tie stuff onto modern cars without a luggage rack, which rentals generally don't have. Renting a minivan, which *will* fit all your gear, can be quite expensive. While prices range widely by market and season, minivans generally command double the going rate of an economy car, and at least 50% more than a full-size car. Renting an RV costs two to five times as much as renting a car: around $1,000 a week, plus mileage, for a midsize unit (see "Practicalities: The RV Advantage," on p. 24, for details; advice on how to pack for a flying-camping vacation is on p. 32). And then there's the ongoing worry of gas prices.

GATEWAYS

If you plan to fly and then rent a vehicle, you often have choices about where to land. Airfares and car-rental rates can vary widely among different towns that are within a day's drive of a park. I've listed the reasonable options for each park under "Arriving" in each park chapter. Starting with that list, use either a good travel agent or the Internet to shop the airfare and car-rental rates to each town, and then determine which one will save most overall. (Don't forget to ask about car-rental taxes and airport fees, which in some communities are 30% or more—enough to erase any savings you think you're getting.) Often there's a small airport near the park, served by propeller-driven planes and usually one or two small car-rental agencies. These generally are the most expensive choices; the largest cities are the cheapest. If you plan to rent an RV, it's especially important to shop around for prices and cities.

BY RAIL

Trains let you cover a lot of ground without having to strap the kids into their seats. To some extent, they can roam up and down through the train, and seats allow much more room to spread out than a plane or car. Unfortunately, train travel is usually impractical for a family national park trip. Trains can be very late on long runs, often don't have stations near parks (Glacier and Grand Canyon are notable exceptions), and many trains and stations are dirty. Luggage is a major problem; few trains have baggage-checking service, and even if they do, you end up at a depot that's usually far from any car-rental agency. Rail fares don't save much on routes with significant airline competition.

While rail travel can save time over driving and allow you to go much farther in a day, you have to balance that with the hassles at each end of the trip. For these reasons, outside of Grand Canyon and Glacier national parks I haven't included rail options for visiting the parks in this book; you can get **Amtrak** information directly at ℂ **800/USA-RAIL** or www. amtrak.com.

5 Tips on Dining

Food can be the toughest issue when traveling with children. Here are ways to make it easier.

CONSISTENT MEALTIMES
Anyone who has traveled with children knows the value of regular mealtimes. I know of no more important rule for keeping a family on an even keel. Letting lunch slip just an hour gets everyone tense, leading to whining, snapping, and temper tantrums. As everyone's mood gets worse, stopping for lunch gets harder—you can't agree on a restaurant or picnic area, and the kids' behavior deteriorates to the point that you don't want to take them into a restaurant. After many hard lessons, we've made strict rules about stopping for meals at certain times, even if lunchtime comes at a bad time for whatever else we are doing. We also keep emergency provisions so that we can quickly slap together peanut-butter-and-jelly sandwiches or some other simple, nonsnack food at the appointed hour. Snacks and junk food don't cut it; they make you feel worse a little while later.

RESTAURANTS & KIDS
Many travelers, not just families, get tired of eating out for every meal on a trip. There's the stress of keeping your kids in line at the restaurant; the queasy feeling of never getting simple, low-fat foods; the expense; and the time wasted, which can amount to much of your day. If you're camping or have a cottage with cooking facilities, the problem is solved. Otherwise, keep a stocked cooler and picnic basket so that you can have breakfast in your room and frequent picnics for lunch or dinner.

We have to eat in a lot of restaurants to review them for the book, including long, expensive meals with white tablecloths. We've found that the children's behavior, even the babies', gets better through the course of a trip as they learn what's expected of them. The key is to set clear rules at the start and enforce them without exception. For example, our children never, ever get out of their chairs during a meal; otherwise, we've found, they're soon under the table or walking around the dining room. When bad behavior hits, we're always ready to haul a kid out to the parking lot; other times, a threat of that embarrassing march is enough. (This starts at home: If you have no discipline there, you can't expect to start when you go on vacation.) Positive conditioning is important, too: Always bring small toys and crayons to the table, and offer treats after a successful meal.

Of course, if you eat only at McDonald's and the like, you don't have to worry so much about behavior. But fast food is poor nutritionally and often makes us feel ill afterward. Children may think they want to eat at their favorite burger joint every day, but our family ends up happier after picnics and sit-down meals.

6 Tips on Accommodations

A national park vacation can be one of the cheapest or one of the most expensive you can choose. Tenting and hiking with a map as your guide costs next to nothing; renting a beach house or a room in a luxury resort and taking guided outings can cost more than most of us have. Often, cheaper is better. We prefer a mix of camping and lodge rooms, which provides the best of both worlds. Here are some of the considerations in deciding how you want to visit.

Where possible, I have listed exact prices in the park chapters. Although many rates will change, these listings can help you calculate approximate costs and compare choices. Except where noted, prices do not include tax.

TENT CAMPING

When you camp, you spend more relaxed time together, less time in restaurants, in the car, or in proximity to diversions like the TV that tend to draw the family apart. A campground is an infinite playground for children, one where you don't have to tell them not to run or jump on the bed. Kids often make friends in camp, too. For the grown-ups, the best park campgrounds put you in glorious places where you can experience nature by touch and smell as well as sight (some others are crowded and stark; each is reviewed in the park listings). Superb campgrounds are waiting at almost every park in the book, and absolutely amazing ones at Great Smoky Mountains, Grand Teton, Sequoia/Kings Canyon, and Olympic national parks.

Camping wins on price, too. Driving to a national park in the family car with the family tent may be the least expensive vacation you can take besides a trip to Grandma's house. Typical park campground fees are less than $20 a night, and groceries cost little more than you'd spend at home anyway.

The downside is that you won't be as clean at a campground as you're used to being at home—trying to get a shower every day is inconvenient and wastes a lot of time, and washing young children in public showers is downright difficult. You're also at the mercy of the weather. If the going gets tough, give up. Check into a motel for the night, clean up, dry out gear, eat in a restaurant, and watch TV. Don't forget, a vacation is supposed to be fun.

Camping with an RV is another subject, which is covered in detail under "Practicalities: The RV Advantage," on p. 24.

HOTELS

You can vacation in the parks by staying in hotels every night, but it takes more planning and money than camping and allows less freedom. The attractive hotels in the parks generally have to be reserved far in advance for the summer season. They typically don't have telephones or TVs in the rooms, or swimming pools, although there are some significant exceptions to that rule. Some unique and wonderful places can make your vacation: The Sol Duc Hot Springs at Olympic, the Jackson Lake Lodge at Grand Teton, and the LeConte Lodge at Great Smoky come to mind. More often, park lodgings offer no better than average, out-of-date rooms, and some are truly terrible (see the park listings for details). Usually, it's much easier to get a room with a pool and other amenities outside the park in one of the gateway communities, although these too tend to book up in the high season. If possible, choose a place where you can cook, at least for part of your trip. Eating out for all your meals can get tiresome and expensive.

COTTAGES

Renting your own home near the park combines the comfort of hotel stays with the independence and relaxation of camping. Cottages or homes with cooking facilities are available at or near Acadia, Cape Cod, Cape Hatteras, Great Smoky, Olympic, and Yellowstone (limited choices are available at other parks). At the national seashores and Acadia, a summer cottage tradition makes it the best way to visit. Generally, cottage rentals require that you commit to a full week, reserve many months in advance, and put down a big deposit. By the night, they tend to be more expensive than hotels, but you offset some of that price difference by cooking your own meals rather than eating out.

CAMPING & HOTEL RESERVATIONS

More people want to sleep in the national parks in the summer than the parks can accommodate. To ration campground sites and backcountry permits, the National Park Service has reservation systems that reward those who know the rules and know when to call or log on. You can't buy your way around these systems or get an agent to reserve for you; the race goes to the prepared.

THE NATIONAL RECREATION RESERVATION SERVICE

The National Recreation Reservation Service (www.recreation.gov) described below currently handles most, but not all, campgrounds in Acadia, Bryce Canyon, Cape Hatteras, Glacier, Grand Canyon, Great Smoky, Olympic, Rocky Mountain, Sequoia and Kings Canyon, Yosemite, and Zion parks. Some or all campsites in many parks can't be reserved in advance. All of Grand Teton's sites are doled out on a first-come, first-served basis, while at Yellowstone the park concessionaire handles reservations through a system described on p. 283. Through the National Recreation Reservation Service you often can choose your own site when making a reservation. Even if you can't, rangers at the campground will give you your choice if you arrive early enough.

When to Reserve

Timing is everything. At all parks in the system, other than Yosemite and Yellowstone, reservations can be made up to 6 months before your visit. For example, starting on January 1, you can reserve through June 1. Then, starting February 1, you can reserve the period through July 1. Popular campgrounds on popular dates fill as soon as they become available, so you need to make your move on the day of the month 6 months before your trip. The system is similar for Yosemite, except that the magic date is the 15th of the month and you can only reserve 5 months ahead of your visit. Yellowstone's system is entirely separate, as I mentioned in the previous paragraph.

Whom to Contact

One-stop shopping for reservations on the nation's public lands is the mission of the **National Recreation Reservation Service** (© 877/444-6777; www.recreation. gov). Operated by ReserveAmerica, the site began offering reservations at many of the national park campgrounds in February 2007. You also can make reservations via the website at thousands of campgrounds in many of the national forests as well as at U.S. Bureau of Land Management and U.S. Bureau of Reclamation recreation areas. Via the site you can learn about national parks, find areas throughout the country specific to your interests, such as biking, boating, and climbing, even book interpretive tours in national parks. You do have to create a member profile at the site, a process that is used to deliver reservation information, confirmation numbers, and, if you choose, newsletters and surveys. Again, not all park campgrounds are included in the system, so even though the system might indicate a particular park's campgrounds are sold out there could be sites available if the park also has first-come, first-served campgrounds; you just need to show up early enough in the day to snag a site. The reservation line (℡ 877/444-6777) is open from 10am to midnight Eastern Time daily March 1 through October 31, and from 10am to 10pm the rest of the year. Online reservations can be made 24 hours a day. The site has details on each campground, online listings of how many sites are available for each date, and a way to make reservations. At Yellowstone, most campgrounds are managed by a concessionaire, Xanterra Parks & Resorts (www.travelyellowstone.com). Currently, the company does not handle online campground reservations, instead requiring you to call their central reservations desk (℡ 866/GEYSERLAND).

How to Pay

You pay for your campsite when you reserve. Some of the camping fees, which are typically a few dollars more than at a first-come, first-served campground, also include a nonrefundable reservation fee, which was $9 in 2007. You can charge your reservation on American Express, Discover, MasterCard, or Visa. You may use certified, personal, or traveler's checks when paying in person at the campground.

Using a Reservation

Once you pay for your reservation, you'll receive a voucher either via mail or e-mail to present at the campground. If you arrive after the campground office closes, your site is posted on a bulletin board and you can set up camp. Come back to the office to check in the morning, however, or your reservation for your entire stay likely will be canceled. Each campground has a phone number to call in case you will be late. Get the number and open times for that campground when you reserve (on the website, the information comes up before you reserve). If you cancel or change your reservation, you're charged a $10 service fee. If you do not cancel your reservation and do not show

up, you'll be charged a $20 service fee and forfeit the first night's fee. If you need to cancel up to the day before the first night of the reservation, call ℡ 877/444-6777. On the day of the reservation, you have to call the park directly; then you pay the cancellation fee and lose the first night's camping fee. These are not large amounts of money. It makes sense to reserve and pay for as many nights as you think you might use; the insurance is worth it at busy parks.

BACKCOUNTRY CAMPING PERMITS

You almost never need a permit for a day hike, but you usually do for overnight camping in national park backcountry, whether you get there by backpacking, by canoe, on horseback, or by other means. Sometimes you need a backcountry permit in national forests as well. Getting a permit is different at every park; sometimes it's as simple as filling out a form at a trail head, and sometimes you have to do it many months ahead at just the right time. I've covered those details in each park chapter in the "Campgrounds" section under "Family-Friendly Accommodations." If you plan a backpacking trip to the Grand Canyon or the high country camps at Yosemite, the permit should be your first priority, with other arrangements revolving around the dates you're able to get. If your dates are flexible, you improve your chances of going where you want to go.

PARK HOTEL RESERVATIONS

The systems to reserve hotel rooms are different at each park. Generally, reserving rooms is similar to booking any hotel room, except that you need to call early to get one. The best places can book up to a year early, whereas less desirable lodgings may be open a few months out. Sometimes, calling on a certain day makes all the difference. Details are in each park chapter in "How Far to Plan Ahead" under "Planning Your Outings" and under "Family-Friendly Accommodations."

7 The Adventurous Family's Vacation Planner

SUMMER CAMPS & FIELD INSTITUTES

All the parks have ranger programs for children and adults during the summer months, and some will even take the kids off your hands for an hour or two; but for an in-depth learning vacation, consider joining a field institute or camp. Park educational institutes offer outdoor seminars and multiday programs for adults or families on subjects such as art, science, and outdoor skills. You'll find these in-depth educational programs at Cape Cod, Glacier, Great Smoky, Grand Canyon, Yellowstone, Rocky Mountain, Yosemite, Sequoia, and Olympic (see "Kid-Friendly Programs," in each chapter for details). You can also split up by entering the children in an education program or a summer camp while you visit the park. I've also included summer camps with sessions of a week or less, including day camps and residential camps, at Acadia, Cape Cod, Cape Hatteras, Grand Teton, Great Smoky, and Rocky Mountain. At Sequoia/Kings Canyon, there's even a camp, Montecito-Lake Resort (see chapter 15, "Sequoia & Kings Canyon National Parks"), that children and parents attend together: While the kids join in structured outdoor activities, parents enjoy the park or otherwise amuse themselves, and then the family reunites for meals and evenings in family dorms. For any of these opportunities, you must plan well ahead.

8 Show & Tell: Getting the Kids Interested in the National Parks

READING UP

The most important book you can take along is a first-aid or medical guide; I've listed two good ones under "Dealing with Hazards" (p. 38). Each chapter in this book lists books for both kids and grownups that relate to the subject at hand, under the heading "Reading Up."

OUTDOORS SKILLS

Unless you're anxious or have spent little time in the outdoors, you don't need a book about how to camp with children, a fact underlined by the painfully obvious advice most of these books include. But if it will make you feel better, or if gaps in your knowledge exist, here are the best we've found.

Parents' Guide to Hiking & Camping, by Alice Cary (Norton, $19), is a fun, readable book full of photos, boxes, quotations, and tidbits of advice from real parents that make it easy to browse for ideas. The book is durable, with a plastic cover and thick, shiny pages, and has an index. The emphasis is on beginners setting out with small children, and it's somewhat superficial.

Camping and Backpacking with Children, by Steven Boga (Stackpole Books, $20), contains more information and has some value for more experienced backpackers, with its detailed sections on health and safety and on survival. Unfortunately, there is no index, and finding a particular piece of information is difficult. The book is cheaply made, with poor layout and gray photos.

CHILDREN'S NATURE STUDY

Teddy's Travels, America's National Parks, by Tedrick De Bear and Trefoni Michael Rizzi (TdB Press, $20), is a wonderful, kid-specific guide to the national parks. Within this book kids ages 8 to 12 can learn a little about the parks they visit, learn how to protect wildlife, compile a scrapbook of postcards and National Park Passport cancellation stamps (p. 32), and be quizzed on what can be found in the parks. Kids can join Teddy's CubClub at www.teddystravels.com and sign up to receive quarterly newsletters and follow Teddy's blog.

A great set of natural-history books for children are from the "Let's-Read-and-Find-Out Science" series (HarperCollins). These inexpensive paperback picture books take on serious subjects like evolution, the water cycle, or oil spills at a level kids in primary grades can read and understand, without dumbing down the material. We haven't found natural-history books of similar quality for older children.

Fieldtrips: Bug Hunting, Animal Tracking, Bird-watching, Shore Walking by Jim Arnosky (HarperCollins, $17) is a great informative and fill-in-the-blanks book for kids from about 5 to 8. Older kids might like the beautifully illustrated and designed *Keeping a Nature Journal: Discover a Whole New Way of Seeing the World Around You* by Clare Walker Leslie and Charles E. Roth (Storey Publishing, LLC, $19).

FIELD GUIDES

The National Audubon Society field guide series (Knopf) is an extraordinary collection, with color plates and loads of interesting facts on every species, as well as plenty of help in identification. One volume or another covers just about anything you might be interested in: trees, birds, and wildflowers of the East or West; seashore creatures; rocks and minerals; and even the weather, stars, or fossils. The disadvantage is that they are so heavy that you can't pack more than one or two in your luggage. Also, Audubon's own *Sibley Guide to Birds* (Knopf, $35), with David Sibley's painted plates rather than photos, is easier to use (published in 2000, it was an instant classic). An alternative is regional field guides, which Audubon publishes for the Pacific Northwest, New England, California, and so on. You carry one book on each trip, but they're not as easy to use. Smaller field guides also solve the weight problem but can be frustrating: There's a very good chance that the plant or animal you are looking at isn't in the book.

PARKS PASSPORT

No family should visit a national park without picking up a National Park **Passport to Your National Parks.** These pocket-size books let you record your park visits with a cancellation stamp that reflects the date and the name of the park you're visiting. The passports, along with providing space for the cancellations and commemorative postage-size stamps you can attach, provide snippets of park history. You can find the passports in park visitor centers, which also offer the cancellation tools.

9 What to Pack

When you're camping far from home, especially if you get there by air or in a small car, you try to do without anything that's heavy, bulky, or hard to carry. At the same time, you may need to be ready for hot, frosty, wet, or buggy weather. This section sums up some of what we learned about balancing those two needs on many flying-camping trips.

WHEN IT'S COLD & WET

Whether your trip takes you to the Sierra Nevada or the Rocky Mountains or to one of the coasts, you need to be prepared for cold. It's simple to prepare for inactive time in the cold: You just need heavy parkas, snow pants, boots, and so on. The real challenge is staying warm while active and potentially wet and in situations with changing temperatures. Perspiration is your biggest enemy, so choose layers that stay warm when wet: synthetics and wool—**never wear cotton.** Quickly change layers whenever you start to get sweaty or chilled. Our everyday inventory includes synthetic thermal long underwear; wool socks, hats, and mittens; fleece pants and coats; breathable wind-resistant outer

Packing Basics

- **Start with a list.** I include sample packing lists below. A list keeps you from forgetting things, and makes it easier to decide what *not* to take.
- **Figure out your limits.** Will you need to be able to move everything by hand all at once, to get on a train or boat, for example? If so, assign bags to each person in the family. If you fly and then drive, you don't have to carry everything at once, but it does have to fit in the trunk of the rental car.
- **Start packing early.** You won't believe how much space all your stuff takes until you see it all together. If you start early enough, you'll have time for alternatives, such as buying smaller gear, mailing some of it ahead, or arranging to rent gear at your destination.
- **Use big, flexible bags.** Duffel bags are inexpensive, hold a lot, and get smaller when there is less in them.
- **Bring an extra collapsible bag** for items you pick up on the way, for dirty clothes, or for mailing items back home that you don't need to carry with you.

jackets and pants; and warm boots. A wool sweater adds even more warmth. For summer in the mountains, add nylon shorts and poly-mix T-shirts, swap the wind layer for a rain layer, and leave the fleece pants (but not the fleece top), wool mittens, and warm boots behind. The underwear layer is the most important, great for sleeping on cold nights.

On temperate nights, sleep in light, summer-weight bags or fleece bag liners, then deal with cold weather by putting on your thermal long underwear or warm pajamas, hats, and a single large winter-weight bag that you can unzip and spread over all of you while you snuggle up.

TOYS

Bring only a few toys, those you need for the first leg of the trip, then send them back or give them away and buy more. This saves space, and new toys are a lot more fun to play with and make good mementos of the trip.

PACKING CHECKLISTS

We keep a packing list on the family computer that we print out before each

trip, marking off the items as we pack them. During the trip, we edit the list, adding or deleting items as we find out whether we need them, then type those changes into the computer when we get home.

CAR CAMPING

This packing list probably has more than you need; it's a starting point to whittle down. I've left off food, clothing, rain gear, footwear, toiletries, diapering supplies, and other givens. Items for the first-aid kit are listed on p. 39.

Kitchen Supplies

    baby bottles and formula
    bottle brush
    bottle opener
    camp stove
    can opener
    cooler and ice packs
    corkscrew
    cutting board
    dish soap
    dish towel
    fish knife
    garbage bags
    large spoon

Packing 101: Gear

Lots of magazines and websites (www.gorp.com in particular), and the Steven Boga book mentioned on p. 31, offer more advice for buying stuff. Here are a few of our family discoveries:

- **A high-quality baby-carrying backpack is worth the money.** The less expensive models (under $100) tire you and the child more quickly and wear out fast. With a heavy-duty pack, you can carry much larger children and carry them farther, greatly extending your freedom in the toddler years. Kelty makes good ones.

- **Bring an inexpensive umbrella stroller** for trips to town and while traveling; baby backpacks don't belong in crowds, shops, or airports. Jogger strollers are impractical, as they take up too much space and weigh too much for longer trips.

- **A portable crib enhances safety** for toddlers. This is a dangerous age when they can wander into trouble.

- **A reliable camp stove is not optional.** You need to be able to heat drinks and meals fast in damp weather when hypothermia or fatigue threatens.

- **Sleeping pads are as important as bags.** Everyone in the family needs a good pad. The ground can sap a child's body heat at night. In the summer you can get by with thin, compact bags (we use fleece sleeping bag liners) if you have good pads and one large bag to spread over all of you on cold nights. **Folding, waffle-pattern sleeping pads,** called Therm-a-Rest Z-Rest pads ($30 at Campmor), take much less packing space than pads that roll up.

- **A car-camping tent** should be big enough to be your home, where you can comfortably change clothes or take a sponge bath. It also needs a rain fly to keep you dry and should be strong enough to withstand windstorms. It doesn't need to be light; you can save a lot of money by buying a sturdy car-camping tent that's not light.

- **A backpacking tent** *does* need to be light, but it need only be large enough to lie down in. In the backcountry, you don't have to worry about privacy: You can change or bathe outside. Strength and a waterproof fly are still important.

- **A screen tent** protects your picnic-table area from bugs and rain. It can serve as your living and dining room, a place to write in journals, play cards, and eat meals when, without it, you would be miserable.

- **Waterproof your tents** before you set out. Buy your tent's "footprint" ground sheet if available. If not, bring a plastic ground sheet. Fold it

lighter	pots, pans, and kettle
matches	salt and pepper
measuring cup	sharp cooking knife
paper cups	silverware
paper towels	spatula
plates, cups, and bowls	sponge with scrubber
potholder	stove fuel

under so the edge of the outer fold is 3 inches from the outer edge of the tent floor. This will prevent the sheet from channeling water into the tent.

- **Get wide, long aluminum tent stakes** designed for snow. The inch-wide, spadelike blades hold in sand and loose soil and don't break. You can purchase them at mountaineering stores such as REI (www.rei.com). Warn your kids that they're there; you don't want any stubbed toes.

- **Bring a nylon tarp and lots of cord.** You can create a shelter outside the tent, or cover gear overnight in case of rain.

- **A cellular phone is reassuring to have** in the event of an emergency or even a minor crisis (especially when boating or hiking), but don't count on coverage in the backcountry; most big western parks don't have good coverage.

- **A collapsible fabric cooler** works almost as well as a hard-sided cooler and takes up much less space.

- **For water in the backcountry,** one solution is a pump water filter and plastic water bottles to store clean water. A filter will handle bacteria such as E. coli and protozoan cysts such as Giardia. A more expensive purifier also uses a chemical to kill viruses, such as hepatitis A, which are much less common in water because they don't reproduce there. A nice alternative to pump filters, because it's smaller, is the MIOX Purifier sold by MSR. This device, about the size of a small flashlight, basically turns salt water into an oxidant-rich solution that kills viruses, bacteria, Giardia, and Cryptosporidium, a nasty parasite that causes diarrhea. The MIOX does not, however, filter the water, and it can leave a chlorine taste. Boiling works, too, but you end up with hot water and you have to carry a lot of fuel. Iodine tablets produce odd-tasting water and are not recommended for use with children. See "Giardia in Water" (p. 42) for information on the risk of drinking untreated water, and water treatment.

- **Light is important.** When you're car camping, a propane lantern extends the day. Battery-powered headlamps should go car camping or backpacking; they allow you to work with both hands and to read without holding the light.

- **Don't buy** until you know what you need and like. Everyone has different tastes in gear. If you're just starting out, rent or borrow the gear you need to get an idea of what you like and what kind of stuff you should buy later.

strainer
tablecloth (plastic)
plastic containers (for washing and storage)
water jug
zippered plastic bags

Camping Supplies
bath towel
blanket
bungee cords
camping knife
campsite reservations
clothespins

cord
duct tape
extra tent stakes
fire starters
flashlight batteries
flashlights or headlamps
ground cloth (plastic)
newspaper
nylon tarp
pillowcases
pliers
propane lantern
safety pins
saw
screen tent
screwdriver
sewing kit
sleeping bags
sleeping pads
sleeping tent
soap
soap box
Super Glue
toilet paper
travel alarm clock

People Needs
art and writing supplies
baby carrier
binoculars
camera
cellphone
day packs
field guides
first-aid kit (see "Health & Safety,"
below)

fishing gear
grown-up books
guidebooks
insect repellent
portable crib
stroller
sunglasses
sun hats
sunscreen
tissues
toys and kids' books
water bottles
whistle

BACKPACKING

The most common mistake beginning backpackers make is taking too much. It's hard to have fun when you're carrying an uncomfortably heavy pack. After you're comfortable with your car-camping skills and have your own list of essentials, pare it down to the bare necessities, then add items you may need from this list.

backcountry permit
backpack
bear deterrent spray
compass
Global Positioning System receiver
mirror for signaling
trail maps
trowel
water bottles
water filter pump
waterproof bags

10 Words of Wisdom & Helpful Resources

Our children seem to be happy anywhere as long as they're healthy, rested, and fed; feel secure; and have challenges for their minds and bodies. As parents, we're responsible for providing those things. With practice, it's not hard, even on the road. Here are a few ideas that work for us. You'll find more tips throughout the book, including the "Keeping Safe & Healthy" section in each park chapter.

FEELING SECURE

Children feel secure when their parents are relaxed and they have a reliable place to retreat and find their favorite things. If you're camping or renting a cottage, it's easy to establish such a home base for children. We try to set up camp or get into rooms early in the day so that no one worries about where we're sleeping that night. If you're moving around a lot, your car becomes that reassuring home base. The problem with that is: Sometimes kids and adults don't want to get out of the car to see the places they are visiting. We avoid staying anywhere less than 2 nights; 3 or 4 is much better, a week best. Anything less, and you can get that uncomfortable, nomadic feeling of never really being anywhere, and the pictures passing by in the car's windows can become as hypnotic as a TV screen.

EXERCISE & REST

A national park trip should be physically exhausting but mentally relaxing. This is a chance to find out how much you can do and to feel the satisfying weariness in your muscles afterward. Nothing makes sleep come faster. If you spend all your time in the car, on the other hand, the kids drive you crazy with pent-up energy, and bedtime becomes a struggle. Bedtime rituals can be difficult to maintain when you're traveling. When we're camping, darkness settles everything down (in Alaska, where the sun doesn't set in the summer, children stay up very late). If you're staying in hotels, it's more important to enforce a set bedtime, avoiding the seductions of the TV, which, for some reason, seem more attractive away from home.

PACING & FLEXIBILITY

People who know how to slow down and enjoy themselves don't need to be told, and people who don't know aren't likely to learn by reading about it here. Still, we have made some practical discoveries that are worth sharing.

An obvious piece of advice that's often ignored is to spend adequate time in each place in a park rather than rushing around to see everything. The times we remember from our trips aren't the 20-minute sightseeing stops; they're the happy, daylong periods of relaxing when memorable things happen all by themselves. When planning your trip, be sure to set aside unstructured time when you can unwind and make your own discoveries—time to play in a stream, check out a newly found trail, or look at shells on a beach. Instead of trying to "do" a park in a few days, try to really know one manageable part of it in the time you have.

Children need time to do nothing. I've listed places for relaxed play in each park chapter, including playgrounds, but a campsite or grassy lawn is all you really need for downtime. Adults need time to do nothing, too, although sometimes we read a magazine or putter around while doing it. On the other hand, there's no reason for the most active and ambitious member of your family to be limited by what the least able or energetic can do. Don't be afraid to split up if you want to take a long, fast hike, while your spouse would rather explore little towns, shops, and museums. Break into two groups, taking the kids to different activities that fit their ages. They are happy to have one parent at a time, just to play, go to a nature center, or romp down an easy nature trail, while the other parent is off doing something grown-up. As long as you're fair about who gets to go off alone and you still spend plenty of time together, the system works well.

KEEPING CLEAN

Unless you stay only in commercial campgrounds, showering every day when you're camping at the national parks is a time-consuming and difficult proposition. But keeping clean is important to enjoying yourself. Usually, one spouse doesn't like camping as well as the other does, and being dirty is often a big part of the dislike; if the more enthusiastic member of the team wants to go camping again, it's wise to attend to this issue. A box in each park chapter lists the location of showers and coin-op laundries.

You can easily wash your hair and face every morning in camp with a pot of warm water poured over the head. Nothing does more to make you feel clean. A quick sponge bath and change of clothes in the tent also works wonders. Don't skip brushing your teeth just because you are camping. Keeping hands clean is important for your health, especially at campgrounds without running water in the bathroom. We always keep soap and water out and handy in camp. Today's ubiquitous "wipes" work well for cleansing sticky little hands and faces when water isn't handy.

11 Health & Safety

I'm no expert on healthcare, but I've culled advice from various sources to repeat here and in the park chapters, on the theory that some information is better than none. We've also listed advice on avoiding outdoor hazards.

PREPARING FOR PROBLEMS

If you're taking your kids into the wilderness, many hours from help, you need to know what to do in an emergency. Taking a course is best, and having a book on first aid is perhaps the least you should do. (I've recommended two good ones under "Dealing with Hazards," below.) I always try to know in the back of my mind how I would get help from wherever we are.

You can avoid most emergencies by using your common sense. Many people who have bad things happen to them in the national parks are doing something stupid. That's why there are signs at the top of the huge waterfalls at Yosemite telling you not to swim there. Rangers call it "the Disneyland effect." Our society protects us so carefully from hazards that some people unconsciously believe that this is the normal state of nature. In fact, in the natural environment, survival of the fittest still prevails, even for our species, which is the only explanation for some national park accidents. For example, at the Grand Canyon, which the *Wall Street Journal* rated the third-most-dangerous park, a man posing for a picture in 1999 climbed over a guardrail and then walked backward over the rim, falling to his death.

DEALING WITH HAZARDS

Here are some tips on avoiding and dealing with some common outdoors hazards. Each park chapter also lists hazards particular to that area under "Keeping Safe & Healthy." Don't look to this book for advice for injuries and illnesses you're just as likely to encounter at home, such as cuts, broken bones, and the like. Always consult a doctor immediately if there's a problem.

I recommend taking a good first-aid book or medical guide in your first-aid kit. Many are available, but I like the books by Dr. William Forgey, president of the Wilderness Medical Society, who devotes much of his time to perfecting outdoor medicine. His *Wilderness Medicine, Beyond First Aid, 5th Edition* (Globe Pequot, $15) is an extraordinary book, designed for people far from medical help, that goes deeply into diagnosis and treatment for a huge range of problems in clear, nontechnical language. Another good one is Dr. Eric Weiss's *Comprehensive Guide to Wilderness and Travel Medicine, 3rd Edition* (Adventure Medical Kits, $15). This pocket-size book is easy to carry and offers advice and techniques on just about every imaginable medical emergency.

ALTITUDE SICKNESS

Altitude sickness is common at elevations above 10,000 feet, where the body needs time to adjust to getting less oxygen in each breath. Spending a few days in the mountains before high-elevation hikes helps, as does drinking lots of water. Symptoms include headache, nausea,

Medical Kit

We have split our medical kit into two parts, each in its own zippered pouch. The large kit is for overnight trips away from potential help, in the wilderness or on a boat, or for long vacations. From the larger kit, we fill the smaller kit with whatever emergency supplies we need for a particular day hike or short outing, and it goes with us everywhere. These are what work best for us.

You can buy first-aid kits that contain most or all of the items you need, but they tend to be very expensive compared to just going to the pharmacy and buying the items individually. Those I list here cover most contingencies.

adhesive tape	anti-inflammatory pain reliever
antacid or other stomach settler	instant ice pack
antibiotic ointment	(chemical pouch)
antihistamine	iodine
antiseptic wipes	ipecac syrup
bandage assortment	latex gloves
Band-Aids	laxative
benzocaine burn spray	magnifying glass
blister pads	measuring spoons
calamine lotion	petroleum jelly
children's acetaminophen	rubbing alcohol
diarrhea medicine	scissors
carsickness medicine	splint
elastic bandages	thermometer
eyewash	toenail clippers
first-aid book	Tums
gauze pads	tweezers
Ibuprofen or other nonsteroidal	waterless hand sanitizer

Also:

- Add prescription medications to the kit, even those you don't use at the moment but might need on a long trip; filling out-of-state prescriptions can be difficult.
- A snakebite kit may be a good idea if you will be in snake country, but you must follow the directions; improper use can cause serious infections.
- We bring a prescription epinephrine injector called EpiPen Jr. for allergic emergencies like the near-fatal bee-sting reaction I had as a child. We don't know if any of our kids are sensitive to stings, but it's best to be ready.

fuzzy thinking, and fatigue. Watch children, especially those being carried in backpacks, for lethargy, which could indicate a problem. Dizziness and poor judgment, leading to accidents, may be the main dangers at elevations family hikers are likely to attain. The cure is to return below 8,000 feet.

A life-threatening buildup of liquid in the lungs or brain caused by high elevation normally occurs only above 14,000 feet, but can happen at lower elevations in people who are especially susceptible. Symptoms include coughing, breathing trouble, and poor coordination. Serious altitude sickness can kill fast, so you should get down as soon as possible.

BURNS

In a campsite, sources of burns aren't as well isolated from children as they are at home. Kids can fall into the campfire, tip the camp stove, or spill hot drinks on themselves. Be conscious of this risk and set up camp to be as safe as possible, establishing clear rules about how to behave around the fire. In case of a burn, cool the skin as quickly as possible with cold water, then check your first-aid reference for treatment, which depends on the severity of the burn.

CRIME

The parks are busy, open places, and serious crimes sometimes happen there. A survey by the *Wall Street Journal* in 2000 showed that many parks had more serious crimes in a year than search-and-rescue operations. The pattern wasn't what you would expect: Cape Cod National Seashore had 155 search-and-rescue incidents and only 13 serious crimes, whereas Yellowstone had 35 searches and 119 crimes. Do the same things to protect yourselves as you would do at home: Keep your children with you, lock the car, and so on. You can't avoid all exposure to theft while camping, but you can make it more difficult. For example, when you have to leave stuff in camp, don't leave it in plain sight.

DANGEROUS WILDLIFE

All wild animals are potentially dangerous, even little squirrels. Don't ever approach or try to touch a wild animal of any kind. They can carry anything from rabies to bubonic plague, and even a minor bite is serious business.

Bears

Black bears are common in many parts of the U.S. Grizzly or brown bears (two names for the same species) live only in the Rockies, from Grand Teton north, and in Alaska. Either species can be dangerous, but advice about how dangerous black bears are varies in different parts of the country. They are smaller than grizzlies, reaching a few hundred pounds, and in natural conditions live primarily on plants. Unfortunately, many black bears in the national parks, especially in California, have come to rely on food and garbage from human beings. A black bear killed a hiker in Great Smoky National Park in 2000, the first such fatality in the history of the National Park Service.

The most important precaution is to store food securely. **Never, ever take food, dirty clothing that smells like food, or even pungent soap or lotion into your tent.** And make sure your kids wash their hands after they eat. Follow National Park Service instructions at the campground. At some parks, storing food in the trunk of the car is sufficient, but black bears in California's Sierra Nevada know how to tear cars open to get to the food. At these parks you're provided with steel "bear boxes" to store your food. At Tuolumne Meadows in Yosemite I watched once as a black bear popped out of the woods and went from box to box, trying to find one that was unlatched. Don't even leave loose papers in your car there, because a bear may mistake them for food wrappers. If there's a food storage locker at your campsite, keep all food you aren't eating at the moment in the locker, with the latch closed. Don't leave food unattended for any amount of time. In California, rangers advise that if a bear comes while you're eating, you should try to scare it off, but don't try to take food away from a bear. In the Rockies, where black bears are wilder, that doesn't happen as much, and you should steer clear of them at all times.

Before heading into the backcountry for a backpacking trip, you'll receive plenty of advice about bears from the Park Service. Follow it. In some areas hanging your food and pungent items from a long tree branch is sufficient, but anywhere in the Sierra and above the tree line in the Rockies, only bear-proof containers will do. California bears have learned to get food out of the trees, and they can destroy the tree in the attempt. You can inexpensively rent canisters at the parks where they are required (they cost $67–$80 each at www.backcountry.com), but be sure to plan your rations and toiletries so that everything fits. A typical canister is a cylinder a foot long and 8 to 9 inches in diameter that weighs about 3 pounds. Another option is the "Ursack," a bear-resistant bag made out of a "bulletproof" fabric that is gaining more appeal because of its packability and performance. (www.ursack.com; $50–$80). Where food hanging is the recommended technique, such as at Yellowstone, be prepared with plenty of cord and a sack. At Great Smoky, many campsites have food-hanging cables. Whatever the storage method, always set up your tent away from your cooking and food storage area.

When hiking, make plenty of noise to avoid startling a bear, especially in brush or thick trees; wearing a bell, singing, or carrying on a lively conversation helps. Keep children nearby, because their small size makes them vulnerable. If you meet a bear in the woods, make a lot of noise, wave your arms, and keep your group together in a knot to look like a larger animal. The bear usually will walk away. Don't walk or run away, because that may make the bear interested in following, but do retreat slowly, keeping your face to the animal.

Also good to have in bear country is a deterrent spray made of capsaicin pepper. If a bear is aggressive, a fog of the burning spray is supposed to deter it (except in wind or rain). A can costs about $40, plus $10 for a holster. One good brand is **Counter Assault** (© 800/695-3394; www.counterassault.com). This dangerous stuff must be kept away from children.

We've camped and hiked a lot in the western U.S., and while we've seen bears from a distance, we've never had to use the spray to defend ourselves. Bears are scary to think about, but don't let the fear deter you from enjoying the outdoors, because the actual hazard is slight compared to others you face every day.

Mountain Lions

These great cats live in small numbers in several western states. Sightings are rare and attacks even rarer; however, a child was killed on a hike at Rocky Mountain National Park a few years ago. Attacks happen near brush, where a lion can hide and pounce, and are unlikely if your group is together and noisy. The boy who was killed had run ahead of his family and was the size of a lion's normal game.

Bison, Moose & Deer

Large mammals are dangerous even if they aren't predators. These animals can move lightning fast and kick and trample a person who approaches too close and appears to be a threat. Each of these species has killed people. Always watch from a distance. Don't try to get closer for a picture. Even gentle-looking deer can be dangerous if you don't respect their space.

DEHYDRATION & HEAT EXHAUSTION

The body normally uses 2 or 3 quarts of water a day, and in the desert you need four times as much. If you lose just 2% of the water in your body, you can suffer weakness, headaches, and nausea, and you may stop thinking clearly or become irritable. This can happen in any climate, and it's dangerous. If your urine isn't light-colored, you're probably not drinking enough water. The cure is to drink, even if you aren't thirsty. Also make your kids drink, especially when you are hiking. Beverages with caffeine or alcohol are counterproductive. Juice is okay, but when children drink enough for good hydration they also get a lot of sugar, which can spoil their appetite for nutritious food.

In sunny conditions, especially in the desert, eating and sun protection are very important. Caps with cloth flaps that hang down work well for kids, as do broad-brimmed caps. Wear light, loose clothing. If you drink a lot of water but don't eat, your body leaches out nutrients, contributing to dangerous conditions, including heat exhaustion and heat stroke. Both conditions happen when your body loses its ability to get rid of heat because of dehydration, not enough nutrition, or overexertion in the sun.

Symptoms of heat exhaustion include weakness, cramps, dizziness, or nausea; the skin becomes pale and damp. Give the victim food, water, and rest, and apply a wet cloth until the feeling passes. Heat stroke is the same condition, but much worse. Now the victim has similar symptoms, plus an elevated temperature; fast pulse and breathing; hot, dry skin; and mental symptoms such as confusion and passing out. The person's life is at risk, and he or she needs shade, cooling damp cloths applied directly on the skin, water, food, and quick medical attention.

DROWNING

These tragedies happen incredibly fast, so you need to keep a sharp eye on your kids whenever you're near water. You should hold on to toddlers or have them on a leash. Swim in pairs, and make sure someone onshore in your party is keeping track of you. I've included some information on ocean swimming in "Practicalities: Swimming Safely in Surf," in chapter 5, "Cape Hatteras National Seashore." River swimming and inner-tubing are highlights of visits to some parks, but ask a ranger first if water conditions are right, and have a grown-up go in before the kids to get a feel for the current. It doesn't take much to carry away a little person.

FALLS

Many people are killed or injured in the parks when they fall into canyons or off mountains. They're often young adults attempting dangerous sports without proper training or safety gear, but people have also simply gotten dizzy at the edge of the Grand Canyon and fallen in. Keep a hand on your children, and don't hike where a fall could lead to disaster. Enroll teenagers who want to climb in programs where they can learn to do it safely. With luck, such a class will teach respect for the dangers of climbing, and contempt for those who take risks without knowing what they're doing.

GIARDIA IN WATER

In the past 20 years, streams all over the North American wilderness have become polluted with a protozoan cyst from feces called *Giardia lamblia,* which causes chronic diarrhea. You can also pick up various nasty bacteria and, less frequently, viruses in some areas. Drinking untreated water from any water body is a risk not worth taking. ("Packing 101: Gear," on p. 34, covers how to treat water.) Giardia is difficult to diagnose and can last for years if untreated. Symptoms usually show up a week to 10 days after exposure and last 1 to 3 weeks, but can return for repeated bouts. If you come down with diarrhea within a month or so of an outdoors trip, ask your doctor for a giardiasis stool test.

HYPOTHERMIA

Dangerous loss of body heat, also called exposure, is a common killer in the outdoors. It happens when your body gets too cold to warm itself. You must be especially vigilant with children because their smaller bodies cool faster, and they may not notice how cold they're getting. Hypothermia can occur on a 50°F (10°C) summer day if you get damp and it's windy, especially if you are physically exhausted. Avoid hypothermia by eating well, being aware of how everyone is feeling, avoiding getting wet or sweaty, and wearing wool or synthetics that stay warm when wet.

Watch out for shivering, sluggishness, lack of communication, and irrational actions. If a person shows symptoms of hypothermia, get him or her indoors, out of damp clothes, and warm as soon as possible. Shivering is a key symptom. If the victim can still shiver, the body should be able to warm itself with warm, dry clothes and shelter. If the victim is too cold or physically exhausted to shiver, that is a sign that you must add heat from outside the body. Putting on more clothing won't help at this point. In the field, get the victim undressed and into a sleeping bag, skin-on-skin, with one or two warm people. Unless the victim is showing signs of shock, give plenty of warm liquids.

INSECTS
Sting Allergies
Extreme allergic reactions to bee and wasp stings can be life-threatening. Watch children carefully, and head for emergency help at any sign of breathing trouble, fainting, stomach pain, or hives. If you suspect that one of you has a sting allergy, or if it runs in the family and the kids have never been stung, it's wise to prepare with a prescription epinephrine injector kit such as EpiPen Jr. Antihistamines help with swelling from mild bug bites. Ask your doctor first.

Poisonous Spiders
Bites by poisonous spiders are rare but require an immediate trip to the doctor. Symptoms of a black widow spider bite include severe abdominal pain and hardness, and difficulty breathing.

Mosquitoes
West Nile virus has made mosquitoes a newly worrisome concern. While only 20% of people infected develop any illness, and only 1 in 150 develops a severe form of the disease, it's still worthwhile to avoid the small chance of such an illness. Tips to avoid bites: Use repellent that contains DEET (see "The Dirt on DEET," below, for advice on repellent), wear long sleeves and pants, use a screen tent at the picnic table, choose a windy campsite over one in the brush or near standing water, and burn mosquito repellent coils in camp. The period from infection to the onset of disease symptoms is usually 3 to 14 days. Symptoms of the mild disease can be tough to tell from common fever and headache. Symptoms of a severe infection include headache, high fever, neck stiffness, stupor, disorientation, tremors, convulsion, and muscle weakness. See the CDC's West Nile virus website (www.cdc. gov/ncidod/dvbid/westnile) for more information. The site also contains a current map of where the virus is found. Teach children not to scratch bites. If you can resist for 30 minutes to an hour, they stop itching; if not, they get worse and can even cause skin infections.

Ticks & Lyme Disease
Ticks can carry Lyme disease, especially in the Northeast and Northern California (cases have turned up in 48 states). It starts with flulike symptoms and can affect the neurological system and heart if not treated with antibiotics. Ticks in the Rocky Mountains, the Southwest, and the Carolinas and neighboring states can also carry Rocky Mountain spotted fever, which causes fever, vomiting, and a measleslike rash, among other symptoms, and is fatal in 30% of cases.

Ticks attach to people by brushing off grass or undergrowth we walk through. Stay on the trail. Wear light-colored, long-sleeved shirts and pants tucked into your socks for hikes. Apply DEET-based insect repellent (see below). After a hike, at bed or bath time, check everyone for ticks, especially on the scalp. Ticks are black and roughly the size of a pinhead. It takes about 48 hours for the tick to pass on the disease. Pull it out with pointed tweezers, taking a little of the skin at the insertion point, and apply alcohol and antibiotic ointment to the wound. If a bull's-eye rash or flulike symptoms arise, see a physician. Rocky Mountain spotted fever shows up in about 6 days and progresses quickly. If you suspect something, see the doctor as soon as possible.

LIGHTNING

About 100 people a year die from lightning strikes in the United States, and many more are injured, making lightning a leading outdoor danger. In mountain areas where afternoon thunderstorms are common, especially the Rockies, plan hikes or boating for the morning so that you can get below the tree line and off the water by afternoon, when storms usually hit. Storms move faster than you do, so you can't count on getting to shelter once a storm appears. If you can, get inside a building; if you're already inside, stay there until the storm passes.

Lightning doesn't have to hit you directly to kill; an area around a strike becomes electrified. The most dangerous place is near a lone tree or another upright object. Standing on top or on the side of a mountain of alpine tundra is also dangerous. A thick forest is a good place to be, but not near the tallest tree.

If you're stuck above the tree line in a storm, squat with your hands on your knees and your feet on the ground in a depression in the ground, and keep your head down. Don't lie down. Stay away from tall rocks, cliff edges, cracks, rock debris, water, or anything that could conduct a strike to you through the ground.

Here are the six most deadly common activities in lightning storms, in order: working or playing in open fields; boating, fishing, and swimming; working on heavy farm or road equipment; playing golf; talking on the telephone; and repairing or using electrical appliances.

POISON IVY & POISON OAK

Poison ivy grows on the East Coast, poison oak on the West. They are closely related, and the sap of both contains a highly allergenic substance that causes an itchy rash, or worse symptoms in sensitive people. I repeat the following chant to my children: "Stay on the trail."

If you think you have come into contact with either plant, wash the contact area with alcohol and soap strong enough to remove tree sap. The sap sticks to clothing and remains active for a long time, so wash anything that might have touched the plant. The rash takes 12 hours to 2 days to appear. Once it does, you have up to 2 weeks of misery ahead, longer if you scratch and it gets infected. Try hot baths and showers—as hot as you can stand—for up to 8 hours of relief from itching. Calamine lotion, acetaminophen, Aveeno oatmeal baths, and antihistamines may help. Get medical treatment for extreme reactions.

SEASICKNESS & MOTION SICKNESS

Being seasick or carsick is one of the worst feelings in the world. We've found Dramamine to be effective. The product as currently marketed is labeled for children as young as 2, but you have to break the tablets into ever-smaller pieces to get the right dosage. For convenience, we buy the orange-flavored chewable variety—original Dramamine tastes terrible and so requires lots of water to get down. You have to take the medicine an hour before you get on the boat or start the drive for it to be effective. It does make you sleepy—potentially a good thing for kids.

SNAKEBITES

Usually, people are bothering a snake when they get bitten. Be careful turning over rocks, reaching into dark places, and

The Dirt on DEET

Since the arrival of West Nile virus, pediatricians have changed their advice about the use of the most effective insect repellents, which contain the active ingredient DEET. Adverse reactions to using DEET are extremely rare and confined to situations where the product was not used in accordance with the label instructions. The risk of the virus or of Lyme disease from ticks is much greater than any risk from using DEET. On the other hand, there is no reason to use repellents with very high concentrations of DEET. More DEET doesn't keep mosquitoes away better; it just makes the protection last longer. We've gotten good results even among thick, Alaskan mosquitoes from DEET-based repellents made for children with a 7.5% concentration, reapplying every couple of hours. However, the American Academy of Pediatrics now says even 30% concentrations are safe on kids when used correctly. But you must be careful: Have an adult apply the repellent, and keep it away from ears, eyes, mouth, or fingers the child might put in his or her mouth. Experts disagree on using it on very young children. Some say it is acceptable on babies over 2 months in low concentrations; others say 2 years. There is a good alternative, especially with babies: netting. For more advice on DEET, see the Centers for Disease Control's West Nile Virus website, www.cdc.gov/ncidod/dvbid/westnile and call your local doctor.

Early in 2005, though, the CDC also approved the use of non-DEET repellents that contained picaridin, a chemical long used in Europe and Latin America, or oil of lemon eucalyptus, a plant-based compound. Cutter makes a product, called Advanced, that contains picaridin, while the makers of Burt's Bees products have a repellent with oil of lemon eucalyptus. I've tested this in the Yellowstone backcountry and found it to stand up well to mosquitoes—and it smells a lot better than DEET! Your children may have allergies, so, as always, consult your own doctor before using anything new.

gathering firewood. If you are bitten, symptoms quickly follow, starting with a funny taste in your mouth. You may want to bring a snakebite kit, but in any event, get medical attention as soon as possible, keeping the bitten limb below the heart. Carry a person who has been bitten on the leg or foot.

SUNBURN

Most skin cancer in adults is caused by overexposure to the sun decades before, as a child, whether tanning or burning. Severe sunburns can also ruin your trip. Wear sun hats with flaps or wide brims. Always apply sunblock with an SPF of at least 15, even on an overcast day. This is especially important at high elevations or on the water. An SPF higher than 15 doesn't offer much additional protection—just a few percentage points. Applying it heavily and often is much more important.

TRAFFIC

Your children are a lot more likely to be hit by a car than eaten by a bear on a national park trip. Many drivers are in unfamiliar vehicles, such as rented RVs. Pedestrians and cyclists have even been hit by big rearview mirrors. Don't let your guard down in parking lots and on roadsides.

3

Acadia National Park

From atop Acadia's Cadillac Mountain, you can see for miles along the glistening Gulf of Maine. The bumpy bedrock landscape, shaped like a lumpy bedspread over a sound sleeper, is filled in by the sea—a rounded green island pokes above the surface here and there like an elbow or a shoulder. You can gaze at it for hours, finding new details. This small national park has mountains and forests, ponds and marshes, rocky and sandy shores, marine and land animals. And people. By the time Acadia became a national park, the land and seashore already had been in use for centuries. On each island, behind every ridge, there are colonies of life.

Compared to other parks, Acadia gives us a different way to understand nature—with people as part of the picture. Most of the famous Western national parks protect sprawling landscapes for us to visit and look at, preserved as much as possible to be as they were before settlers arrived. To feel a part of those places—and not just a viewer of a natural show—we have to leave our cars behind and hike into the wilderness. Acadia is different. People have been here long enough to have become threads in the fabric of the place. From the top of Cadillac Mountain, the scene all fits together: the forests, the tiny islands, and the waterside villages with their boats passing back and forth.

Acadia doesn't have great wilderness areas or backpacking, but its partly tame natural places are so inviting and easy to reach that the park may be the best of all for families. You don't need to be a sturdy hiker to get away from the car. Here you can easily bike (with or without a bike trailer) to quiet woodland ponds. Anyone who enjoys a boat ride or a shore ramble can have a close encounter with the natural world. You will find plenty to do at Acadia; our family is still well short of doing everything we want to there.

Best Things to Do in Acadia National Park

- **Bike the unpaved carriage roads** that wind through the woods of Mount Desert Island, around placid ponds, and over arching bridges of cut stone.
- **Canoe the lakes.**
- **Learn to sea-kayak** in Frenchman Bay.
- **Go sailing** in lovely Great Harbor and Somes Sound.
- **Explore tide pools,** the rocky shores where the tide leaves behind pools of water full of strange little animals.
- **Take a lobster boat** to see wildlife and a tiny, historic island.
- **Hike to the top of Cadillac Mountain,** pick blueberries along the way, and buy a lemonade at the top.

For more information, see "For the Active Family" (p. 66).

Acadia Address Book

Acadia National Park P.O. Box 177, Eagle Lake Road, Bar Harbor, ME 04609-0177. Ⓒ **207/288-3338** and TDD 207/288-3338. www.nps.gov/acad. For some park ranger programs (see "Kid-Friendly Programs," on p. 70), you need to sign up as much as a week beforehand. Check the website or call ahead for a printed schedule.

Eastern National 470 Maryland Dr., Suite 2, Ft. Washington, PA 19034. Ⓒ **877/NAT-PARK**. Fax 215/591-0903. www.eparks.com. For books and maps.

Bar Harbor Chamber of Commerce P.O. Box 158, 1201 Bar Harbor Rd., Trenton, ME, 04605. Ⓒ **888/540-9990** or 207/288-5103. www.barharbor maine.com.

Mount Desert Chamber of Commerce P.O. Box 675, Northeast Harbor, ME 04662. Ⓒ **207/276-5040**. www.mountdesertchamber.org. Northeast Mount Desert and Somes Sound.

Southwest Harbor/Tremont Chamber of Commerce P.O. Box 1143, 204 Main St., Southwest Harbor, ME 04679. Ⓒ **800/423-9264** or 207/244-9264. www.acadiachamber.com.

Other useful websites for planning a Maine vacation: www.mainetourism. com and www.downeastguide.com.

1 History: Putting a Park Together

The map of Acadia National Park shows a patchwork of parkland stitched across Mount Desert Island, with lots of holes in between. It looks that way, and the park feels so civilized, because of the island's unique history as a resort for fabulously wealthy families who lived a life of luxury here. Those visitors were even rich enough to buy a national park: Acadia was put together from gifts of land they bought and then donated to the government.

High society first found out about Mount Desert Island in the 1840s and 1850s, when artists such as Thomas Cole returned to New York with paintings of glorious rustic scenes. Curious visitors began coming from the large cities of the East Coast, and big hotels were built to take care of them. Steamships carried the tourists north in comfort. As time passed, wealthy summer visitors bought the land that made up the island's pretty views and began building houses like palaces, which they called "cottages." By 1880, the island was becoming the fashionable place to be for the richest of the rich, including the Rockefellers, Morgans, Vanderbilts, Fords, and Carnegies. Their cottages had dozens of rooms—one had 80—and armies of servants tended to their whims. These people didn't come just for nature walks. They were more interested in tennis, teas, golf, horse races, society balls, and private clubs.

In 1901, some of the island's major owners and summer people started thinking about protecting its natural beauty permanently. They feared that private owners might eventually cut down the trees for wood, spoiling the views. George Dorr of Boston became the project's main supporter. He dedicated much of his life to buying up Mount Desert Island and creating the park. He worked so hard on it that he didn't

The Maine Coast

attend to his own textile business and lost the fortune he had inherited. A richer man, John D. Rockefeller, Jr., probably contributed the most money. After coming to the island for the first time in 1900 and summering near Seal Harbor, Rockefeller began buying large parcels of land. He eventually donated one-third of today's park area. (He also helped start Grand Teton [p. 310], and Great Smoky Mountains [p. 135] national parks, and others.)

Rockefeller built Acadia's carriage roads. Horseback riding and horse-drawn carriages were an important part of the royal lifestyle the wealthy summer people enjoyed. Even after cars became popular, the summer residents persuaded the Maine legislature to outlaw them on the island. The year-round residents didn't like that and finally won the right to drive in 1915. Rockefeller responded by building his own carriage roads where he could ride horseback without cars to bother him. These lovely forest ways, with granite walls and bridges, snake among the valleys, ponds, and hills. By agreement with Dorr, who ran the new national park he had helped create, Rockefeller built carriage roads over the public lands, too. He paid for and helped design the Park Loop Road and the road to the top of Cadillac Mountain. By the time he died in 1960, Rockefeller had built and maintained 57 miles of carriage roads with 16 beautiful granite bridges all over the eastern side of the island.

For Rockefeller, these special roads were a gift to the public, and building them was an interesting hobby. But many wealthy summer people opposed them because they didn't want to share the island with new visitors who weren't like them. As the years passed, the kind of people who came to the island did change. The outrageously rich lifestyle of Mount Desert's golden age ended during the Great Depression of the 1930s, with higher taxes on the rich, a sour economy, and new ways of looking at how people should relate to each other. The rich couldn't just do whatever they wanted anymore. A huge fire in 1947 wiped out many of the great houses and estates, so today you can't see how the island looked then. But the Rockefeller family stayed, and they still have their property near Seal Harbor, where their private carriage roads are open to walkers and horseback riders, but not bicyclists. The ordinary people that their very rich neighbors didn't want on the island *do* visit Acadia and enjoy the carriage roads by the millions.

2 Orientation

Acadia National Park takes up much of Maine's **Mount Desert Island** (called MDI by locals), a little point to the east called the **Schoodic Peninsula,** and a smaller island to the southwest called **Isle au Haut.** Most of the park and the things to do are on MDI.

Somes Sound, a lovely 7-mile-long fiord, divides the island in two. The best of the park is on the eastern, Bar Harbor side, including the carriage roads, most of the publicly owned shoreline, the botanical gardens, and Cadillac Mountain. Less of the western side belongs to the park, but there are many pretty and less-visited spots, plus a swimming lake and some relatively unspoiled towns.

ARRIVING
BY CAR & RV

The fastest way to drive to Acadia is up Interstate 95 to Bangor, then southeast on Route 1A to Ellsworth and Route 3 into the park. This typically dull but speedy drive takes about 5 hours from Boston.

The other way to go is slow and potentially frustrating, but it's scenic and full of places to stop along the Maine coast. It turns the drive from Boston into a 1- or 2-day affair. Divert from I-95 at Brunswick (exit 22) or later, and take mostly two-lane Route 1 through a series of cute, tourist-choked towns on the sea.

If you take an RV to Acadia, also take a car to get around in. RVs don't belong on these narrow, congested roads, and parking is difficult.

BY PLANE

The Hancock County Airport in Trenton, on Route 3 just off the island, is served from Boston by US Airways via **Colgan Air** (© **800/428-4322** or 207/667-7171; www.colganair.com). Airline rates go up and down like a yo-yo. When last checked, a round-trip ticket cost around $630. **Hertz** (© **800/654-3131** or 207/667-5017; www.hertz.com) and **Enterprise** (© **800/736-8222;** www.enterprise.com) rent cars there.

If you want to save money and don't mind driving a bit farther, have your travel agent shop around for the best car-rental and ticket deals at different cities. **Portland,** a 3-hour drive away, and **Bangor,** a 1-hour drive away, receive the most flights in Maine; Portland has the most car-rental agencies. Or fly to Boston for the greatest number of choices—and possibly the greatest savings—and drive 5 hours.

BY BOAT

The Cat, a futuristic, high-speed car ferry, runs daily between Bar Harbor and Yarmouth, Nova Scotia, mid-May through mid-October. Traveling over the water at 55 mph, the 300-foot catamaran makes the trip in under 3 hours, saving a 630-mile drive. One-way fares are $105 to $152 for large cars, $63 for adults, $58 for seniors, $43 for children, and free for those under 6. One-day round-trip excursion fares are about the same as one-way passenger fares. Reserve at ℭ **877/359-3760** or 207/288-3395, or online at www.catferry.com. (As gas prices fluctuate, so will these. Call for the most up-to-date information.)

VISITOR INFORMATION
NATIONAL PARK VISITOR CENTERS

Each of the visitor centers is seasonal. If you come in winter, stop at the park head-quarters on Route 233 west of Bar Harbor.

Hulls Cove Visitor Center   The main Park Service visitor center is atop a hill at Hulls Cove, off Route 3 north of Bar Harbor. It's a good idea to stop here when you arrive to pick up maps and sign up for ranger programs. Fifty-two granite steps lead up from the parking lot. The center itself is small, but rangers are on staff to answer questions and facilitate program sign-up. Also on-site: a small bookstore, a large relief map of the park, and an auditorium where a 15-minute film on the park shows every half-hour.

Rte. 3 north of Bar Harbor. ℭ **207/288-3338.** July–Aug daily 8am–6pm; mid-Apr to June and Oct daily 8am–4:30pm; Sept daily 8am–5pm. Closed Nov to mid-Apr.

Thompson Island Visitors Center   The Park Service and the island's chamber of commerce run this small information center. Located in the middle of Thompson Island as you cross the bridge from the mainland to MDI, the center offers information on lodging and activities, as well as the park.

Rte. 3, on the bridge to Mount Desert Island. ℭ **207/288-3411.** Mid-May to mid-Oct hours vary. Closed mid-Oct to mid-May.

COMMERCIAL VISITOR CENTERS

Each town has its own printed visitor guide, and three have walk-in centers where you can ask questions and get referrals.

Bar Harbor: Bar Harbor Chamber of Commerce, 1201 Bar Harbor Rd., Tremonton. This facility, on the right side of Route 3 approaching the island, also houses the Acadia Information Center.

Southwest Harbor: Southwest Harbor/Tremont Chamber of Commerce, 204 Main St., Southwest Harbor.

Northeast Harbor: Mount Desert Chamber of Commerce, Sea Street at the marina, Northeast Harbor. Open seasonally.

Acadia Information Center   This commercially operated center offers information on its many clients and maintains an updated lodging vacancy board and an extensive website.

Located in Trenton on the right side of Rte. 3 approaching the island. ℭ **800/358-8550** or 207/667-8550. www.acadiainfo.com. Early May to mid-Oct daily 9am–6pm. Closed Nov–May 1.

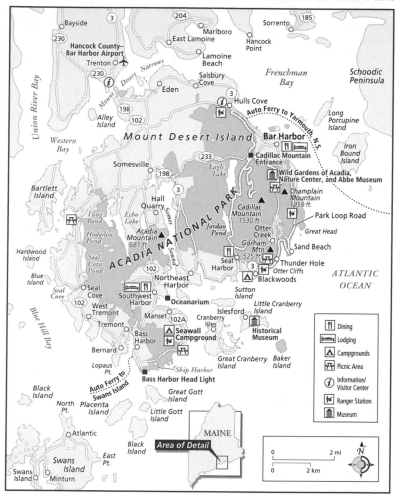

Acadia National Park

READING UP

Each of these books is available from **Eastern National,** listed at the beginning of the chapter, or at the **Hulls Cove Visitor Center.** Down East Books (© **800/685-7962;** www.downeastbooks.com) publishes the handy "Pocket Guide" series of little biking, hiking, and carriage-road books.

Biking: A Pocket Guide to *Biking on Mount Desert Island,* by Audrey Shelton Minutolo (Down East, $8), has maps and descriptions of carriage path tours rated by time, distance, and difficulty, as well as clear directions.

Hiking: A Pocket Guide to *Hiking on Mount Desert Island,* by Earl Brechlin (Down East, $8), is a straightforward trail guide with the right amount of detail to get you where you're going; buy a good map separately.

Maps: National Geographic's Trails Illustrated (www.trailsillustrated.com) publishes the best map of the whole island; it has an amazing level of detail and is printed on plastic ($10).

THE NATIONAL PARK IN BRIEF

Bar Harbor

The largest town on the island is **Bar Harbor,** an attractive and historic seaside community that's been overrun by tourists. It's a center for activities, but it can be crowded and congested; we prefer the other, still-quiet towns and villages.

Other Villages

Their names, in clockwise order around the island from Bar Harbor, are Seal Harbor, Northeast Harbor, Southwest Harbor (the largest after Bar Harbor), Bass Harbor, and Tremont. The villages of Northeast Harbor and Seal Harbor are in the town of Mount Desert.

The Roads

Unless you're on a boat, you'll approach Acadia along **Route 3.** The road leads from the town of Ellsworth (a good place to stop at a large grocery store) south through a gantlet of water parks and minigolf courses, past the airport, and across the bridge to MDI. From the bridge, **Route 102** leads straight to the western part of the island and the town of Southwest Harbor; Route 3 leads 8 miles to the main visitor center at Hulls Cove (see above), another 3 miles to Bar Harbor, and beyond that to the rest of the east side of the island.

Park Loop Road

From the visitor center or Bar Harbor, you can join the **Park Loop Road,** which circles many of the scenic points on the eastern shore of the island and passes through a fee station (the only time you're asked to pay the park fee except at the campgrounds).

3 Getting Around

BY CAR OR RV

Although the distances aren't great, traffic is slow on these scenic, winding roads. Plan your days to spend as much time as you can in one area. Parking in Bar Harbor can be tough; try at Main and Park streets, near the big park. Trail-head parking is a problem, too; if you don't get there early, you might not be able to use the trail. RV sites with hookups are available at some commercial campgrounds, but if you bring an RV, plan to leave it in the campground and use a passenger car or the shuttle to get around, because the narrow, congested roads are not suitable for big vehicles.

BY SHUTTLE BUS

The free **Island Explorer shuttle** (© 207/667-5796; www.exploreacadia.com; summer only) runs eight routes all over the island and to the airport late June through Labor Day, and less frequently through mid-October. By using it, you avoid parking problems in Bar Harbor and at trail heads. The shuttle also allows one-way hikes on some of the park's trails and has bike racks. Service covers all the park campgrounds and attractions and most commercial campgrounds, with all lines connecting at Bar Harbor's Village Green. Service is frequent near Bar Harbor, but becomes impractically far apart as you get farther afield. A shuttle schedule is published in the park newspaper and available at hotels, campgrounds, and visitor centers. Electronic signs at shuttle stops let you know when the next bus is due to arrive.

BY BOAT

Mail and tour boats take passengers to park sites in the Cranberry Islands. See "Boating" (p. 67) for details.

4 Planning Your Outings

WHEN TO GO

July and August are the most popular months to go to Acadia, during the summer break from school but after the worst of the bug season. Temperatures tend to be comfortable, with average highs in the mid-70s (mid-20s Celsius); days in the 90s (30s Celsius) are rare. Rain comes in the form of thunderstorms or longer episodes of drizzle, and you're likely to get wet at least once in any 3-day stay. The popular carriage roads and the streets of Bar Harbor fill with people, hotels and excursions charge their highest rates, and traffic is at its worst during these months. If possible, avoid arriving on a weekend, especially the Independence Day and Labor Day weekends, which are the park's busiest times.

June is a calmer month, when many hotels advertise lower prices and crowds are tolerable. June weather is slightly cooler than later in the summer, and mosquitoes and black flies are more plentiful. To avoid crowds and pay even less, go in May or September, when average temperatures are 10° cooler than in July and rates drop to bargain levels. Bugs are worse in May, less of a problem in September.

In winter Bar Harbor shuts down and visitors are few. Snow is unpredictable; the winter of 2004–05 was very snowy and the cross-country skiing on the carriage roads fantastic, but it's hard to predict that weather. Spring break isn't a good option, either.

HOW MUCH TIME TO SPEND

It takes time to get to Acadia from most places—too long to justify less than 3 or 4 days. A week is best. There's plenty to do, and staying a week gives you access to weekly rentals.

Don't underestimate the time it takes to get around Acadia. Although the distances on the island are small, the traffic is slow and the roads are winding. They were built for sightseeing, not for getting anywhere quickly. Plan your time carefully so that you spend the whole day in one general area and drive across the island only once a day.

HOW FAR TO PLAN AHEAD

To get the dates and places you want, make hotel reservations for anywhere on the island by April for a July or August visit. June is easier to book. Cottages should be booked by early winter for the following summer. The **Blackwoods campground** requires reservations in advance through the national system (see "The National Recreation Reservation Service," in chapter 2). The **Seawall Campground** is first-come, first-served, but it's hard to get a site during busy months. Several excellent private campgrounds mentioned below take reservations.

Commercial activities such as whale-watching, carriage rides, and sea kayaking usually have openings on the same day, but call ahead to make sure. There are plenty of bikes to rent, but it's a good idea to reserve special equipment such as trailers or tandems a day in advance.

Weather Chart: Bar Harbor

	Avg. High (°F/°C)	Avg. Low (°F/°C)	Precipitation (in.)	Ocean Temp. (°F/°C)
December–February	34/1	17/–8	19.7	39/4
March	41/5	25/–4	4	38/3
April	53/12	34/1	4.2	43/6
May	64/18	43/6	3.8	50/10
June	72/22	51/11	3.2	55/13
July	78/26	57/14	3	59/15
August	76/24	56/13	2.7	62/17
September	68/20	50/10	4.3	58/14
October	58/14	41/5	4.6	54/12
November	47/8	32/0	5.9	52/11

WHAT TO PACK
CLOTHING

You'll want to bring clothes for warm, cool, and rainy weather. You should do some boating while at Acadia; out on the water, you'll probably need sweaters and jackets, and even hats and gloves. Evenings on land can be cool, too, and rain and fog come often. Bring breathable rain gear so that you can get out in the woods during drizzle or light rain, and heavy, waterproof gear if you plan on serious boating. Bring a swimsuit for the lakes and pools. Good walking shoes will suffice for the island's well-tended trails. When you're exploring the tide pools and shoreline, tall rubber boots increase your freedom.

GEAR

Bring insect repellent for flying insects and to keep off ticks that might transmit Lyme disease. Campers should bring good, waterproof gear, including a tarp or other roof for the picnic table. Summer nighttime lows are in the 40s and 50s (single digits to mid-teens Celsius).

Tip: If you're driving all the way from home, bring your bicycles and helmets. Fat-tired bikes are best for the unpaved carriage roads, but any touring bike will make it, because the surface is smooth and packed.

KEEPING SAFE & HEALTHY

See "Dealing with Hazards," in chapter 2, for tips on poison ivy, sunburn, seasickness, and Lyme disease. Here are other things to watch out for at Acadia:

BIKE SAFETY

Keep to the carriage roads with children, carrying bikes from the rental agency to the trail head on your car (you can rent a rack) rather than riding through the streets. These busy roads aren't suitable for children.

FALLS

Tide pooling and exploring on the rocky shorelines can be dangerous because of the steep, slippery rocks. Sometimes you can't tell whether a rock you're about to step on is slimy with algae. Make sure the kids have shoes that are not slippery when wet. Keep your children under control, and don't venture into areas with drop-offs or moving waves.

5 Family-Friendly Accommodations

CAMPGROUNDS

NATIONAL PARK CAMPGROUNDS

Besides camping fees listed here, campers also must pay the park entrance fee (see below). The Park Service allows gathering of dead, downed wood for fires, but you won't find much; pick up a couple of bundles at a roadside shop or grocery store. All campgrounds, except Duck Harbor, which is on Isle Au Haut, are on the Island Explorer bus route.

Blackwoods   This huge campground at the southeast end of the island, near Seal Harbor, doesn't feel so big because the sites are thickly wooded—indeed, little direct sun makes it through the trees. You can quickly walk to the steep, rocky shore of Otter Cove, on the Ocean Loop Drive, or join a long trail up Cadillac Mountain (see "Natural Places: Mount Desert Island," p. 61). Although you're close to several of the park's other best spots, a lack of trails or sidewalks means that with kids you'll have to drive or take the free Island Explorer shuttle. Blackwoods is the only reserved campground at Acadia, and sites go quickly (see "The National Recreation Reservation Service," in chapter 2, for details on the national reservation system).

Rte. 3, Otter Creek (between Bar Harbor and Seal Harbor). (℃ 877/444-6777. 306 sites, tents or RVs. May–Oct $20 site; Nov and Apr $10 site; Dec–Mar free (restrooms closed, chemical toilets only). **Amenities:** Cold-water restrooms (flush toilets, showers nearby), dump station. No hookups.

Seawall   This well-wooded campground is on the southwest end of the island, far from the bustle of Bar Harbor and the carriage roads. Sites are well separated on mossy ground. It's near a cobbled beach and seaside nature trails, and a short drive from sailing at Southwest Harbor and swimming at Echo Lake. Half the sites are walk-in, requiring 100 feet or so of effort.

They don't take reservations, so a line forms early in the morning for sites in July and August. As someone leaves, the first in line can take the site.

Rte. 102A, Manset (south of Southwest Harbor). (℃ 207/244-3600. 214 sites, tents or RVs. $20 drive-in site; $14 walk-in site. Closed Oct to late May. **Amenities:** Cold-water restrooms (flush toilets, no showers), dump station.

COMMERCIAL CAMPGROUNDS

Mount Desert Island has some of the best private campgrounds anywhere.

Bar Harbor Campground   Situated with other campgrounds in the touristy area on Route 3 as you approach Bar Harbor, this place is more of a resort than an ordinary campground. Besides the good-size pool, facilities include basketball, an arcade, shuffleboard, and blueberry picking. Campers choose their own sites, either in an open, grassy area with a great view across Frenchman Bay, or more secluded sites surrounded by trees. A grocery store, restaurants, and other tourist businesses are nearby.

Tips Camping Supplies Maine-Style

Just east of the Seawall campground, **Seawall Camping Supplies** (℃ 207/244-3753) offers showers, laundry, food, supplies, canoes, and other country-store goods—plus lobster! Open Memorial Day through October, with limited hours after Labor Day.

Campgrounds in the Acadia Area

Campground	Total Sites	RV Hookups	Dump Station	Toilets	Drinking Water
Bar Harbor	300	Yes	Yes	Yes	Yes
Blackwoods	306	No	Yes	Yes	Yes
Mount Desert	150	Yes	No	Yes	Yes
Seawall	214	No	Yes	Yes	Yes
Smuggler's Den	100	Yes	Yes	Yes	Yes

409 State Rte. 3, Salisbury Cove (RFD 2, Box 1125), Bar Harbor, ME 04609. ☎ **207/288-5185.** www.thebarharbor campground.com. 304 sites, tents or RVs. $26 tent; $36 full hookup tax included. No credit cards. No reservations. Closed mid-Oct to Memorial Day. **Amenities:** Hot showers, laundry, play area, heated pool, store, ATM.

Mount Desert Campground   This family-operated campground is a favorite. Sites lie among tall trees at the head of glittering Somes Sound, the long fiord that divides MDI, where the restricted tidal flow allows the water to warm to a temperature suitable for hearty swimmers (there's no lifeguard). At the dock, kids catch crabs with a piece of string, and rental canoes wait for exploration of the placid waters. The sites are larger than those at the Park Service campgrounds, and many have wooden platforms to help keep you dry (these and the waterfront sites cost a few dollars more). A real sense of community prevails among many campers who have been coming for years, blossoming in the evening at the Gathering Place, where you can buy ice cream or coffee and visit. On the practical side, the restrooms are clean and comfortable and water is always nearby. The campground is at the center of the island, 5 miles from Bar Harbor, Northwest Harbor, or Southwest Harbor, just west of the intersection of routes 198 and 233.

516 Sound Dr., Somesville, Mount Desert, ME 04660. ☎ **207/244-3710.** www.mountdesertcampground.com. 150 sites, tents or RVs under 20 ft. only. $30–$45 site, up to 2 adults and 2 children. $5 additional adult over 18, $2 additional child under 18. MC, V. Closed mid-Sept to mid-June. **Amenities:** Hot showers, water and electricity at some sites, ocean swimming and fishing, canoe and kayak rentals.

Smuggler's Den Campground   Attractive for RVers, but also great for tenters with kids who need room to run, this campground has lots of amenities, and it's within walking distance of the park's west-side hiking trails and the Echo Lake swimming beach. The campground is in a clearing in the woods just to the south on Route 102, with a huge, 4-acre mowed field for play. RVs camp out in the open, and tents hide back in the trees along the edge of the field. Hot showers are included in your fee. The swimming pool has a small slide and a shallow area for toddlers. A camp store sells the basics. Camp cabins rent for about $500 a week in July and August.

Rte. 102 (P.O. Box 787), Southwest Harbor, ME 04679. ☎ **877/244-9033.** www.smugglersdencampground.com. 100 sites, tents or RVs. $28–$32 tent; $39–$49 full hookup for 4 people. $7 per additional person over age 12. MC, V. Closed mid-Oct to Memorial Day. **Amenities:** Hot showers, laundry, playground, heated pool, store.

Showers	Fire Pits/Grills	Laundry	Public Phones	Reservations	Fees	Open
Yes	Yes	Yes	Yes	No	$26–$36	Memorial Day to mid-Oct
No	Yes	No	No	Yes	$20	Year-round
Yes	Yes	No	Yes	Yes	$30–$45	mid-June to mid-Sept
No	Yes	No	No	No	$14–$20	mid-May to Oct
Yes	Yes	Yes	Yes	Yes	$28–$49	Memorial Day to mid-Oct

HOTELS, MOTELS & INNS

If you don't want to camp or spend a whole week in a cottage rental, you can stay in a hotel in Bar Harbor or one of the other towns. Expect to pay $130 a night or more for your room in July and August. Rates may be lower in June and are much lower in May and September. Most hotels are in and around Bar Harbor, where crowds and traffic take something away from the national park experience. I've also listed one in quiet Northeast Harbor.

The Acadia Hotel   This is a rare property: a historic inn that accepts children. It has three rooms large enough to accommodate a family (lower rates than those listed here apply for other rooms), and an apartment with cooking facilities. The classic New England house, with a wraparound porch, faces the town-square park in Bar Harbor. Inside, the 11 rooms carry a light, Victorian theme, appropriate to its period. The proprietor, active in the community, is a great resource for guests. Rooms lack telephones but have TVs and air-conditioning.

20 Mount Desert St., Bar Harbor, ME 04609. ℂ 888/US-MAINE or 207/288-5721. www.acadiahotel.com. 11 units. No rollaway beds or cribs. High season $129–$149 double; low season $59–$79 double. $10 extra person (child or adult). MC, V. *In room:* A/C, TV, some whirlpool baths.

Bar Harbor Regency Holiday Inn   This luxurious resort of stone-faced buildings on the water near Bar Harbor could tempt you to stay on the well-tended grounds or in your large, quiet room rather than visiting the park. The diversions include an attractive, heated outdoor pool with a toddler pool and hot tub, tennis courts, a sauna and fitness room, and several choices for dining, including the elegant Edenfield, with water views. Rooms, decorated in a Colonial style, have high-end amenities, including refrigerators and big TVs.

123 Eden St., Bar Harbor, ME 04609. ℂ 800/23-HOTEL or 207/288-9723. Fax 207/288-3089. www.barharborregency. com. 221 units. High season $152–$279; low season $99–$179. Airbed $20, Pack 'n Play cribs. AE, MC, V. Closed Nov–Apr. **Amenities:** 2 restaurants; poolside bar; outdoor pool; putting green; tennis courts; fitness room; Jacuzzi; sauna; courtesy car (in season only); self-service laundry; boat hookups. *In room:* A/C, TV, fridge, coffeemaker, hair dryer.

Harborside Hotel & Marina   This is a good family choice, if it fits your budget. Fronting Frenchman's Bay, the hotel has a seaside feel, with a large swimming pool and

---

⌒Tips Park Camping Basics: Toilets, Showers & Laundry

Park Service campgrounds have rudimentary restrooms; the visitor center adds the innovation of hot water. Otherwise, count on restaurants and the kindness of strangers. There are commercially operated public showers across Route 3 from Blackwoods campground and at Seawall Camping Supplies (℃ **207/244-3753**), near Seawall Campground. Coin-op laundry facilities are in Bar Harbor at Bar Harbor Laundry (38 Holland Ave.; ℃ **207/288-9064**), in Northeast Harbor below Pine Street Market on Main Street, and in Southwest Harbor on Main Street.

---

hot tub on the shoreline, yet it's also right in the middle of Bar Harbor, on the main waterfront street where some of the whale-watching boats dock. There's a marina just outside, a restaurant, La Bella Vita, that opened in 2007 and a spa that opened in 2006. Regular hotel-style rooms here are light in decor, but the real attraction is the assortment of studio and two- and three-bedroom suites with luxurious bathrooms and big televisions that are gradually replacing the older rooms. The more expensive units have combinations of balconies, fireplaces, Jacuzzis, and water views. Two three-bedroom suites have full kitchens and dining rooms. Some have pullout beds, too.

55 West St., Bar Harbor, ME 04609. ℃ **800/328-5033** or 207/288-5033. www.theharborsidehotel.com. 187 units. $289–$409 double; $1,200–$1,800 suite. Airbed $20, Pack 'n Play cribs free. AE, MC, V. Closed Nov–Apr. **Amenities:** Restaurant; heated outdoor pool; fitness room; self-service laundry; marina. *In room:* A/C, TV, minifridge, coffeemaker, hair dryer, iron/ironing board; Jacuzzi, fireplace, and full kitchen (suites).

Kimball Terrace Inn   Northeast Harbor retains a lot of the charm Bar Harbor has lost to crowds and traffic congestion, and this comfortable motel overlooking a lawn that slopes down to the harbor is an easy place to enjoy it. The rooms, in three levels with exterior entrances, are large and well kept. Private balconies on the upper levels have a fine view, while the ground-floor patios open onto the lawn, with its good-size pool and tennis courts. A lobby sitting room is stocked with games, there is a quiet restaurant, and a short trail leads to Main Street.

10 Huntington Rd. (P.O. Box 1030), Northeast Harbor, ME 04662. ℃ **800/454-6225** (reservations), or 207/276-3383. Fax 207/276-4102. www.kimballterraceinn.com. 70 units. High season $167–$187 double; low season $68–$77 double. Extra person over age 5 $10, 5 and under free in parent's room. Rollaway bed $10. Cribs $5. AE, DISC, MC, V. Closed late Oct to May. **Amenities:** Restaurant; outdoor pool; tennis courts (across from Inn); game lounge; marina nearby. *In room:* A/C, TV, hair dryer; iron/ironing board, fridge for $10 per day.

The Villager   This is a friendly, basic motel with reasonable prices (for Bar Harbor) and ample parking right in town on a strip of good restaurants. The rooms, opening on the parking lot or an upstairs walkway, are nondescript in a style you might call 1970s motel anonymous. Yet they're comfortable, with two double beds and room for a crib, and there is a heated swimming pool by the parking lot.

207 Main St., Bar Harbor, ME 04609. ℃ **888/383-3211** or 207/288-3211. Fax 207/288-2270. www.barharbor villager.com. 63 units. High season $89–$138 double; low season $69–$98 double. $10 extra person, children under 5 stay free in parent's room. Rollaway bed or crib $20. AE, MC, V. Closed Nov to mid-May. **Amenities:** Heated outdoor pool; free local transportation (in season only). *In room:* A/C, TV, Wi-Fi.

COTTAGES

If you're planning to stay for at least a week, renting a cottage makes more sense than staying in a hotel. Besides getting a place more like home, where you can relax and don't have to worry so much about making noise, you'll be able to cook for yourself, saving a lot on restaurant dining and avoiding the tension of eating every meal out. That said, take caution in selecting a cottage, as some are no bigger than a postage stamp.

Summer rentals go from Saturday to Saturday. Most of the attractive houses run $1,700 and more a week, but you can get into a two-bedroom house for around $1,300 during high season. During the low shoulder seasons prices drop by about a third. Prices depend on size and location—rentals closer to the beach or in more fashionable neighborhoods cost more. Repeat visitors book a year ahead, often as they're checking out, and to have a full range of choices, you should book by early winter for July and August. You will have to send a deposit—typically a third of the total rental—but agents here aren't as tough about requiring references as those at some other summer house areas. You will not be able to use a credit card for a house rental. Most houses provide linens and utensils, but check ahead for particulars on what to bring. Make sure to inventory any damage when you move in and when you leave to avoid unwarranted charges.

Below are a few of the agents on the island; you can contact others through the chambers of commerce (see "Acadia Address Book," on p. 47). The Internet helps in finding a cottage; you can browse by area and price, and view pictures of each property.

Acadia Cottage Rentals These friendly folks have cottages all over the island and in towns along the coast.

77 Mount Desert St. (P.O. Box 949), Bar Harbor, ME 04609. ✆ **866/288-3636** or 207/288-3636. Fax 207/288-5855. www.acadiarental.com.

The Davis Agency This agency specializes in the Southwest Harbor area but has properties all over the region.

363 Main St. (P.O. Box 1038), Southwest Harbor, ME 04679. ✆ **207/244-3891**. Fax 207/244-9454. www.daagy.com.

Mount Desert Properties This agency has properties all over the island, including some that are near one another for reunions or groups of families.

P.O. Box 536, Bar Harbor, ME 04609. ✆ **207/288-4523**. www.barharborvacationhome.com.

6 Family-Friendly Dining
LOW-STRESS MEALS

There are no fast-food franchises on MDI, but you can get quick, familiar food in each town.

BAR HARBOR

A popular neighborhood pizza place, with the menu on the wall, is on Cottage Street, near the intersection with Main. **Epi's Subs and Pizza,** 8 Cottage St. (✆ **207/288-5853**), charges under $5 for a sub, around $13 for a large pizza. It's open daily in summer 10am to 10pm, winter Monday through Saturday 10am to 7pm.

Cottage Street Bakery and Deli, 59 Cottage St. (✆ **207/288-3010**), serves omelets, blueberry pancakes, popovers, bakery items, sandwiches, burgers, salads, and good coffee indoors and on an outdoor patio covered by a red-and-white awning. There's a fun children's menu, and box lunches are available. Open every day from 6:30am to 10pm. Closed mid-November to mid-May.

NORTHEAST HARBOR

The **Docksider Restaurant,** in a rough-hewn building on the way down to the harbor at 14 Sea St. (© 207/276-3965), serves a broad and inexpensive choice of seafood, sandwiches, and desserts (PB&J $2.50, lobster rolls $18). Eat in a small dining room hung with fishing nets or outside, or order takeout. It's very casual; in fact, service can be scattered. The restaurant serves lunch and dinner from 11am to 9pm. Closed mid-October to mid-May.

For pizza, try the **Colonel's Deli** (© 207/276-5147), an airy deli and bakery with indoor or outdoor tables and takeout, down a walkway from Main Street. It's open daily in summer from 6am to 9pm.

SOUTHWEST HARBOR

Beal's Lobster Pier (© 207/244-3202 or 207/244-7178), on a dock at the end of Clark Point Road, is a classic Maine lobster pound, where your lobster, clams, and corn on the cob are served on wooden picnic tables with a harbor view. While waiting for your meal you can watch lobster boats unload their catches. It's open 9am to 8pm daily in summer.

BEST-BEHAVIOR MEALS

Each of the following establishments accepts credit cards.

IN THE PARK

Jordan Pond House *(Moments* A meal here is a part of the Acadia experience. The historic 1870s restaurant, rebuilt as a huge brick-and-cedar structure after the original burned down in 1979, is a traditional stop on a park tour, and the experience remains pleasing and relaxingly genteel—after you get past the crowds. During the high season, make reservations for any meal or expect to wait up to an hour. Parking can also be a problem. You can dine in partly or fully enclosed dining rooms, or sit out on the lawn by the pond. The traditional afternoon tea and popovers is $8.75 to $10 per person, depending on whether you have tea, coffee, cappuccino, or chai.

On the Park Loop Rd. at Jordan Pond. © 207/276-3316. www.jordanpond.com. Kids' menu, highchairs, booster seats, crayons. Lunch $11–$20; dinner $16–$24; kids' menu around $5. AE, DISC, MC, V. Mid-May to late Oct daily 11:30am–8pm.

BAR HARBOR

Mama DiMatteo's This is a favorite of people in Bar Harbor, who make it one of only a few restaurants popular enough to stay open year-round. First comes the attitude: The staff makes diners feel like honored guests at a celebration. The dining room is small, and high-backed booths keep your kids from bothering anyone else. The house specialty is Tuscan tenderloin, a hand-cut filet rubbed with garlic, rosemary, sage, and pepper and served with a Gorgonzola butter. The menu changes frequently, allowing the chefs to push their creativity. The result is entrees such as salmon and asparagus wrapped with prosciutto, lobster ravioli, crab- and spinach-stuffed shells, and a wide range of inventive pasta dishes. The children's selections are also very good.

34 Kennebec Place, Bar Harbor. © 207/288-3666. www.mamadimatteos.com. Kids' menu, highchairs, booster seats, crayons. Dinner $7–$23; kids' menu $7. Summer daily 5–10pm; winter daily 5–9pm.

Poor Boy's Gourmet Poor Boy's is just plain fun. Voices ring off the plank floors of the various rooms and porches of a big white frame house, the light and jollity spilling into Main Street. Servers pop in and out of doors, zooming around with big plates of pasta, lobster in one of 10 ways, or one of the 14 nightly desserts, baked in-house. Stop in before 6pm and you can benefit from the "early bird specials." Coming in at just $8.95 per entree, this menu offers just about everything that's on the regular menu, except for lobster and beef. All that said, the food was good but not memorable, the service rather ad hoc.

300 Main St., Bar Harbor. ℂ 207/288-4148. www.poorboysgourmet.com. Kids' menu, highchairs, booster seats. Dinner $9–$23; kids' menu $6. Daily 4:30–10pm. Closed Nov–Apr.

Rupunini   Rupunini, a trendy bar and grill on a busy corner, allows parents to order from a long list of microbrews, wines, and other adult beverages as well as a varied menu while their kids color, order from a good children's menu, and sit in indestructible outdoor iron furniture or well-contained inside booths. You don't have to worry about being too noisy in this pub atmosphere. Not only is the menu expansive and creative, but I particularly like the owners' efforts to seek local, organic sources for their menus.

119 Main St., Bar Harbor. ℂ 207/288-2886. www.rupinini.com. Kids' menu, highchairs, booster seats, crayons. Lunch $6–$18; dinner $12–$27. Daily 11am–1am.

7 Exploring Acadia National Park with Your Kids

ENTRANCE FEES   Acadia charges entrance fees at a station on the **Park Loop Road,** ½ mile from Sand Beach, at the two park campgrounds, and at the visitor center. Vehicles are $20 for 7 days during the high season, $10 during the off season. You can pay the fee at the Thompson Island Information Center, the Hulls Cove Visitor Center, park headquarters, the Blackwoods and Seawall campgrounds, and the Bar Harbor Village Green. The fee supports park improvements and the free shuttle bus system. You can also use the America the Beautiful Pass to gain entry. For details, see chapter 2.

NATURAL PLACES: MOUNT DESERT ISLAND
CADILLAC MOUNTAIN 𝕽𝕽𝕽

A bald granite peak on the east side of MDI, Cadillac Mountain is the tallest mountain on the eastern shore of North and Central America. It's 1,530 feet tall—not much of a mountain compared to most places, but glaciers and weather have worn down this old coast for so long that Cadillac Mountain is the highest thing left, so from the top you can see a long way. It's said to be the first place the sun rises in the United States. The name came from a French aristocrat who tried to colonize the area in 1688, later founded Detroit, and even later got a car named for him. (See p. 62 to learn about the forces that shaped Cadillac Mountain.)

You can drive to the top of the mountain, where there's a small store, but consider hiking instead (you can always do it one-way—down—with the kids). The trails across the barren granite have fantastic views of the island-studded Gulf of Maine and are fun places to hike as you pick your way from one rock cairn to the next and step over small ledges. These open areas are good for birding, too.

Trails climb the mountain from all directions. The **West Face Trail,** from Bubble Pond, is the shortest, at 1.4 miles, and the steepest (you can get to the trail head on the loop road or the carriage roads). The easiest is the **North Ridge Trail,** paralleling the road 2.2 miles from just outside Bar Harbor. The **Cadillac South Ridge Trail** is one of Acadia's longer hikes and our favorite, leading 4.2 miles from the Blackwoods campground gradually up the mountain (you can save .7 mile by starting from Rte. 3).

Fun Fact Acadia's Ice Age

Instead of saying **"ice age,"** scientists now use the words **"glacial period,"** because they understand that the coming of glacier ice to cover much of the planet is a regular cycle, not a one-time event. Our current 10,000-year period of relatively good weather is an **interglacial period**. Based on the movement of the earth in space, the shortest glacial cycle lasts 21,000 years, so we're about halfway to the next glacial period. When that period comes, colder temperatures and increased snow could bring glaciers back across North America.

The granite mountains of **Acadia National Park** were once taller and connected to each other, before glaciers a mile thick piled up behind and plowed over them. Signs of this grinding collision show up all over the landscape. The bald granite mountaintops were cut from bedrock, which has not gathered enough soil since then to fully cover the peaks with trees and plants. The mile-thick ice layer pushing across the rock also explains the mountains' rounded shape. On top of **Cadillac Mountain,** where you can drive or hike, you can see the scratch marks that the glacier left on the rock. A huge boulder brought from about 20 miles north sits where a glacier left it upon melting (such a boulder is called a "glacial erratic"). Between places like Cadillac Mountain, with the hardest rock, the glaciers carved out channels of softer rock where they could flow through more easily. These became the valleys that now hold **Eagle Lake, Jordan Pond, Echo Lake,** and **Long Pond**—notice on the Acadia map (p. 51) how all of these point north and south, the direction the glacier flowed. The largest of the valleys that the glacier gouged became **Somes Sound,** the long, narrow bay that splits Mount Desert Island in half. It's the only true fiord, or glacier-carved bay, on the East Coast of the United States.

The rock that the glaciers ground away from Mount Desert Island ended up far to the south, at the southern end of the glacier. That pile of rock now is known as the **Georges Banks.** The world's sea level was about 400 feet lower back when the glaciers were here, because so much water was frozen in glacier ice. Today the Georges Banks are an underwater shoal and fishing grounds.

ALONG THE PARK LOOP ROAD

The shoreline from Sand Beach around the southeast corner of the island to Seal Harbor is scenic and full of interesting places to stop. Traffic goes one-way, and you have to pay at the fee station. At **Sand Beach** you can join trails that climb .5 mile up to rocky **Great Head,** or walk along the fairly level **Ocean Trail** that leads 1.8 miles to Otter Point, getting a closer look at the dramatic coast than is possible from the parallel road. **Thunder Hole,** where waves boom into a cave, is along the way, as are the impressive **Otter Cliffs.**

Caution: Older children and teens who like challenges will get a thrill hiking to the top of the Beehive. Though less than a mile, round-trip, this trek requires some scrambling, with great exposure, along iron rungs driven into the granite.

THE PONDS

Like the claws of a great animal scratching across Mount Desert Island's granite back, ancient glaciers left deep north-south gouges in the stone. Filled with water, they are the park's intricate ponds and **Somes Sound fiord** (it's like the ponds, but open to the sea). Some of these ponds hide in the mountain clefts, accessible only by carriage roads or footpaths—**Bubble Pond, Aunt Betty Pond, Witch Hole Pond.** Gracious carriage roads encircle **Eagle Lake** and **Jordan Pond,** finding glittering views under a canopy of broad shade trees. At Jordan Pond's grassy southern lawn, the famous teahouse serves popovers and visitors lazily examine a numbered nature trail (see "Family-Friendly Dining," p. 59). On the western side of the island, **Long Pond** branches in complexity, inviting exploration by canoe, and **Echo Pond** sounds with the voices of swimmers (see "For the Active Family," on p. 66). These are places of childhood adventure!

FRENCHMAN BAY & GREAT HARBOR

The water off Bar Harbor, with its many small islands, is **Frenchman Bay,** a rich ground for watching seals, osprey, and other wildlife. It is busy with sea-kayaking excursions, fishing, and wildlife-watching boat trips (see "For the Active Family," on p. 66). You can even walk to one of the alluring little islands. For 90 minutes on each side of low tide, the sandbar path to wooded **Bar Island** is exposed, starting at Bridge Street, off West Street. Just be sure you don't misjudge the tides and find yourself stranded.

Great Harbor, site of the Cranberry Isles, lies south and east of Mount Desert Island, faced by Southwest Harbor and Northeast Harbor. It is a lovely area where small passenger ferries bound for the islands pass seals, birds, and quaint marine scenery (see "Boating," p. 67, and "Kid-Friendly Programs," p. 70). These islands are inhabited— you can rent a cottage here for a week—and there's a little park museum in the village of Islesford, on Little Cranberry Island (see "Places for Learning," p. 64). The area is the essence of coastal Maine, bright and windy and full of life.

SEAWALL AREA

This is a peaceful area, off the park's beaten track, where you can get down to the wild seashore and see some classically picturesque Maine scenery. The seawall itself (near the picnic ground across from the campground) is a natural barrier of cobblestones built by the ocean, at one time removed from the beach to pave city streets in the northeastern United States. Just to the west, two flat paths lead over sandy ground about 1.5 miles round-trip to a rocky shore, great for exploring and seeing birds; they're both fun, easy kid hikes. The **Wonderland Trail** ends at an exposed point with plenty of room to spread out; a little to the west, the **Ship Harbor Nature Trail** traces the edge of the tiny harbor in a loop, with interpretive signs on the way.

Less than a mile farther west, a lighthouse stands on Bass Harbor Head, with steps down the rocky point that allow you to get down in front and see the waves come in and to get a good picture of the light. This working Coast Guard station is not open to tours and does not justify a special trip.

NATURAL PLACES: ISLE AU HAUT

Much of the southern half of Isle au Haut some 20 miles southwest of MDI falls under the park's jurisdiction, but few visitors make it here. Its relatively undeveloped lands are a different experience from the main part of the park; this is a place for solitude and contemplation in the woods and on the seashore, without cars or many tramping feet.

To get to Isle au Haut, take the passenger ferry from Stonington (Rte. 172 and Rte. 15 from Ellsworth). On the island you'll find a small village, a ranger station, and a campground with five lean-tos, open mid-May to mid-October. Eighteen miles of trails follow the coast and cross the rounded, wooded hills in the center of the island.

Despite what some Park Service handouts say, you don't need a permit to visit the island unless you are bringing a large group. But you will need reservations for the campground, which is open from mid-May to mid-October. Reservation requests must be postmarked no earlier than April 1 and include a $25 fee; from those postmarked on or after that day, the Park Service picks in order who will get reservations during the whole summer. If your request is not filled, your $25 is refunded. You can obtain the reservation form either by calling ✆ 207/288-3338 or by downloading it from the park's website **www.nps.gov/acad** (click "In Depth," then "Site Map," then "Isle au Haut"). A 3-night maximum stay applies between June 15 and September 15, 5 nights in the shoulder seasons.

NATURAL PLACES: SCHOODIC PENINSULA

About 45 miles east of Bar Harbor by road, but less than 10 miles over the water, this part of the park takes in a rocky mainland point that you can see from Great Head or Otter Point on MDI. Most visitors just go for the 7-mile, one-way loop drive around the point. There are also a picnic area, a ranger station, and a few short trails to the 440-foot summit of Schoodic Head. To get here, take Route 1 east from Ellsworth, then go south on Route 186.

PLACES FOR LEARNING

Museum of Natural History, College of the Atlantic   Children will certainly enjoy an hour or two of a rainy day spent in this superb little museum on the grassy campus of the environmentally inclined college. Students have built wildlife dioramas that capture an entire story in the life of an animal: raccoons getting into garbage, voles emerging from a snowy burrow observed by a hungry hawk, a honey-raiding bear swarmed by bees. An excellent touch tank allows you to explore a living tide pool indoors, learning about the creatures you can hunt for on the shore later. There are activities for children and adults, the museum offers interpretive programs, and a summer field study program leads children to the island's shores, forests, and ponds for ecological education.

105 Eden St. (just north of Bar Harbor on Rte. 3). ✆ 207/288-5395. www.coa.edu/nhm. Admission $3.50 adults, $2.50 seniors, $1.50 teens, $1 children 3–12, free for children under 3. Mon–Sat 10am–5pm; Thanksgiving–Jan 1 by appointment only.

Mount Desert Oceanarium   These two privately owned facilities focus on teaching and entertaining children with facts and demonstrations about the Maine shore and its marine life. The Bar Harbor facility offers a lobster hatchery and museum, and a marsh nature walk. The Southwest Harbor museum is in a well-worn waterfront building, with aquariums, huge lobsters, a boat kids can climb on, a tide-pool touch tank, and demonstrations. It's well done, with hands-on, personal attention. Pricing varies on how much you want to do, as there are three ticketing options: One gets you into just the lobster hatchery and museum, another into those facilities plus the marsh walk, and the third includes all of the above plus entry to the Southwest Harbor site.

Rte. 3, Thomas Bay, Bar Harbor. ✆ 207/288-5005. Also at 172 Clark Point Rd., Southwest Harbor. ✆ 207/244-7330. www.theoceanarium.com. Bar Harbor admission $10–$15 adults, $6–$9.75 children 4–12, free for children

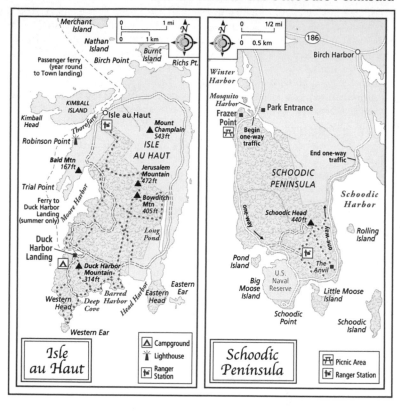

Isle au Haut

- △ Campground
- ☀ Lighthouse
- 🏠 Ranger Station

Schoodic Peninsula

- 🏕 Picnic Area
- 🏠 Ranger Station

under 4; Southwest Harbor admission $8 adults, $6 children 4–12, free for children under 4. Discounts available to visit both sites. Mid-May to mid-Oct Mon–Sat 9am–5pm. Closed mid-Oct to mid-May.

Islesford Historical Museum   The neat thing about this little museum, located on Little Cranberry Island, is that you take a 40-minute mail-boat ferry ride to get there. Islesford is a tiny island village with a restaurant and store and the museum, in an odd brick building. An island summer resident (who's buried out back) started the collection of ship models, dolls, nautical items, and antiques in 1927. The Park Service now runs it.

Islesford, Little Cranberry Island. Free admission. Mid-May to Sept Mon–Sat 9am–noon, Sun 10:45am–noon, daily 12:30–3:30pm. Closed Oct to mid-June. See "Boating" (p. 67) for ferry information.

The Abbe Museum   The Bar Harbor location shows a fine collection of baskets and other artifacts of Maine Indians and teaches about their lives today. The small museum in the park operates seasonally. Its exhibits, while of interest to adults and teenagers, are unlikely to hold the attention of younger children for long.

26 Mount Desert St. and Sieur de Monts Spring. ✆ 207/288-3519. www.abbemuseum.org. Bar Harbor: Admission $6 adults, $2 children 6–15, free for children under 6. Early Nov to Memorial Day Thurs–Sat 10am–4pm; Memorial Day to early Nov daily 10am–6pm. Sieur de Monts (see below for directions): Admission $2 adults, $1 children 6–15, free for children under 6. Memorial Day to early Oct daily 9am–4pm.

Wendell Gilley Museum of Bird Carving ⟨★★⟩   This museum, which tracks the career of noted bird carver Wendell Gilley, is a great rainy-day adventure for kids. Not only can they see dozens of miniature carvings of eagles, ducks, osprey, chickadees, and many other bird species, but they can watch the carver-in-residence at work. Workshops also are offered.

4 Herrick Rd., Somesville. ℂ 207/244-7555. www.wendellgilleymuseum.org. Admission $5 adults, $2 children 5–12, free for children under 5. June–Oct Tues–Sun 10am–4pm (5pm July–Aug); May and Nov–Dec Fri–Sun 10am–4pm. Workshop open to museum members on Friday afternoons, groups by appointment.

SIEUR DE MONTS SPRING AREA

This area, the original core of the park, contains three places to learn about the island: a botanical garden, a nature center, and a branch of the Abbe Museum (covered above). Take Route 3 or the Park Loop Road about a mile south from Bar Harbor and follow the signs. Pick up the free guide booklet to follow the nature trail through the area.

We most enjoyed the **Wild Gardens of Acadia.** Volunteers planted this small botanical garden to show Mount Desert Island's native plants in their natural habitats. A complex of gravel paths and a brook divide 12 habitat types where labels teach the names of plants and trees you encounter while biking or hiking. Our children were delighted with the garden's map-reading, exploring, and imaginative opportunities.

The **Nature Center** is a room with animal and bird mounts and displays explaining natural processes and park management. It's a good place to get questions answered and to find out what the animals you may see look like up close. It is open July through August daily from 9am to 5pm, sometimes shorter hours off season; closed late September to mid-May.

8 For the Active Family

BIKING ⟨★★★⟩

Acadia arguably is the best national park for family biking, and biking is one of the best ways for a family to get into the woods. All of the carriage roads are free of cars, giving kids wonderful new freedom. You gently swoop over mountains and past lakes; riding here is like a dream. Most of the island's regular roads aren't safe for families to ride, but there are some spectacular exceptions, such as the Park Loop Road, for more advanced riders.

Some planning will improve your ride. We saw some out-of-shape riders who were suffering greatly on the carriage roads. All the trails are somewhat hilly—that makes them interesting—so sedentary people may have a hard time. The good guidebook listed under "Reading Up" (p. 51) can help you choose a ride at your ability level, as can your rental agency. Even without the book, you will need a map. The Park Service and rental agencies hand out basic maps free, but because navigation is a big part of the fun for children, you may want to buy a better one with topographic lines (see "Reading Up").

Try not to start your ride in Bar Harbor. The ride out of the city to the nearest carriage road trail head is a bit steep and can be scary with kids. Also, avoid the crowded Eagle Lake trail head. Some prefer to rent a bike rack (for less than $10 at many of the rental shops; the park shuttles also have bike racks) and start at Jordan Pond House, which is on the Park Loop Road; at the Parkman Mountain Trailhead on Route 198 near Northeast Harbor; or at the Brown Mountain Gatehouse near Lower

Haddock Pond. You will have these trails more to yourself than other trails, and they are among the park's most beautiful.

Don't let small children hold you back; they can ride a trailer or trailer bike (also called tag-alongs). Trailer bikes attach to the back of an adult's bike to make it into a tandem that's sized for a kid. They bridge the gap when kids are too big for trailers but not ready to keep up with grown-ups on their own bikes—roughly ages 4 through 7. You feel like a real team riding together. Take it easy at first, however, because the parent often has to counterbalance a wobbly beginning rider. A trailer, carrying a baby or toddler, also can carry your picnic and jackets.

Bike-rental agencies include **Acadia Bike and Canoe** (a sister company to Coastal Kayaking Tours), 48 Cottage St. (© **800/526-8615** or 207/288-9605; www.acadia fun.com), and **Bar Harbor Bicycle Shop,** 141 Cottage St. (© **207/288-3886;** www. barharborbike.com). Adult bikes are around $21 a day (more if you opt for a full suspension model), kids' bikes around $13, with discounts for half-day, multiple-day, or weeklong rentals. Trailers and trailer bikes are $12 to $15 a day; car racks, about $10 a day.

BOATING

With the sailing, whale-watching, canoeing, and sea-kayaking opportunities covered below, the waters around Mount Desert, with their wildlife and many islands, are a paradise. An afternoon boat ride can take you to a quaint island village or just to see the seals, osprey, and incomparable scenery.

The least expensive choices are the passenger ferries and excursions that run from Northeast and Southwest harbors to the Cranberry Islands (see "Frenchman Bay & Great Harbor," p. 63), including Islesford Historical Museum (p. 65). A typical round-trip fare to Islesford or Great Cranberry Island is $20 to $22 for adults, $10 to $14 for children 3 to 11. **Beal and Bunker, Inc.** (© **207/244-3575**), runs many times a day from the municipal pier in Northeast Harbor. **Cranberry Cove Boating Co.** (© **207/244-5882** or 207/460-1981) goes from the upper town dock at Southwest Harbor. Others offer similar service, or rides to islands farther afield; check with the visitor center.

Guided tours run daily, too. A ranger program explores these waters, making a stop at Islesford (see "Kid-Friendly Programs," p. 70). **Sea Princess Cruises** (© **207/276-5352**) offers a tour of almost 3 hours, with 45 minutes on Little Cranberry. Both the morning trip, with a ranger, and the afternoon cruise, which features a retired naturalist, run $25 per person. **Bar Harbor Whale Watch Co.** (see below under "Whale-Watching") also offers Frenchman Bay wildlife tours that are great for kids. Some include pulling lobster pots and inspecting undersea creatures.

CANOEING

Acadia is an excellent setting for beginning canoeists. The park's smooth, long ponds are safe, interesting places to paddle and learn the advantages of silent travel for watching birds and animals. The best way to go is to rent from **National Park Canoe and Kayak Rental** (© **207/244-5854**), which has an outlet at the north end of Long Pond, on Route 102 (Pretty Marsh Rd.) on the west side of the island. Three-hour rentals run $25, 6 hours $35, and all day $45 for a canoe. For a tandem kayak the rates are $27, $44, and $52, while solo kayaks go for $24, $34, and $40. There's also a self-guided sunset tour that costs $16 per person. It's a big lake with a swimming float and lots of bays and channels to explore. You can also take your own canoe or one you rent in Bar Harbor with a car-top carrier to any of the other lakes. Echo Lake has the added advantage of the swimming beach, Jordan Pond has fish and gravel beaches for picnicking, and Somes Sound offers protected marine waters (easily accessible only if you stay at Mount Desert Campground; p. 56). Launch spots are marked on the official park map. For a book with details on all the choices, see "Reading Up" (p. 51).

CARRIAGE & HORSEBACK RIDING

Younger children will enjoy carriage rides along the carriage roads that Rockefeller originally built for horses, not bikes. The carriages are carts with rows of seats, pulled by a team of two horses. Drivers offer a little commentary on the passing scenery, but mostly you just go for the ride. It's fun to watch the passing bicyclists below you, but perhaps not enough of a thrill for older children. **Wildwood Stables,** ½ mile south of Jordan Pond House on the Park Loop Road, is the park concessionaire (℡ **207/276-3622;** www.acadia.net/wildwood). One- and 2-hour rides leave several times a day in the summer. An hour is plenty; that tour, which circles Day Mountain, costs $22 for ages 13 and up, $9 for ages 6 to 12, $6 for ages 2 to 5, and is free for children under 2. Two-hour tours go farther afield, allow better views, or stop for tea and popovers at Jordan Pond House. Call ahead for times and to make reservations with a credit card—a good idea to avoid disappointment. Don't be late, and bring small bills to tip the driver. No horses are for rent in the park, but if you bring your own horse, you can board it at Wildwood Stables.

HIKING

Acadia offers more good family day hikes in a smaller area than anywhere else I know. The park has more than 120 miles of trails, but few of them are more than a few miles long. Many cover wonderful terrain, passing through tall, quiet woods; rounding fresh, bright ponds; and mounting bare granite highlands. Old trails have granite steps or iron climbing rungs. I mentioned some easy and popular choices under "Natural Places," earlier in this chapter, including the **Cadillac Mountain trails, Ocean Trail, Bar Island, Wonderland,** and **Ship Harbor.** But with such a wide range of choices, there's no reason to limit yourself to these. The Park Service gives away a list of trails rated by difficulty, which essentially means steepness. The book mentioned earlier under "Reading Up" provides much more information for planning a hike. Or, to take another approach, just get on a trail and start walking: There's a trail head every time you turn around, and the distances are short.

SAILING

You couldn't ask for prettier waters for a day sail than those of Great Harbor and Somes Sound, which is probably why Southwest Harbor's unique **MDI Community Sailing Center** (℡ **207/244-7905;** www.mdisailing.org) exists. Members who demonstrate their sailing knowledge can use the center's fleet of sailboats all summer. A $425 family membership also includes a week of the Junior Sailing Program. You can also contact the center through **Harbor House Community Center** (℡ **207/244-3713;** www.harborhousemdi.org). For just 1 day's sailing, **Mansell Boat Co.,** in Manset, just south of Southwest Harbor on Shore Road (℡ **207/244-5625;** www.mansellboatrentals.com), rents sailboats starting at $195 a day, and offers 2-hour lesson sails for $195. It rents powerboats, too.

If you want to sail but don't want to handle your own boat, you can take one of several excursions aboard larger vessels that make short day trips from Mount Desert Island. **Downeast Windjammer Cruises** (© 207/288-4585 or 207/288-2373; www.downeastwindjammer.com) operates a four-masted schooner, the *Margaret Todd,* on 90-minute to 2-hour Frenchman Bay cruises from the Bar Harbor Inn Pier. The ticket office is at 27 Main St. The trips cost $32 for adults and $22 for children under 12.

SEA KAYAKING

Sea kayaking is a terrific family sport, with a child in the front of a two-seat kayak and a parent in back. As long as you can trust your child not to freak out, you should be fine. With a hull larger and flatter than a river kayak and a center of gravity lower than a canoe, a sea kayak is the most stable of the three. You skim silently along the surface of the sea, perhaps just inches off the shore. It's the closest thing to walking on water. On the other hand, tall people and those with back problems can find sea kayaking uncomfortable, so it is wise to try a short outing your first time.

Beginners should go with a guide. **Coastal Kayaking Tours,** part of Acadia Bike and Canoe, 48 Cottage St. (© **800/526-8615** or 207/288-9605; www.acadiafun. com), offers several daily paddles, including a 4-hour outing for families with children as young as 8. The company has its act together; our guide was professional and friendly without being intrusive. Where you go depends largely on which way the wind is blowing, although other weather conditions can factor in as well. It's nice to go right in Frenchman Bay, but because fog or wind often makes that too risky, you may have to ride a van to the northern side of the island. We had a great half-day trip from Bartlett's Landing on the west side of the island south past Hardwood and Moose islands to Seal Cove. Joining us for part of the trip were some harbor porpoises. It costs $46 per person. Other trips range from 2½ hours to 3 days—trips that could include island camping or traveling from inn to inn. For kayak rentals, try **Acadia Outfitters** at 106 Cottage St. (© **208/288-8118**). They rent solo kayaks with rudders for $45, tandems for $55, solo kayaks without rudders for lake use for $25, and canoes for $30. Rates are for all day.

SWIMMING

The ocean waters of Mount Desert Island are generally too cold for swimming, but there's a good beach where even young children can swim on **Echo Lake,** with changing rooms and a lifeguard. The beach is very gradual. Hiking trails to Beech Mountain and other peaks connect to the parking area, so some of you can have a more vigorous day while others swim, wade, and sun. Canoeing is permitted on the lake, too. To get there, turn right off Route 102 south toward Southwest Harbor.

TIDE POOLING

If you don't know how to go tide pooling, perhaps your children can teach you. It's all about climbing over wet rocks to find strange little animals; all you need is curiosity. You can bring an identification key and a magnifying glass if you want, but we've had more fun with a pail in which to temporarily imprison tiny fish and crabs. Do wear shoes with good traction that you can get wet. And do choose a time when the tide is low and still has some time to go out; there's a tide table in the *Beaver Log,* the free park newspaper.

At Acadia the difference between low and high tide is around 12 feet: That's a lot of sea floor to explore. **Otter Point,** on the Park Loop Road, is one of the best spots, with a large parking lot and plenty of uneven rocky shore where tide pools can collect. Be careful of slips and falls—the rocks can be steep and slippery. Don't let squeamishness deter you—the creatures may be slimy, but there's nothing there to hurt you. Turn over rocks and brush aside seaweed to see what's underneath; but put everything and everyone back where you found them, and be careful not to trample living things. The Park Service offers good ranger-led tide-pool excursions; check the schedule in the *Beaver Log.*

WHALE-WATCHING ☆☆

On an evening boat ride from Bar Harbor, you motor out of sight of land 30 miles into the Gulf of Maine and, as if by prior arrangement, chance upon meeting a pod of 20 or more humpback whales lunge-feeding close on either side of the boat. When humpbacks feed, they spin a circular net of bubbles to contain schools of herring, then lunge upward through the school with open mouths to swallow the fish. Their upward momentum carries them explosively through the surface of the ocean, a startling and awesome sight.

Now the downside: Children under 7 may get bored, especially if the whales don't show up quickly. Indeed, these Gulf of Maine waters, because of their size, can be a hard place to find whales compared to predictable areas such as Cape Cod's Stellwagen Bank. This big open water also always has ocean swells, which can bring on seasickness. Don't go if the weather is rough. Also, bundle up very warmly in sweaters, jackets, hats, and gloves. Prime time for whale-watching is mid-May to late August.

Bar Harbor Whale Watch Co. (© **888/WHALES-4** or 207/288-2386; www.bar harborwhales.com) offers 3- to 3½-hour whale-watching trips from 1 West St. in Bar Harbor. It costs $49 for adults, $26 for kids 6 to 14, and $8 for kids under 6. Reserve a day or two ahead if possible. Other tours by the same company add birding for puffins or use a different boat. The company also offers a "lobster fishing and seal watching" trip during which the crew pulls in lobster traps. Other companies offer whale-watching in Bar Harbor, and you can easily compare their offerings and prices by checking their storefront offices.

9 Kid-Friendly Programs

Acadia National Park has some ranger-led programs that go beyond the lectures or short walks that parks often offer. For some, you need to sign up in advance (a maximum of 3 days) at the Hulls Cove Visitor Center, so be sure to pick up the *Beaver Log* park newspaper or log on to the website (www.nps.gov/acad) and be ready to make some decisions when you arrive. While many interpretive programs are free, more and more require a fee these days.

CHILDREN'S PROGRAMS

The park offers a nice variety of programs every week aimed at children 5 to 12. In June and September a popular program is the free **Life Between the Tides** outing, a 3-hour adventure from the Ship Harbor parking area that leads children along the coast where they can explore tide pools and the life they contain. During July and August the **Beyond the Beach** program ($10 for adults, $5 kids 5–12) follows a similar path, starting at Sand Beach. The children's programs require advance sign-up at the Hulls Cove Visitor Center to prevent overcrowding. A parent has to go along on the outing.

> ## *Tips* Places for Relaxed Play & Picnics
>
> At times Acadia feels like a huge city park; it's easy to find safe places to play or picnic. Families make good use of the **Village Green** in Bar Harbor, at the corner of Main and Mount Desert streets, which has a fountain, a gazebo, and a lawn to romp on. A much bigger park, with a fenced playground, is at Park and Main streets, near the YMCA. **Sand Beach** and **Echo Lake Beach** are also great spots to lie back and let the kids do whatever they want. Seal Harbor has a modest ocean beach and a village green.

The park's **Junior Ranger program** uses booklets that cost $1.95 at the visitor center, the Sieur de Monts Spring Nature Center, or the campgrounds. Kids complete the worksheets and attend ranger programs to win a Junior Ranger pin, which you pick up at one of the visitor centers. The booklets, one for 7 and younger and one for 8 and older, are mostly rainy-day activities to do with a pencil. They will take time but won't be too hard for the intended ages with a little reading help.

FAMILY & ADULT PROGRAMS

Programs start as early as 7am (for a 3-hr. birding outing) or as late as 9:30pm (to watch the stars on Sand Beach). The lineup changes annually, but usually includes a couple of choices of outings by boat to see wildlife, scenery, and historic places. The Islesford Historical Cruise lasts almost 3 hours, with a stop on Little Cranberry Island. The fare is $24 for adults, $15 for children 5 through 11, and $5 for children under 5; check the schedule for where to reserve your place and catch the boat. Most programs are free, and most adult programs don't require prior sign-up.

Campfire programs take place every night during July and August at Blackwoods and Seawall campgrounds. The topics, such as natural history, conservation, culture, and even singalongs, are posted on park bulletin boards, where you can also get the time, which changes through the year. Anyone can come—you don't have to be camping.

SUMMER CAMPS

Acadia is a place where, if you schedule a long enough vacation, parents and kids can split up for part of that time, each doing what they most enjoy.

Camp Cadillac, operated by the Mount Desert Island YMCA, 21 Park St. (P.O. Box 51), Bar Harbor, ME 04609 (© **207/288-3511;** www.mdiymca.org), offers a tremendous array of nature, outdoors, learning, art, and sports activity camps for children ages 3 to 14. Besides using the more-than-a-century-old Y's impressive facility in Bar Harbor, the camps roam over the national park and island. The day programs last from late June to late August and cost about $170 for a week of full days. Reserve well ahead.

Harbor House Community Center, P.O. Box 836, Southwest Harbor, ME 04662 (© **207/244-3713**), offers day camps for kids 3 to 17. Groups up to age 9 go on field trips to museums and outdoor activities each day. Sailing camp, for ages 6 through 17, costs about $185 a week. Camps run mid-June to mid-August, and you need to reserve by mid-May. The center also operates the **MDI Community Sailing Center** (p. 68).

10 Entertainment outside the Park

A section of lower-quality tourist development lies along Route 3 leading north and west from the Hulls Cove Visitor Center to Ellsworth, off the island. If you decide on an afternoon of empty-calorie fun, this is where you'll find minigolf courses, water slides, and go-carts. Take a look on your drive to Acadia to decide what you want to do, then set aside time for the outing. It's 20 miles of slow driving from Bar Harbor to Ellsworth.

If you run into a rainy day and want to stay dry, see what's playing at the **Criterion Theater,** 35 Cottage St., Bar Harbor (© **207/288-3441;** www.criteriontheater.com). This gorgeous Art Deco theater offers a mix of live music, theatrical productions, and first-run movies.

Kids can create their own Acadia souvenirs at **All Fired Up,** a wonderfully creative shop at 44 Cottage St., Bar Harbor (© **207/288-3130;** www.acadiaallfiredup.com). They can choose a piece of pottery, such as a frog, bowl, or plate; paint it as they see fit; and then glaze it before it's fired in one of the shop's kilns. Kids can also make their own mosaics, as well as stuffed animals.

FAST FACTS: Acadia National Park

Area Code The area code is **207.**

ATMs Banks in Bar Harbor have **ATMs.**

Emergencies For emergencies, dial **911** from anywhere on Mount Desert Island. For emergencies on the water, the **U.S. Coast Guard** unit at Southwest Harbor is at © **207/244-5121.**

Hospitals & Clinics **Mount Desert Island Hospital and Health Center** in Bar Harbor, 10 Wayman Lane (© **207/288-5081;** www.mdihospital.org), offers 24-hour emergency care. The affiliated **Community Health Center** in Southwest Harbor is at 9 Village Green Way (© **207/244-5630).**

Information For information, write Acadia National Park, P.O. Box 177, Eagle Lake Road, Bar Harbor, ME, 04609-0177; call © **207/288-3338,** or check the website www.nps.gov/acad.

Pharmacies You can find pharmacies in Bar Harbor.

Post Office The main post office in Bar Harbor is at 55 Cottage St., across from the grocery store. Villages across the island also have small post offices.

Time Zone The park is on **Eastern Standard Time.**

Weather Updates For weather updates, call the local weather line (© **207/677-8910**) or call the park (© **207/288-3338**).

4

Cape Cod National Seashore

Trying to paint an emblematic portrait of a Cape Cod vacation is akin to counting all the shells on the beach. Okay, perhaps it's not that difficult, but it's not easy. Should your painting focus on a lighthouse rising above the crashing surf or on a clambake? A hike across the dunes or a walk through an old-growth forest? Do you want to picture a sailing excursion or a trip to watch whales? A trip to "the Cape" offers so many possibilities that, unless you plan properly, you can go crazy, which is what you hoped a vacation would help you avoid in the first place, right?

Cape Cod is so famous, you might think you don't need an introduction to it. You probably know what a weathered Cape Cod cottage looks like, and you don't need instructions on how to enjoy the beach.

But Cape Cod is a big, complicated place. It has long, lonesome places as well as traffic jams. You can go there to learn about an amazing variety of wildlife habitats, or to shop at an amazing variety of stores. On a busy Provincetown street, the Cape sometimes seems to be sinking under the crush of people, yet just across the highway lie miles of shifting sand dunes at the edge of the sea's pounding waves. There are 40 miles of beaches within the national seashore alone, some of them deserted all the time, and patches of marsh, cranberry bogs and forest, privately managed nature preserves, a state park, and many other historic and interesting places. The famous side of Cape Cod is only the surface.

BEST THINGS TO DO ON CAPE COD

- **Go to the beach** to swim, hike, fly a kite, build a sand castle, or just lie on warm sand.
- **Canoe in Nauset Marsh** or one of the other salt marshes full of wildlife.
- **Go sailing** on the protected coves facing Cape Cod Bay.
- **Take a nature walk** in the coastal woods or bike one of the paved paths there.
- **Visit a nature center** or kid-friendly history museum.
- **Go whale-watching** by boat.
- **Sign up the kids** for a fun (and educational) day or residential camp. Parents, have a little time alone together.

For more information, see "For the Active Family" (p. 94) for details.

Cape Cod Address Book

PARK & NATURE INFORMATION

Cape Cod National Seashore Headquarters   99 Marconi Site Rd., Wellfleet, MA 02667. ℂ 508/349-3785. www.nps.gov/caco. Some of the best ranger-led activities require advance sign-up, so contact the park before your visit to make your reservation by credit card.

Eastern National   470 Maryland Dr., Suite 2, Ft. Washington, PA 19428. ℂ 877/NAT-PARK. Fax 215/591-0903. www.eparks.com. For books and maps.

Nickerson State Park (and Cape Cod Rail Trail)   Route 6A, Brewster, MA 02631-1521. ℂ 508/896-3491. www.mass.gov/dcr/parks/southeast/nick.htm. Reservations ℂ 877/422-6762. www.reserveamerica.com.

Cape Cod Museum of Natural History   869 Rte. 6A (P.O. Box 1710), Brewster, MA 02631. ℂ 508/896-3867. www.ccmnh.org.

Wellfleet Bay Wildlife Sanctuary   Massachusetts Audubon Society, 291 State Hwy., Route 6 (P.O. Box 236), South Wellfleet, MA 02663. ℂ 508/349-2615. www.wellfleetbay.org.

CHAMBERS OF COMMERCE

Cape Cod Chamber of Commerce   5 Shoot Flying Hill Road, Centerville, Junction of Route 6 and Route 123 (P.O. Box 790), Hyannis, MA 02601. ℂ 888/33-CAPECOD or 508/362-3225. www.capecodchamber.org.

Eastham Chamber of Commerce   P.O. Box 1329, Eastham, MA 02642. ℂ 508/240-7211. www.easthamchamber.com.

Provincetown Chamber of Commerce   307 Commercial St. (P.O. Box 1017), Provincetown, MA 02657. ℂ 508/487-3424. Fax 508/487-8966. www.ptown chamber.com. (Also see www.provincetown.com.)

Wellfleet Chamber of Commerce   P.O. Box 571, Wellfleet, MA 02667-0571. ℂ 508/349-2510. www.wellfleetchamber.com.

1 History: Finding the "Real" Cape Cod

More than many places, the idea of Cape Cod stands for a whole way of living, not just a spot on the map. For summer people, it is slow days of sun amid the scent of salt water and pines, grains of sand always stuck to your feet, and the feeling that, even though it's an old place and you are a short-time visitor, you belong. Here, you can take the time to really see things: a bike leaning against a gray beach cottage, the sun through a roof of shade trees on a narrow Colonial street, a great blue heron on one foot in calm marsh water while the surf roars beyond a barrier beach. Protecting Cape Cod means more than keeping places from changing. It also means protecting the special way of living that produces these moments.

Of course, the Cape is different for everyone, and as time passes, it changes for each of us. Our easy summer days here would seem very strange to the hardworking farmers, boat builders, and whalers who built the towns where we play. As more and more people come to the Cape now, with their cars and new buildings, that Cape Cod is disappearing.

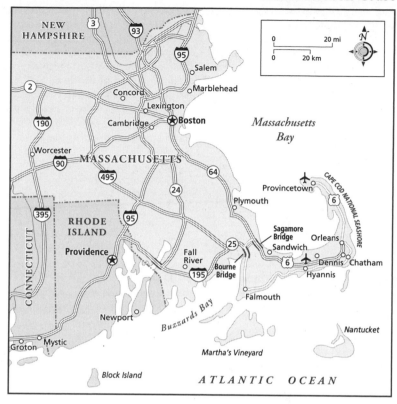

Every wildlife habitat has a carrying capacity—it can support just so many animals, and no more—and the Cape Cod I love may have reached its carrying capacity for people. Each summer, more visitors on shorter trips bring more traffic. Route 6 around Eastham turns into a slow-moving parade of cars. When it's sunny, everyone takes to the beach, where parking lots can fill and cars sometimes form lines to get in. On rainy days, the museums and other indoor activities get crowded. Reservations for summer houses fill while the snow is still falling the winter before. In Provincetown's narrow, historic streets pedestrians gather so thickly that they spill from the sidewalks and take over the lanes, making a solid river of people from wall to wall.

The Cape the Pilgrims found was wild, barely populated by the survivors of bands of Native Americans who had been killed off by diseases brought by the first European explorers. Unlike the Cape today, which is mostly covered by short pitch pine and open, grassy dunes, the Pilgrims found old forests of towering oaks, maples, and cedars. After exploring, however, they decided that the sandy, windy land wouldn't be good for farming and went on to Plymouth, on the other side of Cape Cod Bay.

Later, colonists did settle the Cape, clearing forests for wood and land they could plant. They were the first to build the classic Cape Cod house, a simple, rectangular building, easy to expand and to heat with central fireplaces, and without a lot of expensive glass windows. Shingles of local cedar covered its outside, and its steeply pitched roof shed snow. Farming lasted only a few generations, however, because without the trees and other native plants, the sun dried up the soil and the wind blew it away. Farmers' sons turned to fishing, whaling, boat building, shipping, and salt-making—work that used the rest of the Cape's forests until they too were almost all gone.

Whalers made fortunes sailing from Wellfleet and Provincetown on voyages that lasted years and covered most of the world. They harpooned whales for oil to burn in lamps and for baleen, a material from some whales' mouths. Whales use baleen to filter food from water. People used it much as plastic is used today, for flexible items such as umbrella spokes and stiff parts in ladies' underwear. Cape Cod shipyards also built some of the world's fastest sailing ships, trading along routes up and down the East Coast, especially between Boston and New York.

Many sailors on those voyages died on the shores of Cape Cod—3,000 shipwrecks have been recorded since the arrival of the *Mayflower,* which itself briefly got into trouble in those waters. The shifting sand that makes up the Cape's beaches extends far offshore underwater, creating dangerous shoals. Sailing ships attempting to round the Cape were often caught in northeast winter winds that drove them toward the shore and up on the sandbars, where they got stuck and the surf bashed them to pieces. The Cape's lighthouses and the U.S. Life-Saving Service prevented many deaths. The brave surf men of the service patrolled the beach, launching rowboats into the waves to save sailors. Or, if the surf was too high, the surf men would fire a line to the ship with a Lyle gun and then pull victims ashore in an aerial contraption called a breeches buoy. The digging of the Cape Cod Canal in 1914 allowed ships to cut through rather than round the Cape and saved many more lives.

When Henry David Thoreau's book about the Cape was published in 1865 (after his death), it was still a lonely place. The tourism industry hadn't started yet. And it was difficult to travel around the Cape. Thoreau explored all over, walking from Eastham to Provincetown and meeting the solitary scavengers, called wreckers, who collected driftwood and cargo that washed ashore from shipwrecks. He admired the simple towns and people and wrote philosophically of the wild, ancient sea. "The time must come when this coast will be a place of resort for those New Englanders who really wish to visit the seaside," he wrote.

That change began in 1873, when the railroad reached Provincetown, opening the Cape to visitors. Hunters and wealthy vacationers began to build large summer homes. Around 1900, Provincetown began to develop into an artists' colony, and dramatists, writers, and visual artists started coming to the Cape for the summer to create and share their work. The great playwright Eugene O'Neill joined the Provincetown Players in 1915 and saw his first Pulitzer Prize–winning play produced there. With the construction of highways, many more people came.

After World War I and even more after World War II, family car vacations took over Cape Cod. People who could afford only a week or two came to stay in simple vacation cottages. Today the trend of more people on shorter visits continues. Instead of a week, more visitors come for long weekends. And instead of simple, weathered-board cottages, more people want standard hotel rooms, condo units, or fully equipped modern houses. They want convenient shopping centers and state-of-the-art things to do when they're not at the beach.

The Cape's communities have come to recognize that only so many people can fit on this hook of land before it will be spoiled for everyone. New zoning laws require larger pieces of land for building, so fewer houses can be built. But only wealthy people can afford houses built on large lots of such valuable land. As limits on development limit the supply of vacations and more people want to come, prices are rising. Some families have seen their favorite rental houses get too expensive and sadly moved on to other summer vacation spots. Cape Cod has long been a place where ordinary people can come from hot, dirty cities for family vacations in the outdoors. Will they still be able to afford to come?

We can't capture and preserve the perfect Cape Cod. It's hard even to say what the "real" Cape Cod looks like. Certainly, it doesn't look like a typical American strip mall or condo resort. On the other hand, Thoreau's Cape Cod was missing something, too. As beautiful and desolate as it must have been, there were no scenes of children splashing in the surf or paddling in canoes to learn about the salt marshes.

Even if we can't preserve Cape Cod, we can savor its natural smells and sights, have simple fun, and let tension drift away. Each family can help make Cape Cod the ideal place to visit. Plan enough time to really enjoy it, avoid unnecessary driving, and go to natural places rather than commercial centers. Don't add to all the crowds, traffic, and bustle. Our way of living here now could help set the future so that families can continue to summer the same way for a long time to come.

2 Orientation

The national seashore is 40 miles long, running from Race Point, at the northern tip of Cape Cod, to the thin barrier beaches of Nauset Beach, near the Cape's elbow. Our focus, however, is only on the Cape's forearm, the main part of the national seashore from Eastham north. On the park-managed ocean-facing beaches here, you'll find fine, white sand; high bluffs and dunes; crashing waves; and relatively cold water for swimming. On the opposite, Cape Cod Bay side of the Cape, the water tends to be calmer and warmer, the sand coarser and muddier, and the beaches controlled by towns or private parties. In between, private and park land mix around salt marshes, ponds, and forests.

Towns mix smoothly into one another, but you need to know their names, because that's how people give directions and define the part of the Cape they are talking about. We will cover towns from Eastham north, with a few sites in Orleans and Brewster, towns on the inside of the Cape's elbow.

ARRIVING
BY CAR
The route is simple, but read on for information that could save you hours of frustration.

From the south, split from Interstate 95 onto I-195 in Providence, then take Route 25 to Route 6. From the north, Route 3 takes you straight to Route 6. Head for the **Sagamore Bridge** over the Cape Cod Canal and follow 6 the rest of the way to the national seashore (you can also take the **Bourne Bridge,** a little farther south, with slight added complication). Tie-ups occur at the bridges. Weekly rentals on the Cape turn over on Saturdays, so a large portion of the summer population tries to get across the bridges all at once. Backups can be 3 hours or more. The worst congestion occurs 2 to 8pm Friday and 8 to 11am Saturday. Avoid those hours. If you're not on a weekly rental, try not to arrive or leave on a weekend at all. Eastham is 5½ hours from New York, 2 hours from Boston or Providence, assuming no traffic.

BY PLANE

Commuter planes go to **Hyannis** and **Provincetown.** Fly to Hyannis (also called Barnstable) airport from Boston, New York, or Providence. Carriers include **Cape Air** (*©* 800/352-0714 or 508/771-6944; www.flycapeair.com) and **US Airways Express** (*©* 800/428-4322; www.usairways.com). Fares can range from around $200 to more than $500 from Boston round-trip. Car-rental agencies at the airport include **Avis** (*©* 800/331-1212 or 508/775-2888), **Budget** (*©* 800/527-0700 or 508/790-0163), **Enterprise** (*©* 800/736-8222 or 508/778-8293), and **Hertz** (*©* 800/654-3131 or 508/775-5825).

BY BOAT

Three passenger ferries operated by two companies connect Provincetown to Boston. If you have the time, this can be a fun trip. The boats make day trips from Boston, but you can take it one-way to the Cape, missing the Cape traffic and seeing finback whales and dolphins on the way (if you're lucky!). Where the *Provincetown II* lands, Commonwealth Pier on Seaport Boulevard (Northern Ave.), is a short cab ride from South Station, Amtrak's last stop in Boston. It's a large vessel, but also the oldest and slowest of the choices. It takes 3 hours each way, but the boat has lots of open space, and a children's entertainer was playing music and making balloon animals during our ride. The operator, **Bay State Cruise Company** (*©* 877/783-3779 or 617/748-1428; www.baystatecruises.com), also runs the *Provincetown III,* which makes the run in 90 minutes. **Boston Harbor Cruises** (*©* 877/733-9425 or 617/227-4321; www.boston harborcruises.com) takes only 90 minutes to get from Long Wharf (on State St. in Boston) aboard a 600-passenger, high-speed catamaran. Each boat has a snack bar. Fares on the slowest are $19 one-way, $33 round-trip (free for children up to 12). Prices are higher for the faster service. Bikes cost $5 one-way, $10 round-trip. Expect sparse or nonexistent service on any of these boats in the off season.

VISITOR INFORMATION
NATIONAL SEASHORE VISITOR CENTERS

Salt Pond Visitor Center   The center, the main point of contact as visitors enter the seashore, has a theater where five different films are available for orientation, restroom facilities, and an overall fresher look thanks to a recent $3-million renovation. It is a large center, and has a fascinating little museum of Cape history and nature. When the building is in full operation, it features an information desk, a bookstore, and an outdoor amphitheater for evening ranger programs. Trails and canoeing excursions starting here are covered below under "Nature Walks" (p. 97) and "Canoeing & Kayaking" (p. 97).

Rte. 6, Eastham. *©* 508/255-3421. Daily 9am–4:30pm; later in summer.

Province Lands Visitor Center   This hexagonal building has an upstairs viewing deck with vistas in all directions that take in the surrounding dunes, the sea, and Provincetown. Besides the information desk and a selection of films in the auditorium, there are a few interesting displays that tell how to recognize different kinds of ships. During July and August there are weekly demonstrations of how crews in the early part of the 20th century used a "Lyle gun" to help rescue passengers from ships that ran aground off the Cape.

Race Point Rd., Provincetown. *©* 508/487-1256. Daily 9am–5pm; later in summer. Winter closures vary, usually around Halloween to May.

Cape Cod National Seashore

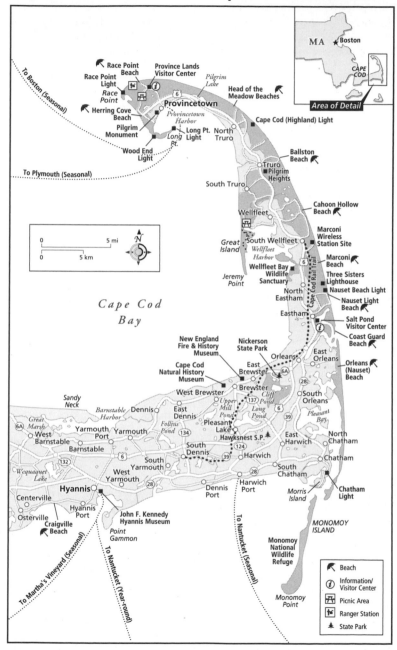

PROVINCETOWN VISITOR CENTER

Provincetown Visitor Center   Run by the Provincetown Chamber of Commerce, the center helps find lodgings and serves as the ticket office for the ferry to Boston.

MacMillan Wharf, 307 Commercial St. ℭ **508/487-3424.** June–Sept daily 9am–5pm; shorter hours off season.

READING UP

Eastern National (ℭ **877/NAT-PARK;** www.eparks.com) operates the visitor-center bookstores and carries a selection of books online or by telephone order.

Nature: The Seaside Naturalist, by Deborah A. Coulombe (Simon & Schuster, $16), is clearly written and illustrated for children and adults.

THE NATIONAL SEASHORE IN BRIEF

Provincetown

This historic town of narrow streets sits at the tip of the Cape. It's clogged with people and best avoided on high-season weekends and afternoons, when day-trippers from Boston add to the mob. Parking is terrible. Resign yourself to paying as much as $10 and pulling into a lot as you enter the town rather than getting stuck in traffic looking for a better spot. Avoid the municipal parking lot, which charges $2.50 an hour. If you visit the Pilgrim Monument, however, it has ample free parking near downtown. Provincetown has many hotel rooms, museums, tour boats, and other activities, and is the only choice if you want to forgo a car during your stay, but I think the crowds spoil it.

Truro

Quiet Truro is made up mostly of cottages along country roads with tree-branch canopies. There's hardly any town center, but you'll find lots of national seashore land and great beaches.

Wellfleet

Grown-ups will enjoy a walk around the town. Its shops, art galleries, and narrow, tree-lined streets look like a movie set of a Colonial New England town. It's the Cape's best mix of town and outdoors. Parking is a problem, so you may need to walk several blocks to the town center.

Eastham

This rural town with no well-defined city center has several interesting historic sites and nature trails, plus the park visitor center.

3 Getting Around

BY CAR

Learning your way around is simple, but you'll need a good map for the details. Route 6 is the north-south spine of the area, running from the traffic circle at the south end of Eastham to Provincetown. Because the Cape is relatively thin, everything is close to Route 6. At the Eastham traffic circle, Route 6 becomes a limited-access two-lane road leading off the Cape. Taking 6A south from the traffic circle leads you through Orleans to Main Street in Brewster. Splitting from 6A to Route 28 in Orleans takes you eventually to Chatham.

Traffic is a big enough problem at the Cape that it can ruin days of your vacation if you're not careful. Route 6 north of Orleans—the national seashore area—is the only way to get anywhere, and most of the way it's a two-lane country road with numerous intersections, traffic lights, and driveways, sometimes becoming a long, slow line of cars. The solution is to reduce your trips. Plan to spend an entire day on visits to the opposite end of the area, such as going to Provincetown from Eastham or to Brewster from Truro, by putting together activities. Plan detailed menus before your trip so that you can do all your shopping at once when you arrive. There is no large grocery store between Orleans and Provincetown, so you don't want to be running to the store. If you plan to put your child in a day camp or spend a lot of time anywhere, get accommodations nearby. Use bikes for short hops.

BY BIKE

The distances are too great and Route 6 is too dangerous to rely on bikes as your primary transportation. You can, however, bicycle for many of your shorter trips—to the beach, to a village center, or for outings along the Cape Cod Rail Trail, a bike path that follows the old railroad route for 30 miles from Wellfleet to Dennis. Several stores in each town rent bikes, with good bikes available for $15 to $20 a day. Reservations during the height of summer wouldn't be a bad idea.

- **Provincetown:** Ptown Bikes, 42 Bradford St. (© 508/487-8735; www.ptown bikes.com).
- **Wellfleet:** Idle Times Bike Shop, Route 6, Wellfleet (© 508/349-9161; www.idle timesbikes.com).
- **Eastham:** Idle Times Bike Rental, 4550 Rte. 6, N. Eastham (© 508/255-8281; www.idletimesbikes.com); Idle Times Bike Rental, 188 Bracket Road, N. Eastham (© 508/255-5070); Little Capistrano's, 30 Salt Pond Rd. (© 508/255-6515; www.capecodbike.com).

4 Planning Your Outings

WHEN TO GO

Summer vacation is the busy season on Cape Cod, beginning solidly at Memorial Day and lasting through Labor Day. Crowds are somewhat smaller in June, when the water is cold for swimming. In May, rates are low and crowds few. If you're coming in the summer and plan to spend less than a week, avoiding weekends matters more than what month you come.

Rates go down before and after the summer season. September and early October are relatively quiet, and the weather is still okay. Many businesses shut down in the winter, especially on the Outer Cape, where the national seashore lies. A winter trip is romantic for couples, but not much fun for families.

HOW MUCH TIME TO SPEND

From the Boston area, it may make sense to go to the national seashore for a weekend or even a day trip, but for anyone from farther afield, a week is the minimum. The best accommodations—houses, cottages, and some campgrounds—rent by the week, from Saturday to Saturday. Besides, Cape Cod isn't the kind of place where you can go and quickly hit the high points. There is a lot to see and do, and you should not do it quickly—relax and forget your cares for a while.

HOW FAR TO PLAN AHEAD

Rental cottages and houses book up for summer in February. Many people go to the same place every summer, and they have certain properties sewn up years in advance. Try making your lodging reservations first, before you set your vacation dates—that way, you have a better shot at getting a good place. Hotels and motels don't fill up as quickly. The best places fill for July and August 2 months ahead, but for midweek lodgings you often can find something without much lead time. If you need a car, reserve that well ahead, too, to avoid paying an outrageous rate.

WHAT TO PACK
CLOTHING
The summer high is typically 10° colder than on the mainland, averaging in the 70s (low to mid-20s Celsius), although occasional high humidity can make it feel muggy. During the day, people wear shorts and T-shirts. In the evening, they dress a little better than at most beach places or national parks—perhaps a skirt or khaki trousers and a cotton sweater for going out to dinner at a nice restaurant. Hats, sunglasses, and sunblock are necessities. Also, bring raincoats for foggy days and occasional drenching rains and don't forget insect repellent. A fleece for cool nights might also be good.

GEAR
At one of the beach shops on Route 6, you can pick up a beach umbrella and sand toys upon arrival. If you have a toddler, bring a backpack or jogger stroller so that you can go far enough down the beach to get away from the crowds. Bring your own bikes to save on renting. Conditions are mild for summer camping.

Weather Chart: Provincetown

	Avg. High (°F/°C)	Avg. Low (°F/°C)	Precipitation (in.)	Ocean Temp. (°F/°C)*
December–March	42/6	28/–2	3.8	37/3
April	53/12	37/3	3.6	46/8
May	64/18	46/8	3.3	55/13
June	73/23	56/13	3.1	55/13
July	79/26	62/17	2.4	71/22
August	78/26	61/16	3.4	72/22
September	71/22	55/13	3.5	67/19
October	62/17	46/8	3.7	59/15
November	52/11	38/3	4.5	50/10

* Water temperatures are for Woods Hole, Massachusetts.

KEEPING SAFE & HEALTHY
For general health and safety tips on sun, seasickness, poison ivy, and Lyme disease, see "Dealing with Hazards," in chapter 2. Info on other issues specific to Cape Cod follows.

DROWNING
Water on the ocean-side beaches at times can be too rough for children under age 8 (or older kids who don't feel comfortable in the water), and on some days swimming there is not safe even for older children and adults. The national seashore swimming beaches have lifeguards, who stand watch near the water when riptides occur to keep swimmers away, but not some town beaches or beaches away from the parking lots. Alternatively, the water is usually calm at the Bay beaches, and little ones can wade far out on the gently sloping shore. Beach details are covered under "Beachgoing" (p. 94). Also see "Practicalities: Swimming Safely in Surf," in chapter 5.

TRAFFIC

Cape Cod's lovely, narrow country roads leave little room for pedestrians and bicycles. In the towns, people often walk in the street. As a driver, take it easy. As a parent, hold your child's hand. Don't plan to bike on Route 6 or other major roads.

5 Family-Friendly Accommodations

CAMPGROUNDS

Cape Cod is great for camping. You'll find no campgrounds in the national seashore itself, but nearby are several superb commercial campgrounds and an extraordinary state park. In addition to the commercial campgrounds below, you can get a list of more campgrounds from the **Cape Cod Chamber of Commerce** (⌀ **888/33-CAPECOD;** www.capecodchamber.org), some of which are on the website. As with everything at the Cape, campsites require reservations well in advance. Also, minimum stays often apply. Backcountry camping requires a high-clearance vehicle and a special permit; see "Off-Road Driving" (p. 98).

Atlantic Oaks Campground   This gated, well-wooded campground, with pull-through sites among shade trees, is intended for RVs. The price includes cable TV hookups. The location is ½ mile from the Salt Pond Visitor Center and right on the Cape Cod Rail Trail (p. 96). The campground requires minimum stays on many weekends. Unlike some others, this property allows campfires.

3700 Rte. 6, Eastham, MA 02642. ⌀ **800/332-2267** or 508/255-1437. www.capecamping.com. 100 sites, tents or RVs. $26–$36 tent; $40–$53 full hookup for 2. $9 each extra adult, $3 each extra child 6–17, free for children under 6. DISC, MC, V. **Amenities:** Hot showers, laundry, playground, game room, evening movies.

Dunes' Edge Campground   This is a simple, old-fashioned campground with large, well-screened sites similar to those at the better national park campgrounds. The hilly, overgrown dune terrain and thick oaks and pitch pine help. Race Point is a couple of miles away by bike, a reasonable ride for kids. Provincetown is just across the highway. The campground has a nice family feel and well-kept facilities, but no resort stuff—there's no playground other than the woods. Tenters will be happiest here, because only 15 sites accommodate trailers, and the 20-amp service at 11 of the 15 sites won't support high-wattage gear. Four sites do have 30-amp service, but it won't drive air conditioners. Also, generators are banned. Campfires are not allowed.

East side of Rte. 6 (P.O. Box 875), Provincetown, MA 02657. ⌀ **508/487-9815.** www.dunes-edge.com. 100 sites, tents or RVs. $30–$38 site for 2. $10–$14 each extra adult, $3 each extra child; $8 extra for electric and water hookup. MC, V. **Amenities:** Hot showers, dump station, laundry.

Nickerson State Park   Nestled among towering white pine in seven groups, the sites here are thoughtfully arranged around the park's lovely kettle ponds so that it feels like wilderness. Few more appealing places to camp exist anywhere. There's more to do at this state park than at a lot of national parks: swimming and sailing in the ponds, long bicycle trails, and ranger programs and children's programs at the nature center (see "Natural Places," p. 91, and "Kid-Friendly Programs," p. 99).

Reservations for summer are essential, and are hard to get (mid-Oct to mid-Apr it's first-come, first-served). Availability opens 6 months ahead, and you should book your dates as soon as they are available. Often scattered openings of a day or two remain after most of the time is booked, so still it's worth a try later.

3488 Main St. (Rte. 6A), Brewster, MA 02631-1521. ⌀ **508/896-3491.** www.mass.gov/dcr/parks/southeast/nick/htm. Reservations ⌀ **877/422-6762.** www.reserveamerica.com. 418 sites, tents or RVs; 6 Yurts. $17 site (with $9.25 reservation

Campgrounds in the Cape Cod Area

Campground	Total Sites	RV Hookups	Dump Station	Toilets	Drinking Water
Atlantic Oaks	100	Yes	Yes	Yes	Yes
Dunes' Edge	100	Yes	Yes	Yes	Yes
Nickerson	418	No	Yes	Yes	Yes
North of Highland	237	No	No	Yes	Yes

charge). AE, DISC, MC, V (through www.reserveamerica.com). **Amenities:** Flush toilets, free hot showers, dump station. No hookups. Bathrooms closed late-Oct to mid-Apr.

North of Highland Camping Area   Intended for tents, this campground (owned by the Currier family since 1954) sits on 60 sandy acres of twisted scrub pine, surrounded on all sides by the national seashore. Head of the Meadow Beach is a short walk down a dirt road, and from there a secluded bike trail leads to Pilgrim Heights. The location is probably the most natural and isolated you'll find on the Cape, allowing you to forget about the car for a while. During the peak season, weeklong minimum stays apply, with shorter minimums at other times. Call well ahead to reserve.

52 Head of the Meadow Rd. (P.O. Box 297), North Truro, MA 02652. (C) **508/487-1191.** www.capecodcamping.com. 237 tent sites. $30 site for 2. $11 each extra adult, $3 each extra child. DISC, MC, V. **Amenities:** Hot showers, laundry, recreation building, store. No hookups. No trailers over 17 ft.

HOTELS, MOTELS & LODGES

A startling number of places, including all but a few historic hotels and B&Bs, are off-limits to kids under age 12. Start looking for a room early, and be sure to ask about age limits right off. Prices are high for good rooms, generally over $100 a night. I've listed only high-season rates; after Labor Day and before mid-June, they drop 25%, and in winter are up to 40% lower. If you're staying a week, a cottage is a better bet for quality and price; cottages rent for a week at a time in the summer.

EASTHAM

Beach Plum Motor Lodge   An old-fashioned place with small rooms, this motel has something no other can claim: proprietor Gloria Moll, who loves her guests, especially children. She does it all, baking the breakfast goodies (rates include continental breakfast), keeping up the blazing glory of the gardens, cleaning the rooms, and sometimes even producing cakes for kids who happen to be here on their birthdays. The rooms are cute and well maintained but have only showers, no tubs, and there's no room to spare. There are a small pool and room to play outside, where a rabbit roams, and the Salt Pond Visitor Center is nearby.

2555 Rte. 6 (P.O. Box 282), Eastham, MA 02642. (C) **508/255-7668.** www.beachplummotorlodge.netfirms.com. 5 units, all with shower only. $76–$140 unit. Rollaway $12. Rates include continental breakfast. AE, MC, V. Closed mid-Oct to mid-May. **Amenities:** Pool.

Showers	Fire Pits/Grills	Laundry	Public Phones	Reservations	Fees	Open
Yes	Yes	Yes	Yes	Yes	$26–$53	May–Nov
Yes	Yes	Yes	Yes	Yes	$30–$38	May–Sept
Yes	Yes	No	Yes	Yes	$17	Year-round
Yes	Yes	Yes	Yes	Yes	$30	Memorial Day to mid-Sept

WELLFLEET

The Even'tide   The owners of this Route 6 motel know how to make families comfortable. A play area in the courtyard has a miniature golf course for kids, and there's also a basketball court as well as some picnic tables with barbecues. Inside, there's a huge, immaculate indoor swimming pool for rainy days. Refrigerators, coffeemakers, and other useful features for families, such as lots of counter space and practical floor coverings make this a good choice. Large family rooms are in their own building to reduce the chances you will disturb anyone. Although the motel fronts the highway, it backs up to the national seashore, and Marconi Beach is .75 mile away on a forest trail. The rustic cottages are in the woods, by the Cape Cod Rail Trail. And if you can't escape work, Wi-Fi is available. You must reserve many months ahead for the high season.

650 Rte. 6 (P.O. Box 41), South Wellfleet, MA 02663-0041. © 800/368-0007 or 508/349-3410. www.eventidemotel. com. 31 units, 8 cottages. $65–$225 double; $850–$2,350 per week cottages. $15 extra adult, $8 extra child in motel rooms. AE, DC, DISC, MC, V. Closed late Oct to Apr 28. **Amenities:** Indoor pool; 5-hole miniature golf course for kids; horseshoe pits; basketball court; shuffleboard court; Ping-Pong table; barbecue grills; Wi-Fi. *In room:* A/C, TV, fridge, coffeemaker, hair dryer.

Inn at Duck Creeke   Standing a little out of the town center on 5 acres along a tidal creek, the inn's main white clapboard house was built around 1810 and has operated as an inn since the 1940s with the same furnishings, many of them antiques. Although creaky and rough in places, the place has loads of period atmosphere, with plank floors, quilts, lace curtains, and charming, old-fashioned wallpaper, faded by the years. There are no TVs or telephones, and air-conditioning is in the top floor only; these are far from standard accommodations and not a good choice if you want a modern hotel room. Room rates include a light breakfast. The award-winning Sweet Seasons Restaurant is on the grounds.

70 Main St. (P.O. Box 364), Wellfleet, MA 02667. © 508/349-9333. www.innatduckcreeke.com. 26 units, 18 with bathroom. $85–$135 double. $15 extra person, $5 children under 5, $10 moving fee for cribs or cots. AE, MC, V. Closed Nov–Apr. **Amenities:** Restaurant. *In room:* A/C (some rooms only), no phone.

Wellfleet Motel and Lodge   The motto is "squeaky clean," and, indeed, this roadside hotel has a pristine, almost antiseptic feel. Rooms come in two sets, the lodge and motel, in three buildings on large lawns screened from the highway by pines. The large rooms have a cool, solid feel. Although they're without character, they lack nothing that you would find in any midscale chain hotel. Indoor and outdoor pools are on-site. Internet access is available for a fee.

Rte. 6 (P.O. Box 606), South Wellfleet, MA 02663. ℂ 800/852-2900 or 508/349-3535. Fax 508/349-1192. www. wellfleetmotel.com. 65 units. $70–$275 double. $10 each additional person. AE, MC, V. **Amenities:** Restaurant; indoor and outdoor pools; Jacuzzi; video game room; barbecue grills. *In room:* A/C, TV, fridge, coffeemaker, hair dryer, Wi-Fi.

NORTH TRURO & PROVINCETOWN

Kalmar Village   On the edge of Cape Cod Bay just south of Provincetown, Kalmar Village is a collection of trim, white cottages separated by green lawns, hedges, and roses. In the evening adults barbecue and socialize while their kids play on the broad private beach and splash in the outdoor pool. Motel rooms and efficiencies rent by the night, but the self-contained cottages are the thing. Airy and cozy, with wood floors and glass doorknobs, they seem to have been beamed to the present from an ideal past. They have TVs but no phones. Everything is provided, including clam rakes. For July and August, the weeklong cottage stays book up in February.

674 Shore Rd. (P.O. Box 745), North Truro, MA 02652. ℂ 508/487-0585. (Winter: 56 Toxteth St., Boston, MA 02116; ℂ 617/277-0091.) www.kalmarvillage.com. 40 cottages, 15 efficiencies, 3 motel rooms. $70–$145 motel rooms; $69–$205 efficiencies double; $630–$2,545 cottages per week. $25 extra child or adult, rollaway beds and cribs free, in efficiencies. DISC, MC, V. Closed mid-Oct to mid-May. **Amenities:** Pool; coin laundry; barbecue grills; beach; Wi-Fi in common area. *In room:* TV, kitchen, no phone.

COTTAGES & HOUSES

The traditional and still the best way to visit the Cape is to rent a place of your own for a week or two. You'll be able to settle in, play without bothering others, and cook relaxed family meals. You can rent a cottage in a compound, a house or cottage off by itself, or even a house where the resident family has gone on vacation. Two of the motels listed above also rent cottages.

The price range extends from rough little places that cost as much as a motel room to palaces renting for more in a week than many people make in a year. The least expensive one-bedroom cottages far from the water start at around $800 a week during the peak season, and a three-bedroom house goes for $1,800 a week. But prices quickly escalate: Some lavish and sprawling waterfront rentals in Wellfleet actually fetch more than $8,000 a week. It's a renter's market, and prices are rising as much as 10% a year. In the area we cover, prices are highest in Provincetown, lowest in Eastham, and about the same in Wellfleet and Truro (my favorite areas). A bigger factor in price is proximity to the beach or a cute Colonial town center, which costs more.

Starting early—preferably by January—is critical. Not much is left by March. Develop an idea of what you want and how much you can pay; looking at houses on the Internet will help, but don't get attached to one house you see. You have to talk to an agent (such as the ones listed below) to find a place that fits your desires, dates, and budget. If you're flexible about where and when, you can get a better deal and better choice. Remember, there's nothing wrong with bare board walls and a bike ride to the beach—that, not a fancy condo, is the real Cape Cod. Staying 2 weeks also broadens your choices. Be sure to find out about the house's surroundings so that you don't end up on a busy street or otherwise undesirable spot.

Before you go, find out exactly what linens, appliances, kitchen items, telephone service, and other necessities the price includes. Plan all your meals in advance so that you can do one major shopping trip when you arrive. There are no large grocery stores between Orleans and Provincetown, and daily shopping wastes a lot of time in traffic. When you arrive, inventory any problems in writing, and do it again when you leave, to make sure you don't get hit for any unwarranted damages.

For cottages at motels, you can call directly and reserve with a credit card, but real estate agents handle most rentals. They will request references, preferring a previous vacation rental. You'll likely have to pay a large deposit upfront, or even the whole amount, by check, just to make a reservation.

Dozens of agents are listed on the website of the **Cape Cod & Islands Association of Realtors** (© **800/442-0006** or 508/957-4300; www.cciaor.com), with links to agencies' sites, some of which have pictures of houses. You can also find an agent through the chamber of commerce in the town you're interested in (see "Cape Cod Address Book," p. 74). Two of the larger agencies follow.

Cape Cod Realty   This agency has many listings in Wellfleet, with a scattering in Truro and Eastham.

P.O. Box 719, Wellfleet, MA 02667. © **800/545-7670** or 508/349-2245. www.capecodrealty.net.

Duarte/Downey Real Estate Agency   These knowledgeable folks represent as many as 300 homes, mostly in Truro but also spanning the area from Eastham to Provincetown.

12 Truro Center Rd. (P.O. Box 2016), Truro, MA 02666. © **508/349-7588**. www.ddre.com.

6 Family-Friendly Dining
PICNICS & TAKEOUT

Box Lunch, with three locations in our area and more elsewhere, packs meals to go. The emphasis is on healthy ingredients and creative preparation. Most items are around $5 to $6; a kid's sandwich is $3, and the menu tops out at $11 for a lobster salad. The original location is in Wellfleet, just off the town center at 50 Briar Lane (© **508/349-2178;** www.boxlunch.com); also in Provincetown at 353 Commercial St. (© **508/487-6026**); and Eastham on Route 6 (© **508/255-0799**). All locations are open 7am to 7pm daily.

In Truro, a summer-only country store and deli, **Jams Gourmet Grocery,** is at 14 Truro Center Rd., just off Route 6 (© **508/349-1616**). Although the prices will convince you not to do all your shopping there, the rotisserie chicken, gourmet pizzas, and baked goods make for an unforgettable picnic or great takeout for dinner.

LOW-STRESS MEALS
EASTHAM

Arnold's   Long dinner lines form under the yellow canopy at Arnold's, a mainstay since 1976 that proudly points to its humble clam shack beginning. Drawing accolades from Maine to New York for its clams, scallops, lobsters, raw bar (open 5–8pm), and other seafood, Arnold's is great for lunch or dinner. A mile south of the Salt Pond Visitor Center on Route 6, Arnold's also is adjacent to the Cape Cod Rail Trail. Kids can choose hot dogs, burgers, chicken fingers, spaghetti, or macaroni and cheese and then enjoy soft ice cream afterward.

1 mile east of Salt Pond Visitor Center on Rte. 6, Eastham. © **508/255-2575**. www.arnoldsrestaurant.com. Kids' menu, highchairs, booster seats, crayons. Reservations not accepted. Lunch $3–$13; dinner main courses $10–$38; kids' menu $2.25–$5.25. No credit cards. Mid-May to mid-Sept, with expanded hours June 20 to Labor Day daily 11:30am–9pm; closes an hour earlier in spring and Sept.

The Ferro Family Lobster Pool   This place perfects a type: the rough-edged New England seafood joint. The floor is concrete and crab pots hang from an unfinished ceiling, but the fish is as good as you will find anywhere. The downside is you're away from the water and along busy Route 6. For families, the side benefit is that it's hard to bother anyone. The service is fast and relaxed. The children's menu includes a lobster for $19 and other items for $2.95 to $8.50. The grown-ups' menu changes every day, according to fish availability and the chef's whim, but always includes the lobsters swimming around near the front of the place. It gets crowded, so dine early.

4380 Rte. 6, North Eastham. © **508/255-9706**, takeout 508/255-3314. Kids' menu, highchairs, boosters, crayons. Reservations not accepted. Lunch $8.50–$21; dinner main courses $17–$34; kids' menu $2.95–$19. AE, MC, V. Mid-Apr to mid-Oct daily 4–10:30pm. Closed mid-Oct to mid-Apr.

WELLFLEET
The Lighthouse   This diner is the place for a traditional, filling meal, especially breakfast, which offers sweets such as blueberry muffins and raisin French toast as well as omelets. This is a classic small-town diner, with friendly, familiar service, a bulletin of local events, and enough noise to drown out the children.

317 Main St., Wellfleet. © **508/349-3681**. www.mainstreetlighthouse.com. Kids' menu, highchairs, boosters, crayons. Breakfast $2.80–$8; lunch $4–$11; dinner $6–$23; kids' menu $2.50–$10. DISC, MC, V. Daily 7am–9pm (until 10pm in summer).

Moby Dick's   This big family-run and -oriented fish place has a long history. It serves lobster, sandwiches, and fried fish. Kids who don't like seafood can choose hot dogs, PB&Js, or grilled cheese.

Rte. 6, Wellfleet. © **508/349-9795**. www.mobydicksrestaurant.com. Kids' menu, highchairs, crayons. Lunch $9–$13; dinner $15–$44; kids' menu $3.30–$8. AE, MC, V. Daily 11:30am–10pm (closes earlier in spring and fall).

PROVINCETOWN
Clem & Ursie's Food Ghetto   Near Route 6, Clem & Ursie's is a masterpiece in chaos. It's noisy, you have to negotiate lines, and there are confusing arrangements of counters and fast-food-style tables, but you'll love it once you get your bearings. And the food! Sophisticated seafood prepared in styles from all over the world for shockingly low prices, simple fresh fish, barbecue, home cooking, and even a $6 kids' meal with a prize. Grab a table, then figure out the menu and order at the counter, where you pay and get a number. The food comes quickly.

85–87 Shank Painter Rd., Provincetown. © **508/487-2333**. www.clemandursies.com. Kids' menu, highchairs, booster seats. Breakfast $3–$7; lunch $3–$9.50; dinner $6–$25; kids' menu $6. MC, V. Daily 7am–10pm year-round.

BEST-BEHAVIOR MEALS
Adrian's   Dining on the deck, you can watch a glorious sunset unfold far below on Cape Cod Bay while enjoying wonderful regional Italian cuisine. It includes a lot of seafood but also Italian-style pizzas with ingenious combinations of ingredients. The service is quick and the atmosphere light and friendly. Children need to behave themselves, but the meal won't be tense.

535 Rte. 6, North Truro. © **508/487-4360**. www.adriansrestaurant.com. Kids' menu, highchairs, boosters, crayons. Breakfast $6–$15; main courses dinner $8–$28; kids' menu $6–$7. AE, MC, V. Summer daily 8am–noon and 5:30–9pm. Closed mid-Oct to mid-May.

The Lobster Pot   This place is an institution, its narrow and lively dining rooms overlooking MacMillan Wharf humming like a town nerve center. Arrive early, because it doesn't take reservations, and children won't stand for the wait it requires to get a table. Other aspects do make sense for families, however, including the long and varied menu (served all day), which allows one diner to have an inexpensive burger while another orders blackened tuna sashimi. It's a good choice for a special lobster dinner. Kids averse to seafood can go back to the basics: hot dogs, burgers, fish and chips, or chicken fingers.

321 Commercial St., Provincetown. © 508/487-0842. www.ptownlobsterpot.com. Kids' menu, highchairs, boosters, crayons. Reservations not accepted. Lunch or dinner $10–$28; kids' menu $5–$8. AE, DC, DISC, MC, V. Summer daily 11:30am–10:30pm; off season daily 11:30am–9:30pm.

7 Exploring Cape Cod National Seashore with Your Kids

ENTRANCE & USE FEES   In the summer, the national seashore charges visitors to use the beaches it manages. Fees are $15 per day, or $45 for a season pass, for each vehicle. See "Beachgoing" (p. 94) for more details. You also can use one of the forms of the America the Beautiful Pass. For details, see chapter 2.

REGULATIONS   Don't climb on the dunes and bluffs except on a marked path, because this speeds erosion. You need a permit from a visitor center (see earlier in this chapter) for an open wood fire. Charcoal grills and camp stoves are okay in picnic areas and on ocean beaches. Pets must be kept on a short leash and are not allowed on bike or nature trails, on beaches with lifeguards, in shorebird nesting areas, or, from May 15 to October 15, in freshwater ponds.

NATURAL PLACES: CAPE COD NATIONAL SEASHORE
PROVINCE LANDS

The tip of the Cape, set aside early on as a common area for the people of Plymouth Colony, is a broad lowland of **sand dunes** and a few **woods,** a kind of desert on the sea. It's a strange, unfamiliar place, where forests of weathered trees fight a slow-motion war with the dunes that are trying to smother them. The area is strung with bike and nature trails, and it has great ocean beaches for swimming or walking. See "For the Active Family" (p. 94) for biking and beachgoing here.

Everything north of Pilgrim Heights, including Provincetown and all the Province Lands, is nothing more than a huge sandbar. For around 6,000 years, since the sea level rose high enough for waves to lick the Cape's bluffs, currents running north along the shore have washed sand from those higher shores and dropped it here. Early settlers stripped the area of trees (of a forest, really) and recovery has taken a long time. Photographs at the **Province Lands Visitor Center,** on Race Point Road (p. 78), show how the landscape has changed in a few generations.

A rare stand of **beeches** off Race Point Road near Route 6 is one of a few surviving patches of the kind of forest that covered much of the Cape when the Pilgrims arrived. In the long history of a piece of sandy ground, different kinds of plants follow each other as the capabilities of each match and change the soil. The beech forest is the last step in this process of plant succession. The **Beech Forest Trail** winds for miles through this peaceful and shady environment, over steep dunes long ago locked down by roots and around a pair of ponds carpeted by lily pads. There are some steps, but it should be an easy walk for anyone over age 4.

An interesting building, the **1898 Old Harbor Lifesaving Station** (© 508/487-1256), stands at the east end of the Race Point Beach parking lot. A one-room display of lifesaving equipment is worth a look if you're at the beach anyway but doesn't justify a special trip. During July and August there are demonstrations of the Lyle gun (see "History: Finding the 'Real' Cape Cod," p. 74, to learn about the lifesavers' work) every Thursday at 6pm.

> ⌒ *Fun Fact* **A Glacial Mess**
> _____
>
> Cape Cod is another glacial moraine—a glacier's pile of leftovers (see "Aca-dia's Ice Age," p. 62). Looking at a map of the Massachusetts coast, let your imagination fill in where the tongue-shaped glacier must have been, where Cape Cod Bay is now. As glaciers plowed the landscape, they bulldozed sand and rock in front of them. The east-west, upper-arm-shaped part of Cape Cod is as far south as the glaciers came during the last glacial period. When the glaciers were melting, the area still stood well above sea level, so the sand and rock piled up on the ground as a long hill. When the water rose, much later, that hill became the southern Cape. The northern, forearm-shaped part of the Cape, where the national seashore is, grew from crushed rock left between two glaciers. A river flowed here, spreading the rock and sand flowing from the glaciers; when the glaciers melted, the riverbed was the ridge that is the Cape. Buried inside it were huge pieces of glacier ice that hadn't melted. When that buried ice melted, it left big holes called ket-tles. Some kettles filled with water, forming freshwater ponds like those at Nickerson State Park, or saltwater bays, such as Salt Pond at the national seashore visitor center in Eastham.

PILGRIM HEIGHTS

This is an unusual place to see a sharp break between two kinds of land. The heights are the northern end of the Cape's **glacial highlands** (turn right from Rte. 6 as you head north from Truro); north of here the land has all been built by sand washing around in the ocean. It's also a historic spot, where the Pilgrims, on their scouting expeditions from Provincetown, first found water in the New World. A **short nature trail** leads to that spot. Another, the **Small's Swamp Trail,** crosses a swamp that was used for farming by Native Americans and by white farmers, with signs to explain the archaeological sites (pick up a trail guide brochure at information centers or at the trail head).

Looking over the bluff from the heights, you can see an area of salt meadow extend-ing far to the sea, a field of dunes covered with beach grass and decorated by oddly shaped little ponds. A **picnic area, restrooms,** and an **information kiosk** are by the parking lot, and a bike trail leads to **Head of the Meadow Beach.**

OUTER BEACHES

Walking along the Atlantic Ocean side of the Cape is like walking in a watercolor painting: a strip of beach, a strip of sea, a blue sky, and a bluff. The pale sun-washed sand, the cool ocean breeze, and the jagged sparkling water rumbling into froth—everything is so bright, it all seems to vibrate.

These beaches are inspiring, a high-energy shoreline—that means **big ocean waves** with a lot of power behind them. The battering waves move the sand around and keep most plants and animals from being able to live here.

Swimming on the outer beaches is for fit adults and big kids only. The beaches with bluffs extend from Wellfleet to North Truro. Look for more low-profile beaches at the Province Lands and from Eastham south. See "Beachgoing" (p. 94) for advice on where to go and what to do, as well as access issues.

BAY BEACHES

Although as little as a mile from the Atlantic-facing beaches, the shoreline along Cape Cod Bay feels completely different. The waves are smaller, the water warmer, and the sand often is coarser, with more seaweed, clams, snails, and other creatures. This is a lower-energy beach. Waves don't have enough room on Cape Cod Bay to pick up much wind energy compared to waves on the wide Atlantic Ocean. Because the waves hit with less force, the sand moves around less, creating **flatter beaches** and allowing **more plants and animals** to flourish. Towns control most of the shore on this side (see "Beachgoing," p. 94), except the wonderful area east of Wellfleet Harbor, site of the **Great Island Trail** (see "Nature Walks," p. 97).

SALT MARSH

The salt marsh is a safe harbor for all kinds of life. Because it is completely protected from waves, it's the lowest-energy shoreline and produces the most **plants, animals,** and **insects.** (See "How a Salt Marsh Is Made," in chapter 5.) Water slowly flows in with the tide, bringing food and sediment to feed grasses, seaweed, crabs, clams, snails, fish, mice, voles, otters, and many varieties of birds, including herons and egrets. It can be a mysterious place, a maze of watery channels among the grasses where you feel as though you might find anything. The best way to explore the salt marshes is by **canoe** (see "Canoeing & Kayaking," p. 97), but you can get a sense for the areas and scope for birds on nature trails, among the best of which is the **Nauset Marsh Trail** (see "Nature Walks," p. 97).

LIGHTHOUSES

Six lighthouses stand out on bluffs and sandy points from Chatham to Race Point. Starting in 1798, passengers on ships from Europe to America saw the first sign that they had arrived at our continent in a flash of the **Highland Light** (also called Cape Cod Light), above the sea cliffs in Truro. The lights are generally not open for tours, but the **Highland House Museum** (✆ **508/487-3397;** open daily 10am–4:30pm in summer) stands near Highland Light on Light House Road, off South Highland Drive. **Chatham Light** dates to 1878; a light has stood on that point since 1808. **Nauset Light** is also relatively easy to get to, off Route 6, and may be open in summer on Sunday evenings. **Race Point Light** is a good walk several miles west down Race Point Beach from the parking lot, and **Wood End** and **Long Point** lights are on Long Point, an island in Provincetown Harbor that you can reach by pontoon boat that leaves from MacMillan Wharf every half-hour, operated by **Flyer's Boat Rental** (✆ **508/487-0898;** $15 round-trip). You can also walk out to Long Point along the breakwater, a long jetty made up of boulders. This is a substantial hike, about 90 minutes on soft sand. The Cape Cod Museum of Natural History leads day and overnight trips to **Monomoy Island** off Chatham and the light there, which it controls (see "Kid-Friendly Programs," p. 99).

NATURAL PLACES
NICKERSON STATE PARK

The park is a great place for camping, biking, hiking, lake swimming, and messing around in small boats, which are for rent by the hour. The 1,900-acre park surrounds a set of ponds created by big chunks of buried ice that were left behind when the glaciers melted. When these chunks melted, the ground caved in around them, forming **kettle ponds.** The area belonged to the wealthy Nickerson family until they donated it to Massachusetts in 1934. Civilian Conservation Corps workers during the Great

Depression planted long rows of white pine, which have grown tall and grand. More recently, the state added a small stretch of bay beach and salt marsh. The park is in Brewster at 3488 Main St. (© **508/896-3491**); take Route 6A west from Orleans. Also see "Biking" (p. 96) and "Campgrounds" (p. 83).

WELLFLEET BAY WILDLIFE SANCTUARY

The **Massachusetts Audubon Society** maintains 5 miles of **trails** that weave through a lovely 1,100-acre preserve of wetlands, woods, and meadows around the south end of Wellfleet Bay. The sanctuary, which began as a private bird research station in 1928, is a great place for a family ramble. Learn about the plants and the birds while exploring paths well designed to unfold views and hidden places. Several trails get a close look at the salt marsh. Stop at the **nature center** to look at the aquarium and pick up a free map and, if available, a printed trail guide that explains what you see. The society also offers naturalist-guided walks, guided outings elsewhere on the Cape, and a summer day camp (see "Kid-Friendly Programs," p. 99). The sanctuary is off West Road in South Wellfleet (© **508/349-2615;** www.wellfleetbay.org); there's a sign on Route 6. The trail fee is $5 for adults, $3 for children. The visitor center is open daily 8:30am to 5pm in summer, the trails 8am to dusk all year. An exceptional campground (20 sites, $260 per week from the third Sat in July until the Sat before Labor Day; $35 per night outside those dates) is only for people who have been members of the society for at least 1 year before booking a site.

PLACES FOR LEARNING
IN PROVINCETOWN

Provincetown Museum & Pilgrim Monument   The large, homegrown museum houses a lot of items that children will enjoy: a doll collection, a horse-drawn fire truck, and many models, including a large *Mayflower,* among other things. It's an old-fashioned place showing off the work of local people representing their own history. You could spend a couple of hours looking at the exhibits while those who lose interest play outside on the broad lawn or climb the monument. It's a 252-foot tower of massive granite blocks, the tallest all-granite structure in the United States. It was completed in 1910, commemorating the Pilgrim's landfall at Provincetown on November 11, 1620. The tower can be seen from far out to sea and down the Cape, and the view from the top is amazing. The climb is not excessively scary, but the 116 stairs and 60 ramps should burn some excess energy; and it's fun to see the stones donated by different towns set in the walls of the stairwell. The museum has plenty of free parking, making it a good starting point for a visit to Provincetown. To avoid the pedestrian-dominated downtown streets, turn left from Route 6 north onto Shank Painter Road, left again on Jerome Smith Road, right on Winslow Street, and left on High Pole Hill Road into the lot.

High Pole Hill Rd. © **800/247-1620** or 508/487-1310. www.pilgrim-monument.org. Admission $7 adults, $5 students and seniors, $3.50 children 4–14, free for children under 4. July–Aug daily 9am–7pm; Apr–June and Sept–Nov daily 9am–5pm. Admission stops 45 min. before closing. Closed Dec–Mar.

Expedition Whydah Sea Lab and Learning Center   This small commercial museum displays the discoveries of ongoing treasure hunts from two real pirate ships. The Whydah (pronounced *wid*-dah) was driven onto the outer beach in a nor'easter storm in 1717 while returning from plundering the Caribbean. The survivors were hanged in Boston. The same expedition team recently uncovered the remains of Captain Kidd's flagship on an island off Madagascar. The museum is intriguing because it

Provincetown Notes

When you visit Provincetown to take a boat ride, go whale-watching, or visit the museums, try to time your visit to avoid the crowds. In summer on weekends and at midafternoon the streets are choked with people. Also, expect to see a lot of homosexual couples showing affection and people who may be dressed outrageously in the evening. Think ahead about how to explain this to any children who may be confused by it.

preserves the mystery of underwater archaeology instead of cleaning everything up. You can see lumps of material still waiting to be taken apart. The museum's office also sells tickets for the fast ferry to Boston.

16 MacMillan Wharf. 🕾 **508/487-8899**. www.whydah.com. Admission $8 adults, $6 children 6–12, free for children under 6. High season daily 10am–8pm; low season daily 10am–5pm. Closed Nov–Apr.

IN EASTHAM & WELLFLEET

Paths at each of these two sites are covered under "Nature Walks" (p. 97).

Marconi Station Site *(Overrated)*   From this high ocean bluff on January 18, 1903, Guglielmo Marconi started the era of instant radio communication with the first meaningful wireless message between America and Europe by Morse code. Most of the ruins either eroded into the sea or were dismantled after the station was shut down in 1917. Located 6 miles north of the Salt Pond Visitor Center off Route 6, the site offers an information kiosk, incredible views over the bluff and clear across the Cape, and access to the Atlantic White Cedar Swamp Trail. A free guide brochure explains the site.

Marconi Site Rd., off Rte. 6, South Wellfleet. No phone.

Penniman House   Captain Edward Penniman used whaling profits to build his fanciful yellow house with a cupola in 1868. The gate is a whale's jawbone. Penniman went to sea at age 11 and rose through the ranks to make his fortune. Inside the house you can see the interesting records of the voyages he took with his wife, each of which lasted years. The rooms are mostly bare, however, and will likely hold your interest for no more than 20 minutes.

Fort Hill Rd., off Rte. 6 south of the Salt Pond Visitor Center, Eastham. 🕾 **508/255-3421**. Free admission. July–Aug Tues and Fri 1–4pm; ranger tours Mon and Sat at 10am. Closed Sept–June.

IN BREWSTER

Cape Cod Museum of Natural History   The museum has good exhibits, such as tanks of tide-pool animals and fish, mounted birds for identification, and simple, clear teaching tools on ecological concepts. It's more of an educational center than a static museum. The enthusiastic staff and volunteers lead visitors outdoors to learn about the museum's extensive marsh and bayfront grounds. (For more on the outings and children's day camps, see "Kid-Friendly Programs," p. 99.) Call or write ahead for the extensive calendar of shows, events, and trips. On rainy days the museum organizes informal talks, microscope viewing, and the like. The winter closure is a new plan at this writing; some trails may remain open while the museum is closed.

869 Rte. 6A. 🕾 **508/896-3867**. www.ccmnh.org. Admission $8 adults, seniors $7, $3.50 children 3–12, free for children under 3. June–Sept daily 10am–4pm; Oct–Mar Wed–Sun noon–4pm; Apr–May Wed–Sun 10am–4pm.

8 For the Active Family

BEACHGOING

ACCESS & FEES   The beach itself is public everywhere on the Cape, but beach access is not. Beaches managed by the national seashore are open to all. Town beach access often is restricted to people living or renting a cottage or a motel room within town limits.

The Park Service charges $15 a day or $45 a season for a beach pass that's good for everyone in the car. National passes cover the fees (see "Entrance Fees" and "Passes," both in chapter 2, for details).

Some town beaches are open for daily use for fees listed under "Town Beaches," below; others require a beach sticker on your car that only renters in the town can get. Renters buy the sticker for around $50 a week by showing a lease or a special form from a hotel at the town office. Get details from your host or landlord or the local chamber of commerce (see "Cape Cod Address Book," p. 74).

CHOOSING A BEACH   The beaches on the eastern, outer side of the Cape have fine sand for sand castles, limitless distances for beach walks, crashing waves to body-surf in and to watch and listen to, relatively cold water, sea-polished shells, and some shorebirds. The beaches on the western, Cape Cod Bay side of the Cape are tamer and safer for young children to wade and swim in. The waves are smaller, the water is warmer and calmer, and the beaches are more gradual—waders don't have to worry about getting in too deep. At low tide, the beach widens and you can look for sea crea-tures and watch shorebirds feeding. The sand is coarser, and there's more seaweed and gunk.

AVOIDING CROWDS   The most crowded beaches are the national seashore beaches and the town beaches that are open to the public. Beaches in Provincetown and Orleans are usually more crowded than those in Truro and Wellfleet, with East-ham in between. Town beaches restricted to residents and renters in Truro and Well-fleet may be least crowded of all—a good reason to rent there and get access. These towns control many miles of pristine beach, usually without lifeguards, that are uncrowded even at the height of the season. Some of the parking lots fit only a cou-ple dozen cars. The gatekeeper is a teenager in a lawn chair, or no one at all in the morning or evening, when you may be able to go without a permit. Also, no permit may be required in early June or in September.

When national seashore parking lots fill, cars form a line at the gate waiting for someone to leave. If the line is long, try another beach. But once you get in, you can be as solitary as you want by walking away from the access point. Most people either are lazy or like crowds, because they pack together tightly rather than take a short walk. If you have a good way to carry small children and you limit your beach bag-gage, you'll be able to go farther. Also, go to the beach in the morning before the crowds arrive and while the sand isn't as hot as it is in midafternoon, or wait until late afternoon when most folks are heading home.

NATIONAL SEASHORE BEACHES

The national seashore beaches, which generally are on the outer shore, have showers, bathrooms, and lifeguards, and, with a single exception, don't sell food or have any commercial services. You need to bring everything with you, including beverages.

Fun Fact **The Mysterious Tides**

Invisible forces from outer space caused the glacial periods, and they control the daily cycle of life on the shore every day. Just watch the tide rise and fall.

The tides are caused by the gravity of the moon and sun pulling on the surface of the ocean. Because the oceans are very large and the water flows freely, even a tiny pull of gravity tends to pile up water in the spot nearest the thing that's pulling. As the moon passes over the ocean, that bulge of water follows along with it, growing a couple of feet high in the middle of the ocean. When the bulge of water reaches shore, however, it piles up much deeper against the barrier of land. The tide rises.

At Acadia National Park, the difference between the high and low tides, or the tidal range, averages 12 feet. At Cape Cod National Seashore, it's about 7 feet, and at Cape Hatteras it's only 2 feet or less. Some days the tide rises higher, and sometimes not so high. When you go to bed at night, you can predict whether the next day's tides will be big or small by looking at the moon. Big tides, called spring tides because the water springs up higher, happen when the moon is full or just a sliver (called a new moon). Little tides that don't come as high or fall as low are called neap tides. They come when the moon is half full.

To understand why this is so, you have to imagine the earth, sun, and moon in space. The sun pulls on the ocean the same as the moon does, but because the sun is so much farther away, its pull is a bit less than half as hard as the moon's. When the moon and sun both pull together, either because they are on the same side of the earth or because they are on opposite sides, their gravity and centrifugal force add together, and pull the water higher on those two sides. That's when we get spring tides. But when the moon is crossways to the sun compared to the earth, the two pull the water in different directions. With the two pulling against each other, not much water moves, so we get neap tides.

The sun, moon, and earth also wobble and tip as they fly through space. Their paths in orbit, never a perfect circle, constantly change shape. All these motions alter the tides, too. By studying the motions, scientists found that the same pattern of tides repeats every 18.6 years. Using that knowledge, and measuring how high the tide comes at each point in the cycle in many different places, they have learned to predict how high the tide will be at any one time in any one place. The predictions are printed in tide books and even in the newspapers in coastal communities, where mariners and clam diggers need the information every day. (For more information or to get tide predictions, visit http://co-ops.nos.noaa.gov.)

- **Coast Guard Beach** *(Kids Kids Kids)*, one of our favorites, is near the Salt Pond Visitor Center in Eastham. Most summer days you have to park a distance from the beach and take a free shuttle. The beach forms a thin barrier around Nauset Marsh. Walk south to the end of the beach and you might spot seals frolicking just off the shoreline.

- **Nauset Light Beach** is just a mile north of Coast Guard Beach on Ocean View Drive near the famous lighthouse. If you don't want to mess with the shuttle at Coast Guard Beach, it's a good alternative, and it's usually less crowded than Coast Guard Beach.
- **Marconi Beach,** in south Wellfleet, is isolated at the end of a longish park road, with no other beach access over the towering cliffs for miles in either direction.
- **Head of the Meadow Beach,** down an unpaved road in North Truro, may be the least used of the national seashore beaches. A town beach is right next to it, and a park bike trail leads to the interesting Pilgrim Heights area (p. 90).
- **Race Point** is a wide, north-facing, white-sand beach in the midst of the busy Province Lands area, and it has the historic **Old Harbor Lifesaving Station** (p. 89). The beach is popular, and many people bike there on the trails from Provincetown.
- **Herring Cove Beach,** near Provincetown at the southwest tip of the Province Lands, is the only national seashore beach facing west, toward Cape Cod Bay. It's halfway between a fine-grained, high-energy ocean beach and a calm, coarse, gradual bay beach. A food stand offers snacks. The parking lot often fills.
- **Remote Beaches,** tens of miles of them, are waiting, if you can get to them. One way is by off-road vehicle (p. 98). Another is on a shuttle boat across Provincetown Harbor to Long Point (not part of the national seashore; see "Lighthouses," p. 91).

TOWN BEACHES

Below I've listed other town beaches open to everyone (not those that require a sticker), along with the daily nonresident fee at each beach:

- **Eastham** (bay side): **Cooks Brook Beach** off Massasoit Road and **First Encounter Beach,** off Samoset Road. Daily fee $15, $50 per week.
- **Wellfleet** (bay side): **Mayo Beach,** on Kendrick Avenue by the town pier. Free. Outer side: **White Crest Beach,** Ocean View Drive, and **Cahoon Hollow Beach,** Cahoon Hollow Road. Fee for 3 days $30, 1 week $60.
- **Truro** (bay side): **Corn Hill Beach,** Corn Hill Road. Daily fee $10.

BIKING

The Cape has several recreational bike trails. The longest is the 24-mile **Cape Cod Rail Trail** 𝕬𝕬𝕬, a state park path on the old rail line between Dennis and Wellfleet. The path is flat and has long, straight sections through scrub pine, but it also passes ponds, bay beaches, and Marconi Beach. It runs near the Salt Pond Visitor Center, where a 1.7-mile bike trail leads to Coast Guard Beach. At its midpoint, the rail trail crosses part of Nickerson State Park, where it meets an 8-mile bike trail that passes through the woods and past the campground and ponds. The park manages the rail trail (see "Nickerson State Park," under "Natural Places," p. 91), and a detailed trail guide and map is widely available.

An 8-mile bike trail, the **Province Lands Trail,** explores the strange area of dune and forest at the tip of the Cape (see "Province Lands," p. 89). The path starts at the visitor center or any of several other spots and leads to Race Point Beach, the Beech Forest Trail, and Herring Cove Beach. This is a fun and interesting ride over steep, rippling hills and around sharp corners, but it's heavily used. The Park Service also maintains a less-used 2-mile trail that connects Head of the Meadow Beach to the Pilgrim Heights picnic area and High Head Road, a beautiful area (see "Pilgrim Heights,"

p. 90). The Park Service gives away a map of its three trails at the visitor centers, where you can also buy an inexpensive booklet, *The Cape Cod Bike Book,* which covers all the trails on the Cape and the connecting roads. Bike-rental agencies are listed under "Getting Around" (p. 80).

CANOEING & KAYAKING

To quote Kenneth Grahame's *The Wind in the Willows,* "There is nothing—absolutely nothing—half so much worth doing as simply messing about in boats." The salt marshes and tidal estuaries of Cape Cod are the best sort of place for that. Paddling through the braided waterways, you can easily imagine that you're discovering hidden places for the first time. This also is the best way to see a lot of birds, animals, and sea life, from snails and crabs to impressive great blue herons, egrets, and osprey. The marsh is biologically rich and the canoe is quiet. Canoeing here is easy over smooth, shallow water; but the currents can be strong, and occasionally you run out of water and need to drag the canoe. Wear water shoes or rubber boots. (Read more in "How a Salt Marsh Is Made," in chapter 5.)

We had a great day, despite rain, exploring part of the huge **Nauset Marsh,** in Eastham. A launch spot and parking lot is near Salt Pond on Route 6, just before the turn for the Salt Pond Visitor Center. Paddling out a narrow channel puts you in the marsh, still more than a mile from the outer, barrier beach. Paddling into the channels from here, you are soon out on your own in a landscape of green grass and water, sand, and mud, frequently encountering wildlife. The **Pamet River,** in Truro, also offers placid paddling and easy access.

Canoes and kayaks are for rent all over the Cape. **Goose Hummock Shop** on 6A in Orleans is a good rental shop (© **508/255-2620;** www.goose.com) and also offers kayak lessons. Several organizations offer guided paddles to learn about canoeing and nature. The **Park Service** offers trips almost every day in midsummer in Nauset Marsh from the visitor center, in Pleasant Bay in Orleans, or in ponds, for adults and children (age limits depend on the trip). For most of the paddles, you need some idea of how to paddle a canoe, but one is for beginners. A list of current offerings appears in the park newspaper or on the website (www.nps.gov/caco). Tickets are $20 for adults, $12 for children 16 and under for paddles ranging up to 3 hours, and you need to reserve up to a week in advance. The best plan is to call the week before you go, because the trips fill fast. Reservations are taken in person at the Salt Pond Visitor Center starting at 9am 7 days before the trip, or starting at 9:30am by telephone (© **508/255-3421**). Pay when you register, by credit card only if by phone.

The **Audubon Society's Wellfleet Bay Wildlife Sanctuary** also offers paddles for families with kids 12 and up. See "Cape Cod Address Book" (p. 74) for contact information for either organization.

NATURE WALKS

The Cape's trails are short. Only the **Great Island Trail** (see below) extends more than a couple of miles. Several make good outings with children, showing off a varied environment. Among the best walks are those on the 5-mile network of trails at the **Wellfleet Bay Wildlife Sanctuary** (p. 92). The **Beech Forest Trail** is truly lovely (see "Province Lands," p. 89). The **Small's Swamp Trail** tours thick woods (see "Pilgrim Heights," p. 90). Here are some other choices:

- **Atlantic White Cedar Swamp Trail:** Starting from the parking lot for the Marconi Station Site (p. 93), at the end of Marconi Site Road in Wellfleet, the flat

1-mile trail crosses from the sandy shoreline habitat of scrub pines to a mossy, shady grove where, from a looping boardwalk, you can find frogs in swamp pools. Notice the different kinds of plants that grow near the sea and farther back in the swamp, and ask your kids why.

- **Buttonbush Trail:** Across the parking lot from the Salt Pond Visitor Center in Eastham (p. 78), the trail is designed to teach children what the outdoors is like to the blind. A grown-up can read the guide brochure while the kids close their eyes and feel their way along the guide rope. It's fun.

- **Fort Hill and Red Maple Swamp trails:** From the grounds of the Penniman House in Eastham (p. 93), the Fort Hill Trail circles 1.5 miles through red cedar along Nauset Salt Marsh, to Skiff Hill. It offers good views of the marsh and beaches and an old Indian sharpening stone. It's a great birding trail. The trail joins the Red Maple Swamp nature trail, a short boardwalk loop where you can look for frogs, turtles, woodpeckers, and catbirds (a little gray bird that mews like a cat and may come out of hiding if it hears you mewing).

- **Great Island Trail:** The national seashore's only substantial hike is this glorious 4-mile (one-way) trail along the sandy strip of land that separates Wellfleet Harbor from Cape Cod Bay. The trail head is near the end of Chequessett Neck Road, west of the Wellfleet town center. The woods and wild beaches feel like primeval Cape Cod, but, in fact, a village once stood here, where people would beach whales to cook out their oil over wood fires. They cut all the trees to build the fires, and without trees, erosion washed away the village. Archaeologists turned up ruins of a tavern in the forest that has recovered (there's nothing there to see), but the hike's main allure is its wildness. The final section is above water only at low tide.

- **Nauset Marsh Trail:** Starting from the Salt Pond Visitor Center (p. 78), the 1-mile loop trail rounds the shore of the pond and then overlooks the marsh from a bluff. With a scope or strong binoculars, it would be a good vantage for birding. You also get to pass through thick shoreline vegetation of oak and eastern red cedar.

OFF-ROAD DRIVING

A section of the outer beach at the end of Cape Cod from Race Point Light to Head of the Meadow Beach is open for over-sand driving during the summer and even beach camping in RVs with the right equipment. If you own a high-clearance four-wheel-drive vehicle (rentals are prohibited) and aren't afraid to put some accelerated wear and tear on it in the salty sand, this can be a fun way to get to fishing or remote beach walks. But call ahead (© **508/487-3698**) or check the website (www.nps.gov/caco/planyourvisit/oversand.htm), because you will need one of a limited number of permits, which run $50 a week just to drive on the beach, $75 a week if you plan to camp in your RV. You must also comply with various regulations and an inspection (most vehicles lack the right tires, for example). The **Race Point Ranger Station** (© **508/487-3698**) manages the system.

SAILING

I doubt there are many places in the world like Provincetown's **MacMillan Wharf,** where you can shop for your choice of wooden schooners, as well as various other vessels, for day trips. The trips last a couple of hours and leave several times daily. Ticket booths and vessels are side by side on the dock, so you can choose the boat and the price you want. Fares range from $18 to $24 for adults, roughly half that for kids. If you want to plan ahead, call the schooner *Bay Lady II* (© **508/487-9308;** www.sail capecod.com).

You can have even more fun sailing your own boat for an afternoon. We had a won-derful time on a 19-foot boat in Wellfleet Harbor, a large, protected, but not too calm body of water. **Wellfleet Marine Corp.** (© **508/349-2233**) offers boats from a booth at the town dock—prices range from $45 for the first hour to $125 a day for motor boats—and has skiffs for fishing. In Provincetown Harbor, **Flyer's Boat Rental,** 131A Commercial St. (© **508/487-0898;** http://flyersrentals.com), offers a wide range of sail- and powerboats, plus rowboats and kayaks. Sailboats are $45 for the first hour to $150 a day. Flyer's also offers sailing lessons by reservation.

WHALE-WATCHING ★★

Migrating humpback, finback, and right whales show up every day off Cape Cod, in **Stellwagen Bank National Marine Sanctuary** or **Cape Cod Bay Critical Habitat Area,** where the Pilgrims first saw whales and later colonists invented whaling. The whales stop here to feed on their way north for the summer, and the area has become a center of whale research and a popular place to see whales. All whale-watching is from boats. It's hard to grasp how big these animals are until you're with them. Chil-dren are as impressed as adults, although young children may not have the patience to watch the whales for as long as grown-ups want to. And some don't like being on small boats.

The **Center for Coastal Studies,** P.O. Box 1036, Provincetown, MA 02657 (© **508/487-3622;** www.coastalstudies.org), works to study and protect the whales, especially the dwindling right whales, by untangling them from fishing nets and diverting ships that might hit them. The center has named more than 1,000 hump-back whales and keeps track of their life stories—staffers can recognize individuals by the white markings on their tails that show when they sound. Contact the center if you want to learn more, or pick up a copy of the "Whale Sighting Guide" chart sold by the Park Service, at the Center for Coastal Studies office, and elsewhere.

Several competing companies send boats from Provincetown's MacMillan Wharf several times a day to see the whales, competing fiercely on price and service on trips that last 3 to 4 hours. We went with **The Dolphin Fleet** (© **800/826-9300** or 508/240-3636; www.whalewatch.com). The boat was large and stable, with ample deck room. More important, the guide was a naturalist from the Center for Coastal Stud-ies who really knew his stuff and gave a fascinating commentary, including his first-hand stories of rescuing net-entrapped whales. The Dolphin Fleet has worked with the center for years, using these commercial whale-watching trips to count and identify the whales as part of its scientific work. Onboard you can consult a huge catalog con-taining the life story and ancestry of every whale you see. They run mid-April through late October, as often as nine times a day in midsummer. The peak-season fare is $33 for adults, $25 for children 5 to 12, and free for children under 5. Discounts often can be found on the group's website. Reservations aren't needed. To avoid seasickness, avoid going in rough weather; also see "Seasickness & Motion Sickness," in chapter 2.

9 Kid-Friendly Programs

Four organizations schedule naturalist offerings in the national seashore area, includ-ing the National Park Service, Nickerson State Park, Cape Cod Museum of Natural History, and the Audubon Society's Wellfleet Bay Wildlife Sanctuary. The last two of these also offer summer day camps for children. Each place is described earlier in this chapter, and contact information for all four is listed under "Cape Cod Address Book" (p. 74). I've also listed Cape Cod Sea Camps, which has day and residential camps. Many of the activities and all the camps require planning and advance reservations, so request details before your trip.

CAPE COD NATIONAL SEASHORE

The national seashore offers one of the most extensive schedules of **ranger programs** in the national park system. Choices are listed in the park newspaper and on the website (www.nps.gov/caco). They start at many points. **Campfires** take place on the beaches after a walk away from the access point. **Walks** on the tidal flats and in the salt marshes teach about the plants and creatures there. **Tours** of historic houses and musical and literary programs take place in various locations. Some **programs** teach new skills and sports, including surf-casting, canoeing, and shellfishing. Several programs are aimed specifically at families with children, and kids are welcome with their families on most. The best programs require reservations and often carry a fee. *Tip:* I recommend mapping it all out before you come, planning your days to minimize driving and to make sure you get reservations for what you want to do.

The Park Service produces a good **Junior Ranger** booklet intended for children ages 8 to 12, which you can get for free at either visitor center. Younger children would enjoy some of the matching exercises and illustrated check-off lists of different kinds of Cape Cod architecture and animals, if not the writing activities. The booklet is designed for use at home as well, recognizing that you don't want to sit inside doing workbooks if the weather is good. To earn a Junior Ranger patch, children ages 8 to 12 complete six workbook activities, attend two ranger programs, and visit and write about park sites—not easy, but doable. Kids ages 5 to 7 have a separate list of requirements to meet to earn a patch.

NICKERSON STATE PARK 🏕🏕🏕

The state park's **Junior Ranger** program comes with an excellent book of outdoor activities aimed at school-age children who read well and have a good attention span. After completing 8 of the 12 activities and an evaluation form, kids get a patch and certificate from the Massachusetts Department of Environmental Management.

A kids' **nature center** near the park entrance has activities for children 6 to 14 just about every day of the summer. It's a casual, drop-off arrangement with a ranger who takes the children for a couple of hours for walks, games, and activities—they were making a pond when I visited. Parents can take off on their own. The park also has programs for families together, including guided nature walks, campfires, and the like.

CAPE COD MUSEUM OF NATURAL HISTORY

The museum has day camps and **programs** for families. Contact them ahead for times and registration (see "Cape Cod Address Book," p. 74). **Day camps** for children as young as preschool and as old as seventh grade last through July and August. Many are just one or two sessions of a few hours, a chance for the family to split up and pursue individual interests without a huge investment of time. Sessions include nature encounters, artistic inspiration, and science skills—they might dig in the tidal mud or make casts of animal tracks. A typical session for kids 6 to 7 lasts 2 hours and costs $115 per three-session week. The museum also offers a day camp of 5 full days for grades one to six and a field school for grades seven to nine. Tuition is about $180 to $250.

Tips Places for Relaxed Play & Picnics

You're never far from a picnic area in the national seashore. The Pilgrim Heights picnic area is mentioned on p. 90. A picnic ground is at Doane Rock, a boulder the size of a house left by a glacier, near the Salt Pond Visitor Center. Others are at the starting points of the Great Island Trail in Wellfleet (p. 98) and the Beech Forest Trail in the Province Lands area (p. 89). I've listed places that pack picnics under "Family-Friendly Dining" (p. 87). The towns generally have small public libraries and school playgrounds for downtime.

WELLFLEET BAY WILDLIFE SANCTUARY

The **Audubon Society** offers programs at its sanctuary and afield focused on adults, families, and kids, and day camps for age 4 through ninth grade. Reservations are necessary for most programs, so request the catalog in advance (see "Cape Cod Address Book," p. 74).

During the high season many programs a day are in session, on many subjects other than birding. **Children's programs** cost as little as $5 or $7—the cost of the aquarium tour, nighttime bug and critter prowl, or nature crafts, and many others. **Family and adult programs** include guided walks at the sanctuary for birding, shoreline study, and the like. Other appealing outings go afield, including the superb boat cruises: birding through Nauset Marsh, pulling up sea creatures from under Wellfleet Bay, or watching gray seals off Chatham. There are several other choices, some aimed specifically at families. Prices are $40 or less for adults, less for children under 13.

The Audubon Society's July and August **day camps** are in five age groups, starting with 4-year-olds, who spend 5 fun mornings at the sanctuary learning about nature for a tuition of $195 for nonmembers, $145 for members. The next two age groups have similar programs, while groups of grades three through five and grades six through nine might concentrate on a particular scientific topic all week and stay busy with activities such as snorkeling and sea kayaking, or day cruises. Tuition is up to $285.

CAPE COD SEA CAMPS

This highly regarded camp with low staff-to-camper ratios is right on Cape Cod Bay. It has been in business since 1922. It offers all kinds of summer camp activities, but the specialty is **sailing.** Residential, day camp, or combination options are available for periods of as little as 5 days or up to 7 weeks between late June and mid-August, for children ages 4 through 17. Prices start at $545 for a week of day camp. Most fill up by January 1, and you can register as early as October. Contact info: P.O. Box 1880, Brewster, MA 02631-0062 (© **508/896-3451** or 508/896-3626; fax 508/896-8272; www.capecodseacamps.com).

---

10 Entertainment outside the Park

Rainy weather can ruin a day at the beach for youngsters. Fortunately, the Cape has lots of diversions, from museums to playhouses to indoor arcades. **The Cape Play-house,** 820 Rte. 6A, Dennis (© **877/385-3911** or 508/385-3911; www.capeplayhouse. com), offers a children's theater with shows to delight youngsters. If you're merely looking for a diversion from the beach, **Adventure Isle,** 343 MacArthur Blvd., Bourne (© **800/53-KARTS** or 508/759-2636; www.adventureislecapecod.com), boasts a 25,000-square-foot indoor entertainment center with roller skating, laser tag, bumper cars, miniature golf, and other great rainy-day activities. **Pirate Adventures,** 191 Queen Anne Rd., Harwich (© **508/430-0202;** www.pirateadventurescape cod.com), gives kids a chance to play pirate and search for treasures during a short cruise on a pirate ship.

FAST FACTS: Cape Cod National Seashore

Area Code The area code is **508.**

ATMs There are banks with ATMs in most of the towns.

Emergencies For emergencies, dial **911.**

Hospitals & Clinics **Cape Cod Hospital** is in Hyannis at 27 Park St. (© **508/771-1800). Outer Cape Health Services,** a clinic with 24-hour on-call service as well as regular office hours, is at 49 Harry Kemp Way in Provincetown (© **508/487-9395). The Wellfleet office,** at 3130 Rte. 6 (© **508/349-3131),** is open daily year-round.

Information For information, write Cape Cod National Seashore, 99 Marconi Station Site Rd., Wellfleet, MA 02667, or call © **508/349-3785.**

Pharmacies Pharmacies can be found in many of the towns.

Post Office There are post offices in all the towns.

Time Zone The seashore is on **Eastern Standard Time.**

Transit Info Coast Guard Beach uses a shuttle system during busy summer days.

Weather Updates For weather updates, look on the Internet at www.nps.gov/caco.

5

Cape Hatteras National Seashore

Driving along Hatteras and Ocracoke islands on a narrow strip of sand with the ocean close on both sides, you may think that the Outer Banks are a geographic miracle. Why should this razor-thin rim of sand persist far out in the sea? How wild it seems, a land of windy beach with no end, always in motion, always vulnerable to the next, slightly larger wave. There's so much here to see and learn, and so much solitude to enjoy.

The parts of the Outer Banks protected by the national seashore and other nature preserves are wild and beautiful. Being here, it's easy to imagine what it was like when the first English colonists landed more than 400 years ago, or when the Wright brothers flew the first airplane over a century ago. Both events are well interpreted at their sites.

The area is fascinating ecologically, too. Here, north and south meet—it's a great mix of ocean currents, climate, fresh and salt water, and geography. The result: a fabulous diversity of bird and plant life at places like the Pea Island National Wildlife Refuge (p. 127) and Nags Head Woods Ecological Preserve (p. 127). And for children, the national seashore is a huge sandbox.

Oddly, some people don't see Cape Hatteras this way. They think of the Outer Banks and conjure up Nags Head or Kill Devil Hills, towns where tourist development has pushed right up to the edge of the sea and, in many places, gotten really ugly. The suggestions in this chapter will lead you to the beautiful places, the places visitors come to again and again to escape the damp heat of the southern summer, to where the cooler winds blow.

BEST THINGS TO DO AT CAPE HATTERAS

- **Be alone with your family** on a hot, sunny beach, where everyone can look for crabs and shells and swim in the warm surf.
- **Visit Wright Brothers National Memorial,** where the first flight occurred in 1903, and Fort Raleigh National Historic Site, where the first English colonists to the New World built a village (that disappeared in the 1580s).
- **Ascend one of the nation's highest lighthouses,** visit the aquarium, and climb aboard a 16th-century ship replica.
- **Hike a wetlands trail** and look for interesting birds.
- **Catch crabs** in shallow Sound waters or go fishing, sailing, or sea kayaking.

For more information, see "For the Active Family" (p. 129).

Outer Banks Address Book

Outer Banks National Park Service Group Headquarters   Mailing address for all area national park units: 1401 National Park Dr., Manteo, NC 27954.

Cape Hatteras National Seashore   ✆ 252/473-2111. www.nps.gov/caha.

Wright Brothers National Memorial   ✆ 252/473-2111. www.nps.gov/wrbr.

Fort Raleigh National Historic Site   ✆ 252/473-5772. www.nps.gov/fora.

Eastern National   470 Maryland Dr., Suite 2, Ft. Washington, PA 19034. ✆ 877/NAT-PARK. Fax 215/591-0903. www.eparks.com. For books and maps.

North Carolina Ferry System   113 Arendell St., Morehead City, NC 28557. ✆ 800/BY-FERRY (eastern U.S. only) or 252/726-6446. Ocracoke ✆ 800/345-1665 or 252/928-3841; Hatteras ✆ 800/368-8949 or 252/986-2353; Cedar Island ✆ 800/856-0343 or 252/225-3551; Swan Quarter ✆ 800/773-1094 or 252/926-1111. www.ncferry.org.

Outer Banks Visitors Bureau   1 Visitors Center Circle, Manteo, NC 27954. ✆ 877/629-4386 or 252/473-2138. www.outerbanks.org.

Outer Banks Chamber of Commerce   101 Town Hall Dr., P.O. Box 1757, Kill Devil Hills, NC 27948. ✆ 252/441-8144. www.outerbankschamber.com.

Ocracoke Civic and Business Association   P.O. Box 456, Ocracoke, NC 27960. ✆ 252/928-6711. www.ocracokevillage.com.

1 History: Islands in Time

As you drive south along the **Outer Banks** from Nags Head, heading down Hatteras Island and crossing to Ocracoke on a ferry, you might imagine you're driving backward in history toward a more isolated, more natural time. The drive starts in **Nags Head,** where the seasonal shopping centers and rows of beachfront houses crowd the ocean. Farther south, the highway enters the national seashore, with its miles of wild, windy dunes and empty sand. On **Ocracoke Island,** the quiet town of Ocracoke sits among the trees in the wider part of the island, while the beachfront along the highway remains pretty much wild.

History set these patterns. Over hundreds of years, people decided which places to fill or leave open based on the jobs they had, the roads and bridges they built, and what they wanted to save for the future.

After **Sir Walter Raleigh's Lost Colony** disappeared in the 1580s, several generations passed without Europeans on the Outer Banks. The islands were too remote and sandy for most people. Just getting there was difficult. On the stormy outer shore, surf constantly beat the beaches, making this a dangerous place to sail and an impossible place to land a ship. On the calm, Sound-side shore, the water was too shallow for all but small boats, and only experienced sea pilots could find the way through channels that constantly shifted in the sand. These conditions were perfect, however, for one group of residents: people who didn't want anyone to find them. The Outer Banks became a hide-out for **pirates** and other fugitives.

North Carolina Coast

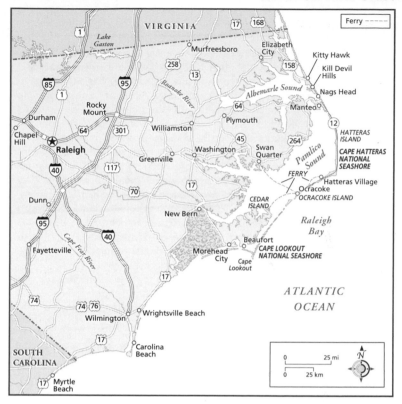

During wars, European kings and queens would allow private ship captains to attack any vessel from an enemy nation and keep whatever they could take. This was called privateering. But when the War of the Spanish Succession ended in 1713, many of the privateers kept right on attacking and robbing other ships. With no war for an excuse, this became plain piracy—and if you got caught, the punishment was death. In 1718, in a battle near Ocracoke, the British navy killed Blackbeard, the most notorious pirate of his day, and the age of piracy ended. No one ever found his treasure.

The village of Ocracoke became a home for **pilots** who knew the shipping channels well enough to safely guide vessels through Ocracoke Inlet and across Pamlico Sound to larger towns on the North Carolina mainland. Just as pilots still do in many parts of the world, an Ocracoke pilot would take a small boat out to meet a ship, steer the ship through the channels, and then travel home in the small boat. As the town was settled and built by pilots and their families, others settled there, too. People lived by piloting, fishing, carrying cargo in boats, grazing cattle and sheep on the beach grass, growing food in their gardens, and gathering valuables that washed up on the beach from shipwrecks.

Many ships sank on the Outer Banks and off **Cape Hatteras.** Sometimes ships wrecked trying to get through the dangerous inlets. Sometimes they wrecked just trying to get around the cape. Look at a map: Cape Hatteras forms a turning point for

First Encounters

Imagine living on the edge of a sea no one you know of has ever crossed. No one knows what's on the other side. One day a ship arrives, larger and more technologically advanced than any your society has the ability to build. The people who get off look completely different from your people and carry tools you've never seen that can do things you never imagined possible. And they settle down to stay, forever, and to change your land in terrible and unexpected ways. It's hard to imagine how it would feel, so think of it this way: Tonight you see on the evening news that space aliens have arrived in a big, high-tech ship more advanced than anything humanity could build, carrying strange and powerful tools and weapons. They announce they'll settle down to live here and change the earth completely. And they don't really care if anyone already lives here. For the Native North Americans, the arrival of European colonists on the eastern seaboard 400 years ago must have felt much like the arrival of space aliens would to us today. The Native Americans' courage and initial hospitality is amazing, when you think about it that way.

What was it like for the first settlers? Their courage is amazing, too. For them, going to America must have been like going to another planet would be for us. They traveled in small wooden ships that often disappeared without a trace on long ocean voyages. If they ran into trouble or got sick, there was no one to help them, and if a few people died on a trip, that was good luck, because usually even more died. Once they left port, there wasn't any way to communicate with family back home. And they were going to a place that no one knew anything about. Out of this new, strange, and completely unknown land, they planned to make a home and a new country.

ships traveling up and down the East Coast. If the wind was blowing the wrong way for a sailing ship to get around the corner, the captain would have to wait for the wind to change, sailing back and forth until it did. If he sailed too far out, he might get caught in a current that carried his ship the wrong way. But if he made a mistake sailing in the shallow water near shore, especially if a storm blew in that direction, the ship could hit the bottom and get stuck. The waves would then destroy the ship— sometimes miles offshore, sometimes right on the beach. Ocracokers and other Bankers (as year-round residents of the islands were called) would help those sailors lucky enough to wash up on the beach alive—but that didn't stop them from gathering the valuable cargo that also washed up, and using or selling it.

The dangerous waters helped towns grow on the Outer Banks. The first Cape Hatteras Light was built in 1802 to guide ships past the hazards. The **lighthouse** that stands in the village of Ocracoke today was finished in 1823; it's the oldest still standing in the area. Over the next 50 years, more great lighthouses were built on the islands. The current Cape Hatteras Light, the second, was finished in 1870. It's the tallest brick lighthouse in the United States, and probably the most famous. The Bodie Island Lighthouse was knocked down by Confederate soldiers during the Civil War—the Outer Banks were the site of furious sea battles—and was rebuilt after the war.

In the 1870s, the U.S. Life-Saving Service built stations along the islands to rescue sailors and passengers from shipwrecks. When a wreck was spotted, horses pulled a boat down the beach, and if the waves weren't too rough, lifesavers rowed to the grounded ship. Sometimes the lifesavers themselves drowned. When the waves were too big to even try rowing out, rescuers fired a cannon that shot a brass ball with a rope attached. With that line fastened to the ship, the sailors could slide across to safety on shore one at a time. (See "Chicamacomico Lifesaving Station," p. 129.)

Even after steamships began to replace sailing ships, many people died on the Outer Banks when they made mistakes in navigation, lost engine power, or suffered storm damage to their vessels. In the world wars, the German navy took advantage of this "Torpedo Junction," the best spot on the East Coast to attack American shipping by submarine. In the first half of 1942, while the U.S. Navy concentrated on fighting in the Pacific Ocean and left Cape Hatteras almost undefended, German U-boats sank about 80 ships within sight of the Outer Banks. The British sent ships to defend against the submarines, and on May 11, 1942, a British ship went down with all hands in a torpedo attack. Four British sailors washed up on Ocracoke and were buried by the islanders, who dedicated their little plot to England forever. You can see it on a walking tour of the village; it's an emotionally moving place.

The Outer Banks had a part in many wars. During the American Revolution, the Ocracoke pilots captured a British ship in their harbor and helped supply General Washington at Valley Forge by guiding ships of supplies. When the first U.S. Census was taken in 1790, 25 families were listed on Ocracoke and Portsmouth islands. Through the generations, the island's founding families have maintained their foothold. Among Ocracokers, the names are all still familiar, for the same families live there today. Over more than 200 years, they developed their own ways of doing things, and even their own accent and words that were spoken nowhere else. When babies were born, a local midwife attended, and when people died they were buried in family plots next to their homes. As you walk around the village, you can see the tiny cemeteries all around.

On the Outer Banks, where towns have come and gone and the population explodes every summer weekend, the permanent community of Ocracoke is rather special. Nags Head is more typical. There, summer visitors built the town, starting in the 1830s. The North Carolina mainland nearby is swampy, and at that time people believed that in the summer, it gave off a poison gas called "miasma" that caused malaria. The deadly fever killed many people, but it seemed that if they went to the Outer Banks, breathed the salty air, and spent a lot of time in the ocean, the miasma wouldn't make them sick. The truth is that malaria is caused by tiny parasites in blood carried from person to person by mosquitoes. Malaria wasn't a problem on the Outer Banks because mosquitoes can't fly in windy places.

The Outer Banks began to wash away soon after the summer visitors arrived. Grazing animals ate and trampled beach grass that helps hold the sand in place. As the sand moved, it buried woods and flattened the barrier dunes that keep the waves back. By the 1930s, the wind had flattened the dunes so much that with each hurricane, waves swept across large areas all along the Outer Banks. Some areas were just bare beach all the way across.

At the suggestion of a newspaper editorial, people started talking about a way to save the Outer Banks from washing away. They proposed a park for the areas that hadn't yet been developed and a program to rebuild the dunes and to plant beach grass.

Elizabeth's Explorers & the Roanokes

In 1584, Sir Walter Raleigh sent the first English colonists to the New World to settle on Roanoke Island, just inside the Outer Banks. The Croatoan Indians greeted the Englishmen with gifts and feasts. The English also offered gifts and traded copper objects, highly valued by the Croatoans, for furs. Captain Arthur Barlowe wrote: "We found the people most gentle, loving and faithful, void of all guile and treason, and such as lived after the manner of the Golden Age." The Native Americans worked hard and traveled far to grow their crops, fish, and hunt for their food. And their tribes often fought over land and honor, warring with surprise attacks and ambushes, just like the Europeans.

The Native Americans' impression of the English was wrong, too. Some thought they were dead people who had returned to earth with supernatural powers—explaining their incredible wealth, ships, and guns. Wingina, chief of the Roanoke Indians, may have thought the English were possible allies to attack his enemies and make him more powerful. He even sent one of his people back to England with the explorers.

The English Outstay Their Welcome

At first, the English settlers were welcomed generously by Wingina and his people, who gave them a place to build a fort and planted a field of corn for them. John White and Thomas Harriot, a painter and a scientist, worked to learn the natives' languages and ways, traveling from village to village to study the wildlife and geography of the area. The studies they produced were the best record ever made of Native American societies before contact with European ways.

But problems developed. The English governor, Colonel Ralph Lane, was a hotheaded military man. Instead of trying to build a colony that could support itself, he relied on Wingina to help catch fish and sell him corn. But the tribe members didn't have enough to feed the English, too.

After a year, the colonists were short of food; a ship they expected to bring supplies was late. The Roanoke Indians didn't want to trade their food for the pretty but useless items the English offered, because their own food supplies were running out. Wingina's people left their villages at times to avoid Lane, perhaps fearing that the English would take the corn by force. The governor heard rumors that Wingina was plotting to attack the colony, and he decided to attack first, killing Wingina and his leading men in an ambush. Not long after, Sir Francis Drake arrived, planning to bring more colonists, but Lane grabbed the opportunity to leave for home with his entire group. When the expected supply ship arrived 2 weeks later, no one was at Roanoke. The 18 men left behind were never heard from again. After the sneak attack by the Englishmen who had just left, it seems likely the Native Americans killed this next group.

Families to Settle America

Raleigh tried one more time, in 1587, to build a community, with 120 skilled colonists (families, not military men). White led the new colony; he brought his pregnant daughter and her husband. They set to work building homes, farming, and fishing. Virginia Dare, White's granddaughter, was the first English child born in the New World.

Before the ships that had brought them left for England, the colony had serious problems. Lane's warlike way of dealing with the Native Americans had made enemies of most of the tribes, and fighting broke out as soon as the new colonists arrived. With the help of Manteo and the Croatoans, who were still friendly, White tried to set up peace talks, but the other tribes no longer trusted the English. The leaders of the colony got together and convinced White to go back to England on the ships that were still waiting in the harbor to get more help. He didn't want to go, but he finally agreed.

White made it back to England and set up a convoy of ships to bring back supplies. But at the same time, Spain attacked England. Its navy, the Spanish Armada, was the largest ever built. All of England's ships had to join the war, including the vessels intended to resupply the colony. White still tried to make it with two small vessels but was attacked and had to give up. In 1588, the English beat the Armada but it took White 2 years to return. He had to go as a passenger on a vessel whose real job was to attack Spanish ships and steal their cargo.

The Lost Colony

When White arrived at Roanoke, he found the colony deserted, the houses gone, and a strong wooden fort built where none had been before. On one of the logs, someone had carved the word CROATOAN. White thought some of the colonists had gone to Croatoan Island, the home of the friendly tribe, and he intended to look for them. But he had more bad luck: The ship was out of fresh water and lost its anchor in a storm. The captain decided to sail south for supplies. In the Caribbean, the ship faced the Spanish and never went back to the Outer Banks.

Over the years, others tried to find the missing colonists, with no luck. In 1653, a visitor to Croatoan, which had become Hatteras Island, found Native Americans there who looked different from others—some had gray eyes— and who said they were partly descended from Englishmen. When no one came, perhaps they married Native Americans and lived out their lives as Croatoan Indians.

White thought most of the colonists went to the Chesapeake Bay to form a settlement there. When the Jamestown colony was formed in 1607, its leader, John Smith, tried to find the earlier colonists. His settlement was struggling with Powhatan, a fierce chief, whose daughter, Pocahontas, twice saved Smith's life. Powhatan told Smith that his warriors had killed off the Lost Colony. Some historians believe that the colony split up, with some people staying at Croatoan to wait for White and others moving to the Chesapeake, where they joined with the Chesapeake tribe and were killed when Powhatan massacred the Chesapeakes. But no one really knows what happened. Good material at a children's level is on the Web at www.nps.gov/fora/voyage.htm.

When you visit, you can see where this happened, explore two good museums about it, go onboard an Elizabethan ship, and attend an evening performance about the story (p. 128). What if the first colony—the one led by the soldier Lane—had tried to supply its own food and live peacefully with the Native Americans?

The changes came fast. The Wright Brothers and Fort Raleigh sites were set aside, and in 1937 Congress authorized the creation of the national seashore by buying up land along the Outer Banks south of Nags Head, except places that were already towns. It was done, and the national seashore started, in 1952. That is why we can drive back in time today, back to the village lanes of Ocracoke.

2 Orientation

Cape Hatteras National Seashore is a stretch of barrier islands off the coast of North Carolina, 75 miles long and as narrow as a few hundred feet in some spots. The protected seashore begins on the southern end of **Bodie Island** and includes most of **Hatteras** and **Ocracoke** islands, although small towns pop up along the way. **Pea Island National Wildlife Refuge** takes up the northern part of Hatteras Island. The bodies of water protected by the barrier islands include wide, shallow Pamlico Sound near Hatteras and Ocracoke islands, and freshwater Albemarle Sound inside Bodie Island. The Sound water is fairly calm, good for crabbing and for wading toddlers; the ocean side has great beaches and big surf. **Roanoke Island** lies between Albemarle and Pamlico sounds, protected by Bodie Island on the ocean side; it's where the Lost Colony was, and where you'll find **Fort Raleigh National Historic Site. Wright Brothers National Memorial** is north of the national seashore, on Bodie Island. **Cape Lookout National Seashore** starts at the next island south of Ocracoke, protecting rugged barrier islands without visitor development.

ARRIVING
BY CAR

From the **north,** you leave I-64 or U.S. 13 in Norfolk, Virginia. Two parallel routes from there—Highway 168 and U.S. 17/158—are about equal. Either way, you end up taking U.S. 158 across Currituck Sound to Kitty Hawk, then south to Whalebone Junction and the start of the national seashore.

From the **west or south,** U.S. Highway 64 leads east from I-40 at Raleigh or from I-95 at Rocky Mount to Roanoke Island and Whalebone Junction. Or, if you are headed to Ocracoke, split from U.S. 64 at Highway 45 and follow it to the ferry at Swan Quarter.

To **Ocracoke,** the main route is to drive through the national seashore on Highway 12 and then take the free ferry from Hatteras Village. If you are coming from the south or west, take the ferry across Pamlico Sound. You can stay in your car, parked on the deck, getting out to watch the water and scenery pass by from the rail; there's also a small indoor seating area. From the west, split from U.S. 64 onto Highway 45 to Swan Quarter. From the south, wend your way up the country roads to Cedar Island. The crossing from either point to Ocracoke is about 2½ hours, and the fare is $15 per car. Reserve in advance, because the ferries are small. Contact information is under "Outer Banks Address Book" (p. 104).

BY PLANE

You need a car to get around the national seashore here. If you want to fly there and then rent a car, the nearest major city airport is in **Norfolk, Virginia,** about 100 miles north. Major car-rental agencies are located there. To shop car-rental prices or airfares, Richmond, Virginia, and Raleigh, North Carolina, are each around 190 miles from the national seashore.

Cape Hatteras National Seashore

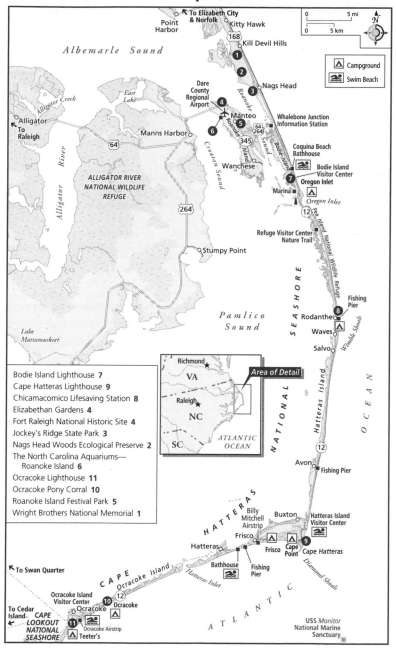

Bodie Island Lighthouse **7**
Cape Hatteras Lighthouse **9**
Chicamacomico Lifesaving Station **8**
Elizabethan Gardens **4**
Fort Raleigh National Historic Site **4**
Jockey's Ridge State Park **3**
Nags Head Woods Ecological Preserve **2**
The North Carolina Aquariums—
　Roanoke Island **6**
Ocracoke Lighthouse **11**
Ocracoke Pony Corral **10**
Roanoke Island Festival Park **5**
Wright Brothers National Memorial **1**

VISITOR INFORMATION
NATIONAL SEASHORE VISITOR CENTERS
Wright Brothers National Memorial, in Kill Devil Hills (p. 129), and Fort Raleigh National Historic Site, on Roanoke Island near Manteo (p. 127), are good first stops for national seashore information. Both are open year-round.

Bodie Island Visitor Center   This small center 6 miles south of the seashore's northern entrance occupies the keeper's quarters for the lighthouse here and has an exhibit on lighthouses. The 156-foot-tall lighthouse itself is open intermittently, when volunteers are present, and then only the base is accessible.

Near the Bodie Island Lighthouse, west of Hwy. 12, 5 miles south of Whalebone Junction. ℰ 252/441-5711. Summer daily 9am–6pm; off season daily 9am–5pm.

Hatteras Island Visitor Center and Museum of the Sea   The national seashore's main center, found 50 miles south of the seashore's northern entrance, occupies a small, historic building, moved from the eroding shore along with the famous lighthouse. Displays found within the two-story "Cape Hatteras Lighthouse Double Keepers Quarters" cover the history of industry and war in the area with artifacts and written placards at an adult level. An information desk and a good little bookstore are downstairs. Many ranger programs start here; for details, see the park newspaper and "Kid-Friendly Programs" (p. 133). Information on climbing the lighthouse is under "The Lighthouses" (p. 125).

Near the Cape Hatteras Lighthouse, Buxton. ℰ 252/995-4474. Summer daily 9am–6pm; off season daily 9am–5pm.

Ocracoke Island Visitor Center   The center mostly is a place to ask questions and join ranger programs, and has a few exhibits.

Near the ferry dock in Ocracoke Village. ℰ 252/928-4531. Daily 9am–5pm.

TOWN VISITOR CENTERS
Outer Banks Chamber of Commerce Visitor Center   If you're coming from the north, this may be the most convenient source of information on businesses.

101 Town Hall Dr., Kill Devil Hills. ℰ 252/441-8144. Mon–Fri 9am–5pm.

The Outer Banks Welcome Center   This is the county visitor bureau's large information stop in Manteo, providing information on offerings for the whole region, including Ocracoke, which doesn't have its own center. Besides staff to answer questions, there are touch-screen kiosks and a drive-in dump station for RVs.

1 Visitors Center Circle, Manteo. ℰ 877/298-4373 or 252/473-2138. www.outerbanks.org. June–Aug daily 9am–6pm; Sept–May daily 9am–5:30pm.

READING UP
The National Park bookstores have good selections in history, nature, and the outdoors. You can order some of these by phone or online from **Eastern National** (ℰ 877/NAT-PARK; www.eparks.com).

Nature: The best nature guidebook I've found on this or any other area is *The Nature of the Outer Banks,* by Dirk Frankenberg (University of North Carolina Press, $19). It explains seashore concepts in understandable terms using mile-by-mile commentary on what you see as examples. You can order directly from the publisher (ℰ 800/848-6224; www.uncpress.unc.edu).

Fishing: The visitor centers sell an excellent 40-page booklet by Ken Taylor, *Fishing the Outer Banks,* for $4, a good purchase for any angler who doesn't know the area.

THE NATIONAL SEASHORE IN BRIEF

Kitty Hawk, Kill Devil Hills & Nags Head

These three towns make up the generally unattractive tourist development that runs together along the road immediately north of the national seashore. There are some interesting places to visit in the area, however, plus large grocery stores and other services—and many motels and rental houses.

Manteo

A pleasant, year-round town on Roanoke Island with a variety of services, a nicely redeveloped waterfront, major historic sites, and an aquarium.

Rodanthe, Waves & Salvo

Heading south through the national seashore, the towns get progressively more attractive as you go away from Nags Head. This trio of tourist towns on the northern part of Hatteras Island shows the wear of years.

Avon, Buxton & Hatteras

Avon is a bit more upscale, but still mostly just a strip of beach houses. Buxton, at the corner where the island turns west, is a larger town on a wider piece of island, with houses back in the woods. The small village of Hatteras, at the south end of the island, has a harbor and some newer hotels.

Ocracoke

The village of Ocracoke, on an island you can reach only by ferry, is the one town on the Outer Banks with real charm. Cut off from the rest of the world for hundreds of years out on this strip of sand, the people, called Ocracokers, developed their own island ways and a unique form of English. The differences are fading with time, but Ocracoke still feels like an island.

3 Getting Around

BY CAR OR RV

Driving is the only practical way around the national seashore. Traffic flows pretty well on **Highway 12,** but don't count on getting anywhere fast. Be careful stopping or trying to turn around on the highway; many vehicles get stuck on the sandy shoulders every day. For off-road driving, see p. 132.

Whalebone Junction is a major landmark, and mileage along the cape is often counted from there.

BY FERRY

To get to **Ocracoke Island** from the rest of the national seashore, you have to take the free state ferry from **Hatteras Village,** a fun, 40-minute ride that's part of what makes the place special. In the summer, the ferry runs from 5am to midnight, leaving on the hour and half-hour during the day, on the hour in the early morning and evening. If you time your arrival at the ramp perfectly to catch the boat, you may find that it's full and you have to wait for the next one. Contact information for the North Carolina Ferry System is under "Outer Banks Address Book" (p. 104).

BY BIKE

Highway 12, the national seashore's main road, with its fast traffic and lack of shoulders, is not safe for children on bikes. If you're spending a week, you or the kids may enjoy taking a bike to the beach, or around the campground or cottage. Bikes can also come in handy in **Manteo,** where a paved bike trail leads from the village to the Fort Raleigh National Historic Site and elsewhere. In the village of **Ocracoke,** traffic is slow and there are quiet lanes safe for biking. The **Pony Island Motel** in Ocracoke (p. 120) rents bikes for $2 an hour or $10 all day.

4 Planning Your Outings

WHEN TO GO

The **visitor season** here falls from Easter (late Mar to late Apr) to Columbus Day (the second Mon in Oct). The area is busiest in July and August, followed by June. The temperatures in midsummer are cooler than on the mainland, but still quite hot if you're not used to it, with highs averaging in the mid-80s (high 20s Celsius) and often going into the 90s (30s Celsius). The trick is to stay in the wind, which is almost always blowing, and in the shade—even the hottest days don't feel that bad if you're under a beach umbrella and there's a strong sea breeze. Wind also helps with mosquitoes, which can be bad all summer, depending on the year. Weather is changeable during spring break, with highs in the 60s and 70s (teens–20s Celsius), but the water then is too cold for swimming. The ocean water is warmest on Ocracoke. **Swimming** starts there around Memorial Day and on the east-facing islands in mid-June.

The best time to go—if you don't have to go during a school break—is September and October, when the weather is cooler, birds and fish are plentiful, the bugs and crowds are gone, and the water is still fine. You'll also save on accommodations after Labor Day and find campsites easy to obtain. Midwinter is stingingly cold on the Outer Banks; not much is open.

Hurricane season runs June through November, with the most likely time for storms mid-August to the first week in October. If one comes, you may have to evacuate and forget about your whole trip.

HOW MUCH TIME TO SPEND

The Outer Banks draw millions of people from nearby states for weekends of beach-going and fishing, but I'd recommend at least a week at the national seashore. You'll want plenty of time to enjoy the beach and other outdoor activities, a couple of days for the historic sites, and time to get down to Ocracoke Island to catch the slow

---

Tips Hurricanes

The **storm surge,** a bulge of water brought by the low pressure and wind of a hurricane, can submerge large parts of the Outer Banks. You really don't want to be here when it happens. **Hurricane season** is June through November, although hurricanes are most frequent mid-August through the first week of October. Keep tuned to a local station for forecasts, or check the **National Hurricane Center** at www.nhc.noaa.gov. A **hurricane watch** means that hurricane conditions (winds over 74 mph) are expected within 36 hours; a **hurricane warning** means 24 hours. County officials give the word if it's time to go. Leave as soon as you can. **Evacuation routes** are published in the park newspaper and posted along the road, but they're pretty obvious, leading off the islands on U.S. Highway 64 or 158. Ocracoke Islanders go north on the ferry to Hatteras, then north by road.

rhythm of life there. Avoid arriving on weekends, especially for camping or sightsee-ing, because of the crowds. During the week, even in the high season, there aren't many people around.

HOW FAR TO PLAN AHEAD

Summer weekends are busy; weekdays are not. For motels, 4 weeks should be enough lead time to reserve, and in the middle of the week there's a good chance of finding vacancies on the same day as your stay. For weekends, especially during summer holi-days, book months ahead, if you can. Make reservations for summer weekly cottage rentals by February or March. People who come back every year reserve a year ahead. Less notice is needed for all accommodations in the off season.

For national seashore camping, only the Ocracoke Campground takes reservations, handled through the national system described in chapter 2, "Planning a Family Trip to a National Park."

Weather Chart: Cape Hatteras

	Avg. High (°F/°C)	Avg. Low (°F/°C)	Precipitation (in.)	Water Temp. (°F/°C)
December–February	54/12	39/4	14	49/9
March	60/16	44/7	4.3	52/11
April	67/19	51/11	3.5	59/15
May	74/23	59/15	4	68/20
June	80/27	67/19	4.1	74/23
July	85/29	72/22	5	77/25
August	85/29	72/22	6	80/27
September	81/27	68/20	5.3	76/24
October	72/22	59/15	5	70/21
November	65/18	49/9	5	58/14

Cape Hatteras averages; precipitation is for the entire period covered.

WHAT TO PACK
CLOTHING

During the summer season you'll spend most of your time in shorts, T-shirts, swim-suits, sandals or beach shoes, and sun hats. Also bring long pants and shirts for pro-tection against insects, walking shoes for the historic sites and scratchy nature walks, and windbreakers or raincoats. If you come in the off season, bring more warm cloth-ing. There aren't many places to wear formal clothing.

GEAR

Prepare for wind, sun, and bugs. Bring mosquito repellent and strong sunblock. You can buy a beach umbrella to get away from the sun, and sand toys for the kids, at surf shops all along the highway. If you have a toddler, bring a backpack or rent a sand cart to carry him or her over sand. You often have to hike over a dune to get to the water, and once there you may want to walk along the beach. A portable radio to keep track of the weather forecasts is a good idea, too.

If you're camping, bring lots of rope or cord. Camping on a windy sand dune requires you to tie your tent to the picnic table, the bumper of the car, or anything else that won't move. Short, skinny tent stakes won't work; instead, you need metal, blade-shaped stakes, and plenty of them (see "Packing 101: Gear," in chapter 2). Also, shade is rare at any of the campgrounds, so canopies and screen-house tents that can go over a picnic table are popular.

KEEPING SAFE & HEALTHY

In addition to these tips, see the information on sunburn, dehydration, insects, poison ivy, and seasickness under "Dealing with Hazards," in chapter 2.

DROWNING

The fact is, people do drown every year in the surf of the national seashore, and that's why you see warnings posted every time you turn around. Some of the advice is easy, but also easy to forget: Don't swim in big surf, and don't let small children swim in little surf, which is proportionally much larger than they are. Have someone watching everyone in the water. Go to beaches that have lifeguards. Red flags mean swimming is dangerous, so stay out of the water if you see one. In any weather the gradual beaches and calm water on the Sound side of the islands are better for little ones. For more tips, see "Practicalities: Swimming Safely in Surf" (p. 130).

FOOT INJURIES

You can run into cacti, burrs, sharp shells, and hot sand unexpectedly, and they can cause great anguish and even injury. Tiny prickly pear cacti grow all over Wright Brothers National Memorial, so heed the signs that tell you to stay on the path. Plants called sand spurs aren't dangerous, but they can hurt and upset kids. They are common in the seaside campgrounds. The spurs stick to socks and soft shoes but don't seem to be as bothersome if they don't have fabric to cling to. Be cautious at the beach and at the very least carry shoes with you. The sand can burn, and sharp shells and washed-up debris can cut.

5 Family-Friendly Accommodations

CAMPGROUNDS

Camping is wonderful at Cape Hatteras, surrounded by wind and sand and close enough to the ocean to stroll from the tent to the water. But you do need shade and wind to escape the heat, and mosquitoes can be vicious near the marshes and when the wind is low. And life is gritty. Despite the cold showers, which are heaven on a hot day, you're always sandy.

NATIONAL SEASHORE CAMPGROUNDS

There are four National Park Service campgrounds in the national seashore, all just behind the dunes on the ocean beach. The facilities generally are more modern and cleaner than those at most national parks. All the campgrounds have **cold showers** in booths—fine on a hot afternoon—and cold-water restrooms with **flush toilets.** While the campgrounds are open to RVs, there are **no hookups** at any of the campgrounds; a **dump station** is at Oregon Inlet.

Only Ocracoke takes **reservations;** the other three are **first-come, first-served.** On Sundays through Thursdays, that system works well, but on Friday and Saturday nights and holiday weekends, getting a site is difficult. The campgrounds often fill on Friday before noon; a waiting list is kept for Saturday in case someone leaves early. During the week, arrive before noon for your choice of prime sites, but even in late afternoon there's usually something left.

Tips Park Camping Basics: Toilets, Showers & Laundry

The national seashore campgrounds and beach restrooms have only **cold water,** although the visitor centers do have **hot water** and soap. The campgrounds offer cold-water showers in booths, and look for open-air showers just for getting sand off at Coquina Beach and Sandy Bay Day Use Area. Places to wash your clothes are not convenient to the national seashore, so bring a good supply. You can drop off laundry at **Outer Banks Cleaners,** 414 S. Hwy. 64/264 in Manteo (© **252/473-5185**).

Campgrounds are listed here by their distance from Whalebone Junction, at the north end of the national seashore. For information on any of the four, call park headquarters, © **252/473-2111.**

Oregon Inlet   Right across the highway from the marina and fishing center, where you can shop for food and fishing supplies, these grassy and sandy sites sit on the edge of and among the dunes. Many informal paths lead through a series of dunes to the broad beach, which is heavily traveled by off-road vehicles. It's an attractive campground, and a good place to stay if you want to be within the national seashore but still close to the historic sites. Coquina Beach, which has lifeguards, is several miles north.

On Hwy. 12, at the south end of Bodie Island. 120 sites, tents or RVs. $20 tent or RV. Closed Columbus Day to Easter.

Cape Point   This campground occupies a big grassy lawn behind the dunes near the point where the Outer Banks make their sharp turn from north-south to east-west. The walk to the very end of the point is about 1.5 miles each way. Of the four National Park Service campgrounds, this one is the nearest to a beach with lifeguards. The Buxton Woods Nature Trail and the big lighthouse also are nearby, as is the town of Buxton, but the campground is at the end of a quiet road. It operates during a shorter season than the others.

46700 Lighthouse Rd., Buxton. At the Cape Point Beach access, near Cape Hatteras Lighthouse. 202 sites, tents or RVs. $20 tent or RV. Closed Labor Day to late May.

Frisco   A few miles west of Cape Point, the Frisco campground has an isolated, wilderness-like feel. Bushy dunes rise around the sites, many of which have good privacy (arrive early to get one of those, not those that are packed close together). From atop the dunes, there are sweeping views all the way to the lighthouse. The seaside is near, too. A mile away, on Highway 12, are the Frisco Market, Frisco Rod and Gun, a post office, and a Texaco that stocks everything a camper could need.

53415 Billy Mitchell Rd., off Hwy. 12, Frisco. 127 sites, tents or RVs. $20 tent or RV. Closed Columbus Day to Easter.

Ocracoke   A grassy area stands behind a single dune, close to long, empty Ocracoke Beach. Don't set up camp on the other side of the campground near the road, where marshy, mosquito-ridden brush grows. To escape the bugs, you have to be in the wind. Reserve through the national system (see chapter 2), but because you choose your site on arrival, it pays to be early. Groceries are available in the village.

4352 Irvin Garrish Hwy. On Hwy. 12, about 4 miles east of the village. 136 sites, tents or RVs. $23 tent or RV. www.recreation.gov. Closed Columbus Day to Easter.

Campgrounds in the Cape Hatteras Area

Campground	Total Sites	RV Hookups	Dump Station	Toilets	Drinking Water
Camp Hatteras	400	Yes	Yes	Yes	Yes
Cape Point	202	No	No	Yes	Yes
Cape Woods	130	Yes	Yes	Yes	Yes
Frisco	127	No	No	Yes	Yes
Frisco Woods	250	Yes	Yes	Yes	Yes
Ocracoke	136	No	No	Yes	Yes
Oregon Inlet	120	No	Yes	Yes	Yes
Teeter's	24	Yes	Yes	Yes	Yes

COMMERCIAL CAMPGROUNDS

All rates listed here are for the high season; they drop somewhat in the off season. Unless noted, all campgrounds have hot showers and flush toilets.

Camp Hatteras   You won't see many places quite like this, although a similar KOA campground is right next door. Covering 50 acres all the way across the cape, with long frontages on both shores, it has indoor and outdoor pools, hot tubs, tennis courts, and more—three stocked fishing ponds, for example. RVs couldn't do better for this kind of place; tenters may not be as happy.

   The area is a bit tacky, with a lot of roadside tourist development, including amusement parks, minigolf courses, and the like—a place for a fun kid trip, but not what you might think of as a national park trip.

24798 Hwy. 12 (P.O. Box 10), Waves, NC 27968. ☎ 252/987-2777. www.camphatteras.com. 400 sites, tents or RVs. $52 tent; $70–$76 full hookup up to 2 people. $6 extra adult, $4 extra child 6–18, free for children under 6. **Amenities:** Full hookups, hot showers, laundry, playground, clubhouse, Wi-Fi, indoor and outdoor pools, store, hot tubs, tennis, sailing, minigolf.

Cape Woods Campground   In the woods next to a pond in Buxton, more than a mile from the ocean, this is a nicely landscaped, family-run campground. The sites are wooded and shady and have a natural feel. There's even a covered pavilion with picnic tables.

47649 Buxton Back Rd. (P.O. Box 690), Buxton, NC 27920. ☎ 252/995-5850. www.capewoods.com. 130 sites, tents or RVs. $30 tent; $42 full hookup up to 2 adults and 2 children. $5 extra adult, $3 extra child under 15. **Amenities:** Full hookups, hot showers, laundry, playground, game room, pool.

Frisco Woods Campground   This is an exceptional campground, combining a natural setting with enough activities to make you want to spend plenty of time here. Set among trees and on lawns with lots of frontage on Pamlico Sound, the family-run campground has a beach and offers gear rental for playing on the water—even windsurfing lessons. Air-conditioned cabins are also available, but you need to provide your own bedding.

Showers	Fire Pits/Grills	Laundry	Public Phones	Reservations	Fees	Open
Yes	Yes	Yes	Yes	Yes	$52–$76	Year-round
Yes	Yes	No	No	No	$20	Memorial Day to Labor Day
Yes	Yes	Yes	Yes	Yes	$30–$42	Mar–Dec
Yes	Yes	No	No	No	$20	Apr to mid-Oct
Yes	Yes	Yes	Yes	Yes	$36–$54	Mar to mid-Dec
Yes	Yes	No	No	No	$23	Apr to mid-Oct
Yes	Yes	No	Yes	Yes	$20	Apr to mid-Oct
Yes	Yes	No	Yes	Yes	$20–$30	Mar–Nov

53124 Hwy. 12 (P.O. Box 159), Frisco, NC 27936. ✆ **800/948-3942** or 252/995-5208. www.outer-banks.com/frisco woods. 250 sites, tents or RVs. $36–$50 tent; $48–$55 full hookup up to 2 adults and 2 children, $6 extra adult, $3 extra child under 12; $69–$89 cabins Memorial Day to Labor Day, less other times of year. Open Mar 1 to mid-Dec. **Amenities:** Full hookups, hot showers, coin-op laundry, playground, pool, convenience store, charcoal grills, Pamlico Sound beachfront, watersports rentals, cable TV, phone, Wi-Fi.

Teeter's Campground   If you want to hook up your RV or camper in Ocracoke, or absolutely must have a hot shower, this campground under shade trees right in the village is the place to go.

200 British Cemetery Rd., Ocracoke, NC 27960. ✆ **800/705-5341** or 252/928-3135. 24 sites. $20 tent; $30 full hookup. $2 extra child over 6. **Amenities:** 2 full hookups, hot showers, charcoal grills.

HOTELS & MOTELS

Motels are ubiquitous. They generally have pools—an advantage over most cottage arrangements—and some rent cottages, too. Read the section below if you are considering that option. Rates are highest in July and August, often declining in June and into the off season. Some places have five or six levels of rates depending on the season. Here I've listed just a few of the better places, going from north to south, with peak weekday rates only. Higher rates may apply for weekends or holidays. All rooms have TVs, phones, and air-conditioning. You can easily find cheaper accommodations in the area's many motels. The **Outer Banks Visitor Bureau**'s website (www.outer banks.org) contains links to accommodations, including rental houses, with updated vacancy information.

Roanoke Island Inn   A huge, perfectly proportioned country house on elaborately landscaped grounds stands right on the waterfront in Manteo, with good restaurants within walking distance. Use the bikes provided to explore the historic parks or aquarium. The house still belongs to the family that built its first section in 1860; the current owner, an architect, remodeled and made it feel just right. Guest rooms are comfortable and stylish, with wood floors, quilts, antique furniture, and reproductions. There are even family suites that have a small, adjoining room with one or two twin beds. The parlor, site of the included continental breakfast and snacks, looks like a movie set, with a stunning ceiling mural painted by an artist from Fort Raleigh's Lost Colony show. Several rooms and the bungalow out back are big enough for families. Through the inn you can even book a house on an island that sleeps four, if you have your own boat, or a cottage within a national historic district that sleeps six.

305 Fernando St., Manteo, NC 27954. (✆) **877/473-5511** or 252/473-5511. Fax 252/473-1019. www.roanokeisland inn.com. 9 units. $198 double; $238 suite for 3; $278 bungalow for 4. AE, DISC, MC, V. Closed Nov–Mar. **Amenities:** Bikes; private boat dock. *In room:* A/C, TV, bungalow has fridge, wet bar w/sink.

First Colony Inn   This lovingly restored wooden building, with its large rooms and Colonial-style antiques and reproductions, doesn't quite fit the neighborhood. Dairy Queen and Blackbeard's Mini Golf are across the street, and so is the beach, with the national seashore and Manteo a short drive away. The large rooms have every amenity, from the usual ones such as VCRs and refrigerators to more exotic additions, including individual climate control, dedicated hot-water heaters, even a safe. Children are welcome and well provided for, with an upstairs library stocked with games and an elegant, wooden-deck pool. Rates include a hot breakfast. Reserve well ahead, because some dates book up a year in advance.

6720 S. Virginia Dare Trail, Milepost 16, Nags Head, NC 27959. (✆) **800/368-9390** or 252/441-2343. Fax 252/441-9234. www.firstcolonyinn.com. 26 units. $189–$299 double. $20 extra person, children under 12 stay free in parent's room. Rates include continental breakfast. No rollaway beds; cribs free. AE, DISC, MC, V. **Amenities:** Pool; croquet. *In room:* A/C, TV, VCR, kitchenette in some semisuites, fridge, coffeemaker, hair dryer, safe, heated towel rack.

Lighthouse View Motel–Cottages   The large, modern, sun-drenched motel rooms feel like a beach house, with the sound and sight of surf ever present just beyond the dune. Standing on pilings, the weathered shingle buildings rise several stories around a sandy, grassy compound with an outdoor pool. Many rooms have decks, and there are many steps to climb. Some of the cottages are real showplaces: luxurious, current, and large; one contains five bathrooms. Check the complex rate card on the website; rates are substantially lower in most of June and August, with the rates listed here applying only for the 6-week summer peak. Off peak, some of the cottages rent by the night as well. If you can't get in here, just down the street is the **Comfort Inn** ((✆) **877/424-6423** or 252/995-6100; www.outerbankscomfortinn.com), with very nice rooms in an attractive building.

Hwy. 12 (P.O. Box 39), Buxton, NC 27920. (✆) **800/225-7651** or 252/995-5680. Fax 252/995-5945. www.lighthouse view.com. 50 units, 28 cottages. $139–$198 double; $515–$850 efficiencies weekly; $850–$2,250 cottages weekly. $5 extra person in motel rooms. No rollaway beds; portable cribs free. AE, DISC, MC, V. **Amenities:** Heated pool; hot tub; coin-operated laundry facilities. *In room:* A/C, TV, kitchen in cottages, fridge, microwave.

Pony Island Motel   There are other, more historic hotels on Ocracoke, but the rooms at this place on the edge of the village are just about perfect for families. In the "newer" building, a three-story wing with 23 rooms opened in 1996, each of the large, airy rooms includes a microwave, refrigerator, a small counter area with small sink, and coffeemaker. The suites are like homes, and the prices aren't out of line. Most of the remodeled, older rooms sport wainscoting or other details, have fridges, but are small compared to those in the newer section. A good-size pool is in front by the highway. There also are four cottages that rent by the week. The popular on-site restaurant serves some of the best breakfasts in town, and the hotel rents bikes for $2 an hour, $10 for the day, or $35 for the week.

Hwy. 12 (P.O. Box 309), Ocracoke, NC 27960. (✆) **866/928-4411** or 252/928-4411. Fax 252/928-2522. www.ponyisland motel.com. 54 units. $98–$164 double; $900 cottages weekly, lower in shoulder seasons. $5 extra adult, $2 extra child under 12 in motel rooms. Limited rollaway beds and cribs free. DISC, MC, V. **Amenities:** Restaurant; pool. *In room:* A/C, TV, VCR, full kitchen in suites, fridge, coffeemaker, whirlpool tub in suites, microwave, washer/dryer in some cottages.

COTTAGES & HOUSES

If you plan to stay a week or two, renting a summer house is the best way to enjoy the Outer Banks. You can relax and spread out, you don't have to worry about eating out with the kids, and you'll have a secure home base with a place to play. An added bonus: You'll have privacy from each other and from the rest of the world. The downside: You have to rent by the week, you usually won't have a pool, and prices can be high, especially if you want to be on the beach. Add the work of cooking, cleaning, shopping, and possibly bringing housewares and linens from home. During the season, the weekly rentals are for a full week, and turn over on Saturday or Sunday. You might be able to negotiate shorter periods during the off season, when more places are empty.

Agents usually ask for references. You often must choose based on a photo and put up a lot of money before you even arrive. Ask plenty of questions, get a complete listing of what the rental comes with and what you need to bring, and make sure you understand the lease conditions. When you arrive, inventory any preexisting damage, so you don't get stuck with a bill for it when you leave.

Most agencies sell insurance against unavoidable cancellations. It costs 4% to 7.5% of the rental cost, depending on the agency and the time of year—hurricane season costs most. Your cash deposit often amounts to half of the rental cost and generally is not refundable if the owner can't rent to someone else—even in case of a hurricane—so the insurance seems like a good bet. For even greater security, consider third-party trip-cancellation insurance. **Access America** (© **800/284-8300;** www.accessamerica.com) is a reputable firm, or shop at www.insure.com and click on the "Travel" tab.

Rates are highest in July and early August, in some cases going down 10% to 20% in June and late August, and dropping as much as half in the spring and fall. Size, location, and view determine how much you pay; beachfront properties command the highest premiums. High season rentals for beachfront houses range from about $1,300 a week for a two-bedroom condo to more than $11,000 for a large place. On the Sound side, prices are on the lower end of that range, sometimes as low as $995 for a three-bedroom house. Real-estate agents publish catalogs and websites that detail their summer rental listings, often with pictures of the houses, rates, and enough information to allow you to make a choice. The three agencies listed below offer just about everything from cottages to castles; the chamber of commerce (see "Outer Banks Address Book," p. 104) can tell you about many others.

Hatteras Realty This agency lists hundreds of houses from Avon to Hatteras Village in a detailed catalog of almost 300 pages. A bonus: Renters get free use of Club Hatteras, a facility in Avon with a large pool, tennis courts, and a summer camp drop-off program for kids. Nonrenters can use the pool for $5 a day.

41156 Hwy. 12 (P.O. Box 249), Avon, NC 27915. © **800/428-8372** or 252/995-5466. www.hatterasrealty.com.

Ocracoke Island Realty This Realtor offers nearly 200 houses in Ocracoke, with high-season prices ranging from $625 to $3,300 a week. Although the island has no oceanfront housing, it does have some houses on the Sound, a few with their own docks, and some where you can bring a pet.

1055 Irvin Garrish Hwy. (P.O. Box 238-A), Ocracoke, NC 27960. © **252/928-6261** or 252/928-7411. Fax 252/928-1721. www.ocracokeislandrealty.com.

Outer Beaches Realty   This agency has an extraordinary selection of more than 500 properties on Hatteras Island, all listed with interior and exterior photos in a catalog you can obtain by calling or going online.

P.O. Box 280, Avon, NC 27915; local offices in Avon, Waves, and Hatteras. © **800/627-3150** or 252/995-4477. Fax 800/627-3250 or 252/995-6137. www.outerbeaches.com.

6 Family-Friendly Dining

The strip of highway north of the national seashore, including Kitty Hawk, Kill Devil Hills, and Nags Head, has every fast-food joint you can think of, often all right next to each other. Just drive the highway until you find your favorite flavor. Below I have included some of the better restaurants to the south, in the national seashore and Manteo.

MANTEO & ENVIRONS

Manteo's redeveloped waterfront area, facing the Roanoke Island Festival Park across a small bay, is a pleasant place to walk, window-shop, take boat tours, and eat. There are a few delis, such as the **Magnolia Grill** (© **252/475-9877**) and **Poor Richard's Sandwich Shop** (© **252/473-3333**) where you can find a quick sandwich or burger. Also on the waterfront, on Queen Elizabeth Street across from the courthouse, the **Full Moon Cafe** (© **252/473-6666**; www.thefullmooncafe.com) serves tasty cuisine that combines southwestern and southeastern influences—a shrimp-and-crab enchilada, for example. Lunch is $6 to $17, dinner $7 to $20, with children's items $5. The cafe is open daily 11:30am to 9pm.

The Lone Cedar Café   Known locally as Basnight's, for its state senator owner, this is a good-time southern seafood place surrounded by Roanoke Sound. Friendly waitresses in shorts quickly bring big plates of fish, shrimp, and shellfish to tables with plastic tablecloths in a dining room rocking with noise and cheer. The preparation is generally simple, but the chef gets a chance to shine with a rich crab lump dip appetizer and tasty crab cakes. Kids will enjoy it, too, except for the wait for a table at popular hours.

On the U.S. 64 causeway between Manteo and Nags Head. © **252/441-5405**. www.lonecedarcafe.com. Kids' menu, highchairs, boosters, crayons. Lunch $7–$19; dinner $15–$31; kids' menu $5–$8. DISC, MC, V. Daily 11:30am–3pm and 4:30–10pm. Closed Dec–Feb.

HATTERAS ISLAND

There are casual eateries in each town along the island, places where families slip out of the beach house for a pizza when they don't feel like cooking. One is **Nino's Pizza** on Highway 12 in Avon (© **252/995-5358**). It's open daily 11am to 10pm and delivers; it closes an hour earlier in the off season, and closes altogether in January and February. On Highway 12 in Buxton, **Angelo's** (© **252/995-6364**) serves pizza and delivers in the evening. Its hours in summer are daily from 11am to 10pm; winter daily 4:30 to 9pm. The game room here keeps youngsters entertained before and after dinner.

Fish House Restaurant   Among all the touristy stuff, here's an authentic-feeling old fish house turned long ago into a Sound-side restaurant. (The floor slopes because it once was used for draining water from fish boxes.) The specialty is locally caught seafood, prepared simply, and it's done right and is served quickly. There's a decent kids' menu and a beer-and-wine list. The plastic tableware adds to the funky southern seaside feel and conserves water.

On Hwy. 12 overlooking Buxton Harbor, Buxton. ✆ 252/995-5151. Kids' menu, highchairs, boosters, crayons. Lunch $3.25–$9; dinner $9–$20; kids' menu $4.25–$7. AE, DISC, MC, V. Daily 11am–2:30pm and 5–9pm. Closed Thanksgiving to 1 month before Easter.

OCRACOKE

Captain Ben's Restaurant   If you've spent much time in East Coast seaside towns, this old-fashioned, nautical-themed place, in business more than 30 years, will be familiar as soon as you walk in. The service is fast and friendly, with a long menu that includes lots of seafood, prime rib, chicken, pasta, burgers, sandwiches—basically something for everyone in the family.

Hwy. 12, Ocracoke. ✆ 252/928-4741. Kids' menu, highchairs, boosters, crayons. Lunch $7–$25; dinner $7–$25; kids' menu $5.50–$8. Mon–Sat 11:30am–9pm. Closed Dec–Mar.

Howard's Pub and Raw Bar Restaurant   If you can get past the feeling that you're taking your children into a bar, this is a great place for families. You can eat away from the smoke on a screened porch or in a light, air-conditioned dining room with a wood floor that's been worn down by sandals and beach sand. Toys and games are stored on one side—as the proprietor said, it's the kind of place where the kids can get up and run around. The menu offers beef, seafood, and items from an in-house smoker as well as sandwiches and pizza. There's a generous kids' menu. The beer list includes more than 200 brews. Howard's boasts that it stays open even for hurricanes, but if the county tells them to shut down due to a storm, they shut down.

Hwy. 12, Ocracoke. ✆ 252/928-4441. www.howardspub.com. Kids' menu, highchairs, boosters, crayons. Lunch and dinner $5–$24; kids' menu $7–$9. Sun–Thurs 11am–10pm; Fri–Sat 11am–midnight.

7 Exploring Cape Hatteras National Seashore with Your Kids

ENTRANCE FEES   There are no entrance fees or beach fees at Cape Hatteras, but historic sites might charge fees (see "Places for Learning," p. 127). For those fees, you might be able to use an America the Beautiful Pass. For details, see chapter 2.

REGULATIONS   Camping is permitted only in formal campgrounds. **Fires** are allowed below the high-tide line, below the dunes. Put them out with water, not sand. **Fireworks** are not allowed anywhere on the national seashore, including the beaches along the towns, because they cause too many fires. **Pets** have to be on a leash and aren't allowed at beaches with lifeguards.

NATURAL PLACES
OUTER BEACHES

The entire length of the Outer Banks, 75 miles of it in the national seashore, is all brilliant sand and roaring waves. You really can be alone, getting over the dune from the highway at any of many deserted ramps and then walking until you drop in the sand. Even without swimming there's plenty to do and discover on the beach. (Beachgoing and off-road driving are covered later, under "For the Active Family.") **Collect seashells:** The best places are at the end of the barrier islands, where the current wraps around. **Hunt for sand crabs:** This is great fun at night, with a flashlight and a sand bucket, but be sure to release all the crabs when you're done. See how close to the waves you can **build a sand castle:** What design holds up best against the waves? Walk back in the dunes, staying on trails so that you don't trample the beach grass, and see what kinds of birds and plants you can identify. Watch the water and see if you can find the three kinds of breakers. Cape Point, at the very tip of Cape Hatteras near the lighthouse, is a great place to do this. Think about how the sand shapes the waves and how they shape the sand.

SOUND SIDE

The inner coast of the national seashore, mainly facing the Sound, differs from the outer shore in many ways, most of which have to do with the energy of the waves that hit the coast. On this side the waves don't have much distance to build, so they're smaller. Without being battered by large waves, the coast can develop into **marshes** full of delicate birds and animals.

Two kinds of marsh grow on the shore: freshwater marshes on Albemarle Sound, to the north, and saltwater on Pamlico Sound, to the south. Many of the saltwater marshes also have freshwater parts nearer land, where rainwater trapped in the sand pushes out against the salt water. You can see examples of both kinds, with excellent birding, on the **Bodie Island Dike Nature Trail,** on the same road that leads to Bodie Island Lighthouse and Visitor Center. A guide brochure, available at the start of the trail or at the nearby visitor center, matches numbered posts. The trail loop is 6 miles long; don't overexert yourself on a hot day. This marsh and those just north on Highway 12 grew upon deltas of sand left behind by the flow of water through inlets that have since filled up with sand. Four inlets existed at one time or another along here, including the one Sir Walter Raleigh's ships came through in 1585. Where the cape is wider, it's often because a former inlet allowed the tide to move sand into the Sound. Sand finally filled the inlet completely, connecting islands with the dry land we see today. Other great trails for marsh exploration are at **Nags Head Woods Ecological Preserve** (p. 127) and the **Hammock Hills Nature Trail** on Ocracoke Island (p. 132).

You also can explore the marshes and channels along the Sound shore by sea kayak, rowboat, or other craft. Go crabbing along the way, about the most fun a kid can have.

Barrier Island Behavior

Cape Hatteras, which is lower, narrower, and more vulnerable to the waves than Cape Cod, hasn't washed away with the rising sea level—it has moved closer to the mainland to make up for the rise. North of Cape Hatteras Lighthouse, the Outer Banks are moving toward the mainland at a rate of 5 feet a year. Geologists have measured the movement from old maps and aerial photographs and figured out how the sand is making the move from the outer side to the inner side. Currents carry sand around the islands, storms wash sand over the top, and wind blows it across. Unlike Cape Cod, which was made partly by glaciers, the Outer Banks are purely barrier islands, created and maintained only by the way the sea acts on moving sand. They have survived this way for thousands of years.

Scientists aren't sure exactly when or how the Outer Banks got started, or even why they stand so far into the ocean. Most of the world's barrier islands are close to the mainland, but the Outer Banks are 10 to 40 miles off the mainland, across a huge expanse of shallow, sandy water—Pamlico and Albemarle sounds. As you drive along Bodie, Hatteras, and Ocracoke islands, it can be hard to imagine how such narrow, low strips of land could survive over time. But they have.

How a Salt Marsh Is Made

Salt marshes often form behind barrier islands and barrier beaches. At Cape Hatteras National Seashore, the whole place is a barrier island, and salt marsh runs pretty much the whole length of the Sound side of the islands.

Salt marshes are like huge tide pools, filling and draining twice a day, but protected from waves by their sand barrier. The calm, slow-moving water makes a good home for grasses, insects, birds, small fish, snails, crabs, and other members of a unique system of plants and animals. Over many years, the living things die and sink into the water, building up its flat floor with rich muck that plants and worms love. As the bottom of the marsh slowly rises, it may become drier, or the rise may match the rise in the ocean level so that the marsh can thrive for a very long time.

Since the water is so shallow, warm, and gentle, these waters are relatively forgiving, a good place to learn to sail or windsurf, kayak, or try other new watersports (see "For the Active Family," below).

Swimming is different on the Sound side, too. The sand is coarser and the bottom is gradual—so gradual that an adult probably could walk miles out into the Sound in places. Waves tend to be small. There are beaches, without lifeguards, at Haulover, just north of Buxton; Sandy Bay, between Frisco and Hatteras village; and Jockey's Ridge State Park (p. 127).

THE WOODS

You could easily visit the Outer Banks without ever noticing the woods, but two notable pockets of ancient forest survive amid the sand, making refuges of quiet and shade, marsh and ponds, and homes for wildlife. **Nags Head Woods** is described on p. 127 and **Buxton Woods** under "Nature Walks" (p. 132); they're both well worth a visit. Before people caused increased erosion here by grazing sheep and cattle on the beach grass, woods covered much more of the barrier islands; without the beach grass, sand dunes buried some of the woods. The oak and pine of the woods grow where a large area is sheltered from salt spray by sand dunes and by plants that can handle salt. Over time, falling leaves and pine needles and dying plants build a layer of soil that can nourish generations of larger and more varied plant life. Finally, the woods grow thick and green, but you can still see the shapes of sand dunes underneath, sometimes holding ponds in between their ridges. Depending on how the islands move, these peaceful places, full of birds and animals, can last for thousands of years.

THE LIGHTHOUSES

The most impressive lighthouse you're ever likely to see is the great **Cape Hatteras Lighthouse** 🎇 at Cape Point. At more than 200 feet tall, it's the tallest brick lighthouse in the United States; in clear weather, it's visible 20 miles out to sea. Visitors can climb 257 steps up an iron spiral staircase right to the circular balcony at the top for an amazing view, but it's a long, hot, and potentially scary climb. Children under 13 can go only with an adult, and children under 38 inches are not allowed; I wouldn't recommend it for children under 5 or for anyone with a fear of heights. Carrying a child or any kind of backpack is rightfully prohibited. To climb, you need to buy a ticket and join a tour with 30 visitors in a group. During the summer the ticket booth opens at 8:15am for tours that day only, and they usually sell out by noon. The ticket indicates the tour time; they start at 9am and run every 10 minutes until 4:40pm. Admission is $7 for adults, $3.50 for children under 12 and seniors 62 and older. The lighthouse is open Easter to Columbus Day.

The lighthouse was built well back from the beach in 1870, but erosion moved the shoreline closer, and by 1935 the Coast Guard gave it up for lost, with waves crashing at its foot. After 60 years of struggle to stop the erosion, the National Park Service moved the light 2,900 feet in 1999, placing it back in the woods 1,600 feet from the beach. Today, the light looks as if it has always been there, but you can see where the tracks lay that over the course of a summer very slowly inched the tower to its new home, without a crack—an amazing engineering achievement.

The **Bodie Island Lighthouse,** at the Bodie Island Visitor Center, and the **Ocracoke Lighthouse,** in Ocracoke Village, are picturesque historic buildings, but they lack the drama and scale of Hatteras, and you can't go inside except irregularly at Bodie Island, when volunteers let visitors into the base.

OCRACOKE PONY CORRAL

In 1585, Sir Richard Grenville picked up some Spanish ponies in Haiti along with other supplies to help establish the colony at Roanoke Island. On June 23, one of his ships, the Tiger, ran aground, and the ponies and other goods were put off. More than 400 years later, their descendants are still running around Ocracoke Island, today confined to a large fenced pasture off Highway 12 north of the village. At least, that's the most plausible explanation for how wild Spanish ponies got here. You can see them from a 600-foot boardwalk, and sometimes the rangers saddle them and ride them on beach patrol. For more on the colony, see "First Encounters" and "Elizabeth's Explorers & the Roanokes," earlier in the chapter.

PARKS & PRESERVES

Cape Lookout National Seashore (Finds) The Outer Banks continue southwest of Ocracoke Island along 56 miles of wild, uninhabited barrier islands in Cape Lookout National Seashore. Visit to experience true wilderness and see a real ghost town. Portsmouth, on the island nearest Ocracoke, existed from 1753 until the last two residents left in 1971, when it was abandoned to the wind. In Portsmouth, ships would stop and unload their cargo to be stored and loaded into smaller boats that could cross Pamlico Sound to the mainland. It was once the largest and busiest town on the Outer Banks, with 500 people, a post office, a school, and a hospital. But on the night of September 7, 1846, a hurricane washed over a dune on Ocracoke Island, parting the sand to make a new inlet and washing away an old man's fig and peach orchard and potato patch. The new opening was Hatteras Inlet, now the northeast end of Ocracoke Island, and it allowed ships to sail right into Pamlico Sound. Portsmouth was no longer needed.

On a day trip, taking everything you need with you, especially mosquito repellent, you can explore the town and go into a couple of buildings, now preserved as a historic site by the National Park Service. The islands themselves are mostly just low dunes and bare beaches extending for mile after mile. Family-operated **Austin Boat Tours** ((© 252/928-4361; www.austinboattours.com) offers day trips to Portsmouth from Ocracoke. The ride takes half an hour each way, and you stay onshore, self-guided, for 4 hours. It costs $20 for adults, $10 for children 6 to 12, $5 for children under 6. At least three adults must sign on for the excursion. You can also arrange your own, special tour at a group rate.

131 Charles St., Harkers Island. ℂ 252/728-2250. www.nps.gov/calo.

Jockey's Ridge State Park   As you drive through Nags Head on Route 158, you can't miss the state park's towering sand dune system, the tallest on the East Coast. The wind blows northeast and southwest here, gathering the sand and moving it back and forth across the crest, but not spreading it out much. The main attraction is a fun and bizarre walk and slide on the shifting and cascading sands. It's a place where you just can't help playing. The view at the top, about 100 feet up, is terrific. If you want to get serious, there is a route (not a trail, because it would soon disappear in the sand) with numbered posts corresponding to a nature guide. On the Sound shore of the park are a calm swimming beach, a couple of feet deep on Roanoke Sound, and another nature trail; take Soundside Road, the first turn south of the main park entrance. The park offers kids' programs on various natural topics. Adults and kids can even learn to hang glide at a school at the park (p. 132).

U.S. 158, Milepost 12, Nags Head. ℂ 252/441-7132. www.jockeysridgestatepark.com. June–Aug daily 8am–9pm; Apr–May and Sept daily 8am–8pm; Mar and Oct daily 8am–7pm; Nov–Feb daily 8am–6pm. Visitor center closes a little earlier.

Nags Head Woods Ecological Preserve   The Nature Conservancy protects this uniquely diverse 1,092-acre forest, a shady mosaic of wetlands tucked between dunes that shield it from the salt spray on three sides. Five miles of nature trails with superb printed guides weave through the woods past ponds, sand dunes, orchids, herons, river otters, and ancient oaks, peaceful places a world away from the fast-food ghetto out on the highway. The place is poorly marked. Southbound on U.S. 158 near milepost 9.5 a small brown sign says NATURE CONSERVANCY, pointing west on Ocean Acres Drive toward the Sound. Take it about a mile to the parking lot on the left. Besides the trails, there is a small visitor center.

701 W. Ocean Acres Dr. (see directions above), Kill Devil Hills. ℂ 252/441-2525. Trails open daylight hours.

Pea Island National Wildlife Refuge *(Finds)*   This 10-mile-long refuge at the north end of Pea Island, within the national seashore 10 miles south of Nags Head, protects an exceptional bird habitat, the best for birding in the area. The cape's unique geography has contributed to an amazing 400 identified species. The refuge encompasses a Sound-side salt marsh and freshwater ponds in the middle of the island. A few exhibits and bird mounts, and a spotting scope, are inside the visitor center. Outside, superb trails, with boardwalks, tour the wetlands and reach across a dike between the ponds with built-in spotting scopes. You can also see turtles.

Hwy. 12, north end of Hatteras Island. ℂ 252/473-1131; visitor center 252/987-2394. http://peaisland.fws.gov. Visitor center summer daily 9am–5pm; winter hours vary.

PLACES FOR LEARNING

Roanoke Island has several exceptionally interesting sites to visit. They take at least 1 full day and can be reached by bicycle from Manteo, mostly on a separated trail. The Wright Brothers National Memorial, in Kitty Hawk, is a short drive from there. There are other museums on the Outer Banks, but they hardly bear mentioning compared to this complex of attractions.

Fort Raleigh National Historic Site   This is where the Lost Colony likely stood, and the mounds of earth you can walk around may be the remains of a fort built by Colonel Ralph Lane, the leader of the first group of English colonists who tried to settle America (see "First Encounters," earlier in the chapter). Or maybe not—archae-ologists can't pin down exactly who built the fort, but it surely had something to do with Sir Walter Raleigh's project. The area was also a Civil War–era colony set up by the Union Army for escaped and former slaves.

A good little museum in the visitor center concentrates on the Lost Colony, with arti-facts, ship models, costumes, armor, and other interesting exhibits. The grounds have quiet, shady lawns, a picnic area, and several miles of walking and nature trails with exhibits that explain how people used the area's natural resources. This is a good place to rest and play during a break from a day of sightseeing. Most of it is navigable by strollers.

The Lost Colony (📞 800/488-5012 or 252/473-3414; www.thelostcolony.org), a summer performance that has played on the grounds of the historic site since 1937, tells the story of the colonists and Indians with music, dance, and re-creations of the events in a large outdoor amphitheater facing the water. It's a local institution, a required part of a trip to the Outer Banks, and popular with kids. The season runs from early June through late August; performances start at 8:30pm Monday through Saturday nights. Tickets are $16 for adults, $8 for children under 12; reserve a week ahead if possible, and ask about nights with special ticket deals for children.

Also at the historic site are the **Elizabethan Gardens** (📞 252/473-3234; www.elizabethangardens.org), with 11 acres of flower beds, well-trimmed hedges, and for-mal lawns Sir Walter Raleigh might have admired. The shady, symmetrical paths and fountains are charming and provide a window on the time. Those interested in gar-dening or the historical period should stop, but children may not relish the genteel setting or find enough to amuse them. The good little gift shop stocks decorative gar-dening items and plants grown from the garden's own cuttings. Picnicking is not allowed. Admission to the garden is $8 for adults, $5 for children 6 to 18, and free for children under 6. Hours are daily in summer from 9am to 8pm (until 7pm on Sun), spring and fall 9am to 6pm, and winter 10am to 4pm.

U.S. 64/264, 3 miles west of Manteo. 📞 252/473-5772. www.nps.gov/fora. Free admission. Summer daily 9am–6pm; low season daily 9am–5pm.

Roanoke Island Festival Park

This remarkable state historical park, across a channel from the waterfront shops and restaurants in Manteo, is the Outer Banks' best cultural attraction and should not be missed. It has several parts. A fanciful but highly informative museum of the area's history will entrance children, who can learn to use an astrolabe, put on Elizabethan clothing, and listen to a mechanical pirate, among many other experiences. Docked on the water is the *Elizabeth II,* a superb replica of a 16th-century sailing ship. As you stroll the decks you encounter sailors in period cos-tume who stay in character; nearby, a small camp is similarly staffed, showing what the Lost Colony was like. An amphitheater stages performing-arts events all summer, and a gallery contains visual-art shows. Indoors, a 45-minute film, showing all day, tells the story of the Native Americans who lived here.

1 Festival Park, Manteo. 📞 252/475-1500. www.roanokeisland.com. Admission $8 adults, $5 children 6–17, free for children under 6. Apr 1–Nov 1 9am–6pm; off season daily 10am–5pm.

The North Carolina Aquariums—Roanoke Island

This aquarium on the edge of the Sound engagingly re-creates the local marine and aquatic environment in miniature. It's a place to learn about the habitat and animals you'll see on the Outer Banks and the Sounds, why they live where they do, and how they live. Everything is in context. An atrium seems to put you right in the marsh with river otters, alligators, turtles, and other animals. Other displays are dramatic, too—divers sometimes swim in the shipwreck tank, as large as a baseball infield and 17 feet deep. Children will love all of it, and the area especially for them is terrific, too. Programs included in the price of admission, for adults and children, happen as often as seven times a day in summer. The gift store is among the best in the area for natural-history books and toys. The grassy grounds and waterfront area are suitable for a picnic.

374 Airport Rd., west of Manteo on U.S. 64/264. ⓒ 866/332-3475 or 252/473-3493. www.ncaquariums.com. Admission $8 adults, $6 children 6–17, free for children under 6. Daily 9am–5pm.

Wright Brothers National Memorial   The Wright Brothers' story is truly inspiring: A pair of bicycle mechanics with no more than a high school education studied and worked hard, and, by careful observation of nature, figured out how to fly. There was no luck involved. This is where they did it, in December 1903. A century later, a celebration commemorating the event added to facilities already deemed historic (the visitor center has been named a landmark of 1960s architecture). A vinyl-covered pavilion was erected for the centennial with plans to let it remain for 5 years; it contains exhibits and a large theater. At the site you can also see the tall dune where the brothers tested a glider in the process of developing their successful plane, which is topped with a huge marker. On the flat, a replica of their launch track and markers show the takeoff and landing points for the four successful powered flights. The Wrights' bunkhouse and workshop are also replicated here.

The memorial's fascinating visitor center contains a mock-up of the plane and a museum on the Wrights' accomplishments. The exhibit, too, has been deemed a historic landmark, so it won't be changing. Ranger talks take place frequently in the summer, and other flight-related programs, such as learning to make kites, happen at various times during the week. Check the website for a schedule.

On U.S. 158, Kill Devil Hills. ⓒ 252/441-7430. www.nps.gov/wrbr. Admission $4 adults, free for children under 16 and seniors 62 or older. Summer daily 9am–6pm; winter daily 9am–5pm.

Chicamacomico Lifesaving Station   Local historical society volunteers support this complex of buildings that date from 1874. Lifesavers once waited here for shipwrecks so they could launch boats into the surf to save the victims. The museum contains their equipment and uniforms, objects from the wrecks, and other maritime artifacts, and there are programs in the summer such as knot-tying lessons and storytelling.

Hwy. 12, Rodanthe. ⓒ 252/987-1552. www.chicamacomico.net. $6 general admission, $15 families, $4 students. Mid-Apr to mid-Nov Mon–Fri noon–5pm.

8 For the Active Family

BEACHGOING

Surely this is how you'll spend most of your time at Cape Hatteras National Seashore. The 75-mile strip of sand is one of the best beaches anywhere, and the water is terrific for swimming. There are no fees for any of the beaches and none is really crowded. You can always be alone if you're prepared to walk a bit or drive to a remote ramp. National Park Service lifeguards generally watch over Coquina Beach, near the north end of the seashore on Bodie Island; Lighthouse Beach in Buxton, near the big lighthouse; and Ocracoke Beach, just north of the village of Ocracoke. Coquina Beach has a bathhouse for changing, and cold, outdoor showers, as does the unguarded Sandy Beach Day Use Area, on the Sound side southwest of Frisco. Each of the campgrounds is within walking distance of the beach, too, with showers in stalls but no lifeguards.

Practicalities: Swimming Safely in Surf

Only strong swimmers should swim in ocean surf, and that never includes younger children, whose size makes them vulnerable to even small waves. Even the strongest swimmers will be safer with some knowledge of how the waves work.

Ocean water is always moving, sometimes faster than you can swim. A **rip current** pulls directly away from the beach. It forms where water running back to the sea funnels through a channel in a sandbar. Rip currents are narrow and ease up as soon as the water gets deeper, so if you find yourself in one, don't swim against it. Instead, swim along the beach until you escape the flow of the rip current. Your biggest risk is fighting the flow and getting tired. Currents along the shore can move fast, too. To guard against them, always be aware of where you are, checking landmarks on the beach, and return to the beach before you're too far into waters you haven't observed carefully from shore. Never swim near piers or jetties, where the currents can be very strong. And don't swim near inlets, where the currents created by the tide rushing in and out of the Sounds could sweep you away.

By paying attention to how the water moves you in the surf, you can learn how to take advantage of the waves. Developing that awareness also helps keep you from getting hit by a falling breaker, which can be scary and even dangerous. Dive into breaking waves. Go with the flow rather than fighting rushing water. For example, a backwash current, or **undertow,** is the water of receding waves pulling back into the surf. If you don't fight it, you're carried a short distance from the beach and then back toward shore with the next wave; if you swim against it, you can end up getting smashed down by the next breaking wave. When you do get tumbled in the froth of a breaking wave, try to relax and curl up rather than fighting it. The water will leave you on the beach or the undertow will carry you to calmer water, where you can surface.

Finally, remember that in case of trouble, you're on your own unless the beach has a lifeguard. That's why you should always swim with a buddy.

All along the seashore, ramps for off-road vehicles lead over the dunes, providing access to long areas of rarely visited beach. You can use these ramps to walk to the beach in remote areas, but be careful about parking, because many people get stuck. North of the national seashore, various town beaches have lifeguards. I've described some other ocean and Sound beaches, and some of the things to do here, under "Natural Places" (p. 123); safety information is under "Drowning" (p. 116) and "Practicalities: Swimming Safely in Surf" (see above).

BIRDING

The Outer Banks' tremendous variety of bird sightings results from its location and variety of habitat types. The islands are on the **eastern migratory flyway.** They stick out into the Atlantic, making a resting place for exhausted birds that have accidentally wandered far from their homes. The habitat includes placid salt and fresh water of the Sound and the marshes, rough ocean beaches and offshore water, the Nags Head and Buxton woods, and the ponds at the **Pea Island Refuge** (p. 127). The refuge is birding central, where you can meet other birders and get advice from rangers.

CRABBING

First you take chicken necks and leave them out in the sun until they get really stinky. Then you tie the bait to a string and dangle it in the water in a marsh where you think a blue crab might be sniffing around. When you see a crab, you hold the bait near it in a tempting way. When the crab grabs hold, you scream and wave your arms, then pull it in on the string, net it, and drop it in a bucket, trying not to get pinched. Back home, steam or boil it and eat it.

For children, crabbing is a lot more fun than fishing, because you can see the crabs walking around in the shallow, marshy waters at the edge of Pamlico Sound from a rowboat or even on foot. You don't need a license, but get size-and-take regulations from a visitor center. The Park Service sometimes teaches this fine art in a ranger program that starts from the **Bodie Island Visitor Center**—check the park newspaper for details. Get the bucket and net at any sporting goods store (**Frisco Rod and Gun,** a sportsman-oriented sporting goods store, is on Rte. 12 in Frisco; ✆ **252/995-5366**), and buy chicken necks—or any other kind of meat—at a grocery store.

FISHING

There are lots of ways to fish, places to go, and kinds of fish to catch at the national seashore, from common, pan-size spot fish to the challenging 40-pound red drum. For children and beginners, the best choice may be one of the fishing piers along the outside beach. Anglers pay a fee, rent gear, and buy bait at the booth, where you can also get tips on how to fish. Fishing piers stick out all along the shore. Several are north of the national seashore and within its boundaries; piers are at Rodanthe, Avon, and Frisco (the latest hurricane permitting).

For more accomplished fishermen, surf-casting allows more of a solitary, natural experience. Pick anyplace you like along the islands away from swimmers; the best spots are in sloughs and holes, which smart fishermen scope out at low tide and come back to later. Fish on an incoming tide when wind and waves are light, casting just to the other side of the breaking waves. Tide tables run in the park newspaper. A good place to get gear is **Frisco Rod and Gun** on Route 12 in Frisco (✆ **252/995-5366**).

There are several places to charter a boat with a guide. The **Oregon Inlet Fishing Center,** on Highway 12 on the north side of the bridge (P.O. Box 2089, Manteo, NC 27954; ✆ **800/272-5199** or 252/441-6301; www.oregon-inlet.com), has a huge fleet. Charter rates, which the Park Service controls, range from just over $350 for a half-day on the Sound in a small open boat (a good choice with kids) to over $1,400 to go offshore all day for trophy fish. For peak weekends, you may have to book a year in advance. The center also sells fishing gear, supplies, and deli sandwiches. **Hatteras Harbor Marina,** P.O. Box 537, Hatteras, NC 27943 (✆ **800/676-4939** or 252/986-2166; www.hatterasharbor.com), offers trips in a similar price range, rents inexpensive apartments by the night, and has a deli. On Ocracoke the **Anchorage Marina,** P.O. Box 880, Ocracoke Island, NC 27960 (✆ **252/928-1101;** www.theanchorageinn.com), represents a few boats for offshore fishing and rents small boats and bicycles. It also has a cafe on the dock.

The biggest fishing trips from the Outer Banks are full-day, offshore voyages 20 miles out to the Gulf Stream for tuna, dolphin, sailfish, marlin, and the like. For beginners and children, choose a short, easy trip on the Sound instead. It costs much less and will probably be more fun with kids. Renting your own boat and messing around in the shallow waters can also be a lot of fun.

HANG GLIDING

Jockey's Ridge State Park (p. 127) is the only place I've run across that makes hang gliding a family activity. The school there, run by **Kitty Hawk Kites** (© 877/FLY-THIS or 252/441-4124; www.kittyhawk.com), takes children regardless of age as long as they weigh at least 85 pounds, as well as people with disabilities. It claims to be the world's largest hang-gliding school, in operation since 1974. Three-hour beginner classes take five flights from 5 to 15 feet high on the dune and cost $89.

NATURE WALKS

The .75-mile **Buxton Woods Nature Trail,** starting from the road to the swimming beach just south of the Cape Hatteras Light, is a pleasant walk over wooded rises and past swamp ponds that formed on the sand dunes and dips that the woods now cover. Excellent interpretive signs explain the landscape. The **Hammock Hills Nature Trail,** on Ocracoke Island across the road from the campground, shows each of the typical ecological areas of the Outer Banks: forest, dunes, and salt marsh, with signs describing what lives there. Bring mosquito repellent. Other trails include the **Bodie Island Dike Nature Trail** (p. 124), **Pea Island Trail** (p. 127), and **Nags Head Woods Ecological Preserve** (p. 127).

OFF-ROAD DRIVING

Large stretches of the national seashore on both sides are open to four-wheel-drive vehicles, if you follow rules designed to save the dunes, nesting birds, and sea turtles. Those rules are changing, too, as seashore officials were working late in 2007 on producing a management plan for off-road use. Driving on the beach can be a lot of fun, and it's a practical way for families to get to beaches of their own that would be too far for little ones to walk. A map given away by the visitor centers tells you where you can drive, what the regulations are, and what equipment you'll need, and provides important tips on how not to get stuck—you can't really do without it. Find the information online at www.nps.gov/caha/planyourvisit/off-road-vehicle-use.htm. Ask about seasonal closures before you go.

More than 20 dune ramps, from the Bodie Island area to the south tip of Ocracoke, allow vehicles access to the beach. They are marked by numbers that represent the mileage from Coquina Beach, with those farther south having higher numbers. On the Sound side, drive only on designated trails.

SAILING/BOATING

The Sound side's calm, warm water and steady winds are just right for day sailing. The **Waterworks,** on the causeway between Roanoke Island and Whalebone Junction (© 252/441-6822; www.waterworks.ws), and at other locations, rents all kinds of motorboats and other craft and offers guided tours to see dolphins, and lessons. **Hatteras Watersports,** on the Sound side in Salvo (© 252/987-2306), offers sailing equipment, parasailing, fishing, and kayaks at a big lawn, beach, and picnic area; kids were catching crabs when I visited. **Kitty Hawk Kites** also has kayaks and kayaking programs.

Sailboat rides on schooners are available, too. The 55-foot *Downeast Rover* (© 866/SAIL-OBX or 252/473-4866; www.downeastrover.com) sails three times daily on 2-hour cruises from the Manteo waterfront. They cost $30 for adults, $15 for children 2 to 12, or $40 for adults or children on the evening trip. They're often full in summer, so reserve ahead.

SEA KAYAKING

The shallow coastal salt marshes on Pamlico Sound are prime sea-kayaking areas, where the silent craft can sneak up on birds and animals. Unlike those in areas farther north, most rental agencies and guides on the Outer Banks use open kayaks, which are like low canoes, not traditional closed-deck kayaks. You get wetter in this kind of craft, but with the water so warm, it usually doesn't matter.

Most agencies offer rentals, guided trips, and classes. **Kitty Hawk Kites** (© 877/ **FLY-THIS** or 252/441-4124; www.kittyhawk.com) offers guided kayaking, rentals, and a kayaking camp of a couple of hours for kids 8 to 15. It takes children as young as 5 on tours with parents. On Ocracoke, **Ocracoke Adventures/Wave Cave,** at the intersection of Highway 12 and Silver Lake Road (© **252/928-7873**), offers kayaking and educational outings run by a former ranger and a real Ocracoker. The school also teaches kids (and adults) surfing; you can leave your kids for lessons.

9 Kid-Friendly Programs

The National Park Service offers programs at **Cape Hatteras National Seashore, Wright Brothers National Memorial,** and **Fort Raleigh National Historic Site.** Other organizations have programs at Jockey's Ridge State Park, Pea Island National Wildlife Refuge, and North Carolina Aquariums—Roanoke Island. All are covered under "Parks & Preserves" (p. 126) and "Places for Learning" (p. 127).

CHILDREN'S PROGRAMS

The three National Park Service units on the Outer Banks give patches or badges to kids who complete a list of tasks in their Junior Ranger programs, but the instructional booklets they do to earn the patches emphasize rote learning—mostly just finding facts and filling them in on a piece of paper. Besides the paperwork, kids attend ranger programs to earn the award. While the ranger programs are certainly worth attending, judge how much time you want to spend on this before committing to do it with your child.

The **Sand Castle Environmental Education Center** at Coquina Beach gives kids something meaningful to do while apart from their parents. The 30- to 60-minute activities have included shirt printing, low-tide beach walks, and studying seashells. They take place frequently on summer days. Check the bulletin board at the beach or ask at a visitor center for details, because the program changes annually.

FAMILY & ADULT PROGRAMS

The schedule and a description of programs at up to six sites appear in the national seashore newspaper. In addition to guided walks and lectures, which you can join by showing up at the appointed time and place, rangers also lead hands-on sessions on

---

Tips **Places for Relaxed Play & Picnics**

The beach is the best place for relaxed play, but if you want a change, you also could stretch out a blanket on the lawns of Fort Raleigh, around the North Carolina Aquarium, or at the Roanoke Island Festival Park. For active play, there's a great ship-theme playground on the Manteo waterfront, Kill Devil Hills has a city park playground at 1634 N. Croatan Hwy. (U.S. 158), and a school playground is at the north end of the town of Buxton.

snorkeling on the Sound, net fishing in a salt marsh, fish printing, boogie boarding, and the like, with the lineup changing annually. If you want to join one of these programs, which may be for limited numbers of people, be sure to contact the applicable visitor center in advance.

10 Entertainment outside the Park

Change your perspective, and take a look at Cape Hatteras from the back of a horse via a 2-hour ride with **Equine Adventures**, 52193 Piney Ridge Rd., Frisco (© **252/ 995-4897;** www.equineadventures.com). These rides, suitable for all ages, lead you through woods and out onto the beaches. This outfit also offers horse-drawn carriage rides through historic Hatteras Village.

Kids who like speed will find the **Colington Speedway,** 1064 Colington Rd., Kill Devil Hills (© **252/480-9144**), perfect, as it offers three levels of motorized carts for negotiating miniature racetracks. More go-carts and an 18-hole championship miniature golf course can be found at **Frisco Mini Golf and Go Karts,** Highway 12, Frisco (© **252/995-6325**). Indoors, the kids'll get lost among the arcade games.

FAST FACTS: Cape Hatteras National Seashore

Area Code The area code is 252.

ATMs ATMs are in towns up and down Highways 12 and 158 and in Manteo and Ocracoke Village.

Emergencies For emergencies, dial © **911.**

Hospitals & Clinics The **Regional Medical Center** (© 252/261-9000) at Milepost 1.5 on Highway 158 in Kitty Hawk has a wide range of services and is open for urgent care 9am to 9pm. **Outer Banks Hospital** at 4800 S. Croatan Hwy., Nags Head (© **877/359-9179** or 252/449-4555), has a 24-hour emergency room. On Ocracoke the **Ocracoke Health Center** (© **252/928-1511** or 252/928-7425 after-hours) is on Back Road by the school playground. Follow the sign off Highway 12 by the ferry terminal.

Information For information, write Cape Hatteras National Seashore, 1401 National Park Dr., Manteo, NC 27954; or call © **252/473-2111.**

Pharmacies CVS Pharmacies can be found in Kitty Hawk at 5547 Croatan Hwy., in Kill Devil Hills at 1101 Colathan Hwy., and in Manteo at Highway 64 Chesley Mall.

Post Office Each town along the national seashore has a post office on Route 12. In Nags Head the post office is on U.S. 158, in Manteo at 212 B. South U.S. 64/264.

Time Zone The seashore is on **Eastern Standard Time.**

Transit Info There is no public transportation in the park.

Weather Updates For weather updates, look on the Internet at www. monitor.noaa.gov/hatteras/hatteras.html.

6

Great Smoky Mountains National Park

The deep woods of the Smokies are closer to my idea of an enchanted forest than anywhere else I've ever been. The place I'm thinking of has tall, graceful trees, a nearly solid roof of green, brightly flowering rhododendron, and a babbling stream of clear, clean water on a leafy bed of black rock. My senses are filled: the sound of the birds and water; the scent of green, growing things; the sensation of warm, moist air; and then the delicious chill of a mountain stream as I plunge into one of its glassy pools, feeling totally alone in a fairy-tale wilderness.

It's a feeling you might not expect in the busiest of all the national parks, which you share with about 10 million other visitors a year. But it's a big park, and fewer than a third of the visitors ever get away from their cars. One out of six never even turns off the engine, touring only places like Cades Cove and the Roaring Fork Motor Nature Trail with many other cars, looking at the old buildings, fall foliage, and animals like visitors at a museum or a game park.

The park protects big, unique natural places within a half-day of most of the population of the eastern U.S. Fortunately, the park isn't completely criss-crossed with pavement. Most of it is hidden from view if you're on the cozy side of a windshield. And many travelers who do leave their cars hike only the five most popular trails. Those trails become crowded strings of people, but many other beautiful trails remain rarely used and can even become overgrown. On foot or by horse, you use your senses, feel the rewarding weariness from a long day on the trail, and have the trail mostly to yourself.

BEST THINGS TO DO IN GREAT SMOKY MOUNTAINS NATIONAL PARK

- **Hike a trail** in the deep woods to a waterfall, old-growth forest grove, or mountaintop.
- **Play in a creek** on a hot day or go tubing downstream just outside the park.
- **Put on a pack** to camp out a few miles into the backcountry, or use a long-haul trail for an expedition as long as you like.
- **Ride horseback** through the forest.
- **Visit the historic abandoned communities** of Cades Cove and Cataloochee and other sites that reveal what backwoods life was like.
- **Take in the museum** and other Cherokee Indian attractions in their reservation just south of the park.

For more information, see also "For the Active Family" (p. 159).

Great Smoky Address Book

Great Smoky Mountains National Park 107 Park Headquarters Rd., Gatlinburg, TN 37738. ✆ 865/436-1200. www.nps.gov/grsm.

Great Smoky Mountains Association 115 Park Headquarters Rd., Gatlinburg, TN 37738. ✆ 888/898-9102. www.smokiesstore.org. For books and maps.

National Forests in North Carolina 160A Zillicoa St., Suite A, Asheville, NC 28801. ✆ 828/257-4200. www.cs.unca.edu/nfsnc. For the Nantahala and Pisgah national forests.

Cherokee National Forest 2800 Ocoee St., Cleveland, TN 37312. ✆ 423/476-9700. www.southernregion.fs.fed.us/cherokee.

Cherokee Tribal Travel and Promotion 498 Tsali Blvd. (P.O. Box 460), Cherokee, NC 28719. ✆ 800/438-1601 or 828/497-9195. www.cherokee-nc.com.

Gatlinburg Chamber of Commerce 811 E. Parkway (P.O. Box 527), Gatlinburg, TN 37738. ✆ 800/588-1817. www.gatlinburg.com.

Swain County Chamber of Commerce 16 Everett St., P.O. Box 509, Bryson City, NC 28713. ✆ 800/867-9246 or 828/488-3681. www.greatsmokies.com.

1 History: Whose Land Is This?

Before Europeans arrived in this area, Cherokee warriors controlled land across a great part of the Southeast that's now in eight states. The Smokies were a small part of that land. The Cherokee patrolled their borders and fought sometimes to expand or protect their territory. When the settlers from the Old World arrived, the Cherokee were wary.

Cherokee customs were quite different from European ways. In contrast to European culture, women among the Cherokee were equal to the men in their families. Mothers owned the family home. When Europeans first met the Cherokee, they were impressed by how civilized they seemed. By "civilized," the whites meant that the Cherokee's organized way of life reminded them of their own society. The Cherokee were serious and dignified, they had age-old laws and met to discuss problems together, and everyone in their communities had jobs. Looking back, they seem more civilized than the white traders, trappers, and settlers. Unlike the Cherokee, whites on the frontier often didn't respect any law and took whatever they could.

The British and French fought over the Appalachian Mountains in the 1750s in the French and Indian War. The Cherokee, like other tribes, got caught up in the war after being threatened by both sides. They fought on the British side against the French; but the Cherokee and British soldiers didn't get along, and soon they were fighting each other. When the war with the French was over, the British came into Cherokee country with a large army and destroyed all their villages, all their crops, and everything they had, and left them to starve in the cold.

LEARNING TO SURVIVE

Over the years of war, some Cherokee leaders came to believe that the only way they could survive was to get some of the special powers the whites had. George Washington met with Cherokee leaders and agreed that they should be protected on their own land. He promised to give them what they needed to assimilate: plows, seed, and men to teach the Cherokee how to farm the land; and spinning wheels and looms so that they could make cloth from the cotton they grew. The Cherokee built churches and schools where the children could learn to read and write. John Ridge, the son of one of the most important chiefs, became a lawyer and married a woman from Connecticut who came back to live in the Cherokee Nation.

The Cherokee believed that if they became as "civilized" as the white Americans, they might be left alone and allowed to keep the land that hadn't already been taken from them. John Ridge helped create a government for the Cherokee that was like the U.S. system: It had a constitution, two elected bodies like the two houses of Congress, a head chief who was like the president, and a supreme court. Sequoyah, an uneducated Cherokee man, created a language with 86 letters so that the Cherokee language could be written and read as well as spoken. (Sequoia trees in California, the world's largest, were named for him.)

PRESSURE TO LEAVE

As time passed, more and more white settlers came to Georgia, North Carolina, and Tennessee, surrounding the Cherokee. The Cherokee had worked hard and succeeded in the ways of the whites. They owned mills, schools, miles of roads, tens of thousands of livestock, houses, ferries, sawmills, cotton-weaving machines, and even slaves. But there were a lot more whites in Georgia than Cherokee, and many of the whites were poorer. They wanted the Cherokee's land, no matter what the law said and no matter how well the Cherokee had taken on white ways. In 1828, the Georgia legislature passed a law saying that all the Cherokee land within the state belonged to the state.

That same year the Cherokee's old war comrade, Andrew Jackson, was elected president. They turned to him for help and protection from the whites in Georgia. But Jackson declared that all Indians should be taken from land east of the Mississippi River and moved out West. He told the Cherokee to go and offered them land in Arkansas and money if they would agree to leave. Georgia and the other states surrounding the Cherokee did more to force them out. The states changed their laws so that they would not protect the Cherokee, and they threw Christian missionaries and teachers in jail if they helped protect the Cherokee. Without the law to stop them, whites began stealing from the Cherokee, attacking them, and taking their land. The Cherokee, having accepted white ways, tried to fight back using the whites' rules. They took Georgia to court. In 1832, the U.S. Supreme Court, the highest law in the land, ruled that the Cherokee were in the right and that Georgia had no right to take their land. But President Jackson, whose job it was under the U.S. Constitution to enforce the court's order, simply ignored it and told the Cherokee they had to leave anyway.

TRAIL OF TEARS

Most Cherokee refused to go, so Jackson sent the U.S. Army to force them out. Soldiers would show up at a house and tell the family to grab what they could carry—they had to leave immediately. Whites were waiting to steal everything that was left behind the moment a Cherokee family was gone. Georgia raffled off the land and houses to whites, including the big plantations of the richest Cherokee. About 12,000 Cherokee people of all ages were forced to walk to Arkansas, more than 1,000 miles, and hundreds died on the way. The route was called the Trail of Tears. Later, when the whites in Arkansas decided that they wanted that land, too, the Cherokee were sent to Oklahoma. A small number of Cherokee managed to stay behind in North Carolina because of a difference in the laws relating to their land. Their small reservation remains just south of Great Smoky Mountain National Park. In the town of Cherokee, you can see their museum, tour a re-created village, and take in an outdoor performance on their history (p. 159).

BUYING THE PARK

People started talking about a national park in the Smokies in the 1880s; city folk and state legislatures quickly supported it. Even more people joined in to help create the Park after 1900, when logging companies began to destroy trees in the mountains. The lumbermen—rich and influential—persuaded Congress not to set aside the parkland for many years. Finally, in 1925, Congress approved the park, but they didn't set aside money to buy the land—that would have to come from private sources and neighboring states.

The children of Knoxville, Tennessee, collected $1,391.72 to help. It fell a little short of the $10 million needed to pay for the land. John D. Rockefeller, Jr., gave the largest chunk—$5 million—to give the project momentum. Eventually, the U.S. government set aside some funds, too. The park's proponents had yet another obstacle to overcome: The lumber companies kept cutting trees as they went to court to try to stop the land sale. Almost 60 years passed between the time the park was conceived and when it was dedicated, in 1940. In that time, the mountain people's way of life had become like a living museum. Some of their homes remain and can be toured (in Cades Cove, Cataloochee, and a few other places within the park).

2 Orientation

Great Smoky Mountains National Park is a rectangle roughly 60 miles by 20 miles that runs east and west in the southern Appalachian Mountains. The high ridgeline running the length of the park divides Tennessee and North Carolina. The tops of the mountains are more open than the thick forests below, but because the Smokies' tallest 6,000-foot peaks are still below tree line, big views open only at special places. Valleys in the lowlands on the north and south sides of the mountains are called **coves;** this is where the largest and most diverse forest grows.

ARRIVING
BY CAR

Interstates run close to the park from every direction, with **I-40** touching the east side. Navigation is simple, but if you want to make time, stay off the country roads until you are as close to your destination as possible.

The **Blue Ridge Parkway** is the ultimate scenic route. The two-lane road follows the top of the Blue Ridge Mountains 469 miles from Shenandoah National Park, in Virginia, to the south entrance of Great Smoky. There's a lot to see and do on the way. Contact the Blue Ridge Parkway, 199 Hemphill Knob Rd., Asheville, NC 28803-8686 (© **828/298-0398;** www.nps.gov/blri). Get business information from the **Blue Ridge Parkway Association,** P.O. Box 2136, Asheville, NC 28802 (www.blueridge parkway.org), which has a comprehensive website. The road is closed in the winter.

BY PLANE

Knoxville's **McGhee Tyson Airport** (www.tys.org), south of the city and 48 miles northwest of Gatlinburg, is the easiest place to fly in and rent a car. It's served by five

Western North Carolina

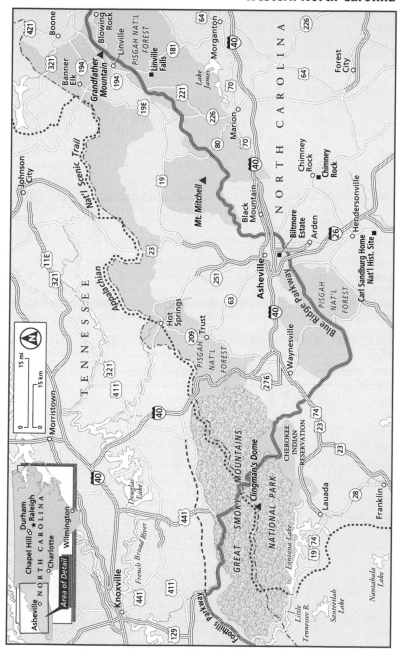

major airlines, including **Delta** (✆ 800/221-1212; www.delta.com), **United** (✆ 800/ 241-6522; www.united.com), **Northwest** (✆ 800/225-2525; www.nwa.com), and **Continental** (✆ 800/525-0280; www.continental.com). Most of the national car-rental agencies operate there. If you want to shop for ticket and car prices, Charlotte and Atlanta are each around 4 hours from Cherokee.

VISITOR INFORMATION
NATIONAL PARK VISITOR CENTERS

Besides these visitor centers, museums and the center at Cades Cove are listed later under "Places for Learning."

Sugarlands Visitor Center   The park's main visitor center has a natural-history museum where you can learn about the different life zones and plant communities, with specimens, animal mounts, and written explanations. It can be quite crowded. A 20-minute film in the high-tech theater covers the park's highlights and scenery. It shows on the hour and half-hour. A well-stocked bookstore and the main backcountry office are here, too.

Newfound Gap Rd., 2 miles from Gatlinburg. ✆ 865/436-1291. High season daily 8am–7pm; winter daily 8am–4:30pm.

Oconaluftee Visitor Center   The visitor center has a small exhibit space and a bookstore. A backcountry office is in an adjoining building, and the Mountain Farm Museum is nearby (p. 158).

Newfound Gap Rd., 1½ miles from the south entrance. ✆ 828/497-1904. High season daily 8am–7pm; winter daily 8am–4:30pm.

COMMERCIAL VISITOR CENTERS

Besides these centers at the park's main entrances, welcome centers are in Townsend on U.S. 321, and on I-40 at Highway 66 (exit 407) east of Knoxville.

Gatlinburg Welcome Center   Before you plunge into Gatlinburg, you can stop here to pick up information about the park and accommodations in town. A board lists available rooms. There are also a 15-minute orientation film and a bookstore. A trolley runs into Gatlinburg in the summer.

Hwy. 441 between Pigeon Forge and Gatlinburg. ✆ 865/436-0519. Daily 10am–6pm.

Cherokee Welcome Center   Pick up brochures and information about attractions and rooms in Cherokee and the rest of the reservation here.

Main St. (Hwy. 19), Cherokee. ✆ 800/438-1601 or 828/497-9195. Summer daily 8am–7pm; winter daily 8am–6pm.

READING UP

The **Great Smoky Mountains Association (GSMA)** operates the visitor center bookstores and sells online and by phone (✆ 888/898-9102; www.smokiesstore.org). The exceptionally good material it publishes on the park includes a collection of $1 map-guides on topics such as wildflowers, day hikes, and waterfalls. Your best deal, though, is the Smokies Explorer Packet. This $20 item includes a 154-page road guide, a 128-page guide to the park, a waterfalls guide, and a day hiking guide.

   Hiking: *Hiking Trails of the Smokies,* edited by Don DaFoe, Beth Giddens, and Steve Kemp (GSMA, $20), is an extraordinary trail guide, covering every hike in exquisite detail and rating trails in various ways, including degree of crowding. It comes with a map. Another remarkable hiking guide is *History Hikes of the Smokies,* by Michal Strutin (GSMA, $13). Here, good, long hikes are narrated like nature trails, with historical essays keyed to sites every few tenths of a mile along the way.

Maps: The maps sold by the park for $1 or included with the book mentioned above are adequate, but a finer-scale map with topographic lines makes it easier to figure out exactly where you are. The waterproof Trails Illustrated edition ($10) is up-to-date and loaded with information.

Field Guides: The GSMA publishes a series of field guides, with titles on birds, reptiles and amphibians, and trees and wildflowers of the Smokies. These award-winning books are as good as any full-color field guide you can buy, with the added bonus that they cover this park only and indicate exactly where you can find the flower or other species described. They cost $10 to $13 each.

THE NATIONAL PARK IN BRIEF

North Side
Gatlinburg

This is the park's main northern gateway, near the headquarters at the Sugarlands Visitor Center. It's easy to see how Gatlinburg, laid out on winding streets in a narrow valley, was once an attractive community. Tourist development has spoiled it entirely, turning the streets into carnival midways of wax museums, gift shops, indoor minigolf, and anything else you can imagine. The largest choice of hotels and restaurants is here.

Pigeon Forge & Sevierville

What they couldn't fit in Gatlinburg, tourism boomers built along a four-lane strip a few miles north, erasing the villages above with a solid strip of schlock that goes on for miles. You can find anything you want except beauty or serenity. East of Gatlinburg on U.S. 321, cabins and other businesses typical of a rural highway extend to the east side of the park.

Townsend

This sparsely developed town near Cades Cove is pleasant but shows early signs of the same disease as Pigeon Forge, with franchise businesses busily digging up the pastures for new stores.

Still, it remains a relatively attractive and mostly rural community, with a beautiful commercial campground and a quiet motel (p. 151 and 152).

South Side
Cherokee

The highways around the town center of the Cherokee reservation at the park's main southern entrance hold old-fashioned roadside motels and Indian curio shops, new chain motels, and a huge video-gaming casino. But there are some cultural attractions of significant interest. Outside town, Big Cove Road has a collection of good commercial campgrounds.

Bryson City

Although it lacks a direct connection to the main park roads (you have to drive 10 miles east to reach Newfound Gap Rd. in Cherokee), Bryson City does have a fine back door on the park. It's a charming, old-fashioned southern town with plenty to do. There are waterfall trails, a park campground, and inner-tubing.

Maggie Valley

Along U.S. 19 near the southeast end of the park, the Blue Ridge Parkway, and the Cataloochee area, this is a small, relatively quiet highway town.

3 Getting Around

BY CAR

A car is the only practical way to tour the park for most families. Be patient and allow plenty of time, though, because driving is very slow. Plan your visit carefully to group your activities. On a longer trip, stay in two different places, using each as a home base for a different park area.

Roads surround and thread through the park, allowing travelers to access lesser-used points on all sides, including Cosby, Big Creek, Cataloochee, paths near Fontana, and Abrams Creek, in addition to the four gateway towns mentioned above. Many of these country ways are slow and winding, including the madly twisting U.S. 129 west of the park, which motorcyclists come from all over the world to try out (averaging no more than 45 mph). The major exceptions are **I-40,** which passes by the east side of the park, and the isolated sections of the **Foothills Parkway,** a round-the-park route begun in 1951 that stalled in 1986 by environmental concerns. Most useful of its three fragments is the spur from U.S. 441 that allows you to bypass Gatlinburg from Pigeon Forge to the Sugarlands Visitor Center. The parkway portion on the western side of the park is spectacular.

Newfound Gap Road and **Sugarlands to Cades Cove Road** are the park's major travel routes. They were built for slow traffic, and sightseeing brings them to a crawl. Although speed limits are faster, count on driving no more than 25 mph.

The 32-mile **Newfound Gap** drive is the park's centerpiece. It crosses the back of the mountains, more than 5,000 feet high, and allows travelers to see how the elevation affects the plants and trees on the way. The road itself is interesting, too, as it snakes and even crosses itself with a bridge on the way up the mountain. Despite the slow traffic, this road is the quickest way across the park. In fact, it's the only way across. It runs from Gatlinburg to Cherokee.

The winding **Sugarlands to Cades Cove** route leads from the Sugarlands Visitor Center, near Gatlinburg, to Cades Cove, where a loop circles the valley and its historic buildings. From the visitor center, the scenic drive to Cades Cove on Little River and Laurel Creek roads totals 25 miles. The **Cades Cove Loop** itself is only 11 miles long (p. 157), but congestion can make the tour very slow.

Unpaved roads also penetrate the park at several points, often following the narrow roadbeds of abandoned logging railroads. These mostly seasonal, usually one-lane routes have narrow wooden bridges; you may even ford through streams. While generally passable by passenger cars, they are really more suitable for mountain bikes (p. 161). A very handy map and route guide called *Auto Touring* is for sale at visitor centers or online from the Great Smoky Mountains Association (see "Great Smoky Address Book," earlier) for $1.

BY TROLLEY

Various trolleys run routes in Gatlinburg and Pigeon Forge, with fares ranging from as little as 25¢ to as much as $1 per trip. You can pick up route maps at the welcome center. Gatlinburg is congested, and parking can be difficult.

BY BIKE

There are quite a few appealing mountain biking routes in and near the park (although not on park trails), and from May through September on Saturday and Wednesday mornings until 10am you can bike Cades Cove without cars, but traffic

Great Smoky Mountains National Park

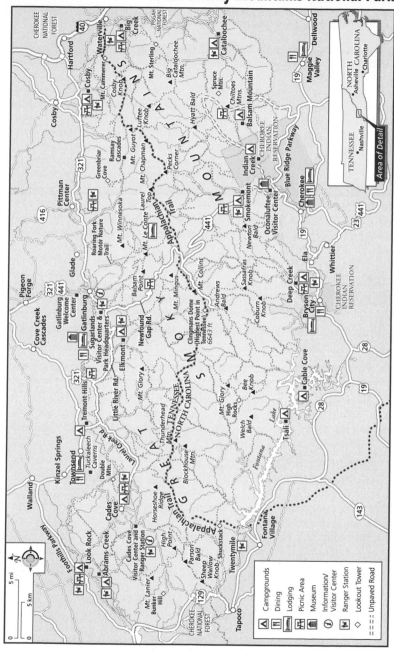

congestion on the park's main roads limits the utility, and safety, of bikes for transportation. See "Mountain Biking" (p. 161) for recreational biking.

4 Planning Your Outings

WHEN TO GO

The visitor season at Great Smoky is long, starting with spring break and running through October, when the leaves flutter red, orange, yellow, and brown. Summer and the fall foliage season are the busiest times, with weekends heavier than weekdays, often commanding a premium hotel rate. The Smokies are rainy all year, with precipitation just shy of rainforest proportions: 87 inches a year at Clingmans Dome. The midsummer months and early spring are wettest.

The park is a good choice for spring break. Roads and other facilities start to open in the second half of March. The weather can still be changeable, with occasional snowstorms at the top of the mountains. Farther down you'll need sweaters in the evening. Snow is gone from trails in April and May, when wildflowers arrive with the warming temperatures. Hotel rates don't rise until June at many places. These are the quietest of the good weather months.

Locals prize the cool summer weather, but that's mainly in comparison to the unbearable temperatures at lower elevations in the region. At Gatlinburg, around 1,500 feet, summer highs average in the upper 80s (upper 20s/low 30s Celsius), with high humidity. Up in the mountains, highs in the mid-60s (upper teens Celsius) make for a delicious break and perfect hiking weather. July is the park's most crowded month, and its rainiest, with an average of 13 rainy days. June is less busy. For inner-tubing, spring through early summer is best, because water levels can dwindle from July on.

A drier, crisper fall weather pattern sets in starting sometime in September. Leaves change in early October in the mountains, late October down below. People out to see the bright foliage clog park roads, and hotel rates shoot up to their annual peak. Reservations are hard to get. Snow hits the highlands in November and is heavy through the winter; little snow falls in the valleys. Hotels are empty and inexpensive during the winter season.

HOW MUCH TIME TO SPEND

The many folds and surprises of the Smoky Mountains make a large area seem even larger. Few people can hope for a comprehensive visit. A week would be adequate to explore a couple parts of the park and see the main highlights. A 3-day visit would allow you a couple of hikes or activities in one area and some sightseeing. Anything less than 3 days will be mostly a drive-through.

HOW FAR TO PLAN AHEAD

The reservation campgrounds often fill up from Memorial Day into the fall. Call as soon as you can after the system opens for your dates (chapter 2 covers the national reservation system). Several out-of-the-way campgrounds, on the other hand, often have sites unclaimed except on summer holiday weekends.

You'll never see more motel rooms in a concentrated area. A week ahead is often enough to reserve motel rooms during the week, but weekends book up earlier, especially in the busy fall foliage season. Plan farther ahead if you want to stay in a cabin or country inn.

Weather Chart: Gatlinburg & Clingmans Dome*

	Avg. High (°F/°C)	Avg. Low (°F/°C)	Precip. Gatlinburg (in.)	Precip. Clingmans Dome (in.)
December–February	51/11	28/–2	4.4	8.6
March	61/16	34/1	5.5	8.8
April	71/22	41/5	4.5	6.5
May	78/26	49/9	4.9	5.4
June	84/29	71/22	5.4	7.8
July	86/30	74/23	6.2	8.4
August	85/29	60/16	5.1	6.3
September	80/27	54/12	3.7	5.1
October	71/22	42/6	3	5.5
November	60/16	33/1	4.2	7.8

* Temperatures are about 20° cooler at Clingmans Dome than in Gatlinburg.

WHAT TO PACK
CLOTHING

The Smokies are famous for rain, so you should come well prepared at any time of year. The dampness comes as mists and haze, steady showers, and ferocious thunderstorms. Up in the mountains, it can be chilly in the spring and fall, and expect blizzards in midwinter. Down in the valleys, northerners will find the weather mild on all but cold winter days, and sometimes warm and muggy in summer. Bring a variety of clothes, from short sleeves for down below to wool sweaters, fleece, and raincoats for the mountains. Even in nice restaurants in Gatlinburg dress is generally casual. Bring good hiking shoes or boots because the trails are often rough.

GEAR

Make sure your camping gear can handle rain. Bring a couple of extra plastic tarps if you have room. A screen tent for the picnic table will make eating and sitting more comfortable with rain or summer bugs. Bring floating toys for the creeks.

KEEPING SAFE & HEALTHY

In addition to the particulars below, see "Dealing with Hazards," in chapter 2, for information on Giardia, hypothermia, lightning, Lyme disease, and poison ivy. A black bear killed a hiker at Great Smoky in 2000, the first such death ever in a national park, so it's time to take bear avoidance seriously here.

CARSICKNESS

If you are susceptible, you're likely to get carsick on twisting, tree-shaded roads such as Little River Road to Cades Cove (avoid some of it by going through Townsend) and many of the country roads. U.S. 129, at the west end of the park, is understandably world famous for its crazy curves. Newfound Gap Road has a few wiggles, too. Other than avoiding these segments, which is only partly possible, use carsickness medicine an hour before setting out (see "Seasickness & Motion Sickness," in chapter 2).

YELLOW JACKET STINGS

These wasps live in the ground, and stepping on a nest can mean a lot of painful stings from a swarm. Stings can cause horrible swelling and, if you suffer enough of them, illness. Antihistamines help with the swelling. Extreme symptoms mean that you need to see a doctor immediately, because allergic sting reactions can quickly be fatal. (See "Sting Allergies," in chapter 2.)

5 Family-Friendly Accommodations

CAMPGROUNDS

The campgrounds listed below are **open year-round** unless otherwise noted.

NATIONAL PARK CAMPGROUNDS

The 10 campgrounds within the park fall into two categories.

Three large campgrounds—Cades Cove, Elkmont, and Smokemont—lie on the main spine of paved roads. Between mid-May and mid-October they are booked through the **national reservation system** (see chapter 2) and are often full during the season. Campers using these campgrounds tend to be visitors from outside the area. Sites are not reserved November through May 15, and rates are lower during that period (which explains the range in the listings below).

The other seven campgrounds, on the fringes of the park and often reached by unpaved roads, don't take reservations. They are seldom all full (Cosby rarely fills) and are used more by locals coming up for a weekend. Some of these campgrounds are idyllic, out-of-the-way discoveries with the feel of backcountry camping.

All campgrounds in the park have **flush toilets,** cold running water, **no showers,** and no electric. Each campsite has a picnic table and charcoal grill. The larger campgrounds hold **campfire programs** in season. Check the park newspaper.

For information on any of these campgrounds, call the main park number at © 865/436-1200.

Campgrounds Accepting Reservations

The reservation system, www.recreation.gov, is covered in chapter 2.

Cades Cove   This large, flat campground among widely spaced shade trees is a center of activity at this end of the park. It has a store (open in the summer only), ranger station, and stable. If you spend a couple of nights here, you can cover the Cades Cove Loop on rented bikes or by car just after dawn or at dusk, when there's little traffic and wildlife is most active. The area also makes a good base for hiking. The sites lack much screening from one another but have gravel tent pads. And the campfire amphitheater is covered—a good idea for rainy nights.

At the western end of Laurel Creek Rd. on Cades Cove. 159 sites, tents or RVs up to 35 ft. $17–$20 site. **Amenities:** Flush toilets, dump station, store w/deli and bike rental, picnic tables, charcoal grills, cold water.

Elkmont   These grassy sites lie along the Little River under shade trees, without much separating them. Riverside sites can be reserved specifically and carry a higher fee during the season, when reservations are accepted. River valley walls enclose the area. A nature trail leaves from the campground, as does the **Little River Trail.** It leads 5.1 miles up the valley, connecting with four other trails on the way, and passes some good swimming holes on the Little River. The first is about .3 mile beyond the gate.

1½ miles up spur from Little River Rd., about 4 miles west of Sugarlands Visitor Center. 220 sites, tents or RVs up to 32 ft. $17–$23 site. Closed Dec to mid-Mar. **Amenities:** Flush toilets, picnic tables, charcoal grills, running water.

Smokemont   Along a rocky, rushing stream (the Bradley Fork of the Oconaluftee River), campsites sit in a narrow valley beneath tall trees. It's a perfect setting. A stable for trail rides is nearby, as are several excellent trails. One is the 5.7-mile **Smokemont Loop,** which comes right back to the campground. It passes by a pioneer cemetery .3 mile back into the woods from the Bradley Fork trail-head end. No other trace remains of the town that once stood where the campground is now.

Newfound Gap Rd. (Hwy. 441), near the south entrance of the park. 142 sites, tents or RVs up to 35 ft. $17–$20 site. **Amenities:** Flush toilets, dump station, running water, picnic tables, charcoal grills, running water.

First-Come, First-Served Campgrounds

Abrams Creek   Not many find their way down the 7 miles of country roads from the extreme west end of the park to this lovely spot under the trees. About half of the sites are right on clear Abrams Creek, a welcoming spot for a dip. The campground also makes a promising spot to start a family backpacking trip, because several loops are possible from two different trail heads with campsites closely spaced. Abrams Falls is about 5 miles away and Cades Cove 7½ miles.

Off Hwy. 72/129, west side of the park. 16 sites, tents or RVs up to 12 ft. $14 site. Closed Nov to mid-Mar. **Amenities:** Flush toilets, picnic tables, charcoal grills, running water.

Balsam Mountain   This is the park's only mountaintop campground, at 5,310 feet. It's an old campground (the bathrooms are built of stone), and the sites, while grassy, are unscreened. The trees are small and bushy. The beautiful **Flat Creek Trail** follows the ridge and creek south, reaching two-tiered Flat Creek Falls after 1.5 miles. The road to the campground from the parkway is paved, but from here onward one-way Balsam Mountain Road is a one-lane adventure, weaving through the woods to meet remote trail heads at the start of some backpacking loops. I thought the road looked like a better mountain-biking route than drive. Open only in summer, the road ends at Big Cove Road, behind Cherokee.

About 7 miles up Heintooga Ridge Rd. from Blue Ridge Pkwy., north of U.S. 19. 46 sites, tents or RVs up to 30 ft. $14 site. Closed mid-Oct to mid-May. **Amenities:** Flush toilets, picnic tables, charcoal grills, running water.

Big Creek   This remote-feeling backwoods campground just off the interstate is quite accessible. All sites are walk-in, but unlike walk-in sites at many campgrounds, these aren't a far walk from the parking lot. Many front on the creek, which has a good swimming spot, and all have gravel tent pads. An unpaved road runs through the mountains south to Cataloochee, a promising mountain-bike ride or slow drive.

Off Rte. 32, near I-40 exit 451. 12 sites, tents only. $14 site. Closed Nov to mid-Mar. **Amenities:** Flush toilets, picnic tables, charcoal grills, running water.

Cataloochee   The winding, partly unpaved, sometimes muddy road and remote location protect this idyllic internal valley from too many visitors; it's my favorite place at Great Smoky. I've covered the historic buildings, hiking, and mountain biking on p. 158. The campground itself is flat and shaded, with large sites, about half of which are along a creek. Be sure to stock up, because it's a long drive to a store. Signs are inadequate: Where U.S. 276 exits I-40, turn northwest on Cove Creek Road, then keep the faith until eventually you reach the park.

11 miles up Cove Creek Rd. from the intersection of U.S. 276 and I-40. 27 sites, tents or RVs up to 31 ft. $17 site. Closed Nov to mid-Mar. **Amenities:** Flush toilets, picnic tables, charcoal grills, running water.

Cosby   This is a quiet, less-visited area of the park, more than 15 miles east of Gatlinburg, and consequently you can almost always find a site at this large campground on a hillside. There's good ground cover, and brush shields the large, well-designed sites from each other, while shade trees shelter all. Most sites have gravel tent pads. A 1-mile nature trail with a guide brochure is at the campground, and many longer trails radiate from here, with loops suitable for family backpacking. The **Gabes**

Campgrounds in the Great Smoky Mountains Area

Campground	Elevation	Total Sites	RV Hookups	Dump Station	Toilets	Drinking Water	Showers
Abrams Creek	1,125	16	No	No	Yes	Yes	No
Balsam Mountain	5,310	46	No	No	Yes	Yes	No
Big Creek	1,700	12	No	No	Yes	Yes	No
Cable Cove	1,620	26	No	No	Yes	Yes	No
Cades Cove	1,807	159	No	Yes	Yes	Yes	No
Cataloochee	2,610	27	No	No	Yes	Yes	No
Cherokee KOA	N/A	400	Yes	Yes	Yes	Yes	Yes
Cosby	2,459	165	No	Yes	Yes	Yes	No
Deep Creek	1,800	92	No	Yes	Yes	Yes	No
Elkmont	2,150	220	No	No	Yes	Yes	No
Indian Creek	3,008	68	Yes	Yes	Yes	Yes	Yes
Look Rock	2,600	68	No	Yes	Yes	Yes	No
Smokemont	2,198	142	No	Yes	Yes	Yes	No
Tremont Hills	1,900	150	Yes	Yes	Yes	Yes	Yes
Tsali	1,620	41	No	No	Yes	Yes	Yes
Twin Creek RV	1,500	85	Yes	Yes	Yes	Yes	Yes

Mountain Trail starts at the campground and passes Hen Wallow Falls after 2.2 miles. A tiny grocery store is a couple of miles away, but generally the area is quite rural. *Note:* Twenty of the sites can be reserved through the national reservation system.

Off Rte. 32 in the northeast corner of the park. 165 sites, tents or RVs up to 25 ft. $14 site. Closed Nov to mid-Mar. **Amenities:** Flush toilets, dump station, picnic tables, charcoal grills, running water.

Deep Creek
The sites in this pleasant campground are on tiers above the creek, like seats in a theater. There are big trees, along with little ones that provide a sense of privacy to some sites. Gravel pads help keep your tent dry. The creek is one of the area's best for inner-tubing, and a superb network of trails, relatively little used, leads from the campground to waterfalls a short distance away and connects to longer backpacking trails. Inner-tube rental outlets are nearby, as is a little country store.

W. Deep Creek Rd., 2½ miles north of Bryson City. 92 sites, tents or RVs up to 26 ft. $17 site. Closed Nov to early Apr. **Amenities:** Flush toilets, dump station, picnic tables, charcoal grills, running water.

Look Rock
This exceptional campground is along the scenic ridge-top parkway west of the park. Sites gain total privacy by their distance from the road or a step down in elevation, a clever design that makes use of the ridge location. The sunset views from the tower, a .5-mile walk away, and from some of the parkway pullouts are unforgettably grand and graceful.

On Foothills Pkwy. 18 miles from Townsend. 68 sites, tents or RVs up to 32 ft. $14 site. Closed Nov to mid-May. **Amenities:** Flush toilets, dump station, picnic tables, charcoal grills, running water.

Fire Pits/Grills	Laundry	Public Phones	Reservations	Fees	Open
Yes	No	No	No	$14	Mid-Mar to Nov
Yes	No	No	No	$14	Mid-May to mid-Oct
Yes	No	No	No	$14	Mid-Mar to Nov
Yes	No	No	No	$10	Apr–Nov
Yes	No	No	Yes	$17–$20	Year-round
Yes	No	No	No	$12	Mid-Mar to Nov
Yes	Yes	Yes	Yes	$30–$50	Year-round
Yes	No	No	Yes	$14	Mid-Mar to Nov
Yes	No	No	No	$17	Apr–Nov
Yes	No	No	Yes	$17–$23	Mid-Mar to Dec
Yes	Yes	Yes	Yes	$22–$26	Late Mar to Nov
Yes	No	No	No	$14	Mid-May to Nov
Yes	No	No	No	$17–$20	Year-round
Yes	Yes	Yes	Yes	$20–$58	Year-round
Yes	No	No	No	$15	Mid-Apr to Nov
Yes	Yes	Yes	Yes	$42	Mid-Mar to Dec

FOREST SERVICE CAMPGROUNDS

The Nantahala National Forest's **Cheoah Ranger District** (© **828/479-6431**) has two campgrounds on the south side of Fontana Lake, west of Bryson City; take Route 19 to Route 28. Sites are first-come, first-served, for tents or RVs.

Cable Cove   This grassy campground is quiet and lightly used, with huge sites, many set far back, that are supplied with tent pads.

Forest Rd. 520, 1½ miles off Rte. 28. 26 sites, tents or RVs. $10 site. Closed Nov to mid-Apr. **Amenities:** Flush toilets, boat ramp, drinking water, picnic tables, fishing.

Tsali   Fifteen miles west of Bryson City, this attractive, grassy campground is set among rhododendrons, maples, and other broadly separated trees. Sites are far apart and have tent pads. The price includes hot showers. Four highly rated single-track mountain-biking trails nearby network 40 miles through the woods; their use carries a $2 per person per day fee. The lake is popular for fishing and boating.

Forest Rd. 521, 1½ miles off Rte. 28. 42 sites, tents or RVs. $15 site. Closed Nov to mid-Apr. **Amenities:** Flush toilets, showers, boat ramp, bike wash, fishing.

BACKCOUNTRY CAMPING PERMITS

To camp along the trail on a backpacking or horseback-riding trip, you need a free backcountry permit. It couldn't be much easier to get. The first step is to get the National Park Service's *Great Smoky Mountains Trail Map*, usually called the Back-country Map, which costs $1 and includes trail mileage, permit rules, and campsite

---

Tips **Park Camping Basics: Toilets, Showers & Laundry**

All the campgrounds have flush toilets, even the small ones, but only the **Tsali Campground** in Nantahala National Forest has showers. In Gatlinburg the Wash House offers showers and laundry machines, east from town on U.S. 321. Cherokee Express Laundromat (*©* **828/497-3499**) is at 700 Cherokee Crossing; it does not have showers.

---

locations. It is for sale online or by telephone or mail order from the Great Smoky Mountains Association (see "Great Smoky Address Book," p. 136). Postage on the item by itself is an additional 75¢, but you should also consider ordering the trail guides and the better map listed earlier under "Reading Up." There are about 80 backcountry sites and 15 three-sided shelters in the park. The shelters, along the Appalachian Trail, are in high demand. You can reserve them and 14 of the campsites—those shown on the map in red—by calling the **backcountry office** (*©* **865/ 436-1231**) up to a month in advance. If you just want information but aren't ready to reserve, call *©* **865/436-1297.** The office is open daily from 8am to 4:30pm.

The great majority of campsites, shown in green on the map, are open without reservations. There's enough room at each campsite for several parties, and no need for rationing. If you plan to use only those sites, you can self-register at any ranger station or visitor center when you arrive. Be sure to read up on the regulations on avoiding bears, storing food, and other issues on the back of the National Park Service map. Also see "Backpacking" (p. 159).

COMMERCIAL CAMPGROUNDS

Unless otherwise noted, all commercial campgrounds take reservations and offer hot showers and flush toilets.

Cherokee

Big Cove Road, which leaves Cherokee to the northeast, has a series of campgrounds in a wooded river valley. You can drive along the road and take your choice. The two I've listed are at opposite ends of the road, and opposite ends of the range between natural and developed camping.

Cherokee KOA Kampground   This is a true camping resort with enough activities to keep you entertained for a good part of your vacation. It has everything found at the fanciest resort campgrounds, plus some I haven't seen elsewhere, such as an adults-only center with a big-screen TV and dataports. The campground is in a nice spot, too, on a river where the family can go inner-tubing. It even serves meals, has a tour desk, and has a bus to town. Don't look here for a natural camping experience, however, because it feels more like a camping city. For not much more than the cost of a campsite, 100 camping cabins and 16 cottages are for rent.

Big Cove Rd. (Mailing address: 92 KOA Kampground Rd.), Cherokee, NC 28719. *©* **800/562-7784** or 828/497-9711. Fax 828/497-6776. www.cherokeekoa.com. 400 sites, tents or RVs. $43–$50 full hookup for 2; $30–$34 tent. $5 extra adult, children under 18 free; $14 extra for riverside site. Lower rates off season. **Amenities:** Full hookups, hot showers, flush toilets, playground, game room, outdoor and indoor pools, store, Wi-Fi, hot tub, volleyball, basketball, activity center, miniature golf, bounce pillow, trout fishing ponds.

Indian Creek Campground   At the confluence of two creeks below steep mountains, with trout fishing right from a few secluded sites, this thickly wooded campground that sprawls over 88 acres is more like what you usually find inside a park than a commercial operation. Ask for the kind of site you want, because they range in quality. It's run by a family and has a relaxed country feel. It's also more than 8 miles from town. Trailers and cabins are for rent, too.

1367 Bunches Creek Rd. (off Big Cove Rd.), Cherokee, NC 28719. ℂ 828/497-4361. www.indiancreekcampground. com. 70 sites, tents or RVs. $23 2-person tent; $29 full hookup for 2 people. $5 extra adult, $3 child 4–17. Closed Nov–Mar. **Amenities:** Full hookups, hot showers, flush toilets, laundry, playground, store, cable TV available in full-hookup area for $2.

Gatlinburg
Twin Creek RV Resort   The campground is near enough to Gatlinburg to be on the trolley route, but the peaceful streamside grounds are a world away from the tourist bustle there. They are lovingly landscaped, more like a pleasure garden than a campground, and each paved site has its own seating deck. Hookups include cable TV. The pool and children's pool are both large. The resort doesn't accept tenters.

1202 E. Pkwy. (2 miles east of town on U.S. 321), Gatlinburg, TN 37738. ℂ 800/252-8077 or 865/436-7081. www. twincreekrvresort.com. 85 sites. RVs only. $42 full hookup for 2. $4 extra person. **Amenities:** Full hookups, playground, Wi-Fi, pool, whirlpool, showers, laundromat.

Townsend
Tremont Hills Campground and Log Cabins   This beautifully maintained 20-acre grassy campground overlooks the Little River right at the park entrance, only 7 miles from Cades Cove. It's an unspoiled area, but close to other businesses. You can go fishing and inner-tubing nearby. The pleasant cabins have full kitchens and fireplaces.

Hwy. 73 at the park entrance (P.O. Box 5), Townsend, TN 37882. ℂ 800/448-6373 or 865/448-6363. www.tremont camp.com. 150 sites, tents or RVs. $26–$52 full hookup for 2 people; $20–$28 tent for 2 people. $3 extra person, children under 5 free. **Amenities:** Full hookups, hot showers, flush toilets, laundry, playground, game room, pool, children's pool, store, basketball.

HOTELS & CABINS
I've listed only weekday summer rates below; off-season rates drop in a somewhat unpredictable pattern. Some places have just two seasonal rate schedules; others have complicated schemes with rates that rise and fall as occupancy changes by the week. Generally, lows are two-thirds to one-half of summer rates. October rates might be $10 higher than summer rates. Weekend rates often carry a premium of $10 to $30.

IN THE PARK
LeConte Lodge   There's no more beautiful or authentic lodging than these log cabins looking out from the top of the park's third-highest peak, but to get here you have to climb the mountain. The spectacular 5-mile hike up the **Alum Cave Trail** is crowded at first, then thins out over the 2,500-foot climb. Trails radiate from the lodge. When I visited, management was getting ready for the season, lowering cases of chardonnay from a helicopter; it's $8 for a bottomless glass. (Llamas also bring in goods.)

The cabins are rugged but perfect, with wooden bedsteads and kerosene lanterns. Flush toilets are in a central building, but there are no showers. Meals are family-style southern cooking—chipped beef and gravy, cornbread, grits, and so on. Reservations open for the following year on October 1 and are full within a few weeks.

On top of Mt. LeConte, 5 miles up the Alum Cave Trail (and other trails). 250 Apple Valley Rd., Sevierville, TN, 37862. ℂ 865/429-5704. www.leconte-lodge.com. 7 cabins, 8 group sleeping lodges that sleep 10–13 people each. $93 adults; $73 children 10 and under. Price includes all meals. No credit cards. Closed mid-Nov to mid-Mar. **Amenities:** Central restrooms; propane heaters; kerosene lamps.

GATLINBURG

This gateway town has 6,500 motel rooms, with some chains represented several times. More are nearby. Except for holiday weekends, you should have no trouble finding a budget room. Cabins are for rent in the area, too, so you can get out of the bustle of town. **B. Whitlock's Cabins,** P.O. Box 1565, Gatlinburg, TN 37738 (© **800/ 972-2246;** www.bwhitlockcabins.com), has cabins east of town with many amenities, including full kitchens and hot tubs, renting for $175 a night in summer.

Best Western Twin Islands Motel   The motel occupies an island, surrounded by the Little Pigeon River, but stands right in the center of town, saving guests parking and traffic hassles. In the middle of the island, the motel's landscaped courtyard has a protected feeling, with a pool, a playground, covered picnic tables, and barbecue grills. Around the edge, kids can play in the water and anglers can catch the regularly stocked trout. Rooms are comfortable and attractively decorated. All have refrigerators, coffeemakers, and other such amenities, and the better rooms are quite posh. There is a restaurant and a coin-op laundry on-site, and more restaurants are a block away.

539 Pkwy., Gatlinburg, TN 37738. © **800/223-9299** or 865/436-5121. Fax 865/436-6208. www.oglesproperties. com. 113 units. $85–$155 for up to 4 people. No rollaway beds; crib $6. AE, DC, DISC, MC, V. **Amenities:** Restaurant; pool; children's playground w/slides and swings; coin-op laundry. *In room:* A/C, cable TV, dataport, fridge, coffeemaker, hair dryer, iron/ironing board, some rooms have microwaves, some have fireplaces.

Garden Plaza Hotel   These are good, standard American hotel rooms, with good-size bathrooms and extras such as small refrigerators, coffeemakers, ironing boards, and hair dryers. Rooms are large and light. The common areas and the program for families are exceptional. The hotel has three pools (two indoors) and a 1-foot toddler pool, an arcade, table tennis, barbecue grills, and picnic tables. A park is nearby, and the on-site pizzeria delivers to the rooms. There's a sit-down restaurant, too.

520 Historic Nature Trail, Gatlinburg, TN 37738. © **800/435-9201** or 865/436-9201. Fax 865/436-7974. www.4 lodging.com. 400 units. High season $130 double. Children under 18 stay free in parent's room. Rollaway bed $10; crib free. AE, DC, DISC, MC, V. **Amenities:** Restaurant, 3 pools; toddler pool; fitness center; laundry facilities; arcade; grills; picnic tables. *In room:* A/C, TV, Wi-Fi, fridge, coffeemaker, hair dryer, iron/ironing board.

Mountainloft Resort   On a hill just east of Gatlinburg, the resort consists of a wooded condo development in free-standing chalets and apartment-like units in larger buildings. It's lavishly furnished and decorated, with the amenities of a quality home, including laundry machines; full kitchen with microwave, blender, and dishwasher; VCR; stereo; whirlpool; and so on. The least expensive units are equivalent to a moderately sized hotel room; the largest sleep 10. A family-oriented clubhouse has a partly covered outdoor pool.

110 Mountainloft Dr., Gatlinburg, TN 37738. © **800/456-0009** or 865/436-4367 Fax 865/277-2251. www.bluegreen rentals.com. 266 units. $150–$350 unit. No rollaway beds; crib free. AE, DISC, MC, V. **Amenities:** Indoor, outdoor, and children's pools; exercise room; hot tub; sauna; massage; clubhouse w/game room; concierge; barbecue grills; playground. *In room:* TV, VCR, CD player, full kitchen, coffeemaker, hair dryer, iron/ironing board, laundry, whirlpool bath, fireplace.

TOWNSEND

Talley Ho Inn   In a quiet town on expansive grounds just outside the park, a family has kept this group of motel buildings well maintained and landscaped for more than 50 years. Accommodations include basic motel rooms, cozy units with big brick fireplaces, others with terraces, plus large cottages. There are an outdoor pool, tennis courts, and a family restaurant, which is open mid-March to Thanksgiving.

8314 State Hwy. 73, Townsend, TN 37882. ℂ 800/448-2465 or 865/448-2465. www.talleyhoinn.com. 46 units, 2 cottages. $49–$175 double. $10 extra person, children under 12 stay free in parent's room. Rollaway $10; crib $5. DISC, MC, V. **Amenities:** Restaurant; heated pool; tennis court; picnic area. *In room:* A/C, TV, coffeemaker, some rooms have kitchenettes, some rooms have Jacuzzis, some have fireplaces.

CHEROKEE

Near the park entrance on U.S. 441, the **Best Western Great Smokies Inn** (ℂ 828/497-2020) has a nicely landscaped courtyard with a pool and children's pool and large rooms for $100 double weekdays during the high season, $119 to $159 on weekends. Some of the best rooms in Cherokee are at a group of chain hotels on Highway 19 west of town. The **Comfort Inn** (ℂ 800/228-5150 or 828/497-2411; www.comfort inn.com) has rooms overlooking the Oconaluftee River for $70 to $80 in the high season ($40–$50 more on weekends). The **Holiday Inn of Cherokee** (ℂ 800/HOLI-DAY or 828/497-9181), across the road, has large indoor and outdoor pools, a laundry, and rooms with lots of extras. Rates vary widely, but in general rooms go for $90 on summer weekdays, $125 on weekends.

BRYSON CITY

This town has a lot of authentic southern character and plenty to do nearby. The kids will have to behave if you stay at one of these historic inns, but unlike most of what you find around the park, it won't be a plastic experience.

Folkestone Inn   This welcoming old farmhouse full of antiques stands in a peaceful country setting ¼ mile from the little-used waterfall trails and inner-tubing at the Deep Creek entrance to the park, 2 miles north of Bryson City. Charming rooms have quilts, wood floors, and claw-foot tubs. The inn takes children over 10 only. The library has a phone.

101 Folkestone Rd., Bryson City, NC 28713. ℂ 888/812-3385 or 828/488-2730. Fax 828/488-0722. www.folkestone inn.com. 10 units. $79–$158 double. $12 extra adult or child. Rates include breakfast. DISC, MC, V. *In room:* A/C, hair dryer, some rooms have electric fireplace, no phone.

Fryemont Inn   On a hill above Bryson City, thickly shrouded in eastern hemlock, the bark-covered exterior immediately takes you back to 1923, when the inn started operation. Inside, a nostalgic sense hangs over the wood floors and walls. Each room is different, with furniture that ranges from antique to just plain old. Most are spacious, especially a four-bed suite. The 37 units in the main building lack air-conditioning or television. Eight suites in separate buildings do have those amenities; more modern and more expensive, each is equipped with a living room, fireplace, and wet bar. There's an outdoor pool among the trees. Best of all, sophisticated and traditional southern meals from an extensive menu come with the room; there's a good kids' menu too. You save a lot by staying here. Nonguests are also welcome for dinner.

Fryemont Rd., off Veterans Blvd. (P.O. Box 459), Bryson City, NC 28713. ℂ 800/845-4879 or 828/488-2159. www.fryemontinn.com. 45 units, 1 cabin. $125–$145 double. Extra adult $36, extra child 2–10 $20. Rates include breakfast and dinner. Rollaway bed $6; crib free. DISC, MC, V. Main lodge closed Thanksgiving to mid-April; suites and cabin open year-round. **Amenities:** Restaurant; heated pool. *In room:* Suites have wet bar, fireplace, living room.

MAGGIE VALLEY

Jonathan Creek Inn   Twelve miles east of Cherokee on the way to Cataloochee or I-40 on Highway 19, an industrious couple has transformed this roadside motel into a delightful country inn. The rockers, wreaths, decorative borders, quilts, and other warm touches give it a cozy feeling, and the large rooms are a real bargain. Refrigerators, microwaves, coffeemakers, big TVs, wireless Internet, and other amenities are standard; some rooms have fireplaces and Jacuzzis. Kids can play in a playground or the trout-stocked creek that flows out back by the hot tub, or swim in the glass-enclosed pool by the parking lot. For a longer stay, luxurious houses on the other side of the creek rent by the week for $750 to $1,400.

4324 Soco Rd. (P.O. Box 66), Maggie Valley, NC 28751. ℂ 800/577-7812 (reservations) or 828/926-1232. Fax 828/926-9751. www.jonathancreekinn.com. 44 units, 7 villas. $70–$145 double. $5 extra adult, kids stay free in parent's room. Rollaway bed $10; crib free. AE, DISC, MC, V. **Amenities:** Pool; hot tub; laundry; playground w/slides and play-houses for young children; picnic area w/grill. *In room:* A/C, TV, Wi-Fi, fridge, coffeemaker, hair dryer, iron/ironing board, microwave.

6 Family-Friendly Dining

NORTH SIDE OF THE PARK
LOW-STRESS MEALS

In Gatlinburg and Pigeon Forge, you can get any kind of franchise fast food you might want. On U.S. 441 as it enters Gatlinburg, you'll find **Pizza Hut, McDonald's,** and **Applebee's,** a chain pub restaurant that also treats children well. In addition, pancake houses and barbecue restaurants are in good supply.

BEST-BEHAVIOR MEALS

The Park Grill   Inside this heavy log structure you find a menu that ranges from big, hickory-smoked steaks and lamb chops to seafood and chicken. For a truly local dish "from the still to the grill," try the "Moonshine Chicken"—a skinless chicken breast marinated in orange juice, sweet lime, and real moonshine. Kids will get a kick out of the waitstaff, which is outfitted in uniforms meant to resemble park ranger uni-forms. The children's menu requires grown-up tastes, with steaks, chicken fingers, prime rib, and even trout. Pricing is innovative, though: 75¢ times the child's age. Crowds can back this eatery up on weekends. Reservations aren't taken, but if you call ahead they'll place your name on a waiting list and give you an idea of what time they can seat you.

110 Pkwy., Gatlinburg. ℂ 865/436-2300. www.parkgrillgatlinburg.com. Kids' menu, highchairs, boosters, crayons. Dinner $18–$38; kids' menu 75¢ multiplied by child's age. AE, DC, DISC, MC, V. Sun–Fri 5–10pm; Sat 4:30–10pm.

SOUTH SIDE OF THE PARK
CHEROKEE

Cherokee has plenty of places to get fast food, including **Dairy Queen, McDonald's,** and **Big Boy** restaurants just outside the park, and there are many casual coffee shops; but I never found a place that got me excited. **Myrtle's Table,** in the Best Western Great Smokies Inn (ℂ 828/497-2020), is a comfortable place decorated with squared log walls. **Pizza Inn** (ℂ 828/497-9143), near the center of town on U.S. 441 North, is a typical family pizzeria and has a lunch buffet. The **Holiday Inn,** on Route 19 heading west (ℂ 828/497-9181), has a pleasant restaurant called the Chestnut Tree, with good grown-up and children's menus, including pizza.

BRYSON CITY

The restaurant at the **Fryemont Inn** (ℂ 828/488-2159) is one of the best in town (p. 153). There are lots of choices for fast or casual food, too, including **McDonald's, Hardee's, Arby's,** and **Pizza Hut.** But my favorite was a place on the east side of town, **Na-Bers Drive-In,** at 1245 Main St. (ℂ 828/488-2877). This is a real, unrecon-structed, old-fashioned drive-in, where cars pull into stalls, the driver orders through an intercom, and someone carries the food out. There's also a small dining room decorated with 1970s country music album covers (Glen Campbell, for example).

MAGGIE VALLEY

Joey's Pancake House, at 4309 Soco Rd. (U.S. 19; © **828/926-0212**), is the best of its kind I've ever dined at. The pancakes are fluffy and delicious (the mix is fantastic, too, and needs only water); the dining room is light and comfortable, with many booths; and the service is quick, friendly, and old-fashioned. People come from afar for breakfast here. It's open only for breakfast. Hours are Friday through Wednesday 7am to noon except Sunday, when it closes at 1pm. November through February, it's open Friday through Monday. Joey's closes the entire month of March.

7 Exploring Great Smoky Mountains National Park with Your Kids

ENTRANCE FEES   The National Park Service charges no fees to enter the park.

NATURAL PLACES
THE COVE HARDWOODS

The coves, or valleys, at the foot of the Smokies feed their forests with the perfect mixture of dampness, warmth, and soil to grow trees and plants fast and fancy. The trees are tall, roofing over the land with a high green canopy, and come in an amazing variety. If you're not from around here, hiking through these woods is full of surprises and wonder. You'll see brand-new trees and plants, or kinds that you have seen before only in botanical gardens, not wild woodlands. In the spring everything seems to flower. Near openings and streams, the brush is thicker than in the full shadow of the trees, with huge rhododendrons, twining wild grapes, and other junglelike growth. The forest can feel truly enchanted.

The handy *Trees & Forests* map-guide published by the Great Smoky Mountains Association (see "Great Smoky Address Book," p. 136) shows where old-growth and selectively cut forests survive in the park, and which trails lead through them to the different forest types. It costs $1. There are lots of ways into the rich cove hardwoods. Five miles up Newfound Gap from the north end, the **Cove Hardwood Nature Trail** is a loop less than 1 mile long.

A 4-mile trail rises 2,000 feet through some huge old-growth tulip trees and other cove hardwoods to Ramsay Cascades, the park's highest waterfall. The **Ramsey Cascade Trail** also leads past swimming holes on the Little Pigeon River. The trail head is on Greenbrier Road, off Highway 321, 6 miles east of Gatlinburg. Like other waterfall trails, it is among the park's busiest. One less-used trail leads to an old-growth forest of enormous cove hardwoods, including a tulip tree 25 feet around: the **Albright Grove Loop.** The loop starts about 3 miles up the Maddron Bald Trail, 15 miles east of Gatlinburg on Highway 321 (turn on Laurel Springs Rd.). After hiking along an old farm road and past a farm cabin and overgrown fields, you reach the ancient primeval forest of huge mossy trees, a natural spiritual refuge.

You needn't stick to these trails to see cove hardwoods, however; indeed, they cover much of the park, and many trails pass through them for great distances.

THE PINE-OAK FOREST

Higher in the hills above the cove hardwoods, where the weather is a bit colder and the soil drier on the western and southern slopes, a forest of oaks and pines grows.

Pines are the first trees to grow on land disturbed by fire. Trees like the Table Mountain pine open their cones in the heat of fire and need soil cleared by flames to get started. After 50 or 60 years, if not renewed by fire, these trees grow old and oaks begin to fill in where they decline.

Trails in the southwestern part of the park, where the land is driest, pass through more of this kind of forest, but you might encounter it in patches on many trails. The **Abrams Falls Trail,** starting on the west end of Cades Cove and going 2.5 miles one-way along Abrams Creek to the falls, rises and falls gently from pine-oak ridges to thick hemlock and rhododendron by the creek. It ends at the wide, roaring falls. The trail can be crowded.

THE MOUNTAINTOPS & BALDS

High in the Smokies you can look down on ridges that tangle like tree roots, spreading out into the dim distance. Clouds wash against the green mountainsides like a rising flood, white mist seeping into the valleys between the ridges. At the top, the air is crisp and smells fresh—your head clears from the scent of sleepy rot you smelled among the big trees down below—and the sky opens among rocks and small spruce and fir trees. At the grassy, brushy mountain balds, big views open in all directions, and in season, flowers shout out to the sky.

The easiest way to the mountaintops is **Newfound Gap Road.** The **Appalachian Trail** meets the road at the ridge of the Smokies. Drive west to Clingmans Dome on a 7-mile spur road (closed in winter) to see sweeping mountain views from a tower that stands at the highest point in the Smokies, 6,643 feet. The paved, .5-mile walk from the parking lot is steep, but the view is well worth it. Some excellent trails lead from the Clingmans Dome and Newfound Gap roads. The **Alum Cave Trail,** on Newfound Gap Road, is gorgeous, but often quite crowded until the steepness weeds out weaker hikers. For an easy, uncrowded walk, try one of the paths along the road marked Quiet Walkway. These are former road segments.

Reaching the summit of a mountain can be a letdown at Great Smoky when you find that the summit is a thick forest with no view, but the balds are great mountain destinations with fine views. For reasons unknown, these areas stayed grassy and open amid the trees. You can see a long way, feel a cool breeze, and enjoy the sun. The flowers can be extraordinary, especially the flame azaleas blooming in June and July. And, since it takes some work to get there (you can't drive), these areas are not crowded with cars or people.

Andrews Bald is a reasonable family hike, 1.8 miles down a steep and rocky trail from Clingmans Dome Road. The views are sublime and the bald is large and easy to lose yourself in; it's a perfect picnic destination. **Gregory Bald,** above Cades Cove, is an all-day hike or an easy overnight. Two backcountry campsites are nearby. The trail rises 2,500 feet over 4.5 miles from Parson Branch Road on the south side of Cades Cove.

WATERFALLS & STREAMS

Clouds from the Gulf of Mexico float over the south, full of water, then bump up against the Smokies and mist, drip, or slosh down upon its mountainsides. The streams from that water have worn down these mountains from towering peaks into the branched ridges and valleys they are today. On a hot summer day, the streams can be wonderful places to play. Rarely do you find a hole deep or wide enough to swim more than a few strokes, but there are plenty of places to feel the thrill of cold water all over your hot body, splash around, and experience a unique joy. Streams are everywhere; sometimes it's a battle to keep hiking when swimming holes keep presenting themselves so appealingly (see "Inner-Tubing & Swimming," p. 160, for safety and other tips).

Waterfalls happen when a streambed runs from a harder rock to a softer rock. The water wears away the softer rock faster, leaving a drop-off at the place where the harder rock ends. Because of the old and complicated geology of the Smokies, different kinds of rock meet in many places, so there are many waterfalls. They make good destinations for hikes, and the Great Smoky Mountains Association sells a $1 map-guide called *Waterfalls* that has descriptions of each fall and the route to it. The popularity of waterfall hikes also means that these are the most crowded trails in the park. The Ramsay Cascade and Abrams Falls trails are described above in this section. Some easy and less-traveled waterfall hikes start in the peaceful Deep Creek area, near Bryson City. They include **Indian Creek Fall, Juney Whank Falls,** and **Toms Branch Falls. Mingo Falls,** on the Cherokee Reservation, is the highest in the area, with a 120-foot drop; to get there, take the first left on Big Cove Road to Mingo Falls Campground, which is less than .25-mile from the falls. **Hen Wallow Falls** is about 2 miles through old-growth trees from the Cosby Campground, at the east end of the park.

PLACES FOR LEARNING

Cades Cove   Settlers began clearing trees and building farms in this lovely mountain valley in 1819, when the state of Tennessee got the land from the Cherokee in a treaty. As many as 700 people lived here, and some of their churches and hand-hewn log houses have been saved in an **open-air museum,** arranged around the edge of the fields in the center of the cove. Walking through these buildings and cemeteries is fascinating and ghostly. You can almost hear the ordinary people who lived here. The open vistas and grass make this among the park's best places to see wildlife. Animals are most often seen at morning and dusk.

An **11-mile scenic loop** road circles the cove, passing by buildings and trail heads on the way. A 31-page booklet, *Cades Cove Tour,* available for $1 at visitor centers, explains the sites by number; you need it to understand the tour. At the back of the loop, the **Cades Cove Visitor Center** is a place to ask questions about the cove's history and buy a book. The nearby Cable Mill, a gristmill, operates spring through fall. If you have a general question, however, don't make the slow trek to this visitor center; instead, ask at the ranger station at the Cades Cove Campground.

The problem with Cades Cove is crowding. The road is one lane, and people tend to stop traffic while they watch deer or look at a cabin. At peak times the loop can take more than 3 hours, without stops—an unbearably slow pace. The Park Service is studying the problem; for now, the solution is to go early or late in the day, and if the pace is just too slow, take one of the shortcut roads across the pastures. Or rent a bike at the Cades Cove campground. On Saturday and Wednesday before 10am, only bikes are allowed in Cades Cove. Even at other times, you can have more fun and move faster by biking around the cars. Buggy rides or hayrides go through the cove every day, some with rangers along to give commentary (see "Horseback Riding & Hayrides," p. 160). The other alternative, and my preference, is to skip Cades Cove entirely and spend the time instead at Cataloochee, which I cover next.

West end of Laurel Creek Rd. No phone. Free admission. Visitor center spring–fall daily 9am–7pm; winter daily 9am–6pm.

Cataloochee ★★★ *Finds*   Up in the mountains at the end of a rough, twisting gravel road, this ghost village is like a version of Cades Cove without crowds. There are pastures, which are great for wildlife-viewing (particularly shortly after sunrise and just before sunset, when many of the park's elk come to browse), and spooky old buildings you can walk through, including cabins, farmhouses, a barn, a church, and a school. One house holds an interesting little museum. Even better, several hiking trails lead into dark hardwood forest past more buildings, including the extraordinary church at Little Cataloochee, several miles beyond where car-bound tourists can see. The narrow, unpaved roads limit driving, but they look to be good mountain-biking routes, especially the road from Big Cataloochee to the Little Cataloochee trail head, which continues north to Big Creek, on the northeast corner of the park; on maps, it is marked as "Old NC 284."

Cove Creek Rd., off U.S. 276 (complete directions under the Cataloochee listing under "National Park Campgrounds," p. 146).

Mingus Mill   This working mill grinds corn under a stone powered by creek water passing through a cast-iron turbine propeller that dates from 1886. When I visited, a couple of old guys in overalls were running the machinery and passing the time, much as workers might have 100 years ago. It was an interesting and authentic country experience.

Newfound Gap Rd., across from Oconaluftee Visitor Center. Daily 9am–5pm. Closed Thanksgiving to mid-Mar.

Mountain Farm Museum ★   Buildings saved from around the Smokies have been set up in a pasture to show what a pioneer farm might have looked like. When the government bought the land for the park, there were about 1,200 mountain farms in the Smokies. Each was mostly self-sufficient, with family members working together to raise and store grains, vegetables, fruit, and meat. Today, when we rely so much on others to survive, it's interesting to see how you might be able to do it alone. Get the inexpensive guide booklet at the visitor center before starting.

Newfound Gap Rd., behind the Oconaluftee Visitor Center, at the park's south entrance.

CHEROKEE SITES

The Cherokee have created an oasis of meaning in the midst of the exploitative roadside tourist businesses outside the park. These three sites are on the reservation just outside the south park entrance.

Museum of the Cherokee Indian ★★   The museum uses technology and artifacts to effectively put you in a place and time, following the Cherokee story from the deep past and through the Trail of Tears. I'd be surprised if the experience of the exhibit doesn't inspire tears in many visitors. It starts with a 5-minute film on the creation myth in a mock campfire circle, so you may have to wait a few minutes.

589 Tsali Blvd. (Hwy. 441 and Drama Rd.), Cherokee. © 828/497-3481. www.cherokeemuseum.org. $9 adults, $6 children 6–13, free for children under 6. Daily 9am–7pm. Closed Christmas, Thanksgiving, and New Year's Day.

Oconaluftee Indian Village   Cherokee guides lead visitors on a 1-hour tour through a shady re-creation of a 1750s village, stopping to look in the buildings and see demonstrations of traditional crafts and life ways; the kids on our tour were fascinated by the blowgun. It's nicely done and well worth the hour, although the expense of admission may exclude those without a particular interest in the Cherokee.

Off U.S. 441 N., Cherokee. © **828/497-2315,** or 828/497-2111 off season. www.cherokee-nc.com/oconaluftee_main.php. $13 adults, $6 children 6–13. Daily 9am–5:30pm. Closed late Oct to mid-May.

Unto These Hills This is a huge summer outdoor drama telling the story of the Cherokee from the arrival of De Soto in 1540 to the Trail of Tears (see "History: Whose Land Is This?" on p. 136). The drama has run since 1950.

Off U.S. 441 N., Cherokee. (C) **866/554-4557** or 828/497-2111. www.cherokee-nc.com/oconaluftee_main.php.com. Reserved seating $22 adults, $10 children 6–10, free for 5 and under; general admission $18 adults, $8 ages 6–12. Performances early June to mid-Aug Mon–Sat 8:30pm.

8 For the Active Family

BACKPACKING

Great Smoky is a good place for beginning or advanced backpackers. Beginners can plan short days, because there are plenty of campsites, many of them close together. Backcountry permits are easy to get without advance reservations (p. 149). Cold weather is rare in summer and fall, and although climbing a mountain with a backpack on a hot summer day is sweaty work, you can usually stop and dunk yourself in a creek to cool off. Spring-break temperatures are perfect for backpacking, although it's often muddy at the top. In any season, count on rain and mist, and be prepared to hike through it. The park's trails include many loops, so you can plan a trip that returns to your car without covering the same trail twice. The Great Smoky Mountains Association (see "Great Smoky Address Book," p. 136) publishes a $1 map-guide called *Backpack Loops,* which provides planning and trail details on 12 routes of 1 to 3 nights. Volunteer rangers in the backcountry office are helpful in choosing a route, too, but I recommend preparing before you leave home. A superb trail guidebook is mentioned under "Reading Up" (p. 140). Opportunities for guided backpacking in groups with naturalists and outdoors experts are described under "Kid-Friendly Programs" (p. 162). However you go, read up on how to avoid black bears, which are common in the Smokies and can be dangerous. The park uses food-hanging cables at the backcountry campsites, so you will need a bag to put your food in and a way to attach it to the hook. Keep everything with any odor hanging on the cable. See "Dangerous Wildlife," in chapter 2, for more on bear safety.

FISHING

Anglers go for rainbow, brown, and rare southern brook trout in Smoky's streams. The truth is, the fishing isn't very productive. Experienced locals might do well, but tourists spend a lot of time flogging the water. That's okay if you enjoy standing for hours on the edge of a sparkling mountain stream under huge, waving trees, but children might lose patience. A fishing license from either Tennessee or North Carolina is good anywhere in the park. If you're going to fish in waters outside the park, you'll need a special permit from either the Cherokee reservation or the town of Gatlinburg, depending on where you head. Get a list of regulations at a visitor center. Licenses are widely available. Gear can be found in Gatlinburg at the **Smoky Mountain Angler,** 466 Brookside Village Way, Suite 8 ((C) **865/436-8746**).

HIKING

Smoky is one of the great hiker's parks, with more than 850 miles of trails through fairy-tale forests and few other people in evidence. Despite the great numbers of visitors, only 30% ever leave their cars, and only 5% of that number go beyond certain popular trails that total about 20 miles—famous routes and short paths to waterfalls. Starting out on a hike early one morning, I had the Alum Cave Trail to myself, returning around midday to the trail head surrounded by dozens of people struggling upward in the hot sun in an almost solid line. After the delicate scent of spring flowers and mountain air up the trail, I thought I would choke on the thick odor of after-shave and perfume. On another trip, I chose a more obscure trail and never encountered another hiker; indeed, at points the trail was overgrown. Yet the hike was beautiful. I came to a gorgeous waterfall, an abandoned rail trestle, and many more swimming holes than I could use. The lesson: Hike early on popular trails or choose less-known routes. Choosing an uncrowded trail is made much easier by a book called *Hiking Trails of the Smokies* (see "Reading Up," p. 140), which indexes hikes by popularity as well as other ways. It's the best trail guide I've ever come across. Each trail description is a thoughtful essay on its area's nature and history, as well as a lode of practical advice. You'll also need a map, also covered under "Reading Up," and a trail guide, especially for those interested in the history along the way.

I've described several trails elsewhere in this chapter: the **Little River Trail** at Elkmont Campground (p. 146), the **Smokemont Loop** trail at the Smokemont Campground (p. 146), the **Flat Creek Trail** at Balsam Mountain Campground (p. 147), the **Gabes Mountain Trail** at Cosby Campground (p. 147), the **Alum Cave Trail** under LeConte Lodge (p. 151), the **Ramsey Cascade Trail** and **Albright Grove Loop** under "The Cove Hardwoods" (p. 155), **Abrams Falls Trail** under "The Pine-Oak Forest" (p. 155), **Andrews Bald** and **Gregory Bald** trails under "The Mountaintops & Balds" (p. 156), and Cataloochee trails (p. 158).

HORSEBACK RIDING & HAYRIDES

About half of the trails at Smoky are open to horses, and stables offer scheduled day trips in the park for families with children over age 4. Charges are approximately $20 for 1 hour, $39 for 2 hours, $75 for 4 hours, $100 for all day. Not all stables offer all lengths of rides. At **Cades Cove,** 1-hour rides, 20-minute horse-drawn buggy rides, and 2-hour tractor-drawn hayrides let you see, with younger children or nonriders, some of the area as the settlers did. Some hayrides have rangers along to give commentary. Hayrides are $6 to $8 per person, buggies $7.50 per person. The cove's trails are flat, so the stable allows children under 5 to ride on the same horse in front of their parents as long as their combined weight is less than 250 pounds. Call the **Cades Cove Stables,** at the General Store at Cades Cove (⟨ 865/448-6286), for reservations.

The **Smokemont Stables,** which offers 1-hour, 2½-hour, half-day, and full-day rides, are near the campground of the same name on the North Carolina side (⟨ 828/497-2373). **Smoky Mountain Riding** (⟨ 865/436-5634) is a few miles east of Gatlinburg on Highway 321. It offers 1- and 2-hour rides in the park, its weight limit is 225 pounds. A third option is **Sugarlands Riding Stables** (⟨ 865/436-3535), which is just 1 mile south of the park's Gatlinburg entrance. All close for the winter months.

INNER-TUBING & SWIMMING

Few ways of spending a hot summer afternoon could be more fun than floating down a creek on an inner-tube—or "tubing," as they call it around here. There are no rules about where you can swim or tube in the park, but use your common sense. In fact, the park discourages swimming and tubing, pointing out that drowning is one of the main causes of death in the park. If you must go, for tubing it's wisest to go where you see others; even at popular spots you can get banged up, so going where you aren't sure of the conditions is foolhardy. Many businesses and campgrounds outside the park rent or sell tubes on streams where you can jump right in. You'll need a swimsuit, lifejackets for kids, and shoes you can get wet. Perhaps the best spot for really wild tubing is at **Deep Creek,** near Bryson City. The lower portion near the campground is reasonable, but if you want real white water, losing your tube, and getting bumped around, you can hike a mile higher. The **Deep Creek Tube Center** (© **828/488-6055;** www.deep creekcamping.com) is one of the operators there, with tubes and changing rooms, charging $4. As the summer wears on and water levels subside, tubing becomes more difficult; at Deep Creek the best tubing is in May and June, but tubing can continue through Labor Day.

For swimming, almost any inviting pool or hole in a slow-moving river will do. I've mentioned swimming holes all through the chapter, especially with the campgrounds, but it's not necessary to plan around a particular spot. Few spots are big enough to really swim, but many creeks have holes as big and deep as a large hot tub, enough to cool down and splash around. The season does make a difference, however, so it's a good idea to stop at a visitor center and ask about water conditions. Never swim in the seemingly appealing pools under waterfalls, because they often have strong currents that can pull you into danger. Of course, there are no lifeguards.

MOUNTAIN BIKING

Bicycles are not permitted on trails, but the park is rich in one-lane dirt roads through the mountains where you can ride as sunlight flashes through the leaves of overhanging trees. I've mentioned **Balsam Mountain Road** with the Balsam Mountain Campground (p. 147) and the route in the east of the park known as **Old NC 284** in Cataloochee (p. 158). A route over Forge Creek and Parson Branch roads leads from the south side of the Cades Cove Loop, in the west end of the park, over Hannah Mountain to twisty U.S. 129. On any of these rides, you will need to backtrack or have someone pick you up on the other end, because families shouldn't ride in the traffic of the paved roads. The most unusual of the park's bike routes is the scenic **Lake View Drive,** better known as "the road to nowhere." It leads from Bryson City partway around the north side of Fontana Lake and through a 1,100-foot-long tunnel before ending at the point construction had reached when environmental concerns halted the project in the 1960s. I've covered biking in Cades Cove itself on p. 142. Outside the park the national forests have famous single-track trails where bikes are allowed. The **Nantahala National Forest** near Bryson City offers many choices, including the 40-mile trail network near the Tsali campground (p. 149). The **Nantahala Outdoor Center,** 13077 Hwy. 19 W., west of Bryson (© **888/905-7238;** www. noc.com), offers bike rentals and guided outings.

RAFTING

There's no rafting within the park, but you'll find good rides outside its boundaries. The **Nantahala Outdoor Center,** 13077 Hwy. 19 W., west of Bryson City (© **888/ 905-7238;** www.noc.com), is the region's best-established service and something of an institution in the Bryson City area. It offers trips on seven different rivers every day during the season. Relatively easy floats on the Nantahala and Pigeon rivers are for beginners but still have Class III rapids; children must weigh at least 60 pounds on the Nantahala, at least 70 on the Upper Pigeon. You can rent a raft and gear for the run for around $22 per person. The guided 3-hour trips start around $40. You can ride one-way on the **Great Smoky Mountain Railroad** (© **800/872-4681;** www. gsmr.com) and raft back on the Nantahala River for $74 adults, $57 under 13. At the other end of the spectrum, ferocious water and overnights on the Chattooga River are

Tips **Places for Relaxed Play & Picnics**

The woods and stream banks are places to play together. If you're looking for play facilities, there's a **city park** in Gatlinburg on the hill above Historic Nature Trail; take that road uphill, turn right on Cherokee Orchard, and then turn right again on Asbury Way. In Bryson City the **Swain County Recreation Park** is a family facility on the way to the park's Deep Creek Campground. It has a pool, playgrounds, tennis, basketball, skateboard park, and soccer field. The pool fee is $2.50 per person above 5, $2 for 2- to 5-year-olds. For information, call the county parks department (© **828/ 488-6159**). There are many picnic grounds in the park, marked on the map on p. 143 and on the official park map. Some of them, on the main roads, are huge areas with dozens of tables and restrooms with flush toilets.

for fit adults and teenagers only and cost considerably more. The center also offers canoe and kayak instruction and mountain-bike rentals and trips; rents cabins; and has showers, laundry, and three restaurants on-site.

WILDLIFE-WATCHING

The best places to see wildlife are in open areas where you have a wide field of vision and there are grass and undergrowth for animals to eat: **Cades Cove, Cataloochee,** and **the balds.** You're most likely to see deer, woodchucks, other small mammals, and wild turkeys, although elk are fairly visible in the meadows at Cataloochee around sunrise and sunset. More than 1,500 black bears live in the park, more than the natural habitat can easily support. Visitors see the bears mostly in the spring when they're looking for food after hibernating. In June they head into the hills and woods. In October more sightings occur again as the bears fatten up for hibernation. Be careful to avoid attracting bears with food odors. Prepare for bear encounters by reading "Dangerous Wildlife," in chapter 2.

9 Kid-Friendly Programs

CHILDREN'S PROGRAMS

The park has a **Junior Ranger** program for kids ages 5 to 12 based on a booklet of activities sold by the Great Smoky Mountains Association for $3. Buy it at a visitor center or through the contacts listed under "Great Smoky Address Book," earlier in this chapter. After completing the activities in the booklet, participants earn a Junior Ranger badge from the Park Service. The award-winning booklet is well beyond the blah materials some other parks produce: Printed in full color, it comes with a magnifying glass and trading cards. There are 11 activities to do in the booklet.

FAMILY & ADULT PROGRAMS
PARK SERVICE

During the summer and fall, rangers lead an extensive program of hikes; talks on flowers, forests, birding, and other natural-history topics; history walks and talks; films; and so on. Children can go along, if you think they'll be interested in the topic.

Many programs start from the Sugarlands Visitor Center; something's always about to start during the visitor season. Others start at trail heads or other areas around the park. The schedule appears in the *Smokies Guide* park newspaper, available at the visitor centers, and online (visit www.nps.gov/grsm, click "Things to Do," then "Schedule of Events"). The programs are free, and there's no need to sign up in advance. Rangers also offer evening campfire programs at most of the larger campgrounds. Check the park newspaper for times.

Smoky Mountain Field School   The University of Tennessee and the National Park Service offer a large catalog of 1-day classes and multiple-day outdoor learning expeditions March through October. Most are open only to adults, but on many summer weekends, there are programs especially for families. Sessions might cover subjects like mountain life and song or reptiles and amphibians. They cost $29 to $35 for adults, $19 to $25 for children 6 to 12. Check the catalog online to find out what's on when you'll be visiting and sign up—all programs are limited, and they do fill. Registration is available online, by phone, by fax, or in person.

The University of Tennessee Professional and Personal Development, 313 Conference Center Building, Knoxville, TN 37996-3181. (☎ 865/974-0150. www.outreach.utk.edu/smoky.

SUMMER CAMPS

Great Smoky Mountains Institute at Tremont   The institute, with dormitories and classrooms in a mountain valley in the northwest part of the park, offers intensive sessions for adults all year, and residential summer camps for ages 9 to 17 during the summer. Campers backpack in the park, do fun activities, study science, and become naturalists. The tuitions are a bargain: 5-day camps, for ages 9 to 12 or 13 to 17, are $440 or less. Reserve well ahead.

9275 Tremont Rd., Townsend, TN 37882. (☎ 865/448-6709. www.gsmit.org.

10 Entertainment outside the Park

GATLINBURG

The Gatlinburg area is a prime habitat for water parks, country music theaters, freak museums, go-cart tracks (outdoor and indoor), bumper boats, bungee jumping, an aerial tram, and the most amazing variety of minigolf courses I've ever seen. The attractions are unlimited, and I don't doubt many are fun, but they're just a distraction from the park. I found it a relief to escape the carnival atmosphere. Get information at the welcome center or the Gatlinburg Chamber of Commerce (see "Great Smoky Address Book," p. 136).

CHEROKEE

The museums and performance operated by the Cherokee are covered on p. 158.

BRYSON CITY/DILLSBORO

The **Great Smoky Mountains Railroad** (☎ 800/872-4681 or 828/586-8811; www.gsmr.com) operates excursion trips around the mountainous countryside every day of the season. Many are pulled by a steam engine. Special options include dinner trains and a river-rafting train that goes to the Nantahala Outdoor Center (see "Rafting," p. 161). Summer fares start at $40 for a 4-hour ride, half price for children 2 to 12. Timetables and reservations are available online.

FAST FACTS: Great Smoky Mountains National Park

Area Code The area codes are **865** and **828**.

ATMs There are banks with ATMs in most of the towns.

Emergencies For emergencies, dial ℂ **911**.

Hospitals & Clinics **Fort Sanders Sevier Medical Center** (ℂ **865/429-6100**) is in Sevierville on Middle Creek Road, 15 miles north of Gatlinburg. **Swain County Hospital** (ℂ **828/488-2155**) is in Bryson City.

Information For information, write Great Smoky Mountains National Park, 107 Park Headquarters Rd., Gatlinburg, TN 37738; or call ℂ **865/436-1200**.

Pharmacies Pharmacies can be found in many of the towns.

Post Office In Gatlinburg, the post office is on East Parkway (U.S. 321) near Newman Road. In Cherokee it's on 441 North (which becomes Newfound Gap Rd.). The Bryson City post office is on Slope Street.

Time Zone The national park is on **Eastern Standard Time.**

Transit Info There is no public transportation in the park.

Weather Updates For weather updates, look on the Internet at www.nps.gov/grsm.

7

Grand Canyon National Park

Nothing prepares you for it. The first sight of the Grand Canyon is overwhelming, no matter how many pictures you've seen. Coming from the south, you've been driving through desert and pines, eyes focused at the usual distance on the world around you. Then, all of a sudden, the earth in front of you disappears.

There's nothing but air for 1 mile down and 10 miles, on average, across. It's hard to take in all that you're seeing at once: all the layers of rock, carved into so many shapes, shadow and searing brightness, tiny and massive rocks fitting together. The very fact that this park is centered around an incredibly large crack in the earth makes the Grand Canyon a bit difficult to visit with young children. Outwardly, there doesn't seem to be much for them to do besides look at the canyon. While there are hiking trails, the variety is pretty small. Some are nice, flat, paved paths along the rim that offer great views. Others are brutally steep descents into the furnace of the canyon, too tough for young kids. The famous mules serve fewer than 100 visitors a day—1 in 1,000 visitors get to go. Most trails are terribly crowded during most of the day. As a result, many people make short visits to the park, just driving in, taking a look, and passing on. The average stay is 4 hours. In the summer, visitors clog the South Rim area with cars. Not surprisingly, as you find yourself either idling in lines or jockeying for a parking spot, the incredible summer crowds diminish the experience of this extraordinary place.

Fortunately, if you plan carefully, you can avoid these pitfalls and have a great visit. And the park isn't as kid-unfriendly as it might seem on first glance. No matter how much you try to describe the size of the canyon to your kids, you'll never do it justice. Count on them being floored by the sheer enormity of the canyon when they stand along its rim. Point out to them the scurrying lizards, too. If you visit the North Rim, the kids will love running through the forests, and some wonderful trails there—that aren't too strenuous for youngsters—lead out to the rim. If your family likes backpacking, well, there's plenty of that at the Grand Canyon, too. Just be sure to plan far in advance to obtain the necessary permits so that you can get away from the throngs.

And regardless of whether you find yourself on the South or North Rim for your stay, plan at least 1 day to rise before dawn to beat the heat and the crowds on canyon trails and to catch the spectacular morning vistas.

BEST THINGS TO DO AT THE GRAND CANYON

- **See the canyon at dawn or sunset,** when the angle of the sun picks out the folds in the rock.
- **Rise before dawn to hike** at least a little way down into the canyon, seeing how its extraordinary walls look from close up.

Grand Canyon Address Book

Grand Canyon National Park   P.O. Box 129, Grand Canyon, AZ 86023. ✆ **928/ 638-7888.** www.nps.gov/grca.

Grand Canyon Association   P.O. Box 399, Grand Canyon, AZ 86023. ✆ **800/ 858-2808** or 928/638-2481. www.grandcanyon.org. For books and maps.

Tusayan Ranger District   Kaibab National Forest (South Rim). P.O. Box 3088, Grand Canyon, AZ 86023. ✆ **928/638-2443.** www.fs.fed.us/r3/kai.

North Kaibab Ranger District   North Kaibab Ranger District (North Rim). 430 S. Main St. (P.O. Box 248), Fredonia, AZ 86022. ✆ **928/643-7395.** www. fs.fed.us/r3/kai.

Xanterra Parks & Resorts (park concessionaire)   6312 South Fiddlers Green Circle, Suite 600N, Greenwood Village, CO 80111. ✆ **928/638-2631.** www. grandcanyonlodges.com. For reservations: ✆ **888/297-2757.** Fax 303/297-3175. www.xanterra.com.

Grand Canyon Field Institute   P.O. Box 399, Grand Canyon, AZ 86023. ✆ **866/ 471-4435** or 928/638-2485. www.grandcanyon.org/fieldinstitute.

- **Get a backcountry camping permit** so that you can hike farther, away from the crowds.

For more information, see "For the Active Family" (p. 188).

1 History: The Struggle for Preservation

The Grand Canyon's human history revolves mostly around how people tried to get across it or down it. The canyon is so long, so deep, and so steep that it divides the Southwest. It has blocked animals and plants as well as people. Many living things couldn't survive in the heat at the bottom of the canyon. People also had to deal with the steepness of the sides. Even today, with bridges and dams that help us go around the canyon and over the Colorado River, the area to the north is remote, and not many people live there.

Those who do live on the strip of Arizona that lies north of the canyon connect more with southern Utah than with the rest of their own state. Native Americans who lived here long ago didn't use written language, so archaeologists must piece together a history from the things they left behind: ruins of houses, tools, baskets, and so on. Explorers of hard-to-reach caves have found models of animals made of willow and cottonwood twigs that were split, bent, and tied together. These could be at least 4,000 years old, dating from before the time when Southwestern natives learned about farming or settled in villages. Scientists think that hunters might have imbued these shapes with magical powers and used them to help their hunt.

Later, after they learned to farm, Native Americans lived in the canyon and on the rim in small villages, but the Grand Canyon area never was a center of large, complicated villages like the great stone pueblos farther south and east. This area was the edge of the Ancestral Puebloan (also called Anasazi) territory, where they mixed with other, simpler cultures. You can see one of their villages at the Tusayan Museum and ruin

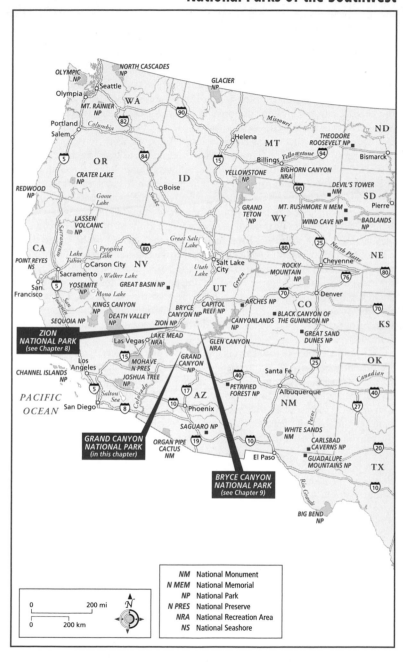

OLYMPIC NP
NORTH CASCADES NP
GLACIER NP
Seattle
Olympia
WA
MT. RAINIER NP
Portland
Salem
Columbia
Missouri
Helena
MT
THEODORE ROOSEVELT NP
ND
Bismarck
OR
CRATER LAKE NP
ID
Boise
Billings
Yellowstone
YELLOWSTONE NP
BIGHORN CANYON NRA
DEVIL'S TOWER NM
SD
Pierre
REDWOOD NP
Goose Lake
Snake
GRAND TETON NP
MT. RUSHMORE N MEM
WIND CAVE NP
BADLANDS NP
LASSEN VOLCANIC NP
Great Salt Lake
WY
CA
Lake Tahoe
Pyramid Lake
POINT REYES NS
Carson City
NV
Salt Lake City
Utah Lake
ROCKY MOUNTAIN NP
NE
Cheyenne
Sacramento
Walker Lake
Green
Denver
San Francisco
YOSEMITE NP
Mono Lake
GREAT BASIN NP
UT
CO
KINGS CANYON NP
DEATH VALLEY NP
BRYCE CANYON NP
CAPITOL REEF NP
ARCHES NP
BLACK CANYON OF THE GUNNISON NP
KS
SEQUOIA NP
ZION NP
CANYONLANDS NP
GREAT SAND DUNES NP

ZION NATIONAL PARK (see Chapter 8)
LAKE MEAD NRA
Las Vegas
GLEN CANYON NRA

Los Angeles
CHANNEL ISLANDS NP
MOHAVE N PRES
JOSHUA TREE NP
GRAND CANYON NP
Santa Fe
OK
Canadian
PACIFIC OCEAN
Salton Sea
San Diego
Colorado
AZ
Phoenix
PETRIFIED FOREST NP
NM
Albuquerque
Pecos

GRAND CANYON NATIONAL PARK (in this chapter)
SAGUARO NP
ORGAN PIPE CACTUS NM
WHITE SANDS NM
CARLSBAD CAVERNS NP
El Paso
GUADALUPE MOUNTAINS NP
TX

BRYCE CANYON NATIONAL PARK (see Chapter 9)
Rio Grande

BIG BEND NP

NM	National Monument
N MEM	National Memorial
NP	National Park
N PRES	National Preserve
NRA	National Recreation Area
NS	National Seashore

0   200 mi
0   200 km

N

(p. 187). Native Americans today still use the canyon; the Havasupai still live along Havasupai Creek, to the west.

Spanish explorers first saw the Grand Canyon in 1540, but they couldn't find a way down. No one figured out how to get across until 1776, when a group led by a pair of Spanish missionaries set out to find a route from Santa Fe, New Mexico, to Monterey, California. They crossed the Colorado River in Glen Canyon and also discovered, but did not use, the crossing at Lees Ferry. Later travelers used those routes, but the Grand Canyon still wasn't explored even after Mexico gained independence from Spain. In 1846, the United States attacked Mexico; in the 2-year Mexican War the U.S. won most of what is now considered the American West (south of Oregon and west of Santa Fe). The U.S. government sent explorers to map the area, looking for routes for railroad lines. In 1857, one of the military groups found the Grand Canyon and decided it was impossible to survey. The party reported back that it was beautiful but useless, and said there was no reason for anyone else to go back.

A member of that group convinced the Grand Canyon's most famous explorer, John Wesley Powell, to float down the Colorado in 1869 with 10 others. Powell took wooden boats from the Green River in Wyoming to towns below the Grand Canyon. Think about his courage: No one knew whether the trip was possible. There might be huge waterfalls. If he ran into trouble with the boats, there might be no way out, up the canyon walls and across the desert. At one point three of his group said they'd had enough and tried to hike out, and when they reached the canyon rim they were killed, probably by Native Americans. But Powell made it, then did it again 2 years later. He was a geologist, and he carefully wrote down his exciting discoveries, which are still studied.

Prospectors explored the canyon and found valuable metals in the 1870s and 1880s, but they didn't make much money mining because it was too expensive and difficult to get the ore from inside the canyon to where people could use it. In the 1890s, the miners started to realize that they could make more money showing the canyon off to tourists, and they began building hotels and trails. In 1901, a railroad punched through, and President Theodore Roosevelt came in 1903. In 1908 he made the canyon a national monument, protecting it for visitors to enjoy.

Since then, the history of the park has been about protecting it from human needs. The people of the Southwest need the water in the Colorado River, so dams catch it in a series of lakes. The Glen Canyon Dam, holding back Lake Powell above the Grand Canyon, controls the wild flow of the river. That changed the nature of the canyon in ways scientists still study. Environmentalists defeated a plan to build a dam that would have backed up water in the Grand Canyon itself.

Perhaps most difficult of all, the canyon suffers from too much love. More than four million tourists come each year, crowding beautiful places and bringing their garbage and other waste. Down in the canyon, the dry weather preserves anything that's left behind—early films show rotting trees that are still in the same places 100 years later. Garbage lasts just as long, so the Park Service works hard to keep any from being left. For example, backpackers are encouraged to carry out their bowel movements in plastic bags, and rangers haul the contents of some backcountry toilets up to the rim on mules.

In the mid-1990s, the Park Service decided to limit the number of cars coming to the South Rim, announced plans for a light rail system, and talked about rationing the number of people who could come in. The U.S. Congress stopped those plans. The

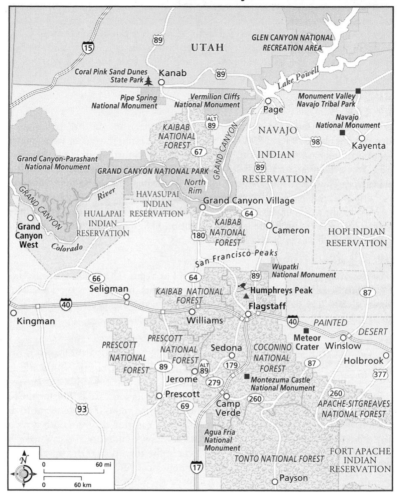

only part that was built was a visitor center for people getting off the shuttle train; now it looks as though the train itself will never be built. But while the discussions went on in Washington, D.C., history marched on. Visitors helped solve the crowding problem. Those who felt the experience was ruined in the summer started coming in the spring and fall, or not coming at all. The Park Service still aims to keep the Grand Canyon as close as possible to the way it was when Powell first floated down the Colorado by using mass transportation rather than cars. You can help by using the voluntary shuttle buses or bicycles in the South Rim area and leaving your car parked, by planning your visit to avoid the peak season, and by seeking out alternatives, such as the North Rim.

2 Orientation

The Grand Canyon has three main areas for visitors: the South Rim's **Grand Canyon Village**, the **Desert View area** on the eastern end of the South Rim, and the **North Rim**. **Tusayan** is the touristy highway town just outside the south entrance near Grand Canyon Village.

ARRIVING

BY CAR

If you're coming **from the north** by way of the other parks in this section, see the descriptions of U.S. 89 and 89A later in this chapter. From the east or west, Interstate 40 runs through northern Arizona. **From the east,** turn north from Flagstaff on Route 180. **From the west,** turn at Williams on Route 64. **From the south,** I-17 leads 140 miles from Phoenix to Flagstaff; stop off at Montezuma's Castle National Monument or camp in Oak Creek Canyon and see Sedona.

It's typically a 5-hour drive from the Grand Canyon Village to the North Rim. Go east to Desert View on Route 64, then north on U.S. 89 to 89A, then west to Jacob Lake, and south to the rim on Route 67.

BY PLANE

The closest major airports are in **Phoenix** and **Las Vegas.** The Grand Canyon Airport (© 928/638-2617) in **Tusayan** has commuter flights from Las Vegas on **Scenic Airlines** (© 800/634-6801; www.scenic.com). Scenic and others offer packages and air tours from Las Vegas.

BY TRAIN

A good, fun alternative to driving to the South Rim is to park in Williams, Arizona, on I-40, and take the train. The run isn't particularly scenic, but the staff works hard to make it entertaining for families, using historic equipment on this, the last of the original railroads that once were the main ways to the national parks. During the summer the machinery includes a steam engine to pull the train. If all you want to do is look at the canyon for a few hours and leave, you can ride the train both ways in 1 day. The railway also offers lodging packages at Maswik Lodge, or you can make your own overnight reservations and just buy tickets; the train does offer baggage service. The train leaves Williams at 10am for a 2¼-hour ride; you should check in earlier. It spends 3¼ hours at the canyon and gets back to Williams at 6:15pm. Round-trip coach-class tickets are $65 for adults, $40 for youths 11 to 16, and $30 for kids 2 to 10 (babies under 2 sit on their parent's lap free); higher classes are $30 to $105 more, plus the park entrance fee and sales tax. The **Grand Canyon Railway** depot is at 233 N. Grand Canyon Blvd. in Williams (take exit 163 from I-40); call © **800/843-8724** or 928/773-1976, or check www.thetrain.com for more information.

VISITOR INFORMATION

NATIONAL PARK VISITOR CENTERS

Questions for all visitor centers should be directed to the park's main phone number, © **928/638-7888.** Hours for the park's visitor centers vary seasonally, but generally are 7:30am to 6:30pm throughout the summer and 8am to 5pm off season.

South Rim

Canyon View Information Plaza   This visitor center was built as the initial stop for a mass transit system, which now is indefinitely postponed. Use it as your first stop to ask questions, get maps and hiking guides, and sign up for programs. Outdoor displays explain what to do in the park. The Mather Point overlook and a paved path leading to the Rim Trail are nearby, and you can bike on trails from here 2 miles to the South Rim village.

Near Mather Point.

Desert View Information Center   A small, one-room station with a ranger to answer questions and a few books for sale serves as the visitor center at the east entrance.

Near the east entrance, at the Watchtower.

North Rim

Kaibab Plateau Visitor Center   The exhibits and ranger programs at this U.S. Forest Service facility about 44 miles north of the North Rim are the most extensive you'll find in the area.

U.S. 89A and Rte. 67, Jacob Lake. 🕻 **928/643-7298.** Closed Oct to mid-May.

North Rim Visitor Center   This small visitor center, with restrooms behind the building, has a few exhibits but primarily is a place to ask questions.

Just north of Grand Canyon Lodge. 🕻 **928/638-7864.** Closed mid-Oct to mid-May.

READING UP

The **Grand Canyon Association** (🕻 **800/858-2808** or 928/638-2481; www.grand canyon.org) operates park bookstores at the visitor centers; you can also order online or by phone.

Maps: The $3.95 *Earthwalk Press Hiking Map Guide* offers adequate detail; the plastic Trails Illustrated map ($10) is more durable. The association also sells $3 map guides to each park trail.

Trail Guides: I used and liked Scott S. Warren's *100 Classic Hikes in Arizona* (The Mountaineers, $20), which gives details on hikes and backpacking trips in the canyon, and many other alternative hikes beyond the park that are easier and less crowded. It is not listed on the association's website.

THE NATIONAL PARK IN BRIEF

The South Rim: Grand Canyon Village

The Grand Canyon Village area is the traditional center of visits, with the main entrance at the tourist town of **Tusayan.** In the village area are historic hotels, the area's largest campground, several trail heads that lead along and down into the canyon, and the Park Service headquarters.

Desert View

This area is 25 miles east of Grand Canyon Village on a highway that runs along the rim. It has the Route 64 entrance, a campground, a store, and a few miles to the west the **Tusayan Ruin and Museum.** It is a quieter place to camp than the village, but you spend more time driving to the trail heads.

The North Rim

The North Rim of the canyon is open only from mid-May to mid-October, depending on weather. It's a heavier-treed, more rustic area, with a lodge, store, visitor center, and campground. The North Rim is a 5-hour drive from the South Rim. Zion National Park is closer to the North Rim by road than the Grand Canyon's own South Rim.

Grand Canyon National Park

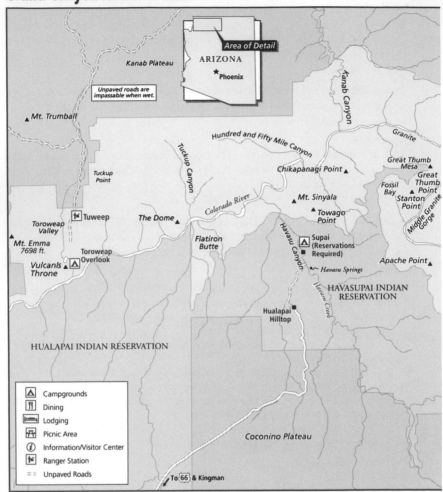

Area of Detail

ARIZONA

★ Phoenix

Unpaved roads are impassable when wet.

Kanab Plateau

Kanab Canyon

▲ Mt. Trumbull

Hundred and Fifty Mile Canyon

Granite

Tuckup Canyon

Chikapanagi Point ▲

Great Thumb Mesa ▲

Tuckup Point

Colorado River

Mt. Sinyala ▲

Great Thumb Point ▲

Fossil Bay

▲ Towago Point

Stanton Point

Middle Granite Gorge

The Dome ▲

Havasu Canyon

Supai (Reservations Required) 🔺

Flatiron Butte

▲ Tuweep

Toroweap Valley

Havasu Springs

Apache Point ▲

Mt. Emma 7698 ft.

Toroweap Overlook

HAVASUPAI INDIAN RESERVATION

Vulcan's Throne 🔺

Havasu Creek

Hualapai Hilltop ■

HUALAPAI INDIAN RESERVATION

Coconino Plateau

🔺	Campgrounds
🍴	Dining
🛏	Lodging
⛱	Picnic Area
ⓘ	Information/Visitor Center
🔺	Ranger Station
= =	Unpaved Roads

To ⟨66⟩ & Kingman

3 Getting Around

BY CAR

The current driving and parking arrangements in Grand Canyon Village are difficult at all times except in the dead off season; help yourself and the park by parking your car and leaving it. You can get around by shuttle bus and, to some extent, by bike. West of the village, to Hermits Rest, and on the short road to Yaki Point and the South Kaibab Trail, you have to take the shuttle March through November. There were plans to repave the road to Hermit's Rest beginning early in 2008. If things proceed as planned, around April 1 the road will be closed to all vehicles, including shuttle buses, west from Mohave or Hopi Point. By midsummer, the entire road could be closed from the village west. The work should be completed by November.

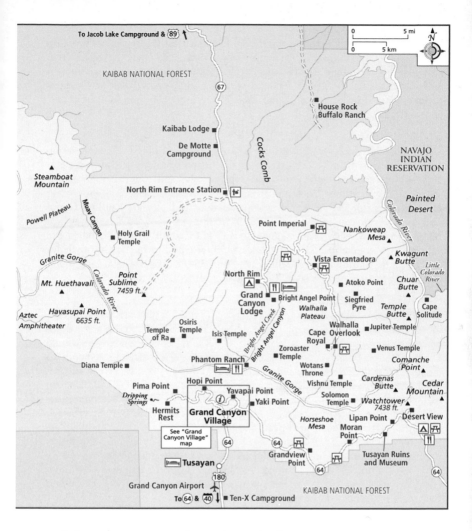

Only a car can get you to the North Rim (see "Arriving," above).

The park's most spectacular drive for private cars is on the South Rim from the village east along Route 64, to Desert View and out of the park.

BY SHUTTLE BUS

Once you get the hang of it, the excellent shuttle system makes getting around the park easy. It allows one-way hikes along the canyon rim without a car at each end. It's a good idea to carry the map of shuttle-bus routes, widely available at the park or downloadable at www.nps.gov/grca (click "Plan Your Visit," then "Maps," or, for more information, "In Depth"). Having the map also will update you on changes in the system. At this writing, shuttles were running on three loops: the blue **Village Route,** which circles the developed village area; the green **Kaibab Trail Route,** which links to the Village Route at the Canyon View Information Plaza to Yaki Point and the South Kaibab Trail and back; and the red **Hermits Rest Route,** which runs from the west end of the village area to Hermits Rest and back. The Village and Kaibab Trail routes operate year-round. The Hermits Rest Route currently operates March through November only. When it's not running, the road is open to private vehicles. The shuttles run frequently, with service varying through the seasons. The buses are free to ride, and no tickets are needed.

BY HELICOPTER OR SMALL PLANE

Helicopters and small planes from the Grand Canyon Airport in Tusayan swoop across the canyon many times a day. Seeing the canyon from the air gives you a better sense of its size and allows you to take in more angles and areas that you wouldn't see otherwise. But the experience is expensive for families and far from indispensable—it's just a fun add-on. Among companies offering flights are **Papillon Grand Canyon Helicopters** (© 800/528-2418 or 928/638-2419; www.papillon.com), which runs flights all day. A 30- to 40-minute tour is $135 for adults, $105 for children 2 to 11, with a 50-minute tour $195 for adults, $159 for kids 2 to 11. Fixed-wing flights are offered by **Grand Canyon Airlines** (© 866/235-9422 or 928/638-2463; www.grandcanyonairlines.com), with a 50-minute tour for $99, $79 for kids 2 to 11.

BY MULE & HORSEBACK

SOUTH RIM   Only about 60 people a day get to ride a mule from the South Rim into the canyon; many more than that would like to, because it's the only way down other than your own two feet. Reserve with Xanterra, the concessionaire (see "Grand Canyon Address Book," p. 166). Tickets book up on the first day of the month 23 months before the ride; they're all booked before the end of the day except for rides in midwinter. You could get lucky, because there are cancellations. Put your name on the waiting list at the transportation desk in the Bright Angel Lodge. The outings are sold as day trips or overnight stays at Phantom Ranch, the dormitory and cabins at the bottom of the canyon. Day trips are $148 and include a box lunch; overnights are $401 for one person, $710 for two, $321 for each additional person, all-inclusive. Riding the mules is hard on your behind and not for people afraid of heights—you're just along for the ride while the mule picks his way down the trail over steep dropoffs. Children under 4 feet, 7 inches, pregnant women, and people over 200 pounds (including everything you are carrying) are not permitted.

KAIBAB NATIONAL FOREST   Just outside the park, **Grand Canyon Apache Stables,** based outside the south entrance station to Grand Canyon National Park (© 928/638-2891; www.apachestables.com), offers **horseback and wagon rides** in the Kaibab National Forest. Half-day rides include a canyon view. Prices for horseback rides range from $46 to $86 and wagon rides cost $26; call for details.

NORTH RIM   These are easier to book than the South Rim trips. **Grand Canyon Trail Rides** (© 435/679-8665; www.canyonrides.com) offers mule trips into the canyon from the North Rim and along the rim. Hour-long rides along the rim for adults and kids as young as 7 are only $30, and half-day rides along the rim or into the canyon for those 10 years old and up are $55. The longest, full-day rides go as far as Roaring Springs on the North Kaibab Trail for $105 per person. Riders on that excursion must be at least 12 years old and less than 200 pounds.

BY BIKE

The park is slowly developing bike trails to help solve the traffic problems at the South Rim, but there is still much work to do. Trails link the Canyon View Information Plaza to the edge of the village area, but not across it to the Bright Angel Trail (the Rim Trail is closed to bikes). The roads are narrow and not designed for bikes; families may not be safe riding on them. Moreover, you have to bring your bike from home, because no rentals are available in the park or nearby. See also "Mountain Biking" in "For the Active Family" (p. 188).

BY RAFT

See "Rafting" in "For the Active Family" (p. 188).

BY FOOT

In the village, if you stay at Maswik Lodge or one of the hotels right on the rim, you can walk most places, but it's too far to walk from Yavapai Lodge or the campgrounds. See also "Hiking" in "For the Active Family" (p. 188).

4 Planning Your Outings

WHEN TO GO

For families with school obligations, only a winter holiday break offers much chance of avoiding crowds. It can be a delightful time to visit the South Rim, but snow and ice can make hiking tricky. Spring break (mid-Mar to Apr) can be just as busy as midsummer. You might get snowed on even through May on the South Rim, and the North Rim is closed until mid-May. Spring-break high temperatures in the canyon are often in the 70s (low to mid-20s Celsius), the best hiking weather. An added bonus of off-season visits: more sleep, because you don't have to get up as early to see the sunrise in the canyon and avoid canyon heat.

Summer down in the canyon is very hot, with temperatures frequently topping 100°F (38°C), and high temperatures along the rim usually in the 80s (upper 20s to low 30s Celsius). Those conditions aren't suitable for hiking the steep canyon trails, and backpacking is miserable. Of the summer months, June is best and July hottest. The Park Service asks hikers to avoid midday hiking in the summer because so many people get into trouble. Because the rim is typically 15° to 20° cooler than the inner gorge, summer can be pleasant at the top, but the crowds are heavy.

HOW MUCH TIME TO SPEND

On a 1-day visit to the park, you can enjoy the spectacular views and take a walk. In view of the distance you have to drive, you'll want to spend a night somewhere relatively near, such as Flagstaff, 77 miles to the south; Williams, 56 miles to the south; or just outside the park's south entrance in Tusayan.

For a family that isn't up to strenuous hiking, 2 or 3 nights should be enough time for a complete visit to the South or North Rim, including seeing the canyon at different times of the day, which is important. More time could be boring for the kids. If you're up to a backpacking trip, a few days of rugged day hiking, or a rafting trip, you'll need more time.

HOW FAR TO PLAN AHEAD

If you can plan your trip to the Grand Canyon a year or two ahead, you have a better chance at some of the special activities, like taking a mule ride or staying at Phantom

Ranch, in the canyon bottom. River-rafting outings also book a year or more ahead (see "Rafting," p. 189). For hotel rooms, you need 6 months for a decent selection in the summer, less for the off season. Reservations for blocks of rooms may be canceled close to the date, so keep calling. Campgrounds book up for the high season soon after they become available on the national reservation system (see "The National Recreation Reservation Service," in chapter 2). Off season, you might find mud or snow, but you'll also have more choices.

Weather Chart: Canyon Temperatures & Daylight

	South Rim Elev. 7,000 Avg. High/Low (°F/°C)	North Rim Elev. 8,400 Avg. High/Low (°F/°C)	Canyon Floor Elev. 2,600 Avg. High/Low (°F/°C)	Sunrise/Sunset Time (1st day of period)
December–January	43 (6)/19 (–7)	39 (4)/18 (–8)	56 (13)/37 (3)	7:21/5:14
February	46 (8)/22 (–5)	40 (4)/18 (–8)	64 (18)/42 (6)	7:29/5:26
March	50 (10)/24 (–4)	44 (7)/22 (–5)	72 (22)/48 (9)	6:58/6:24
April	59 (15)/29 (–2)	52 (11)/28 (–2)	82 (28)/55 (13)	6:14/6:51
May	70 (21)/37 (3)	62 (17)/33 (1)	92 (33)/63 (17)	5:36/7:16
June	80 (27)/46 (8)	73 (23)/40 (4)	103 (39)/73 (23)	5:13/7:40
July	85 (29)/53 (12)	77 (25)/47 (8)	106 (41)/77 (25)	5:15/7:49
August	82 (28)/52 (11)	74 (23)/46 (8)	103 (39)/75 (24)	5:36/7:33
September	75 (24)/45 (7)	69 (21)/39 (4)	96 (35)/69 (21)	6:00/6:56
October	64 (18)/36 (2)	58 (14)/31 (–1)	83 (28)/58 (14)	6:24/6:12
November	51 (11)/27 (–3)	46 (8)/25 (–4)	68 (20)/46 (8)	6:51/5:32

WHAT TO PACK
CLOTHING

Pack for two climates, the desert of the lowlands and the cooler high country. You'll need light-colored, lightweight, breathable clothing and sun hats for hiking trips into the canyon or in the desert outside the park. In the spring and fall, you'll also need sweaters and jackets for cool nights on the rim. Bring clothes you can layer to adjust to changes in elevation and temperature. In the summer, the canyon is too hot for much hiking, and while nighttime lows on the rim are in the 40s and 50s (single digits to midteens Celsius), you'll mostly need hot-weather clothes.

A shirt with a collar and long pants will do nicely at all the park restaurants. For hiking in the canyon, you need sturdy footwear, such as hiking boots, not sneakers. In the winter and spring you'll likely encounter snow and mud at the rim and ice on the high parts of the trails. Instep crampons, which are ice-walking spikes that attach to your shoes, are sold at the store in the South Rim Market Plaza. They're a necessity on the canyon trails in case of ice.

GEAR

Tent camping on the rim during spring break is iffy. It could be comfortable, or you might be buried in snow. Weather changes are quick and extreme. The temperatures are good for tenting in the canyon in the spring, but that's only for backpackers. The unpredictable conditions make RVs an especially attractive choice for this region; see "Practicalities: The RV Advantage," in chapter 2, for tips on renting one. In the summer, tent camping at the rim is great, but it's very hot down below. Bring gear to stay warm if the temperature drops to freezing on spring nights, and light gear for summer.

If you need a crib, ask when you're making reservations. Not all the available cribs fit every room, so you may want to bring a portable crib from home.

For day hiking, bring hats, water bottles, a small backpack, and the footgear described above. Strollers can manage most walks at the rim, particularly the paved portions of the Rim Trail, but a baby backpack will give you more options.

See "Linking the Parks," later in this chapter, for advice on traveling to and around this part of the Southwest and linking a Grand Canyon visit with a trip to another park.

KEEPING SAFE & HEALTHY

In addition to the tips here, see "Dealing with Hazards" (chapter 2) for information on dehydration, elevation, hypothermia, sunburn, and snake and insect bites.

FALLING

People are killed every year falling into the Grand Canyon, sometimes for very stupid reasons. Visitors have fallen in while sitting on a railing, getting dizzy on a precipice, or backing up to have their picture taken. There are no guardrails along much of the Rim Trail, so one wild move could be the last. No child has ever died from a fall from the rim, but teens have died from falls within the canyon. Make sure to hold hands whenever you are near the edge or on steep portions of canyon trails with kids.

HEAT EXHAUSTION

Most people who die or have to be rescued at the Grand Canyon (250 a year, on average) overestimate their ability to climb out. Walking down into the canyon is easy and alluring; going back takes twice as long and much more energy. For a strenuous 3-hour hike, you have to turn around after an hour. In the summer, rangers see dozens of people a day, usually casual day hikers, who need treatment or rescue because they went too far down and didn't bring enough water or food. The most common victim is a young adult male; strength doesn't protect you from sun and heat. Every year some die. Preparation and knowing your limits are key to hikes here. Don't hike in the heat of a summer day. Always take and drink plenty of water and wear a broad-brimmed hat. Eat plenty of energy-rich, salty foods; the water can leach nutrients from your system, another way to get into danger. Know the symptoms of and treatment for heat exhaustion and heat stroke (see chapter 2). The park also distributes lots of good information; see www.nps.gov/grca/grandcanyon/dayhike.

KNEE PROBLEMS

A friend who backpacked into the canyon found the steep descent the hardest part because walking downhill all day is so hard on knees and hips. Know your limits if you have joint problems. A good hiking staff or stick is handy, too, to ease the downhill pounding on knees; one for each hand is better!

5 Family-Friendly Accommodations

CAMPGROUNDS

NATIONAL PARK CAMPGROUNDS

Except for the **car camping** campgrounds listed here, all other campgrounds and campsites are for **backpackers** and are below the rim, including the Bright Angel Campground, allocated through the backcountry permit system (p. 180). Trailer Village is the only campground within the park offering hookups for **RVs.**

Campgrounds Accepting Reservations

Permits for Mather and North Rim campgrounds should be reserved when sites become available on the national reservation system covered under "The National Recreation Reservation Service," in chapter 2.

Mather   This large, partly shaded campground sits among the pinyons back from the rim and commercial area in Grand Canyon Village. You can walk to the store, showers, visitor center, and rim, but you'll need to use the shuttle or a bike to get to trail heads and restaurants. There's little ground cover, so sites don't have much privacy.

Grand Canyon Village, behind the commercial area. 320 sites, tents or RVs. $18 site, $15 off season. Open year-round; reservations accepted Apr–Nov. Pets accepted. **Amenities:** Flush toilets, grills, coin-op laundry and showers nearby.

North Rim   This is the only Park Service campground on the North Rim. It's near the store and gas station, and within walking distance of most of the trails. After mid-October, some sites remain open on a first-come, first-served basis until snow closes the area.

Bright Angel Point, Rte. 67 at North Rim. 82 sites, tents or RVs. $18 site. Closed mid-Oct to mid-May. Pets accepted. **Amenities:** Grills, coin-op showers and laundry nearby.

Trailer Village   Although the long-range plan calls for improvement, there isn't much to this RV park at present—just a line of paved parking spaces with a few scattered shade trees. It's conveniently in the park, near Mather campground, and has hookups for your rig, the only ones you will find in the park. You'll need to use bikes or the shuttle to get to restaurants and trail heads. Xanterra takes reservations up to 23 months in advance; call as far ahead as possible.

East of Yavapai Lodge at Grand Canyon Village. Reserve through Xanterra, the park concessionaire: © **888/29-PARKS.** www.grandcanyonlodges.com. 84 sites, RVs only. 30- and 50-amp service. $28 for 2. $2 per extra person. DISC, MC, V. Open year-round. **Amenities:** Full hookups, cable TV, coin-op showers and laundry nearby.

First-Come, First-Served Campgrounds

Desert View   The eastern end of the park is more open and desertlike than the village, quieter and farther from the center of things. But the major trail heads at the village are 26 miles away, and other than the Watchtower and Tusayan Museum, which take less than half a day, there's not much to do in the Desert View area. The campground doesn't take reservations, but at busy times you need to get there well before noon for a chance at a site; as people leave, those in line take their sites.

Rte. 64 at east entrance to the park. 50 sites, tents or RVs. $12 site. Closed mid-Oct to mid-May. No reservations. Pets accepted. **Amenities:** Flush toilets.

FOREST SERVICE CAMPGROUNDS

The Kaibab National Forest has several campgrounds near the park. Each can accommodate **tents or RVs.** None have hookups. The Forest Service campgrounds don't take reservations. At busy times you need to get there early for a chance at a site; as

---

Tips **Park Camping Basics: Toilets, Showers & Laundry**

The National Park Service campgrounds have unheated, cold-water bathrooms. You'll find the best public bathrooms at the Canyon View Information Center and in hotel lobbies and restaurants. The Tusayan Museum has only portable toilets. Showers and laundry facilities are at the Mather campground and near the North Rim Campground.

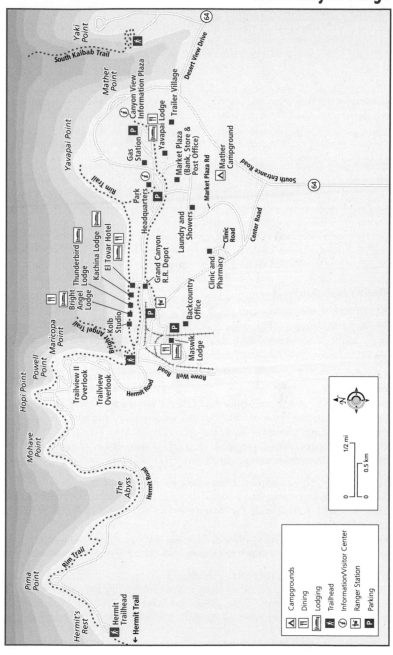

Campgrounds in the Grand Canyon Area

Campground	Rim	Total Sites	RV Hookups	Dump Station	Toilets	Drinking Water	Showers	Fire Pits/Grills
DeMotte Park	North	23	No	No	Yes	Yes	No	Yes
Desert View	South	50	No	No	Yes	No	Yes	No
Jacob Lake	North	53	No	No	Yes	Yes	No	Yes
Mather	South	320	No	Yes	Yes	Yes	Yes	Yes
North Rim	North	82	No	Yes	Yes	Yes	Nearby	Yes
Ten-X	South	53	No	No	Yes	Yes	No	Yes
Trailer Village	South	84	84	Nearby	Yes	Yes	Nearby	Yes

people leave, newcomers take their places. For more information, contact the Kaibab National Forest (www.fs.fed.us/r3/kai) on the North Rim at the **North Kaibab Ranger District** (✆ **928/643-7395**), which operates a visitor center at Jacob Lake daily from mid-May to mid-October; for the South Rim, contact **Tusayan Ranger District** (✆ **928/638-2443**).

South Rim
Ten-X Campground   This is the Forest Service campground nearest to the park's main, south entrance, which is 8 miles away. Situated at an elevation of 6,650 feet, ponderosa pines shade the sites. In the summer, rangers offer campfire programs.

2 miles south of Tusayan on Rte. 64/180. 70 sites, tents or RVs. $10 site. Closed Oct–Apr. **Amenities:** Pit toilets, grills.

North Rim
Demotte   The closest campground outside the north side of the park, this woodsy facility is at a higher elevation of 8,500 feet. Tents, trailers, and RVs are allowed, but there are no dump stations or hookups.

Rte. 67, 5 miles outside the park boundary. 38 sites. $16 site. Closed mid-Oct to mid-May. **Amenities:** Vault toilets, grills, picnic tables, running water, concessions nearby.

Jacob Lake   This campground was scheduled to be closed through 2008 to allow for road work, installation of an improved water system, and so larger RVs could be accommodated. Check with the **Forest Service** (✆ **928/643-7395**) for a 2009 reopening date.

Rte. 89A and Rte. 67, about 30 miles from the North Rim. 53 sites, tents or RVs. $12 site. Closed mid-Oct to mid-May. **Amenities:** Flush toilets, picnic tables, grills, running water, access for those w/limited mobility, concessions nearby.

BACKCOUNTRY CAMPING PERMITS
You need a backcountry permit to camp in the canyon. The only other way to sleep in the canyon is to spend the night at **Phantom Ranch** (p. 183). You don't need a permit to day hike, but the bottom of the canyon is too far for a family to do a round-trip in a day.

Planning ahead and knowing the system is important at the Grand Canyon because so many people are chasing so few permits (each year the park averages 30,000 permit requests, and 13,000 are issued). Begin planning in the fall for a spring-break hike. First, figure out where you want to go (see "Backpacking," p. 188). Get a trail guide,

Laundry	Public Phones	Reservations	Fees	Open
No	No	No	$12	Mid-June to mid-Sept
No	No	No	$12	Mid-May to mid-Oct
No	No	No	$12	Mid-May to mid-Oct
Nearby	No	Mar–Nov	$18 (Apr–Nov), $15 (Dec–Mar)	Year-round
Nearby	Yes	Yes	$18	May 15–Oct 15
No	No	No	$10	May–Sept
Nearby	Nearby	Yes	$28 plus $2 each add'l person	Year-round

a topographic map, and the Park Service publication *Backcountry Trip Planner.* It's a newsprint guide with good advice, a map of the permit areas, and a form to request a backcountry permit. Order the planner from the park (see "Grand Canyon Address Book," p. 166), or download the information and permit form from the very complete website, www.nps.gov/grca/backcountry. **Backcountry rangers** answer questions by phone (© **928/638-7875**) Monday through Friday from 1 to 5pm.

Permits cost $10 plus $5 per person, per night; you can pay by check, American Express, Diners Club, Discover, MasterCard, or Visa. The permits are issued starting the first day of the month 4 months before the trip, so permits for all of March start to disappear on November 1 of the preceding year. **Applications** are taken by mail (use the main park address), by fax (© **928/638-2125**), and in person at the **Backcountry Office,** at the Backcountry Information Center across the railroad tracks from Maswik Lodge. Applications postmarked before the first of the month are discarded. Overnight deliveries are accepted, but faxes with a credit card number make the most sense—you can get ahead of the day's mail by faxing first thing in the morning or right after midnight. In-person applicants are taken as they come in, giving them priority, but that isn't practical for most people.

If you arrive without a permit, show up at the backcountry office in Grand Canyon Village before 8am; that's when permits that aren't picked up are given away to people on a standby list. You can usually get a permit through a cancellation within 2 or 3 days, but you have to be at the office at 8am each morning or your name is dropped from the list.

HOTELS, MOTELS & LODGES

Besides the hotels within the park, a strip of motels lies along the road just outside the entrance in Tusayan. Options include the **Grand Hotel** (© **888/634-7263** or 928/638-3333; www.grandcanyonhotel.com), a **Holiday Inn Hotel and Suites Grand Canyon** (© **888/473-2269** or 928/638-3000; www.gcanyon.com), a **Quality Inn and Suites Canyon Plaza** (© **800/228-5151** or 928/638-2673; www.grandcanyon qualityinn.com), a **Best Western** (© **800/622-6966** or 928/638-2681; www.grand canyonsquire.com), and a **Red Feather Lodge** (© **800/538-2345** or 928/638-2414).

The hotels described below are in the park, operated by **Xanterra** (see "Grand Canyon Address Book," p. 166). By staying near the rim, you can gaze into the canyon just after sunrise and just before sunset, when it is at its most beautiful. The most desirable rooms, such as the rim cabins at Bright Angel, go a year in advance. Some dates in the high season book up 6 months ahead all over the park. If you're flexible with dates and choices or travel in the fall or winter, you can find rooms 1 or 2 months in advance. Because Xanterra allows cancellations without penalty up to 48 hours in advance, you can sometimes grab a room at the last minute, even at the busiest times, by calling the Xanterra switchboard (© **928/638-2631**). This is also the number to call to contact lodging guests. All rooms have TVs and telephones, except at Phantom Ranch and some Bright Angel Lodge rooms. Only El Tovar and Yavapai East (at Yavapai Lodge) have air-conditioning; most of the others have swamp coolers (a unit that blows hot air across cool water to lower the air temperature). In-park lodging has free rollaways and cribs (first-come, first-served), but not every one fits into every room configuration. If it's important to you, ask when you're making your reservation. Children under 16 stay free with their parents, and Xanterra takes all major credit cards.

SOUTH RIM

Bright Angel Lodge   This is one of my favorite national park hotels, not because of the luxury or style, but for the incomparable location on the canyon rim and the quirky and unmistakable character of the buildings and rooms. The hotel is of stone and logs, strange angles and disconnected lines, spartan backpacker rooms, and charming little cabins with views that would make a vacation by themselves. Among these 12 units, the Bucky O'Neill Cabin is the oldest structure in the park. The lobby, with a huge stone fireplace, can be quite busy—it serves as the center of activity in the area, with a desk that books mule rides. The accommodations range from crude to delightful; some have no amenities at all, while others have telephones and televisions.

© **928/638-2631.** www.grandcanyonlodges.com. 39 units, some with shared bathroom, 50 cabins. $58–$239 double. $9 extra adult. Rollaway beds and cribs free. AE, DISC, MC, V. **Amenities:** Restaurant; ice-cream fountain; lounge; gift shop. *In room:* TV in cabins.

El Tovar   This big log structure on the rim dates from before the canyon was set aside as a park. Although not likely to be confused with a luxury hotel or resort elsewhere, it has a rustic elegance fitting to the park, and the location along the canyon rim couldn't be better. The suites and deluxe rooms are spacious, although the standard rooms can be small for families, and you may worry about making too much noise. Some rooms accommodate rollaway beds.

© **928/638-2631.** www.grandcanyonlodges.com. 78 units. $142–$205 double; $258–$322 suite. $14 extra adult. Rollaway beds and cribs free. AE, DISC, MC, V. **Amenities:** Restaurant; lounge; shops; newsstand. *In room:* A/C, TV.

Kachina and Thunderbird Lodges   These ugly concrete buildings look and feel like something from a 1970s community college campus, yet they occupy some of the world's best real estate, on the canyon rim. The rooms are inviting, and those on the canyon side, which cost $10 more, have extraordinary views. Rooms in either lodge are nearly identical.

© **928/638-2631.** www.grandcanyonlodges.com. 104 units. $139–$152 double. $9 extra adult. Rollaway beds and cribs free. AE, DISC, MC, V. *In room:* TV, fridge, coffeemaker, safe.

Maswik Lodge   These two-story wooden buildings—Maswik North and Maswik South—are set back from the rim in the village area but are still convenient to most of what you'll want to see. The rooms in the newer and more attractive northern section are large, with high ceilings, tables, and two queen-size beds. They cost $61 more than the south rooms, which are comfortable but unmemorable. The cabins are rustic.

☎ 928/638-2631. www.grandcanyonlodges.com. 250 units, 28 cabins. $78–$139 double; $80 double in 4-plex unit. $9 extra adult. Rollaway beds and cribs free. AE, DISC, MC, V. **Amenities:** Cafeteria; lounge w/TV; activities desk; shops. *In room:* TV.

Yavapai Lodge   Near the Market Plaza with its market, post office, and bank and a mile away from the historic part of the village, these buildings offer basic motel rooms a step below the best at Maswik, but still quite serviceable. Yavapai East is at the higher end of the range and has standard rooms with air-conditioning in two-story wooden buildings. Rooms in Yavapai West, in one-story brick buildings where you can drive right up to your door, cost $18 less. They're out-of-date, and certainly unattractive from the outside, but inside they're more than adequate and might be just the kind of low-key place you want.

☎ 928/638-2631. www.grandcanyonlodges.com. 358 units. $98–$127 double. $9 extra adult. Rollaway beds and cribs free. AE, DISC, MC, V. Closed Nov–Mar. **Amenities:** Cafeteria; shops; Market Plaza nearby. *In room:* TV, Yavapai East rooms have A/C, Yavapai West rooms have ceiling fans.

NORTH RIM
Grand Canyon Lodge   The only hotel on the North Rim stands out on a point above the canyon, with basic motel units and cabins that range from rustic to almost luxurious. The only accommodations for this area of the park, it's a center of activity, with a gift shop, bookstore, restaurant, and snack bar. The attractive stone building is in the rustic national-park style.

North Rim. ☎ 928/638-2611. www.grandcanyonnorthrim.com. 40 units, 168 cabins. $100–$145 double. $10 extra adult. Cribs/rollaways allowed in some rooms. AE, DISC, MC, V. Closed mid-Oct to mid-May. **Amenities:** Restaurant; coffee shop; deli; lounge; gift shop; camper store; laundry.

IN THE CANYON
Phantom Ranch is a famous and charming lodge at the bottom of the canyon. The only ways to get there are on foot, by mule, or on a raft. If you manage to book an overnight mule ride (p. 174), a night in a cabin is included in the reservation and price. Hikers sleep in single-sex dorms and can reserve meals in the dining hall, but those slots book more than a year in advance through **Xanterra** (see "Grand Canyon Address Book," p. 166). Reservations open 23 months ahead, and that's when you need to act to be sure of a space; however, you can sometimes snag a cancellation on the day of the stay by calling ☎ **928/638-2631.** A dorm bed is $34 (including tax) per person per night; a four-person cabin costs $93, a 10-person $195.

6 Family-Friendly Dining

You don't go to the Grand Canyon for food, but you will find a couple of good fine-dining rooms, plus good family restaurants and relaxed cafeterias where you can eat inexpensively. The concessionaire, Xanterra, manages the restaurants inside the park; the cost for a kid's meal runs about $3 to $6, if he or she orders from a kids' menu. Outside the park in Tusayan, you can find familiar fast food such as Wendy's, McDonald's, and at the National Geographic Visitor Center a small version of Pizza Hut.

LOW-STRESS MEALS
Large cafeterias at **Maswik** and **Yavapai lodges** serve thousands of meals a day in the quick, low-key style that families often want. Maswik is in the village, back from the

rim; Yavapai is just east of Market Plaza. Both dining rooms are light and airy. The food is perfectly adequate, with burgers, pizza, pasta, Mexican entrees, and other familiar foods. There's also a fresh salad bar deep with veggies and fruits, and both cafeterias sell packaged carrots and fruits. Yavapai is especially popular among park employees for its definitely un-heart-healthy fried chicken. Both cafeterias are open daily from 6am to 10pm.

Located on the canyon rim at Bright Angel Lodge, the **Bright Angel Fountain** sells hot dogs, prepackaged sandwiches, soft drinks, ice cream, and the like for takeout only. Hours vary with the season, and payment must be in cash.

PICNICS & TAKEOUT

The deli in **Canyon Village Marketplace,** a concessionaire-operated grocery store near the south entrance in the village, makes sandwiches for picnics. A **snack bar** with a very limited menu operates from a window at Hermits Rest at the end of Hermit Drive. Also, see the **Bright Angel Fountain,** above.

BEST-BEHAVIOR MEALS

These concessionaire-operated restaurants accept all major credit cards.

Arizona Room This beef place, which also offers several chicken and seafood dishes, sidles right up to the South Rim. Though it's largely aimed at adults, older children who can behave themselves might enjoy it for the view. I had a great meal, and a great view out over the South Rim. Reservations aren't taken. Instead they take your name when you arrive and call you when a table opens. Arrive early for a window seat.

Facing the rim at the Bright Angel Lodge, Grand Canyon Village. ☎ **928/638-2631**. Kids' menu, highchairs, boosters, activity books, crayons. Reservations not accepted. Lunch $8–$12; dinner $15–$27. Lunch 11:30am–3pm; dinner 4:30–10pm. Closed Nov–Feb for lunch, Jan–Feb for dinner.

Bright Angel Restaurant This bright, bustling family restaurant with a Southwest theme knows how to treat kids, giving parents a chance to have real food brought by a real waiter without having to worry about the children getting bored (there are games on their menus) or not being able to eat what they want. The food is predictable.

At the Bright Angel Lodge, Grand Canyon Village. ☎ **928/638-2631**. Kids' menu, highchairs, boosters, activity books, crayons. Reservations not accepted. Breakfast $4–$11; lunch $5–$10; dinner $11–$25. Daily 6am–10pm.

El Tovar Dining Room This restaurant in the historic El Tovar hotel tries for formality to match the setting. The service is accommodating; but a meal with kids can take a long time. I wouldn't choose it for a family dinner for anything less than a special occasion. It's worth arriving early for a window seat for lunch, with views of the passing crowds and the canyon.

In the El Tovar hotel, Grand Canyon Village. ☎ **928/638-2631**, ext. 6432. Kids' menu, highchairs, boosters, activity books, crayons. Advance dinner reservations recommended by phone or e-mail (eltovar-dinner-res-gcsr@xanterra.com). Breakfast $5.50–$13; lunch $11–$16; dinner $19–$32. Daily 6:30–11am, 11:30am–2pm, and 5–10pm.

7 Exploring Grand Canyon National Park with Your Kids

NATURAL PLACES

THE SOUTH RIM

The South Rim of the Grand Canyon is a great spot to see a vast and amazing natural place, but the rim itself is crowded and developed. You can find overlooks and

Reading Rock Layers

When you see the layers in the sides of the Grand Canyon, you're looking at a step-by-step record of the earth's history going back about halfway to the original formation of the planet. Nowhere else on earth can you see such a thing. The bottom layers were laid down first, the next-highest layer next, and the top layer last. At the base of Zion Canyon, the bottom layer is the same kind of rock as the top layer at the Grand Canyon, so the story continues up through the top of Zion. At Bryce Canyon, Zion's top layer of rock shows up at the bottom; Bryce's layers finish the story (p. 186).

Geologists use the layers to figure out the order in which things happened—what the area was like first, next, and so on. For example, looking into the Grand Canyon, you can see a steep red wall called the Redwall Limestone, which makes one of the most noticeable stripes along the canyon wall (actually, the red is a stain from the rocks directly above). Limestone is made of calcium and carbon, or calcium carbonate, the same stuff bones and shells are made of, and this Redwall Limestone layer has many fossils of coral and other sea animals with shells. When this layer was being made, the area must have been underwater. The calcium carbonate must have fallen to the bottom of the ocean from seashells, dead animals, and other sea sediment. Judging from what we know about the oceans today and what kinds of fossils are in the rocks, it must have been a warm, shallow sea, like the ones in the Tropics today.

The next layer higher on the canyon, which looks like a flatter ledge of red rocks, is completely different. It is sandstone and siltstone—rock made of sand and silt or clay that was pressed together and heated inside the earth. The fossils here are of moss, ferns, and the footprints of amphibians—animals like frogs, toads, and salamanders that live on land and in the water. This area must have been swampy and damp, but not underwater. With these clues, a story starts to develop: The area was under the ocean, then it rose enough so that it became land, but it still was low, warm, and moist.

pathways without many people, but they are the exception. That doesn't mean you can't have fun; you just have to ignore or enjoy the other people and plan ways to avoid the thickest crowds. Use the less-known trails, such as the **Hermit Trail** (p. 189), and get out at sunrise, one of the prettiest and least crowded times of day. Sunset is also very beautiful, but then the overlooks are most crowded. Other fun things to do: Take picnics to different places along the rim, and walk the Rim Trail at different times to see how the sun changes the canyon as the day passes; enjoy meeting other families at the campground or hotel; try to figure out the many foreign languages being spoken.

BELOW THE RIM

Everyone who visits the Grand Canyon should go at least a little way over the edge. The cliffs look completely different from down there, because you're walking across

Bryce Canyon And
Cedar Breaks Area

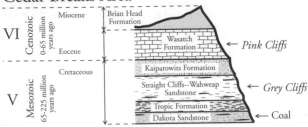

VI | Cenozoic 0-65 million years ago | Miocene | Brian Head Formation
| | | Eocene | Wasatch Formation ← *Pink Cliffs*

V | Mesozoic 65-225 million years ago | Cretaceous | Kaiparowits Formation
| | | | Straight Cliffs--Wahweap Sandstone ← *Grey Cliffs*
| | | | Tropic Formation
| | | | Dakota Sandstone ← Coal

Zion Canyon Area

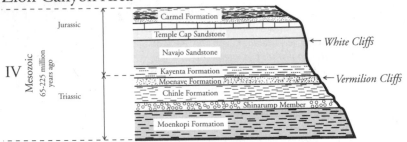

IV | Mesozoic 65-225 million years ago | Jurassic | Carmel Formation
| | | | Temple Cap Sandstone
| | | | Navajo Sandstone ← *White Cliffs*
| | | Triassic | Kayenta Formation
| | | | Moenave Formation ← *Vermilion Cliffs*
| | | | Chinle Formation
| | | | Shinarump Member
| | | | Moenkopi Formation

Grand Canyon

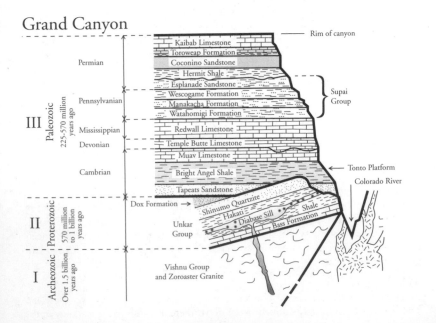

III | Paleozoic 225-570 million years ago | Permian | Kaibab Limestone — Rim of canyon
| | | | Toroweap Formation
| | | | Coconino Sandstone
| | | | Hermit Shale
| | | Pennsylvanian | Esplanade Sandstone
| | | | Wescogame Formation — Supai Group
| | | | Manakacha Formation
| | | | Watahomigi Formation
| | | Mississippian | Redwall Limestone
| | | Devonian | Temple Butte Limestone
| | | Cambrian | Muav Limestone
| | | | Bright Angel Shale — Tonto Platform / Colorado River
| | | | Tapeats Sandstone

II | Proterozoic 570 million to 1 billion years ago | Dox Formation → Shinumo Quartzite
| | | Unkar Group | Hakati Diabase Sill Shale Bass Formation

I | Archeozoic Over 1.5 billion years ago | Vishnu Group and Zoroaster Granite them on the trails. You get a better perspective when you see the individual rocks and folds of the canyon, and a better grasp of its sheer size. Also, as soon as you're on the exposed rock of the canyon side, you can feel the climate change. The air gets warmer, and yuccas and twigs of desert plants start to disappear until you're in a sterile landscape of broken, sun-heated rocks. It's hard to believe how quickly the change happens. See "Hiking" (p. 188) for ideas on where and when to go.

THE NORTH RIM

One-tenth as many visitors go to the North Rim as to the South. The area is quieter and more relaxed, and facilities intentionally have been kept rustic. Getting there takes time, so people who just want to drive through stay away. Only one trail from the developed area descends into the canyon, but more explore the pine woods at the rim and lead out onto points that extend a bit into the canyon and offer fantastic views. That allows families who can't tackle a steep canyon trek to have a good hike—something that's lacking on the South Rim. If you want to get away from the crowds, **Cape Royal Road** and **Point Imperial Road** connect with various overlooks and trails with fantastic views.

The North Rim is usually open only from mid-May to mid-October for overnight visitors. People can keep coming in just for the day until the snow flies, as late as December, but you have to be ready to leave quickly in case of a storm. The higher elevation—over 8,000 feet—makes the air thinner and cooler at the North Rim, and the forest of ponderosa pine is thicker and has more shade and more wildlife.

PLACES FOR LEARNING

Kolb Studio   The Kolb brothers were early photographers of the canyon, and this house over the Bright Angel Trail was their studio and shop. A good bookstore is on the upper level, and there are frequent art exhibits down below.

Grand Canyon Village at the Bright Angel Trailhead. ℂ **928/638-2481**. Free admission. Daily 8am–5pm (until 7pm in peak season).

Tusayan Museum *(Finds*   The small museum and nearby Ancestral Puebloan (Anasazi) ruin make up the park's best cultural display. The museum occupies a single room in a small stone building, with artifacts from the site displayed to show how the native people of the region lived and used their environment. The 14-room ruin amounts to low lines of stones where a pueblo stood for about 30 years 800 years ago. Signs do a good job of helping you imagine what it was like. The bathrooms are limited to portable toilets, but Desert View has full facilities. There are regular ranger-led tours of the ruin.

Rte. 64, 3 miles west of Desert View. ℂ **928/638-2305**. Free admission. Daily 9am–5pm.

Yavapai Observation Station   This historic station, rededicated in 2007 after a thorough renovation, today serves as an excellent geologic museum and a great outpost to gaze across the canyon and compare its layers to a geological cross section displayed on wall panels. Along with installing a new roof and heating and cooling system, crews installed artworks and interpretive panels that explain the surrounding geology. There's even a three-dimensional carving of the canyon. Located just 1 mile east of Market Plaza, the station also has a well-stocked bookstore.

Yavapai Point, on the rim between Canyon View and Mather areas, east of the village. Daily 8am–5pm.

8 For the Active Family

BACKPACKING

To get into the canyon overnight and really see it, you'll probably need to hike in carrying your gear. For first-timers, it's a good idea to stick to the corridor of the Bright Angel and South Kaibab trails, which have campgrounds and water and can be connected into a 2- or 3-night loop. (Trails are described below, under "Hiking.") For example, hike down the South Kaibab, camp at the Bright Angel Campground at the bottom of the canyon, take the Bright Angel Trail to Indian Garden Campground, halfway up, and then complete the final leg back to the top. It's a good spring-break trip for a family with children in elementary school. See "Backcountry Camping Permits" (p. 180) for information about reserving your trip and getting necessary advice.

Wherever you choose to go, remember that this steep desert hiking is different from what you might be used to. Especially in the summer, plan short days you can cover in the early morning and evening to avoid the midday heat. You also can lighten your load by having a **pack train** haul some of your stuff back up the canyon. The service costs $61 one-way for 30 pounds; contact **Xanterra** (see "Grand Canyon Address Book," p. 166). Information about getting a bed at **Phantom Ranch,** at the bottom of the canyon, is on p. 183.

HIKING

The best way to see the Grand Canyon is to walk in and around it. Unfortunately, the main trails are strenuous and can be very, very crowded. The Park Service understandably tries to scare off unprepared hikers with extreme warnings. But if you're cautious and follow some simple advice, there's no need to let the warnings stop you from enjoying the park.

During the hot months, hikers get into trouble with heat and exhaustion in the middle of the day. Experienced desert hikers stay put during the hot hours. If you start down at 6am and hike 90 minutes into the canyon, you can be back by 10:30am.

Here are some of the main park trails:

Rim Trail: In the Grand Canyon Village area, the trail along the top of the canyon is paved and suitable for strollers. To the west of the village, it's rougher but still basically level, extending all the way to Hermits Rest, 8 miles away. There, or at points along the way, you can catch a shuttle back.

Bright Angel Trail: This is the main foot highway into the canyon from the heart of the south rim's Grand Canyon Village. It's an incredible trail, with switchbacks and holes blasted in the rocks, but also incredibly crowded, and can be smelly from the manure from the mule trains that use it. There are good places 1.5, 3, 4.6, and 6.1 miles down to get water (during the warm months) and turn around. **Bright Angel**

⌐*Tips* **Proceed with Caution**

Remember, you have to allow twice as long to come up as to go down. Hikers going any distance over the rim should bring along ½ to 1 gallon of water per person per day, salty snacks, a sun hat, sunglasses, and sunblock. If you want a long hike, especially on a less-used trail, buy a topographic trail map and trail guide (see "Reading Up," p. 171). Bring a flashlight, a mirror for signaling, a jacket, and a first-aid kit.

Campground, across the Colorado, is 9.5 miles and more than 4,500 vertical feet from rim to river, too far for a round-trip day hike.

South Kaibab Trail: The two Kaibab trails (North and South) link the two sides of the Canyon. The South Kaibab Trail descends from Yaki Point, a few miles east of the village. The trail itself is beautiful, an engineering masterpiece blasted out of the rock. A good goal for day hikers is Cedar Ridge, 1.5 miles and less than 1,140 feet down; it's enough to give you a sense of the canyon but makes a manageable day for younger or less fit hikers. I've seen dozens of kids make this stretch of the hike. The next major stop is Bright Angel Campground, at the bottom, 6.4 miles away—again, the round-trip is too much for a day hike. No water is available on the trail.

North Kaibab Trail: Go 14 miles down this trail, and you'll come to the Bright Angel Campground, where you can hook up with the trail up to the South Rim. For a day hike, start from the North Rim, and hike at least part of the way down. Roaring Springs is 4.7 miles and 3,400 vertical feet down from the rim, a tough but rewarding day hike.

Hermit Trail: For a hike that's not too tough but still gets you below the rim to great views, this is the route to choose. The trail leads into the canyon from Hermits Rest, at the west end of Hermit Road. Board the shuttle from the village before dawn to be at the trail head at sunrise. Because it is out-of-the-way, the trail is less crowded than the others; it's also not as steep in the early going, although it is rugged and unmaintained. You descend through a basin. The views are good, but not the sweeping vistas of the Bright Angel and South Kaibab trails. Santa Maria and Dripping Springs are possible goals, 2.5 and 3 miles down; bring your own water or treat what you find.

Other Trails: There are eight other trails in the North Rim area; the park newspaper that covers that part of the park lists them. Several, such as the **Ken Patrick Trail** and **Widforss Trail,** offer good, long day hikes in the woods and canyon rim without huge elevation changes.

MOUNTAIN BIKING

Biking isn't allowed on the hiking trails. Dirt roads in the North Rim area and adjacent Kaibab National Forest offer some long rides with lots of solitude and the advantage of high altitude, which means cooler temperatures. A strenuous 42-mile round-trip ride with sweeping canyon views leads from Highway 67 near the park's north boundary, ending at Sublime Point. At this writing, there was no bike shop or rental agency near the park, so you must bring your own bike.

RAFTING

If your children are 12 or older and you want a long white-water expedition with extraordinary scenery, the Grand Canyon may be a good choice. But you must be patient. River-rafting trips with commercial operators book a year or more in advance, and going on your own is impractical unless you are very committed and an experienced river-runner. A new weighted lottery system for noncommercial trips requires you to first create a "profile" within the park's permitting system, and then you file a permit application, which costs $25, a nonrefundable fee. Under the program, the lottery is conducted a year ahead of your actual trip. So if you wanted a permit for 2010, you'd apply during the 2009 lottery, which typically gets underway in February of that year. For details of this system and floating the Colorado River through the canyon in general, visit www.nps.gov/grca/planyourvisit/whitewater-rafting.htm.

Commercially guided trips last around 1 to 3 weeks. More than a dozen companies have permits to offer the trips; the park can give you a list and has links to them online (see www.nps.gov/grca/planyourvisit/river-concessioners.htm). Some go by motorized raft, which speeds the time between rapids, others on quieter oared or paddled rafts, dories, or kayaks. Generally, the company provides everything. Most floats begin at Lees Ferry. A weeklong float costs around $2,300 for adults, about $1,845 for kids 16 and younger. I've had great experience with O.A.R.S. (© **800/346-6277;** www. oars.com), which was one of the first companies to use oar-powered rafts on the Colorado, and they offer family-specific trips through the canyon.

9 Kid-Friendly Programs

CHILDREN'S PROGRAMS

The Park Service has a series of ranger programs aimed at children. Pick up a schedule at the visitor center.

The **Junior Ranger program** is aimed at kids ages 4 through 14, with an activity booklet, divided into three age levels, that you obtain at a visitor center. To earn Junior Ranger awards, kids complete worksheet activities in the booklet and attend a ranger program. They receive a badge and a certificate that entitles them to buy a patch at a park bookstore. The material for the younger children is good, but the program offers much more exciting educational opportunities for children ages 9 to 14 who can join special ranger-led programs and earn additional patch awards. The Dynamic Earth program includes a guided geology walk near Hermits Rest, while the Discovery Pack program starts with a 90-minute ranger program, and then kids set off independently (with parents, of course) with a set of real naturalist's tools and a field notebook. These two programs are offered only in summer. A year-round program is the Phantom Rattler Junior Ranger program offered at Phantom Ranch. It's available only to children 4 to 14 who make it to the bottom of the canyon. Information on all the programs is at www.nps.gov/grca/pphtml/forkids.html. *Tip:* Given the time and effort involved, it's a good idea to plan your involvement into the schedule for your trip.

FAMILY & ADULT PROGRAMS

Rangers offer walks and talks every day during the summer and some other busy times at the North Rim, Grand Canyon Village, and Desert View/Tusayan Museum. Schedules appear in the park newspapers and online. Some walks range as far afield as Cedar

---

Tips **Places for Relaxed Play & Picnics**

Formal picnic grounds are marked on the park map you'll receive when you arrive, along Desert View Drive, and all over the North Rim area. Places where kids can just blow off steam aren't so common. If you're camping, they can play at your site, and some hotels—Yavapai and Maswick lodges, for instance—have small grassy areas or slices of ponderosa pine forest comfortably away from the canyon rim where they can expend any energy they didn't use up touring the park.

Evening programs take place in the North Rim Campground and Lodge. On the South Rim, evening programs are in the Shrine of the Ages Auditorium in the colder months, and in the Mather Amphitheater after it gets warmer in May.

Linking the Parks

The Southwest has many wonderful national parks, recreation areas, and monuments fairly close together. Most people visit more than one. I have covered a number of parks in the chapters and nearby state parks and national monuments below in this chapter, but I haven't included other parks a bit farther away, such as **Capitol Reef, Canyonlands,** and **Arches.** It's possible to visit them all in one trip, and many people do, driving through quickly for the star attractions. We believe in slower visits to fewer parks.

Bryce Canyon National Park is the farthest north, on scenic Route 12, the path east to Capitol Reef, Canyonlands, and Arches national parks. (For details on these three parks, which this book does not cover, see *Frommer's Utah*, Wiley Publishing, Inc.) Zion, Bryce Canyon, and the **North Rim of the Grand Canyon** roughly form a triangle. The **South Rim** is off to the south and west. The highways connecting these parks are two-lane roads. They're straight and you can make good time, but expect no services along the way.

U.S. 89

Route 89 is the main highway linking these parks. Interstates 17 and 40 meet U.S. 89 in **Flagstaff,** which is a hub for the Grand Canyon. Route 180 is the most direct route from there to the South Rim. U.S. 89 is the main road north, passing **Wupatki** and **Sunset Crater** national monuments, then crossing the **Painted Desert** to the town of Page at Glen Canyon National Recreation Area.

From Page, 89 turns west to the funny little tourist town of **Kanab,** then north to access routes to Zion and Bryce Canyon national parks (from the U.S. 89 side, the entrance to Zion involves a low-clearance tunnel on the Zion–Mount Carmel Hwy.; see p. 211). U.S. 89 finally meets I-70 near I-15 on the way to Salt Lake City. Other than the Painted Desert portion, the scenery along 89 isn't memorable.

U.S. 89A

This older, alternate route branches off from U.S. 89 south of Page and goes west, past **Lees Ferry** and the **Vermilion Cliffs.** It climbs to the **North Rim** of the Grand Canyon, at over 8,000 feet, then descends to Kanab and rejoins 89. Lees Ferry and the standing rocks are worth a visit, and the forests of the North Rim are special and not as mobbed as the South Rim. If you're going both ways, take the spectacular drive on 89A at least one-way.

Ridge on the South Kaibab Trail—a good day hike. Programs on fossil finding, archaeology, and geology will interest older kids. Walks aimed specifically at children are mentioned above.

Grand Canyon Field Institute   This nonprofit organization, affiliated with the Park Service, offers a catalog of multiple-day workshops, backpacking, and float trips, all with educational themes about the canyon or learning backcountry skills. Difficulty ranges from stationary workshops to trekking beyond the trails for more than a week. Most classes are for adults only, but the institute also has a series of family

Stops along the Way

TOWNS

Flagstaff

This attractive college and skiing town also serves as a hub for the Grand Canyon, the nearby national monuments, and northern Arizona. It's at the junction of I-17, I-40, and U.S. 89, about 2 hours north of Phoenix. The drive to the Grand Canyon, about 77 miles away, takes a bit over an hour.

You could spend a couple of days here, or more if you want to ski. Among the attractions are the **Arboretum** at Flagstaff, 4001 S. Woody Mountain Rd. (© 928/774-1442; www.thearb.org); the **Museum of Northern Arizona,** 3 miles along Route 180 on the way to the Grand Canyon (© 928/774-5213; www.musnaz.org); **the Lowell Observatory,** 1400 W. Mars Hill Rd. (© 928/774-3358; www.lowell.edu); and, 35 miles east on I-40, the **Meteor Crater** (© 800/289-5898; www.meteorcrater.com), a private attraction with a museum and theater around a well-preserved impact site that *Scientific American* called the world's best for visiting. The **Flagstaff Visitors Center** (© 800/842-7293 or 928/774-9541), operated by the city, is in the train station at 1 E. Rte. 66. Information from the Flagstaff Convention and Visitors Bureau is at www.flagstaffarizona.org.

Kanab

On the way to Zion or Bryce Canyon, just north of the Arizona border on U.S. 89, this funny little cattle and tourist town has a few Western-style attractions of interest to younger children. It's a good stop for groceries or fast food. A visitor center offering regional information is at 78 S. 100 E., Kanab, UT 84741 (© 800/733-5263 or 435/644-5033; www.kaneutah.com).

PARKS & MONUMENTS

Walnut Canyon National Monument

You can explore Sinagua cliff dwellings built in cave ledges. Pace yourself, because the air is thin, and coming back out of the canyon requires climbing more than 200 steps. The visitor center includes a museum and ranger talks. Guided hikes to off-trail cliff dwellings and other usually off-limits sites are offered from June through August by reservation only.

About 7 miles east of Flagstaff on I-40; take exit 204 and drive 3 miles south to Walnut Canyon Rd. Tight turnaround for large trailers. © 928/526-3367. www.nps.gov/waca. Admission $5, free for children under 17. Visitor center hours: May to October daily 8am to 5pm; November to April daily 9am to 5pm.

Wupatki and Sunset Crater Volcano National Monuments

These two monuments lie on a 36-mile road that loops from U.S. 89 through **Coconino National Forest** and next to **the Navajo Indian Reservation. Sunset**

Crater Volcano National Monument is to the south, closer to Flagstaff. A 1-mile nature trail crosses a lava flow from the volcano that blew in 1064; another ascends a cinder cone. Interesting exhibits at the visitor center explain the site. Depending on your interest, you could spend 30 minutes to 2 hours here.

Wupatki National Monument is extremely interesting. The main ruins of a Sinagua pueblo are behind a first-rate visitor center, about 20 miles north of Sunset Crater. As you walk among the rooms and ball court, you really can imagine what it was like to live here 800 years ago. A natural rock formation called the blowhole—which appears simply as a hole in the ground—sucks or blows air harder than a vacuum cleaner into and out of hidden caves in the underlying Kaibab Limestone. The monument has a Junior Ranger program with a good workbook, if you want to spend the time. There are pleasant picnic grounds at Doney Mountain, northwest of the visitor center, where a trail leads to a high overlook for views of the area and the Painted Desert.

On Route 89, 12 miles north of Flagstaff. Wupatki: (℅ **928/679-2365.** www.nps.gov/wupa. Sunset Crater: (℅ **928/526-0502.** www.nps.gov/sucr. Admission to both $5, free for children under 17. Wupatki visitor center open daily 9am to 5pm year-round; Sunset Crater visitor center daily 8am to 5pm May to October, 9am to 5pm November to April.

Coral Pink Sand Dunes State Park

These sand dunes are popular among off-road vehicle enthusiasts, but there are also hiking trails, and kids will enjoy playing in the sand. Stop for a picnic on the way. Off Route 89 north of Kanab, Utah. (℅ **800/322-3770** (camping reservations) or 435/648-2800; www.utah.com/stateparks/coarl_pink.htm. $5 day-use fee; $15 camping fee, $7 reservation fee.

Pipe Spring National Monument

This monument represents American Indian cowboy and Mormon history that revolved around a rare and valuable water source in this arid region. A ranch of red sandstone was built here as a fort to defend against Navajo raiders and to raise cattle. Park Service guides lead tours of the ranch house every half-hour, or you can use a self-guided map to tour the grounds. There are often living-history demonstrations, such as pioneer cooking and blacksmithing, during the summer. 14 miles west of Fredonia on Route 389, Fredonia, Arizona; 21 miles from Kanab, Utah. (℅ **928/643-7105,** ext. 18. www.nps.gov/pisp. Admission $5 (includes $1.50 tribal fee), free for children under 16. Daily June to August 7am to 5pm (guided tours 8:30am–4:30pm); September to June 8am to 5pm (guided tours 9am–4pm).

classes, for adults and children over 7, including short day hikes along the rim, multiday camping and river trips, and photography workshops. Rates for the family classes range from $95 to $415 per person. Reserve well ahead.

P.O. Box 399, Grand Canyon, AZ 86023. ℂ 928/638-2485. www.grandcanyon.org/fieldinstitute.

10 Entertainment outside the Park

Other than the tourist strip of Tusayan and other rather desolate highway-side attractions, there's not much near the Grand Canyon. The one major temptation: the National Geographic Visitor Center in Tusayan (ℂ **928/638-2468**; www.explorethe canyon.com). It is open daily March through October 8:30am to 8:30pm; November through February 10:30am to 6:30pm. Admission is $13 adults, $9.60 children 5 to 10, and free for children under 5.

You'll find a super-big-screen IMAX theater that shows a 34-minute historical film about the Grand Canyon, starting on the half-hour all day. The movie tells the story of the Powell expedition and has lots of spectacular aerial photography of the canyon. Children over 7 should enjoy it. On the other hand, why not skip it and go see the real thing a few miles down the road? The food court in the building includes a Pizza Hut.

FAST FACTS: Grand Canyon

Area Code The area code is **928.**

ATMs You can find an ATM on the South Rim at Market Plaza at the bank; in Tusayan at the National Geographic Visitor Center. The closest ATM to the North Rim is at Jacob Lake, 44 miles north on Arizona 67.

Emergencies For emergencies, dial ℂ **911** or ℂ **9-911** from hotel rooms.

Hospitals & Clinics The area sports a clinic known as the North Country **Grand Canyon Clinic** on the South Rim. Look for it at 1 Clinic Rd., southeast of Grand Canyon Village (ℂ **928/638-2551**). It's open all year Monday through Friday 9am to 6pm and Saturday 10am to 2pm, with additional hours in the high season.

Information For information, write Grand Canyon National Park, P.O. Box 129, Grand Canyon, AZ 86023; or call ℂ **928/638-7888.**

Internet Access & Cybercafes You will find Internet access at the Grand Canyon Tourist Center, Highways 180 and 64, Tusayan (ℂ **928/638-2626**).

Pharmacies There are no pharmacies in the area, but the clinic (see "Hospitals & Clinics," above) has some medicines.

Post Office The local post office can be found at the Grand Canyon Village at the Market Plaza (ℂ **928/638-2512**).

Taxis For a taxi call ℂ **928/638-2631**, ext. 6563.

Time Zone The park is on **Mountain Standard Time;** Arizona doesn't observe daylight saving time.

Transit Info Shuttle schedules for the South Rim are located in the park's newspaper, *The Guide.*

Weather Updates For weather updates, call ℂ **928/638-9552** or look on the Internet at www.nps.gov/grca.

8

Zion National Park

Zion Canyon is a sanctuary of stone, an amazing sandstone landscape even when compared to the Grand Canyon to the south. Zion just feels so intentional, as if it had been made specifically to say something spiritual. In fact, the Virgin River made the canyon by cutting down through layers of rock for millions of years—there's no reason to believe that God had more of a hand here than anywhere else. But that's not how it feels when you stand in the quiet evening shadows under the ash and cottonwoods and see, through their broadly spreading branches, the corners of white cliffs catching the setting sun far up in a deep blue sky. At those moments, this valley floor is like a garden in a great cathedral. It's peaceful and gentle, a place of respite after the severe and pitiless desert.

In the summer it's also a place of crowds. Like other parks with a single star attraction, Zion attracts many visitors who just want to stop by, look around, and move on. The average visit is about 2 hours. Over the years day-trippers have clogged the two-lane roads into Zion Canyon with cars. Thankfully, the Park Service has gotten most cars out of the canyon itself, using buses to shuttle people in and saving it from feeling like a huge parking lot. You also can escape the crowds by hiking, sightseeing early or late, and visiting less-known park areas.

BEST THINGS TO DO IN ZION NATIONAL PARK

- **Hike!** Spend a few days climbing the trails and testing your limits. Steep, challenging routes lead to cooler mountain air, a change to a different plant-and-animal community, and incredible views.
- **Mountain bike** along some good routes in the lands outside the park.
- **Go by horseback** along the Virgin River in the canyon.
- **Float down the river** on an inner-tube in Springdale, just outside the park.

For more information, see "For the Active Family" (p. 213).

Zion Address Book

Zion National Park   SR 9, Springdale, UT 84767-1099. ☏ **435/772-3256.** www.nps.gov/zion.

Zion Natural History Association   Zion National Park, Springdale, UT 84767. ☏ **800/635-3959.** www.zionpark.org. For maps, books, DVDs, Junior Ranger program materials.

Zion Canyon Visitors Bureau   P.O. Box 331, Springdale, UT 84767. ☏ **888/518-7070.** www.zionpark.com.

1 A Spiritual History

Zion Canyon made people think of God from the start. The first white explorer who came to the area, a Mormon missionary named Nephi Johnson, and a later visitor, Methodist minister Frederick Vining Fisher, both gave places here spiritual names—West Temple, Pulpit, Angel's Landing, and Great White Throne, among others. The name of the canyon comes from a Mormon settler; he supposedly called the mountains temples, as good for worship as the temples of Zion, the Promised Land in the Old Testament.

But we don't know what the first people here thought of the place. The earliest remains that archaeologists have found were left by Ancestral Puebloan (also called Anasazi), people who farmed the riverside bottomlands and hunted in the highland forests. Sites of houses, granaries, and rock art are scattered around the park (but very few are open to the public). From the evidence, archaeologists believe that only a small community lived here, and those who did were on the fringe of their people's region and a little behind the times. About 700 years ago, when the Ancestral Puebloans left their pueblos elsewhere in the Southwest, they abandoned Zion, too. Southern Paiute used the canyon now and then for the next 600 years, until the Mormons pushed them out.

The Mormons were members of the Church of Jesus Christ of Latter-day Saints, a religious group that started in upstate New York and later settled in the Midwest but was forced to leave by people who didn't like the Mormons' beliefs. They came to Utah in 1847 when the area hadn't been explored and was still part of Mexico—the U.S. won it from Mexico in a war that ended in 1848. Mormons settled along the Virgin River from the beginning, and the church's leader, Brigham Young, sent Nephi Johnson upriver to explore the Zion Canyon area in 1858. Other settlers followed, founding the town of Springdale and building farms in the canyon, including the flat area where the Zion Lodge is now.

John Wesley Powell, the explorer who first floated the Grand Canyon, came to Zion Canyon in 1872. With other scientists, he made maps and wrote descriptions of the area. Their reports drew others, including artists who painted the canyon. The St. Louis World's Fair of 1904—dedicated to showing many wonders from the West—displayed paintings of the canyon that people simply could not believe. A government survey party visited in 1908, and its report on the area was so enthusiastic that President William Howard Taft made the canyon a national monument the next year. Zion became a national park in 1919.

2 Orientation

Zion has two main parts: the Zion Canyon area, and Kolob Canyons and the high country. Zion Canyon and the approaches to it, on the south side of the park, draw most visitors.

ARRIVING
BY CAR

Zion is just east of Interstate 15. **Las Vegas** is 158 miles away on fast roads. Zion is also on the way from the Grand Canyon and Bryce Canyon National Park and other parks and attractions to the north. **Bryce** is 86 miles north along U.S. 89, or a bit farther up I-15 by way of **Cedar Breaks National Monument** (p. 233). The **Grand**

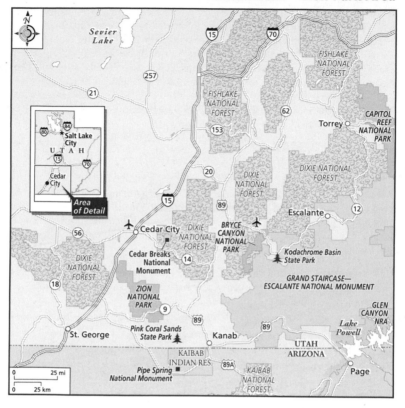

Canyon's North Rim is 120 miles, and the South Rim is 250 miles. If it's at all possible and you have the time, plan to take U.S. 89—the not-to-be-missed Zion–Mount Carmel Highway—through the east entrance of the park (see p. 211 for a description of the drive).

BY RV

If you're coming from the other parks to the east on U.S. 89, you'll need to take Route 9, the Zion–Mount Carmel Highway, through a long, narrow tunnel. Vehicles over 11 feet, 4 inches tall or 7 feet, 10 inches wide—almost any RV or bus—have to drive down the middle of the tunnel to fit through the arched ceiling. If yours is over 13 feet, 1 inch tall or over 40 feet long, you can't go through at all. To allow RVs to drive down the middle of the road, rangers have to radio ahead and stop oncoming traffic from the other end. To do this, you pay a $15 fee when you enter the park. Save the receipt, which is good for the return trip in the same vehicle up to 7 days later. The tunnel is staffed only from 8am to 8pm daily, April 1 through October; if you're late, you can't go through. In the winter, RV drivers must call ahead (© **435/772-3256**) to arrange for passage through the tunnel.

BY AIR

The nearest major airport is McCarran International (www.mccarran.com) in **Las Vegas,** within a few hours' drive. You can rent a car or RV there (see p. 24 for tips on RV rentals). **St. George, Utah,** less than an hour west, has a small airport served by **Delta/SkyWest** (© **800/221-1221;** www.delta.com) to Salt Lake City and **United Express** (© **800/864-8331;** www.united.com) to Los Angeles. Car rentals at the airport are available from **Avis** (© **800/230-4898** or 435/627-2002; www.avis.com), **Hertz** (© **800/654-3131** or 435/652-9941; www.hertz.com), and **Budget** (© **800/527-0700** or 435/673-6825; www.budget.com).

VISITOR INFORMATION
NATIONAL PARK VISITOR CENTERS

The **Zion Nature Center** is listed under "Children's Programs" (p. 215).

Zion Canyon Visitor Center   The visitor center contains a ranger desk, a large bookstore, a few natural-history exhibits, and many outside displays. It's a good first stop but by no means indispensable.

Rte. 9, just inside the south entrance station along the road to Watchman Campground. © **435/772-3256.** Summer daily 8am–7pm; winter daily 8am–5pm. Closed Christmas Day.

Kolob Canyons Visitor Center   This tiny center answers questions and offers orientation about the park's high country. It has geology exhibits, a bookstore, and a backcountry-permit desk.

At the northern park entrance, exit 40 off I-15. © **435/586-9548.** Summer daily 7am–7pm; off season daily 8am–4:30pm.

READING UP

Zion Natural History Association (© **800/635-3959;** www.zionpark.org) operates the park bookstores and sells its wares online.

    Maps: A topographic trail map printed by the Zion Natural History Association covers the park in good detail and costs $4.

    Hiking: The association carries several trail guides, of which the most in-depth may be *Hiking Zion & Bryce Canyon National Parks,* by Eric Molvar and Tamara Martin (Falcon, $17).

THE ZION CANYON AREA IN BRIEF

Zion Canyon Scenic Drive

A 6-mile-long dead-end road, the red-asphalt **Zion Canyon Scenic Drive** leads to the lodge, pullouts, and trail heads on the canyon floor. Most hikes and activities start there. Except for November through March, only shuttle buses and bicycles are allowed on this road (p. 200).

Route 9

Route 9 leads across the south of the park and meets the scenic drive. Campgrounds, the visitor center, the main entrance, and the town of

Springdale are on the southern edge of the park along Route 9. Farther west, this road reaches Interstate 15 north of the city of St. George. To the east, Route 9 becomes the amazing **Zion–Mount Carmel Highway** on the way to the tiny town of Mount Carmel and U.S. 89. See p. 197 for restrictions on RVs on this road.

Kolob Canyons Road

The northern area of the park is in the high country, where summers are a touch cooler, spring is snowy, and the trees are pinyon, juniper, and ponderosa

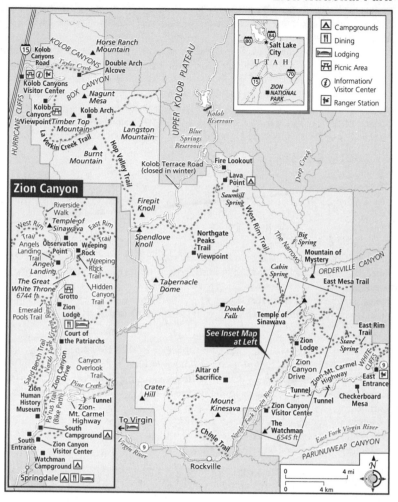

pine. There are no commercial services. A pair of scenic drives leads among the steep-walled, red-rock **Kolob Canyons.** To reach this area of the park, take I-15 north from St. George. To hike there from the Zion Canyon area is a significant backpacking trip.

Kolob Terrace Road

The Kolob Terrace Road crosses the center of the park and is another way into the backcountry. The long, partly paved route branches north from Route 9 west of Springdale. It cuts across the middle of the park's high country and meets several remote trails, leading ultimately to dirt roads north of the park and the primitive campground at Lava Point. The road is closed in the winter.

3 Getting Around

BY CAR OR RV

You'll need a car to get to Zion, to experience the Zion–Mount Carmel Highway, and to get to the Kolob Canyons area of the park, 45 miles from the Zion Canyon Visitor Center by way of Route 9 and I-15. In season, you can't drive the Zion Canyon Scenic Drive in your own car, unless you've booked a room at the lodge. In the off season, the Drive is open to vehicles, but if you're steering an RV, you'll find it difficult because of the narrow roadway and limited parking. RVs also have special restrictions on the Zion–Mount Carmel Highway, the eastern portion of Route 9 (p. 197).

BY SHUTTLE BUS

The shuttle-bus system in Zion Canyon reduces traffic congestion, pollution, and noise. The system has two loops, one in the town of Springdale and the other along Zion Canyon Scenic Drive. The loops connect at the Zion Canyon Visitor Center near the south park entrance. While the shuttle is operating, from early April through the end of October, you must use the shuttle or go by foot or bike to travel the Zion Canyon Scenic Drive (off Rte. 9), unless you're an overnight guest at the lodge. Parking is terrible even outside the canyon, so it is best to use the shuttle (or bikes) and leave your car at your hotel or campground in Springdale or in the park. Shuttles run frequently—up to every 6 minutes at peak times—over a long daily schedule. Hours and frequency change through the year, and are posted at each stop. You can bring packs, coolers, and strollers, plus two bicycles; eating, drinking, smoking, and pets are not allowed.

BY BIKE

During high season, when the Zion Canyon Scenic Road is closed to private vehicles, bikes are a great way to explore the park. A paved bike trail, the **Pa'rus Trail,** leads through the woods along the Virgin River from the campgrounds and main entrance near Springdale roughly 2 miles to the intersection of Route 9 and the Scenic Drive. From there, you can bike into the canyon trail heads and viewpoints. During the off season, when the road is open to private vehicles, biking is appropriate only for older and more experienced cyclists.

Bike rentals are listed on p. 215.

4 Planning Your Outings

WHEN TO GO

Summer is busy and hot at Zion. Thunderstorms are frequent in July and August, with daytime highs in the canyon almost always in the 90s (30s Celsius) and often over 100°F (38°C). The rim is 10° to 15° cooler. Rangers might swear the park is over-crowded from May to October, but the 3 summer months are heaviest. The fall is perfect, with bright yellow leaves on the cottonwoods (foliage in the canyon peaks in late Oct), reasonable temperatures, and fewer crowds. Heavy snow is unlikely before November, and then only in the high country, not the canyon.

We've visited in the spring and early summer, and both visits were glorious. There were plenty of people, but it wasn't hard to find a parking space or campsite, and the easier trails were busy but not too crowded to be fun. Down in the canyon, daytime temperatures were in the low 70s (low 20s Celsius) in the spring and low 80s (high 20s Celsius) in June, and evenings were cool. Because early spring weather is unpredictable and can be severe with snow squalls, a later spring break would be better than one in March. The final disappearance of snow is different each year, but all trails should be clear by early May.

Weather Chart: Zion National Park

	Avg. High (°F/°C)	Avg. Low (°F/°C)	Days/Month over 90°F (32°C)
December–February	52–57/11–14	29–31/–2 to –1	0
March	63/17	36/2	0
April	73/23	43/6	1
May	83/28	52/11	8
June	93/34	60/16	21
July	100/38	68/20	30
August	97/36	66/19	28
September	91/33	60/16	18
October	78/26	49/9	3
November	63/17	37/3	0

HOW MUCH TIME TO SPEND

Zion lends itself to day trips, and that's how most people see it. In that case, you won't have time for any but the easiest hikes and a trip down the scenic road—not enough, in my opinion. If you can spend 3 days, you'll be able to take a couple of day hikes and perhaps enjoy some bicycling, inner-tubing, and a trail ride. With even more time and plenty of planning, Zion is spectacular for backpacking.

HOW FAR TO PLAN AHEAD

Zion is crowded during the summer and early fall, and Zion Lodge reservations should be made 3 to 6 months ahead. The best Springdale rooms book up 2 or 3 months early. Most of the park's campsites can be reserved from spring to early fall through the national reservation system (see p. 29 for details).

WHAT TO PACK
CLOTHING

Bring good hiking shoes or boots. Up-and-down hiking can really chew up your feet in sneakers. That goes for kids, too. Remember to have the kids wear their new boots or shoes for a few days before the trip. When you're planning on doing a lot of walking, you don't want complaints that their shoes aren't properly broken in.

In the summer pack for hot, bright days in the canyon, with hats, sunglasses, and light, reflective clothing. Evenings are pleasant. Up on top, you can wear light clothing in the summer, but you might need a sweater in the evening. Thunderstorms come often in the summer, so pack jackets or ponchos, especially if you plan longer hikes.

For spring and fall visits, bring light clothing as well as layers of sweaters and jackets to make the transition from hot days in the canyon to cold evenings, especially higher up. You won't need clothing more formal than a clean pair of long pants and a shirt with a collar.

GEAR

In the summer, light camping gear will do. In the spring and fall, be prepared for chilly nights with heavier sleeping bags or a layered arrangement. If it's convenient, bring your bikes to use on Zion Canyon Scenic Drive (and its one paved path that's open to bikes); otherwise, you can easily rent. Hiking in the high country in early spring or winter might require snowshoes.

KEEPING SAFE & HEALTHY

The blazing summer heat in the canyon and chilly spring and fall weather on the rim demand caution. Please read the sections on dehydration and hypothermia in "Dealing with Hazards," in chapter 2. Also review the notes on lightning and snake and insect bites. Below are a couple of specific things to be aware of at Zion.

FALLS

Many trails run along precipices, some of them with sheer drop-offs of more than 1,000 feet. Carelessness has been fatal in the past. Also, knocking rocks off these high places endangers people below. Even if your route is safe, be aware of the fears of other members of your party. Have them turn back before they freeze in a frightening spot.

DROWNING

The swift-flowing river helps give the park its wonderful sense of life, and kids will enjoy playing near it. But be careful, especially in the spring, because they easily can fall in and be swept away. Don't let kids near water without supervision. Flash floods are terrifyingly fast and violent in the park's slot canyons. Get advice from a ranger before setting out on a canyon trek. The park's website (www.nps.gov/zion/Backcountry/Flashfloods.htm) explains flash-flood risks and has links to forecasting resources.

5 Family-Friendly Accommodations

CAMPGROUNDS

NATIONAL PARK CAMPGROUNDS

Reservations are accepted spring through early fall for Watchman Campground's 145 sites, but never for the 126 sites at South Campground or the six sites at Lava Point Campground. (See "Camping & Hotel Reservations," in chapter 2.) In the busy season, getting a first-come, first-served site can be difficult. Many people camp at a commercial campground outside, then show up at the park campgrounds early in the morning in hopes of getting a site when someone leaves. General information on the campgrounds can be obtained by calling the park's main number, © **435/772-3256.**

Lava Point Campground   This remote campground at the end of a dirt road is near high-country backpacking trails. The campground is on a plateau point at about a 7,900-foot elevation. Vehicles over 19 feet are not recommended, and any creek water you find should be treated before drinking.

At the end of Kolob Terrace Rd., 40 miles from the Zion Canyon Visitor Center. © **435/772-3256.** 6 sites. No fee. Closed mid-Oct to May. **Amenities:** Vault toilets, no water.

Watchman and South Campgrounds   These lovely campgrounds next to one another along the Virgin River are shaded by Fremont cottonwoods and other trees, but there's not much to shield some sites from one another. The most coveted sites are along the water, but the whole place has a special feel, under the chiseled stone peaks on either side of the valley. The slightly smaller South Campground closes in the winter; Watchman is open all year, takes reservations in season, and might have slightly larger sites. In addition, Watchman has two loops with electric hookups. It's an easy walk or bike ride on the paved trail to town, where you can buy firewood from a stand just outside the park or at a handy grocery store. The **Watchman Trail** leaves from the service road near the Watchman Campground registration station, climbing a few hundred feet over 1 mile to a viewpoint of the valley. The **Zion Nature Center,** which has a Junior Ranger program (see "Kid-Friendly Programs," p. 215), is at the entrance to the South Campground.

Rte. 9 near the Springdale entrance. ℭ 435/772-3256. 357 sites, tents or RVs. $16 standard site; $18 site with electric hookups; $20 riverside site. **Amenities:** Flush toilets, dump station, picnic tables, fire pits, drinking water.

BACKCOUNTRY CAMPING PERMITS

Heavy use of certain canyons in the backcountry at Zion has led to a rationing system that requires a lot of planning, but most of the backpacking trips appropriate for families with kids are still easy to put together. You need a permit, issued at either visitor center, to camp anywhere outside a campground. Fees are $10 for parties of 1 or 2 people, $15 for 3 to 7 people, and $20 for parties of 8 to 12. Slot canyon hikers may need permits even for day hikes. For some of those canyon hikes, reservation requests are taken 3 months ahead and entered in a lottery, which costs $5. Otherwise, permits are given out only in person, starting 3 days before the hike for backpacking trips and the day before for canyon trips. They're often in high demand, so being in line when the permit desk opens may be necessary if you have your heart set on certain rationed trips. On the other hand, some areas that are easier for families—such as the La Verkin Creek Trail in the Kolob Canyons area of the park—remain available without competition up to the day before the hike. In some areas, you must use designated campsites, but in others camping is allowed anywhere off the trail. Rangers at the **Backcountry Desk** (ℭ 435/772-0170) will help you figure out where to go at your group's ability level, and help you through the permit process. A book such as the one recommended under "Reading Up" (p. 198) is almost essential. Some information is available on the park's website (www.nps.gov/zion/Backcountry/Backcountry.htm). The Park Service's informative *Backcountry Planner* includes all the regulations, a map of sites and camping areas, and essential advice (see "Zion Address Book," p. 195).

COMMERCIAL CAMPGROUNDS

In addition to the two RV-oriented campgrounds listed here, tent campers should read about **Zion Ponderosa Ranch Resort** (p. 206).

Mukuntuweep RV Park and Campground   Along the sparsely developed highway east of the park toward U.S. 89, this campground is on a large plot of mostly open ground. Its best feature is its proximity to the park entrance. There are also, for $25 a night, six basic but comfortable log cabins, a hogan, and a tepee that share the campground's bathhouse.

East of the park on Rte. 9 (P.O. Box 193), Orderville, UT 84758. ℭ 435/648-3011. www.xpressweb.com/zionpark. 150 sites, tents or RVs. $15 tent; $22 full hookup for 2. $3 extra person, $1.50 extra child under 11. AE, DISC, MC, V. **Amenities:** Full hookups, hot showers, laundry, video arcade, recreation hall, store, restaurant.

Zion Canyon Campground and RV Park   This grassy campground with shade trees and a duck pond is far more pleasant than many arid, parking-lot-style RV parks that dot the region. Sites with picnic tables descend from the main street in Springdale to the edge of the Virgin River, where kids can splash around with inner-tubes. Dogs are permitted at RV sites but not at tent sites. The same couple has run the campground for more than 30 years. It's a popular place, and reservations are important for the busy season. Try to make them at least a month in advance.

479 Zion Park Blvd. (P.O. Box 99), Springdale, UT 84767. ℭ 435/772-3237. www.zioncamp.com. 220 sites, tents or RVs. $22 tent; $27 full hookup for 30 and 50 amp for 2. $3.50 extra person, $2 extra child 4–15. Extra car $1.50.

Campground	Elevation	Total Sites	RV Hookups	Dump Station	Toilets	Drinking Water
Lava Point	7,900	6	0	No	Yes	No
South	4,000	127	0	Yes	Yes	Yes
Watchman	4,000	145	63	Yes	Yes	Yes
Mukuntuweep	6,000	150	30	Yes	Yes	Yes
Zion Canyon	3,800	220	102	Yes	Yes	Yes

DISC, MC, V. **Amenities:** Full hookups, hot showers, laundry, playground w/swings and slides, picnic tables, fire pits, game room, Wi-Fi, heated pool, store, ATM, river swimming, restaurant.

HOTELS, MOTELS & LODGES

Only **Zion Lodge,** described below, is within the park, but Springdale has delightful hotels and is so close you might as well be in the park. With a population of about 550, Springdale is developing fast, gaining new hotels and tourist businesses, but thoughtful planning has helped it retain the atmosphere of a charming mountain resort community. Try to reserve a couple of months ahead for the busy season. In addition to the choices listed below, **Driftwood Lodge** (© **888/801-8811** or 435/ 772-3262; www.driftwoodlodgeandsuites.com) is nice, and **Best Western Zion Park Inn** (© **800/934-7275** or 435/772-3200; www.zionparkinn.com) has lots of good standard accommodations. High-season rates run from March or April to October, with low-season rates about 25% less.

Canyon Ranch Motel This is an excellent budget choice. Although the stucco duplex and fourplex cottages look a bit old-fashioned, inside they're well kept. They sit on a grassy compound with a pool and swings. Kitchenettes are available, pets are permitted with a one-time $15 fee, and you can drive right to your door. Free Wi-Fi is available.

668 Zion Park Blvd. (P.O. Box 175), Springdale, UT 84767. © **866/946-6276** or 435/772-3357. Fax 435/772-3057. www.canyonranchmotel.com. 22 units. High season $74–$99 for 2–5 people. Rollaway bed $15, crib $10. DISC, MC, V. Pets permitted for $15 (flat fee). **Amenities:** Pool; Jacuzzi; picnic area; free Wi-Fi. *In room:* A/C, TV, kitchenettes available for an extra $15, fridge, hair dryer.

Cliffrose Lodge and Gardens *Finds* On 5 beautifully landscaped acres along the Virgin River, this lodge has good standard hotel rooms with balconies and large bathrooms. Most units sleep two or four; four upscale suites sleep six people each. The buildings have long, pitched roofs and warm wood siding above stone foundations. The lodge, which is on the shuttle bus route, has flower gardens, a playground, a sandbox, a hot tub, and a swimming pool.

281 Zion Park Blvd., Springdale, UT 84767. © **800/243-UTAH** or 435/772-3234. Fax 435/772-3900. www.cliffrose lodge.com. 40 units. Apr–Oct $139–$209 per unit; Nov–Mar $89–$149 per unit. Rollaway bed $10, crib $6. AE, DISC, MC, V. **Amenities:** Heated pool; Jacuzzi; hammocks and swings; laundry; basketball court; riverside beach. *In room:* TV, Wi-Fi, suites have fridge, VCR, free movie rentals, microwave, wet bar sink.

Showers	Fire Pits/Grills	Laundry	Public Phones	Reservations	Fees	Open
No	Yes	No	No	No	Free	June–Oct
No	Yes	No	Yes	No	$16	Mar–Oct
No	Yes	No	Yes	Yes	$16–$20	Year-round
Yes	Yes	Yes	Yes	Yes	$15–$22	Year-round
Yes	Yes	Yes	Yes	Yes	$22–$27	Year-round

Flanigan's Inn   Flanigan's combines a rare set of qualities and is one of my favorites. The stylish, handcrafted small hotel feels like a resort and is more than friendly to families—it positively courts them. The grounds are a small paradise of stone walls and hedges, with a swimming pool on a terrace, an ornamental pond, a children's play area with a treehouse, and a nature trail that snakes off into the desert. The rooms are large and have features such as vaulted ceilings and original art. All have coffeemakers and some have kitchenettes; some of the nicely appointed "suites" are actually separate houses. All units are nonsmoking. Flanigan's also has two "extended stay" villas; Villa II is perfect for families of four. It has a bedroom upstairs with a king-size bed and bathroom, and downstairs are two twins and another full bathroom, a living room, and a kitchen. This villa runs $265 a night or $1,450 a week. The Spotted Dog Café, which offers patio and inside dining, is not a particularly good option for restless toddlers or kids raised on fast food. See p. 207 for details.

428 Zion Park Blvd. (P.O. Box 100), Springdale, UT 84767. ✆ **800/765-RSVP** or 435/772-3244. Fax 435/772-3396. www.flanigans.com. 34 units. $109–$139 double; $149–$259 suite. $10 extra person over age 12. Cribs free, rollaways $10. AE, DISC, MC, V. **Amenities:** Restaurant; bar; heated pool; hot tub; spa services available including massages, facials, and body wraps. *In room:* TV, Wi-Fi, kitchenette in some, fridge in some, coffeemaker, fireplace in some.

Zion Lodge   The park lodge, a collection of buildings with massive stone foundations, spreads over a large campus under shade trees in the middle of Zion Canyon. The lobby, restaurant, and auditorium building is a center of activities where you can reserve horseback rides, eat at the snack bar, browse in the large gift shop, and play on the big lawn. The modern motel rooms are in a pair of brown wood-framed buildings; each has a balcony and two beds. The rooms lack TVs but have air-conditioning, telephones, and tubs with showers. The cabins, in duplex and fourplex buildings, have a national park atmosphere, with vaulted ceilings, light wood moldings, and gas-burning stone fireplaces. Suites have a sitting room with a queen-size hide-a-bed, a wet bar, and a separate bedroom with a king-size bed. The Red Rock Grill, on the second floor, is a great place for kids to recharge on familiar foods like burgers, pastas, and chicken nuggets. See p. 207 for details.

Zion Canyon Scenic Dr., inside Zion National Park. ✆ **435/772-3213**. Fax 435/772-2001. www.zionlodge.com. ✆ **888/297-2757** or 303/297-2757. www.xanterra.com. 40 cabins, 81 units. $151 double; $161 cabin; $171 suite. $10 extra person over age 16. Rollaway bed $12, crib $5. AE, DISC, MC, V. **Amenities:** Restaurant. *In room:* A/C, hair dryer, cabins have gas fireplaces.

⸜Tips⸝ Park Camping Basics: Toilets, Showers & Laundry

The nicest public restrooms are in the visitor centers and at Zion Lodge. There are also toilets in Zion Canyon at the Temple of Sinawava, Weeping Rock, and Grotto Picnic Area, and outside the canyon at the Zion Museum. The campground bathrooms have cold water, and Lava Point Campground has no water at all. There's a coin-operated laundry in Springdale at the Zion Canyon Campground and RV Park (p. 203). It also offers hot showers to the public for $4 for 8 minutes.

Zion Ponderosa Ranch Resort   High-energy families no doubt will want to consider this resort, which expends great amounts of its own energy to keep guests active. Located in a remote area on the East Rim only a couple of miles from Zion Canyon, the resort handles everything from running a shuttle to collect you at the end of a long hike to offering trail rides, mountain biking, horseback riding, skeet and trap shooting, fishing, rappelling, climbing, and numerous other activities. In the summer a day camp keeps kids busy for up to 8 hours while adults tackle more ambitious activities. The resort has a pool and hot tub, tennis courts, and other sports equipment. Rates vary greatly based on the type of cabin—they come from spartan, one-room log cabins with log-built bunk beds and no bathrooms to spacious five-bedroom, three-bathroom homes outfitted with everything from gas fireplaces and surround-sound television to formal dining rooms, laundry facilities, and even a treehouse—you choose. Large cabins and homes have TVs and full bathrooms, smaller cabins do not. There are no telephones except in the largest unit, and only some of the cabins have air-conditioning. For kids, they offer twin-size mats instead of rollaway beds. For meals, there's an on-site restaurant that serves three meals a day.

East of Zion National Park (2 miles east of the park entrance, then 5 miles north on North Fork Rd.). P.O. Box 5547, Mount Carmel, UT 84755. ⓒ **800/293-5444** or 435/648-2700. www.zionponderosa.com. 53 cabins and mountain homes, 10 tent sites, 5 RV sites. Lodging $60–$545 double. Tent sites $10 per person per site, RV sites $55 full hookup for up to 4, $10 each additional. Cribs and mats free. DISC, MC, V. **Amenities:** Pool; tennis; hot tub; game room w/foosball, billiards, table tennis; massage; basketball court; volleyball; climbing wall; mountain biking; horseback riding; ATVs; rappelling. *In room:* Larger cabins and homes have A/C, TV, kitchen, fireplace, laundry facilities.

6 Family-Friendly Dining

LOW-STRESS MEALS

Neither Zion Park nor Springdale has name-brand fast-food franchises, but you'll find plenty of places to get sandwiches and takeout. In the park, the Castle Dome Café at **Zion Lodge** serves burgers, sandwiches, pizza, salads, and the like. You can sit under a patio umbrella or take your food out to the lawn (kids' menu prices range from $4.95–$9.95).

A great place to gather picnic necessities is the **Springdale Fruit Co.** located 3 miles south of town at 2491 Zion Park Blvd. (ⓒ **435/772-3222;** www.springdalefruit. com). Inside the gorgeous timber building, which is bordered by orchards, you'll find scrumptious trail mixes, fresh breads, organic fruits, cheeses, and sandwich fixings. Kids love the fruit smoothies. In Springdale you can get good homemade pizza to eat in or take out at **Zion Pizza & Noodle,** in a former church with a turquoise steeple at 868 Zion Park Blvd. (℘ **435/772-3815;** www.zionpizzanoodle.com). It's open daily from 4pm, with reduced hours in winter, and closed January and February. Deli sandwiches, fresh-baked muffins and cinnamon rolls, gourmet coffee, and such are for sale at **Zion Park Gift & Deli,** 866 Zion Park Blvd. (℘ **435/772-3843**), open Monday through Saturday 8am to 9pm in summer, with shorter hours in winter. There's a deli at the **Zion Canyon Giant Screen Theatre** complex, 145 Zion Park Blvd. (℘ **435/772-2400**); see below for hours.

BEST-BEHAVIOR MEALS

None of these places are really formal, but because you do sit down and get waited on, some patience is required. All the dining options below accept credit cards, unless otherwise stated.

Bit and Spur Restaurant & Saloon

Despite the Western saloon ambience, the sophisticated Mexican and southwestern cuisine here is popular with families. They sit in their own dining room or on the patio. The fare—Mexican standards like burritos, fajitas, flautas, and chiles rellenos along with more creative dishes such as smoky chicken (think a smoked, charbroiled game hen with sourdough stuffing and a chipotle sauce) and mushroom-stuffed poblano with a smoky cheddar-cheese sauce—have garnered praise from the folks who produce the Zagat's guide.

1212 Zion Park Blvd. ℘ **435/772-3498.** www.bitandspur.com. Kids' menu, highchairs, boosters, crayons. Reservations recommended. Dinner $11–$26; kids' menu $5–$6.25. Daily 5–10pm; limited winter hours.

Red Rock Grill

Zion Lodge's huge main dining room, upstairs in the main building, is decorated with lots of handsome wood and rock, including a stone fireplace, and offers an unforgettable view of the canyon walls. The room and service are formal, but the customers aren't. The menu changes periodically, but usually includes slow-roasted prime rib, broiled Utah red trout, and the always-popular fudge lava cake, a chocolate cake with melted chocolate in the center, for dessert.

At Zion Lodge, Zion Canyon Scenic Dr. ℘ **435/772-3213.** www.zionlodge.com. Kids' menu, highchairs, boosters, crayons. Dinner reservations required in summer. Breakfast $6–$8.95; lunch $6–$8.50; dinner $14–$22. Daily 6:30–10am, 11:30am–3pm, and 5:30–9pm.

Spotted Dog Café

The creative cuisine here uses fresh local ingredients, including vegetables from the inn's garden. The food is served on a sidewalk patio or in a light, tiled dining room with high ceilings and original art. While the toasted-pumpkin-seed-encrusted trout is a year-round favorite, the menu includes many goodies, including vegetarian selections—try the Navajo eggplant with a tomatillo cream sauce—and prices are reasonable. The children's menu is comprehensive and inexpensive. Microbrews are on tap.

At Flanigan's Inn, 428 Zion Park Blvd. ℘ **435/772-3244.** www.flanigans.com. Kids' menu, highchairs, booster seats, crayons. Reservations recommended. Breakfast $3–$9; dinner $15–$28. Daily 7–11am and 5–9:30pm; reduced hours in winter. Closed Jan to mid-Feb.

7 Exploring Zion National Park with Your Kids

ENTRANCE FEES The entry fee is $25 per vehicle. Entering by bicycle (from Springdale this makes sense) costs $12 per person, with a maximum of $25 per family. America the Beautiful passes are accepted and a good buy if you will visit other parks in the region. RVs pay an added $15 fee for traveling through the tunnel on the

Zion–Mount Carmel Highway; see an important note on that under "Arriving" (p. 196). You also can gain entrance with one of the America the Beautiful passes. For details, see chapter 2.

NATURAL PLACES
TEMPLE OF SINAWAVA & THE NARROWS 𝖌𝖌

The Temple of Sinawava is at the heart of the park, at the head of the Zion Canyon Scenic Drive. Here Zion Canyon becomes too narrow for the scenic road to continue north. It ends in a magical space, nearly encircled by vertical cliff walls 1,600 feet high.

How did it get this way? The Virgin River made it. At this point on its path, the river jogged, making a bow that remained as its bed eroded and left a towering cliff that reaches around and blocks the view down toward the mouth of the canyon. The Virgin River starts high on the Markagunt Plateau, at 9,000 feet. It ends 200 miles south and 8,000 feet lower in Lake Mead, a part of the Colorado River held back by the Hoover Dam. Water flows fast over its steep course, especially in spring floods fed by snowmelts in the high country and summer thunderstorms. When that happens, water roars down the canyons and chips away at the soft rock with harder rock it picks up along the way. Currently, water is wearing away about a foot of canyon every 1,000 years.

North from the parking lot, a flat, paved trail, **Riverside Walk,** runs along the Virgin River between the narrowing walls of the canyon. This corridor through rock shrinks and twists until it feels as though you're walking down a secret passage into the heart of the earth. Wildflowers grow from cracks in the walls where water seeps out. Signs along the way explain what you're seeing.

After 1 mile, the canyon runs out of room for a trail. This is the start of the **Narrows,** a 16-mile-long route, much of which is a slot canyon that's as little as 30 feet wide and 2,000 feet deep. Why is Zion Canyon so narrow here and wider back toward its mouth? The steep cliffs are mostly Navajo sandstone, a grainy rock of light tan to red that wears away easily a grain at a time but stays in one piece as it is being carved up. Just below the layer of sandstone lies shale from the Kayenta Formation, which breaks into bigger pieces than the sandstone and doesn't hold together as well in cliffs. In the Narrows, where the canyon is only as wide as a large hallway, the river is still wearing through the sandstone and hasn't reached the shale, so it carves only a thin, deep crack. Where the canyon gets wider, the river has reached the layer of shale. There the river washes shale away from underneath the sandstone, which then falls down, making the canyon much wider but still just as tall.

There's no trail through the Narrows, because water covers the canyon floor, but people do hike it by wading in the river. Because it's so difficult to hike against the current, most go downstream to traverse the whole thing, which requires a permit. But starting from the bottom, you can explore upriver without a permit, being careful not to overextend yourself and checking for flash-flood warnings first (see "Keeping Safe & Healthy," earlier in this chapter). The river bottom is slippery, and a walking stick is a good idea. Just start wading. The scene is amazing right from the start. About 2 miles upstream, you come to the meeting of the Orderville Canyon, among the most beautiful spots on the river and a good turnaround destination. Of course, wading against a stream is only for strong hikers.

Going downstream the whole 16 miles is a unique and exceptionally challenging hike that's only for strong hikers. You need a permit, which is priced depending on how many are in your party. Hikers must be at least 12 years old and 56 inches tall.

Experiment: How Far Away Is Lightning?

Many times, lying in a tent at night, I've watched the flash of lightning, heard the roar of thunder, and tried to judge how far away the thunderstorm was. I've figured if the storm was getting nearer or going away, and estimated how long before I would get wet. Not that knowing helps in any way, but it's more fun than just waiting.

The longer the time between a flash of lightning and a thunderclap, the farther away the lightning is. If the light and noise are getting farther apart with each lightning strike, the storm is moving away. If they're getting closer together, it's coming toward you. If both come at the same time, the storm is quite near. You can even figure out roughly how fast the storm is moving.

The reason this works is that light travels very fast and sound travels much slower. Light is made of photons, the fastest things in the universe, with a speed of about 186,000 miles per second. Light from a lightning bolt gets to you practically instantly. Sound, on the other hand, is like a wave on the ocean. The thunderclap moves the air, the air moves your ear, and you hear. (That's why you can feel the deep rumble of thunder and other loud noises, and it's also why there is no sound in outer space, where there is no air.) The speed of sound depends on the temperature and moisture of the air. For a round number, call it ⅕ (or .2) miles per second (720 mph).

Let's say you see a flash of lightning and hear the thunder 5 seconds later. You know the light got to you instantly and the sound took 5 seconds to come from the same spot. So if you figure out how far sound can travel in 5 seconds, you will know how far away the lightning struck. The figuring is pretty simple: Sound travels ⅕ mile per second, so in 5 seconds it travels 1 mile (⅕ × 5 = 1). The lightning must be 1 mile away. In 10 seconds, sound will travel twice as far, or 2 miles. The simple rule to remember is 5 seconds per mile. Start counting when you see the lightning, stop when you hear the thunder, and divide by 5.

You can even figure how fast a storm is approaching or moving away (although you can only get its actual speed if it is on a line over your location). Just compare the distances you get with your counting. If the first strike is 2 miles away, and 5 minutes later a strike is a 1 mile away, then it has come closer by 1 mile in 5 minutes, and you probably have 5 minutes or less before you get wet.

For many more details, including information on one-way transportation between the two ends of the hike and how to get a permit, see the information sources under "Backcountry Camping Permits," p. 203. For outdoor gear (for sale or rental) and advice, visit **Zion Adventure Company** behind Zion Pizza Noodle at 868 Zion Park Blvd., Springdale (© **435/772-0990;** www.zionadventures.com). These friendly young guys make a specialty of outfitting and teaching skills for the park and the surrounding outdoors. Stop in and talk with them, especially if you plan a canyon trek.

Layers of Life Zones

I'll never forget climbing the West Rim Trail in Zion Canyon in March. Down below, the morning sun was T-shirt warm. The canyon around the Virgin River was a green oasis, but the desert was near at hand. The path, climbing through switchbacks and steep ledges chipped from the sandstone, rose 1,500 feet upward. I stayed warm enough with a hard climb, but I could feel the air cooling around me. In a narrow side canyon, pine trees appeared in the shade of the rocks—I hadn't seen any of those down below. On top, the crisp freshness of the air, the light, and the views from 1,000-foot cliffs made me feel like an eagle. As I hiked on into the mountains, the pines and rock outcroppings reminded me of the high country at Yosemite. And then, turning into a shaded valley, I ran into deep snow. In a couple of hours, I had hiked from spring back into winter.

Elevations of Life Zones

One of my favorite things about traveling in this part of the country is seeing how the habitat changes with elevation. More often than not, there are no exact lines between the life zones, and plants from two zones frequently mix. (See "A Little Field Guide," p. 470, for pictures and descriptions of some of the plants and animals.)

Below 4,500 feet: You're in the desert. In the Painted Desert, east of the Grand Canyon on the drive to Glen Canyon along Route 89, broad landscapes with almost no plants pass by your window. In other desert places, you might see plants such as prickly pear and cholla cacti, and creosote bush. These plants have roots that can gather what little water is available in the ground and store it in their stalks through long droughts. Near year-round

They also rent dry suits for walking in the water of the Narrows and can provide a trail-head shuttle.

Whichever direction you hike in the Narrows, the water level and temperature in the river determine the difficulty of the hike—or if it is even possible—and what equipment you'll need. The water usually drops to a reasonable level in mid-June. From late July through early September, thunderstorms create the risk of deadly flash floods.

WEEPING ROCK

The most common rock formations at Zion are from the 2,000-foot-thick layer of Navajo sandstone and the Kayenta Formation of shale that lies right under it. The sandstone was made from huge dunes that were buried about a mile under the earth and pressed and heated into rock. The Kayenta rocks started out as mud and silt in a swampy environment, forming shale and siltstone when they became rock. An important difference between the two kinds of rock is that water seeps through the sand grains of the sandstone but can't get through the finer grain of the shale. Where the layers meet, water from the sandstone flows on top of the shale until it finds a way out. That's what happens at Weeping Rock. A spring coming out of the rock feeds hanging gardens of wildflowers (in season) that seem to grow from the cliff. It's only rivers at the bottom of Zion Canyon and similar places, Fremont cotton-woods and other lush plants grow.

4,500 feet to 6,500 feet: You're in a zone called the Upper Sonoran zone, or the pinyon-juniper belt. A lot of these parks and the surrounding land are at this level. The ground is rocky and dry, and rain and snow bring only about 10 inches of water a year. It's hot in the summer, but not as hot as the desert. This is a halfway stage between desert below and forest above, and it's half of each. The pinyon—a small, twisted pine tree—and the Utah juniper grow with plenty of space between. Yuccas and other desert plants, like sagebrush and the twiggy ephedra, commonly grow at this level, too.

6,500 to 8,000 feet: You're in the pine-oak belt, or the transition zone. The ground is sandy but gets more moisture—20 to 25 inches of water a year in rain and snow. This is truly a forest, with a variety of leafy plants and trees. The main tree is the ponderosa pine—the great, straight, tall pine that towers over much of the West. The big trees often stand far apart, allowing light to reach the forest floor, where bushes can grow.

8,000 feet or more: At these high elevations, sometimes called the Canadian life zone, the forests become thick with fir, aspen, and, above 9,500 feet, spruce. The rain and snow amount to three or more times the amount that falls in the pinyon-juniper belt, helping lots of bushes, plants, and trees grow in the topsoil that is created when they drop their leaves. Snow, wind, and cold challenge even the hardy trees, and above about 11,000 feet, trees can't grow at all. This is the alpine zone, with low tundra plants similar to those found in the Arctic.

¼ mile from the nearest parking lot on the scenic drive. More ambitious trails climb the canyon from the parking lot here, too.

THE ZION–MOUNT CARMEL HIGHWAY

The red asphalt highway that enters the east side of the park is a wonder because of the strange and beautiful land it passes through, and because of the amazing effort it took to build the road. Plan to use this road on your way into or out of the park, allowing plenty of time to enjoy the scenery and take a walk. If you need to use the western entrance to come and go, plan a half-day excursion to the Zion–Mount Carmel Highway. (Practical information about the highway, also known as Rte. 9, is covered on p. 198.)

Starting from the east, on the way into the park you go through a mountain valley of ponderosa pines and rounded sandstone outcroppings of white, tan, orange, and red, known as **slickrock country.** These rocks were sand dunes in a vast desert more than 150 million years ago, during the Jurassic Period, the age of dinosaurs. Many of the shapes look like sand dunes or huge waves of blowing fabric. Even more interesting, many of the mounds of rock have patterns of lines. These lines show the way the sand was arranged by the wind during the Jurassic Period.

How exactly did this happen? When wind blows over sand dunes, it picks up grains of sand from one side and moves them across the top to the other side. When the sand piles up more steeply than the "angle of repose" (34 degrees in this case), it avalanches down the side of the dune. As sand is buried deep, it starts to stick together, and the patterns of lines left by the little avalanches are preserved. When the wind changes, the pattern changes, leaving a different set of lines. You can still see those lines clearly, crisscrossing on **Checkerboard Mesa** and many other places along the road.

This bedrock is inviting for walking, but be careful, because it's easy to slide off the steep slopes. A single trail branches off the road between its two tunnels. The .5-mile **Canyon Overlook Trail** leads to an impressive view of Zion and Pine Creek canyons. Get a guide booklet at the trail head or visitor center.

The second tunnel along the highway is more than a mile long; on the other side you pop out in completely new terrain, perched high on the side of a deep canyon. The road was built in 1930, and it's fun to imagine how they managed it. On the way down, you'll want to stop and take in the view a few times (don't want the driver taking his or her eyes off the road!).

THE CANYON RIM

Zion Canyon is a notch in the White Cliffs, a step in the Grand Staircase that leads up a series of plateaus from northern Arizona to Bryce Canyon National Park and Cedar Breaks National Monument, north of Zion in Utah. Few other places allow you to see so clearly how elevation affects the habitat of plants and animals. As you go higher, the weather gets cooler and damper, just as it does when you go north. By one estimate, 1,000 feet up equals 400 miles north in this area of the country. In a day hike at Zion, you can climb what would be the equivalent of 800 miles north—from the desert Southwest on the canyon floor to pine forests more like those in Idaho. It's fun and easy to identify a few plants at the bottom, to note when they disappear on the way up, and to note the appearance of new plants as you rise. For an idea of what to look for in each elevation zone, see "Layers of Life Zones," above.

KOLOB CANYONS AREA

The northern area of the park, an hour's drive from Zion Canyon on Route 9 and I-15, includes canyons at the edge of the high Kolob Terrace. The red rock cuts steeply along narrow canyons, with many odd and interesting formations. A 5-mile scenic drive leads from the visitor center in front of the cliffs and up to a high overlook. Pick up a copy of the road guide at the visitor center (p. 198). Two trails lead into the area; both are described below under "Hiking."

PLACES FOR LEARNING

Besides the museum listed here, the visitor centers listed earlier and the nature center under "Children's Programs," below, also have exhibits.

Zion Human History Museum   If you have aspiring historians or geologists in your group, this is a great stop during a particularly hot, or rainy, afternoon. Located on the shuttle route inside the park's former visitor center, this museum chronicles the area's pioneers and natives. Permanent exhibits explain how the area's water, wildlife, plants, and geology relate to how humans used Zion through history. Temporary exhibits change a few times a year. When I visited, they had a great exhibit on members of the Civilian Conservation Corps who cut a lot of the trails in the park during the 1930s. The museum also has an information desk; small book, postcard, and poster section; and an auditorium that shows the park's orientation video on the hour and half-hour.

1 mile from the south park entrance on Rte. 9. Free admission. Daily 8am–5pm.

8 For the Active Family
BACKPACKING
Zion's trails link to create a network from one end of the park to the other. By carrying your gear and camping in the backcountry, you can take advantage of this land and really get away from people. Below, under "Hiking," I've described some of the main routes. Before your trip, get advice—and a backcountry permit—from a backcountry ranger (p. 203) and a topographic map (see "Reading Up," p. 198).

HIKING
Setting out on Zion's trails is the best way to see the park. Unlike the Grand Canyon, with its risk of getting exhausted and stuck at the bottom, Zion hikes mostly start out going steeply uphill, and if you tire, you just walk back down again. Be sure to wear good shoes or boots, and in hot weather take sun-protective clothing and plenty of water. A handy list of trails—with mileage, elevation gain, and the Park Service's conservative estimates of time and difficulty level—appears in the park map and newspaper you get when you arrive. Here are some of your choices, listed by area in order of difficulty. In addition, the **Riverside Walk** and hiking through **the Narrows** are covered under "Temple of Sinawava & the Narrows," p. 208; **Weeping Rock** is on p. 210; and the **Canyon Overlook Trail** is under "The Zion–Mount Carmel Highway," p. 211.

Zion Canyon
Emerald Pool Trails: The lower pool trail is a 1.2-mile paved loop; the upper pool trail adds another .8 mile that's a bit rougher (the latter is not good for kids with vertigo). A stroller is possible but not easy on the lower trail, and impossible on the upper trail, but this is a great hike for young children. It leads to interesting places, they can manage the whole thing, and it isn't just another flat nature trail—there's some challenge to it. The trail crosses the Virgin River on a footbridge and then climbs a short way up the east side of the canyon to a series of pools, a lovely stream, and a pair of glorious waterfalls—part of the trail passes behind one of these. Go early to avoid crowds and the heat. Swimming in the pools is not allowed.

Sand Bench: It's possible to hike much of the length of Zion Canyon on the west side of the river, away from the road, without much elevation gain. This 3.6-mile loop trail is the south end of that network. It gradually gains about 500 feet. The horseback-riding concessionaire uses it for trail rides in summer (p. 214), making it a bit less attractive to hikers.

East Rim (& Hidden Canyon)
East Rim Trail: Starting from the Weeping Rock parking lot in the canyon, the **East Rim Trail** is one of two that climb to the canyon rim (the other is West Rim, discussed below) up a spectacular and challenging series of switchbacks. It joins a network of high-country trails and ultimately leads to the east entrance station on the Zion–Mount Carmel Highway, 12 miles away. Or you can opt to do only part of the trail, to then hook up with the Hidden Canyon Trail (see below).

Hidden Canyon Trail: From the Weeping Rock parking lot, this trail climbs 850 feet into a side canyon. At the top, you can strive for incredible lookouts on Observation Point or Cable Mountain. The 2-mile-round-trip trail has many scary points, with long drop-offs; it's steep and hard work, but the rewards are great. Fit, energetic grade-school children should be able to make it.

West Rim (& Angel's Landing)

West Rim Trail: The incredible **West Rim Trail** has even more elevation gain than East Rim, climbing steeply over 3,500 feet. Join it from the footbridge across the river at the Grotto picnic area on the scenic drive. The trail is a wonder, especially the flurry of switchbacks (21 to be exact!) near the top built out of cut stone. They're called **Walter's Wiggles** after the park superintendent who built them. The awesome views start at the beginning, so this is a good trail to try even if you're not sure you'll make it to the top.

Angel's Landing: For this hike, you'll start as you would for Walter's Wiggles, then branch off for Angel's Landing. This trail climbs 1,488 feet to a final half-mile scramble along a knife-edged ridge with vertical drops of more than 1,000 feet on each side. There's a chain to cling to, but I wouldn't take children or anyone who isn't completely fearless.

Connecting Trails: You can keep going up the West Rim to the high country of ponderosa pine and exposed sandstone. Ultimately, the trail leads 14 miles to Lava Point, at the end of Kolob Terrace Road. From there it joins other trails that cross all the way to the Kolob Canyons entrance, a backpacking trip of several days.

Kolob Canyons Area

Taylor Creek Trail: The trail follows the middle fork of the creek into one of the canyons, a round-trip of 5.4 miles, with less than a 500-foot elevation gain. It offers a chance to see the steep-walled canyon up close as well as some early homesteaders' cabins. The trail head is a few miles beyond the visitor center on Kolob Canyons Road.

La Verkin Creek Trail: The trail leads to 310-foot Kolob Arch—thought to be the largest natural arch in the world—after a one-way walk of 7 miles. It's an ambitious day hike, descending into hot canyon bottoms, but a good family backpacking trip (permits are not hard to get). For a longer trip, various trails branch, creating the possibility of a multiple-day backpacking trip all the way back to Zion Canyon.

HORSEBACK RIDING

Canyon Trail Rides (✆ **435/679-8665;** www.canyonrides.com) offers two rides a day, starting at the corral across the road in front of Zion Lodge. The reservation desk is in the lodge. The guides offer commentary on plants and the history of landmarks on the way. Children as young as 7 can join the 1-hour ride along the Virgin River, which costs around $30 per person. It starts by fording the river and goes as far as the Court of the Patriarchs. Children who are at least 10 years old are welcome on the half-day trip, which uses the Sand Bench Trail and costs approximately $65 per person. Riders must be no heavier than 220 pounds. Book ahead in the busy season; you can reserve up to a year ahead, but a few days are probably enough.

Tips   Relaxed Play & Picnics

The grassy lawns under shade trees near **Zion Lodge** reminded me of a campus. You can spread out, throw a ball, and walk over to the snack bar when you get hungry. Come evening, wild turkeys occasionally spend time on the lawn. Just up the canyon is the well-shaded **Grotto picnic area,** with plenty of running-around room and raised grills. In Springdale, you'll find a **city park** with a playground, tennis courts, and volleyball, on Lion Boulevard, behind Flanigan's Inn.

INNER-TUBING

When the Virgin River slows down and the weather heats up, families play in the water, especially where it passes through Springdale. In the past, competing shops have rented tubes and shuttled floaters between the start and end points, both of which are outside the park. Both businesses closed down shortly before we went to press, but by the time you reach the park someone else will have picked up the service. You'll need a bathing suit and shoes that can get soaked.

MOUNTAIN BIKING

See "By Bike" (p. 200) for details on road biking in the park. Bikes aren't allowed off pavement within the park, but the nearby Bureau of Land Management territory has many exceptional mountain-biking routes, some good for kids and some very challenging **Zion Cycles,** 868 Zion Park Blvd., #2 (© **435/772-0400;** www.zioncycles.com), rents high-quality bikes, kids' bikes, trailers, and racks, and leads tours. A half-day rental ranges from $20 to $35 for an adult bike, $10 for a kids' bike or trailer.

9 Kid-Friendly Programs

CHILDREN'S PROGRAMS

Zion Nature Center (© **435/772-0169**), at South Campground, is a miniature natural-history museum for kids and their families. It's open only in the summer. The exceptional **Junior Ranger Explorer Program** operates here in the summer for children 6 to 12. Parents leave their kids with the rangers for active half-day educational sessions. Morning and afternoon sessions are different, so you can come back at midday, feed your children, then leave them for the afternoon session. They'll learn a lot and have fun, and it may be the cheapest child care in the world ($2). By attending one session, children earn a certificate and pin; after two sessions (or a session and another ranger program) they get a patch. You must sign the kids in personally. Registration for the 9-to-11:30am program is at 8:30am, and for the 1:30-to-4pm program at 1pm. Call for details or check www.nps.gov/zion/forkids/index.htm or the park newspaper.

Children under 6 can become Junior Ranger Helpers by completing an activity sheet with their parents and receive a decal. Off season, the program for the older kids is self-guided, too. Get the materials at the visitor centers.

FAMILY & ADULT PROGRAMS

Ranger-led programs in various areas of interest, including guided hikes, are available from April to October. You can find out when and where only by checking the bulletin boards at the campgrounds and the visitor center.

10 Entertainment outside the Park

THE BIG VENUES

Dixie State College presents performing arts in the 2,000-seat outdoor **O. C. Tanner Amphitheater** (© 435/652-7994; www.dixie.edu/tanner), on Lion Boulevard just off Zion Park Boulevard in Springdale. Concert offerings range from the Utah Symphony Orchestra to country bands to barbershop quartets. Performances begin at 8pm every Saturday from Memorial Day through Labor Day. Tickets are $9 for adults, $5 for children under 19. Check the website or call for the schedule.

MOVIES

The **Zion Canyon Theatre,** 145 Zion Park Blvd. (© 435/772-2400; www.zioncanyon theatre.com), shows films on a big screen in a complex that also has a deli, shops, a photo processor, and an ATM. The regular offering, *Zion Canyon—Treasure of the Gods,* presents the cliffs, rushing water, and spectacle of the place, plus a little pop history, in 37 minutes. Shows start on the hour all day. During the high season the theater is open from 11am to 8pm; winter hours are shorter and inconsistent. Admission is $8, $6 for seniors, $5.50 for children 3 to 11, and free for babies under 3.

FAST FACTS: Zion National Park

Area Code The area code is **435.**

ATMs There are ATMs in Springdale at **Zion Bank** (921 Zion Park Blvd.), **Sol Foods Market & Deli** (95 Zion Park Blvd.), and at the **Zion Canyon Theatre** (145 Zion Park Blvd.).

Emergencies For emergencies, dial © 911 or call © 435/772-3322 to reach the Park Service.

Hospitals & Clinics The **Zion Canyon Medical Clinic** is in Springdale, 120 Lion Blvd. (© 435/772-3226). The nearest hospital to Springdale is **Dixie Regional Medical Center,** 1380 E. 480 S. (south on River Rd. after the freeway), St. George (© 435/251-1000).

Information For information, write Zion National Park, Springdale, UT 84767; call © 435/772-3256; or check the website www.nps.gov/zion.

Pharmacies The local drug store is **Zion Drug** in Hurricane, 72 S. 700 W. (© 435/635-4456).

Post Office A post office is at 624 Zion Park Blvd. in Springdale (© 435/772-3950).

Time Zone The park is on **Mountain Standard Time.**

Transit Info No taxis are available. From April through October shuttle buses operate from 6:30am until 11pm linking Springdale to the park's South Entrance where you can board shuttles into Zion Canyon.

Weather Updates For weather updates, call © 435/772-0120 or look on the Internet at www.zionpark.com/weather.htm.

9

Bryce Canyon National Park

Each park in the Southwest's Grand Staircase region has its own character, and Bryce is the most intimate. The other, bigger canyons impress you with their hugeness, which turns a single person into only a speck. Bryce, on the other hand, is a land of details you can walk right into. At the Bryce Amphitheater, red-rock statues sit up like spectators in a great half-bowl, watching the sky's eternal show of drifting clouds. Paths draw you down into tiny canyons like aisles in a theater full of stone giants. With each step, the scene changes. Each tower has a different weird shape; each narrow alley twists to show a newly framed view of an unearthly landscape. A pair of fir trees reaches from the bottom of a canyon called Wall Street, just wide enough for their trunks and the pathway. A red rock balances high on a tall, skinny stone needle that looks as if a strong wind would topple it. The place is huge, but the size isn't what amazes me—it's the feeling that no matter how carefully I explore, no matter how closely I look, there always will be something smaller and finer to discover.

The statuelike pillars of stone are called **hoodoos.** They and the other strange shapes at Bryce were created and are still being carved by water as it works on ground where hard and soft rocks are mixed together.

The park and other nearby public lands—**Dixie National Forest, Kodachrome Basin State Park,** and **Cedar Breaks National Monument**—include habitat that ranges from the hot, dry desert to the alpine zone, above 10,000 feet (see "Layers of Life Zones," in chapter 8). In a little time in the car, or a bit more on foot, you can go from winter to spring to summer. On the plateau at Bryce, you stand at 8,000 feet amid tall ponderosa pines and look out on land where not much grows and snow can stick well into spring. If it's cold at Bryce, you can go down to Kodachrome Basin at 5,800 feet and warm up. If it's hot, head up over 10,000 feet to Cedar Breaks.

BEST THINGS TO DO IN BRYCE CANYON

- **Hike the bewitching hoodoos,** an activity well within the reach of school-age children (and strong preschoolers).
- **Ride horseback** through the rock formations and on the desert plateau outside of the park.
- **Cross-country ski.** Winter is long at this elevation. Ski trails span much of the rim area.
- **Go stargazing.** Most nights the thin, clear air allows for visibility of more than 100 miles. Each June the park offers its own Astronomy Festival.

For more information, see "For the Active Family" (p. 233).

Bryce Address Book

Bryce Canyon National Park   P.O. Box 640201, Bryce Canyon, UT 84764-0201. ✆ **435/834-5322**. www.nps.gov/brca.

Bryce Canyon Natural History Association   P.O. Box 170002, Bryce Canyon, UT 84717. ✆ **888/362-2642** or 435/834-4601. www.brycecanyon.org. For maps and books.

Best Western Ruby's Inn   1000 S. Hwy. 63, Bryce, UT 84764. ✆ **866/866-6616** or 435/834-5341. Fax 435/834-5481. www.rubysinn.com. Commercial and activity center outside park entrance.

Cedar Breaks National Monument   2390 W. Hwy. 56, #11, Cedar City, UT 84720. ✆ **435/586-9451**. www.nps.gov/cebr.

Dixie National Forest   1789 N. Wedgewood Lane, Cedar City, UT 84720. ✆ **435/865-3700**. www.fs.fed.us/dxnf.

Kodachrome Basin State Park   P.O. Box 238, Cannonville, UT 84718-0238. ✆ **800/322-3770** (campground reservations) or 435/679-8562. www.utah.com/stateparkskodachrome.htm.

Garfield County Travel Council   55 S. Main, Panguitch, UT 84759. ✆ **800/444-6689** or 435/676-1160. www.brycecanyoncountry.com.

1 History at the Edge of Civilization

Bryce Canyon was never used much by people before it became a park. Like other high-elevation parks in the West, the cold, snowy land was harder to live on than nearby lower areas that were warmer and free of snow during more of the year. The Ancestral Puebloans (also called Anasazi) and Fremont people visited only for summer hunting or gathering, and they didn't build much for anyone to find later. After they were gone, the Southern Paiute came to the area on occasion. Their legends said that the hoodoos were ancient people who were turned to stone by the powerful Coyote, an animal spirit from early times.

In the 1870s, government explorers, including the famous John Wesley Powell, found the canyon, named the area with Paiute words, and reported their discoveries to the world. Around that time, Mormon settlers forced out the Southern Paiute and tried to settle near Bryce, but they couldn't overcome the hard weather and poor land. Among them, Ebenezer and Mary Bryce arrived around 1875. Besides his name, which stuck to the canyon when he built a logging road, Ebenezer also left behind a famous comment that helps you imagine how hard it must have been to ranch here; he said it was "a hell of a place to lose a cow." Later settlers were able to make it by building a 10-mile ditch to bring water over the plateau. As you drive east from the park, you can see the dry little towns they built. The biggest, grandest, and most lasting buildings remain the churches of the (Mormon) Church of Jesus Christ of Latter-day Saints.

Bryce Canyon itself became a place to live and work only when people started coming to see it. A road was built in 1915, and in 1919, Ruby and Minnie Syrett built a tourist rest lodge near the rim. The Union Pacific Railroad developed tourism, building the beautiful lodge that stands today near the rim of the Bryce Canyon Amphitheater.

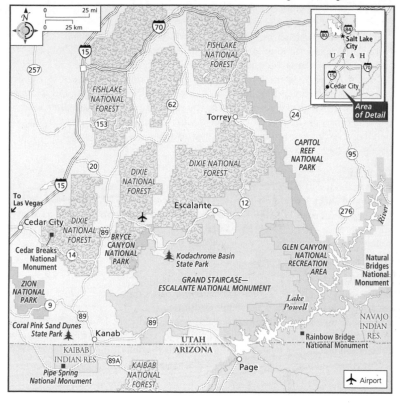

In 1923, Bryce became a national monument and 5 years later it gained parkhood. The Syrett family still owns Ruby's Inn, a huge hotel, campground, and activity complex just outside the park entrance. But the plateau remains mostly empty land, a place where human history hasn't really taken root.

2 Orientation

Bryce Canyon National Park is a long, narrow strip of land. It takes in the cliffs and bluffs of the eastern edge of the Paunsaugunt Plateau, with a rim at around 8,000 feet elevation. These Pink Cliffs are the highest step on the Grand Staircase that descends to the south. There's no canyon, really—just this edge and the places where erosion has dug notches. The biggest notch is the 5-mile-wide, 3-mile-long, 800-foot-deep **Bryce Amphitheater.**

The park's one 18-mile road carries visitors to more than 15 scenic overlooks.

ARRIVING
BY CAR

The park road intersects with scenic **Route 12,** which meets **U.S. 89,** running north-south just west of the park. **Interstate 15** is about 40 miles farther west. If you're coming from Zion National Park, 80 miles away, or the other parks in this section, U.S.

89 is the backbone you will follow (see "Linking the Parks," in chapter 7). The Grand Canyon's North Rim is 160 miles away, the South Rim 300 miles.

If you're coming from the southwest, or you want to pass through Cedar Breaks National Monument (56 miles away) or the Kolob Canyons area of Zion, take I-15, then cut east on **Route 14,** one of the most scenic roads in the area.

East of the park, Route 12 is a beautiful drive through sections of Grand Staircase–Escalante National Monument to Capitol Reef National Park, and it connects with other state highways to some of the region's other parks. Visitors often link them with the others in this section in a Grand Circle route. Unless you have a long vacation, however, going to so many parks over so many miles will mean a lot of driving broken by short, superficial visits to the parks.

BY AIR

Bryce is about 240 miles from **Salt Lake City** and 250 miles from **Las Vegas.** If you want to fly closer, **Cedar City** airport is 87 miles from the park, served from Salt Lake City by **US Airways** (© 800/428-4322; www.usairways.com). Rental cars are available there from **Avis** (© 800/331-1212 or 435/867-9898; www.avis.com) or Enterprise (© 435/865-7636; www.enterprise.com).

VISITOR INFORMATION
VISITOR CENTERS
Bryce Canyon Visitor Center   This is the park's only visitor center. Besides the usual bookstore and desk where you can ask questions, the center also has an exceptional little museum about the history and nature of the area. A topographical model and graphic display explain the Grand Staircase, and an award-winning 22-minute orientation video plays in an auditorium every half-hour.

Near the entrance station. © 435/834-5322. Summer daily 8am–8pm; spring and fall daily 8am–6pm; winter daily 8am–4:30pm.

Cedar Breaks National Monument Visitor Center   The center has a bookstore, rangers to answer questions, and exhibits on the geology, history, and biology of the monument.

Rte. 148, south entrance of monument. © 435/586-0787. Mid-May to mid-Oct daily 8am–6pm. Closed mid-Oct to mid-May.

READING UP
Bryce Canyon Natural History Association (© 888/362-2642; www.bryce canyon.org) operates the visitor center bookstore and lists its catalog online.

Auto and Trail Guide: The association's $4 *Bryce Canyon Auto and Hiking Guide,* by Tully Stroud, hits all the high points, but, with its lavish illustration, it is pitched as more of a souvenir book than a practical hiking guide. It lacks useful maps.

Trail Guides: The association offers various hiking guides for day hikes or backpacking for less than $2.

Maps: The plastic Trails Illustrated topographic hiking map of the park ($10) contains adequate detail to plan day hikes or a backpacking trip without any other resource.

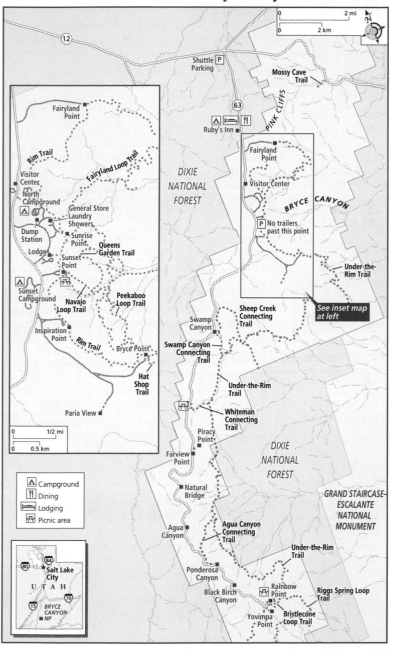

Bryce Canyon National Park map

Legend:
- Campground
- Dining
- Lodging
- Picnic area

THE NATIONAL PARK IN BRIEF

Visitor Center Area

The lodge, campgrounds, and Bryce Amphitheater are all within a few miles of the visitor center. **Ruby's Inn,** the area's commercial center, is just outside the park on Route 63.

Route 63 Extension

An 18-mile dead-end road, the extension of **Route 63** that branches south from Route 12, runs most of the length of the park. It goes from the visitor center near the only entrance, at the north end, to Rainbow and Yovimpa points.

Rainbow & Yovimpa Points

These two 9,100-foot overlook points are at the south end of the park. From there you can see all the way to the Grand Canyon's Kaibab Plateau and Navajo Mountain, south of Glen Canyon. Overlooks and trail heads are all along the way.

3 Getting Around

BY CAR OR RV

The park road overlooks all face east, so it makes sense to drive from the north entrance all the way to the south end and then make your stops on the way out so that you make only right turns. Parking and traffic are a problem at the overlooks during the middle of the day from May to September, especially for RVs, which cannot use spaces marked for buses. Vehicles over 25 feet are not allowed at the Paria Overlook. If you're pulling a trailer, you have to leave it in your campsite or parked at a designated trailer turnaround area while you tour the park.

BY SHUTTLE BUS

From late May to early September a voluntary, free **shuttle service** carries visitors into the park to reduce congestion. Buses run about every 12 minutes from Ruby's Inn and travel down to Bryce Point and back. To reach Yovimpa Point you will have to drive your own vehicle.

BY BIKE

There are no bike trails in the park, and mountain bikes aren't allowed on hiking trails. If you're bringing bikes anyway, you'll find them useful in the campgrounds and around the lodge. Mountain bikes are for rent at **Ruby's Inn,** just outside the park. There's great mountain biking in the region (p. 234).

4 Planning Your Outings

WHEN TO GO

Summer is glorious—not too hot for hiking at this high elevation—but crowds fill the trails and hotels. My favorite season in Bryce is fall, when the park is less crowded and spectacular with glowing aspen leaves. While the weather stays reasonable into October, September snowstorms are not unheard of.

Winter can bury Bryce in snow, making it a great cross-country ski destination. While the park lodge is closed, Ruby's Inn remains open. The clear, clean air allows exceptional star viewing and expansive vistas. The views of the red-rock formations, highlighted by snow, make the setting spectacular, but most of the hiking trails become impassable. Cross-country ski and snowshoe trails cover much of the plateau portion of the park, and Ruby's Inn offers winter activities and events.

Spring break is marginal but feasible. Snow and very cold nights last through March. The lodge opens around April 1. Snow and ice sometimes don't leave the trails completely until mid-May, but they can be passable much earlier. Spring offers cool days and a lack of crowds.

HOW MUCH TIME TO SPEND

Most visitors just drive through the park, which is possible to do in a few hours if you don't care about seeing it in-depth. But I recommend spending a minimum of 2 full days and 3 nights, and I would enjoy staying 5 days. For a 2-day stay, you could spend a day getting oriented and driving the park road, and a day hiking or horseback riding. With more time, you could take more and longer hikes or go backpacking, and add visits to nearby Kodachrome Basin, Red Canyon, and Cedar Breaks National Monument.

HOW FAR TO PLAN AHEAD

For a midsummer visit, people who want to stay in rooms at the lodge or Ruby's Inn start reserving more than a year ahead. Make plans 6 months in advance to ensure a good selection. But don't give up. Large tour groups routinely cancel at Ruby's 1 month ahead. On the day of a visit, you may also snag a last-minute cancellation by calling around checkout time. It's far easier to find rooms at other motels, less attractive and farther from the park. The Park Service takes reservations at one of Bryce's two campgrounds, and campsites are almost always available at Ruby's Inn if you can't find one in the park.

Weather Chart: Bryce Temperature & Snowpack

	Avg. High (°F/°C)	Avg. Low (°F/°C)	Avg. Snow Depth (in.)
January	36/2	9/–13	11
February	39/4	12/–11	15
March	46/8	17/–8	11
April	56/13	25/–4	3
May	66/19	31/–1	0
June	76/24	31/–1	0
July–August	80–83/27–28	45–47/7–8	0
September	74/23	37/3	0
October	63/17	29/–2	0
November	51/11	19/–7	2
December	37/3	10/–12	6

WHAT TO PACK
CLOTHING

Be ready for a great range of temperatures. Evenings are cool all year. Even in midsummer the temperature can drop to freezing at night at Bryce, and just a few miles away, off the plateau, the next afternoon is over 100°F (38°C). Typical summer days are in the 70s and 80s (20s Celsius). The best way to deal with this variability is with layered clothing. You'll want cool clothing for hot weather, plus long sleeves, pants, sweaters, and jackets you can add when it gets colder. Thunderstorms are frequent in July and August. The sun is powerful at high elevations at any time of year, so bring sun hats, sunglasses, and sunscreen. Good walking shoes or boots will help you enjoy the steep trails. There's never a need for formal clothing.

In winter, spring, and fall, Bryce is often cold and snowy. It's a beautiful time, with good cross-country skiing and snowshoeing, but cold for camping or inactive time outdoors. Warm winter clothing may be necessary October through April.

GEAR

For summer tent camping, prepare for cool nights. Most of your camping at other parks in the region will be at lower, warmer elevations, so you may want to prepare with layers, which could include sleeping-bag liners, summer bags, thermal long underwear, and a single heavy bag to use as a comforter over you all. Tent camping before May or after October is only for the hardy, because the nights can be frigid. If you come in the winter, you can bring cross-country skis or rent them at Ruby's Inn for reasonable rates. The Park Service lends snowshoes whenever the snow is at least a foot deep (you have to leave a deposit or credit card charge). See "When It's Cold & Wet," in chapter 2, "Planning a Family Trip to a National Park."

KEEPING SAFE & HEALTHY

The main risks at Bryce are from weather and falls. To protect against falls, you need good shoes, common sense, and control of your children. For tips on dehydration, hypothermia, and lightning, see "Dealing with Hazards," in chapter 2.

5 Family-Friendly Accommodations

CAMPGROUNDS

NATIONAL PARK CAMPGROUNDS

There are two campgrounds in the park; North Campground offers limited reservations in the summer through the system operated for recreation on America's federal lands (see chapter 2). Without a reservation, you need to arrive at the campgrounds before 1pm for a chance of getting a site; the earlier you arrive, the better your chances. The two campgrounds have a total of 208 sites. For camping questions, call headquarters (© **435/834-5322**).

North The campground is extremely convenient, within walking distance of the visitor center and the canyon rim, yet the design makes it feel remote and woodsy. Sites are well separated among ponderosa pines, and some have little terraces built up with stone blocks. There are four loops—A, B, C, and D—with C and D restricted to tent campers. **Loop A,** nearest the visitor center, is open all winter, for those few who care to camp in the snow.

Tips **Backcountry Camping Permits**

To camp along the **Under-the-Rim Trail** or **Riggs Spring Loop** you need a backcountry permit that can be purchased at the visitor center. These permits cannot be reserved; they are available up to 48 hours before the hike from 8am until 2 hours before the visitor center closes. The number of permits issued is limited, but park officials say they seldom run out. There are eight campsites along the Under-The-Rim Trail and another four along the Riggs Spring Loop. See "Backpacking," p. 233, and check www.nps.gov/brca/hiking.html, where you can download a free map and brochure.

Tips Park Camping Basics: Toilets, Showers & Laundry

The Park Service provides flush toilets in the campgrounds, at the visitor center, and at Sunrise, Sunset, and Rainbow points. Showers for $3 can be obtained at the campground at Ruby's Inn. Ruby's also maintains a large year-round coin-op laundry. If you're near Kodachrome Basin State Park, you can use the showers for $2.

Entrance across from the visitor center and near Sunrise Point. © **435/834-5322.** 107 sites. $10 site plus $10 reservation fee. Reservations accepted for 32 sites during summer through www.recreation.gov (see chapter 2). Open year-round, dump station closed in winter. **Amenities:** Flush toilets, dump station, coin-op laundry and showers nearby, running water.

Sunset   This campground, about 1½ miles south of the visitor center, has sites separated by ponderosas and shrubs. It's back from the rim across the main park road, making it a little quieter than North. There are three loops—A, B, and C—with B and C reserved for tent campers.

Across main park road from turnoff to Sunset Point. © **435/834-5322.** 101 sites. $10 site. Closed mid-Oct to mid-Apr. **Amenities:** Flush toilets, running water, 2 wheelchair-accessible sites.

OUTSIDE THE NATIONAL PARK

Besides these campgrounds, **Cedar Breaks National Monument** (see "Natural Places Just Outside the National Park," p. 232) has a 28-site campground that does not take reservations. Typically open from mid-June through September, the campground has flush toilets and evening ranger programs. Camping fees are $14.

Kodachrome Basin State Park _Finds_   The sites here are separated and screened, well maintained and grassy, with concrete pads. When we visited, the bathrooms were remarkably clean and had showers without the usual coin-fed meters. In the spring, when it's too cold to camp at Bryce Canyon National Park, this lower, desert area is warmer and free of snow. I've described this wonderful little park more on p. 232. From Bryce, drive about 14 miles east to Cannonville, then turn south, following the signs 7 miles to the park.

South of Cannonville, east of Bryce Canyon National Park on Rte. 12 (P.O. Box 180069), Cannonville, UT 84718-0069. © **800/322-3770** (campground reservations) or 435/679-8562. www.stateparks.utah.gov/parks/kodachrome. 27 sites, tents or RVs. $15 site. **Amenities:** Flush toilets, free hot showers, ranger station and store, activities.

Ruby's Inn RV Park and Campground   This is an exceptional commercial campground, on the edge of a pond among small pine trees. It's next to the activity center of Ruby's Inn, where you can use the indoor pools, laundry, and other facilities, or watch the rodeo. The campground also has its own outdoor pool. RVers who need hookups should reserve ahead, but I've been told that there's almost always room for more self-contained campers, in tents or vehicles. In the winter, RVs can plug in behind the hotel, where the employees live.

On Rte. 63 just outside the park entrance (P.O. Box 22), Bryce, UT 84764. © **866/866-6616** or 435/834-5301 summer, or 435/834-5341 winter. Fax 435/834-5481. www.rubysinn.com. More than 200 sites, tents or RVs. $20 tent for 2; $31 full hookup. $2 extra person over age 5. AE, DC, DISC, MC, V. Closed Nov–Mar. **Amenities:** Full hookups, showers, dump station, laundry, game room, swimming pools, hot tub, activities, propane.

Campgrounds in the Bryce Canyon Area

Campground	Elevation	Total Sites	RV Hookups	Dump Station	Toilets	Drinking Water
North	7,700	107	No	Yes	Yes	Yes
Sunset	8,000	101	No	No	Yes	Yes
King Creek (USFS)	8,000	37	No	Yes	Yes	Yes
Red Canyon (USFS)	7,400	37	No	Yes	Yes	Yes
Ruby's Inn RV Park	7,600	227	Yes	Yes	Yes	Yes
Kodachrome	5,800	27	No	Yes	Yes	Yes

DIXIE NATIONAL FOREST

See "Bryce Address Book" (p. 218) to contact the national forest. Both of these campgrounds accept reservations through the national system described under "The National Recreation Reservation Service," in chapter 2. The months of operation are minimums: The campgrounds remain open in the winter when weather permits.

King Creek Campground   This campground is at the end of a 7-mile gravel access road, on the Tropic Reservoir, a popular fishing hole along the Sevier River. Two trails run from the campground among big pines.

Rte. 087, west of Bryce. 37 sites, tents or RVs. $10 site. No reservations. Closed mid-Sept to mid-May. From Rte. 12 west of Bryce, follow gravel road south at sign for campground and Tropic Reservoir. **Amenities:** Flush toilets, dump station, grills, running water, boating, swimming, fishing.

Red Canyon *(Finds* This is a well-developed campground among ponderosa pines near the canyon of red rocks on Route 12. The striking rock here is from the same formation that makes Bryce so beautiful. There are good trails from the campground, with some mountain-biking opportunities.

Rte. 12, west of Bryce. 37 sites, tents or RVs. $12 site. Closed Oct to mid-May. **Amenities:** Flush toilets, showers, dump station.

HOTELS, INNS & LODGES

Best Western Ruby's Inn   The visitor complex built by the park's pioneering Syrett family dominates the landscape just outside Bryce's gates. In fact, in 2007 the family gained approval to incorporate the area into a town of its very own. Ruby's has huge motel buildings, a prominent Chevron service station complete with auto shop, the pond around which the family homes are located, the spread-out campground, and a row of false-front businesses across the road. Inside are two pools, a grocery and gift store, an art gallery, and a sort of mall for tours and activities. It's a remarkably well-run place. The rooms lack much character but are loaded with amenities—some have VCRs, there's Wi-Fi throughout the complex, and Jacuzzis, for example. People start to reserve more than a year in advance, but because many tour groups cancel 1 month ahead, you often can get rooms then. Rates vary many times through the year; I've listed only the highs and lows.

Showers	Fire Pits/Grills	Laundry	Public Phones	Reservations	Fees	Open
Yes	Yes	Yes	Yes	Yes	$10	Year-round
Yes	Yes	Yes	Yes	Yes	$10	Mid-Apr to mid-Oct
No	Yes	No	No	No	$10	Mid-May to
Yes	Yes	No	No	No	$12	Mid-May to Oct early Sept
Yes	Yes	Yes	Yes	Yes	$20–$31	Mid-May to Oct
Yes	Yes	Yes	No	Yes	$15	Year-round

1000 S. Utah 63, Bryce, UT 84764. (C) **866/866-6616** or 435/834-5341. Fax 435/834-5265. www.rubysinn.com. 368 units. High season $130–$195 double; low season $59–$125 double. Children under 18 free in parent's room. Roll-aways $10, cribs free. AE, DC, DISC, MC, V. **Amenities:** Restaurant; indoor pool; laundry; post office; shops; ATM; 1-hr. photo; currency exchange; liquor store; automobile repair shop; Internet kiosks. *In room:* A/C, TV, tea-/coffeemaker, hair dryer, iron/ironing board, Wi-Fi.

Bryce Canyon Inn
Just down the road, this establishment offers 18 charming log cabins and eight motel rooms. The rooms feature cozy quilts atop the beds, 27-inch TVs, refrigerators, and even wireless Internet if you can't leave work behind.

21 N. Main St., Tropic, UT 84776. (C) **800/592-1468** or 435/679-8577. Fax 435/679-8888. www.brycecanyoninn.com 18 cabins, 8 motel units. High season $65–$85 double; low season $45–$60 double. Rollaway bed $10. MC, V. **Amenities:** Restaurant. *In room:* A/C, TV, microwave, fridge, iron/ironing board, Wi-Fi.

Bryce Canyon Lodge
The lodge and cabins built by the Union Pacific Railroad under the guidance of renowned architect Gilbert Stanley Underwood in 1924 are among the most beautiful examples of the rustic national-park style. The huge pine logs and long, cedar-shingled roofs give an eternal feeling to the perfectly proportioned lodge building, which sits among towering ponderosa pines. The location is ideal, too, right in the center of things, just back from the Bryce Canyon rim.

The 40 historic cabins, which have been restored to their 1920s appearance, aren't large but have high ceilings, stone gas-burning fireplaces, two double beds, and interiors that tastefully balance comfort and the rustic park tradition. The 70 motel rooms are standard, with two queen-size beds and a balcony or patio. The most expensive lodgings are the three suites. All units have phones but no TVs. Reserve 6 to 8 months ahead for the high season, or call or stop in to try for a cancellation.

1 Bryce Canyon Lodge, Bryce Canyon, UT 84717. (C) **435/834-5361.** Fax 435/834-5464. www.brycecanyon lodge.com. (Reservations: c/o Xanterra Parks and Resorts, 14001 E. Iliff Ave., Suite 600, Aurora, CO 80014. (C) **888/ 297-2757** or 303/297-2757. www.xanterra.com.) 73 units, 40 cabins. $115–$159 double; $149 double cabin. $10 extra person over age 16. Cribs $5, rollaways $12. AE, DISC, MC, V. Closed Nov–Mar. **Amenities:** Restaurant; gift shop. *In room:* Cabins have fireplaces.

Bryce View Lodge
This basic motel consists of four two-story modular buildings, set back from the road and grouped around a large parking lot and attractively landscaped

area. Rooms are simple but comfortable and quite quiet. Owned by the same company that operates the Best Western Ruby's Inn, it offers guests access to the swimming pools and other amenities across the street at Ruby's.

991 S. Utah 63 (across from Best Western Ruby's Inn), Bryce, UT 84764. ℂ **888/279-2304** or 435/834-5180. Fax 435/834-5181. www.bryceviewlodge.com. 160 units. $52–$83 double. $2–$3 extra person over age 12. Rollaway bed $10, crib free. AE, DC, DISC, MC, V. **Amenities:** Guests have access to Ruby's Inn facilities. In room: A/C, TV.

World Host Bryce Valley Inn   In the tiny town of Tropic, 10 miles east of the park on Route 12, this motel is a group of large wooden buildings with good, standard rooms, each with two queen-size beds or one king-size. A 24-hour laundry facility is on-site, as is Clarke's Restaurant, a pleasant but typical Western roadside cafe, as well as Coyote Collectibles, which offers a gift shop, deli, bakery, and ice-cream shop.

199 N. Main St., Tropic, UT 84776. ℂ **800/442-1890** or 435/679-8811. Fax 435/679-8846. www.brycevalleyinn.com. 65 units. High season $75–$85 double; low season $50–$105 double. $5 extra person over age 12. Rollaway bed $10, cribs free. AE, DISC, MC, V. **Amenities:** Restaurant; gift shop; laundry. In room: A/C, TV, dataport, coffeemaker, hair dryer, iron/ironing board, microwave and refrigerator on request ($5).

6 Family-Friendly Dining

One drawback of a long stay at Bryce is the lack of restaurants. Still, the chefs strive to make up for that with creative entrees built largely around seafood, poultry, beef, and vegetables.

Bryce Canyon Dining Room   Located inside the park's lodge, this is the best restaurant in the region, and you certainly can't beat the setting. As with most restaurants in national parks, the chefs have made a real effort to upgrade their menu beyond simple steaks and chicken. You'll find innovative entrees such as Fairyland Crème Brie and Apple Stuffed Chicken, Red Canyon Grilled Trout Almandine, and Gorgonzola Ravioli, a vegetarian dish featuring raviolis stuffed with three cheeses and wild mushrooms and topped with tomatoes and Gorgonzola sauce. For lunch they roll out a soup, salad, and taco bar along with the ubiquitous burgers and sandwiches, while breakfasts are best built around the buffet that features hot and cold cereals, French toast, waffles with fruit toppings, and egg dishes.

Bryce Canyon Lodge. ℂ **435/834-5361.** www.brycecanyonlodge.com. Kids' menu, highchairs, boosters, activity book with crayons. Reservations required for dinner. Breakfast $4.25–$10; lunch $7.25–$15; dinner $12–$22. AE, DC, DISC, MC, V. Apr 1–Oct 31 daily 6:30–10:30am, 11am–3:30pm, and 5:30–9:30pm. Closed Nov–Mar.

Canyon Diner   Really nothing more than a fast-food outlet, the diner exists for those in a hurry, or with kids who are satisfied with the likes of burgers, sandwiches, pizza, and chicken.

Ruby's Inn, 1000 S. Hwy. 63, Bryce, UT. ℂ **435/834-5341.** www.rubysinn.com. Kids' menu, highchairs, boosters. Entrees $3–$15. Apr–Oct daily 6:30am–9:30pm. Closed Nov–Mar.

Cowboy's Buffet and Steak House   Inside Ruby's Inn, this is a comfortable family restaurant with a heavy Western theme and plentiful, reasonably priced meals built around beef, chicken, and fish. Dinners are $13 to $30. The service is good, but the food is more institutional than subtle. It's a good place for a grown-up, sit-down meal where you don't have to worry about the kids. It serves three meals a day all year. Hours are daily 6:30am to 10pm in summer, daily 6:30am to 9pm in winter.

Ruby's Inn, 1000 S. Hwy. 63, Bryce, UT. ℂ **435/834-5341.** www.rubysinn.com. Kids' menu, highchairs, boosters. Breakfast $3–$13; lunch $5.50–$15; dinner $13–$30; kids' menu $4–$10. AE, DC, DISC, MC, V. Daily 6:30am–9pm (to 10pm in summer).

Tips **Places for Relaxed Play & Picnics**

Rainbow and Sunset points both have formal picnic areas with restrooms. Rainbow Point is at the end of the park road, a good goal for a day-trip picnic. The park is isolated, so there's no town and no town playgrounds, but the Ruby's Inn complex, just outside the park, has basketball courts and other recreation areas. There's also plenty of room to play under the pines around the lodge.

World Host Bryce Valley Inn   East of the park, in Tropic—a small town developing character—is World Host Bryce Valley Inn, a lodging alternative to Ruby's Inn. Here you'll find Clark's Restaurant, a good place to take breakfast, lunch, and dinner. It's not fancy. Just hearty Western fare built around steaks, trout, pork chops, pasta, and chicken. Lunches are simple affairs cobbled around hamburgers, sandwiches, and salads.

World Host Bryce Valley Inn, 199 N. Scenic Byway 12, Tropic, UT, 84776. ℭ **800/442-1890** or 435/679-8811. www. brycevalleyinn.com. Kids' menu, highchairs, boosters, crayons. Breakfast $3.50–$9.95; lunch $5–$10; dinner $8.95–$30. AE, DISC, MC, V. Daily 6:30–10am and 5–10pm.

---

7 Exploring Bryce Canyon National Park with Your Kids

ENTRANCE FEES   Park admission is $25 per vehicle. You also can gain entrance with any of the various iterations of the America the Beautiful Pass. For details, see chapter 2. National park passes apply (see p. 18 for details).

NATURAL PLACES IN THE PARK
BRYCE AMPHITHEATER

The park is a strip of land along cliffs that form the eastern edge of the Paunsaugunt Plateau, which itself is a portion of the Pink Cliffs, the top step in the Grand Staircase. The Bryce Amphitheater is a dent in the cliff, the largest natural amphitheater among many along the park road. No river made this canyon. As you walk down through passages among the many fins of rock, you'll see that a river couldn't have done it, because a river would have made one deep channel rather than many. Instead, the water from melting snow and thunderstorms parted the rock as it trickled down from the plateau. Soft layers wore away fast and made slots between hard layers.

Lots of other trails wander through the hoodoos, allowing hikers to match a route to their energy levels and time. You will need a map of some kind, because it's easy to get mixed up. The trails start from three of the four overlooks on the amphitheater's rim (the exception is Inspiration Point). A fairly flat, 11-mile **Rim Trail** connects the overlooks and Fairyland Point to the north.

Sunset and Sunrise points lie in the park's front parlor, between the amphitheater and the lodge, campgrounds, and services. The .5-mile section of the rim trail between these points is paved and okay for strollers, but to go much beyond the crowds here, you'll need a way to carry toddlers. Both points have picnic areas, and Sunset Point has bathrooms. Climb down the **Queen's Garden Trail** ⁂ or **Navajo Loop Trail,** both less than 2 miles in length and descending 300 to 500 feet from Sunrise and Sunset points, respectively. A superb 2.8-mile hike links the two trails and takes you through some of the park's best highlights; any fit school-age child can manage it.

Bryce Point is farthest south in the amphitheater. The **Peekaboo Loop Trail** connects it to Sunset or Sunrise points, extending the Navajo Loop or Queen's Garden trails and allowing access to some more amazing terrain (add 3.5 miles to the connecting trail to get the total distance). You have to share the way with horses on this trail (see "Horseback Riding," p. 234). Also from Bryce Point, the 4-mile round-trip **Hat Shop Trail** is a relatively challenging path that's less crowded than most of the park's hikes and leads to some balanced rocks. That route continues as the backcountry's **Under-the-Rim Trail** south into a portion of the park with less fanciful topography.

Trail guides and maps at the park are inexpensive (see "Reading Up," p. 220), and the park website has a remarkable trail guide feature with topographic and relief maps (go to www.nps.gov/brca and click "In Depth").

THE PARK ROAD

The road south through the park and the overlooks off the plateau to the east are a main feature of the park. Beyond Bryce Point, however, erosion has worked down through the red Claron Formation that makes the strange shapes in the Bryce Amphitheater. Cliffs south of there tend to be steeper and not as fancy, because the layer below the Claron Formation is softer and washes away more easily. That undercuts the Claron rock and breaks it off before it has a chance to erode into long rows of hoodoos.

Here are some highlights from north to south, the way the road goes. If traffic is bad, you may want to take the overlooks from south to north so that you make only right turns. Stop at the visitor center for a map and possibly the guidebook mentioned under "Reading Up" (p. 220).

Farview Point

The road rises from the park entrance at about 7,800 feet, where ponderosa pines in the transition life zone take over from the treeless high desert. Here, at 8,800 feet, the transition zone gives way to the higher, moister Canadian life zone, with spruce and fir trees. That zone extends up to 9,115 feet at Rainbow Point, the beginning of the alpine zone.

Natural Bridge

This 85-foot-long, 125-foot-high arch was formed by water expanding inside an eroded fin of rock and splitting away the opening below a harder layer above. Later, running water made it deeper.

What Makes Rocks Red?

You may wonder, but your kids will really wonder what makes all the colors that appear in the canyons, especially Bryce. It's like looking into a fire. It's not just red; here you'll see pinkish red, yellow, purple, and white.

A geologist could tell you that the red and pink rocks contain hematite, which is mostly iron. Pure hematite is an ore that is mined for the iron we use in cast-iron skillets and steel beams. Iron rusts and when it does, it turns red. (That's why Mars appears red to us in the sky, too.) In these sedimentary rocks—rocks made of sand, mud, bones, and other sediment—the red color often comes from just a tiny amount of the mineral that holds together the grains.

It works the same for other colors. Something like rust produces yellow rocks, such as limonite, and purplish manganese oxide. Copper turns green (like the Statue of Liberty) and green desert rocks often have copper in them.

Hoodoos

Flowing rivers explain the deep canyons—the Grand Canyon, Glen Canyon, and Zion Canyon—but not Bryce Canyon, which is really just a notch in the Pink Cliffs. **The Bryce Amphitheater,** the park's main attraction, is a rounded gap in the cliffs 12 miles wide and 800 feet deep. When you walk down into it, you can see there's no river there, and no way a river could have made the delicate red shapes.

Here's how geologists believe Bryce came to be and is still being carved.

- Snow that falls above the cliffs in the winter melts on warm spring mornings into water that trickles down through cracks in the rocks. As the weather changes, cooling at sunset or during a cold snap, water that seeped into the cracks freezes. Frozen water takes up more space than liquid water, so the ice pushes the sides of the cracks apart, making them larger. When the morning sun again thaws the ice in a crack, a big hunk of rock might fall off a cliff. Water trickling through the rocks can make them weaker in warm weather, too. Some kinds of rock dissolve in water, as salt does. Other rocks might slowly come apart when the water seeping down brings acids from rotting plants or other chemicals from the air. Finally, melt water and runoff from thunderstorms wash away the broken rocks and gravel.
- Water and ice could have made a straight cliff at Bryce, but instead it wore down in strange and amazing shapes because of the way different kinds of rocks are mixed up here. These pink and red rocks started out as sediment that fell to the bottom of lakes. The lakes came and went over time, getting deeper and shallower and sometimes drying up completely. The water in the lakes came from rivers that started in many different places and brought sediment from many different kinds of rock.
- The hoodoos are an easy example to understand. Hoodoos are the skinny towers of red rock along the edge of the Bryce Amphitheater. On the trails near Sunset and Sunrise points, you can walk among the hoodoos, feeling as though you're walking in a forest of stones. Each hoodoo started with layers of softer rock under a layer of harder rock. Water and ice carved down through cracks in the harder rock until it reached the softer rock, then started carving much faster. Pieces of the hard rock above stayed solid, like a hat protecting the soft rock underneath it from water. Those protected rocks stayed tall, forming fins or sharp ridges. Then cracks in the sides of the ridges eroded the same way, cutting them off from the cliff. But where a piece of hard rock stayed on top, the soft rock under the hat still stood tall, like a column. You can still see the hat on some of the hoodoos. The mixture of different kinds of rocks of different hardness works in other ways all over the park, making odd shapes.

Ponderosa Canyon

Here you can see how elevation makes different kinds of habitats. Where you stand is a forest of spruce and fir of the Canadian life zone, and over the rim of the canyon you can see warmer, lower ground that supports ponderosa pine of the transition or pine-oak zone. The 1.6-mile **Agua Canyon Connecting Trail** leads down to the Under-the-Rim Trail.

Rainbow Point, Yovimpa Point

From the park's high point, over 9,100 feet, you can see all the way back down the Grand Staircase. The view stretches over 100 miles to the south, to the high Kaibab Plateau, site of the North Rim of the Grand Canyon, and Navajo Mountain, on the south shores of Lake Powell. The jagged pink cliffs here are the top step. Look for high-elevation alpine plants and trees, including short, twisted bristlecone pine trees up to 1,800 years old. The 9-mile **Riggs Spring Loop Trail** is a popular backpacking route with several backcountry campsites, but strong hikers can do it as a day hike. It leaves from Yovimpa Point and descends gradually some 1,600 feet through forest with views of the pink cliffs. The **Under-the-Rim Trail,** which runs 23 miles to Bryce Point, ends at Rainbow Point. You can escape the crowds to a gorgeous setting by taking this trail, but in late summer and fall water can be scarce.

FAIRYLAND CANYON

This relatively small canyon at the northern end of the park is full of strange rock shapes. It's less visited because the spur road to the overlook is a mile long and splits off from the main road north of the visitor center. The area along the rim here is a central part of the cross-country skiing loops because it connects the Ruby's Inn trails with the park trails. The **Fairyland Loop Trail,** usable only in the warm months, descends 900 vertical feet into the canyon, climbs back up to Sunrise Point, and then returns along the rim trail, a total distance of 8 miles. You will see fewer people than on the easiest trails right in the Bryce Amphitheater and will pass through lots of interesting rock shapes and a forest of pinyon and juniper.

NATURAL PLACES JUST OUTSIDE THE NATIONAL PARK
KODACHROME BASIN STATE PARK

East of the national park, Route 12 descends steeply from the plateau into hot semi-desert, past arid ranches and tiny towns, 14 miles to Cannonville. There, a 7-mile spur road leads south to this wonderful little state park. In the spring, when it's chilly in the national park, the weather is warm here, at 5,800 feet elevation, in the Upper Sonoran life zone of pinyon and juniper. Spring highs average in the 70s (low to mid-20s Celsius), summer highs in the 80s and low 90s (mid-20s to mid-30s Celsius). The whole park is on a comfortably small scale, perfect for families. The day-use fee is $6 per vehicle. The campground is covered on p. 225. Park contact information is under "Bryce Address Book" (p. 218).

The National Geographic Society named the basin in 1949. It sits in a desertlike landscape below pastel-colored sandstone cliffs. The rocks have many odd shapes (although nothing to compete with those at Bryce Canyon). The narrow columns of rock are called chimneys because they stand as straight and round as a chimney. (Before *National Geographic* came along, the area was called Chimney Rocks.) The chimneys were probably formed by sediment that filled hot water vents like the geysers of Yellowstone National Park. When the softer surrounding rock eroded away, the shape molded by the vent remained.

Six **nature trails** ranging from .25 mile to 3 miles meet the paved and dirt park roads. South and east of the park, dirt roads for mountain bikes and four-wheel-drive vehicles continue 10 miles to the 99-foot Grosvenor Arch, in Grand Staircase–Escalante National Monument. From there, they run down the Cottonwood Canyon and Paria River all the way to Glen Canyon National Recreation Area. Get advice from the state-park ranger station before attempting that trip.

Also in the park, **Trailhead Station** (© **800/592-1468** or 435/679-8502) operates a small store with camping supplies, food items, and the like, and also offers horseback and stagecoach rides. Trailhead Station operates March through October; store hours are daily from 9am to 5pm, later in midseason. You can join horseback rides there ($20 for 1 hr., $40 for 2 hr., $60 for 3 hr.; minimum age 5, 225-pound weight limit), and 1-hour stagecoach rides that cost $16 for anyone over 2. The company also rents six cabins with full bathrooms, refrigerators, and microwave ovens for $87 per night for up to four people. MasterCard and Visa are accepted.

CEDAR BREAKS NATIONAL MONUMENT

The monument rises to over 10,000 feet west of Bryce Canyon and north of Zion National Park. A spectacular 2,500-foot-deep amphitheater of multicolored limestone falls from the edge of the plateau. At this elevation, there's alpine life that you might recognize from the Rockies: Engelmann spruce, subalpine fir, quaking aspen, and meadows of wildflowers. You'll also find some wonderful stands of bristlecone pines, the Methuselahs of the tree world. There are a couple of hiking trails, a tiny visitor center (p. 220), and a campground (p. 225). The entrance fee is $4 per person, free for children under 17. To reach the monument, take Route 14 east from I-15 or west from U.S. 89, then Route 148 over the scenic 5-mile drive through the monument. Monument contact information is under "Bryce Address Book" (p. 218).

8 For the Active Family

BACKPACKING

Carrying your gear into the backcountry for 1 to 3 nights is the best way to get off by yourself in the park. Campsites are along the Under-the-Rim Trail that dives off the plateau at Bryce Point and runs to Rainbow Point. The Riggs Spring Loop Trail, mentioned under "Rainbow Point, Yovimpa Point" (p. 232), below Rainbow Point also has some sites. Getting below the plateau onto the trails offers a unique perspective of the colorful cliffs, and peacefulness you won't find on top. Of course, water is scarce in these parts, and you'll need to carry a lot to get you from spring to spring. You'll need a Backcountry Camping Permit from the visitor center (p. 224). Pricing ranges from $5 for 1 or 2 people up to $15 for 7 to 15; the permits are valid for 7 days. Backcountry camping isn't allowed in the Bryce Amphitheater, but you could hike through on your first or last day. The park is small, and the **Under-the-Rim Trail** that ties together Rainbow Point and Bryce Point is the longest in the park at just 23 miles. The shuttle does not reach Rainbow Point, so you will have to get a ride back to the starting point. You can shorten the route with any of various spur trails that reach up to the park road along the way. The trail has a lot of ups and downs, and because the thin air slows you down, it's easy to overestimate how much ground you can cover if you live at a low elevation.

Without hiking an entire trail, a family can get out under the stars to a not-too-remote backcountry campsite and spend a couple of nights of solitude there, making day hikes and playing during the day. In any event, you'll need a good topographic map (see "Reading Up," p. 220).

FLIGHTSEEING

You can buy tickets for flights over the park in helicopters or a fixed-wing plane in the lobby of **Ruby's Inn.** Various tour operators also have desks there. **Bryce Canyon**

Airlines and Helicopters (© 435/834-8060; ask for the flight desk) charges $59 to $349 for narrated flights lasting 15 to 70 minutes, with discounts for families and groups of eight or more.

HIKING

If you don't hike at Bryce, you're missing a lot. Choose a hike at the Bryce Amphitheater to see the park's most famous and impressive rock formations, trails that also get the heaviest use. They include the Rim Trail, Queen's Garden Trail, Navajo Loop Trail, Peekaboo Loop Trail, and Hat Shop Trail, all covered under "Bryce Amphitheater" (p. 229). From north of the amphitheater, the Fairyland Loop Trail is a longer path with fewer people (p. 232). By going south of the amphitheater, you hike away from the most interesting rock formations, but also away from most of the people. The trails here tend to be longer and more rugged; they're covered under "Backpacking," above. Maps and guides are covered under "Reading Up" (p. 220).

HORSEBACK RIDING

Rides are available from a park concessionaire in the Bryce Amphitheater and from another operator outside the park. The inside-the-park rides feature descents among the weird shapes of the canyon. The outside-the-park outfit offers longer rides.

Canyon Trail Rides (© 435/679-8665; www.canyonrides.com) offers rides that start from the corral near Sunrise Point and descend a horse trail north of the point into the canyon. A 2-hour ride, open to children as young as 7, goes down the trail to the canyon floor twice a day. It's about $40 per person. A half-day ride follows the Peekaboo Trail, which crosses most of the Bryce Amphitheater. It costs about $65 and is okay for children 10 and over. A 220-pound weight limit applies to both rides. Reserve by phone or at the lodge.

Rides offered by **Ruby's Red Canyon Horseback Rides** (© 866/782-0002 or 435/834-5341) leave from Ruby's Inn, where the company has a desk, and explore nearby Red Canyon. Kids must be 7 or older and riders under 220 pounds; half-day rides cost $65 and full-day rides, which include a box lunch, cost $100. Rides of other lengths are available, and Ruby's Inn guests get a discount.

MOUNTAIN BIKING

The trails within the park are off-limits to bikes, but the vast public lands nearby offer great mountain-biking routes. Red Canyon, in Dixie National Forest (see "Bryce Address Book," p. 218), offers the best. Bike rental is available at Ruby's Inn.

SKIING & SNOWSHOEING

The high elevation often makes for a good snowpack on top of the plateau from December to February (it's wise to call about snow conditions before going). The colored rocks are even more beautiful against white snow. There are two connecting sets of trails. Ruby's Inn grooms more than 18 miles of track for both classical and skate skiers. They connect with the Park Service trails, which are set with tracks for diagonal stride skiing but are not regularly groomed. The park's easy trails run to Fairyland Point, hug the rim from near the inn south to Inspiration Point, and then follow a forested 3.5-mile loop near Paria View. Snow machines are allowed on some of the Ruby's Inn trails but can't enter the park. (You have to bring your own snow machine; none are for rent here.) The set trails go over generally gentle terrain. Skiing down into the canyon is usually impossible due to a lack of snow, but skiing is permitted everywhere in the park if you want to break trail. **Ruby's Inn** rents skis and snowshoes for low rates ($10 a day, less for a half-day), offers inexpensive lodging packages, and stages a 3-day winter festival with races, clinics, children's events, and entertainment each February.

The Park Service lends snowshoes free at the visitor center and often leads snowshoe hikes. Snowshoeing is fun and much easier to learn than skiing—it just takes a little coordination and energy.

9 Kid-Friendly Programs

CHILDREN'S PROGRAMS

In summer rangers lead family hikes two or three times a week, depending on staff availability. Check the visitor center's bulletin board for the schedule.

The park's **Junior Ranger program,** mostly based on worksheet activities such as a crossword puzzle and a word hunt, is available free from the visitor center. Kids who do the activities, attend a ranger program, and collect a bag of trash or recycle goods get a badge and certificate.

FAMILY & ADULT PROGRAMS

During the busy summer season, five or six ranger programs run every day. In addition to guided hikes and geology talks, rangers lead evening sky viewing, which is exceptionally good thanks to the clean air, elevation, and lack of pollution. These programs usually wrap up with star gazing through the park's telescopes. If you plan on visiting the park in June, be sure to coincide your visit with the annual Astronomy Festival, which usually falls in mid-month. Throughout the summer months evening talks are offered at Bryce Canyon Lodge, and campfire programs take place nightly at both campgrounds. The schedule of programs is posted at the visitor center.

FAST FACTS: Bryce Canyon National Park

Area Code The area code is **435**.

ATMs You'll find an **ATM** in the lobby of Ruby's Inn.

Emergencies For emergencies, dial ℂ **911**.

Hospitals & Clinics **Garfield Memorial Hospital and Clinic** in Panguitch, 224 N. 440 E (ℂ **435/676-8811**), is the nearest medical facility.

Information For information, write Bryce Canyon National Park, P.O. Box 640201, Bryce Canyon, UT 84764-0201; call ℂ **435/834-5322;** or check the website www.nps.gov/brca.

Pharmacies The local drug store is **Panguitch Drug Co.** in Panguitch, 95 E. Center St. (ℂ **435/676-8850**).

Post Office There's a post office in the park lodge and one in Ruby's Inn.

Time Zone The park is on **Mountain Standard Time.**

Transit Info A free, optional shuttle bus system runs from late May through late September daily between 9am and 6pm, with stops running from a parking area just north of Ruby's Inn to Bryce Point.

Weather Updates For weather updates, the park recommends using www. accuweather.com; once at that site, type in the park's zip code, 84717, for the local forecast.

Glacier National Park

From the air, Glacier National Park seems almost like a layer cake of blues, grays, greens, and more blues jutting into the sky. Blue skies atop gray, granitic peaks atop green forests that sweep down to the shorelines of blue lakes. On the ground, though, the park towers over you as one of the most rugged landscapes in the national park system, a preserve of more than 1 million acres that isn't for the timid, yet one that offers gentle windows for peering across the roof of the Rocky Mountains.

Tucked away in northern Montana hard along the U.S.-Canadian border, Glacier is a tremendous plein-air geological museum, one that showcases erosion, forestry, biology, glaciology, and climate change. Stand atop Logan Pass and as you look about you'll see the results of what happened eons ago when tremendously thick and powerful rivers of ice, much like fingers slicing through mountains of clay, slowly ground through the bedrock. Left in their wake were deep, U-shaped valleys and canyons that later filled with snowmelt to create today's lakes.

Regardless of whether you believe in climate change or global warming, Glacier's namesake glaciers are on the retreat, melting faster than winter's snows can pile up. The meltdown has scientists predicting that midway through the 21st century, possibly as early as 2030, the glaciers could all be gone. But even if they do trickle away, Glacier's riveting landscape will remain, as inviting as ever.

As rich as the park's geology is, so too is its wildlife. Grizzly bears, wolves, mountain lions, and wolverines roam the forests and mountains, as do elk, bighorn sheep, and mountain goats. The park and its surrounding forests and wilderness areas comprise one of the most complete ecosystems in the lower 48 states, a potent reservoir of "wildness" that is a remnant of the 19th century and beyond.

While most of Glacier's landscape above 4,000 feet is accessed only by foot or on the back of a horse, down below along lower sections of the Going-to-the-Sun Road on both sides of the Continental Divide you'll find idyllic way stations for wading into glacier-fed streams and lakes, gazing across meadows to spy elk and bear, or simply pausing to spend a few hours marveling at the park.

BEST THINGS TO DO IN GLACIER NATIONAL PARK

- **Hike, hike, and hike** some more. Glacier offers myriad trails, ranging from short, easy strolls along boardwalks that offer great views to multiday backcountry treks.
- **Rent a boat** to explore Lake McDonald, or sign on for one of the scenic cruises across Lake McDonald, Swiftcurrent Lake, or Two Medicine Lake.
- **Take a full-day excursion** along Going-to-the-Sun Road in one of the park's renowned Red Jammers.
- **Search for wildlife** at Logan Pass.

For more information, see "For the Active Family," p. 265.

Glacier Address Book

Glacier National Park P.O. Box 128, West Glacier, MT 59936. ✆ **406/888-7800** and TDD 406/888-7806. www.nps.gov/glac.

Glacier Natural History Association Historic Depot 12544 Hwy. 2, P.O. Box 310, West Glacier, MT 59936. ✆ **406/888-5756**. www.glacierassociation.org. For books and maps.

Glacier Institute 137 Main St., P.O. Box 1887, Kalispell, MT 59903. ✆ **406/755-1211**. www.glacierinstitute.org. For youth camps, outdoor education courses.

Flathead National Forest 1935 3rd Ave. E., Kalispell, MT 59901. ✆ **406/758-5204**. www.fs.fed.us/r1/flathead.

Blackfeet Tribe P.O. Box 850, Browning, MT 59417. ✆ **406/338-7521**. www.blackfeetnation.com.

Glacier Park, Inc. P.O. Box 2025, Columbia Falls, MT 59912. ✆ **406/892-2525**. Fax 406/892-1375. www.glacierparkinc.com.

Belton Chalets P.O. Box 188, West Glacier, MT 59936. ✆ **888/345-2649**. www.sperrychalet.com. Backcountry chalets.

Sun Tours 29 Glacier Ave., P.O. Box 234, East Glacier, MT 59434. ✆ **800/786-9220** or 406/226-9220. www.glaciersuntours.com.

Glacier Park Boat Co. P.O. Box 5262, Kalispell, MT 59903. ✆ **406/257-2426**. www.glacierparkboats.com.

Whitefish Chamber of Commerce 520 E. 2nd St., Whitefish, MT 59937. ✆ **877/862-3548** or 406/862-3501. www.whitefishchamber.com.

1 History: Going to the Sun

The Great Northern Railway arrived in Glacier country in the early 1890s when tracks were laid over Marias Pass, a saddle low in the mountains at an elevation of 5,220 feet just south of the present-day park. Before the end of the decade, a trickle of tourists was discovering the area and the railroad's trains were making regular stops at Belton, which would later change its name to West Glacier.

At the time there was no road through Glacier. Those who got off the train at Belton took a stagecoach to the toe of Lake McDonald, where they'd board a boat for the trip to the Snyder Hotel, which once existed where the Lake McDonald Lodge now stands. But as more and more people decided they'd like to visit this rugged land in northern Montana, the railroad began to realize there was a market waiting to be tapped. As a result, the Great Northern got into the hotel business, building a string of chalets in Glacier that guests could reach by horseback.

Not long after Glacier officially became a park in 1910, park officials, railroad officials, and other concessionaires began to clamor for a road that would cross the park's jagged, demanding landscape. But they couldn't agree on its path. Some thought it should run on the north side of Lake McDonald, some thought it should head northeast to Waterton Lake in Canada, others wanted it to run past Gunsight Pass, and some thought it should connect Apgar Village to Many Glacier. Louis Hill, president of the Great Northern Railroad, preferred that last option.

"When the road finally goes through," he wrote to Lyman Sperry, the railroad's general passenger agent, "I am inclined to think that it should be farther north for the purpose of enabling travelers to see as much of the mountain country as possible, and to have an ultimate destination in the park, probably in the vicinity of Many Glacier Hotel."

But the U.S. Bureau of Public Roads thought it had the best route, as it surveyed a proposed course over the Continental Divide for the Going-to-the-Sun Road in 1914. This path over 6,664-foot Logan Pass, the bureau noted, provided not only the lowest route across the park's interior, but also the most logical.

While the debate dragged on, J. E. Lewis, who owned a lodge on the east shore of Lake McDonald (which evolved into today's Lake McDonald Lodge), in 1919 built his own road, a 3-mile stretch that jogged along the shore. Two years later, after brushing other proposals aside, the government finally joined the road-building effort when Congress provided the National Park Service with construction funds.

By 1925, not only had work on the western side of the park pushed the road as far as Avalanche Creek, but work on the eastern side saw workers nudging the road toward Logan Pass. Between 1926 and 1933 the bulk of the road was constructed and on July 15, 1933, after an investment of $2 million in federal funds and 3 decades of planning, surveying, and building, the Going-to-the-Sun Road officially opened to traffic.

Though more than 300 men worked on gouging the road out of the mountains, amazingly only one worker, a foreman who fell 60 feet to his death, was killed during the 50-mile-long road's construction.

The road, both a National Historic Landmark and a National Civil Engineering Landmark, is a genius of construction, particularly when you consider that much of the work was done with picks and shovels, dynamite and horse teams. It showcases gorgeous geologic wonders, such as Heaven's Peak, Bird Woman Falls, and Jackson Glacier. U-shaped valleys, evidence of the park's glaciated past, swoop down above and below the road in spots. And the road shows off engineering wonders, such as the West Side Tunnel, which has windows through which you can view Heaven's Peak if you glance quickly enough, and the Triple Arches Bridge.

So magnificent is the road and the landscape through which it passes that at one point in the park's history it was estimated that more than 95% of Glacier's visitors based their visit around the road and its offerings.

But the route is not for the jittery, as it gains more than 1,400 feet in 32 miles and is very narrow in places. Visitors with a fear of heights should take a van or Red Jammer tour or shuttle. Because of the road's narrowness, oversize vehicles and trailers must use U.S. 2.

Today the road is being rebuilt and restored in sections, a process that is expected to run 8 to 10 years and cost between $140 million and $170 million (as of estimates from 2002).

2 Orientation

Sprawling across 1,013,572 acres of mostly pristine wilderness, Glacier National Park is a rugged, remote landscape traversed completely by just one road. In transecting the park, the Going-to-the-Sun Road ties together West Glacier on the western border

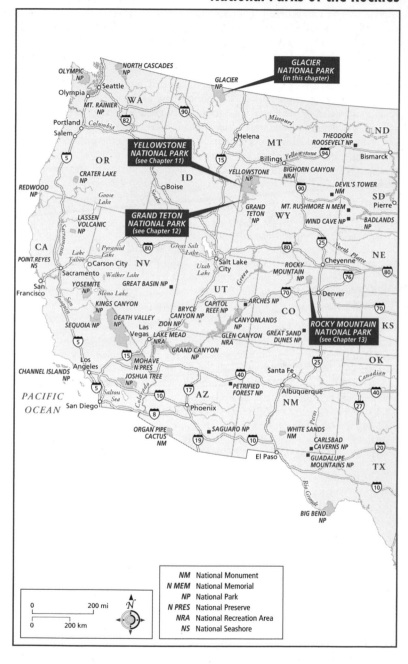

OLYMPIC NP

NORTH CASCADES NP

GLACIER NATIONAL PARK (in this chapter)

GLACIER NP

Seattle

Olympia

MT. RAINIER NP

WA

90

82

Columbia

Portland

Salem

OR

5

Helena

MT

Billings

Missouri

THEODORE ROOSEVELT NP

94

ND

Bismarck

CRATER LAKE NP

YELLOWSTONE NATIONAL PARK (see Chapter 11)

ID

Boise

15

Yellowstone

YELLOWSTONE NP

BIGHORN CANYON NRA

90

DEVIL'S TOWER NM

SD

Pierre

REDWOOD NP

Goose Lake

Snake

GRAND TETON NATIONAL PARK (see Chapter 12)

GRAND TETON NP

MT. RUSHMORE N MEM

WY

WIND CAVE NP

BADLANDS NP

LASSEN VOLCANIC NP

Sacramento

CA

Pyramid Lake

Lake Tahoe

80

Great Salt Lake

80

North Platte

NE

POINT REYES NS

Carson City

NV

Walker Lake

Salt Lake City

Cheyenne

76

80

San Francisco

YOSEMITE NP

Mono Lake

Utah Lake

Green

ROCKY MOUNTAIN NP

25

Denver

Sacramento

San Joaquin

KINGS CANYON NP

GREAT BASIN NP

UT

70

ARCHES NP

70

SEQUOIA NP

DEATH VALLEY NP

BRYCE CANYON NP

CAPITOL REEF NP

CANYONLANDS NP

CO

ROCKY MOUNTAIN NATIONAL PARK (see Chapter 13)

KS

Las Vegas

ZION NP

LAKE MEAD NRA

GLEN CANYON NRA

GREAT SAND DUNES NP

OK

Los Angeles

CHANNEL ISLANDS NP

15

MOHAVE N PRES

JOSHUA TREE NP

Colorado

GRAND CANYON NP

Santa Fe

40

25

5

Salton Sea

17

AZ

PETRIFIED FOREST NP

Albuquerque

40

27

PACIFIC OCEAN

San Diego

10

Phoenix

8

NM

Pecos

WHITE SANDS NM

ORGAN PIPE CACTUS NM

19

SAGUARO NP

10

CARLSBAD CAVERNS NP

20

El Paso

GUADALUPE MOUNTAINS NP

TX

Rio Grande

10

BIG BEND NP

NM	National Monument
N MEM	National Memorial
NP	National Park
N PRES	National Preserve
NRA	National Recreation Area
NS	National Seashore

0   200 mi

0   200 km

N

with St. Mary on the eastern boundary. Between those two towns, it connects the dots of Apgar Village, Lake McDonald, Logan Pass, and a small handful of campgrounds.

Near East Glacier on the park's southeastern corner, a 9-mile-long road dives into the park to reach Two Medicine with its campground, trail heads, and boating possibilities. The Many Glacier region with its historic lodge, campground, and trail heads is accessed by a 12-mile-long road that enters the park just west of Babb.

While most park visitors stick closely to the Going-to-the-Sun Road and its way stations, tremendous backcountry travel exists throughout the park. Narrow, unpaved roads that make short forays into Glacier provide access for some of the campgrounds and trails, while trail heads can be found at various spots along the park's circumference.

Roughly 70% of Glacier's visitors enter through West Glacier and Apgar Village, a small enclave of lodgings, restaurants, and activities on the southwest shore of Lake McDonald.

ARRIVING
BY CAR & RV

There is no quick way to reach Glacier by road, unless you live in the neighborhood. And since Montana is a very big neighborhood, even that could entail quite a drive. You can reach the park from **U.S. Highways 2 and 89.** If you tow a **trailer,** be advised that trailers longer than 21 feet or wider than 8 feet (including mirrors) are prohibited from the steepest sections of the Going-to-the-Sun Road and instead are directed to U.S. 2 that runs along the park's south boundary.

BY AIR

Cities closest to the park with airline service are **Kalispell,** 29 miles southwest of the park, and **Great Falls,** 143 miles southeast of the park. **Glacier Park International Airport** (© 406/257-5994; www.glacierairport.com), just north of Kalispell, is served by Big Sky, Delta, Horizon, Northwest, and United. Rental-car agencies include Avis (© 406/257-2727), Budget (© 406/755-7500), Hertz (© 406/758-2220), and National (© 406/257-7144). **Great Falls International** airport (© 406/727-3404; www.gtfairport.com) has all the same airlines plus Allegiant Air. Rental-car agencies here include Avis (© 406/761-7610), Alamo/National (© 406/727-0273), Dollar (© 406/453-3535), Hertz (© 406/761-6641), and National (© 406/453-4386).

BY TRAIN

On its way between Chicago and Seattle **Amtrak's** *Empire Builder* (© 800/872-7245; www.amtrak.com) stops twice daily at West Glacier, at Essex upon request, and at East Glacier from May 1 to October 1.

VISITOR INFORMATION
NATIONAL PARK VISITOR CENTERS

There are three visitor centers in Glacier, each with its own flavor. Only the Apgar Village center is open year-round; the other two, at Logan Pass and St. Mary, are shuttered through the winter. The open dates are approximate; big storms may delay the opening (or speed the closing) of the centers. Direct questions to park headquarters, © 406/888-7800.

Apgar Village Visitor Center   The main Park Service visitor center is in the middle of Apgar Village at the south end of Lake McDonald. Small compared to most other parks' main visitor centers, this one offers the basics: a small area for guidebooks, maps, postcards, posters, and kids' games; a large raised relief topographic map of the

BRITISH COLUMBIA WATERTON LAKES NATIONAL PARK Milk ALBERTA

CANADA UNITED STATES

GLACIER NATIONAL PARK 89

Cut Bank

Whitefish Browning Box Elder

Kalispell 2

Sandpoint 2 89 15 Ft. Benton

Lake Pend Oreille Flathead Lake Missouri

Coeur d'Alene Polson Great Falls

93

IDAHO Bitterroot Range Missoula 200 MONTANA 87

Helena

Nezperce 12 Deer Lodge

Grangeville Anaconda Butte

Clearwater Mts. 93

95 Bozeman 90

89

Salmon Dillon 191

Bitterroot Range 15

Challis YELLOWSTONE NATIONAL PARK

N 0 40 mi
0 40 km Airport WYOMING

200

park so you can get your bearings; a counter staffed by seasonal rangers to field your questions; and two LCD screens—one that relays hiker shuttle stops and another listing the availability status of the park's campgrounds. There is a tiny public restroom attached to the center. A short walk down a path leads you to the Apgar Transit Center, where you can catch a park shuttle, use interactive kiosks to help plan your day, and view videos of various locations in the park.

2 miles inside the west entrance, just off the Going-to-the-Sun Rd. 𝄡 406/888-7800. May 1–June 23 daily 9am–5pm; June 24 to Labor Day daily 8am–7pm; Sept 4–Oct 31 daily 8am–5pm; Nov 1–Apr 30 Sat–Sun 9am–4:30pm.

Logan Pass This facility atop Logan Pass offers exhibits on the alpine ecosystem that covers the upper third of the park. Plaster casts of animal tracks (see how small your hand is compared to the grizzly's paw!), stuffed birds, and examples of plants such as the delicate glacier lily and tenacious alpine fireweed that grow at this high elevation are on display. You'll also find rangers here to field your questions, a fireplace to warm up next to, and restrooms. Behind the center a boardwalk trail, one of the most popular in the park, leads across flower-dotted meadows to Hidden Lake.

Located at Logan Pass along the Going-to-the-Sun Rd. 18 miles west of St. Mary. 𝄡 406/888-7800. June 1–24 daily 9:30am–4:30pm; June 24 to Labor Day daily 9am–7pm; Sept 4–30 daily 9:30am–4:30pm. Closed Oct to late May.

St. Mary   This small center offers the basics: a counter with rangers where you can arrange backcountry treks; books, postcards and posters; and some geologic exhibits on glaciation.

On Going-to-the-Sun Rd. at the St. Mary Entrance on the east side of the park. © 406/888-7800. May 14–21 and Sept 16–30 daily 8am–5pm; May 22–June 25 daily 7am–5pm; June 26 to Labor Day daily 7am–9pm; Sept 4–15 daily 7am–5pm. Closed Oct to mid-May.

COMMERCIAL VISITOR CENTERS
West Glacier   The Glacier Natural History Association operates a nice center in the old passenger train depot along U.S. 2 at West Glacier across from the Belton Chalet. Inside is a wonderful array of books, guidebooks, maps, posters, postcards, and pins and other park souvenirs. In fact, this was the only place where I could find a large, waterproof USGS topographic map covering the entire park. And it was only $10. The display of early Great Northern Railroad passenger train china also is of interest to railroad buffs.

Historic Depot–Hwy. 2, West Glacier. © 406/888-5756. www.glacierassociation.org. Mon–Fri 8am–4:30pm.

READING UP
Many of these books are available from the Glacier Natural History Association, listed at the beginning of the chapter.

   Natural History: *Crown of the Continent* by Ralph Waldt (Riverbend Publishing, $25) provides a naturalist's voice and outstanding photography to chronicle the beauty of the region considered "the last great wilderness of the Rocky Mountains."

   Hiking: *The Hiker's Guide to Glacier National Park* (Glacier Natural History Association, $11) covers the high, and low, country in the park. Trail descriptions cover elevation changes, point out which topographical maps are needed, and mention camping restrictions. *Hiking Glacier and Waterton Lakes National Parks* by Erik Molvar-Step (Falcon Press, $15) covers not only Glacier, but adjoining Waterton Lakes National Park in Canada.

   Kids: *The Great Yellowstone, Grand Teton, Glacier Activity Book* (Rising Sun, $7.95; www.northlandpub.com) is chock-full of word searches, crossword puzzles, mazes, journals, and other activities to keep young minds busy.

THE NATIONAL PARK IN BRIEF
Apgar Village
In the conifer forest near Glacier's west entrance at the toe of Lake McDonald, this charming, little center of activity arguably is the park's best welcome center. It is home to a visitor center/ranger station where you can get the latest details on campsite availability, backcountry permits, and boat rentals. You'll also find the Apgar Transit Center, where you can catch one of the park's free shuttle buses. These buses run between the village and St. Mary with stops at trail heads and campgrounds along the way. Also there: lodgings, restaurants, groceries, and other shops. Just off the Going-to-the-Sun Road, this village offers a good orientation to the park.

Going-to-the-Sun Road
The only way to cross Glacier without walking or riding a horse is via this historic road that slices east and west across the park's interior between West Glacier and Saint Mary. Along the way it climbs to the roof of the Continental Divide at **Logan Pass,** where you'll find a nice visitor center, great hiking trails, and plenty of mountain goats.

From atop the pass you are afforded expansive views of both high country and U-shaped glacial valleys sculpted thousands of years ago by rivers of ice. At various points along the 50-mile-long road are trail heads to lead you either deep into the backcountry or out on shorter day hikes. **Lake McDonald Lodge** is perhaps Glacier's most popular resting spot thanks to its picturesque hotel on the lakeshore, small complex of shops and restaurants, scenic cruises, and ever-present fleet of Red Jammers. From here you can hike to the **Sperry Chalet** or take a horseback ride into the forest. The road is undergoing a much-needed, end-to-end, rehabilitation, and you could encounter slight construction delays.

Many Glacier

Far removed from the park's main centers of activity, the **Many Glacier** area offers quick access into the park's backcountry via a network of trails and scenic cruises. Perhaps the most breathtaking vistas of any of the park's lodges are had from the **Many Glacier Hotel.** Secluded on the northeastern shore of Swiftcurrent Lake, the majestic lodge is an elegant throwback to when railroads brought visitors to the park. Not far from the lodge are the **Swift Current Motor Inn** and the **Many Glacier Campground.**

The Gateway Towns

Thanks to the park's far-off location in northern Montana along the Canadian border, there are no sizable towns near the park. And only two, **West Glacier** and **St. Mary,** can be considered true gateway towns as they anchor opposite ends of the Going-to-the-Sun Road. West Glacier, near the road's western terminus, is the best-known gateway and welcomes most of the park's visitors. Minutes from Apgar Village, West Glacier offers a small collection of shops, lodgings, and eateries. On the eastern end of the Going-to-the-Sun Road lies St. Mary, a largely seasonal town that shutters its tourist businesses come winter. **East Glacier,** near the Two Medicine Entrance, is roughly 33 miles from Saint Mary and is home to the park's flagship **Glacier Park Lodge.** There's a small outpost at **Polebridge,** which lies across from the entrance of the same name on the park's northwestern shoulder.

3 Getting Around

BY CAR OR RV

A car is about the easiest, most flexible way you're going to navigate this sprawling park, unless you plan to spend your vacation in the backcountry. One main road cuts the park in half: the Going-to-the-Sun Road. Slicing through the park from West Glacier to St. Mary, the 50-mile road takes you past the park's main attractions—Apgar Village with its visitor center (see "Visitor Information," p. 240), campground, and backcountry permit center; Lake McDonald with its historic accommodations, fleet of Red Jammers, and scenic lake cruises; Logan Pass with its visitor center and hiking trails; and St. Mary, which offers more lakeside accommodations and a third visitor center.

Other roads make only a few brief forays into the park: The Many Glacier Road stabs just 12 miles from Babb to Many Glacier; the road to Two Medicine runs 9 miles; the Camas Road spans but 11 miles to connect Apgar Village with the Camas Creek Entrance; the Inside North Fork Road meanders 28 dirt-and-gravel miles from the Fish Creek Campground on the north shore of Lake McDonald past the Logging Creek and Quartz Creek campgrounds en route to Polebridge; the road to Bowman Lake runs 6 miles; and the route between Polebridge and Kintla Lake Road traverses 14 miles.

BY RED JAMMER

A great day, or half-day, can be spent touring Glacier National Park in one of the historic Red Jammer touring cars. These 17-passenger, fire-engine-red buses—which take their name from the way drivers once had to "jam" through the transmission's gears—have removable canvas tops that are stowed away on sunny days. Thick woolen blankets help ward off any chill, while the drivers regale you with park history. Half-day trips typically include visiting Logan Pass from Lake McDonald or Many Glacier, or going into Two Medicine from Glacier Park Lodge at East Glacier. Daylong trips, which might be a bit much for youngsters, traverse the Going-to-the-Sun Road with stops at Apgar Village, Lake McDonald, Logan Pass, Rising Sun Motor Inn, St. Mary, or Many Glacier, depending on your starting point. Trips depart daily from Lake McDonald, Glacier Park Lodge, and Many Glacier Lodge. For fares and times, contact Glacier Park, Inc. (see "Glacier Address Book," p. 237).

BY TOUR VAN

An interesting alternative to the Red Jammer tours are the van excursions offered by **Sun Tours** (© 800/786-9220 or 406/226-9220; www.glaciersuntours.com), a Native American–owned company that provides Blackfeet guides onboard for expert interpretation. To the Blackfeet nation, the mountains of Glacier were known as the "Backbone of the World." Through the guides' perspectives you'll come to know how the Blackfeet used, and revered, this landscape. They share the tribe's philosophical views of the landscape and provide insights into what plants were traditionally relied upon for food and medicine. These enclosed, air-conditioned vans will pick you up at your motel or campground in the East Glacier, St. Mary, West Glacier, and Browning areas.

BY SHUTTLE BUS

In June 2007 the park unveiled a **shuttle bus system** that navigates the Going-to-the-Sun Road between Apgar Village and St. Mary. It's a great addition, for during the busy summer season the road can quickly become backed up with tourist traffic and the stream of Red Jammer tours. The shuttle buses stop at campgrounds and trail heads along the road. Glacier Park, Inc., connects with the park shuttles at the St. Mary's Visitor Center with a convenient **hiker's shuttle** to trail heads into the Many Glacier area. While the park shuttles were free, the Glacier Park shuttles cost $8 per person, one-way.

4 Planning Your Outings

WHEN TO GO

July and August are the most popular months to visit Glacier, during the summer break from school but after the worst of the bug season. Temperatures can be warm, with average highs near 80°F (27°C); days in the 90s (30s Celsius) are rare. While spring can be damp, summer usually is a period of long, dry days with an occasional thunderstorm.

The park remains open year-round, but winter's snows seal off most of the Going-to-the-Sun Road, which closes for the winter on the Monday following the third Sunday in October if snows haven't already shut it down. Still, the road is plowed from Apgar Village to Lake McDonald Lodge, opening up wonderful cross-country skiing and snowshoeing possibilities. In spring the road usually opens across the park by early June.

HOW MUCH TIME TO SPEND

It can take awhile to get to Glacier from most places—too long to justify less than 4 or 5 days. If you want to sample the backcountry, another 2 or 3 days would be great. Because there's only one main road through Glacier, unless you're planning to explore the little-used Inside North Fork Road, head over to Many Glacier, or visit Two Medicine, crossing the park isn't overly time-consuming, and there are plenty of pull-offs for dawdlers.

HOW FAR TO PLAN AHEAD

Even though two million people a year visit Glacier, it's not too difficult to land a room. Just the same, reserving a room 6 to 9 months ahead of your trip isn't a bad idea.

Weather Chart: West Glacier

	Avg. High (°F/°C)	Avg. Low (°F/°C)	Precipitation (in.)
January	32/0	18/–8	3.2
February	35/2	18/–8	1.8
March	43/6	22/–6	2
April	54/12	30/–1	2
May	65/18	38/3	2.7
June	71/22	44/7	3.3
July	79/26	48/9	1.9
August	79/26	47/8	1.3
September	70/21	38/3	1.6
October	55/13	33/1	2.9
November	35/2	25/–4	3.7
December	30/–1	17/–8	3

WHAT TO PACK
CLOTHING

During the summer, bring clothes for warm days and cool evenings, with some rain gear kept handy just in case of a passing thunderstorm. If you take one of the scenic boat cruises, a light jacket wouldn't hurt if a breeze kicks up. Bring a swimsuit for the lakes. Good hiking shoes will help you navigate the trails. Visit in late summer or early fall and you'd be wise to pack some colder outerwear, heavy boots, and even some gloves and a warm hat: An early winter squall on September 12, 2005, dumped 18 inches of snow on Logan Pass.

GEAR

Bring bug repellent for biting insects. If you're planning a backcountry trip, purchase some bear spray when you reach the park. Car campers should bring good, waterproof gear, including a tarp or other roof for the picnic table. Summer nighttime lows are in the 40s and 50s (single digits to midteens Celsius).

KEEPING SAFE & HEALTHY

See "Dealing with Hazards," in chapter 2, for tips on dangerous wildlife, drowning, and lightning. Here are other things to watch out for at Glacier:

BIKE SAFETY

The Going-to-the-Sun Road is narrow, and an ongoing rehabilitation project is going to make bike travel on it tricky for the foreseeable future. This definitely is not a park for family cycling.

FALLS

There are some overlooks along the Going-to-the-Sun Road that feature precipitous drops. Take care to rein in your children.

SNOW & ICE

While frolicking in snow and on glaciers can be fun, it can also be slippery, so take care not to find yourself hurtling out of control down a snowfield and into trees or rocks. Also, snow bridges could collapse under your weight, dropping you deep into a crevasse or an icy stream of snowmelt.

ANIMALS

Most visitors to Glacier won't encounter grizzly bears, even if they head into the back-country. Still, encounters can happen. In late August 2005, a man and his daughter rounded a corner on the Grinnell Glacier Trail in the Many Glacier area and ran smack into a grizzly sow and her two cubs. Both sustained serious injuries, but lived to talk about it. Also, mountain goats abound in the alpine meadows along the Hidden Lake Trail above the Logan Pass Visitor Center. While they seem unfazed by humans and appear tame, these are wild animals with sharp horns and can be unpredictable. Keep your distance.

5 Family-Friendly Accommodations

CAMPGROUNDS

NATIONAL PARK CAMPGROUNDS

Glacier's developed campgrounds offer a wide variety of experiences, from being in tightly knit enclaves with little privacy to near-wilderness experiences in remote settings.

To help you plan, Glacier officials have developed one of the Park Service's most user-friendly and helpful websites. Not only does the site provide basic information such as the cost of a night in a campground and whether there are flush or vault toilets, but it has a handy feature that allows you to tell when a particular campground filled up. For an overview of camping, go to www.nps.gov/glac/planyourvisit/camping. htm. From this page you can click on the "Detailed Camping" link to find information on specific campgrounds and even learn at what time the campground ran out of sites the previous day.

If you can't find all your answers on this website, call park headquarters (© **406/ 888-7800**) with any questions. Once you're in the park, the visitor center at Apgar Village has a handy LCD screen that tracks campground availabilities.

You have a wide range of campground possibilities in Glacier. Some easily accessible, some not so easily accessible. Paved roads lead to campgrounds at **Apgar,** near the West Glacier entrance; **Avalanche Creek,** just up from the head of Lake McDonald; **Fish Creek,** on the west side of Lake McDonald; **Many Glacier,** in the northeast part of the park; **Rising Sun,** on the north side of St. Mary Lake; **St. Mary,** on the east side of the park; and **Two Medicine,** in the southeast part of the park near East Glacier. You get to **Sprague Creek,** near the West Glacier entrance, by way of a paved road; you can't take towed vehicles there. Travel by narrow, dirt roads to five other campgrounds. These sites do not have utility connections, but they do offer fire pits, picnic tables, washrooms (with sinks and flush toilets), and cold running water. Campsites are available on a first-come, first-served basis, payable by cash or check, except for Fish Creek and St. Mary campgrounds, where sites can be reserved by credit card (Discover, MasterCard, Visa) through the **National Recreation Reservation Service** (© **877/444-6777;** www.recreation.gov).

There are a few campsites for **bicyclists** at Apgar, Sprague Creek, Avalanche, Fish Creek, Many Glacier, Two Medicine, Rising Sun, and St. Mary campgrounds, for $5 per person. The sites at Fish Creek and St. Mary can be reserved.

Apgar   This is the park's largest campground, and one of the most conducive to family fun. Nestled in trees just off the south shore of Lake McDonald, it's close to both the water and the amenities of Apgar Village. An amphitheater that fronts the lake offers nightly ranger programs. While there are no shower facilities, a quick dip in the lake will keep you fresh.

Campgrounds in the Glacier Area

Campground	Elevation	Total Sites	RV Hookups	Dump Station	Toilets	Drinking Water
Apgar	3160	194	No	Yes	Yes	Yes
Avalanche	3,200	87	No	No	Yes	Yes
Bowman Lake	4,030	48	No	No	Yes	Yes
Cut Bank	N/A	14	No	No	Yes	No
Fish Creek	3200	178	No	Yes	Yes	Yes
Glacier	3,900	160	Yes	Yes	Yes	Yes
Johnson's	4,500	157	Yes	Yes	Yes	Yes
Kintla Lake	4,010	13	No	No	Yes	Yes
Lake Five	N/A	51	Yes	Yes	Yes	Yes
Logging Creek	3,440	7	No	No	Yes	Yes
Many Glacier	4,880	110	No	Yes	Yes	Yes
Quartz Creek	3,460	7	No	No	Yes	Yes
Rising Sun	4,520	83	No	Yes	Yes	Yes
Sprague Creek	3,160	25	No	No	Yes	Yes
St. Mary	4,520	148	No	Yes	Yes	Yes
St. Mary-Glacier Park KOA	N/A	171	Yes	Yes	Yes	Yes
Two Medicine	5,170	99	No	No	Yes	Yes
West Glacier KOA	N/A	132	Yes	Yes	Yes	Yes
Y Lazy R.	N/A	40	Yes	Yes	Yes	Yes

On the south side of Apgar Village, 2⅓ miles from the West Glacier entrance. © **406/888-7800**. 194 sites, 25 can handle RVs up to 40 ft. $20 site. Closed mid-Oct to early May. **Amenities:** Flush toilets, dump station, nearby to camp store, cold-water sinks, picnic tables, fire pits and grates, amphitheater, boat rentals, horseback rides, bear boxes.

Avalanche Campground   Towering cedar and hemlock trees, some of the park's old-growth forests that escaped the logger's saw, keep this popular campground cool and shady. Nearby is the trail head to Avalanche Lake, a wonderful, family-friendly 4-mile round-trip hike with an incredibly scenic payoff. The Trail of the Cedars, also close by, offers a great primer on the forest. Lake McDonald Lodge is a short drive away.

16 miles from west entrance. © **406/888-7800**. 87 sites, 50 can handle RVs up to 26 ft. $20 site. Closed after Labor Day to mid-June. **Amenities:** Flush toilets, cold-water sinks, picnic tables, fire pits and grates, amphitheater, bear boxes.

Showers	Fire Pits/Grills	Laundry	Public Phones	Reservations	Fees	Open
No	Yes	No	Yes	No	$20	May to mid-Oct
No	Yes	No	No	No	$20	Mid-June to Labor Day
No	Yes?	No	No	No	$15	Mid-May to mid-Sept
No	Yes	No	No	No	$10	Memorial Day to late Sept
No	Yes	No	No	No	$23	June to Labor Day
Yes	Yes	Yes	Yes	Yes	$20–$27	Mid-May to Oct
Yes	Yes	Yes	Yes	Yes	$19–$38	May–Oct
No	Yes	No	No	No	$15	Mid-May to mid-Sept
Yes	Yes	Yes	Yes	Yes	$20–$60	May–Oct
No	Yes	No	No	No	$10	July to Labor Day
No	Yes	No	No	No	$20	Memorial Day to mid-Sept
No	Yes	No	No	No	$10	July to Labor Day
Yes	Yes	No	No	No	$20	Memorial Day to mid-Sept
No	Yes	No	No	No	$20	Mid-May to mid-Sept
No	Yes	No	No	Yes	$23	Memorial Day to late Sept
Yes	Yes	Yes	Yes	Yes	$27–$50	Mid-May to Oct
No	Yes	No	No	No	$20	Memorial Day to mid-Sept
Yes	Yes	Yes	Yes	Yes	$27–$47	May–Oct
No	Yes	No	No	Yes	$15–$18	June to mid-Sept

Bowman Lake   One of the more difficult campgrounds to reach, because of a long, bumpy dirt road, Bowman Lake offers peace and quiet thanks to its remoteness. Fishing, boating, and hiking are right out your tent's front door. Just be sure to pack plenty of bug repellent and mosquito netting to ward off the bugs day and night.

33 miles from the west entrance. (C) **406/888-7800.** 48 sites, RVs not recommended. $15 site. Closed mid-Sept to late-May. **Amenities:** Pit toilets, picnic tables, fire pits and grates, running water, boating, swimming, bear boxes.

Cut Bank   The limited number of tent sites, and the 5-mile-long dead-end access road, ensure that this campground offers solitude. With the few number of well-spaced sites, you don't feel like you're in a tent village. However, unless your family enjoys hiking, this probably is not a great spot to base your visit. Though there are no major lakes nearby, there are trail heads that will quickly lead you into the park's interior.

18 miles from St. Mary entrance, 5 miles from U.S. 89. ℂ 406/888-7800. 14 sites, RVs not recommended. $10 site. Closed late Sept until Memorial Day. **Amenities:** Pit toilets, picnic tables, fire pits and grates, running water, bear boxes.

Fish Creek   Located on the north shore of Lake McDonald, this is one of the most popular campgrounds in the park and one of just two that allow you to reserve a spot. Tall, shady trees keep the campground cool and provide some privacy. Loops C and D offer some great sites that overlook the lake. The trail head to Rocky Point lies in Loop C, and the campground's amphitheater guarantees nightly interpretive programs.

4½ miles from west entrance, 2½ miles from Apgar Village. ℂ 800/365-2267. http://reservations.nps.gov. 178 sites, 18 sites can handle RVs up to 35 ft. $23 site. Closed after Labor Day to May. **Amenities:** Flush toilets, dump station, cold-water sinks, picnic tables, fire pits and grates, amphitheater, boating, swimming, bear boxes.

Kintla Lake   Thanks to this campground's remote location, those who make the trek for one of its sites are rewarded with quiet. If you like to paddle, bring your canoe or kayak along to explore Kintla Lake, which is closed to motorized watercraft. Not only is the trout fishing excellent, but if you're lucky you might hear the baleful howling of wolves at night, a memorable event while you're gathered around your campfire.

14 miles from Polebridge. ℂ 406/888-7800. 13 sites, RVs not recommended. $15 site. Closed mid-Sept to Memorial Day. **Amenities:** Pit toilets, fire pits and grates, running water, boating, swimming, bear boxes.

Logging Creek   Like the Kintla Lake campground, this one is for those in search of serenity. Determined hikers can tackle the 12-mile round-trip hike to Logging Lake with its great views. But this probably is not best for families with young children, due in part to the long drive in over a dusty, washboard-riddled road and the lack of activities. *Note:* This campground was closed in 2007 due to hazardous trees and washed-out campsites. Call the park to check on its availability.

8 miles from Polebridge. ℂ 406/888-7800. 8 sites, RVs not recommended. $10 site. Closed after Labor Day to July. **Amenities:** Pit toilets, picnic tables, fire pits and grates, running water, bear boxes.

Many Glacier   This campground is a very short walk from Swiftcurrent Lake. Well treed in general, many of the spots offer good privacy, although others seem a bit too close to one another for my liking. Still, the setting is one of the most dramatic for developed campgrounds. Right across the street is the Swiftcurrent Motor Inn and down the road 5 minutes is Many Glacier Lodge with its dining room, gift shop, boat dock, and convenience store.

21 miles from St. Mary at the west end of Many Glacier Rd., across from Swiftcurrent Motor Inn. ℂ 406/888-7800. 110 sites, 13 can handle RVs up to 35 ft. $20 site. No reservations. Closed late Sept until Memorial Day. **Amenities:** Flush toilets, dump station, cold-water sinks, picnic tables, fire pits and grates, bear boxes. Restaurants, boat tours, camp store nearby.

Quartz Creek   Like the Logging Creek campground, this tiny campground offers peace and quiet, but limited views and limited activities for youngsters. No water is available, either.

5⅔ miles from Polebridge. ℂ 406/888-7800. 7 sites, RVs not recommended. $10 site. Closed after Labor Day to June. **Amenities:** Pit toilets, picnic tables, fire pits and grates, bear boxes.

Rising Sun   This is a great spot if you want to explore the eastern side of the park. Just across the Going-to-the-Sun Road from St. Mary Lake, this campground is well spaced with plenty of trees to provide shade and keep things cool. The Rising Sun Lodge is nearby with its general store and restaurant, you've got nightly programs at the campground's amphitheater, and scenic boat tours on the lake are launched nearby.

6¼ miles from St. Mary entrance. ✆ **406/888-7800.** 83 sites, 10 sites can handle RVs up to 25 ft. $20 site. Closed mid-Sept until Memorial Day. **Amenities:** Flush toilets, hot-water coin-operated showers, dump station, cold-water sinks, picnic tables, fire pits and grates, bear boxes. Restaurant, camp store, and boat tours nearby.

Sprague Creek   Located on the shore of Lake McDonald, this is a tent-camper's haven since trailers aren't allowed. The location isn't bad; my only gripe is that the campground runs along a sliver of land pinched between the road and the water. Still, land a site along the lake and you're fairly well shielded from the road noise by the thick stand of trees, although you won't enjoy the quiet you'll find in many other campgrounds that are farther away from the Going-to-the-Sun Road. You will enjoy sweeping views of the lake, though, and the Lake McDonald Lodge complex is a short drive away. No towed units are allowed.

9½ miles from the west entrance along the Going-to-the-Sun Rd. ✆ **406/888-7800.** 25 sites, tents only. $20 site. Closed mid-Sept to mid-May. **Amenities:** Flush toilets, cold-water sinks, picnic area, fire pits and grates, running water, fishing, swimming, bear boxes. Camp store, restaurant, Red Jammer tours, horseback rides nearby.

St. Mary   Laid out among low scrub and aspen, this campground can be hot and windy with little shade. If there's a saving grace, it's close to St. Mary with its restaurants and stores.

1 mile from St. Mary entrance. ✆ **800/365-2267.** http://reservations.nps.gov. 148 sites, 25 can handle RVs up to 35 ft. $23 site. Closed late Sept until Memorial Day. **Amenities:** Flush toilets, dump station, cold-water sinks, picnic tables, fire pits and grates, bear boxes. Camp store, restaurants nearby.

Two Medicine   Close to three lakes and a stream, this somewhat remote campground is fairly well shaded. Nearby is a camp store and gift shop that is housed in what once was the Two Medicine Chalet that the Great Northern Railroad built. The sites run along the south side of Pray and Two Medicine lakes, so you're never far from water. The presence of an amphitheater means nightly entertainment courtesy of the rangers.

13 miles from East Glacier. ✆ **406/888-7800.** 99 sites, 13 can handle RVs up to 32 ft. $20 site. Closed late Sept until Memorial Day. **Amenities:** Flush toilets, cold-water sinks, picnic tables, fire pits and grates, fishing, swimming, amphitheater, bear boxes.

CHALETS

Like to head into the backcountry, but dread sleeping on the ground or worrying about a rainstorm in the middle of the night? Then check into either the Granite Park or Sperry chalets. The Great Northern Railway built these rustic, native-rock structures, now listed as National Historic Landmarks, between 1912 and 1914. These days **Belton Chalets Inc.** (✆ **888/345-2649**) runs the chalets to cater to backcountry travelers who don't like to carry tents or meals with them. While picturesque, these chalets are rustic, with light provided either by propane lanterns or your own flashlight. The Sperry Chalet is the more upscale of the two, with running water, meals included in the overnight price, and single or double beds as opposed to the bunk beds you'll find in the Granite Chalet. Both chalets are extremely popular. Reservations are taken beginning in late October and November for the following summer. Wait until May or June and you'll likely be unable to get the exact date you want. If you're limited to travel dates, it's wise to make a reservation no later than January. Youngsters who don't like long hikes or using outhouses best not be brought to the chalets.

Granite Park Chalet   The Granite Park Chalet is a hiker's shelter with few amenities, a place where self-sufficiency is key. Twelve rooms with bunk beds that sleep two to six per room (rooms are assigned by party size) are provided, as are a community kitchen with a cooking stove and a dining room. Belton Chalets offers meals you can order in advance. When you reach the chalet, your ingredients are waiting for you. Just don't forget to order your meal, for there might not be any extras waiting if you forget. If you prefer to bring your own meals, you will have access—along with all the other guests—to the kitchen with its basic set of pots and pans and utensils. You'll need your own plates, bowls, cups and utensils, flashlights, and sleeping bags. You can, though, order bedding for $15, when you reserve your night. No public water is available, although you can buy bottled water at the chalet, and there is a water source a quarter-mile from the chalet. If you plan to rely on that source, be sure to pack a filter and water bottles.

Along the Crown of the Continent Highline Trail, 7½ miles from Logan Pass. © 888/345-2649. www.granitepark chalet.com. 12 rooms. $70 for first person; $68 for each additional in same room. $15 for bedding. AE, MC, V. Closed early Sept to June 29. **Amenities:** Kitchen facilities, dining room, composting toilets.

Sperry Chalet *(Finds* This chalet, which was built in 1913, closed in 1992 and was reopened in 1999 after renovations. It is an impressive stone structure in the center of the wilderness. There are 17 rooms with accommodations from one to five per room. Here you'll get a room (with linens) plus three meals daily, but no bathing facilities except cold water, and the modern composting toilets are in a separate building. This chalet is a tad more kid-friendly, as the trail from Logan Pass down is not too challenging, you don't need to worry about cooking, and the accommodations are more comfortable than those at Granite Park.

Along the Sperry Trail, 6⅗ miles from Lake McDonald Lodge. © 888/345-2649. www.sperrychalet.com. 17 rooms. $160 for 1st person; $110 each additional in same room. AE, MC, V. Closed early Sept to early July. **Amenities:** Meals provided, running water, composting toilets.

COMMERCIAL CAMPGROUNDS

There's a nice variety of campgrounds on both sides of the park, from industrial-strength KOA spreads to smaller, locally owned facilities with more character.

IN EAST GLACIER

Y Lazy R This small campground is conveniently located within walking distance of East Glacier and is the closest to town and its laundry facilities. Plan to arrive early if you want to snag one of the few sites with trees. The Y Lazy R is a great value and an ideal place to plant the RV before heading off to explore the region.

Situated just off U.S. 2. P.O. Box 146, East Glacier, MT 59434. © 406/226-5505. 10 tent sites, 30 RV sites. $15 tent; $18 full hookup. No credit cards. **Amenities:** Showers, laundry, restrooms, water, RV dump, hookups.

IN ST. MARY

Johnson's of St. Mary April through September (depending on the weather), this is where you want to camp if you can get a spot. The campground, located near the southern end of Lower St. Mary Lake, has nice, well-spaced grassy sites scattered throughout an aspen grove on a hillside that offers nice views into the park. It's an inexpensive overnight stop with access to the east side of the park and the tourist facilities at the St. Mary Lodge. The family also offers a handful of cottages. Alcohol is prohibited.

HC 72-10 Star Rte., St. Mary, MT 59417. © 406/732-4207. www.johnsonsofstmary.com. 75 tent sites, 82 RV sites, 42 with full hookups. $19 tent; $21–$38 RV. $5 extra adult, $2.50 extra child beyond 2 adults, 2 children. MC, V. **Amenities:** Showers included in price, dump station, laundry facilities, restaurant, horseshoes, propane.

St. Mary-Glacier Park KOA I'm not overly crazy about KOA campgrounds because of the "small community" atmosphere, but if you're traveling with kids they're a good option. Where else can you find a campground with a game room? Right on the edge of St. Mary Lake, this KOA also comes with hot tubs, a volleyball court, playground, laundry facilities, and a Wi-Fi hotspot.

106 West Shore, St. Mary, MT 59417. ℂ 800/562-1504 or 406/732-4122. www.goglacier.com. 64 tent sites, 107 RV sites. $27 tent; $37–$50 RV; $80–$240 cabin. MC, V. Closed Oct 2 to mid-May. **Amenities:** Laundry, playground w/swings and slides, game room, Wi-Fi, camp store, hot tubs, volleyball court, canoe and paddleboat rentals, mountain bike rentals, gift shop.

IN WEST GLACIER

Glacier Campground   This campground—1 mile west of West Glacier on U.S. 2— is the closest campground outside the park. Set on 40 acres amid a forested area overgrown with evergreens, it's a quiet, comfortable, shady place to retreat. Most sites have water and electric hookups; the balance are perfect for tent camping. Five rather primitive cabins are also available, but furnishings are modest: sleeping beds with mattresses and electricity, but no plumbing or kitchen facilities. Recreational facilities include volleyball, horseshoes, and a basketball court; also on the premises are a laundry and small general store.

P.O. Box 447, 12070 U.S. 2, West Glacier, MT 59936. ℂ 888/387-5689 or 406/387-5689. www.glaciercampground. com. 80 tent sites, 80 RV sites, 5 cabins. $19 tent; $20–$27 RV; $35–$45 cabin. Extra person 5–12 $1, over 12 $1.50. DISC, MC, V. **Amenities:** Showers, dump station, laundry, camp store, video rentals, volleyball, horseshoes, basketball court.

Lake Five Resort   Located 3 miles west of West Glacier and approximately 1 mile from U.S. 2 is this cabin and campground arrangement, an alternative to potentially crowded park campgrounds. Situated on a 235-acre lake surrounded by private homes and summer cottages, the resort is far from the madding crowd (though still close to the park itself). Seven of the nine cabins are on the lakefront, all of them equipped with bathrooms and showers. The only distraction may be the sound of powerboats.

540 Belton Stage Rd., West Glacier, MT 59936. ℂ 406/387-5601. www.lakefiveresort.com. 9 cabins, 6 tepee lodges, 45 sites with electricity and water, 14 of which have sewer hookups. $35–$40 site; $110–$165 cabin; $50–$60 tepee. No credit cards. **Amenities:** Swimming, fishing, horseshoes, canoe and paddleboat rentals, water-skiing lessons.

West Glacier KOA   Not as large as the St. Mary KOA, this facility is set off U.S. 2 in a nice pine wood. Just 2½ miles from the park's west entrance, this campground has all the amenities of its sister facility, plus a swimming pool.

355 Half Moon Flats Rd., West Glacier, MT 59936. ℂ 800/562-3313 or 406/387-5341. www.westglacierkoa.com. 26 tent sites, 106 RV sites, 28 cabins. $27–$29 tent; $27–$47 RV; $58–$72 cabin. Closed Oct 2–Apr 30. **Amenities:** Laundry, heated pool, camp store, hot tubs, horseshoes, mountain bike rentals, ice-cream shop, recreation room, playground.

HOTELS

Lodging in Glacier National Park offers spectacular views, charm, and the benefits of being *in* the park. That said, these accommodations were built decades ago and don't have all the amenities and feel of, say, the Old Faithful Snow Lodge in Yellowstone National Park or the Ahwahnee in Yosemite. They're a tad bit undersize when it comes to the rooms, and TVs and telephones are not standard. All the national park accommodations have a limited number of rollaway beds and cribs, available at $15 per night.

Reserve well in advance. August dates often fill before the spring thaw.

Apgar Village Lodge   The independently owned Apgar Village Lodge is located on the south end of Lake McDonald and is one of two lodgings in Apgar Village. There's a wide variety of lodging available here, and repeat customers are the norm. The best places—reserve early—are along McDonald Creek and on the banks of the lake. Cabin 6 offers the best view—it's at the mouth of McDonald Creek, which drains the lake. There are nine river cabins, and several motel rooms overlooking the creek. The cabins are much nicer than they look on the outside. Inside you'll find knotty pine paneling and rough-hewn beams. Five large cabins offer two bedrooms; most cabins have kitchens with stoves and refrigerators. Some of the small ones tend to be a little dark, and the towels aren't big enough.

2⅓ miles from west entrance on the south end of Lake McDonald. Apgar Village, Box 398, West Glacier, MT 59936. ℂ 406/888-5484. Fax 406/888-5273. www.westglacier.com. 28 cabins, 20 motel rooms. $99–$250 cabin; $89–$108 double motel room. Children 10 and under free in parent's room. No rollaway beds, crib $4. DISC, MC, V. Closed early Oct to Apr. **Amenities:** Lakeside location. *In room:* TV, no phone.

For more information on the following properties or to make a reservation, contact **Glacier Park Inc. (GPI),** P.O. Box 2025, Columbia Falls, MT 59912 (ℂ **406/892-2525;** fax 406/892-1375; www.glacierparkinc.com). For GPI properties, children under 12 stay free with parent, there's a $15 extra person charge, and rollaways cost $15. Rooms do not come with air-conditioning, TVs, coffeemakers, or refrigerators. GPI does not accept pets at any of its facilities.

Lake McDonald Lodge

The Lake McDonald Lodge feels like a genuine backwoods hunting lodge, with mounted elk, antelope, deer, mountain goats, moose, and bighorn sheep, golden eagles, and hawks glaring down from above. Modeled after the Great Northern Railroad's early-20th-century lodges, this two-story building has a warm, cozy feel inspired by its wood construction, stone floors, and exposed rafters.

The lobby's massive fireplace was decorated with Indian pictographs that, legend has it, Charles M. Russell etched into the stone. However, that appears to be just a legend with no truth to it (although it's a good one). Lodge rooms, located on the second and third floor of the lodge (no elevator), are pleasantly decorated and have a historical feel, but are tiny. The showers are so small—the bathrooms are located in what used to be closets—that you'll have a hard time changing your mind in them. Outside the lodge, the motel units are simple but well maintained. The well-preserved cottages, which offer more space than the lodge rooms, are located in multi-unit cottage buildings in a wooded area. Cabins 12 and 13 offer the best lake view and a short trail down to the beach. Curiously, when I was there cabin 12A boasted a picture of the snow-covered Tetons.

On the shore of the park's largest lake, the lodge provides a marvelous central base for exploring the western half of Glacier. It's a center for boating activity; scenic cruises depart throughout the day and canoe rentals are popular. Red Jammer bus tours come and go from here, too. Common lounging areas are furnished with heavy couches, sofas, and chairs that ring the stone fireplace. A post office and general store are also on the grounds. The entire lodge is nonsmoking.

One of the lodge's best features: It has only 100 rooms. Soon after the last Red Jammer tour of the day returns to the lodge, day-trippers and campers vanish and the tiny Lake McDonald complex transforms into a deliciously small neighborhood, with off-duty employees playing football and soccer and guests enjoying the evening quiet and the sunset as it splashes across the lake.

Glacier National Park, MT 59936. ℂ **406/892-2525.** Fax 406/892-1375. www.glacierparkinc.com. 62 units in lodge and motel, 38 cottage units. $162 lodge room; $124 motel unit; $114–$162 cottage. AE, DISC, MC, V. Closed late Sept to late May. **Amenities:** Restaurants; lounge; Red Jammer tours; horseback rides; boat tours; post office; general store. *In room:* Iron/ironing board, hair dryer available from front desk.

Many Glacier Hotel

This vast, sprawling four-story structure on Swiftcurrent Lake is graced by one of the most scenic national-park vistas you'll find. Across the lake rises Grinnell Point, to the north is Altyn Peak, and to the south Allen Mountain climbs 9,376 feet into the sky. It's the most popular lodging in the park, and with good reason. The setting is breathtaking, and there are a wide variety of activities to embark upon: boating, hiking, trail rides, and bird-watching, to name but a few. Most of the rooms are a little larger than those usually associated with a Great Northern Railroad hotel. But this was never a "railroad hotel." Completed in 1915, it was one of a network of chalets—others were Sperry and Granite—that visitors rode to on horseback. The chalets were set a day's ride apart.

The rooms, which are small with dated furnishings, are located in the main lodge off interior balconies that overlook the lobby or in the adjoining annex. The lakeside rooms offer great views of Swiftcurrent Lake. Families are best in the annex, where some fourth-floor units have two connecting bedrooms. Hallways that tie the main lodge structure to the dining room boast small sitting areas, some with fireplaces. The Interlaken Lounge outside the dining room is complete with armchairs facing the lake, a perfect spot to relax after a hike. The main lobby once boasted a stone fountain that was wrapped by a spiral staircase that descended to the St. Moritz Room. Removed in the 1950s, there are rumors it might be returned. All units are nonsmoking.

Glacier National Park, MT 59936. © **406/892-2525.** Fax 406/892-1375. www.manyglacierhotel.com. 208 units. $136–$162 double; $219 family room; $268 suite. AE, DISC, MC, V. Closed late Sept to early June. **Amenities:** Restaurant; 2 lounges, convenience store; boat tours; horseback rides; boat rentals; fishing; family units. *In room:* Iron/ironing board, hair dryer available from front desk.

Rising Sun Motor Inn   Six and a half miles from St. Mary, just off Going-to-the-Sun Road, the Rising Sun consists of a complex made up of the Two Dog Flats restaurant, a motor inn, cottages, a camp store, a gift shop, and a service station. The basic motel rooms are just that—basic, uninspiring motel rooms—but are completely adequate for a good night's rest and in an excellent location for those who want to explore the eastern side of the park from Going-to-the-Sun Road. The cottages (you rent half of a duplex) are more interesting but a bit on the rustic side. All units here are nonsmoking.

Glacier National Park, MT 59936. © **406/892-2525.** Fax 406/892-1375. www.risingsunmotorinn.com. 63 units. $104–$124 double; $114 cottage. AE, DISC, MC, V. Closed mid-Sept to mid-June. **Amenities:** Restaurant; general store; boat tours. *In room:* No phone.

Swiftcurrent Motor Inn   The Swiftcurrent Motor Inn is located about a mile upstream from Many Glacier Hotel, but it attracts an entirely different crowd. Here the guests are younger, less well-to-do, and primarily active types interested in spending lots of time exploring the backcountry trails. Like Many Glacier, the inn is set against a mountain backdrop in what is considered a hiker's paradise. Motel rooms here have standard motel decor—functional but nothing special; cabins are a bit more interesting, with one or two bedrooms, and perhaps a bathroom (communal facilities are nearby). All units are nonsmoking.

The Swiftcurrent was built in 1936 as a motor hotel, the first in the park specifically directed at tourists arriving by car rather than by train. There are three circles of cabins and two motel-style units, all set back in the trees. The inn sits in a wildlife migratory path, so you might see bear, elk, and moose in the parking lot. The Italian Garden Ristorante serves a mean garlic and artichoke-heart pizza. There's also a camping supplies store on the property.

Glacier National Park, MT 59936. © **406/892-2525.** Fax 406/892-1375. www.swiftcurrentmotorinn.com. 88 units and cabins, most cabins without private bathroom. $104–$124 double in motor inn; $53–$79 double in cabin. AE, DISC, MC, V. Closed mid-Sept to mid-June. **Amenities:** Restaurant; general store; laundry facilities. *In room:* No phone; iron/ironing board, hair dryer available from front desk.

Village Inn   Not to be confused with Apgar Village Lodge, the Village Inn is the smallest of the properties operated by GPI in Glacier. Located in Apgar Village, the inn is convenient to the general store, cafes, and boat docks. Like its counterparts throughout the park, the Village Inn is comfortably outfitted with modest furnishings, making it a cozy and convenient place to set up camp. All 36 rooms are located on two floors of the inn and 12 of them have kitchenettes. Apgar Village bustles with activity during the summer and is a great choice for families.

Glacier National Park, MT 59936. (C) **406/892-2525.** Fax 406/892-1375. www.villageinnatapgar.com. 36 units. $121–$164 1-bedroom unit; $147–$189 2-bedroom unit. AE, DISC, MC, V. Closed mid-Sept to June. **Amenities:** Lake views from all rooms; beach, restaurants, gift shops, boat rentals nearby. In room: Coffeemaker, no phone; iron/iron-ing board, hair dryer available from front desk.

COMMUNITIES OUTSIDE THE PARK
IN BROWNING

Lodgepole Gallery & Tipi Village *(Finds*   I enjoyed two of my best night's sleep in one of the tepees that Darrell Norman and his wife, Angelika Harden-Norman, have erected in a field behind their art gallery/home. Dozing off to the gentle flapping of the tepee canvas was wonderful, as was waking to a gorgeous sunrise over the high plains just east of Glacier National Park. Youngsters fascinated by the "Wild West" will enjoy falling to sleep in the full-size tepees. Bring your own sleeping bag or rent one with a sleeping mattress. On cold nights, fight the chill with a fire that is vented through the top of the tepee. In the mornings, look for the Spanish mustangs that you share the field with. Darrell, a member of the Blackfeet Tribe, can regale you with the tribe's history and lore over the excellent meals he prepares for guests.

On U.S. 89 2½ miles west of Browning, MT 59417. (C) **406/338-2787.** Fax 406/338-2778. www.blackfeetculture camp.com. 10 tepees. $40 1st person; $12 each additional; $6 children under 12. Sleeping bag and mattress $6. MC, V. Open May to mid-Sept. **Amenities:** Bathhouse w/restrooms; meals available; art gallery w/Native American works.

IN EAST GLACIER

Glacier Park Lodge   Just outside the southeast entrance at East Glacier, this is the park's flagship inn, an imposing timbered lodge that stands as a stately tribute to the Great Northern Railroad and its early attempts to lure tourists to Glacier. It also hap-pens to be the most family-friendly lodging in or around the park. The carefully mani-cured lawn and ever-blooming wildflowers frame the grounds in colors spectacular enough to rival the mountain backdrop. The day I visited kids were laughing and gig-gling as they rolled down a gentle slope on the front lawn, while parents watched in rocking chairs from the covered front porch. Out back more laughter resonated from the swimming pool. The interior features massive Douglas fir pillars, some 40 inches in diameter and 40 feet tall. In fact, stand in the middle of the lobby and look up— you'll discover beams, carved from massive trees that are the structural supports for the entire building. Skylights, wrought-iron chandeliers, and a desk hewn from a 36-inch-diameter log add to the Old West flavor.

Rooms are simply furnished with beds, a small writing table, and an end table; the showers are elbow-banging small; and sinks are significantly smaller than those found in today's modern hotels and motels. A wooden deck outside the lounge provides an excellent spot for cocktails, reading, or a late-afternoon snooze. A glass-enclosed breeze-way connects the main building to the west wing; the oak chaise longues found there are an ideal spot from which to watch a sunrise. There's even an immaculately groomed executive-style golf course. The Trading Post offers traditional souvenirs, as well as nicely crafted American Indian artwork and clothing. While here, plan to spend an evening around the fireplace as members of the Blackfeet tribe recount their history.

East Glacier, MT 59936. ⓒ **406/892-2525**. Fax 406/892-1375. www.bigtreehotel.com. 154 units. $129–$170 double; $159–$199 family room; $179–$299 suite. AE, DISC, MC, V. Closed Oct 1 to late May. **Amenities:** Restaurant; lounge; pool; golf course; gift shop; convenience store; volleyball; horseback rides. *In room:* Iron/ironing board, hair dryer available from front desk.

Jacobson's Cottages

Located in a nicely wooded area, these quaint cottages are small but comfortable. All have cable TV and one has a kitchen. Entertainment and good food are short walks away with Restaurant Thimbleberry a half-block down the street, and Two Medicine an 11-mile drive. The cottages are available seasonally, and reservations are recommended.

1204 Mont. 49 (P.O. Box 454), East Glacier, MT 59434. ⓒ **406/226-4422**. Fax 406/226-4425. 12 cottages. $50–$75 double. Rollaway bed $6, crib free. AE, DISC, MC, V. Closed Oct–May. **Amenities:** Restaurants nearby. *In room:* TV, 1 room has kitchen.

Mountain Pine Motel

Just a half-mile from the Amtrak station, this property is a one-story, 1950s-style motel that provides clean, well-furnished rooms equipped with cable TV. It is in a shaded, timbered area along Mont. 49. Most standard rooms have two queen-size beds, reading chairs and table, chest, and bathrooms with tub/shower combinations. There is also a large three-bedroom log house available with a view of the mountains. All units are nonsmoking.

Mont. 49, East Glacier, MT 59434. ⓒ **406/226-4403**. www.mtnpine.com. 25 units. $66–$71 double. Rollaway bed $4, crib free. AE, DC, DISC, MC, V. Closed Oct–May. **Amenities:** Restaurants nearby. *In room:* TV.

IN ESSEX

Izaak Walton Inn

Built in 1939, this inn originally housed railway workers. It now has three floors of rooms, a restaurant, and a tavern. The rooms are not large, but they are beautifully kept, with wood-paneled walls and various Western touches. Each has a private bathroom. Some have, in addition to the double beds, futon couches that can be folded out for another bed. The halls are decorated in railroad memorabilia. The converted cabooses are similarly decorated, and what train buff can resist the temptation of spending the night in a genuine caboose? Unlike a lot of Glacier lodging establishments, the inn is booming in winter. Skiers are attracted to its 30 miles of groomed trails, and a covered ice rink. There is also an attractive Finnish sauna that's open 7am to 10pm year-round.

290 Izaak Walton Inn Rd., Essex, MT 59916. ⓒ **406/888-5700**. Fax 406/888-5200. www.izaakwaltoninn.com. 33 units plus 4 caboose cottages. $137–$255 double; $690 caboose for a 3-night minimum stay. Rollaway beds and cribs free. MC, V. **Amenities:** Restaurant; tavern. *In room:* No phone.

IN ST. MARY

St. Mary Lodge and Resort

The best accommodations in or out of the park can be found here on the east edge of Glacier National Park. Overall the accommodations are very nice, those in the Great Bear Lodge are excellent—roomy with large bathrooms, comfortable beds, wet bars, Western- and Arts and Crafts–style decor, and balconies overlooking Divide Creek, whose rippling waters will serenade you to sleep. Suites offer fireplaces and Jacuzzis. The less-expensive units are small but bright, with golden logs. The furniture is lodgepole pine. The six cottages on the hill across U.S. 89—which hold four adults and rent for $450 per night in season—are the best luxury accommodations anywhere in or near the park. They each have a living room, full kitchen, two bedrooms, spacious deck, a good-size bathroom with a tub, and a gas grill. The cottages sit high on a hill, and the view from the decks out over St. Mary Lake is spectacular. Most units are air-conditioned—a rarity in the area. If there's a low point, it's the lack of grassy areas to play on. The lodge's Snowgoose Grille offers elaborate entrees and fantastic views of East Flattop Mountain, Red Eagle Mountain, and Curly Bear Mountain.

U.S. 89 and Going-to-the-Sun Rd., St. Mary, MT 59417. © **888/778-6279** or 406/732-4431. Fax 406/732-9265. www.stmarylodgeandresort.com. 103 units, 19 cabins and cottages. $99–$135 double; $145–$450 cabin or cottage; $160–$350 lodge room or suite. Rollaway beds and cribs $10. AE, DISC, MC, V. Closed Oct–May. **Amenities:** Restaurant (see Snowgoose Grille, below); cafe; pizza parlor; coffee/chocolate shop; lounge; coin-operated laundry; gas station. *In room:* A/C, TV, fridge, hair dryer, wet bar.

IN WEST GLACIER

Belton Chalet and Lodge   A National Historic Landmark, this facility across from the railroad station has been completely restored to the elegance of an early-20th-century hotel. The rooms are small, simple, and old-fashioned. The bathrooms are also small. But the warm feel of the place is comfortable and the staff is very friendly. Many of the rooms have their own balcony looking out over the rounded timber hills in the near distance, the foothills to Glacier National Park. The only drawback—and it could be a huge one if you're a light sleeper—is the dozens of freight trains and two Amtrak trains—that rumble past the lodge day and night.

12575 U.S. 2, West Glacier, MT 59936. © **888/235-8665** or 406/888-5000. Fax 406/888-5005. www.beltonchalet. com. 25 units, 2 cottages. July–Aug $135–$285 double; Sept–July $115–$205 double. No rollaway beds or cribs. AE, MC, V. **Amenities:** Restaurant (see "Family-Friendly Dining," below); bar. *In room:* Hair dryer and iron/ironing board available from front desk, no phone.

Glacier Wilderness Resort   Surrounded by Forest Service lands, the lodges at this year-round resort are as private as you can get. Each lodge is a "home," done in modern Western decor. Families will like the two-bedroom lodges. Kids can play outdoors during the day (there are 23 undeveloped acres) and there are diversions like foosball, indoor pool, and video games in the rec center. Cabins also have their own hot tubs. Hiking trails abound, and some even come up on some surprising waterfalls. For a summer stay, reservations should be made before March.

P.O. Box 295, West Glacier, MT 59936. © **406/888-5664.** Fax 406/888-5664. www.glacierwildernessresort.com. 10 lodges. $175–$200 lodge. 5-night minimum stay. Cribs free. MC, V.

Great Northern Chalet   If you've always wanted that place in the mountains, it'd probably end up looking something like these accommodations. This small, family-oriented resort located near West Glacier offers log chalets that have balconies facing landscaped flower gardens and a pond, with mountain views in the distance. Three types of chalets are offered, the largest being beautifully furnished two-story, two-bedroom units with three queen-size beds, a full bathroom upstairs, and half bathroom downstairs. Smaller chalets have one large upstairs bedroom with two queen-size beds, and a downstairs level with a full-size sleeper sofa and a kitchen with service for six. Interiors are Western—lots of log and rock in the living and dining rooms, while bedrooms are tastefully done with wainscoting, earth-tone hues, and furnishings that reflect the mountain setting. Three-night minimum required during peak season.

12127 U.S. 2, West Glacier, MT 59936. © **800/735-7897** or 406/387-5340. Fax 406/387-9007. www.gnwhitewater. com. 5 units. Apr–May 31 and mid-Sept to Nov $99–$135; June to mid-June and Aug 26 to mid-Sept $175–$235; June 20 to late Aug and Dec 21–31 $260–$295. No rollaway beds, cribs free. AE, DISC, MC. **Amenities:** TV; full kitchen; gas grill.

Tips **Park Camping Basics: Toilets, Showers & Laundry**

Park Service campgrounds have rudimentary restrooms; some have running water, some don't. Only Rising Sun has access to hot showers. You can find commercially operated public showers at Johnson's campground and at Rising Sun.

West Glacier Motel   This property has two locations. Half of the units are in West Glacier on Going-to-the-Sun Road, about a mile from the park entrance, and a second set of units is another mile away on a forested piece of ground that presents panoramic views of the park. This 1950s-style motel has a great location, the prices can't be beat during peak season, and rates drop dramatically the week before Labor Day. The Western-style cabins are better suited to family use, since they come with two or three queen-size beds.

200 Going-to-the-Sun Rd. (Box 410), West Glacier, MT 59936. © **888/838-2363** or 406/888-5662. www.west glacier.com. 32 units, 5 cabins. $82–$102 motel room double; $141–$163 cabin. Children 10 and under stay free in parent's room. Extra person $10. Rollaway bed $10, crib $4. AE, DISC, MC, V. Closed early Oct to Apr. **Amenities:** Flathead River access; walking distance to shops and restaurants. *In room:* TV, kitchen in cabins, no phone.

6 Family-Friendly Dining
LOW-STRESS MEALS

There aren't a lot of dining alternatives outside of the lodges, but the gateway towns offer a few.

IN THE PARK

Eddie's Restaurant   This roadside cafe offers typical cafe fare, from eggs and grill items for breakfast to burgers and sandwiches for lunch and steaks, chicken, and trout for dinner. They'll also fix a box lunch for your hike.

Apgar Village. © **406/888-5361.** Kids' menu, boosters, highchairs, crayons. Breakfast $2.25–$8; lunch $6.75–$11; dinner $14–$20. DISC, MC, V. Daily breakfast 7–11:30am, lunch 11:30am–5pm, and dinner 5–9:30pm. Closed midSept to early June.

Italian Gardens Ristorante   Lunch and dinner feature combinations of salads, sandwiches, pasta dishes such as baked lasagnas, and "create your own" pizzas. Breakfast items come mainly from the griddle.

Swiftcurrent Motor Inn. © **406/732-5531.** Kids' menu, highchairs, boosters, crayons. Breakfast $4.50–$8; lunch and dinner $4.50–$12. AE, DISC, MC, V. Daily 6:30–10am, 11am–3pm, and 5–9:30pm. Closed mid-Sept to early June.

Jammer Joe's   You'll find inexpensive meals and a photo collection that traces some of the park's history at this pizzeria named in honor of those who drive the park's Red Jammers. You can build your own pizzas, as well as your own burgers, pasta dishes, and sandwiches.

Lake McDonald Lodge complex. © **406/888-5431.** Kids' menu, highchairs, boosters, crayons. Lunch and dinner $4.50–$12. AE, DISC, MC, V. Daily 11am–9:30pm. Closed early Sept to late June.

Two Dog Flats Grill   This grill across from St. Mary Lake carries a southwestern theme with its burritos, tacos, and chimichangas, but also offers burgers, wraps, and salads.

Rising Sun Motor Inn. © **406/732-5523.** Kids' menu, boosters, highchairs, crayons. Breakfast $4.50–$8; lunch and dinner $4.50–$15. AE, DISC, MC, V. Daily 6:30–10am and 11–9:30pm. Closed mid-Sept to mid-June.

BEST-BEHAVIOR MEALS
IN THE PARK
Ptarmigan Dining Room   The cavernous dining room has Swiss decor with a Western flair in keeping with the lodge. Large windows that run the length of one wall try to frame the spectacular mountain and lake views. Overhead, wagon-wheel chandeliers hang, while a 6-foot-wide rock fireplace anchors one wall. Meals range from continental fare to Swiss cuisine, such as Wiener schnitzel and bison stroganoff, and there's a sprawling breakfast buffet that includes a waffle station with a variety of fresh fruit toppings. The children's menu offers such lunch and dinner items as grilled cheese, hamburgers, popcorn chicken, and pasta with sauce for between $4 and $6.

Many Glacier also has the **Swiss Room and Interlaken Lounge,** with an afternoon fondue and a bar menu of sandwiches and appetizers, and **Heidi's,** a fast-food counter known for its huckleberry frozen yogurt.

Many Glacier Lodge. © 406/732-4411. Kids' menu, highchairs, boosters, crayons. Breakfast $4.50–$13; lunch and dinner $6–$30. AE, DISC, MC, V. Daily 6:30–10am, 11:30am–2pm, and 5–10pm. Closed late Sept to early June.

Russell's Fireside Dining Room   With its wood-plank walls, flooring, and ceiling, massive support timbers and beams, and large fireplace, this dining room has a distinctive hunting lodge atmosphere. It specializes in American standards, including beef tenderloin, roast duckling, seared mountain trout, roast turkey, Alaskan salmon, and steaks; there's also a full breakfast buffet.

Next to the dining room is the **Stockade Lounge,** which serves a bar menu of sandwiches and appetizers. It's a great option for lunch if the dining room is backed up.

Lake McDonald Lodge. © 406/888-5431. Kids' menu, highchairs, boosters, crayons. Breakfast $4.50–$13; lunch and dinner $6–$30. AE, DISC, MC, V. Daily 6–10am, 11:30am–2pm, and 5–9:30pm. Closed Oct to late May.

EAST GLACIER
Glacier Village Restaurant   This family-owned, seasonal restaurant is one of the few full-service dining establishments in the area that serves three meals. Portions are healthy and prices are moderate, with breakfast standards like yummy waffles and pancakes made from homemade batter. The restaurant's impressive menu also includes pork chops with huckleberry sauce, plus jams and syrups to go.

304–308 Mont. 2, East Glacier. © 406/226-4464. Kids' menu, highchairs, booster seats, crayons. Breakfast $5–$11; lunch $7.95–$16; dinner $7.95–$22. DISC, MC, V. Daily 6:30am–9pm. Closed Oct–Apr.

Great Northern Steak and Rib House, Glacier Park Lodge   Anchoring one end of the massive lobby, this restaurant boasts Western decor and a menu of beef, barbecued ribs, fish, and chicken, plus a full breakfast buffet. The nearby **Sunset Lounge** offers a bar menu of sandwiches and appetizers.

Glacier Park Lodge, East Glacier. © 406/226-5600. Kids' menu, highchairs, boosters, crayons. No reservations. Breakfast $1.25–$8.95; lunch $2.50–$11; dinner $5.95–$29. AE, DISC, MC, V. Daily 6:30–9:30am, 11:30am–2pm, and 5–9pm. Closed Oct 1 to late May.

Serrano's   In East Glacier, if you're going to eat only one dinner, eat it at Serrano's. The farther north you go, the warier you should be of Mexican restaurants. But Serrano's only claims a kind of Mexican-California-Southwest influence, and the food succeeds very well. The seafood enchilada, with shrimp and scallops, is excellent, especially when accompanied by one of the restaurant's fabulous margaritas. Or, if you prefer, have a beer from the large selection of microbrews. Serrano's has an outstanding local reputation, so don't be surprised if you encounter masses of people during the height of summer. Easiest way to land a table is get there as close to 5pm as possible.

29 Dawson Ave., East Glacier. ℂ **406/226-9392**. Reservations not accepted. Main courses $7.95–$17. AE, DISC, MC, V. Daily 5–10pm. Closed Oct–Apr.

Whistle Stop   This low-slung eatery may serve up the very best breakfasts in the area. Omelets and huckleberry French toast are a specialty. Omelets come in seven different styles, including a Spanish omelet with chorizo, lots of peppers, tomatoes, onions, and spinach. French toast dishes are as rich as desserts, with fillings ranging from huckleberries and apple cinnamon to hazelnut vanilla. Definitely a diet buster. Barbecue ribs, steaks, and chicken are popular lunch and dinner dishes. Try the huckleberry pie.

1020 Mont. 49, East Glacier. ℂ **406/226-9292**. Breakfast items $3.95–$7.25; lunch and dinner $4.75–$21. Daily 7am–9pm. Closed late Sept to early June.

POLEBRIDGE

Northern Lights Saloon   Polebridge is where the serious Glacier outdoors people hang out. And the Northern Lights Saloon is where they go to have a beer and a burger. This small restaurant, located squarely in the middle of Polebridge, gets enough customers in summer that you actually may have to wait for a table. The fact that there are only four or five tables exacerbates the problem. The customers are usually folks who have spent the last few days in the backcountry, on the river, or in one of the primitive lodging choices that Polebridge offers. The saloon is a classic Old West–style hangout. You can find your burgers (including turkey and falafel burgers) and pizza here, as well as more creative dishes like chicken in a chipotle cream sauce depending upon who is cooking that day.

Polebridge. ℂ **406/888-5669**. Reservations not accepted. Lunch main courses $8–$10; dinner $10–$15. AE, DISC, MC, V. Late May to mid-Sept daily 4–9pm; mid-Sept to late May Fri–Sat 4–9pm, Sun 9am–3pm. Bar open later.

ST. MARY

Park Café   Housed in a Robin's egg blue building with a deck that wraps half the cafe, this eatery is renowned for its homemade pies (the cafe's motto is "Pie for Strength") that range from blackberry and boysenberry all the way to "razzleberry" (a blend of blueberries, blackberries, and raspberries) and banana cream. Breakfasts come mainly from the griddle, while lunches and dinners are built around burritos, sandwiches, and burgers.

U.S. 89, St. Mary. ℂ **406/732-4482**. Boosters, highchairs. Breakfast $4.50–$9.95; lunch and dinner $6–$15. AE, DISC, MC, V. Daily 7am–10pm. Closed Oct–May.

Snowgoose Grille   Located in the St. Mary Lodge and Resort (p. 257), the Snowgoose Grille is a high-priced alternative to park food. The ambience is upscale for these parts—a glass-enclosed dining room with views of the mountains and the creek. The restaurant specializes in elegant preparation of Montana-style food: beef and wild game plates.

The Resort at Glacier, U.S. 89 and Going-to-the-Sun Rd., St. Mary. ℂ **800/368-3689** or 406/732-4431. Fax 406/732-9265. Kids' menu, highchairs, boosters, crayons. Breakfast main courses $6.75–$9.25; lunch $8–$11; dinner $12–$28; kids' menu $5–$9. AE, DISC, MC, V. Midsummer daily 7–10:30am, 11:30am–4pm, and 5:30–10pm; shorter hours at the beginning and end of the season. Closed Sept. 30 to Memorial Day weekend.

WEST GLACIER

Belton Tap Room and Grille   This restaurant, located in restored buildings that were once the Great Northern Railroad Chalet, serves up respectable food geared toward American tastes—steaks, buffalo, chicken, ribs, trout, and salmon. And although this place is deep within the heart of the meat-and-potatoes Rockies, there are a number of vegetarian selections, such as a grilled vegetable napoleon featuring layers of eggplant, yellow and red tomatoes, zucchini, squash, arugula, and crimini mushrooms. Kids aren't overlooked, either, as their menu offers triple-decker PB&Js, pasta, and chicken nuggets. A large stone fireplace dominates the taproom, which serves several kinds of brewed-in-Montana beers.

12575 U.S. 2, West Glacier (across from the west entrance to the park and from the Glacier Amtrak Station). © 406/ 888-5000. Kids' menu, highchairs, boosters, crayons. Dinner $20–$33. AE, MC, V. Summer daily 5–10pm; shorter hours through winter. Bar open later.

Glacier Highlander Restaurant   This is the spot to satisfy the sweet tooth; a baker is on hand, so the pies are well worth the stop, and the cinnamon rolls are breakfast giants. The Highland Burger is, by any standard, a great hunk of beef, and the fresh trout is a dinner specialty.

U.S. 2, West Glacier. © 406/888-5427. Kids' menu, highchairs, boosters, crayons. Breakfast $4.95–$8.75; lunch $6–$8.50; dinner $8.50–$19. AE, DISC, MC, V. Daily 7am–10pm. Closed Nov–Apr.

---

7 Exploring Glacier National Park with Your Kids

ENTRANCE FEES   Glacier charges entrance fees at both the West Glacier and St. Mary entrances. Vehicles are $25 for 7 days, but if you live in the region a yearlong pass specific to Glacier is just $30. You also can gain entrance with one of the America the Beautiful passes. For details, see chapter 2.

NATURAL PLACES
GOING-TO-THE-SUN ROAD

Going-to-the-Sun Road cuts a paved pathway across the heart of Glacier National Park and, in doing so, showcases the park perhaps better than any other road through any other park that I know of. A near second is the Grand Loop that draws a figure eight in the heart of Yellowstone, weaving past geyser basins, along lakefronts, through forests, and over mountain passes. But while you don't have to navigate the entire loop to come away with the feeling that you "know" Yellowstone, such a journey must be taken on the Going-to-the-Sun Road if you are to become truly familiar with Glacier.

Though just 50 miles long, the "Sun Road" skirts lakes, enters and exits dense forests, and climbs nearly to the top of the Continental Divide at Logan Pass before dropping quickly back down to Glacier's eastern entrance at St. Mary. Along the way, you pass dozens of trail heads, a handful of lakes begging to serve as backdrops for picnics or to wet a fishing line, and enough overlooks to expose all the film you're carrying.

Among the notable stopping points are Upper McDonald Creek Falls, at mile 14.5 from West Glacier; Trail of the Cedars, at mile 16.2; the "Loop," at mile 24.6 from where you can hike to Granite Park Chalet; and Sunrift Gorge, at mile 39.4.

These and other points of interest are clearly marked along the road and correspond to the park brochure *Points of Interest Along the Going-to-the-Sun Road,* which is available at visitor centers.

Through the years, this road has seen a lot of traffic, and in places its surface shows it. As a result, the park is undertaking an ambitious rehabilitation of the road.

LAKE MCDONALD

To many, Lake McDonald is the epitome of Glacier National Park. The largest, most accessible, and most beloved of the park's lakes, it has been the final destination for travelers since the 1890s. Charles Russell, the well-known Western artist, liked the setting so much that he and his wife, Nancy, summered year after year in a cabin not far from Apgar Village.

Today the small compound surrounding Lake McDonald Lodge is a hive of activity during the day, with Red Jammer tours coming and going, scenic cruises being launched off the dock, and day-trippers stopping by for a meal, directions to nearby trail heads, or simply to take in the view. At night that frenetic setting is transformed into a quieter, less hectic one.

But the complex is more than merely a front-country rest stop. It's a kicking-off point for adventures. Directly across from the complex, on the south side of Going-to-the-Sun Road, is a horse corral (which can be smelly when the wind is blowing the wrong way) where you can arrange short and long rides into the mountains, and trails that lead to Sperry Chalet and deeper into the backcountry.

Less than 10 miles east on Going-to-the-Sun Road lies the Avalanche Creek Campground and two popular trails: the **Trail of the Cedars Nature Trail,** and the **Avalanche Lake Trail** 🐾🐾. The quarter-mile-long nature trail is one of Glacier's shortest and easiest trails. The elevated boardwalk loops through a dense forest of cedars and hemlocks that rise 60 to 100 feet into the sky, blotting out most of the sun's rays. The woods here catch moisture barreling out of the Pacific Northwest; proof of that can be found on the leafy forest floor, where the water produces a thick undergrowth of ferns and shrubs while mosses carpet downed tree trunks and rocks kept wet by seeps.

An adjacent trail head leads to Avalanche Lake, one of my favorite destinations in the park due not only to the trail's relatively short length, but also for the picturesque forest of cedar and hemlock that it rolls through and the incredibly scenic payoff at the lake.

About a third of a mile from the trail head the path passes Avalanche Gorge, a moss-covered grotto carved into the bedrock by the pounding flows of Avalanche Creek. The water is a brilliant blue, colored by glacial silt carried out of the high country.

While hiking through the forest, my ears tried to follow the shrill trilling of the varied thrush, a bird that sounds as if it's tweeting harshly on a policeman's whistle. So intent was I on listening for the bird that I practically butted heads with a deer that was rummaging the forest for breakfast.

From the trail head it's 2.3 miles to Avalanche Lake, a pool of water seemingly nestled in the bottom of a stony cauldron with walls roughly 4,000 feet tall. The day I visited at least four cataracts were tumbling out of the high country to feed the lake and its draining creek. The setting is idyllic; a perfect place for a lazy afternoon's picnic. To preview this hike from your home, visit Glacier's website (www.nps.gov/glac), click on "Visit Glacier's Website Visitor Center," and view **eHikes.** This program, viewed best on a high-speed Internet connection, takes you along the Avalanche Creek Trail and provides a natural history lesson. Additional **eHikes** were being planned as this book went to press.

LOGAN PASS

Hunkered down at 6,646 feet near the crest of the Continental Divide, Logan Pass to me is one of the most beautiful places in the Rocky Mountains. Thirty-two miles east of West Glacier and 18 miles west of St. Mary, the pass is like the balance of a gigantic teeter-totter beneath the Going-to-the-Sun Road. Step to the west and you begin a steep descent below the Garden Wall, a towering, 9,000-foot-high rampart of rock that is an unofficial barrier separating the eastern and western halves of Glacier. Step to the east and you dive into the broad, glacially carved canyon that drains Reynolds Creek down to St. Mary Lake.

From this vantage point it's so easy to see how glaciers sculpted this landscape. Beyond the U-shaped canyons that funnel Reynolds Creek to the east and Logan Creek to the west there are the serrated mountaintops and "glacial horns" that survived the rivers of ice.

Once you've fully digested the distant views, look closer at your surroundings. In summer the broad alpine meadows are studded with pink, yellow, white, and blue flowers, and runoff from ice and snow higher up cascades downhill, cutting this way and that. Steely peaks, some dressed still in snowfields in mid-summer, cup the meadows. Mountain goats call this place home, and if you're lucky, you'll find yourself surrounded by them. On my hike along the **Hidden Lake Trail** 🌶🌶, a mostly gentle, 3-mile round-trip that leads you to an observation platform overlooking the crescent-shaped lake, mountain goats crowded the boardwalk to the delight of kids and every adult with a camera. Some were so close it seemed as if they had been paid to pose for the shutterbugs. Others were more skittish and stayed higher up on the talus slopes.

Closer to the ground, indignant pikas chirped loudly at human intruders to this landscape, and then scurried quickly away to hiding places in the rocks.

As you head up the trail, the boardwalk eventually gives way to a gravel path that uses steppingstones to help you past rivulets of runoff. As you go higher, the vegetation clings closer to the ground, unable to make much of a go against the harsh climate that embraces this part of the park much of the year. Trail-side signs explain how glaciers stripped most of the vegetation and soil from the landscape, and how tiny lichens and other pioneering plants eventually managed a tenuous foothold that slowly grew in size.

MANY GLACIER

Driving to Many Glacier Lodge, the landscape does a great job of keeping secret the fabulous setting that awaits you. From Babb, Montana, the 12-mile-long road rolls along the shore of Lake Sherburne, a thin finger of water that rests in the trough between Apikuni Mountain and Boulder Ridge. The view across the water, meadows, and broken forest is nice, but reveals nothing of what you encounter once you reach the pinch point between Allen Mountain and Altyn Peak.

Once past that point, the craggy backcountry of Glacier rears its majestic head, revealing Grinnel Point climbing above Swiftcurrent Lake and Lake Josephine with the much taller Mt. Wilbur and Mt. Grinnell in the background. Look hard and you might see the Ptarmigan Wall and Swiftcurrent Mountain.

In the foreground rests the lodge itself, a four-story construction of wood beams, wood-shingle roofing, and plank exterior, one that's crowded with balconies, stone chimneys that funnel away the smoke of many fireplaces, and windows featuring Swiss-styled jigsaw moldings. Inside, massive hand-peeled logs help support the various floors and ceilings, while chandeliers dangle overhead. A massive circular copper fireplace anchors the middle of the lobby, surrounded by chairs, couches, and end tables.

This structure without a doubt is Glacier's best rendition of stately national-park lodging, and with a view to match. Behind (or in front, depending on your perspective) of the lodge pools Swiftcurrent Lake, a shimmering body of water crisscrossed daily by cruise boats and paddlers in canoes, kayaks, and rowboats. An old bull moose enjoyed the waters the day I visited, standing knee-deep while sinking his bulbous face into the water again and again to pluck vegetation from the lake bed.

Though the lodge's rooms are weary and in need of a serious makeover, it's the location—not the accommodations—that makes a stay in Many Glacier an obligation to park visitors. Trails unravel away from the lodge, leading to glaciers, waterfalls unseen from the front country, and tiny lakes perfect for pitching a tent nearby.

For a daylong hike, the **Iceberg Lake Trail** (9.5 miles round-trip; access at a trail head in a cabin area east of the Swiftcurrent Coffee Shop and Campstore), is one of the park's most beautiful. This is a moderate hike that traverses flower-filled meadows to a jewel of a high lake backed against a mountain wall. Even in summer, there may be snow on the ground and ice floating in the lake. Look for mountain goats or bighorn sheep on the cliffs above. And, as in many of the park's backcountry areas, keep an eye out for the grizzlies.

If all you have is a few hours, the **Swiftcurrent Lake Nature Trail** (2.4 miles round-trip; access is at a picnic area half a mile west of the hotel turnoff) is a fun and easy hike along the lake shore, through the woods, and near a marsh, so you may see deer and birds—keep an eye out for blue grouse.

A longer, 10-mile round-trip trail to Grinnell Glacier, the park's largest, is also accessed from this area.

TWO MEDICINE

Head north from East Glacier on Mont. 49 toward Two Medicine and you'll notice that the earth appears to fall off. The contrast is inescapable—mountains tower in the west, but to the east the High Plains begin, sporting a horizon that extends so far and so flat as to seemingly lend credence and legitimacy to the Flat Earth Society. But round a bend on Two Medicine Road and suddenly you'll find yourself faced with three mountains (Appistocki Peak, Mount Henry, and Bison Mountain) bare of vegetation but as red as their Southwestern counterparts.

The Two Medicine entrance itself is only about 4 miles north of East Glacier Park on Mont. 49, with auto access to Lower Two Medicine Lake and Two Medicine Lake, as well as hiking trails to Pumpelly Pillar and over Pitamakan Pass.

PLACES FOR LEARNING

In Browning at the junction of U.S. 2 and 89 stands the **Museum of the Plains Indian** (© **406/338-2230**), a fairly modest effort that needs some attention yet still features one of the best collections of Indian garb in the West. During the summer months a collection of tepees is set up on the museum lawns, while inside through exhibits you can track the history of Indian tribes, the landscape of the West, and tribal art. Collections also touch on toys, music, and ceremonies, such as the sun dance. June through September there is a suggested donation of $4 for adults, $3 for seniors, $1 for children ages 6 to 12. The rest of the year it's free.

8 For the Active Family

BOATING

During my visit to Many Glacier Hotel, I strolled down to the dock to snap some pictures of Grinnell Point. At the same time, a family was piling into some of **Glacier Park Boat Co.**'s (see "Glacier Address Book," p. 237) kayaks and canoes to explore Swiftcurrent Lake on their own, while the cruise boat headed off in another direction.

With 653 lakes overall, and many of them easily accessible, Glacier is a paddler's paradise. The long lakes offer miles of shoreline to explore, some fairly good fishing, and a great opportunity to leave the crowds behind. And you don't have to be particularly skilled, either, as the Glacier Park Boat Co. (see "Glacier Address Book," p. 237) rents canoes, sit-on-top kayaks, rowboats, and even motorboats. Prices range from $12 an hour for the canoes, kayaks, and rowboats to $22 an hour for 10-horsepower motorboats. The boat company offers rentals at Apgar Village, Lake McDonald Lodge, Two Medicine, and Many Glacier. Of course, those who live within driving distance can simply strap their craft to the top of their rigs.

For those who like their watery excursions to pack a little more punch, there are plenty of opportunities to spend a day white-water rafting (see "Entertainment outside the Park," p. 269).

FISHING

Glacier's streams and lakes are habitat for whitefish, kokanee salmon, arctic grayling, and five kinds of trout. Try the North Fork of the Flathead to fish for cutthroat and bull trout and any of the park's three larger lakes (Bowman, St. Mary, and McDonald) for rainbow, brook trout, and whitefish. State of Montana fishing licenses are generally not required within the park's boundaries, although you will need one on the North Fork and Middle Fork of the Flathead River. Also, keep in mind that since the eastern boundary of the park abuts the Blackfeet Indian Reservation, you may find yourself fishing in their territorial waters. To avoid a problem, purchase a $10 use permit from businesses in the gateway towns; the permit covers fishing, hiking, and biking in the reservation. Fishing outside the park in Montana waters requires a state license; check in at a local fishing shop to make certain you're within the law.

HIKING

Just about anywhere you turn in Glacier you'll come face-to-face with a hiking trail. Overall, there are 151 trails, and while some of those can be grueling thanks to some steep climbs, others are perfect for introducing youngsters to the out-of-doors.

Pick up **trail maps** at outdoor stores in Whitefish and Kalispell or the major visitor centers and ranger stations in the park. Before striking off into the wilderness, however, check with the nearest ranger station to determine the accessibility of your destination, trail conditions, and recent bear sightings. Also note that the trail maps don't show elevation changes or many terrain features beyond lakes and the tallest peaks. If you plan to do any extensive hiking, it is best to purchase a U.S. Geological Survey (USGS) topographic map, available at outdoor sporting goods stores and the USGS website (www.usgs.gov).

The Park Service asks you to stay on trails to keep from eroding the fragile components of the park. Also, don't traverse snowbanks, especially the steeper ones. You should have proper footwear and rain gear, enough food, and, most important, enough water, before approaching any trail head. A can of pepper spray can also come in handy for grizzly habitat.

I've listed some of my favorite hikes under "Natural Places" (p. 262). Here's a look at some of the other possibilities:

The Loop (8 miles round-trip; access is on Going-to-the-Sun Rd., about halfway between Avalanche Campground and Logan Pass Visitor Center) offers a moderate hike that climbs to Granite Park Chalet and back. Many people use it as a continuation of the Highline Trail, but this is the section to do if you're not quite so adventurous (the

Highline Trail is almost 8 miles long). If you want to spend the night in the chalet, contact **Belton Chalets, Inc.,** for reservations (© **888/345-2649**). (See the descriptions of the chalets in "Family-Friendly Accommodations," p. 251.)

The **Sun Point Nature Trail** (1.4 miles round-trip; access is 9 miles west of St. Mary at the Sun Point parking area) is an easy walk on gentle slopes that presents commanding views of Baring Falls.

From the Many Glacier area the 10-mile round-trip trail to **Grinnell Glacier,** the park's largest ice flow, makes for a great daylong excursion with a great payoff, although the elevation gain of 1,600 feet might be too tough for some youngsters. Take the boat cruise across Swiftcurrent Lake and the hike's round-trip length is shortened to 7.6 miles.

The very easy **Running Eagle Falls Trail** (.6 mile round-trip; access is 1 mile west of the Two Medicine entrance) winds through a heavily forested area to a large, noisy waterfall. The popular **Twin Falls Trail** (7.6 miles round-trip; accessed from Two Medicine Campground) is an easy hike to scenic Twin Falls. Hikers can walk the entire distance to Twin Falls on a clearly identified trail, or boat across Two Medicine Lake to the foot of the trail head, and hike the last mile. The **St. Mary Falls Trail** (1.6 miles round-trip; accessed from Jackson Glacier Overlook) is a fairly easy walk that takes you to rushing falls of the St. Mary River. The roar of the cascade is prodigious and satisfying.

HORSEBACK RIDING

Getting onto the back of a horse is a good way to see Glacier's backcountry if you don't have the time for an extended backpacking trek. There's just something inherently "Western" when you mount up, and with the horse doing all the work, you can better enjoy the scenery. Inside the park, **Swan Mountain Outfitters** (© **406/888-5555** at Lake McDonald, © **406/888-5010** at Apgar Village, or © **406/732-4203** at Many Glacier; www.mule-shoe.com) offers rides that last just 1 hour ($32) or run all day ($135) from corrals at Lake McDonald and Many Glacier. Some of the all-day rides from Many Glacier go to Poia Lake and Cracker Lake, where there's an abandoned copper mine. The all-day rides have a minimum age of 9, and on some rides the weight limit is 200 pounds, on others it's 225 pounds. **Glacier Gateway Trailrides** (© **406/226-4408**) runs rides from 1 hour to all day ($25–$175) into areas outside the park, such as the Two Medicine River Gorge, from corrals across from Glacier Park Lodge in East Glacier.

SCENIC CRUISES

As the sun was dipping toward the horizon, the captain of the *DeSmet* clanged the boat's bell and slowly backed the vessel away from the dock at Lake McDonald Lodge. Pulling out into the 10-mile-long lake, he pointed the *DeSmet's* prow toward Apgar Village at the far end and began a slow journey that offered time to bask in the waning sunlight while a naturalist schooled the passengers on some of the park's history and geology. As we cruised smoothly through the lake's small chop, he explained how glaciers long ago scooped the lake bed out of the landscape and pointed to the lateral moraines on both sides of Lake McDonald and the terminal moraine at Apgar Village that dammed McDonald Creek and turned it into a lake.

Cruising slowly along Lake McDonald, Swiftcurrent Lake, St. Mary Lake, and Two Medicine Lake is one of the best ways to enjoy Glacier's dramatic scenery. The sun shines down on you, there's a slight breeze in your face, and there's no traffic to worry about. Kids learn almost by accident, as the naturalists quiz the passengers on what they've learned and answer any questions that surface.

The cruise along Swiftcurrent Lake can be combined with a walk to Grinnel Lake, while the St. Mary Lake cruise offers the option of a short hike to St. Mary Falls. The Two Medicine cruise also offers an optional walk to Twin Falls.

Cruises, which are offered throughout the day during the summer months, range from 45 to 90 minutes. Tickets from the **Glacier Park Boat Co.** (see "Glacier Address Book," p. 237) are about $11 to $17 for adults, half that for kids 4 to 12, while children under 4 ride free. During the season, the following numbers link you directly to the docks: Lake McDonald, ℂ **406/888-5727;** Many Glacier, ℂ **406/732-4480;** St. Mary, ℂ **406/732-4430;** and Two Medicine, ℂ **406/226-4467.**

SWIMMING

Glacier's high-elevation lakes typically are a bit too cold for most to enjoy a nice swim, but they can be refreshing and, if you're camping, a great way to wash some of the dust off. I've seen young and old dash into the water on the beach in front of Lake McDonald Lodge and at Apgar Village, although it's not something that draws crowds.

9 Kid-Friendly Programs

Throughout the summer Glacier National Park has some ranger-led programs, ranging from scenic cruises paired with hikes to day hikes and interpretive talks. The programs are based out of Lake McDonald, St. Mary, Two Medicine, Many Glacier, and Logan Pass. Some of the day hikes are pretty easy—the Avalanche Lake hike is only 4 miles, round-trip, and the trek spans 3½ hours—while others are fairly intensive. The **Siyeh Pass** hike, for instance, covers 11 miles in 8 hours and climbs up the park's highest established trail, not something you'd want to take your youngster on. Check the *Glacier Explorer,* the park newspaper, for times and details.

Additionally, Native American presenters offer talks throughout the summer at Lake McDonald Lodge, the St. Mary Visitors Center, and at some of the campgrounds. Again, check the park paper for specifics.

Naturally, many of the park campgrounds have amphitheaters where evening talks are given around the campfire. Topics might touch on the park's geology and its wildlife, or feature Native American presentations.

CHILDREN'S PROGRAMS

The park's **Junior Ranger** program, aimed at kids between 6 and 12, requires that youngsters complete six described activities that will introduce them to various habitats found in Glacier and either interview a ranger or attend a ranger-led program. The requirements are laid out in the *Junior Ranger* newspaper, which can be found in the visitor centers. Once kids complete five activities and fill out the form in the newspaper you can head back to any visitor center to turn it in and receive a Junior Ranger Badge.

On occasion there are ranger-led programs aimed specifically at kids. Check the park's newspaper, *The Glacier Explorer,* for offerings during your visit.

The **Glacier Institute** ℱ (see "Glacier Address Book," p. 237) conducts field classes in the summer that examine Glacier's cultural and natural resources. These 1- to 7-day courses include instruction, transportation, park fees, and college credit. Instructors are highly skilled in their area of expertise, bringing to each course an intimate knowledge

Tips Places for Relaxed Play & Picnics

While there are countless places to have a picnic—I like **Avalanche Lake**—a great spot is on the Going-to-the-Sun Road at the **Sun Point Lake** parking area. Located about 9 miles east of the Logan Pass Visitor Center, or 9 miles west of the St. Mary Visitor Center, this setting offers great views across the lake to the mountains. This is also the start of the .7-mile round-trip hike that follows the lake's shoreline to **Baring Falls.**

of the region and subject matter. The classroom is Glacier National Park and—during the park's off season—other areas in northwest Montana. Previous courses have covered alpine wildflowers, Glacier's grizzlies, poetry, sketching, weather systems, and nature photography.

There are even **kid-specific** programs, such as the **Wolf Pup Mini Camp** that is designed to introduce 7- and 8-year-olds to their first overnight camp-out; **the Young Naturalist Camp,** a 5-day camp that takes 9- and 10-year-olds to explore the wild lands of Glacier; and **Wild Land Hiking** for 11- and 12-year-olds, who are taught how to find their way through the woods with map and compass.

Contact the institute for a copy of their current catalog. Prices range from $50 to $640 per course.

10 Entertainment outside the Park

RAFTING

Though the waters that are actually in the park don't lend themselves to white-water rafting, the forks of the Flathead River are some of the best in the northwest corner of the state. For just taking it easy and floating on your back in the summer sun, the North Fork of the Flathead River stretching from Polebridge to Columbia Falls and into Flathead Lake is ideal. Portaging in Polebridge can be difficult, however. The same may be said for the Middle Fork of the Flathead, at the southern border of the park.

For white-water voyagers, the North Fork of the Flathead River (Class II, III) and the Middle Fork (Class III) are the best bets. Inquire at any ranger station for details and conditions, since flow rates change dramatically as snow melts or storms move through the area.

The Middle Fork is a little more severe; the names of certain stretches (such as the Narrows, Jaws, and Bonecrusher) are terror-inspiring in themselves. To assuage that terror, several outfitters offer expert and sanctioned guided trips.

The **Glacier Guides and Montana Raft Company** (© **800/521-RAFT** or 406/387-5555; fax 406/387-5656; www.glacierguides.com) offers rafting trips in Glacier and the surrounding area. Prices for an adult range from a half-day for $47 to an 8-day hiking and rafting trip for $1,135 per person. Prices cover equipment and food. Trips are scheduled throughout the season. The full-day trip puts in at Cacadilla about 15 miles up the Flathead River. You'll paddle down the relatively calm upper portion, stop for lunch, then be ready for the Class II and Class III white water below Moccasin Creek.

WALK IN THE TREES

Ever wonder what it *really* looks like at the top of the forest, say 70 feet in the air? If so, head to the **Big Mountain Ski Resort** (P.O. Box 1400, Whitefish, MT 59937; ✆ **800/858-4157**; www.bigmtn.com) in Whitefish 25 miles west of Glacier to Walk in the Treetops. This 2½-hour trek, which includes a half-mile hike through a sub-alpine forest from the resort base to the start of the treetop trail, takes you up onto a boardwalk roughly 70 feet in the sky to stroll along through the forest's canopy. Running 800 feet, the boardwalk includes two observation platforms where you can relax a bit while taking in the views of the Flathead Valley and the surrounding mountains. A guide leads the way, after making sure your safety harness fits and it's securely clipped onto a safety cable system. Participants must be at least 10 years old and 54 inches tall. Tickets are $49.

FAST FACTS: Glacier National Park

Area Code The area code is **406.**

ATMs ATMs can be found at Apgar Village, Lake McDonald Lodge, Many Glacier, St. Mary, East Glacier, Rising Sun, Swiftcurrent, and West Glacier.

Emergencies For emergencies, dial ✆ **911.**

Hospitals & Clinics There are no medical facilities in the park. The **Kalispell Regional Hospital** is in Kalispell (310 Sunny View Lane; ✆ **406/752-5111**), while the **North Valley Hospital** is in Whitefish (Hwy. 93 S., Whitefish; ✆ **406/863-3500**).

Information For information, write Glacier National Park, P.O. Box 128, West Glacier, MT 59936; call ✆ **406/888-7800;** or check the website www.nps.gov/glac.

Pharmacies The closest drug store is **Tidyman's Pharmacy** in Kalispell, 55 1st Ave. (✆ **406/756-5960**).

Post Office There are post offices in West Glacier (110 Going-to-the-Sun Rd.; ✆ **800/275-8777**), Lake McDonald (Lake McDonald complex; ✆ **406/888-9953**), East Glacier (15 Blackfoot Ave.; ✆ **800/275-8777**), and St. Mary (✆ **800/275-8777**).

Time Zone The park is on **Mountain Standard Time.**

Transit Info Summer shuttle-bus service between Apgar Village and St. Mary, with stops at campgrounds and trail heads.

Weather Updates For weather updates, look on the Internet at www.wrh.noaa.gov.

11

Yellowstone National Park

Despite Yellowstone's being 2.2 million acres, the size of a small country, Yellowstone is ridiculously easy to experience up close with little effort. I've driven along the Firehole River and watched hot springs dump their steaming waters into the river while bison graze on the hillsides. Overhead, eagles dart by, occasionally in the pursuit of ducks. Cruising through the Lamar Valley on the other side of the park, I've stopped to watch wolves return to their dens from a morning hunt, spotted grizzly bears frolicking in early summer's waning snowfields, and watched bighorn sheep graze on the hillsides. In the Upper Geyser Basin, you can practically drive by geysers, although it's much wiser to park your car and walk the boardwalks around Morning Glory Hot Spring, along Geyser Hill, or into Black Sand Basin.

With so much to see right by the road, driving can get addictive. But there is a price to pay, in this case traffic and crowding. The trick at Yellowstone is to say "enough," break from the car after seeing some highlights, and go deeper into the country. Fewer than 1% of Yellowstone visitors ever get more than ¼ mile from the road, so it takes little effort to leave people behind. And the payoffs are incredible. Along with my wife and our two sons I've hiked in early October down the paved path to the Lone Star Geyser to watch it erupt during a snowstorm, and my sons and I have visited Solitary Geyser in the Upper Geyser Basin, quickly leaving behind thousands at the Old Faithful complex. Both are short hikes and don't require any special preparation or training. Yet the rewards are rich and memorable.

Yellowstone is the center of the country's largest area of preserved lands outside Alaska. Going there and staying in a car the whole time makes as much sense as going to an art museum and refusing to take off your sunglasses.

BEST THINGS TO DO IN YELLOWSTONE NATIONAL PARK

- **Walk along the geyser basins** in the Old Faithful or Norris Geyser Basin areas and climb over the otherworldly landscapes of Mammoth Hot Springs.
- **See huge herds of bison and elk** wandering the meadows of the Hayden Valley or Northern Range, or watch for wolves in the Lamar Valley.
- **Take a day hike** or an overnight on one of America's best networks of trails.
- **Ride horseback** on Yellowstone's spectacular Northern Range.
- **Come in winter** to see the countryside under deep snow, traveling by snow coach or on cross-country skis.

For more information, see "For the Active Family" (p. 304).

Yellowstone Address Book

Yellowstone National Park   P.O. Box 168, Yellowstone National Park, WY 82190-0168. ℂ **307/344-7381.** TDD 307/344-2386. www.nps.gov/yell.

Xanterra Parks and Resorts, park concessionaire (also known as Yellowstone National Park Lodges)   P.O. Box 165, Yellowstone National Park, WY 82190-0165. ℂ **866/GEYSERLAND** or 307/344-7311. Fax 307/344-7456. www.travel yellowstone.com.

The Yellowstone Association   P.O. Box 117, Yellowstone National Park, WY 82190. ℂ **307/344-2293.** Fax 307/344-2486. Retail sales ℂ **877/967-0090.** www.yellowstoneassociation.org. For books, maps, programs, and the Yellowstone Institute.

Gallatin National Forest   Federal Building (P.O. Box 130), Bozeman, MT 59771. ℂ **406/587-6701.** www.fs.fed.us/r1/gallatin.

Shoshone National Forest   808 Meadow Lane, Cody, WY 82414. ℂ **307/527-6241.** www.fs.fed.us/r2/shoshone.

Cooke City Chamber of Commerce   P.O. Box 1071, Cooke City, MT 59020. ℂ **406/838-2495.** www.cookecitychamber.org.

Gardiner Chamber of Commerce   P.O. Box 81, Gardiner, MT 59030. ℂ **406/848-7971.** Fax 406/848-2446. www.gardinerchamber.com.

West Yellowstone Chamber of Commerce   P.O. Box 458, West Yellowstone, MT 59758. ℂ **406/646-7701.** www.westyellowstonechamber.com.

1 History: A Good Idea

The story of Yellowstone National Park is simple, and it helped to change the world. This is the first national park not only in the United States, but anywhere on earth. Yellowstone kick-started the idea of national parks, and with it the idea that some natural places should be preserved as nature created them.

Just 136 years later, it seems strange that people didn't always value wilderness as we do today. But when Yellowstone was set aside as a national park, much more of the natural world was left unchanged. Explorers were still discovering parts of the planet. To most people, the world seemed limitless. Wild land and animals didn't have the same value they do for us today, partly because there was so much. That feeling probably had something to do with Yellowstone's becoming a park, too. Why not set aside this one special place, when so much of the West was left to settle? Later, creating the smaller Grand Teton National Park, just to the south, was much harder because people wanted the land for other uses.

Native Americans used Yellowstone mostly in the summer. As in other high Rocky Mountain country, they came to hunt when the snow melted, then returned to warmer lowlands when winter arrived. The Crow, Shoshone, Blackfoot, Arapahoe, Flathead, and Nez Percé were all using the area that's now the park when white men arrived. The area has many archaeological sites of primitive Native American camps, some in areas around geysers—disproving stories that the Indians were afraid of them.

A Shoshone band called the Sheepeaters, who lived by hunting mountain sheep, probably used hot water from the geyser basins to straighten the sheep's curled horn for excellent bows. Other ancient tribes, not identified for certain, mined Obsidian Cliff, in the northwest area of the park on the road between Mammoth Hot Springs and Norris Geyser Basin. (Don't break the law and help destroy the park by taking obsidian, or any other rocks. You can buy obsidian from outside the park in rock shops.) Obsidian is a black, glassy rock made by thick lava that comes to the surface and cools very quickly. A natural glass, obsidian breaks in sharp flakes. If you don't have metal, flakes of obsidian make the best possible points for spears and arrows. Native Americans traded rocks from Obsidian Cliff with other tribes that could give them valuable items from other parts of North America. By studying the exact mixture of elements in Yellowstone obsidian, scientists have proven that ancient points found far away came from here. They've found this obsidian in archaeological sites in Ohio, Washington, North Dakota, Colorado, Manitoba, Alberta, Saskatchewan, and other, closer places.

Yellowstone's history of white settlement is unique: No sooner was it officially discovered than it became a park. "Discovered" is a funny word, because what it means always depends on your point of view. Native Americans discovered Yellowstone at least 10,000 years ago. John Colter, a member of the Lewis and Clark expedition, first

Yellowstone National Park

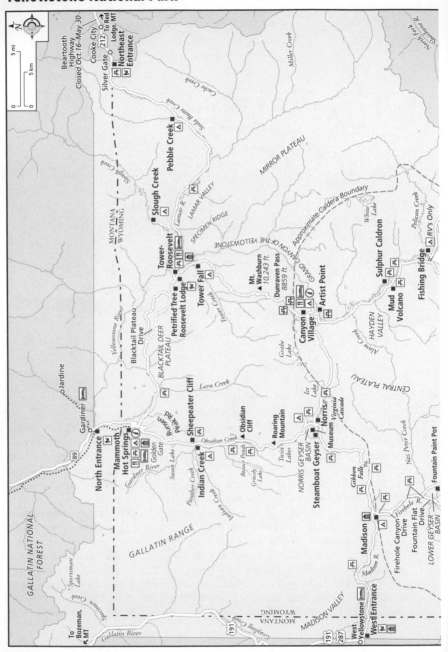

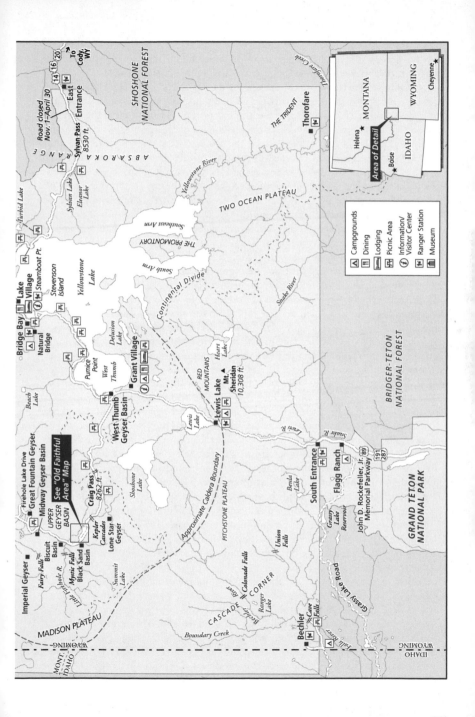

passed through while hunting for furs in 1807. Fur trappers wandered through the area for decades after Colter. But part of discovery means reporting what you find back to people who don't know about it, and having them believe you.

Gold prospectors began to pass through in the 1860s and came across the geysers and hot springs that the trappers and Colter had found before them. That inspired a group from Helena, Montana, to explore the area in 1869. Their report of the canyons and geysers was rejected by East Coast publications as not believable, but it interested Henry Washburn, the official surveyor for the Montana Territory. He visited the next year. Members of his group returned to the East and lectured about what they had seen. Dr. Ferdinand Hayden, director of the U.S. Geological and Geographical Survey, heard one of the lectures in Washington, D.C. His job was to draw the map of America. The next year, 1871, he went out West and "discovered" Yellowstone, bringing back photographs and paintings to prove it.

When you're expecting to see a geyser, it's amazing enough. Imagine how you would feel if you were hiking across the country and saw one shoot off in front of you, completely unexpectedly! Geysers show up in only a few places in the world, and most of them are here. Discovering them was big news. People started thinking right away about how to make money from them. Soon after Hayden returned from his trip, the Northern Pacific Railroad joined him in pushing to have the thermal area protected as a park. The railroad wanted to carry tourists to the area on its trains. The law setting aside the park passed quickly, and President Grant signed it on March 1, 1872.

Yellowstone was not the first land in the United States to be preserved. Earlier, Congress gave California the Yosemite Valley and some areas of big Sequoia trees, with the agreement that the land would not be used except as a state park. California later gave the land back to be a national park (see "History: Fight for the Valley," in chapter 14, "Yosemite National Park"). But Yellowstone was the world's first national park, and here people have fought hardest over the years about what a national park should be.

When Yellowstone became a park, land in the West was pretty much open for people to use as they liked, taking whatever valuable minerals or trees they might find. In the East, most land belonged to someone, and lines on a map showed who owned what. In the West, land was free for the taking. Poor people from the East could move here and get land of their own without much money. They would find a place they liked, mark the boundaries, and file papers at a government office. If they built a farm or ranch and lived on the land for a few years—called "proving their claim"—they normally received permanent ownership of the homestead. The first to arrive homesteaded the best land, closest to a railroad line or in valleys good for farming. The next families might go a bit farther out. Much of the private land in the West was settled this way, one homestead at a time.

At first, creating the national park just meant no one could homestead at Yellowstone. That was easy enough to agree on, because no one wanted to homestead there anyway. The area was too rugged and too far from towns to be worth much. After Yellowstone became a park, people still treated it as open land. They killed animals by the thousands for fur and took away whatever they wanted, breaking pieces off geysers and even plugging them up with coins and garbage. In 1886, the U.S. Army took over control of the park with the mission of protecting it. The army stopped the hunting and patrolled the backcountry to keep out poachers (people who kill wildlife when hunting is not allowed). Strange as it seems to us today, the soldiers thought of wolves, cougars, and coyotes as poachers, too, and killed them to keep them from killing other animals. People soon learned that animals in the park couldn't be protected without also protecting some of their habitat outside the park's boundaries. Forestland was set aside around Yellowstone in 1891, stopping homesteading and uncontrolled hunting there, too. President Theodore Roosevelt made these areas into the first national forests in 1905.

Eventually, all of the West was divided into either private land or government land, each area with a certain purpose. The private land came in homesteads, railroad lands, and other government gifts. The government lands were national parks, national forests, national wildlife refuges, and land controlled by the Bureau of Land Management, called the BLM. Each kind of government land is managed by a different agency with a different purpose. Most of the lands, including the national forests and BLM lands, are managed for multiple uses. That means they aren't just for recreation and wildlife habitat, but also for logging, mining, and livestock range.

The great political debates in the West today are about how each of these lands should be used—if they can be used up, if they should be used in a sustainable way that can go on forever, or if they should be preserved and set aside like the national parks. Lands that are preserved for nature and wildlife are a small part of what's left from the Old West.

2 Orientation

Yellowstone is a square roughly 60 miles on each side straddling the Continental Divide. It's mostly in northwest Wyoming, with a strip of Idaho on the west and Montana on the north. Much of the park is a mountain plateau 7,000 to 8,000 feet high, with mountains over 10,000 feet ringing it. The park's Northern Range is a lower, grassy valley, with grandly rolling terrain. Geysers and other thermal features show up all over the park, but the most impressive are on the western side of the park; at Old Faithful, in the southwest quadrant; Norris Geyser Basin, near the midpoint; and Mammoth Hot Springs, in the northwest corner. On the eastern side of the park, the most notable attractions were created by the water of the Yellowstone River. It flows north from huge Yellowstone Lake, in the southeast part of the park, and through the impressive "Grand Canyon of the Yellowstone" (p. 300) and Tower Fall in the northeast part.

Choose one or two of the series of developed areas in the park for your base. Six areas have lodgings and visitor centers, and several others have campgrounds, museums, or other attractions. Details are in the appropriate sections below (see "The National Park in Brief").

ARRIVING
BY CAR

Yellowstone isn't near any large cities. Salt Lake City is a 350-mile drive, Denver 600 miles, and Seattle 800 miles. The closest interstate east-west highway is I-90, and the nearest north-south route is I-15. Two-lane U.S. highways enter the park at five places on routes that are fairly easy to follow on any highway map. You can enter from Jackson, Wyoming; Cody, Wyoming; Cooke City, Montana; Gardiner, Montana; and West Yellowstone, Montana.

BY AIR

Several towns where you can fly in and rent a car have air links to hubs in Denver, Salt Lake City, or Seattle. Airfares often differ greatly for each portal depending on where you are coming from. If price differences aren't great for your plans, you can choose according to how far you want to drive and where in the park you want to enter.

If you're staying at Mammoth Hot Springs, you can fly into **Bozeman,** Montana's Gallatin Field Airport (www.gallatinfield.com), 79 miles away. Bozeman is served by **Delta/SkyWest** (© 800/221-1212; www.delta.com), **Northwest** (© 800/225-2525; www.nwa.com), **United Express** (© 800/864-8331; www.united.com), **Big Sky Airlines** (© 800/237-7788; www.bigskyair.com), and **Horizon** (© 800/252-7522; www.horizonair.com). You can rent cars there from **Budget** (© 800/527-0700 or 406/388-4091; www.budget.com), **Enterprise** (© 800/261-7331 or 406/586-8010; www.enterprise.com), **National** (© 800/227-7368 or 406/388-6694; www.nationalcar.com), or **Hertz** (© 800/654-3131 or 406/388-6939; www.hertz.com).

If you're staying in Grant Village, Jackson, Wyoming, is 55 miles from the south entrance (you can rent an RV there, too).

Cody, Wyoming, is 53 miles from the east entrance. The Yellowstone Regional Airport (www.flyyra.com) there is served by **United Express** (© 800/864-8331 or 307/587-9740; www.ual.com), **Delta/SkyWest** (© 800/221-1212 or 307/587-9740; www.delta.com), and **Mesa Airlines** (© 800/864-8331 or 307/587-9740; www.mesa-air.com). Car rentals are available from **Hertz** (© 800/654-3131 or 307/587-2914; www.hertz.com), **Budget** (© 800/527-0700 or 307/587-6066; www.budget.com), and **Thrifty** (© 800/367-2277 or 307/587-8855; www.thrifty.com).

West Yellowstone, Montana, is at the west entrance. It's served only during the summer by **Delta/SkyWest** (© 800/221-1212; www.delta.com), with car rentals available from **Budget** (© 800/231-5991 or 406/646-7735; www.budget-yellowstone.com) and **Big Sky Car Rentals** (© 800/426-7669 or 406/646-9564).

If you don't mind driving a little farther, have your travel agent shop for ticket and car rates at Idaho Falls and Billings. Major carriers and car-rental agencies serve both.

VISITOR INFORMATION
NATIONAL PARK VISITOR CENTERS

Each of these centers has a bookstore and a desk where you can ask questions. Canyon and Albright have backcountry-permit desks; otherwise, backcountry offices are usually nearby. Ranger stations, which answer questions and issue permits, are at many other sites around the park. Check the free park map, website, or *Yellowstone Today* park newspaper for locations.

Albright Visitor Center 🖈   Housed in a stone building that once served as bachelor officers' quarters in historic Fort Yellowstone, this large center contains a rich two-story museum. Highlights include the art of Thomas Moran and photographs of William Henry Jackson that first revealed Yellowstone to the world and led to the park's creation. It's worth up to an hour of your day. Films on park history show all day.

Mammoth Hot Springs. © **307/344-2263.** Summer daily 8am–7pm; winter daily 9am–5pm. Open year-round.

Canyon Visitor Education Center   This beautiful new center provides tremendous interpretation on geologic forces, both in Yellowstone and throughout the world. There's a 9,000-pound rotating globe that pinpoints geologic hot spots around the world, a room-size relief map that explains the park's hot spots, volcanic eruptions, lava flows, and even past glaciers. Kids will get a kick out of the lava lamp, one of the biggest in the world, that illustrates how magma rises to the service by heat convection.

Canyon. © **307/242-2550.** Summer daily 8am–6pm; fall daily 9am–5pm. Closed mid-Oct to mid-May.

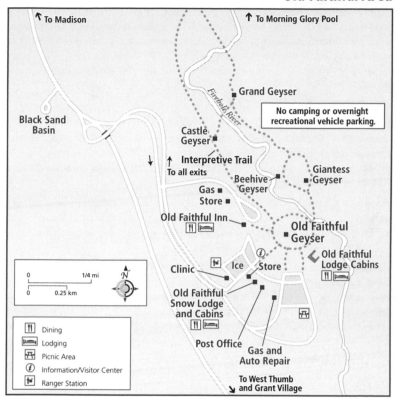

↖ To Madison

↑ To Morning Glory Pool

Firehole River

● Grand Geyser

Black Sand Basin

No camping or overnight recreational vehicle parking.

Castle Geyser ■

↑ **Interpretive Trail**
To all exits

↓

Beehive Geyser

Giantess Geyser

Gas ■
Store ■

Old Faithful Inn

Old Faithful Geyser

Clinic   Ice   Store

ⓘ

Old Faithful Lodge Cabins

Old Faithful Snow Lodge and Cabins

Post Office   Gas and Auto Repair

To West Thumb and Grant Village

0   1/4 mi
0   0.25 km

N

Dining
Lodging
Picnic Area
ⓘ **Information/Visitor Center**
Ranger Station

Fishing Bridge Visitor Center   The two-room museum on the natural history of Yellowstone Lake and its animals isn't that exciting, but the stone-and-timber building is a wonderful architectural piece. The lakeside site is a nice place to play. Go to the ranger stations at the Lake and Bridge Bay areas for backcountry permits.

North side of Yellowstone Lake. ℂ **307/242-2450.** Summer daily 8am–7pm; fall daily 9am–6pm. Closed Oct to mid-May.

Grant Village Visitor Center   The center contains an exhibit on the great fire of 1988 and the natural history of forest fires in general, an explanation of the big areas of standing deadwood you have passed on the road. Most of it is well oriented to children. There's a slide show on the same theme.

On Yellowstone Lake at the southern end of the lower loop. ℂ **307/242-2650.** Summer daily 8am–7pm; fall daily 9am–6pm. Closed Oct to mid-May.

Old Faithful Visitor Education Center   If things go as planned, a new visitor center will open in 2010 and bring with it a wealth of interpretive information on how Yellowstone's geothermal plumbing system works. Also planned are exhibits on microbiology in the park—critters such as extremophiles that can live in the park's hot springs. For now, though, the old visitor center has been razed to make way for the new one and tourists are left with five tiny trailers that are serving as a temporary visitor center. Exhibits have been removed, leaving little but a monitor that displays either the Old Faithful webcam or a seismograph report. There is a small theater, which can hold only about 20, where films on what to do in the park and on Yellowstone's volcanic background are shown. For backcountry permits, go to the combination ranger station and clinic across the west parking lot.

Old Faithful. (℡ 307/545-2750. Summer daily 8am–7pm; fall and winter daily 9am–5pm. Closed Nov to mid-Dec and mid-Mar to mid-Apr.

COMMERCIAL VISITOR CENTERS
Check the "Yellowstone Address Book" (p. 272) for contact information.

Cooke City Chamber of Commerce The center outside the park's northeast entrance has an information desk and brochures.

205 Main Street, Hwy. 212, Cooke City. (℡ 406/838-2495 or 406/838-2272 off season. Late May to mid-Sept daily 11am–6pm. Closed mid-Sept to late May.

Gardiner Chamber of Commerce Stop here for information about businesses outside the north entrance or to use the restroom or the public computer.

222 Park St., Gardiner. (℡ 406/848-7971. Summer Mon–Sat 9am–7pm, Sun 1–5pm; winter Mon–Wed 9am–5pm. Open year-round.

West Yellowstone Chamber of Commerce Visitor Center The center has desks staffed by the local chamber of commerce, the National Park Service, and the U.S. Forest Service. There's room to rest and look at information from many businesses and agencies, and there's free Wi-Fi.

Corner of Yellowstone and Canyon sts., West Yellowstone. (℡ 406/646-7701. Summer daily 8am–8pm; winter Mon–Fri 8am–5pm. Open year-round.

READING UP
All of these items, except for the kids' activity book, are for sale at visitor centers or by mail order or online from the Yellowstone Association (℡ **877/967-0090;** www.yellowstoneassociation.org).

Hiking: *Yellowstone Trails,* by Mark Marschall (Yellowstone Association, $10), is full of useful details and organized to help find a hike at your ability level and near where you are.

Maps: Various maps are available showing the whole park, but I think they try to fit too much on one piece of paper to be satisfactory for hiking. Much better are the quartet of maps covering the park published on plastic by National Geographic's Trails Illustrated, for $9 or $10 each, available as a set of four, from the Yellowstone Association, for $35. They show the locations and numbers of all the backcountry campsites and trail heads compatible with the park's backcountry permit process.

Geology: *Windows into the Earth,* by Robert B. Smith and Lee J. Siegel (Oxford University Press, $30), is a stunningly illustrated and clearly written explanation of the geological processes of Yellowstone and Grand Teton national parks.

Ouch: *Death in Yellowstone,* by Lee Whittlesey (Roberts Rinehart, $17), chronicles more than 300 deaths at the park, including every one that wasn't caused by a vehicle. The morbid fascination doesn't last through all 300, but you will likely end up more cautious.

Kids: *The Great Yellowstone, Grand Teton, Glacier Activity Book* (Rising Sun, $7.95; www.northlandpub.com) overflows with word searches, crossword puzzles, mazes, journals, and other activities to keep young minds busy.

THE NATIONAL PARK IN BRIEF

Mammoth Hot Springs

At the north entrance, near the town of Gardiner, Montana, this historic area includes the park headquarters, two restaurants, a post office, historic lodgings, a museum, a store, a gas station, a clinic, a campground, and the visitor center and commercial services. Nature walks circle the beautiful terraced hot springs. The terrain is relatively low, warm, and open.

Tower-Roosevelt

This quieter, less developed area in the northeast part of the park has a ranger station and rough lodgings in cabins at Roosevelt Lodge. It's a center for horseback riding in the open, grassy land of the Northern Range. There are a restaurant, store, and gas station. Tower Fall and the campground are a few miles south of Roosevelt Lodge.

Canyon Village

Near the falls on the Grand Canyon of the Yellowstone, the village is crowded with more than 500 cabins, a hotel, a huge campground, a general store, three restaurants, a cafeteria, a gas station, a post office, public showers and laundry, and a visitor center. It lies at the eastern connecting point of the upper and lower loop roads.

Fishing Bridge, Lake Village & Bridge Bay

These three areas, within a few miles of one another on the northern shore of Yellowstone Lake, have lots of lodging and camping choices, from fine historic lodgings to claustrophobic cabins. There are restaurants, stores, a post office, and a gas station. The marina and a large campground are at Bridge Bay, and an RV park is at Fishing Bridge.

Grant Village

On Yellowstone Lake along the route to the south entrance, the charmless village has three restaurants, a hotel, a large campground, stores, public showers and laundry, a post office, a gas station, and a visitor center. There's a boat ramp here for anglers or those launching backcountry canoe or kayak trips, and the lakeside West Thumb geyser basin is just to the north.

Old Faithful

The famous geyser is surrounded by a semicircle of hotels, a visitor center, stores, restaurants, a post office, a gas station, and a clinic. Lots of other geysers are nearby on nature walks. This is the only major developed area without a campground, but there's one 16 miles to the north at Madison. The stretch of road in between is the park's richest in geysers and other thermal features.

Norris

There are two museums, a bookstore, and a great campground near the spectacular Norris Geyser Basin, but no lodgings or other commercial services. This is the connecting point of the two road loops on the west side, opposite the other intersection at Canyon Village, 12 miles east.

Gateway Towns

Details on the towns appear below in the appropriate sections. Here's an overview.

West Yellowstone

This Montana enclave at the park's west entrance is the most developed and touristy of Yellowstone's gateways, with large chain hotels, a museum, an IMAX theater, and a wonderful wildlife attraction. The town is cold and snowy in winter. A great trails network through the Gallatin National Forest that lures mountain bikers in summer and cross-country skiers in winter has a downtown trail head. The airport is open only in summer.

Gardiner

Near the north entrance and Mammoth Hot Springs, Gardiner, Montana, is a tourist-oriented town with lots of motels, but it still has some real Western character. Come here for rafting trips on the Yellowstone River, outside the park. The relatively low elevation helps keep deep snow away.

Cooke City

Cooke City, Montana, is a small town in a beautiful setting of forest and mountains, with basic motel rooms but little else in terms of tourist amenities. It stands outside the northeast entrance.

3 Getting Around

BY CAR OR RV

Driving is the only practical way for a family to get around the park. People do tour by bicycle, but the distances are great and I wouldn't recommend taking children on these narrow, heavily trafficked roads except before they open to vehicles in May (see "Biking & Mountain Biking," p. 304). Even in a car, the park is large, and to cover it efficiently takes planning. You can't get anywhere fast, and it's pointless and frustrating to try. Minimize driving by breaking your trip into two or three different areas, exploring each from a home base within a limited radius before moving on to a new home base in another area. Better yet, relax and spend your whole trip in one part of the park. The fact is, after you've seen one geyser basin, you don't need to visit them all.

The road system at Yellowstone has two connected loops, like an "8," with five tails leading to entrances in five directions. Most visitors meander around these loops, park at the overlooks, and stop to watch geysers and take nature walks along the way. At a fast, superficial pace, each road loop takes a day of touring. Even driving across the park without stopping takes half a day, because the roads wind and people looking at wildlife or scenery frequently back up traffic. My advice is to spend a week on one side of the park and get out of the car. In winter one route is open, through the Northern Range from the north entrance, at Mammoth Hot Springs, to the northeast entrance, near Cooke City, Montana. Other roads close in November and reopen in April or May, depending on snow conditions.

4 Planning Your Outings

WHEN TO GO

The park's main visitor season is July and August. At this elevation, the weather seldom is too hot. Brief afternoon thunderstorms are common.

Until mid-June, trails remain snowy or muddy at the 7,000-foot elevation across most of the park, and some facilities aren't open yet. Campgrounds open between mid-May and mid-June, except Mammoth, which is open all year. Yellowstone Lake ice generally clears in May, but sometimes doesn't go out until early June.

Spring break visits aren't practical, with the park still largely snowbound and few facilities open. Campgrounds start closing in early September. In September and October, crowds are gone and hotel rates drop steeply; lodgings start closing in stages in early September. The air gets frosty at night in October, with few campgrounds left open. Roads close with the November snows. The Mammoth Hot Springs Hotel and Old Faithful Snow Lodge are open for the winter and summer seasons, but not in late fall and early spring.

The park is beautiful in snow, and wildlife congregates at the geothermal hot spots and along river bottoms. One of the most popular activities, snowmobiling, remains the subject of controversy, and likely will be permitted on a limited basis at least for the near future. Visitors can also get around in vanlike snow coaches and can cross-country ski or snowshoe. The winter visitor season lasts from late December to the second week in March. For coverage of winter vacations, see "Winter Sports & Sightseeing" (p. 307).

HOW MUCH TIME TO SPEND

Just driving around the park and seeing the highlights takes 3 days, and for a good visit you need at least 5 days and preferably more time for hiking, boating, riding, and other activities away from the road. With 2 weeks, you could try various activities in more than one area of the park, or add a side trip to Grand Teton National Park (see chapter 12, "Grand Teton National Park").

HOW FAR TO PLAN AHEAD

Yellowstone gets nearly three million visitors each year, and virtually all spend the night. Hotels and five campgrounds in the park take reservations up to a year ahead, through the park concessionaire, **Xanterra** (contact information is under "Yellowstone Address Book," p. 272). You can reserve a campsite 6 months ahead of a summer date, but choices start to fill up after that. Seven campgrounds managed by the Park Service give sites away on a first-come, first-served basis, but they can be difficult to get, and you shouldn't count on them. Backcountry sites are easier to get; top choices are awarded in a lottery on April 1 for the whole year, but a good number are held back for walk-in applications 2 days before the trip. If you need lodgings, you should have your rooms booked 3 to 6 months in advance. The Old Faithful Inn books up 6 months out for peak summer dates; most lodgings are still available 2 or 3 months in advance. Reserve a table in the better hotel dining rooms at the same time because they, too, book months ahead (you can always cancel). Hotels outside the park have openings later, but because anything near Yellowstone fills up in the summer, last-minute planning isn't a good option. The concessionaire enforces a 2-day cancellation policy in the summer, 14 days in the winter; you may find a room by checking when those deadlines hit, or by grabbing a room the morning of a stay if a guest doesn't stay over.

Weather Chart: Old Faithful*

	Avg. High (°F/°C)	Avg. Low (°F/°C)	Snowfall (total in.)
December–February	27–33/–3 to 1	–2 to 1/–19 to –17	119
March	40/4	9/–13	33
April	47/8	18/–8	21
May	56/13	27/–3	9
June	65/18	34/1	2
July–August	73/23	36–39/2–4	0
September	64/18	28/–2	2
October	51/11	20/–7	7
November	35/2	7/–14	34

* The elevation of Old Faithful is approximately 7,200 feet.

WHAT TO PACK
CLOTHING

Summer weather may call for short or long pants and shirts, sweaters, or jackets, depending on the day and elevation. Summer highs are in the 70s (20s Celsius), but afternoon thunderstorms are common. Summer lows are typically in the 40s (single digits Celsius), and get lower as you go higher. Everyone will do a lot of walking, even if you don't go on hikes, just to see the geysers and hot springs, so bring good shoes. Two fine restaurants suggest better than outdoor clothing, so if you plan to eat there, bring nice casual clothes.

In the winter West Yellowstone is often the coldest spot in the United States outside Alaska. Temperatures below zero Fahrenheit are no surprise. For outdoor sports such as cross-country skiing, bring layers of synthetic long underwear, fleece pants and tops, and wind-resistant clothes. For more sedentary sightseeing, add heavy winter clothing, including parkas and well-insulated winter boots. Snowmobiling requires special gear for warmth that you may be able to borrow if you rent a machine; figure out this issue with the rental agency before you go—few people own the kind of outfit you need for snowmobiling in cold temperatures.

GEAR

As at all hiking-oriented parks, a good baby backpack makes your group more mobile. A stroller is usable on most nature trails around the geysers and other famous sites. Quality summer-weight camping gear is okay for Yellowstone from June to early September with an extra layer for especially cold nights (long synthetic underwear or a heavy bag to cover all of you). Your tent should be ready for brief, heavy rain. It gets quite chilly in the fall, when you'll need winter-weight gear.

KEEPING SAFE & HEALTHY

In addition to the special tips here, see "Dealing with Hazards," in chapter 2, for information on bears, hypothermia, and lightning.

BISON

Signs are posted everywhere, and still people walk up to bison to take their pictures. These animals are the size of pickup trucks, have sharp horns, and can get mad unexpectedly. They run 30 mph, faster than the fastest sprinter. Use your common sense, and stay safely back.

BURNS

Visitors have been scalded to death in the hot springs. The danger isn't just falling into a pool of boiling water, but also slipping into hot mud that looks like solid ground. Prevention is simple: Stay on the trail when you are near thermal features, and keep good control of your children.

SWIMMING

There's great swimming at Yellowstone (p. 284), but not in hot springs or water running entirely from hot springs, where the water can carry nasty bugs, including potentially fatal amoebic meningitis. The lakes are too cold for swimming.

5 Family-Friendly Accommodations

CAMPGROUNDS

NATIONAL PARK CAMPGROUNDS

Yellowstone is a huge park, covering some 2.2 million acres. Keep that in mind when considering which campgrounds you might want to stay at. If you want to spend the bulk of your visit around the geothermal features, you won't want a campsite in the southern or northeastern areas of the park, as the drive back and forth will chew up your day. Conversely, if you don't want to focus on the geyser basins and want to avoid most of the crowds, those areas should be considered. That said, there are 12 campgrounds in the park, with varying facilities. The concessionaire, **Xanterra** (© 307/344-7311), operates an RV park and the four largest, most developed campgrounds. You can reserve up to a year ahead, and should call 6 months ahead for the high season if you can (see "Yellowstone Address Book," p. 272). The other seven campgrounds, generally quieter, more isolated choices with larger sites, are run by the Park Service and don't take reservations. For many years, people showed up at these campgrounds early in the morning to grab a site from someone leaving during July and August, with the last sites going at the 10am checkout time. That meant these campgrounds were not a good choice for your first night. In the last several years, however, finding a site has not been so difficult; even during high season sites sometimes go begging. I cannot predict how many people will come in the future, so I can only advise caution: Reserve at least your first night.

At six of the more developed campgrounds, RV generators are allowed (noted in the listings below). They can run only from 8am to 8pm, but that's more than enough to drive you crazy if you're tenting next door. Fishing Bridge RV Park is the only campground with hookups; generators there can run from 7am to 10pm.

Campgrounds Accepting Reservations

These campgrounds, managed by Xanterra, resemble Park Service campgrounds in most ways but have more generous features, including soap in the bathrooms and vending machines for ice, newspapers, and soft drinks. All have flush toilets and dump stations, and all allow RVs and generator use. All but Fishing Bridge allow tents.

Bridge Bay   This huge campground, at an elevation of 7,800 feet, has an attractive half and an area to avoid. The good sites have pine trees and sit on a higher bench overlooking Yellowstone Lake across a grassy meadow, including loops E through J (F is best). The other area, with loops A through D, is a large, flat field, completely without screening; full of tents and RVs, it looks like an updated Civil War encampment. You can ask for a certain site when you reserve, but it is not guaranteed; so arrive early if you can. The campground is near the marina and across the road from Yellowstone Lake, making it a good choice for anglers.

At Yellowstone Lake, near the marina. © 307/344-7311. www.travelyellowstone.com. 425 sites, tents or RVs. $17 site. Closed mid-Sept to late May. **Amenities:** Flush toilets, dump station, picnic tables, fire pits and grates, running water, ice, marina, pay showers and laundry within 4 miles.

Canyon   This thickly wooded campground sits on a hillside above the hotel, visitor center, and other services; at 8,000 feet, it's the highest campground in the park and closes early in September. If you want to be near showers, restaurants, and a full general store, it's a good choice. Hiking trails and the Grand Canyon of Yellowstone are nearby.

Campgrounds in the Yellowstone Area

Campground	Total Sites	RV Hookups	Dump Station	Toilets	Drinking Water	Showers
INSIDE THE PARK						
Bridge Bay*	425	No	Yes	Yes	Yes	Nearby
Canyon*	250	No	Yes	Yes	Yes	Yes
Fishing Bridge**	325	Yes	Yes	Yes	Yes	Yes
Grant Village*	400	No	Yes	Yes	Yes	Yes
Indian Creek	75	No	No	Yes	Yes	No
Lewis Lake	85	No	No	Yes	Yes	No
Madison*	250	No	Yes	Yes	Yes	No
Mammoth	85	No	No	Yes	Yes	No
Norris	100	No	No	Yes	Yes	No
Pebble Creek	30	No	No	Yes	Yes	No
Slough Creek	29	No	No	Yes	Yes	No
Tower Fall	30	No	No	Yes	Yes	No
NEAR THE PARK						
Bakers Hole	73	No	No	Yes	Yes	No
Lonesomehurst	27	No	No	Yes	Yes	No
Rainbow Point	86	No	No	Yes	Yes	No
Rocky Mountain Campground	87	Yes	Yes	Yes	Yes	Yes
Yellowstone Grizzly RV Park	191	Yes	Yes	Yes	Yes	Yes
NEAR NORTHEAST ENTRANCE						
Chief Joseph	6	No	No	Yes	Yes	No
Colter	23	No	No	Yes	No	No
Crazy Creek	16	No	No	Yes	No	No
Fox Creek	27	No	No	Yes	No	No
Soda Butte	27	No	No	Yes	Yes	No
NEAR NORTH ENTRANCE						
Eagle Creek	16	No	No	Yes	No	No
NEAR EAST ENTRANCE						
Eagle Creek	20	No	No	Yes	Yes	No
Three Mile	33	No	No	Yes	Yes	No

* Reserve through Xanterra Parks and Resorts.
** Fishing Bridge accepts hard-sided vehicles only.

Fire Pits/Grills	Laundry	Public Phones	Reservations	Fees	Open
Yes	Nearby	Yes	Yes	$17	Late May to mid-Sept
Yes	Yes	Yes	Yes	$17	June to early Sept
Yes	Yes	Yes	Yes	$35	Mid-May to Oct
Yes	Yes	Yes	Yes	$17	Mid-June to mid-Sept
Yes	No	No	No	$12	Early June to mid-Sept
Yes	No	No	No	$12	Mid-June to early Nov
Yes	No	Yes	Yes	$17	May–Nov
Yes	No	Yes	No	$14	Year-round
Yes	No	Yes	No	$14	Mid-May to Oct
Yes	No	No	No	$12	June–Oct
Yes	No	No	No	$12	Late May to Nov
Yes	No	No	No	$12	Mid-May to Oct
Yes	No	Yes	Yes	$14–$19	Mid-May to mid-Sept
Yes	No	No	Yes	$14	Mid-May to mid-Sept
Yes	No	Yes	Yes	$14	Mid-May to mid-Sept
Yes	Yes	Yes	Yes	$25–$44	Apr 15 to mid-Oct
Yes	Yes	Yes	Yes	$25–$53	May to mid-Oct
Yes	No	No	No	$8	June–Oct
Yes	No	No	No	$8	Mid-July to Oct
Yes	No	No	No	$10	May–Nov
Yes	No	No	No	$10	May–Oct
Yes	No	No	No	$9	July–Oct
Yes	No	No	No	$7	Year-round
Yes	No	No	No	$15	May to mid-Sept
Yes	No	No	No	$15	May to mid-Sept

In Canyon Village. ℭ **307/344-7311.** www.travelyellowstone.com. 250 sites, tents or RVs. $17 site. Closed Sept–May. **Amenities:** Flush toilets, showers, dump station, laundry, stores, picnic tables, fire pits and grates, running water, ice, restaurants, gas station nearby.

Fishing Bridge RV Park   This RV park is green and pleasant, but the sites—back-in only—are small and closely spaced, with room for little more than your rig and a lawn chair, and they lack tables or fire pits. The lake is across the highway. The visitor center and other facilities are a little way down the road.

North end of Yellowstone Lake. ℭ **307/344-7311.** www.travelyellowstone.com. 344 sites, hard-sided RVs up to 40 ft. only. $35 full hookup for 4 people. $1 per extra adult. Closed Oct to late May. **Amenities:** Full hookups, flush toilets, showers, dump station, laundry, store, picnic tables, fire pits and grates, running water, ice, museum.

Grant Village   The campground, at 7,800 feet, goes on and on along the shore of the lake. Although closely spaced, the sites are mostly wooded, and some have good lake views. Restaurants, the visitor center, and other comforts are nearby. The location makes some sense if you plan to spend time at Old Faithful, which has no campground (Madison Campground makes even more sense), but Grant isn't close to most of the park's most interesting areas.

At Yellowstone Lake, on the way to the south entrance. ℭ **307/344-7311.** www.travelyellowstone.com. 400 sites, tents or RVs. $17 site. Closed late Sept to late June. **Amenities:** Flush toilets, showers, dump station, laundry, stores, picnic tables, fire pits and grates, running water, ice, restaurants.

Madison   The campground is in a pleasant spot at 6,800 feet among pines on the banks of joining rivers. It's the closest campground to Old Faithful and a good base to explore the geyser basins, but it doesn't have a park village nearby to add crowds and activity. Sites are small and not well screened. The lower elevation means a longer season and warmer air, and the park's best river swimming is from the banks at the campground and nearby on the Firehole River, where the earth warms the water (see "Swimming," p. 284). This campground also is a short ride from West Yellowstone, just in case you need a fix of restaurant cooking or laundry facilities.

Near the west entrance. ℭ **307/344/7311.** www.travelyellowstone.com. 250 sites, tents or RVs. $17 site. Closed Nov–Apr. **Amenities:** Flush toilets, dump station, picnic tables, fire pits and grates, running water, ice.

First-Come, First-Served Campgrounds

These campgrounds, managed by the Park Service, are more primitive than those described above, but I think that adds to their appeal. RVs or tents are allowed at all, but most do not permit generators, a plus for tenters. Be at the gates early to get a site.

Indian Creek   The campground, situated at 7,300 feet, is quiet, well off the park road, and the nearby creek is good for fishing or swimming. The area burned, and pines now screen the many well-separated grassy sites, although some are built too close together.

South of Mammoth Hot Springs. 75 sites, tents or RVs. $12 site. Closed mid-Sept to early May. **Amenities:** Vault toilets, picnic tables, fire pits and grates, no generator use.

Lewis Lake   Most campsites here sit far apart, in thick forest on the edge of a placid mountain lake. Not much else is in the immediate vicinity, which lends solitude to the setting. The lovely lakeside sites are walk-in only. A boat launch and dock make a portal to the backcountry if you bring along a boat, canoe, or kayak.

Near the south entrance. 85 sites, tents or RVs. $12 site. Closed early Nov to mid-June. **Amenities:** Vault toilets, picnic tables, fire pits and grates, no generator use.

Mammoth   The year-round campground at 6,200 feet occupies a bend in the highway that leads down to the north entrance and Gardiner. It's on an exposed hillside below the developed area where the hotel, visitor center, and many services are located. Owing to the low elevation, it can be warm in summer and stays open in winter. Sites are well separated among grass, sagebrush, cottonwood, aspen, and juniper trees. It's a pretty spot, but it can be noisy and not the best place for kids to run free because of the road.

North end of the park, at Mammoth Hot Springs. 85 sites, tents or RVs. $14 site. **Amenities:** Flush toilets, dump station, picnic tables, fire pits and grates, running water, generators permitted.

Norris   Norris is one of my favorite Yellowstone campgrounds. Set at an elevation of 7,500 feet, sites are large and arrayed on a grassy hillside among large pine trees. A creek and the ranger museum are at the bottom of the hill. Ice and firewood are for sale, but there's no busy park village area nearby. The location makes a convenient base; it's near the Norris Geyser Basin, 12 miles from the Canyon area, 21 miles south of Mammoth, 30 miles north of Old Faithful, and near several trail heads.

Near Norris Geyser Basin, west side of the park. 116 sites, tents or RVs. $14 site. Closed Oct to late May. **Amenities:** Flush toilets, picnic tables, fire pits and grates, running water, generators permitted.

Pebble Creek   This is another quiet, out-of-the-way campground, down a gravel spur from the park road.

Near the northeast entrance. 32 sites, tents or RVs. $12 site. Closed Oct–June. **Amenities:** Vault toilets, picnic tables, fire pits and grates, no generator use.

Slough Creek   This isolated campground is tucked away in a river valley several miles up a gravel road from the highway. You're in the middle of wolf habitat here, which lends the possibility of catching some howling at night. Wildlife-viewing in the Lamar Valley down below can be exceptional. Cooke City with its stores and motels is a short drive to the east, while Tower-Roosevelt is a bit farther away to the west.

East of the Tower-Roosevelt area. 29 sites, tents or RVs. $12 site. Closed Nov to late May. **Amenities:** Pit toilets, picnic tables, fire grates and pits, no generator use.

Tower Fall   The campground, at 6,600 feet, is on a steep hillside well above the road in a dramatic area on the edge of the mountains overlooking the Northern Range.

Across from the falls parking lot. 32 sites, tents or RVs. $12 site. Closed Oct to late May. **Amenities:** Vault toilets, picnic tables, fire pits and grates, no generator use.

BACKCOUNTRY CAMPING PERMITS

The best campsites in Yellowstone are away from the roads, reached by hiking trails or, on the lakes, by boat. The 300 backcountry sites have no facilities, just a place to hang your food away from the bears. You must be self-sufficient, but if you're up for it, it's simply magical to be off in your own beautiful place without other people. Some of my favorite visits to Yellowstone have been by canoe to Shoshone or Yellowstone lakes. Backcountry sites are in less demand than hotel rooms or developed campground sites, and you can almost always get one somewhere, without a reservation, 48 hours in advance. But if you have a special area in mind, submit a reservation application in advance.

You'll need permit application forms and a copy of the *Backcountry Trip Planner,* a newspaper full of information and a map showing site locations. To order these documents, write to the Park Service at the address listed under "Yellowstone Address Book" (p. 272); call the main backcountry office at © **307/344-2160;** or visit the park website (click "In Depth," then "Table of Contents," then "Backcountry Camping," or go direct to www.nps.gov/yell/publications/pdfs/backcountry/index.htm). You'll also need detailed topographic maps and a trail guidebook (see "Reading Up," p. 280).

Submit your advance reservations by mail or in person along with a $20 reservation fee. The fee is good for your whole backcountry trip, which is defined as a foray from a trail head. If you return to the road and start at a new trail head, that is considered a new trip and you pay again. Checks, traveler's checks, and money orders are accepted. Have your application in by April 1 to be entered in an initial random drawing for sites with more than one application. Drawings are usually necessary for Slough Creek and Yellowstone and Shoshone lakes. After April 1, sites are assigned as requests come in. The Park Service will send you a confirmation, which you must turn in at a backcountry desk in person to get your actual permit.

Some sites in each area of the park are held back for walk-ins, with no reservation fee, starting at opening time 2 days before your trip. With flexibility, you can always find somewhere to go. Check at any of the 12 backcountry desks at visitor centers and ranger stations all over the park. You can go to any of the desks, which are linked by computer, but you may get better information from rangers closer to where you intend to go. Rangers will help you figure out where to go and what's available, and you'll be required to watch a safety film that's mostly about avoiding bears. One last note: More and more campfires in the backcountry are prohibited, a fact that might disappoint youngsters.

FOREST SERVICE CAMPGROUNDS

Yellowstone National Park is surrounded by national forests that take in millions of acres of land. There's a lot of wilderness to explore, and the campgrounds also take park overflow. They're relatively primitive, with pit toilets and few services, but they're often in wonderful places, with fishing, boating, and hiking opportunities right at your site.

All the campgrounds I've listed are in **Gallatin National Forest** and **Shoshone National Forest;** main contact information appears in "Yellowstone Address Book" (p. 272). Gallatin also has ranger district offices in West Yellowstone (© **406/646-7369** or 406/823-6961) and Gardiner (© **406/848-7375**), and a desk at the West Yellowstone visitor center. I've included campgrounds within 10 to 15 miles of the entrances, listed by the park entrance that is closest. Many other Forest Service campgrounds are farther afield. Reservations are taken only where noted; use the National Recreation Reservation Service explained in chapter 2.

Northeast Entrance

Soda Butte, Colter, and Chief Joseph campgrounds are in Gallatin National Forest, and the Fox Creek and Crazy Creek campgrounds are in Shoshone National Forest. Colter is noteworthy because it's on a mountaintop with great views; Fox Creek is near a fishing stream. More campgrounds are along Highway 212 farther away.

Chief Joseph   Highway 212, 9 miles east of entrance, this is a nicely treed, very quiet setting, due to the small number of sites. Six sites, tents or RVs. $8 site. Closed October to mid-July. **Amenities:** Vault toilets, picnic tables, fire pits and grates, drinking water.

Colter   Highway 212, 72 miles east of entrance. Twenty-three sites, tents or RVs. $8 site. Closed October to mid-July. **Amenities:** Vault toilets, picnic tables, fire pits and grates, drinking water.

Crazy Creek Highway 212, roughly 15 miles east of entrance. Sixteen sites, tents or RVs. $10 site. Closed November to May. **Amenities:** Vault toilets, picnic tables, fire pits and grates, no drinking water.

Fox Creek Highway 212, roughly 10 miles east of entrance. Thirty-four sites, tents or RVs. $20 site. Closed mid-September to May. **Amenities:** Water and electric at each site, vault toilets, picnic tables, fire pits and grates, drinking water.

Soda Butte Located among trees on Soda Butte Creek, Highway 212, 6 miles east of entrance and just 1 mile from Cooke City. Twenty-seven sites, tents or RVs. $9 site. Closed October to July. **Amenities:** Vault toilet, picnic tables, fire pits and grates, drinking water.

North Entrance

Eagle Creek This minimal campground in Gallatin National Forest has corrals if you bring your horse. From Gardiner, take dirt Jardine Road 2¼ miles. Sixteen sites, no parking aprons, tents or RVs. $7 site. Open all year. **Amenities:** Vault toilet, picnic tables, fire pits and grates, no fresh water, no firewood.

West Entrance

These three campgrounds are in Gallatin National Forest, near West Yellowstone. Stop at the visitor center there for information on other campgrounds a little farther afield.

Baker's Hole The campground is convenient to fishing in the Madison River.

Hwy. 191, 3 miles from park entrance. 73 sites, tents or RVs. 33 sites have electric. $14 site; $19 site with electricity. Closed mid-Sept to mid-May. **Amenities:** Vault toilets, picnic tables, fire pits and grates, drinking water, fishing.

Lonesomehurst This lakeside campground offers boating and swimming.

On Hegben Lake, 12 miles from park entrance. From West Yellowstone, go 6½ miles west on Rte. 20 to sign, then 3½ miles to campground. 27 sites, tents or RVs. $14 site. Closed mid-Sept to mid-May. **Amenities:** Vault toilets, picnic tables, fire pits and grates, drinking water, boating, swimming.

Rainbow Point This is a nicely treed site. Guests have access to boating, fishing, and swimming on the lake.

On Hegben Lake, 10 miles from park entrance. From West Yellowstone, take Rte. 191/287 north 4½ miles and follow signs. 86 sites, RVs only. $14 site. Closed mid-Sept to mid-May. **Amenities:** Vault toilets, picnic tables, fire pits and grates, drinking water, boating, swimming, fishing.

East Entrance

These two campgrounds are on U.S. 14/20 in Shoshone National Forest, Wapiti Ranger District (© **307/527-6921**). Grizzly bears are common; observe the food storage rules. Several more campgrounds are along the highway east to Cody.

Eagle Creek 8 miles east of entrance. 20 sites, hard-sided RVs only. $15 site. Closed mid-Oct to May. **Amenities:** Vault toilets, picnic tables, fire pits and grates, drinking water.

Three Mile 4 miles east of park entrance. 33 sites, RVs only. $15 site. Closed mid-Sept to May. **Amenities:** Vault toilets, picnic tables, fire pits and grates, drinking water.

COMMERCIAL CAMPGROUNDS

Rocky Mountain Campground Atop a hill with good views near the lower-elevation north entrance to the park, this family-run park makes sense for RVers who want full hookups, but the tent sites are too exposed for my taste. The Yellowstone River Trail starts here.

> **Tips Park Camping Basics: Toilets, Showers & Laundry**
>
> Campground listings in this chapter describe toilet arrangements. The Canyon and Grant Village campgrounds and Fishing Bridge RV Park have public showers and coin-op laundries. In West Yellowstone **Canyon Street Laundry**, 312 Canyon St. (© **406/646-9733**), has coin-op machines and showers.

14 Jardine Rd., Gardiner, MT 59030. © **877/534-6931** or 406/848-7251. www.rockymountaincampground.com. 87 sites, tents or RVs. $36–$44 full hookup, $34–$42 water and electric; $25 tent for 2 people. $4 per extra person. **Amenities:** Full hookups, showers, laundry, game room, store, miniature golf, cable TV.

Yellowstone Grizzly RV Park   The open, grassy park is right on the south edge of town and a few blocks from the west entrance to the park. It's a trim, modern place, a good choice for RVers looking for full services.

210 S. Electric St., West Yellowstone, MT 59758. © **406/646-4466.** www.grizzlyrv.com. 191 sites, tents or RVs. $43–$53 full hookup; $25 tent. **Amenities:** Full hookups, showers, laundry, small children's playground, game room, store, cable TV, Wi-Fi.

HOTELS, CABINS & LODGES
WITHIN THE PARK

Yellowstone National Park Lodges operates the accommodations within the park; its owner, and more commonly used name, is **Xanterra Parks and Resorts** (see "Yellowstone Address Book," p. 272). Options include some superb rooms in new and historic buildings, but also units that embarrass the site managers who put guests in them. Some cabins seem far less than charming and in dire need of a nail or two and some paint. But if you know that going in, the experience might be tolerable. The situation is slowly improving, but some units still are well below most people's standards. A room doesn't have to be fancy, and I enjoy crude wilderness cabins, but worn-out facilities and peeling paint are unacceptable.

Still, the hotel rooms are far better than the cabins. Some of the cheapest cabins (such as the Roughrider units at Roosevelt) are nice, with bare boards and woodstoves, because they don't try to be anything but old-fashioned frontier shelter. The worst are midrange cabins that are trying to be like motel rooms but have deteriorated into slums (some of these are Pioneer, Economy, or Budget class). Even many of the top "Western" class cabins are drab and out-of-date, while some are charming. The basic problem with almost all is that they were built 50 to 80 years ago with no thought of having them used this long.

Unless I've noted otherwise, rooms and cabins have private bathrooms but no telephones, TVs, or air-conditioning. It's critical to reserve as early as possible. Dinner at some of the hotel dining rooms should be reserved when you reserve your room, months ahead (see "Family-Friendly Dining," p. 296). Xanterra accepts American Express, Diners Club, Discover, MasterCard, and Visa. Rates are for two people in the room; extra adults are $11 each, kids under 12 stay free. Rollaway beds are *not* available, but free cribs are, although they're not guaranteed. You can check availability and reserve online at www.travelyellowstone.com. The rates quoted here include tax.

Canyon Lodge and Cabins   A pair of comparatively new hotel lodges in the classic park style include some really special rooms with coffeemakers, other modern amenities, and exceptional attention to detail. Those buildings stay open until mid-September.

Most people end up in one of the cabins, however, and they are nothing to write home about. The best, Western class, are clean, with newish carpet, drapes, bedspreads, and tub enclosures, but that can't erase the 1950s ranch-style tract-house design, with small bathrooms, cheap wall paneling, and acoustic tile ceilings. Many of the midrange Frontier cabins have been renovated recently. The lower-priced Pioneer units can be drab and depressing, with stained carpet and other signs of long, hard use.

Canyon Village. (C) 307/344-7311. www.travelyellowstone.com. 79 units, 540 cabins. $155 double; $66–$142 cabin. Closed mid-Sept to June. **Amenities:** Restaurant; shops nearby; elevator in some buildings. *In room:* Some rooms have coffeemakers, no phone.

Grant Village   Six two-story gabled buildings, built in the 1980s with plywood siding, face the lake in tiers. The standard motel rooms are modern and well kept. They have telephones. The place lacks character, however; it's something like a generic midrange condo development. Also, noise carries through the lightweight construction, so you will have to keep the kids quiet.

Near Yellowstone Lake on the way to the south entrance. (C) **307/344-7311.** www.travelyellowstone.com. 300 units. $125–$130 double. Closed Oct to late May. **Amenities:** Restaurants; shops nearby; museum. *In room:* Some rooms have no phone.

Lake Lodge Cabins   The 1920s log-and-stone lodge building, full of cane-backed chairs for relaxing in front of the fire, sits by the lake in an area of the park that is pleasantly quieter than most others. Work has been done to improve the cabins, and some of the Western-class units are among the freshest in the park. But the renovations are bringing these cabins up from a very low level, and many need more work or replacement. For example, the 10×10-foot Pioneer cabins will never be more than inexpensive shelter from the elements. Some partially renewed Western units were decently maintained but still out-of-date.

Near the Lake Yellowstone Hotel. (C) **307/344-7311.** www.travelyellowstone.com. 186 cabins. $65–$132 cabin. Closed late Sept to early June. **Amenities:** Near restaurant; shops.

Lake Yellowstone Hotel and Cabins   This yellow 1891 hotel has been carefully restored to 1920s style. The common rooms and lodgings in the main building are as stylish and posh as they were during its golden age, a real experience that adds to your trip. These rooms go for $197 and up, and they have telephones. Rooms in an annex are about $60 less; they are basic and lack phones. The Frontier-class cabins out back are barely acceptable; the bathrooms were renovated, but the rooms themselves are drab and worn out.

Yellowstone Lake. (C) **307/344-7311.** www.travelyellowstone.com. 194 units, 102 cabins. $139–$211 double; $525 suite; $111 cabin. Closed early Oct to mid-May. **Amenities:** Restaurant; shops. *In room:* Some rooms have no phone.

Mammoth Hotel and Cabins   The Mammoth Hotel is an impressive 1930s hotel, with a well-preserved exterior and common areas. The rooms, while not the restored showplaces of the Lake Yellowstone Hotel, are pleasingly old-fashioned and comfortable. Some bathrooms have shower stalls, others old-fashioned tubs without showers. Some rooms share large bathrooms. The rooms have phones. The cabins are better kept than in most of the park while preserving a fun 1930s style. They're set around a grassy compound with picnic tables, and some have hot tubs. The hotel is a base for cross-country skiing, ice-skating, and other winter sports.

Near the north entrance. (C) **307/344-7311.** www.travelyellowstone.com. 97 units, some with shared bathroom, 116 cabins. $110 double with bathroom; $82 double without bathroom; $356 suite; $72–$104 cabin; $182 hot tub cabin. Closed Oct to mid-Dec and Mar–Apr. **Amenities:** Restaurants; shops; gas station; museum.

Old Faithful Inn *(Finds)*   You'll never see a more amazing hotel lobby than the one at this historic landmark. It's made of logs more than 70 feet tall, like a trapper's cabin mated to a Gothic cathedral. It sounds preposterous, but somehow it feels grand and cozy at the same time. In the evening it comes to life on various levels, including kids' programs on the huge balcony. Architect Robert Reamer also designed the lovely Fishing Bridge Visitor Center and other wood-and-stone buildings in the park, helping establish the rustic national park style. The 1904 inn contains an extremely wide range of rooms down long, confusing corridors. The premium rooms, in a 1920s wing, are luxurious and thoughtfully renewed to reflect their period (they have phones). The "Old House," on the other hand, has the fairly crude, shared-bathroom original rooms with log walls and other untouched details. The smallish midrange rooms are comfortable but unmemorable. Many rooms have views of the geysers.

Old Faithful Complex. (℃) **307/344-7311.** www.travelyellowstone.com. 327 units, some with shared bathroom. $117–$198 double with bathroom; $91 double without bathroom; $344–$457 suite. Closed mid-Oct to mid-May. **Amenities:** Restaurants; lounge; shops; geyser basin. *In room:* Suites have fridge.

Old Faithful Lodge Cabins   The lodge building is an impressive example of the rustic park style and a good place to get an ice cream or meal while waiting for Old Faithful to go off. The cabins, once the park's worst, are in the process of improvement, with many of the grimmest gone. A remodeled Frontier-class unit was very clean, with white walls and new carpet and plumbing, although the bathroom remained tiny.

Old Faithful Complex. (℃) **307/344-7311.** www.travelyellowstone.com. 97 cabins. $67–$104 cabin. Closed late Sept to early May. **Amenities:** Restaurant.

Old Faithful Snow Lodge and Cabins   This award-winning lodge contains the park's best standard rooms. They re-create the solid, rustic, communal feeling of the park's best classic architecture. Rooms and common areas have sumptuous current comforts and details, including handcrafted furniture and design touches. All rooms have two double beds and telephones. The cabins are newer than others in the park (14 were built after the 1988 fires) and, like the hotel rooms, are among the best in the park.

Old Faithful Complex. (℃) **307/344-7311.** www.travelyellowstone.com. 100 units, 24 cabins. $184 double; $91–$133 cabin. Closed mid-Oct to mid-Dec and mid-Mar to Apr. **Amenities:** Restaurants; lounge; shops. *In room:* Some rooms have no phone.

Roosevelt Lodge Cabins   Built in 1919 to resemble a dude ranch, the place has returned to standards that really do resemble a good wilderness lodge. Remodeled Frontier cabins are cute, with white walls and wainscoting, while those that haven't had the treatment remain worn and dreary. My choice, however, would be the shared-bathroom Roughrider units, real Old West cabins with plank floors and rag rugs, heated by cast-iron woodstoves. (The bathhouse was remodeled, too.) The central lodge is a fine old building of logs and stone. The beautiful area is great for horseback riding.

In the northeast section of the park. (℃) **307/344-7311.** www.travelyellowstone.com. 82 cabins, some with shared bathroom. $104 cabin with bathroom; $64 cabin without bathroom. Closed Sept–May. **Amenities:** Restaurant. *In room:* Some have woodstoves.

OUTSIDE THE PARK

A normal motel room outside the park rents for about $110 to $125 a night in the summer and winter, much less in spring and fall. I've listed only summer peak rates. Unless otherwise noted, all have TVs, telephones, and air-conditioning.

West Yellowstone

The tourist town of West Yellowstone has the most motels, including national chains. For longer stays, the town also has a good rental pool of cabins, condos, town houses, and full-size houses. Contact the chamber of commerce (see "Yellowstone Address Book," p. 272).

Holiday Inn SunSpree Resort West Yellowstone Conference Hotel   This place strives to be the best in town, with an attractive indoor pool and an activities director at a desk in the lobby to arrange park and fishing outings. The resort also operates its own snow coach. The guest rooms are large and immaculate, with sofas, microwaves, coffeemakers, and other extras. Family suites have a king- and two queen-size beds in two rooms, two TVs, and even, in some, two bathrooms. The railroad-theme decor includes an impressive 1903 VIP railroad car that has been restored, brought indoors, and made into a museum. The hotel's Oregon Short Line Restaurant serves steak, elk, buffalo, salmon, and other entrees for $15 to $25.

315 Yellowstone Ave. (P.O. Box 470), West Yellowstone, MT 59758. © **800/646-7365** or 406/646-7365. Fax 406/646-4433. www.doyellowstone.com. 123 units. $179 double; $219–$229 suite. Children under 19 stay free in parent's room; kids 12 and under eat free in restaurant from kids' menu. Rollaway bed $15, cribs free. AE, DC, DISC, MC, V. **Amenities:** Restaurant; indoor pool; family suites. *In room:* TV, fridge, coffeemaker, hair dryer, iron/ironing board, some suites have fireplaces, microwave, Wi-Fi.

Three Bear Lodge   This is a good, reasonably priced family motel with an outdoor pool. The rooms are large enough for families, with two queen-size beds. A selection of two-room family suites is available. All were nicely kept up on our visits. On-site are a little first-run movie theater, an exercise room, and a Western-style family restaurant.

217 Yellowstone Ave. (P.O. Box 1590), West Yellowstone, MT 59758. © **800/646-7353** or 406/646-7353. www.three bearlodge.com. 73 units. $109 double; $139–$169 suite. No rollaway beds, limited number of cribs $5. AE, DISC, MC, V. **Amenities:** Restaurant; outdoor pool; fitness room; hot tubs; movie theater. *In room:* A/C, TV, hair dryer, iron/ironing board, Wi-Fi.

Gardiner

Absaroka Lodge   This friendly, family-run hotel in a striking building is perched above the Yellowstone River right in town. Each room has a balcony over the water. The well-kept rooms are light and airy, though unadorned by art or decoration and a bit dated. For $10 more, you can get a kitchen suite with a dining table.

Rte. 89 at Yellowstone River bridge (P.O. Box 10), Gardiner, MT 59030. © **800/755-7414** or 406/848-7414. Fax 406/848-7560. www.yellowstonemotel.com. 41 units. $105 double. $5 extra person. Children under 13 stay free in parent's room. Rollaway beds and cribs free (rollaways in rooms with kitchen only). AE, DC, DISC, MC, V. *In room:* A/C, TV, suites have kitchenette, fridge, microwave, Wi-Fi.

Yellowstone Village Inn   This is a good, family-oriented motel, with a good-size indoor pool, a grassy play area, and a basketball court in the large parking lot. The country-sportsman decor carries from the lobby into nice, up-to-date standard rooms and large condos. Rates include continental breakfast, and a coin-op laundry is on-site. All rooms are nonsmoking.

1102 Scott St. (P.O. Box 297), Gardiner, MT 59030. © **800/228-8158** or 406/848-7417. Fax 406/848-7418. www.yellowstonevinn.com. 40 units, 3 condos. $109–$139 double; $169–$219 condo. $10 extra person in motel. Children under 6 stay free in parent's room. Rollaway bed $10, crib $4. MC, V. **Amenities:** Indoor pool; laundry facilities; basketball court. *In room:* A/C, TV, kitchen suites have microwave, coffeepot, utensils.

South Entrance

Flagg Ranch Resort   The log resort lodge and fourplex cabins sit among small pines between Yellowstone and Grand Teton, offering modern, year-round accommodations but lacking proximity to any of the main attractions or trails. The resort offers its own guided outings and rentals for fishing, riding, and rafting. A laundry, store, and restaurant are on-site. The campground, with free showers, is best for RVs but does have tent spaces. You won't find rollaway beds here, although the resort will give you an air mattress to use on the floor while you're there, if you ask in advance.

John D. Rockefeller Jr. Pkwy. (Rte. 89/191/287), between Yellowstone and Grand Teton national parks (P.O. Box 187), Moran, WY 83013. ℂ 800/443-2311 or 307/543-2861. Fax 307/543-2356. www.flaggranch.com. 92 cabins. $165–$175 cabin. $10 extra person. Children under 18 stay free in parent's cabin. Cribs free, air mattresses $15. Closed mid-Oct to mid-May. Campground: 172 sites. $45 full hookup; $20 tent. AE, DISC, MC, V. **Amenities:** Restaurant; store; laundry; fishing; free showers for campground guests. *In room:* Coffeemaker.

6 Family-Friendly Dining

IN THE PARK

I've arranged dining information in this chapter by area, starting from Mammoth and working around the park clockwise.

Reservations make a meal at a formal hotel restaurant something to look forward to all year. You can make them starting in January. Although tables don't book up as fast as rooms, reasonable dining times will be gone well before you start your trip. The best move is to reserve your table when you set up the rest of your trip; you can always cancel later. Less-formal places don't accept reservations.

The children's menu for those 11 and younger is the same at all of the more-formal dining rooms, with breakfast from about $1 to $4, and lunch and dinner $3.25 to $5. It's the bland food most kids like: burgers, grilled cheese, PB&J, chicken or fish strips, or spaghetti with tomato sauce.

The Yellowstone General Stores have old-fashioned soda fountains and grills at several sites, which often are the most convenient and fun places to eat. They are all open roughly 8am to 9pm daily. Besides those mentioned at the villages below, small fountains with limited menus are at Tower Fall and Fishing Bridge.

MAMMOTH HOT SPRINGS

The Terrace Grill is a fast-food outlet, similar to a McDonald's in food, price, and furniture, without the brand names. It is open daily 7am to 9pm in the high season, shorter hours off season.

Mammoth Hotel Dining Room   I especially like this restaurant. Families get to enjoy the airy Art Deco dining room and tablecloths without all the formality and expense of the other big hotel restaurants. You don't need reservations, and the food is good but not ostentatious. Many entrees are served for lunch or dinner, including burgers and items such as Rocky Mountain bison bangers and mashers and Wild Montana Whitefish.

ℂ 307/344-7311. Kids' menu, highchairs, boosters, crayons. Breakfast $4.50–$10; lunch $7.25–$12; dinner $15–$23. AE, DC, DISC, MC, V. Summer daily 6:30–10am, 11am–2:30pm, and 5–10pm; shorter hours off season.

ROOSEVELT LODGE

The Western trail ride cookout is covered under "Horseback Riding" (p. 306).

Roosevelt Lodge   The casual dining room is part of the lobby in the historic main lodge, like a big ranch house. The menu leans to steaks, fried chicken, chili, barbecue, and other cowboy fare, but it includes everything you expect in a typical hotel cafe. This is a good place for a sit-down meal with kids. From 3 to 4pm it serves a limited, light lunch. After your meal, relax in a rocking chair on the front porch.

© 307/344-7901. Kids' menu, highchairs, boosters, crayons. Reservations not accepted. Breakfast $5.25–$8.50; lunch $5.75–$9; dinner $8.50–$25. AE, DC, DISC, MC, V. Daily 7–10:30am, 11:30am–4pm, and 5–9pm. Closed Sept–May.

CANYON

Canyon is too busy and hectic for my taste. It's a huge facility, built in the 1950s and apparently little changed since then. Certain details, like the star-shaped fluorescent-tube chandeliers, are so out they're back in and back out again. The place reminded me of a big student center. It operates June through mid-September.

There are four places to eat, serving more than 5,000 meals a day. In the **Yellowstone General Store,** there is an old-fashioned fountain, with a grill serving burgers. It is open daily 7:30am to 8:30pm; the price range is $5.60 to $7.25. In the restaurant building, a deli shop has a couple of tables and takeout for the picnic tables outside. It serves sandwiches, wraps, and salads ($5–$7.95) and is open daily 11am to 9:30pm, closing at 6pm in September. Next door the cafeteria serves hordes of diners in a setting that was dark and noisy when I stopped in. Breakfast prices top out at $4 for an omelet, lunch is around $5 to $12, and dinner runs $6 to $16. There are stations for pasta and for hot sandwiches. Hours are daily 7 to 10:30am, 11:30am to 2:30pm, and 5 to 10pm.

Canyon Lodge Dining Room   This is an old-fashioned Western steakhouse, with a menu of rib-eye, New York strip, prime rib, top sirloin, and chicken-fried steak to match the authentic 1950s decor. You also can build your own burger, whether that be a Bison Burger, All-American Burger, Wild Alaska Salmon Burger, or Mini Burger. A full-service lounge opens at 3:30pm.

© 307/344-7901. Kids' menu, highchairs, boosters, crayons. Reservations not accepted. Breakfast $5.25–$9.75; lunch $6.50–$13; dinner $8.50–$20. AE, DC, DISC, MC, V. Early June to early Sept daily 7–10am, 11:30am–2:30pm, and 5–10pm.

LAKE VILLAGE

The village has a fountain serving cold sandwiches and ice cream at the Yellowstone General Store, in an interesting and even strange building between the lodge and the hotel. You can also buy sandwiches made to order from a deli in the big yellow hotel building, open daily 10:30am to 9pm.

The main dining choice for families is the cafeteria at Lake Lodge, a huge log building with a rustic, historic feel. Breakfast is traditional and inexpensive. For lunch, two stations operate, for wraps, hot or cold sandwiches, or for hot meals such as pot roast or lasagna ($2.75–$9.50). For dinner, a prime-rib station replaces the wrap station ($6.75–$16). Hours are daily 6:30 to 10am, 11:30am to 2:30pm, and 4:30 to 9:30pm.

Lake Yellowstone Hotel   Lake Yellowstone Hotel offers one of the best meals in the park system, in part because of the gorgeous lakeside setting, and in part because the menus are creative and well executed. One night you might choose the pan-seared elk medallions and broiled lobster tail, another the grilled portobello mushroom with the cabernet vegetable demi-glaze, sautéed spinach, and lyonnaise potatoes. Light pours into the large dining room, with very high ceilings, and over the wood floors and restored 1920s details. Through the windows you have views of Yellowstone Lake, the surrounding mountains, and the occasional bison that strolls by on the yard. All that said, meals are on the expensive side and this probably is not the best choice for families with young children due to the formal atmosphere.

© 307/344-7311. Kids' menu, highchairs, boosters, crayons. Dinner reservations needed. Breakfast $4.50–$11; lunch $7.25–$13; dinner $16–$37. AE, DC, DISC, MC, V. Late May to early Oct daily 6:30–10:30am, 11:30am–2:30pm, and 5–10pm.

GRANT VILLAGE

There are three restaurants. The Village Grill is in the Yellowstone General Store. Furnished like a fast-food restaurant, it has quick counter service for a menu of sandwiches, burgers, soup, and a salad bar ($4.75–$7.25; breakfast $2.50–$5). All in all, it's hard to do better for a hassle-free lunch.

The Lake House is quite casual, too, serving pizza ($11 and up) and a pasta bar ($5 kids, $12 adults) for dinner in a dining room that sits on the lake at a defunct marina. Breakfast is continental or a buffet that costs $4.95 for children, $8 for adults. Hours are daily 7 to 10:30am and 5 to 9pm.

Grant Village   This place most resembles the typical American midrange hotel restaurant. The dining room occupies a modern building with big windows and a high vaulted ceiling. It holds far fewer tables than the park's big, old restaurants. The atmosphere is dim and subdued. The breakfast and lunch menus are traditional, the dinner menu slightly more adventurous, but specializing mostly in beef and trout.

ℭ 307/344-7311. Kids' menu, highchairs, boosters, crayons. Dinner reservations required. Breakfast $4.50–$9.75; lunch $7.25–$11; dinner $11–$22. AE, DC, DISC, MC, V. Late May to early Oct daily 6:30–10am, 11:30am–2:30pm, and 5:30–10pm.

OLD FAITHFUL

There are seven places to eat in the Old Faithful area, not counting all the espresso carts, ice-cream stands, and such. The **Yellowstone General Stores** have two choices, a historic fountain and a pizza place. **Yellowstone National Park Lodges** has two fast-food outlets, **The Pony Express** at Old Faithful Inn (daily 10:30am–7:30pm) and the **Geyser Grill** at the Old Faithful Snow Lodge (daily 8am–9pm), serving burgers and sandwiches for lunch and dinner. At the Geyser Grill, breakfast items such as English-muffin egg sandwiches cost less than $4.50.

The dining room at the cafeteria at the Old Faithful Lodge is memorable, with its construction of huge timbers and stone and the immense windows of many panes looking out on the famous geyser. The choices for lunch or dinner are many, including heavy hot dishes such as meatloaf or lasagna, sandwiches, trout, burgers, or barbecue ($4–$9) with prime rib added in the evening ($12–$15). Just about everything also comes in a smaller and less expensive children's portion. I enjoyed eating there much more than I expected. Hours are daily 11am to 9pm.

Obsidian Room (at the Snow Lodge)   Like the cafe restaurant in any modern high-end hotel, this dining room serves a varied menu in a setting of polished casualness. Fancy breakfasts are served as late as noon, the only such offering for late risers in the park. The restaurant doesn't serve lunch. Dinner offerings include braised bison short ribs, linguine with Tuscan chicken, fish, and pasta. Housed in the gorgeous hotel, it is the most modern restaurant in the park.

ℭ 307/344-7311. Kids' menu, highchairs, boosters, crayons. No reservations. Breakfast $4.50–$11; dinner $14–$23. AE, DC, DISC, MC, V. Early May to late Oct daily 6:30am–noon and 5–10pm.

Old Faithful Inn Dining Room   The restaurant at the inn appears more formal than it is. The staffers wear uniforms, but their behavior is loose and congenial, with something of a sense of controlled crisis as they rush to serve the huge dining room. The cuisine ranges from specialties of prime rib, pork chops, or the park's ubiquitous trout to seared wild Alaska Salmon with citrus beurre and crystallized ginger. Our several meals here have been excellent, okay, and not good at all; there's a lack of consistency year to year. Children should be on good behavior, but the noise and activity will cover most sins. Lunch is casual and includes a Western buffet, while breakfast revolves around a buffet, a very good one at that with various grill items, egg dishes, hot and cold cereals, and fresh fruit.

(C) 307/344-7311. Kids' menu, highchairs, boosters, crayons. Dinner reservations required. Breakfast $10; lunch $7.50–$12; dinner $15–$30. AE, DC, DISC, MC, V. Daily 6:30–10am, 11:30am–2:30pm, and 5–10pm. Closed early Oct to early May.

OUTSIDE THE PARK

Fast food and Western diners are not hard to find in the towns around the park, especially West Yellowstone, which has been invaded by fast-food chains. I've mentioned a couple of restaurants with the hotels that house them (see "Family-Friendly Accommodations," p. 285). A sit-down place, the **Outpost Restaurant,** 115 Yellowstone Ave. (© **406/646-7303**), is quite family-friendly, with a good menu of hearty beef. **Sydney's Mountain Bistro,** 38 Canyon (© **406/646-7660**), is a 10-table eatery that is raising West Yellowsone's culinary stakes, with items such as butternut squash ravioli and pan-seared halibut. **Helen's Corral Drive-In** is a fun choice in Gardiner, on U.S. 89, on the north side of the Yellowstone River (© **406/848-7627**). Some of the burgers are among the biggest you'll ever encounter: The half-pounders have been known to measure 7 inches from top to bottom.

7 Exploring Yellowstone National Park with Your Kids

ENTRANCE FEES   The park admission fee is $25 per vehicle, and it's good for 1 week at both Yellowstone and Grand Teton national parks. You also can gain entrance with an America the Beautiful Pass. For details, see chapter 2.

NATURAL PLACES

I've described the places in clockwise order, starting at the north entrance.

MAMMOTH HOT SPRINGS

Where the springs come to the surface, the flowing water has built high mounds of weirdly contoured rock called travertine. The rock continues to grow, sometimes 2 feet a year, engulfing trees and boardwalks. Scallop-edged pools of pastel stone steam and trickle like fountains in a pleasure garden, but the patterns are so complex and diverse that only nature's randomness could have made them. Elk often come here to bask in the warmth from the earth. A boardwalk nature trail circles the lower area of the springs, and a traffic-clogged one-lane loop road goes through the less active upper area. Strollers can roll on many of the boardwalks, but some amazing areas require a stiff stair climb. An excellent map and guide to the site is on sale for 50¢ at the visitor center; however, the most active and interesting areas change constantly, so you need to explore on your own.

The water for the springs falls as rain and snow, probably coming down 21 miles south near the Norris Geyser Basin. The earth heats it and mixes it with carbon dioxide, making carbonic acid. Then the acidic water flows to Mammoth through an underground crack called a fault. The underground limestone at Mammoth, outside Yellowstone's volcanic rim, started out as seashells and other muck on the bottom of an ancient ocean. Limestone dissolves in carbonic acid. When the acidic water from Norris gets to Mammoth, the acid dissolves the limestone and carries it to the surface. When the carbon dioxide gets to the surface, it floats off into the air, leaving the limestone behind. The limestone sticks back together and forms the travertine rocks you see at the hot springs.

Bacteria growing in the springs give the rocks their colors. Different water temperatures grow bacteria of different colors, and it's possible to find out how hot a pool is by what color it is. See if you can figure out which colors grow in the hottest and coolest pools, then check your answer in the guide map.

THE NORTHERN RANGE

The broad mountain pastures along the northern leg of the park loop are an important wildlife habitat and a good place to find animals in the winter, when these lower elevations harbor thousands of elk and bison. Hiking and horseback riding in this area are glorious because of the open sky and wonderful views, but it can be warm in the summer. Paths lead from several points along the highway between Cooke City and Mammoth across the valleys and into the canyon of the Yellowstone River, routes suitable for a day hike or overnight. Horseback riding starts from the stable at Roosevelt Lodge. See "Hiking" (p. 305) and "Horseback Riding" (p. 306).

TOWER FALL

A short paved walk leads to an overlook, then a steep .5-mile trail gets you to a much better view at the base of the falls. Unfortunately, it's often crowded. The waterfall is a creek spilling over into the canyon of the Yellowstone River. A spur leads farther down to the Yellowstone, a good place for supervised riverside play. The road south from this area to Canyon Village passes through the park's grandest mountain terrain and leads to two trail heads for the popular hike up Mount Washburn, 3 miles one-way from the Crittenden Road or Dunraven Pass parking areas. The alpine trail, leading over 10,243 feet, offers views over much of Yellowstone and a good chance to see bighorn sheep.

GRAND CANYON OF THE YELLOWSTONE

The Yellowstone River has cut up to 1,200 feet deep through yellow rock and mud to create the canyon, which is still deepening. Besides being huge, it is fascinating to look at because the way it looks changes so much from different viewpoints. Each point has a different scene of chaotic shapes of colored, broken rock, gushing water from two huge waterfalls, and trees that grow in seemingly impossible places. The paths and overlooks join the road a mile from Canyon Village, at the eastern midpoint of the loop roads. Many overlooks are crowded near the road, and the less crowded canyon-top trails can be scary for parents. Our strategy was to take a quick look with everyone else, then head out on an uncrowded trail from the Wapiti Trailhead, just south of the canyon, to Clear Lake, a strange body of water fed by hot springs. The terrain there is beautiful rolling meadows. The 50¢ Canyon map and guide explains the natural history of the canyon and shows all the trails; get one at the visitor center.

The canyon's yellow rock is rhyolite, which formed from lava flows. The geologic story of the canyon hasn't been clearly figured out, but we know that various lava flows poured out over thousands of years after the big eruption 600,000 years ago. The volcano also caused the earth to bulge, creating giant cracks that water could widen much later into the canyon. There was once a geyser basin here, too. The hot water helped weaken the rhyolite rock the river could cut easily. You still can see steam plumes in the canyon in places and around Clear Lake. At the end of the last ice age, about 10,000 years ago, a series of ice dams probably formed at the edge of Yellowstone Lake. When the dams broke, flash floods would wash down this way, quickly carving the canyon. Today's waterfalls mark spots where a layer of a harder rhyolite lava flow forms a shelf over a softer flow layer. The softer rock wore away faster, leaving a steep drop. The rock is yellow because it contains iron that is oxidizing, or rusting, in the air.

HAYDEN VALLEY & MUD VOLCANO

On the drive south from the Canyon area to Yellowstone Lake, the Hayden Valley is a spectacular mountain meadow along the Yellowstone River. This is one of the park's best areas to see groups of buffalo and elk from the road, or to hike off the road for more wildlife-viewing (trails here can be tricky because the bison knock down the markers). To the south, Mud Volcano and Sulphur Caldron belch nastiness for the nose, eye, and ear right by a parking lot. They're definitely worth a quick stop, even if they are less impressive than the park's other thermal features (get the 50¢ guide at a visitor center). A .6-mile nature trail loop brings you to other such weirdness on a smaller scale.

YELLOWSTONE LAKE & WEST THUMB

The lake is unique for its size, 20×14 miles, and its elevation, 7,733 feet, but if you could see underneath, you would be much more impressed. Exploration by a robot submarine in 1999 found craters up to ½ mile across, spires of rock more than 110 feet tall, and canyons, including the lake's deepest spot, up to 390 feet deep. It's a wild volcanic scene down there. The lake bed itself is lifting up, tilting more toward the south. On the north, the lake bed is becoming exposed, and on the south, water has flooded former forest. At one time, the lake probably drained that way, flowing down the Snake River and eventually to the Pacific Ocean instead of going down the Yellowstone River and winding up in the Atlantic. Maybe it will switch again someday.

The best place to get an idea of what violence is happening under the water is at the West Thumb Geyser Basin, north of Grant Village. West Thumb is a large bay formed by a volcanic explosion 150,000 years ago. On a map, it looks a little bit like a thumb. At the geyser basin, a nature trail follows mostly flat boardwalks around deep, hot pools that seem to flow with rich, pure colors. The springs and vents are right on the lakeshore, often mingling the hot and cold water. Get the 50¢ trail guide and map. A small information station has a bookstore and a ranger to answer questions.

The hot water coming up underneath helps Yellowstone Lake sustain more life than would normally be found at this high, cold elevation by speeding the growth of algae and bacteria. Insects and other small creatures eat that growth, and they become food in turn for larger creatures, such as trout. The native cutthroat trout in turn get eaten by eagles, white pelicans, bears, and many other animals. Recently, however, lake trout somehow were introduced to the lake, and they threaten to wipe out the cutthroat if they aren't stopped. Rangers net the lake trout every year, and probably always will, and they encourage anglers to take as many as they can. If you fish in Yellowstone Lake, you need to learn to identify the fish accurately, because any lake trout you catch must be killed, but all native fish must be released to swim again. (Always check on current regulations before you fish.) Anglers can rent boats or engage guides at Bridge Bay Marina (see "Fishing," p. 305).

Without fishing, you can get out on the lake in a rented canoe, or get a lift to one of the backcountry campsites on the lakeshore from the concessionaire at Bridge Bay (see "Boating," p. 304). Narrated 1-hour boat tours leave from the marina all day in the summer. Fares are $11 for adults, $6.75 for children 2 to 11. Call ℂ **307/344-7311** for reservations. The tours are expertly done, but there just isn't enough to see to make it worthwhile.

To the south, forested Lewis Lake is on the road to the park entrance. It has a campground and provides access for canoeists and kayakers to take an appealing backcountry trip to Shoshone Lake, which is untouched by roads and has a significant geyser basin on its southwest shore. Backcountry campsites in the area are in high demand, so start planning for this area before April (see "Backcountry Camping Permits," p. 289).

OLD FAITHFUL & NEARBY GEYSER BASINS

Walkways, hotels, restaurants, stores, and parking lots circle halfway around Old Faithful. If it ever stops shooting off hot water, the area will look awfully funny, because everything focuses on that one spot. The time between eruptions has lengthened because of earthquakes, but so far, the geyser is still going strong. It erupts roughly every 70 minutes and shoots up to 180 feet high, as it has at least since it was first described in 1870. The visitor center posts the predicted time of the next eruption for Old Faithful and some other geysers in the area; getting that information and the 50¢ guide map of this and the nearby geyser areas when you arrive will greatly improve your tour. The guide maps also list the usual intervals between eruptions for various geysers. Some of the buildings around the geyser, especially the Old Faithful Inn, also are worth a stop (be sure to check out the inn's lobby). These were the first experiments with designing buildings to fit a national park.

Many other geysers in the area benefit from more natural settings. One-fifth of the world's geysers—140 of them—are within a mile of Old Faithful. You can tour them on a network of trails several miles long that starts from Old Faithful and on the road to the north. Steam and water shoot up from sterile plains of white mud and rock. It always turns my imagination to other worlds. This white material is sinter, or geyserite. Silica in the rocks below dissolves in the geysers' water, then solidifies on the surface into this white or gray rock. The ground all around you hisses and groans unexpectedly. Shoots of steam bloom, and strange mineral smells rise up.

There are more geysers and hot pools in the park than will interest most people, but you can spend a fascinating full day just walking around these basins. Some paths are open to bicycles, too. A drive circles through the Firehole Lake area, with geysers and huge ponds of hot water. Don't worry too much about choosing where to go. The best geyser is one that's going off at the moment, and, with a few exceptions, that's unpredictable; so all you can do is head out to explore and see what you see. If a geyser suddenly goes off next to you, you'll have a wonderful thrill.

NORRIS GEYSER BASIN & MUSEUM 🐸🐸

Looking down on the basin from the museum, you see far across a great, white wasteland spouting steam, a truly hellish vista that seems entirely hostile to life. This view from above gives Norris the best first impression of any of the road-accessible geyser basins. That first impression is pretty accurate. Norris is the hottest and most acidic of all the thermal areas in the park; so hot, in fact, that in 2003 a foot trail had to be closed when the trail itself rose to boiling temperature. The basin also has one of the park's most consistent geysers, Echinus, which goes off roughly hourly, allowing visitors to get close to billowing torrents of highly acidic water. Lots of other interesting geysers and thermal features are here, too, including the world's tallest geyser, the annoyingly inconsistent Steamboat Geyser. It has gone as long as 50 years without erupting, but in recent years has shot off more frequently to a height of 300 to 400 feet, although your chances of catching a performance are probably on the order of winning the lottery. Pick up the 50¢ trail guide, which covers a couple of miles of paths through the gurgling, rumbling basin floor.

The **Norris Geyser Basin Museum** (© **307/344-2812**) occupies two rooms in a log building above the basin. Interesting graphic placards explain how the geothermal features work and will hold your attention for up to half an hour. A roving ranger answers questions. The museum is open daily late May to early October from 10am to 5pm.

PLACES FOR LEARNING
IN THE PARK

Most of the museums in the park are at the visitor centers described above under "Visitor Information" (p. 278). The Norris Geyser Basin Museum is described above under "Natural Places" (p. 302).

Museum of the National Park Ranger, Norris *(Finds)*   This is a charming, relaxing museum of great interest to children. The displays tell the history of the Park Service and how early rangers lived, with uniforms and mock-ups of rooms. The changes in the parks are an interesting window on the changes in society. Best of all, the museum occupies a beautiful old log building by a creek where retired rangers spin yarns about the old days for anyone who asks.

At the Norris Campground. (*C*) 307/344-7353. Free admission. Late May to late Sept daily 9am–5pm.

IN WEST YELLOWSTONE

This tourist town isn't worth sacrificing time in the park to visit, but these sites are of interest if you are already in the area.

Grizzly Discovery Center *(Finds)*   You're not likely to see grizzlies out in the park, but you can see them and wolves here in a nicely landscaped area, like a tiny zoo. The staff does a good job of holding kids' interest while telling them about the animals and their rescue. In fact, for $1 your kids can stash food for the bears and then watch them root it out, an adventure that teaches youngsters not only how bears forage but how dangerous they can be when searching for food. You can view the bears and wolves from decks overlooking both enclosures. A small museum area also is well pitched for kids. The huge gift shop helps support the not-for-profit operation.

Canyon St. (*C*) 800/257-2570 or 406/646-7001. www.grizzlydiscoveryctr.com. Admission $9.75 adults, $9 seniors, $5 children 5–12, free for children under 5. Admission good for 2 consecutive days. Year-round daily 8am–dusk.

Yellowstone Historic Center   This museum in West Yellowstone's old railroad depot opened in 2001. It's the work of a community group seeking to preserve the buildings surrounding the 1908 railroad link to West Yellowstone. Spend 15 minutes here and you can learn all you need to know about the five railroads—the Northern Pacific, Union Pacific, Burlington Northern, Chicago and Northwestern, and Chicago and Pacific—that hauled passengers to Yellowstone early in the 20th century. There also are exhibits on wildlife and the 1988 fires that burned through the park.

104 Yellowstone Ave. (*C*) 406/646-1100. www.yellowstonehistoriccenter.org. Admission $6 adults, $4 children 3–17, $15 families. Summer daily 9am–9pm; Sept daily 9am–7pm. Closed Oct–May 15.

Yellowstone IMAX Theater   Like IMAX theaters that have cropped up outside several of the Western parks, this facility shows movies about Yellowstone, bears, and wolves on a huge screen. The films show gorgeous scenery and wildlife, and tell about early park history, the area's geology, the workings of geysers, and how wildlife survive. It's well done and entertaining to children, but somewhat expensive for less than an hour. The lobby contains fast-food outlets.

101 Canyon St. (*C*) 406/646-4100. Admission $9 adults, $8.50 seniors, $6.50 children 3–12, free for children under 3. Daily 9am–9pm, but with fewer showings outside of summer; shows hourly on the hour.

8 For the Active Family

BACKPACKING

Yellowstone is one of the best parks for backpacking, for many reasons. It's huge, with plenty of room for everyone. The backcountry-permit system is understandable and well managed, and permits are easy to get. You can take long hikes in spectacular places, making destinations of backcountry geysers and seeing lots of bison, elk, and other wildlife. But you don't have to go far to have a backcountry wilderness experience—some beautiful campsites are just a couple of miles off the road. A family with school-age children without prior backcountry experience can handle it with careful planning to avoid excessive packs or long days. You just need to be self-sufficient and to follow carefully the Park Service's bear-avoidance rules, which you'll receive in detail when you get your backcountry permit. Gathering deadwood is permitted in most areas of the park, but fires should be kept in rings at established campsites. Of course, you also need a camp stove.

Details on the backcountry system are explained under "Backcountry Camping Permits" in chapter 2; more hiking information appears below.

BIKING & MOUNTAIN BIKING

Family biking at Yellowstone is quite limited, but there are some opportunities. Hiking trails and boardwalks are off-limits to bikes, and the park's main roads are too narrow and busy to be safe with kids. In the spring, some park roads open to nonmotorized travel, allowing bicyclists to tour the park. This opportunity depends on conditions, so you can't plan very far ahead, and that makes it less practical for families. Optimally, it lasts from mid-March to the third Thursday in April, when vehicle traffic resumes. Call the park for the latest, and check the website for a list of roads affected (see "Yellowstone Address Book," p. 272).

Bikes are not for rent in the park, but there are a few mountain-biking routes if you bring your own; a great one exists at the Rendezvous Trail System that starts in West Yellowstone. In the park are a few longer unpaved routes that are also open to cars, and 13 that are open to bikes and hikers, all but three of them just a mile or two. The Park Service provides route descriptions in the publication *Bicycling in Yellowstone National Park*, which you can also find online (www.nps.gov/yell; click "Activities," then "Biking").

BOATING

Most boating at Yellowstone starts from Bridge Bay Marina, on the northwest corner of the lake. With its straight, steep shores topped by a highway, it's not the most interesting area for paddling. The less-than-thrilling tour-boat ride is covered under "Yellowstone Lake & West Thumb" (p. 301). Xanterra (see "Yellowstone Address Book," p. 272) operates the marina, catering mostly to anglers (see "Fishing," below). But you can also use its service to get to backcountry lakeside campsites on the southern part of the lake, places you otherwise couldn't reach with young or nonbackpacking members in your group. The marina offers shuttle service, and you can take a rented canoe along to provide mobility at the site. The ride costs $72 an hour, and it often is a 4-hour round-trip. Canoe rentals for backcountry trips are $47 a day, and that includes paddles and PFDs. You should reserve well ahead for this service. You'll also need a backcountry camping permit (p. 289). The marina also rents rowboats and skiffs with outboard motors, but they are really just for anglers—you have to stay in a zone near the marina.

For self-guided canoeing and kayaking, you can bring your own boat or rent one in Jackson or another town neighboring the park (see "Canoeing, Kayaking & Boating," in chapter 12). So equipped, you can explore Lewis, Shoshone, and Yellowstone lakes, launching either from the Lewis Lake Campground near the south entrance or, for Yellowstone Lake, from Grant Village. These are true wilderness waters, very beautiful and with interesting shoreline, but not for the inexperienced. Almost every year someone drowns in one of these lakes in a boating accident. Backcountry camping permits are in high demand, so plan early for overnights (see "Backcountry Camping Permits," p. 289). The water is cold, and to be safe you need to stay near shore, wear life jackets, and bring warm clothing in dry bags that you can put on if you get wet. Also, plan to paddle in the morning, because stormy winds can whip up the lakes in the afternoon.

Boats brought from outside the park usually require a boating permit from the Park Service, except that Grand Teton National Park permits are honored as 7-day permits here. Yellowstone permits cost $5 for 7 days for nonmotorized vessels, such as rowboats, canoes, and kayaks, and $10 for a week for motorized vessels. Permits are sold at the south entrance, Lewis Lake Campground, Grant Village Visitor Center, Bridge Bay Ranger Station, and Lake Ranger Station; at Canyon and Mammoth visitor centers you can buy permits only for boats without motors.

FISHING

Thanks to the growth aided by hot water from below, trout in Yellowstone streams can grow as much as four times faster than in cold mountain streams in similar areas without geothermal activity. Catch-and-release regulations have helped keep fishing exceptionally good. The trout can get quite a workout, being caught as many as 10 times a season. On some streams, only fly-fishing is permitted.

Regulations, permits, and gear for sale or rent are available at the Yellowstone General Stores, and you can get permits and guidance at a visitor center or ranger station. A Park Service fishing permit good for 3 days costs $15, for 7 days it's $20, and for the entire season $35. Permits are free for children 12 to 15 years old; children under 12 don't need a permit but must be supervised by an adult. You don't need a state fishing license within the park. Xanterra (see "Yellowstone Address Book," p. 272) offers guided fishing from Bridge Bay Marina, on Yellowstone Lake, for anywhere from $315 to $405 for 4½ hours for a boat that holds up to six people; reserve well ahead. You can rent your own boat, too. A rowboat is $43 a day, and a boat with an outboard is $45 an hour; reservations are not accepted.

HIKING

I love hiking, but even if I didn't, I would hike away from the roads at Yellowstone. That's how you get away from the crowds. After a mile or so, a bubble seems to pop, and you find yourself out under the sky, alone in a world that seems brighter and more real because it belongs to your eyes only. The small part of the universe where people control everything is left behind, and the beauty of Yellowstone seems brand-new.

More than 1,000 miles of trails cross the park, so it isn't hard to find your own place. One of my favorite hikes, one that is great for families, is the stroll to the **Lone Star Geyser.** I say "stroll" because the route runs along a paved trail that parallels the Firehole River. With no noticeable gradient, young hikers can tackle this—and they may even notice the conifer forest and rippling river. From the trail head, about 3½ miles southeast of the Old Faithful complex along the Grand Loop Road, this trail offers a leisurely 5-mile round-trip that samples the park's wonderful backcountry. A spouting geyser, with a cone that towers a dozen feet above the ground, is the payoff.

To help choose other good day hikes, get one of the free handouts the Park Service produces on each park area, or check the park website (www.nps.gov/yell; click "Activities," then "Hiking"). Trail guidebooks and maps are covered under "Reading Up" (p. 280). Some great family trails include these: at Mammoth, the Beaver Ponds Loop, an easy 5-mile route from Liberty Cap, at the springs, leading to a beaver pond (go in the evening or early morning to see the beavers); at Madison, the .5-mile Harlequin Lake trail, with good birding; Tower Fall and Mount Washburn trails (see "Tower Fall," p. 300); and the Clear Lake/Ribbon Lake trails (see "Grand Canyon of the Yellowstone," p. 300).

HORSEBACK RIDING

Yellowstone National Park Lodges (see "Yellowstone Address Book," p. 272) operates stables for trail rides at Roosevelt Lodge, Mammoth Hot Springs, and Canyon Village. The rolling grassland of the Northern Range at Roosevelt is the best setting for a ride, a scene out of your fantasies of the West. It's the only site with the option of a ride on a stagecoach (really a large cart) for the very young, and a fun cookout and singalong every evening. Our kids really enjoyed it. Don't expect anything intimate, however, because the rides often amount to long parades of riders. One-hour rides are $35. Two-hour rides are $54, but are not offered at Mammoth. Children must be at least age 8 and 4 feet tall and, if under 11, must be accompanied by someone 16 or older; riders can weigh no more than 240 pounds. Call ahead to reserve and be sure to arrive early for the ride to sign the paperwork. The Roosevelt stagecoach rides are $9.35 adults, $7.50 children 2 to 11. The cookout stagecoach ride is $53 adults, $43 children 5 to 11; children under 5 are free if they sit on your lap and eat off your plate. Going to the cookout on horseback is $63 adults, $53 children 8 to 11 for a 1-hour ride, $75 and $65 for 2 hours. Note that all these rates go up a little annually.

For more serious riders, dozens of outfitters offer half-day, all-day, and overnight backcountry rides and pack trips with horses or llamas. Typically, outfitters will guide you into remote country on horseback, providing the animals, meals, and gear for around $150 to $300 per person, per day. They usually have minimum age and experience levels for guests. You can go with just your family or join a group. Guided fishing on backcountry streams is a specialty of many of the operators. It seems like a perfect way to the wilderness for families who enjoy horses or want to experience a llama trip. All the licensed operators, with links to many, are listed on the park's website (www.nps.gov/yell/planyourvisit/stockbusn.htm).

RAFTING

Rafting isn't permitted in the park itself, but several companies offer raft rides outside. They run on the Yellowstone River from Gardiner, where it flows north out of the park, and on the Gallatin and Madison rivers, from the western side near West Yellowstone or Big Sky, Montana. You can choose half- or full-day rides on wild or calm water. **Yellowstone Raft Company** (© **800/858-7781;** www.yellowstoneraft.com) is a longtime operator on the Yellowstone River. The company offers trips, kayak instruction, and guided float fishing. The website has good trip descriptions. Children as young as age 6 are accepted. Prices for half-days are $35 for adults, about $10 less for children under 13; full days, which include lunch, are $78 for adults, $58 for kids.

SWIMMING

You can have a wonderful afternoon playing in the river at Madison Campground, where the water is partly warmed by the geothermal water flowing down the Firehole

River. The Firehole itself has popular swimming holes with limited parking on Firehole Canyon Drive, which runs one-way from just south of Madison. River currents can be dangerous, especially for kids, and there are no lifeguards; so be careful and, if in doubt, check with a ranger. Swimming in hot springs is illegal and can be deadly: Don't even think about it.

WINTER SPORTS & SIGHTSEEING

Yellowstone is the best national park for winter sports. Snow is reliably deep in areas above 7,000 feet, which includes all parts of the park except the Northern Range. And in winter the scenery is better. White brings sharper contrasts and cleaner shapes. The geysers and other thermal features seem exaggerated in the cold, and they create strange microclimates of plant and animal life, attracting wildlife with warmth and the absence of snow. Equally important for visitors, the park is well developed for cross-country skiing, snowshoeing, sightseeing, and, to some extent, snowmobiling.

The winter season, when hotels, visitor centers, and other businesses are open, begins in late December and lasts until the second week of March. Most activities revolve around **Old Faithful Snow Lodge** (p. 294) and **Mammoth Hotel** (p. 293), which remain open for the season. Mammoth, at a lower elevation, doesn't get heavy snow, and you can drive there year-round. Old Faithful is the more romantic choice, snowed in all winter and reachable only by snow coach (a small bus or van on caterpillar tracks). Xanterra (see "Yellowstone Address Book," p. 272) runs the **snow coach** to Old Faithful daily from various starting points, such as West Yellowstone or Mammoth. A ride from Mammoth to Old Faithful, or Old Faithful to Flagg Ranch outside the South Entrance, costs $64 one-way for adults, $32 for kids 2 to 11. The trip from West Yellowstone to Old Faithful is $51 one-way for adults, $26 for kids. It's a slow mode of travel. There is commentary and a chance to stretch your legs during the trip, which lasts up to 4 hours. Day sightseeing tours are available as well. Mammoth also has an outdoor skating rink and inexpensive skate rentals and hot tubs. The visitor centers at the two main areas are the only ones open in the winter season. Warming huts, many with snacks, operate at spots all over the park, which are listed in the newspaper. Nature trails remain open, too.

Snowmobiling in the park is among the most controversial of political topics around here. Under President Clinton, the Park Service decided to phase it out entirely due to the air pollution, noise, and disturbance of wildlife the machines produced. Supporters of snowmobile use, which include many tourism businesses in the surrounding communities, sued to stop the plan, and under President Bush the lawsuit was settled with a new decision to allow snowmobiling to continue while additional environmental studies were conducted. The latest proposal called for upward of 540 snowmobiles to be allowed into the park per day beginning in December 2008, but that could easily change before it's implemented. Snow coaches are becoming more and more popular as a means for exploring the park and reaching Old Faithful, although they can be expensive. Round-trip tickets from West Yellowstone to Old Faithful, for example, are around $100 per person. Nordic skiing is a good way to see the park in winter. There are a few groomed trails, and wide-open roads and hiking trails to explore. From Mammoth Hot Springs, you can catch a round-trip shuttle to Indian Creek, a great area for ski touring, for $15 per adult; children pay $7.25. Old Faithful guests can ski from the Old Faithful Snow Lodge or take a snow coach to Fairy Falls or the Continental Divide and ski back; $14 for adults, $6.75 kids. The concessionaire operates ski-rental shops at Old Faithful and Mammoth, which also carry snowshoes. They offer guided tours, too. See "When It's Cold & Wet," in chapter 2, for what to wear.

9 Kid-Friendly Programs

CHILDREN'S PROGRAMS

The visitor centers sell $3 **Junior Ranger** newspapers for ages 5 to 7 and ages 8 to 12. After completing the workbook questions, doing outdoor activities, attending ranger programs, and turning in the newspapers with various signatures, kids get a patch. Take a good look at the newspaper before getting into this, because it's likely to take quite of a bit of your and your child's time and may be difficult if you don't cover a large portion of the park. You'll also need quiet time to do writing activities; if you can't finish while at the park, it's okay to do some of it on the way home and mail in the worksheets for your patch. The winter program costs includes a "Snow Pack" of equipment you check out for use in the field for science activities, such as hand lenses and thermometers. It is available from Old Faithful or Mammoth visitor center; at Mammoth, kids can also borrow snowshoes for the program.

FAMILY & ADULT PROGRAMS

The park newspaper lists ranger programs all over the park, mostly near the most popular natural features. They start every hour or two all day during the height of the summer season. These programs are walks and lectures, not activities or lessons, and are primarily aimed at adults. In the evening during the summer, campfire talks and slide shows are offered every night at many of the campgrounds and some other sites; the exact list of locations depends on annual Park Service budgets.

THE YELLOWSTONE INSTITUTE

One of the best ways to experience Yellowstone is to sign up for one of the programs offered by the nonprofit **Yellowstone Association** (see "Yellowstone Address Book," p. 272), which offers highly regarded educational programs using the park as a classroom. The unique **Yellowstone for Families** program lets families join in an educational experience for 4 days, a sort of science camp that includes grown-ups. Led by experienced rangers, groups of 13 or fewer kids and parents join daily for hiking, painting, science experiments (measuring the temperature of thermal features, for example), a fire ecology scavenger hunt, games, and so on. It's fun, you get to do it together, and you pay very little: around $813 for a single adult or $1,218 for a couple plus $379 per child, including lodging at Mammoth, breakfast and lunch, transportation in the park, and the all-day program itself. A similar program runs out of Grant Village and costs slightly more: $895 for a single adult or $1,298 for a couple plus $379 per child. Two versions are offered every week of the summer, one with

---

Tips **Places for Relaxed Play & Picnics**

There are picnic sites all over the park, clearly marked on the map you receive when you enter. All the hotel restaurants pack box lunches for $7 to $8, and you can get takeout at the deli restaurants listed under "Family-Friendly Dining" (p. 296). There are plenty of places to play, but there's no convenient playground equipment.

hikes of 3 to 5 miles and the other with hikes under 3 miles. The educational program is designed for ages 8 to 12, but other ages can be accommodated. Reserve early, because they always book up.

The institute offers an impressive catalog of intensive programs in natural history, outdoors skills, art, history, photography, backpacking and horse-packing trips, and many other subjects, mostly aimed at adults or mature teens. Each course description includes age limits. Groups are small and leaders are experts in their fields, with college credit available for some of the 1- to 5-day sessions. Prices start around $80 a day for a field course, and quickly go up. The institute is at Buffalo Ranch, in Lamar Valley in the northeast part of the park, near Cooke City, and many of the classes happen there. The catalog is released in January, and popular courses fill fast. Find it at www.yellowstoneassociation.org/institute.

FAST FACTS: Yellowstone National Park

Area Code The area code is 307.

ATMs ATMs are available at Fishing Bridge General store, Grant Village General Store, Lake Yellowstone Hotel, Mammoth General Store, Mammoth Hot Springs Hotel, Old Faithful Inn, Old Faithful Snow Lodge, Old Faithful Upper Store, Canyon General Store, and Canyon Lodge. First Security Bank is at 103 S. Electric St. in West Yellowstone (✆ **406/646-7646**).

Emergencies For emergencies, dial ✆ **911**.

Hospitals & Clinics Three hospitals are available at Yellowstone: **Yellowstone Lake Clinic, Pharmacy and Hospital** is open from late May to late September (✆ **307/242-7241**), **Mammoth Clinic** is open year-round (✆ **307/344-7965**), and **Old Faithful Clinic** is open from mid-May to early October (✆ **307/545-7325**). There's also a year-round clinic at 236 Yellowstone Ave., West Yellowstone (✆ **406/646-0200**).

Information For information, write Yellowstone National Park, P.O. Box 168, Yellowstone National Park, WY 82190; call ✆ **307/344-7381**; or check the website www.nps.gov/yell.

Pharmacies The Lake Clinic, Pharmacy and Hospital is open from late May to mid-September (✆ **307/242-7241**).

Post Office Branches are located at Mammoth Hot Springs (open year-round; ✆ **307/344-7764**), Old Faithful (open mid-May to early Oct and mid-Dec to mid-Mar; ✆ **307/545-7252**), Grant Village (open mid-May to mid-Sept; ✆ **307/242-7338**), and Lake Village (open mid-May to mid-Sept.; ✆ **307/242-7383**).

Time Zone The park is on **Mountain Standard Time.**

Weather Updates For weather updates, call ✆ **307/344-7381**.

12

Grand Teton National Park

The Teton Range is a shock the first time you see it. The gray rock mountains seem impossibly steep and sharp. They stand so tall that you have to take a good look just to get used to how big they are. What also makes them so awesome is how they stand up like a wall from the flat ground on their eastern side. Most mountains have a ramp of foothills in front of them, and usually you have to be a lot farther away to see a whole mountain—that's how the Tetons are on the west side. But on the east side, you can get close to something very big without being on it. From the valley floor to the top of Grand Teton, a distance of about 3 miles, the elevation rises 7,000 feet, or more than a mile, straight up. The mountains fill the sky.

It takes a little longer to appreciate the flat land that you stand on when you look up at the mountains, but the flat is more important for animals and for families traveling to the park. Not much can live up on those rocky mountain peaks in the snow and cold. The valley, called Jackson Hole (*hole* is a word for valley), is a special place, a perfect habitat for elk, moose, and many other animals. The rampart of mountains protects the valley from the worst of the snowy weather. As you drive into Jackson Hole you can sense the way this land is protected, as if it's in the palm of a great hand and the Tetons are the fingers. As you hike, camp, ride, swim, or canoe, the mountains are always there to the west, inspiring you and enclosing the big sky. As you climb into the mountains, you can see how the rich life of the lowlands slips away, and you can feel the thin, cool air of that higher world. When you return, the lowlands seem even more inviting.

Yellowstone is like a three-ring circus, with geysers and canyons and mountain lakes. Grand Teton, on the other hand, is a single grand opera stage. The main show is the Teton Range and Jackson Hole. There's as much or more to do in the outdoors, but not as much sightseeing to keep you on the run, and that gives the park a more relaxed feel. The town of Jackson (often called Jackson Hole) is a fun and bustling resort community with good restaurants.

BEST THINGS TO DO IN GRAND TETON NATIONAL PARK

- **Hike around the ponds** of Jackson Hole to see moose, bison, trumpeter swans, white pelicans, and lovely views.
- **Ride the aerial tram** to the top of Rendezvous Mountain to start a high-elevation hike with sweeping views and cool, thin air.
- **Canoe String and Leigh lakes** or Jackson Lake, and dive in for a swim.
- **Camp in the backcountry,** traveling by canoe or by foot.

For more information, see "For the Active Family" (p. 333).

Grand Teton Address Book

Grand Teton National Park   P.O. Drawer 170, Moose, WY 83012-0170. ℂ **307/ 739-3300.** TDD 307/739-3400. www.nps.gov/grte.

Grand Teton Lodge Company   P.O. Box 250, Moran, WY 83013. ℂ **800/628- 9988** or 307/543-2811. Fax 307/543-3046. www.gtlc.com. Main park concessionaire.

Dornans at Moose   P.O. Box 39, Moose, WY 83012. ℂ **307/733-2415.** www. dornans.com. Center for rentals and activities.

Grand Teton Association   P.O. Box 170, Moose, WY 83012. ℂ **307/739- 3403.** www.grandtetonpark.org. For books and maps.

Bridger-Teton National Forest   P.O. Box 1888, Jackson, WY 83001. ℂ **307/ 739-5500.** www.fs.fed.us/btnf.

Caribou-Targhee National Forest, Teton Basin Ranger District   515 South Main, P.O. Box 777, Driggs, ID 83422. ℂ **208/354-2312.** www.fs.fed.us/r4/ caribou-targhee.

Jackson Hole Chamber of Commerce   532 N. Cache, P.O. Box 550, Jackson, WY 83001. ℂ **307/733-3316.** Fax 307/733-5585. www.jacksonhole chamber.com.

1 History: Rockefeller to the Rescue

John D. Rockefeller, Jr., one of the richest men who ever lived, found a way to use his money to create something that will live on and make future generations grateful. He was born with money; his father started one of the world's largest oil companies. The son's lasting achievement was the way he spent that money. He bought land for some of America's greatest national parks, including Grand Teton, Acadia, and Great Smoky Mountain (all of which are in this book), and many others.

The first superintendent of Yellowstone National Park, Horace Albright, was the impetus behind Grand Teton National Park. Albright, a young man from California, loved spending time in the mountains. He was one of the first members of the National Park Service when it took over the parks from the Army in 1916. The first time Albright saw Jackson Hole and the Tetons, he wanted to add them to Yellowstone. But times had changed since Yellowstone had become a park in 1872. At that time, settlers had barely touched the Rockies; by 1916, people lived on the flat lands of Jackson Hole, and they had worked hard to build ranches there. Engineers had dammed Jackson Lake, raising its level to help water farms.

Later, the Park Service fought plans to dam Jenny Lake and other beautiful waterways. Locals wanted to make their living on this land, not have it made into a park. The representatives they elected to Congress blocked the establishment of the park for many years.

One group in the valley, however, thought it could make money from a park. Jackson became home to dude ranches, and visitors came to ride horses and enjoy the area's beauty. The owners thought their businesses could be more successful if the mountains were protected in a park. Albright got together with this group, and they worked to persuade their neighbors and congressmen to support the park. Still, many residents wanted only the mountains, not the valley, to be in the park. The Teton Range is too steep and rugged to ever be developed into farms and towns. No one had a use for the mountains other than looking at them, so most people agreed to the park plan. In 1929, after Albright's original idea was cut down to just the mountains and six lakes at their base, Congress passed the law that created Grand Teton National Park.

But Albright didn't give up. In 1924, John D. Rockefeller, Jr., and his family visited Yellowstone. Albright set up a special tour for the Rockefellers and made friends with them. He knew that Rockefeller had helped create Acadia National Park in Maine, but he didn't ask for help for Grand Teton right away. Two years later, however, when the Rockefellers returned, Albright drove them to Jackson Hole. They picnicked on the hill next to where Jackson Lake Lodge stands today and saw five moose. The spot is one of the grandest and most beautiful you will ever see, and they had a wonderful day. The next day, they drove farther and saw how human development was spreading into some of Jackson Hole's prettiest areas. Because only the mountains and lakes were in the park, the valley had been left open for businesses. Even in the 1920s, the areas of unplanned roadside tourist development were ugly. The Rockefellers were horrified, and it wasn't long before they agreed with Albright's plan—they would buy the property in the valley and give it to the government to expand Grand Teton National Park.

If you're going to buy a whole valley, you have to be very careful about how you do it. If people knew that one of the richest men in the world wanted to buy their land, they would probably raise the price. In a place like Jackson Hole, where many people opposed expanding the park, buying the land would be even more difficult. So Rockefeller and Albright decided to buy the land secretly. Rockefeller set up a company that hired people to buy land without telling them why they wanted it or who was paying the bills. The buyers just got a list of what property to buy and the money to do it. At the same time, Albright worked secretly in Washington, D.C., to keep more government-owned land in Jackson Hole from being made into private homesteads or otherwise given away. The project worked. Soon, all the land in Jackson Hole that Albright wanted for the park was under the control of Rockefeller or the federal government.

When people in Wyoming found out, they were furious that they had been fooled. They felt their valley and their ability to make a living had been stolen. They accused the pro-park group of breaking the law, and a scandal broke out, with investigations and hearings. Albright resigned to take a better-paying job. No one found evidence he'd done anything wrong.

Rockefeller had hoped to give the land to the park fairly quickly, but the local residents wouldn't give up. Their representatives in Congress stopped the Park Service from accepting the land for years. In 1942, after working on the project for 15 years, Rockefeller wrote a letter to the president saying he would give up on the whole thing if something wasn't done. The next year President Franklin Roosevelt made Jackson Hole a national monument. A national monument is an area like a park; but it's usually smaller, and the president has the power to create it without a vote by Congress. The congressmen who had stopped the park before were so angry that they passed a bill to do away with the monument and take away the president's power to create monuments. Roosevelt vetoed the bill, and the monument survived.

Over the years, many Jackson residents changed their minds. After World War II ended, more tourists came to see Grand Teton. Finally, in 1950, the locals stopped fighting. Congress passed a bill to add the national monument to the old Grand Teton

National Park, making the park the size and shape it is today. To settle the disagreement, the ranchers who were already using parkland to graze their cattle were allowed to stay for as long as they and their children were alive. In the eastern part of the park, you can still see those ranchers' houses and animals. Today, pretty much everyone thinks the park was a good idea. A few ranchers may be left, but most jobs and businesses in the area depend on the visitors who come to the park. They bring in a lot more money than ranching ever could.

2 Orientation

Grand Teton National Park is about 45 miles long and half as wide. It stretches from the south entrance of Yellowstone National Park and the John D. Rockefeller Jr. Parkway, in the north, to the town of **Jackson** and the National Elk Refuge in the south. The **Teton Range** towers along the western side of the park. **Jackson Lake** sits in the mountains' lap in the northern part of the park. Most boating, camping, and lodgings are on the lake's eastern shore. Most hiking trails into the mountains start south of Jackson Lake, near **Jenny Lake.** The **Snake River** flows from the southeast corner of Jackson Lake and runs south through the valley and into a canyon south of Jackson.

Grand Teton National Park

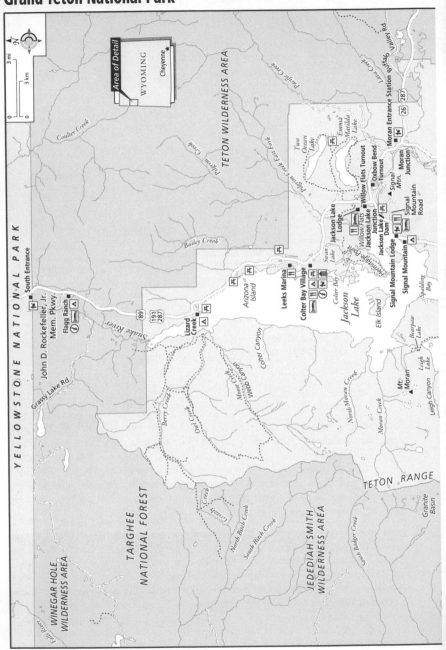

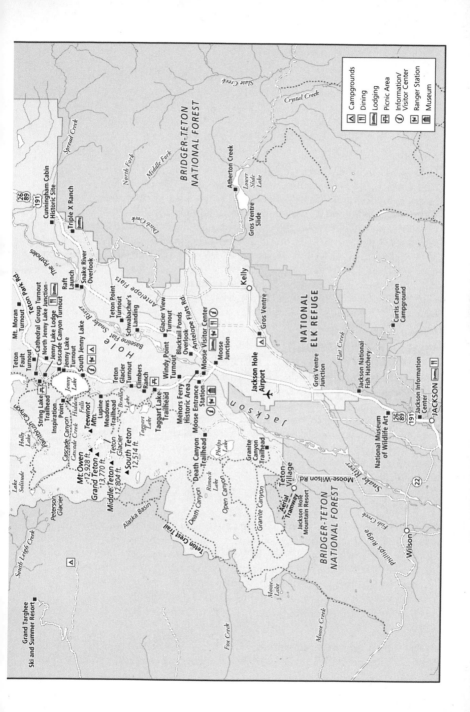

ARRIVING
BY CAR

See "Arriving" in Yellowstone (p. 277) for approaches from the north. If you're coming from the west or south, take I-15 to Idaho Falls and then drive over the back of the Tetons to Jackson on U.S. Highway 26 and state roads 31, 33, and 22 (the way is well marked). From the east, U.S. 26/287 leads to the park from across Wyoming, splitting from I-80 or I-25 on the other side of the state.

BY AIR

Jackson has the area's major airport (www.jacksonholeairport.com), served by jet from Chicago and Dallas by **American** (*©* **800/443-7300;** www.aa.com), from Salt Lake City by **Delta/SkyWest** (*©* **800/221-1212;** www.delta.com), from Denver by **United** (*©* **800/864-8331;** www.united.com), and from Minneapolis by **Northwest** (*©* **800/225-2525** or 307/739-9920; www.nwa.com). Cars are available from **Alamo** (*©* **800/327-9633** or 307/733-0671; www.alamo.com), **Avis** (*©* **800/831-2847** or 307/733-3422; www.avis.com), **Hertz** (*©* **800/654-3131** or 307/733-2272; www. hertz.com), and **Thrifty** (*©* **800/367-2277** or 307/734-8312; www.thrifty.com). You can also rent an RV in Jackson from **Cruise America**'s outlet, Eagle Rent-a-Car (*©* **800/327-7799** or 307/739-9999). See "Practicalities: The RV Advantage," p. 24, for advice. If you want to shop around for airfare or car rentals, try Idaho Falls or Salt Lake City.

VISITOR INFORMATION
NATIONAL PARK VISITOR CENTERS

Colter Bay Visitor Center   In the park's main northern activity hub, 25 miles from Moose, this center bustles with people asking questions and buying books before heading out on the many nearby activities. Inside, the Colter Bay Indian Arts Museum contains a rich collection of Native American art and other objects from all over the country presented in a visually interesting if subdued space. Many of these objects are surprisingly fresh and finely made, but a lack of context reduces the time they will hold children's interest. Native American residents sometimes put on demonstrations and sell crafts.

½ mile west of Colter Bay Junction on U.S. 89/191/287. *©* **307/739-3594.** June to early Sept daily 8am–7pm; spring and fall daily 8am–5pm. Closed Oct to early May.

Craig Thomas Discovery and Visitor Center   Previously known simply as the Moose Visitor Center, this facility opened in August 2007 and was named in honor of the late U.S. Sen. Craig Thomas, R-Wyoming, a passionate advocate for national parks. The 22,000-square-foot building offers displays about the park's natural history, frequent films, useful postings and information for hikers, and a large bookstore. Permits for backpacking and paddling in the park can be obtained here.

Near Moose Junction, at the south end of the park. *©* **307/739-3399.** June–Sept daily 8am–7pm; Oct–May daily 8am–5pm.

Flagg Ranch Information Station   Stop here if you need information on your way south into the park from Yellowstone; otherwise, you can pass by without missing anything.

U.S. 89/191/287, 2½ miles south of Yellowstone entrance. *©* **307/543-2327.** June–Sept daily 9am–4pm. Closed early Sept to early June.

Jenny Lake Visitor Center   This information station, with maps and geology displays, is in a small wooden building on the edge of Jenny Lake. The center, open only during the summer, serves as the most popular starting point for hikes into the mountains and is a good place to stop for trail conditions, advice, maps, and the like.

Grand Teton Park Rd. at Jenny Lake. (C) **307/739-3392**. Mid-May to late Sept daily 8am–7pm. Closed late Sept to mid-May.

COMMERCIAL VISITOR CENTERS

Jackson Hole and Greater Yellowstone Visitor Center   This large interagency facility at the north edge of Jackson overlooks the elk refuge—it has free telescopes to watch the elk—and dispenses information for the local chamber of commerce and all the land agencies in the area, including the national park and national forests. In addition to the rangers and other helpers, the center contains wildlife exhibits and a bookstore, and you can purchase park passes as well as fishing licenses here.

532 N. Cache St. (C) **307/733-3316**. Summer daily 8am–7pm; winter daily 8am–5pm.

READING UP

You can get most of these books and maps at visitor centers, online, or by mail order from **Grand Teton Association** ((C) **307/739-3403;** www.grandtetonpark.org).

Hiking: *Hiking Grand Teton National Park,* by Bill Schneider (Falcon/Globe Pequot, $15), covers all the trails.

Maps: The waterproof Trails Illustrated topographic map ($9.95) is the most detailed and complete map of the whole park. In addition, some of the best day-hike areas are covered in detailed color maps and field guides that cost only a few dollars each, a good buy if you are taking the aerial tram to Rendezvous Mountain or hiking Colter Bay or Cascade Canyon.

History: *Crucible for Conservation: The Struggle for Grand Teton National Park,* by Robert W. Righter (Grand Teton Natural History Association, $9), is a detailed, scholarly, clearly written account for adults.

Kids: The *Great Yellowstone, Grand Teton, Glacier Activity Book* (Rising Sun, $7.95; www.northlandpub.com) is chock-full of word searches, crossword puzzles, mazes, journals, and other activities to keep young minds busy. *The Kid's Guide to Grand Teton National Park* (Grand Teton Association, $4.95; www.grandtetonpark.org) is part field guide and part travel guide to the park.

THE NATIONAL PARK IN BRIEF

Jackson

The pricey resort town of **Jackson** is the gateway to the park and a good entry to the region. It's pretty touristy, but has managed to keep some Western charm and uniqueness.

Teton Village

Teton Village is a ski-resort complex northwest of Jackson where the aerial tram climbs the mountains and there are some restaurants, lodgings, and campgrounds. To get there from Jackson, turn off West Broadway on Route 22, cross the Snake River, and then drive north on Highway 390, also known as the Moose-Wilson Road. Past Teton Village north to Moose this road is rough, narrow, and winding, but very pretty.

Moose

Moose is a small developed area at the southern end of the park, where the main visitor center is.

3 Getting Around

BY CAR

Driving is the only practical way for a family to get around the park. Distances aren't great, but you can eat up a lot of time driving; plan your visit to avoid splitting up your day in park areas.

A two-lane U.S. highway runs the length of the park. It's numbered 89 and 191 all the way along, from Yellowstone to Jackson, but it's known locally as **U.S. 89.** From the east **U.S. 26/287** meets 89 at Moran Junction, halfway up the park. The **Teton Park Road** runs from just north of Moran Junction along the base of the Teton Range to the small lakes and trail heads, ending back on 89 at Moose Junction, near the south end of the park. Entrance stations are located so that you can drive 89 through the park from Moran Junction to Jackson without paying an entrance fee. You do have to pay to drive the park road or to go north from Moran Junction toward Yellowstone.

BY BIKE

Biking in the park has been a touchy proposition, as there has been little room other than narrow shoulders for cyclists to take to. However, in the coming years 40 miles of multiple-use pathways are to be installed. The first, a stretch between Moose and South Jenny Lake, was to be built during 2008. Bikes are not allowed off-road in the park. Mountain-biking options are described under "For the Active Family" (p. 333).

4 Planning Your Outings

WHEN TO GO

Grand Teton's busy season is July and August, when temperatures are warmest, although September is getting more traffic. Snow, outside of perennial snowfields in the very highest elevations, slowly disappears from the mountains and is gone completely in late July or early August. Thunderstorms sweep through the mountains on many afternoons. Nights can be chilly. Popular trails and campgrounds are busy.

June and October are quieter. Daytime weather is still comfortable, but nights can be cold. Mountain trails are still snowy in June. By late May, snow clears out of Jackson Hole. That's where campgrounds are and where families spend most of their time. Ice on the lakes is gone in mid-May.

Almost everything in the park shuts down from October 15 to May 15. The main winter activities are downhill skiing at the two Jackson resorts, cross-country skiing and snowshoeing in the park, and wildlife-viewing at the National Elk Refuge.

HOW MUCH TIME TO SPEND

To get out on the trails, lake, and river, you need at least 3 days, but you could spend a week without getting bored if you enjoy the outdoors. If you're interested only in sightseeing, you can see the mountains while driving through the park on your way to or from Yellowstone.

Weather Chart: Moose Junction

	Avg. High (°F/°C)	Avg. Low (°F/°C)	Snowfall (total in.)
November–March	26–39/–3 to 4	1–14/–17 to –10	160
April	49/9	22/–6	9
May	61/16	31/–1	3
June	71/22	41/5	0
July–August	79–80/26–27	40–41/4–5	0
September	69/21	32/0	1
October	56/13	23/–5	4

Elevation approximately 6,400 feet.

HOW FAR TO PLAN AHEAD

Telephone reservations for accommodations in the park become available in October for the following summer, but written requests are accepted earlier. Traditionally, the best rooms fill by February with other units still available in April. In recent years of lowered tourism, rooms have been available all year. The rougher cabins at Colter Bay are the easiest to reserve. Activities can be reserved starting in the early spring, but reservations aren't always needed before you arrive unless there's something you want to be sure to do. Campgrounds in the park, except the RV park at Colter Bay, do not accept reservations. See "Campgrounds," below, for information on the daily scramble for sites, and to find out about the system to reserve permits to camp in the backcountry.

WHAT TO PACK

The advice on Yellowstone in chapter 11, "Yellowstone National Park," is good for Grand Teton, too. Be prepared for cool nights and afternoon thunderstorms. Remember to bring good hiking shoes or boots; mountain hiking often covers steep, rugged trails. Do bring your swimsuits for the delicious lakes.

KEEPING SAFE & HEALTHY

See "Dealing with Hazards," in chapter 2, for information on dangerous wildlife, elevation, hypothermia, and lightning, all of which are risks here. Be especially well prepared for mountain hikes. Try to start as early in the morning as possible to avoid afternoon thunderstorms. They can bring lightning and damp, chilly conditions that can lead to hypothermia. Bring warm clothing you can wear in layers—it is cool in the mountains even on warm days down below.

5 Family-Friendly Accommodations

CAMPGROUNDS

NATIONAL PARK CAMPGROUNDS

Park campgrounds (other than the Colter Bay RV Park) do not take reservations. Visitor centers and entrance booths post or will report which campgrounds are full as the day progresses, and a sign on the road gives the same information as you leave Yellowstone for Grand Teton headed south. You have to get up early and participate in a stressful process to get a site in one of the more popular campgrounds in the high season, but two larger campgrounds usually have sites as late as early afternoon. The spectacular Jenny Lake tent campground often fills at dawn before people leave and has a 7-day limit (all others have 14-day limits). Signal Mountain goes soon after Jenny Lake. Fill-up times are listed below as a guide; but of course, these vary during the week and by season.

Campgrounds in the Grand Teton Area

Campground	Total Sites	RV Hookups	Dump Station	Toilets	Drinking Water	Showers
INSIDE THE PARK						
Colter Bay	350	No	Yes	Yes	Yes	Yes
Colter Bay RV Park	112	Yes	Yes	Yes	Yes	Yes
Gros Ventre	350	No	Yes	Yes	Yes	No
Jenny Lake	50	No	No	Yes	Yes	No
Lizard Creek	60	No	No	Yes	Yes	No
Signal Mountain	86	No	Yes	Yes	Yes	No
NEAR THE PARK						
Flagg Ranch	175	Yes	Yes	Yes	Yes	Yes
Snake River Park KOA	83	Yes	Yes	Yes	Yes	Yes
Grand Teton RV	205	Yes	Yes	Yes	Yes	Yes
BRIDGER TETON NF						
Atherton Creek	20	No	No	Yes	Yes	No
Curtis Canyon	11	No	No	Yes	Yes	No
Hatchet	9	No	No	Yes	Yes	No
Snake River Park KAO	83	Yes	No	Yes	Yes	Yes
TARGHEE NF						
Mike Harris	12	No	No	Yes	Yes	No
Teton	21	No	No	Yes	Yes	No
Trail Creek	11	No	No	Yes	Yes	No

* *Tents only are allowed here*

Here's the routine for getting a site in one of the popular campgrounds. Arrive at the campground as early as possible; I know folks who got to Jenny Lake at 7am one morning and didn't get a site. Pick up a registration envelope at the entrance and drive around the campground. Each site has a post with a registration slip on it, upon which is written the date of departure of the current occupant. If you find a site with that day's date, stop and ask the people if they are in fact leaving. If the answer is yes, post your own registration marker and leave a member of your party to wave others past, scurry back to the entrance, and register and pay your fee. If you find an unoccupied site, make sure it has no registration paper or other sign of being taken, then leave your own paper plus a lawn chair, an OCCUPIED sign, or one of your offspring, while you go register.

Clearly, you can't manage this early morning registration on the day you arrive at the park, so you will have to stay in town or at one of the less popular campgrounds your first night and move the next morning if you want one of these coveted sites.

These campgrounds are managed by concessionaires. These sites are offered on a first-come, first-served basis.

Fire Pits/Grills	Laundry	Public Phones	Reservations	Fees	Open
Yes	Yes	Yes	Yes	$17	Mid-May to late Sept
Yes	Yes	Yes	Yes	$32–$49	Mid-May to late Sept
Yes	No	Yes	No	$17	Early May to Oct
Yes	No	Yes	No	$19	Late May to late Sept
Yes	No	Yes	No	$17	Early June to early Sept
Yes	No	Yes	No	$17	Mid-May to mid-Oct
Yes	Yes	Yes	Yes	$20/$45	Mid-May to Late Sept
Yes	Yes	Yes	Yes	$35–$39/$53–$55	Mid-Apr to mid-Oct
Yes	Yes	Yes	Yes	$35/$39–$57	Year-round
Yes	No	No	No	$15	Memorial Day to Oct
Yes	No	No	No	$15	Mid-May to mid-Sept
Yes	No	No	No	$15	Mid-May to Oct
Yes	Yes	No	Yes	$35–$55	May–Sept
Yes	No	No	Yes	$10	Mid-May to mid-Sept
Yes	No	No	Yes	$10	Mid-May to mid-Sept
Yes	No	No	Yes	$10	May–Sept

All campgrounds have flush toilets. For answers to any other questions, call park headquarters, © **307/739-3399.**

Colter Bay   Despite its size, this campground is well designed to give good privacy to the sites, set among trees and boulders. Sites don't have lake views. Tenters should ask for a loop where RV generators are not allowed. Tent sites have gravel pads, which does a lot to keep you dry in a storm. The park's primary family-oriented facilities serve the campground; they include restaurants, showers, laundry, visitor center, museum, and store. A swimming beach on Jackson Lake is nearby, as are the wonderful family trails at Swan Lake and Heron Pond (see "Hiking," p. 334).

At Colter Bay Village, north of Jackson Lake Junction. 350 sites, tents or RVs. $17 site, $7 for hikers and cyclists. Fills around noon. Closed Oct to late May. **Amenities:** Restrooms w/flush toilets, showers, dump station, laundry, camp store, picnic tables, fire pits and grates, running water, sinks, restaurants, museum, swimming.

Colter Bay RV Park   This RV park is well wooded with pines and sits near the store and other facilities. Sites have picnic tables, but fires and tents are not allowed. Make reservations well ahead with the Grand Teton Lodge Company (see "Grand Teton Address Book," p. 311).

At Colter Bay Village. 112 sites, RVs only. Spring and summer $45–$49 full hookup; fall $28–$32 full hookup. Closed Oct to late May. **Amenities:** Full hookups, restrooms w/flush toilets, showers, laundry, camp store, picnic tables, running water, sinks, restaurants, museum, bear boxes.

Gros Ventre   This large campground, the closest in the park to Jackson Hole, is the last to fill because it's on the east side of the valley, somewhat distant from the lakes, mountains, and visitor facilities. It's a wonderful campground, with loops of well-separated sites along the Gros Ventre River, among cottonwoods, grass, and sagebrush. Here you should find quiet and space.

Near the south end of the park, between the entrance and Kelly. 360 sites, tents or RVs. $17 site. Fills in the afternoon. Closed mid-Oct to Apr. **Amenities:** Restrooms w/flush toilets, dump station, picnic tables, fire pits and grates, running water, sinks, bear boxes.

Jenny Lake   Lucky campers who arrive early (see tips for getting a site, above) get sites in this spectacular campground, one of the most desirable in any of the national parks. Tents nestle on large, private sites among small pines and little grassy hills at the base of the Tetons. Even the bathrooms fit in. The park's most popular trails and loveliest canoeing and swimming waters are nearby.

At South Jenny Lake. 50 sites, tents only. $19 site. Fills early morning. Closed late Sept to mid-May. **Amenities:** Restrooms w/flush toilets, picnic tables, fire pits and grates, running water, sinks.

Lizard Creek   The campground is on Jackson Lake, among thick pines at the northern end of the park. There are many walk-in sites, with wonderful privacy, and even some with lake frontage. A pizzeria is at the marina up the road (p. 328), but mostly this area of the park is quiet, undeveloped, and often overlooked by other campers.

At the north end of the park on U.S. 89. 60 sites, tents or RVs. $17 site. Fills early afternoon. Closed Sept to early June. **Amenities:** Restrooms w/flush toilets, picnic tables, fire pits and grates, running water, sinks, bear boxes.

Signal Mountain   Some campsites overlook Jackson Lake from a steep hill while others hide among the pines. The views are excellent and the campground is not too large. There's even a small beach for swimming. The campground is well used, and some sites have received much-needed restoration. Signal Mountain Lodge, with its store, marina, and restaurant, is nearby.

On the park road near Jackson Lake Junction. 86 sites, tents or RVs. $17 site. Fills midmorning. Closed mid-Oct to mid-May. **Amenities:** Restrooms w/flush toilets, dump station, store, picnic tables, fire pits and grates, running water, sinks, bear boxes, swimming, restaurant nearby.

BACKCOUNTRY CAMPING PERMITS

To camp along hiking trails or lakes outside campgrounds, you need a backcountry permit, for which you'll be charged a $15 processing fee. (See "Backpacking," p. 333, and "Canoeing & Kayaking," p. 333, for advice on trips.) Campsites and camping zones are shown on a map distributed free by the Park Service. To get a copy, write to the address at the beginning of the chapter, call the backcountry office (© **307/739-3309**), or download it from the website (www.nps.gov/archive/grte/trip/activities/back.htm). You'll also need a topographic map and a trail guide to plan your hiking itinerary; see "Reading Up" (p. 317) for recommendations.

Only a third of the permits are given out by reservation, so plenty are available for walk-in applicants at the Craig Thomas Discovery and Visitor Center and Colter Bay visitor centers 24 hours before the trip begins (be there when the center opens at 8am to get your choice). To be certain of a particular site, or to make sure you match your itinerary to your group's abilities, a reservation is a good idea. Reservations for the summer are taken from January 1 to May 15 by mail, by fax (©/fax **307/739-3438**), or in person—not by phone. Sites are allotted according to whose request gets there first, so a mad rush of faxes comes in on New Year's Day, clogging the machine so that requests are lost. Sending your request a little later might be more effective. No-shows are released at 10am on the day of the trip.

FOREST SERVICE CAMPGROUNDS

Campgrounds in the Bridger-Teton and Caribou-Targhee national forests are helpfully marked on the official park map. Those that accept reservations are noted below. Reserve through the Forest Service's national system, described in chapter 2. All have vault toilets and piped drinking water. For more information, contact the national forests directly (see "Grand Teton Address Book," p. 311) or stop at the visitor center in Jackson, which is staffed by forest rangers.

Bridger-Teton National Forest

These campgrounds are east of the park or Elk Refuge.

Atherton Creek   This campground faces the landslide-created Slide Lake from a steep hillside with aspen and spruce trees and much open ground. It has a dock for swimming and a place to launch canoes and boats. The Gros Ventre Slide nature trail (p. 332) is just down the lake. The road is narrow, with some steep drop-offs. Four and 5 miles farther on the same road, the **Red Hills** and **Crystal Creek campgrounds** are even more remote. Camping at these primitive, tent-only campgrounds costs $10 per site; reservations are not taken. They have 11 sites total and are closed mid-October to mid-May.

On Lower Slide Lake about 6 miles up Gros Ventre Rd. 20 sites, tents or RVs. $15 site. No reservations. Closed Oct to late May.

Curtis Canyon   This inner canyon campground is in an alpine setting above the elk refuge.

8 miles from Jackson over dirt roads; follow Broadway out of town past Elk Refuge, then follow signs. 11 sites, tents or RVs. $12 site. No reservations. Closed mid-Sept to mid-May.

Hatchet   This is a shady campground with good scenery near the highway to the park.

About 8 miles east of Moran Junction entrance station, Hwy. 26/287. 9 sites, tents or RVs. $10 site. No reservations. Closed Oct to mid-May.

Targhee National Forest

The forest, administered jointly with Caribou National Forest, is west of the park, mostly in Idaho. Unlike campgrounds on the other side of the Tetons, you can reserve these sites by calling © **866/444-6777** or via www.recreation.gov.

Tips Park Camping Basics: Toilets, Showers & Laundry

All the Park Service campgrounds have typical cold-water bathrooms. Other public bathrooms (with hot water and soap) are at the visitor centers, restaurants, hotels, and marinas. Within the park, public showers and laundry machines are at Colter Bay Village only. In Jackson, you'll find public showers at the **Jackson Teton County Recreation Center,** 155 E. Gill Ave. (© 307/739-9025; p. 338). **Wagon Wheel Village Coin Laundry,** 435 N. Cache (© 800/329-9279), is across from the visitor center on North Cache.

Mike Harris   Secluded among small pines, the campground is rich in berry bushes.

Rte. 22 west of Jackson. 12 sites, tents or RVs. $10 site. Reservations accepted. Closed mid-Sept to mid-May. **Amenities:** Vault toilets, picnic tables, fire pits, grills, pump water.

Teton Canyon   This campground is a back door to the Teton Range trails most used for backpacking trips and trail rides. Getting there requires a drive on back roads from the Idaho side of the mountains.

12 miles east of Driggs, Idaho. 21 sites, tents or RVs. $10 site. Reservations accepted. Closed mid-Sept to mid-May. **Amenities:** Vault toilets, picnic tables, fire pits, grills, running water.

Trail Creek   Among the spruces right next to the creek and mountain road, the campground suffers from car noise.

Rte. 22 west, 3 miles west of Mike Harris. 11 sites, tents or RVs. $10 site. Reservations accepted. Closed Sept–May. **Amenities:** Vault toilets, picnic tables, fire pits, grills, running water.

COMMERCIAL CAMPGROUNDS

With the great public campgrounds in the area, there's little reason for tenters to camp outside the park or national forests, but if you bring an RV and Colter Bay RV Park is full, here are two choices near the park.

Grand Teton Park RV Resort   This self-contained village is in a great location if you enjoy solitude and want to bounce between Yellowstone and Grand Teton. Located 6 miles east of the Moran Junction entrance station, you can choose from cabins, tent spots, or motoring in with your RV.

Hwy. 26/287, Moran, WY 83013. ℂ **800/563-6469** or 307/733-1980. www.yellowstonerv.com. 205 sites. Year-round $68–$75 cabin; $35 tent; $39–$57 RV. $5.50–$6.50 additional person charge. DISC, MC, V. **Amenities:** Shower house, laundry, playground w/slides, video arcade room, pool, grocery store, camp store, hot tubs, billiards, propane, Wi-Fi.

Snake River Park KOA   Located 13 miles south of Jackson, this campground is bordered by the Snake River on one side, and Horse Creek on another, which is great if you love water. There's a nice, grassy layout with trees. The downside is the distance you have to negotiate to go to and from the park.

9705 S. Hwy. 89, Jackson, WY 83001. **800/KOA-1878** or 307/733-7078. www.snakeriverpark.com. 83 sites. $35–$39 tent; $53–$55 full hookup for 2. $7 extra person over 5, $10 extra vehicle. DISC, MC, V. **Amenities:** Playground, game room, store, showers, laundry, rafting concession, Wi-Fi, restaurant nearby.

HOTELS, CABINS & LODGES
IN THE PARK

Reservations for lodgings in the park require deposits of 2 nights' advance payment, and cancellation carries a fee. Check before you reserve.

Grand Teton Lodge Company

The park's main concessionaire is the **Grand Teton Lodge Company** (see "Grand Teton Address Book," p. 311). I've covered two of its three facilities; the other, the luxurious Jenny Lake Lodge, is not suitable for most families. Rooms lack TVs or cooking facilities. Guests at any of the properties can use the pool at Jackson Lake Lodge. Children under 12 stay free, unless you need a rollaway bed, which comes for a small fee (see listings). The company accepts Visa, MasterCard, and American Express for payment, but does not take American Express for deposits.

Colter Bay Village   These are the park's main family accommodations, at the center of lakeside activities. The metal-roofed cabins are authentic, rough-hewn log structures with dark linoleum floors and rag throw rugs. Many were brought here from original sites where they were built by settlers. Unlike older cabins at Yellowstone, they've been kept in prime condition. They're spacious and remarkably clean and fresh. There are many types, from simple single rooms to places as large as a house. All prices seem a decent bargain, especially for large families that normally need two units. Like real log cabins, they tend to be dark, and the bathrooms have only shower stalls, no tubs. Also, old wiring prevents air conditioners or fans, and so the cabins can be uncomfortably hot during the height of summer.

The tent cabins can be fun for a night or two, but are more than halfway to camping, and rather close together for that. They consist of concrete slabs with log walls and canvas roofs. Small woodstoves and cots are inside, and barbecues and picnic tables are out front. Everyone in the tent cabins uses a shared bathhouse, and showers cost extra.

Restaurants are covered under "Family-Friendly Dining" (p. 327).

166 cabins, 9 with shared bathroom, 66 tent cabins. $45–$165 double cabin with bathroom, $10 extra person over age 11; $41 tent cabin double; $10 extra person. Rollaway bed $5.50, crib free. AE, MC, V. Cabins closed late Sept to late May; tent cabins closed Sept to early June. **Amenities:** Restaurant.

Jackson Lake Lodge   Rockefeller had this built near the spot on Picnic Tree Hill where he first fell in love with the Tetons. I struggle with the architecture of the concrete building; it's not cut from the traditional national-park mold. But some find its straight lines and airy space perfect for the setting. They frame the overwhelming view from the main lobby sitting room. The immaculate rooms are just as good, elegantly decorated in light Western style. For families, the best are cottage rooms with patios that open onto the grass and the moose-filled willow flats. Somehow, these units manage to be tasteful, luxurious, and vacation-casual all at the same time. In the evening, climb the hill for an unforgettable sunset view, probably with moose in the foreground. The lifeguard-protected outdoor pool is large and splendid, with a baby pool. The hotel's several dining choices are covered under "Family-Friendly Dining" (p. 327).

385 units. $189 main lodge double; $269 main lodge double with view; $189–$259 cottage double; $450–$625 suite. $10 extra person over age 11. Rollaway bed $10, crib free. Closed early Oct to mid-May. AE, MC, V. **Amenities:** Restaurants; lounge; heated pool; shops; horseback rides; river float trips; scenic cruises; fishing; medical clinic; Wi-Fi. *In room:* Dataport.

Other Lodgings inside the Park

The **Flagg Ranch Resort** is on the John D. Rockefeller Jr. Parkway north of the park (see chapter 11).

Dornans in Moose Spur Ranch Log Cabins   These are large, well-appointed log cabins on the Snake River near the south end of the park, below the Dornans complex of stores, eateries, and outdoors outfitters. It's a quiet alternative to busy Colter Bay, and the units, with rustic-style furniture sitting on wood floors between log walls, are comfortable and competitively priced. Each has a living room, kitchen, and one or two bedrooms; they sleep four to six. Units have phones and dataports.

Moose Junction (P.O. Box 39), Moose, WY 83012. © 307/733-2522. Fax 307/733-3544. www.dornans.com. 12 cabins. High season $175–$250 cabin; low season $125–$175 cabin. 3-night minimum stay in high season. No rollaway beds or cribs. AE, DISC, MC, V. **Amenities:** Restaurants; boat rentals; mountain bike rentals; shops; camp store; ATM; service station; groceries; rafting; cross-country ski and snowshoe rentals. *In room:* Dataport, fully equipped kitchen.

Signal Mountain Lodge   This is the classic lakeside family resort, with the significant advantages of friendly, professional management and a location in the heart of the park, with trails and boating from the grounds. The accommodations, which can be reserved a year in advance, range from simple cabins to a couple of houses with cooking facilities. But most are on the more modest end. Some are charming old log cabins with stone fireplaces. Lakefront units have porches or decks over the water. All have telephones, but the only TV is in the common room. Rent canoes and boats or book guided fishing, sailboat, and scenic raft trips. There's a coin-op laundry, too. Dining is a short walk away, with offerings ranging from formal dining in the Peaks Restaurant to a pizzeria and short-order grill (p. 328).

South of Jackson Lake Junction on park road (P.O. Box 50), Moran, WY 83013. © **307/543-2831**. Fax 307/543-2569. www.signalmountainlodge.com. 79 cabins. $117–$291 cabin for up to 6 people. Rollaway beds $15, cribs free. AE, DISC, MC, V. Closed mid-Oct to early May. Pets accepted $10 per night. **Amenities:** 3 restaurants; bar; boat rentals; coin-op laundry; camp store. *In room:* Some rooms have kitchenette, fridge, coffeemaker, gas fireplace, microwave.

Dude Ranches

Triangle X Ranch   The original way to visit the area was to spend a week or two at a dude ranch such as the Triangle X Ranch, which has been serving guests since 1926. It's a working ranch, within the park on the east side of Jackson Hole, with a comfortable but authentically rough atmosphere. Summer guests come for weeklong stays in log cabins starting at nearly $1,430 per person. Kids under 6 break off each day for their own supervised activities and even have their own dining room at the lodge. In winter, a quiet and beautiful time to visit, there's a 2-night minimum stay.

2 Triangle X Ranch Rd., Moose, WY 83012. © **307/733-2183**. Fax 307/733-8685. www.trianglex.com. 22 cabins in 1-, 2-, and 3-bedroom layouts. Summer $1,430–$1,790 per person per week, all meals and activities included; winter $110 per person per night, 2-night minimum. Rollaway beds and cribs free. Cash in summer, MC, V in winter. Closed Nov 1–Dec 26 and Mar 15 to last week in May. **Amenities:** Dining room; horseback riding; hiking; swimming; fishing; cross-country skiing; snowshoeing. *In room:* Coffeemaker in winter.

IN JACKSON

Shop around with the help of the chamber of commerce (see "Grand Teton Address Book," p. 311), which has links to many lodgings at www.jacksonholechamber.com.

Best Western The Lodge at Jackson Hole   This well-crafted luxury hotel with a stone-and-log front has large, fresh rooms with microwaves and many other extras. The decoration is warm and dark; the rooms feel solid, so you don't worry about bothering the neighbors. Carved wooden bears are all over the place, peeking out of unexpected places. The pool is cool, too, with doors that can make it indoor or outdoor. Rates include breakfast year-round and appetizers in winter, served from a buffet in a dining room off the lobby. The neighborhood, an area with supermarkets and car dealerships, doesn't match the posh hotel. It's a short walk to downtown Jackson.

80 Scott Lane (P.O. Box 7478), Jackson, WY 83002. © **800/458-3866** or 307/739-9703. Fax 307/739-9168. www. lodgeatjh.com. 154 units. High season $249–$349 double; low season $139–$219 double. Children under 14 stay free in parent's room. Rates include full breakfast. No rollaway beds, cribs free. AE, DISC, MC, V. **Amenities:** Breakfast buffet; pool; exercise room; spa; laundry. *In room:* TV, fridge, coffee/tea maker, hair dryer, iron/ironing board, safe, microwave, free Wi-Fi.

The Virginian Lodge   The hotel's brown, suburban-ranch-style exterior is so out-of-date it's retro, but the prices are right and the large, grassy courtyard, with its large pool, will keep the kids active. The rooms have paneling and some have been used hard, but they were clean. Many were large and had good configurations for families.

Some have microwaves, coffeemakers, and small refrigerators. A restaurant, laundry, and RV park are on-site.

750 W. Broadway (P.O. Box 1052), Jackson, WY 83001. ℂ 800/262-4999 or 307/733-2792. Fax 307/733-4063. www.virginianlodge.com. 170 units. High season $104–$117 double, $134–$205 suite; low season $55 double, $62–$145 suite. $7 extra person, children under 12 free. Cribs and rollaways $7. AE, DISC, MC, V. **Amenities:** Restaurant; heated pool; hot tub; laundry. *In room:* TV, fridge, coffeemaker, microwaves, Wi-Fi.

6 Family-Friendly Dining

IN THE PARK
COLTER BAY VILLAGE

There are two family restaurants at Colter Bay, as well as the store, where you can buy good sandwiches for a picnic.

Chuckwagon This is in a large, windowed dining room—which is hot on a warm day—with many booths and corny Western decor. The service usually is quick and meals such as steak or pasta are satisfying, if uninspired. The children's menu is exceptional.

Colter Bay Village. No phone. Kids' menu, highchairs, boosters. Breakfast $7.50–$11; lunch $7.25–$12; dinner $14–$20; kids' menu $3.50–$6.25. AE, MC, V. Late May to late Sept daily 6:30–11am, 11:30am–1pm, and 5:30–9pm. Closed rest of year.

John Colter Café Court This is a noisy but pleasant cafeteria with reasonable prices under $8. The all-day lunch and dinner menu revolves around Mexican dishes such as burritos, tacos, and quesadillas; sandwiches; hamburgers; and soup. You can also arrange box lunches here for a day out in the park.

Colter Bay Village. No phone. All-day menu $2–$9.25. AE, MC, V. Late May to late Sept daily 11am–10pm. Closed rest of year.

JACKSON LAKE LODGE

The lodge has four places to eat, and each comes with a children's menu with breakfast, lunch, and dinner offerings under $6.50.

You can eat a light breakfast in the Coffee Cart, a quaint cart in the main lobby, daily from 6 to 10am. The **Pool Grill** serves sandwiches, burgers, and pizza daily from 11am to 6pm, and during July and August an all-you-can-eat Western barbecue for dinner Sunday through Friday from 6 to 8pm. The food is unmemorable, but the ultrarelaxed setting by the pool is pleasant. It costs $28 for adults, $14 for children under 13, including tax and gratuity.

Mural Room This is a gorgeous formal restaurant with dinner entrees around $25, and the kids' menu helps contain the final bill for families. Through the floor-to-ceiling windows you have great views of Willow Flats, Jackson Lake, and the jagged Tetons. Inside you'll find rough-hewn oak flooring, comfortable seating and a menu heavy with beef, game such as the "espresso-dusted Rocky Mountain elk loin," seafood, and poultry.

Jackson Lake Lodge (near junction of U.S. Rte. 89/191/287 and Teton Park Rd.). ℂ 307/543-2811. www.gtlc.com. Kids' menu, highchairs, boosters. Reservations recommended. Breakfast buffet $13 adults, $8.50 kids; lunch $8.95–$17; dinner $20–$37. AE, MC, V. May to early Oct daily 6am–10pm. Closed rest of year.

Pioneer Grill Kids feel right at home in this throwback grill that sports a soda fountain and swivel seating around a chrome lunch counter. However, it's not that practical for large families or when it's crowded and you have a hard time finding seats together. But the meals are filling, with the huckleberry pancakes particularly note-worthy. This is a good place to order a box lunch.

Jackson Lake Lodge (near junction of U.S. Rte. 89/191/287 and Teton Park Rd.). ℭ 307/543-2811. Kids' menu, crayons. Breakfast $4.25–$8.25; lunch $7.25–$11; dinner $7.25–$20. AE, MC, V. May to early Oct daily 6am–10pm. Closed rest of year.

SIGNAL MOUNTAIN LODGE

The **Deadman's** bar is family-friendly at lunchtime, and the immense Signal Moun-tain Nachos (chips, beans, chicken, beef, cheese, and so on) will easily feed a family of five for $14. This bar has one of the few televisions in the park, so it can be packed and noisy during broadcasts of major sporting events.

Peaks Restaurant   This full-service dining room, which serves only dinner, has great views of both Signal Mountain and Jackson Lake. The upscale menu boasts a wonderful selection of beef, fish, chicken, and pasta entries made from organic or sus-tainably raised ingredients.

Signal Mountain Lodge (Teton Park Rd. near junction with U.S. Rte. 89/191/287). ℭ 307/543-2831. Reservations accepted only on Mother's Day. Dinner $17–$35; kids' menu under $6.50. AE, DISC, MC, V. Mid-May to mid-Oct daily 5:30–10pm.

Trapper Grill   This is a small, casual restaurant overlooking Jackson Lake. The food was more interesting than that at most family restaurants, but most important for families with kids, the restaurant was professionally run—the food comes quickly, and the staff is friendly and eager to please.

Signal Mountain Lodge (Teton Park Rd. near junction with U.S. Rte. 89/191/287). ℭ 307/543-2831. Kids' menu, highchairs, boosters. Breakfast $5.75–$8.95; lunch and dinner $7.25–$13; kids' menu under $5.50. AE, DISC, MC, V. Mid-May to mid-Sept breakfast 7–11am, lunch 11am–2:30pm, dinner 3:30–10pm. Closed rest of year.

LEEK'S MARINA PIZZERIA

Near the north end of the park, this is a popular place for a pizza, sandwich, salad, or beer overlooking the lake. It's a quieter spot than Colter Bay. The restaurant is open in season daily 11am to 10pm.

IN JACKSON
LOW-STRESS MEALS

In Jackson you can get most kinds of familiar fast food, including **Denny's, Domino's Pizza, Kentucky Fried Chicken, McDonald's, Pizza Hut, Subway,** and **Taco Bell.**

Jedediah's Original House of Sourdough   For breakfast or lunch with a bit more atmosphere, try this old favorite that's located near the town square. Dining rooms are in the small, rough rooms of an old house and on a sunny patio. The atmos-phere is noisy and festive, the service casual to a fault, the menu a step above that of the typical diner with eggs Benedict and buffalo burgers.

135 E. Broadway, Jackson. ℭ 307/733-5671. Kids' menu, highchairs, boosters. Most items under $12; kids' menu under $5.25. Daily 7am–2pm.

BEST-BEHAVIOR MEALS
Calico Italian Restaurant and Bar   Grown-ups will appreciate the sophisticated northern Italian food, rich risotto, and grilled items. For the kids, there's good pizza, a children's menu under $4.50, and a huge lawn where they can play with balls, games, and toys while the food is being prepared. Parents watch from the porch or through big windows and French doors while sipping cocktails and microbrews. The airy dining

room has high ceilings and stained glass, and the decor mixes trendy Italian style and casual Western touches. Unfortunately, the place is so popular that service can suffer.

On Hwy. 390 to Teton Village. © 307/733-2460. www.calicorestaurant.com. Kids' menu, highchairs, boosters, toys. Dinner main courses $11–$32; kids' menu $4.50. AE, MC, V. Daily 5–10pm.

7 Exploring Grand Teton National Park with Your Kids

ENTRANCE FEES   The $25 entrance fee covers both Grand Teton and Yellowstone national parks; it's good for 1 week in both. The fee isn't collected for the highway from Moran Junction to Jackson and the land east of the Snake River, including Gros Ventre campground, but you do have to pay to get into most of the best parts of the park. You also can gain entrance with the America the Beautiful Pass. For details, see chapter 2.

NATURAL PLACES
JACKSON LAKE

The lake sits at the foot of the Tetons in the foreground of a view so dramatic that it seems unreal at first. Sometimes the water reflects the mountains. At other times, afternoon winds turn it silver. The mountains helped make this lake and the other, smaller lakes to the south. The water fills in low spots left behind by glaciers that once cascaded down from the peaks. Once, all the rock and dust that is the flat ground of Jackson Hole was up above. Water—both liquid and frozen—chipped and wore away at the mountains and spread out the broken and powdered rock into a flat valley. Where the last of many glaciers stopped, they left rowlike piles of ground-up rock marking their greatest size, the way a bathtub ring marks how high your bath water came. These low ridges are called moraines. One formed the natural dam that holds back the south end of Jackson Lake.

In 1906, before the area was a park, the government built a dam of its own at the lake's outlet. The human-made dam raised the lake and kept the water level from going up and down, the way it used to when spring melt filled the lake and warm summer days drained it. This more even flow of water made the Snake River, which flows out of the lake, more useful for farmers downstream in Idaho. The park road crosses the dam just south of Jackson Lake Junction. The river below is a prime spot to see white pelicans that are feeding on trout; osprey; and even river otters; human anglers also congregate below the dam.

Enjoy the shores of Jackson Lake. On the east side, at Colter Bay Village or Signal Mountain Lodge, you can swim and toss pebbles in the water while watching the view change. Just south from Colter Bay, the **Heron Pond** and **Swan Lake trails** and other level trails of various lengths trace the lake's edge and then circle wetlands full of waterfowl, including trumpeter swans—easy family loop hikes with the reward of incredible views. The sight of the Tetons across Heron Pond is so perfect it is hard to believe even when you see it. Use the map mentioned under "Reading Up" (p. 317) to figure your route, which can be as long or as short as the combination of paths you choose.

Start a paddle by canoe from the marina at Colter Bay to explore the tiny islands there and in Half Moon Bay, sheltered waters with lots of folds to feed the young imagination. You can see deep into the clear water. Backcountry campsites are within easy paddles of the marinas at Colter Bay or Signal Mountain Lodge, allowing families who can't hike far to get out on their own. Catch dinner from the lake. More accomplished paddlers can head out to Elk Island or to other island sites across the lake (see "Backcountry Camping Permits," p. 322). If you're not up to handling your own boat, tour boats take guests to sit-down meals out on the lake. The concessionaire offers guided fishing, or you can rent a boat to fish. Details on all those choices are under "For the Active Family" (p. 333).

JENNY LAKE & CASCADE CANYON 𝄞

A glacier once flowed down Cascade Canyon, giving it a U-shaped bottom, and plowed into Jackson Hole, digging the dip that's now filled with Jenny Lake. The rounded eastern shore was once the glacier's face. The path up Cascade Canyon is gradual, scenic, and rich in wildlife after a short, initial steep section to the Inspiration Point overlook. Easy trails into the Tetons are few, so this is a very popular route, and quite crowded in summer. Paths circle the lake, and the eastern shore has a visitor center, a campground, and other facilities—a pretty spot, but frequently crowded.

To avoid crowds set out for Cascade Canyon early or late by following the 2-mile path around the lake to the canyon trail head; it's a pretty walk over level terrain. Early morning is the best time for wildlife. You're likely to spot bighorn sheep, moose, possibly black bears, as well as birds and small animals. If you don't want to walk around the lake, the **Jenny Lake Boating** launch runs back and forth from near the visitor center, at the south end of the lake, to the Cascade Canyon trail head, subtracting those 2 miles off each end of the hike. The launches (© **307/734-9227;** www.jenny lakeboating.com, summer only) run on demand from 8am to 6pm May 15 through September. The round-trip fare is $9 for adults, $5 for children 5 to 12, and it's free for children under 5; one-way (if you hike early and use it to come back) is $5 and $4. The company also rents canoes and kayaks for $12 an hour or $60 a day, and offers scenic evening cruises. Departing at 6:30pm, these 90-minute, naturalist-accompanied rides are a great way to enjoy the scenery and learn more about the park. Adult tickets are $14, with kids 5 to 12 charged $7. Reservations are recommended.

STRING LAKE & LEIGH LAKE

You can spend a great day at Grand Teton simply by hiking along the shore of String Lake and Leigh Lake, with the sun glinting off the water, the immense mountains peeping through gaps in the trees. These are the best lakes to swim in, as they warm more so than Jackson Lake does. String Lake is shallow and as narrow as a river, so the sun warms the water. Leigh Lake is large and bright and the water colder; it is far enough from the crowded trail head to get away from other people. Eight backcountry campsites are along its shore, which is easily reached by canoe; a 250-yard portage connects the two lakes. Trails loop String Lake and run north past Leigh Lake to Jackson Lake or up Paintbrush Canyon, or south to Jenny Lake; you can devise a route that matches your abilities. Take Teton Park Road to the North Jenny Lake Junction, then the Jenny Lake Loop Road to the String Lake picnic area; the trail head and canoe-launch beach are there.

THE TETONS

The abrupt way the mountains rise, as improbable as a crayon drawing, rips through habitat zones of elevation that usually change more gradually. In a few miles on a steep hike into the Tetons, you pass from the open, arid range of Jackson Hole, through the pines, across the green tundra and flowers of the alpine zone, and into barren high country where only scattered pinpricks of color grow among fields of misty gray stone. Up here snow lasts too long to allow plant life to reclaim the ancient rock. Hot summer never arrives. There are a few living things here—plucky little pikas, lichens, and

Making the Tetons

There was a mystery about the Tetons' birth. Here are some of the clues. On the east side, the mountains rise out of the flat valley of Jackson Hole as steep as a knife blade, but on the west side, away from the park, they are far less impressive, rising slowly in a ramp of rounded hills. Their age is odd, too. The Tetons are only 7 million years old, quite young as mountains go, but they are made of some of the oldest rock in North America—gneiss—that was laid down about 2.5 billion years ago, when life on earth wasn't much more advanced than single cells.

It took some clever scientific detective work to figure out how the Tetons got here. Geologists looked at the shape of the mountains and tried to imagine what could have made such a sharp break from a flat valley to a nearly straight wall of rock, while the other side of the same mountains looked like a ramp. It made sense if there was a fault at the base of the mountains. A fault is a place where the crust of the earth is cracked. During earthquakes, one side of the crack would rise while the other side would fall, creating a steep cliff. That would explain why one side of the mountains had no foothills and the other side did. Imagine the fault as a partly opened trapdoor in a floor. The open edge of the door is a steep break, but the edge with the hinge is like a ramp.

To test this theory, geologists drilled down into Jackson Hole, looking for the same kinds of rock they had found up in the mountains. If they could find the same layers of ancient gneiss, they would know where the mountains came from. It worked. Far below the valley, the drills hit layers of rock that fit the layers of rock up in the mountains the way two pieces of a broken teacup fit together. But to put the pieces together, the valley would have to be higher, or the mountains lower, by 30,000 feet.

The layers must have been one flat piece before the fault started moving 7 million years ago. A block rose along one side of the fault while the block on the other side sank lower. Rivers and ice wore down the higher rocks and carried broken rock and sand down into the valley, filling it in as it dipped down so that the valley floor came out flat, as it is today. The fault stopped moving, but the mountains, made of hard, old gneiss, resisted wearing away and became sharp and pointed.

miraculous little flowers, for example—but some get a ghostly feeling of standing in an eternal, lifeless realm.

From below, the Teton Range looks so rugged that it's hard to imagine how people climb. Getting to the top requires equipment and training, but families with fit school-age children can get far enough to find out what the alpine habitat is like, and to see dizzying views from high above. Most trails start in the southwest area of the park, from Jenny Lake south to the Teton Village ski area. The Cascade Canyon hike is described above under "Jenny Lake & Cascade Canyon"; other hikes and the aerial tram are described below under "Hiking" (p. 334).

JACKSON HOLE & THE SNAKE RIVER

The valley in front of the Tetons stretches out, amazingly flat. Seen from the mountains, it looks like a huge map: the lakes nearest, then low moraine ridges where trees grow, next the Snake River, then broad sagebrush flatlands to the far mountains. Fine soil in some spots holds enough water for trees to grow in the valley, but across most of it the ground is made of fragments of rock rubbed off the mountains by glaciers. There the water from rain and snowmelt quickly sinks in, so only plants adapted to the high desert can grow. Bison and pronghorn like that habitat, and you can sometimes see them along the roads on the east side of the valley, in the Antelope Flats area. Along the river, cottonwoods stand above a tangle of willows, perfect moose food. The slow part near Jackson Lake Junction, called Oxbow Bend, is the place to see moose and other mammals and waterfowl such as white pelicans, and is a superb spot to launch a canoe in gentle water.

Before towns like Jackson blocked the valley, elk used Jackson Hole as a corridor, migrating from Yellowstone each fall on the way to lower land where they could spend the winter. After the town arrived, the herds stopped here and starved because there wasn't enough winter food. The **National Elk Refuge,** at the south end of Jackson Hole (http://nationalelkrefuge.fws.gov), was set aside well before the rest of the park to help save the elk. Each winter the U.S. Fish and Wildlife Service feeds hay to more than 7,000 elk that group there. Rangers from the service answer questions at the Jackson Hole and Greater Yellowstone Visitor Center at 532 N. Cache St. in Jackson (p. 317), and in winter you can join sleigh rides through the refuge from the visitor center (see "Wildlife-Watching," p. 337). Other hikes, bike rides, horseback riding, canoeing, and river floats are covered below in "For the Active Family."

GROS VENTRE SLIDE

In 1925, in the valley where the Gros Ventre River flows down into Jackson Hole, a piece of a mountain tumbled and made a dam. A brand-new lake filled on top of the roads and ranch land that had been there. In 1927, the top of the dam broke, sending a flash flood into the valley below and killing six people. Today much of the natural dam remains and you can walk on the landslide debris along a nature trail where plants have yet to cover the jagged rock and dead trees that fell that day. The tops of more dead trees still stick through the surface of Upper Slide Lake. The lake and slide are in Bridger-Teton National Forest, on the east side of the park; driving north from Kelly, turn right into the mountains on narrow Gros Ventre Road. Campgrounds in the area are covered on p. 319.

PLACES FOR LEARNING

Cunningham Homestead   South of Moran Junction on U.S. 89, this early homestead ranch with just a single cabin still standing takes a lot of imagination to picture.

5½ miles south of Moran Junction on U.S. Rte. 26/89/191. Free admission. Daily 24 hr.

Menor's Ferry Historic Site   Less than a mile north of the Craig Thomas Discovery and Visitor Center on the park road, a spur leads to this early homestead and Snake River ferry, an important crossing until a bridge was built in 1927 (you also can park at the Dornans complex and take the restored ferry across). It's well worth a stop. Follow the free Park Service guide from building to building, getting a feeling for self-sufficient life here before the automobile. From late May through September, an old-fashioned general store operates with a clerk in costume (hours normally daily 9am–4:30pm). Buy a candy stick from a jar, just as children did a century ago, and see how simple a store was back then. You can also see a display of carriages and ride on the restored ferry, pulled across the river with ropes when river conditions permit, starting in mid-July. Don't miss Maude Noble's Cabin, site of an important early meeting to create the park, which now holds a fascinating display of historical photographs. Nearby, take a look at an old log church, the Chapel of the Transfiguration.

Teton Park Rd., half-mile north of Moose. No phone. Free admission.

National Museum of Wildlife Art *Finds*   Families should not miss this stunning museum. The award-winning sandstone building melds into the cliffs above the Elk Refuge. Inside, galleries contain an arrestingly displayed collection of wildlife art in various styles, from a masterpiece Haida totem pole to hyperrealistic images of big game. There are also a kids' area, a cafe for light meals, an auditorium for films, and a schedule of programs.

On U.S. 89, just north of Jackson. (© 800/313-9553 or 307/733-5771. www.wildlifeart.org. Admission $10 adults, $9 students, free for children 18 and under. Summer and winter daily 9am–5pm; spring and fall Mon–Sat 9am–5pm, Sun 1–5pm.

8 For the Active Family
BACKPACKING

Grand Teton is known for challenging and spectacular backpacking trips. It has some that strong family hikers can handle, too. Trips wind through the rugged canyons of the Tetons, along backcountry camping zones where you can choose your own campsite on the tundra. After you're up there, the network of trails offers lots of choices for side trips. The Park Service's free *Backcountry Camping Zones* map covers 10 routes ranging from 17 to 38 miles (download it from www.nps.gov/grte/planyourvisit/bczones. htm); you will also need a detailed topographic map (see "Reading Up," p. 317). Most of these hikes are for fit adults and teenagers who have already tested their abilities before climbing into this steep, high-elevation setting, where the air is thin and the weather cold. Those are the famous hikes. Grand Teton also has several opportunities for families with younger children to spend time camping on their own away from people at the foot of the mountains along and north of Leigh Lake (see "String Lake & Leigh Lake," p. 330). Get a backcountry permit through the system described on p. 322.

CANOEING, KAYAKING & BOATING
CANOEING & KAYAKING

Exploring the lakes and their islands in a canoe is my idea of fun. Even better, get a backcountry campsite and spend 2 or 3 nights out alone on an island, like the kids in the *Swallows and Amazons,* by Arthur Ransome. Paddling in Jackson, Jenny, String, and Leigh lakes, and in Oxbow Bend of the Snake River is covered above under "Natural Places" (p. 329). If your children are too young for a canoe—meaning you can't trust them not to tip it over—you can rent a motorized skiff or rowboat on Jackson Lake. Rent by the hour or day from **Colter Bay Marina** (© 307/543-3100), **Signal Mountain Lodge** (© 307/543-2831), or **Jenny Lake Boating** (© 307/734-9227). An aluminum canoe or a kayak goes for around $13 an hour; motorboats from the Grand Teton Lodge Co. start at $27 an hour or $155 a day. Signal Mountain rents rowboats for the same price as canoes.

For longer rentals, you can get better equipment at a lower rate by renting away from the water and carrying the canoe on your car. **Dornans at Moose** (see "Grand

Teton Address Book," p. 311) rents canoes and kayaks for $40 a day. Serious paddlers should contact **Rendezvous River Sports/Jackson Hole Kayak and Canoe School,** 945 W. Broadway, Jackson (© **800/733-2471** or 307/733-2471; www.jhkayakschool. com). A paddle-sports specialty store and school, it offers beginner and advanced classes and guided day outings and overnights in the park and in white water outside its boundaries, as well as rentals. Both provide the car carrier with the rental.

If you bring your own craft, get a permit to take it out on the park's lakes or rivers (rental boats should already have permits). Buy the permit from one of the Park Service visitor centers for $10 for nonmotorized craft, $20 for motorboats. It's good for 7 days in both Grand Teton and Yellowstone national parks.

Lake water at Grand Teton is swimmable in late summer, but it is cold and you must be cautious about falling in accidentally. Always wear life jackets and have dry, warm clothing along. Plan trips in the morning to avoid afternoon winds and thunderstorms that can rough up the water and bring the threat of lightning strikes.

TOUR-BOAT RIDES

If you don't want to rent your own boat or canoe, you can get out on Jackson Lake in a comfortable, classy little tour boat operated by the **Grand Teton Lodge Company** (see "Grand Teton Address Book," p. 311). The outing includes breakfast or dinner on Elk Island at a cookout with picnic tables. The trips are sedate fun and do give you some time to look around on your own on the island. They don't often see wildlife. The breakfast cruise is $33 for adults, $21 for children 3 to 11, and free for children under 3; the dinner cruise is $55 for adults, $33 for children. A scenic cruise without food or landings is $21 for adults, $10 for children.

FISHING

The park is known for trout fishing. The Snake River cutthroat is native. In the lakes you can fish for lake and brown trout and whitefish. The Park Service manages the fishery for the wildlife that use it, encouraging catch-and-release for anglers, but you can keep fish taken from certain waters. Carefully check regulations and license information from the visitor centers, or download it from www.nps.gov/grte/pubs/pubs. htm. Fishing tackle, required Wyoming licenses, and advice are available at **Dornans at Moose,** at some general stores, and at businesses in Jackson. The **Grand Teton Lodge Company** offers guided fly-fishing and lake fishing. Contact information for both businesses is under "Grand Teton Address Book" (p. 311).

HIKING
EASIER TRAILS

I've described most of my favorite level-ground hikes above under "Natural Places." The **String and Leigh Lake trails** offer lovely scenery and swimming (p. 330). At the **Gros Ventre Slide,** you can hike over the debris from a natural catastrophe (p. 332). **Inspiration Point** and **Cascade Canyon,** the easiest walk into the mountains, is the park's most popular hike (see "Jenny Lake & Cascade Canyon," p. 330). The **Heron** and **Swan Lake** trails at Colter Bay (see "Jackson Lake," p. 329) have superb views and great waterfowl viewing. For similar wildlife-watching walks, with fewer people, go to Christian Pond, Emma Matilda, and Two Oceans lakes from the east side of the road near Jackson Lake Lodge; as you hike farther, you see fewer people.

HIKES FROM THE AERIAL TRAM

There are plenty of hikes into the Tetons, but if you or your children can't handle a steep 5-mile climb—and many can't, at least enjoyably—you can still get into the high country by taking the aerial tram in Teton Village. Unfortunately, you'll need to wait until 2009 to take the tram, as a new one being built won't be running until the winter of 2008. The new one will follow the old route, though. Designed to serve the challenging Rendezvous Mountain ski area, the tram rises from the resort west of Jackson to an elevation of 10,450 feet, well above the tree line, with stunning views of the surrounding mountaintops and down into Jackson Hole. The ride itself is fun, and you can start some wonderful hikes from here, losing elevation rather than gaining. The easiest one-way trek leads straight down the ski mountain (you pay full fare just to go up, but if you hike up and ride down, it's free). Other routes cover a lot of ground in the Tetons, and you can even use the tram as the start of an overnight (get the special map, covered under "Reading Up," p. 317). With younger children, rambling around the mountaintop will be enough. The rock and tundra seem limitless. Exactly how much the new tram will cost to ride wasn't available as this book went to press, so check with the resort when making plans for your trip. For the summer of 2008, and possibly every summer thereafter, the resort operates the Bridger Gondola. Although it doesn't reach the top of Rendezvous Mountain, the gondola still lifts you 2,800 feet to an elevation of 9,095 feet and some nice hiking terrain, and there are even two restaurants—the Headwall Deli and Couloir—at the top of the ride for a bite of lunch. Tickets for the gondola run about $18 for adults and $9 for kids 6 to 14. Whether you ride the new tram when it opens or the gondola, go early to avoid thunderstorms and to allow plenty of time for hiking. Bring warm clothes, food, and lots of water. The gondola runs daily Memorial Day weekend through mid-October from 10am to 6pm. Call © 888/DEEP-SNO or 307/739-2654 for information. To get there, take Highway 22 west from Broadway in Jackson, then turn right on 390; it's 12 miles from Jackson.

HARDER HIKES

School-age children of tested ability or fit teenagers will enjoy climbing up into the Tetons. Be prepared for a steep, long hike with proper footgear, clothing, water, snacks, and so on. Also, check at the Craig Thomas Discovery and Visitor Center or Jenny Lake Visitor Center for trail conditions. Snow and ice last in the high mountain valleys through June, or even later. South of Jenny Lake, from the Lupine Meadows Parking Area, the **Surprise Lake Trail** is a scenic but very steep climb, rising 3,000 feet over 4.5 miles, one-way. The destination is a small lake in a glacier-carved crater amid the bare, broken rock of the high country. Without going that far, you can enjoy the views and turn back after 3 miles. The **Death Canyon Trail** offers good views at various levels, so you don't feel driven to go farther than you have energy for; the trail head is down the Moose-Wilson Road, west of the Craig Thomas Discovery and Visitor Center. If you have determined teens in your family, consider climbing the **Grand Teton.** It's a breathtaking experience, and one you and your kids will take pride in once you gaze down from the summit. Exum Mountain Guides Inc. (© **307/733-2297;** www.exumguides.com) and Jackson Hole Mountain Guides (© **800/239-7642** or 307/733-4979; www.jhmg.com) are well-experienced and highly reputable outfits that can get you to the top.

HORSEBACK RIDING

This is horse country, and many operators offer trail rides and pack trips in the region. Check with the tourist authorities in Jackson, listed at the beginning of this chapter, for referrals outside the park. Within the park, **Grand Teton Lodge Company** (see "Grand Teton Address Book," p. 311) offers rides and cookouts from Colter Bay or Jackson Lake Lodge. Rides last 1 and 2 hours and cost $33 and $48 per person; 3-hour breakfast rides are $53 for adults, $43 for children, and 4-hour dinner rides $63 and $53. Children must be at least 8 years old and 4 feet tall. Younger children can go on the breakfast and dinner ride cookout in a wagon; that costs less. Call before your vacation to reserve if it is a priority. For a riding vacation, the dude ranch is a fun alternative (p. 326).

MOUNTAIN BIKING

Trails in the park are closed to bikes, but dirt roads are open, and some national forest lands around the park permit bikes on trails. In the park **Snake River Road,** off the park road just south of Signal Mountain Road, is a scenic, 15-mile dirt road with good wildlife-viewing opportunities. The **Shadow Mountain area,** just outside the east border of the park in Bridger-Teton National Forest, has many trails of varying difficulty.

Dornans at Moose (see "Grand Teton Address Book," p. 311) rents adults' and kids' basic mountain bikes and bike trailers, and high-performance models, for $14 to $25 a day.

RAFTING

Snake River rafting is famous, but the legendary rapids are outside the park, south of Jackson. Floats within the park are gentle, mostly for looking at the scenery and listening to the guide's commentary about the passing riverbanks. Such outings always depend on the guide's knowledge and people skills. Most guides go through thorough training on the park's history and what you're likely to see on one of these trips. Floats cover one of two stretches of river: a slower upper stretch, which may be more scenic, and a somewhat faster run from Deadman's Bar to Moose; ask which you will be on. It typically takes 3 to 5 hours to cover 10 miles of water; that's a very gradual ride, so the experience depends a lot on the guide's commentary. **Grand Teton Lodge Company** (see "Grand Teton Address Book," p. 311), which runs many outings each day, including lunch and dinner floats, charges $49 to $65 for adults, $29 to $45 for children 6 to 11. Kids under 6 are not allowed. Check with the visitor center for many other operators.

Rough white-water rafting takes place outside the park, south of Jackson, in the Snake River Canyon along U.S. 89. A lot of operators offer these floats, but **Sands' Wild Water River Trips** (© **800/358-8184** or 307/733-4410; www.sandswhitewater.com) has the singular claim of having taken President Clinton, Chelsea, and the Secret Service through the rapids on a 1995 vacation. A 3½-hour white-water outing over 8 miles of river in an eight-passenger boat costs $54 for adults, $45 for children under 13; prices are $6 less on a 14-passenger boat. Longer trips, including overnighters, are available.

SWIMMING

Most visitors to Grand Teton National Park don't intentionally go swimming. The waters in the lakes and the Snake River are either too cold or two swift and dangerous. That said, two great places for a dip are Leigh and String lakes, which are shallow enough to actually soak up some of the sun's warmth. Both lakes can be accessed from the Teton Park Road, where you'll find a picnic area at the String Lake Trailhead.

WILDLIFE-WATCHING

It isn't necessary to seek wildlife at Grand Teton. If you spend a few days hiking and canoeing, you will have encounters. I've mentioned some animals you can expect to find in different habitats in "Natural Places" in the sections on Jackson Lake (p. 329) and Jackson Hole and the Snake River (p. 332), and under "Hiking" (p. 334). The willow flats, a big marsh between the river and Colter Bay, is one of the park's richest wildlife habitats. Especially at dawn and dusk, a walk out the back of the Jackson Lake Lodge and up Lunch Tree Hill offers sweeping views of the flats, where you can often see moose munching on willows. Hiking farther from the lodge, toward Hermitage Point, you pass beaver dams where waterfowl and other animals gather.

In the winter more than 7,000 elk converge on the National Elk Refuge, right next to the town of Jackson. Join one of the sleigh rides starting from the Jackson Hole and Greater Yellowstone Visitor Center in Jackson for a fun outing and a chance to get quite close to the animals. Rangers usually do the commentary on the sleighs, which carry 15 to 20 passengers. They operate three to four times an hour mid-December through March daily, except Christmas, from 10am to 4pm. The cost is $16 for adults, $12 for children 5 to 12, free for children under 5. Rides are first-come, first-served.

9 Kid-Friendly Programs

CHILDREN'S PROGRAMS

Rangers lead the **Young Naturalist Program** for children ages 8 to 12 every summer afternoon from 1:30 to 3pm at the Craig Thomas and Colter Bay visitor centers. Sign up in advance to assure a space and to be ready with what you need to bring along, then leave the children for their learning experience. Children of any age can win a Young Naturalist patch, similar to the Junior Ranger patch at other parks, by completing a four-page newspaper workbook called *The Grand Adventure* and attending ranger programs—the Young Naturalist program or any other ranger programs—and paying $1 at a visitor center. The workbook is pitched to grade-school children and makes good use of the park to teach about nature—it's not just busywork. You can get the workbook from a visitor center or download it (www.nps.gov/grte; click "For Kids," then click the "Grand Teton Young Naturalist Program" on the right-hand column, and then the link to the "Grand Adventure Activity Book"). First and second graders will likely need help.

FAMILY & ADULT PROGRAMS

The Park Service offers a full schedule of ranger-led programs, including talks, walks, wildlife-viewing, and tours of the Indian Arts Museum at the Colter Bay Visitor Center. Some programs require reservations and fees. There are also campfire talks and slide shows. Check the park newspaper or pick up a weekly calendar at a visitor center.

10 Entertainment outside the Park

The world-famous downhill skiing in Jackson is outside our scope, but I have to mention a couple of fun things to do there in summer. The **Alpine Slide** at the Snow King Mountain (© **800/522-KING** or 307/734-3188; www.snowking.com) is a highlight of many children's visits. It's a sort of summertime luge run, with two tracks that descend 2,500 feet down the mountain. Riders ascend on a chairlift and come down, each on his or her own sled, controlling speed with a brake on a lever. The slide is open 10am to 9pm daily, and single rides costs $12 to $15. There are discounts for multi-ride passes; might as well bite the bullet, because you won't be able to do it only once. The **Jackson Teton County Recreation Center,** 155 E. Gill Ave. (© **307/739-9025;** www.tetonwyo.org/parks), has lots of facilities, including a large pool with a 180-foot water slide, a toddlers' pool, and a hot tub. It's open Monday through Friday 6am to 9pm, Saturday 10 to 9pm, Sunday noon to 7pm. Call ahead to check for open-swim hours. Admission is $6.25 for adults, $4 for children 3 to 12, $5 for those 13 to 17. Families are charged a flat $20.

FAST FACTS: Grand Teton National Park

Area Code The area code is **307.**

ATMs Banks in Jackson, Jackson Lake Lodge, Colter Bay Village, Dornans at Moose, and Flagg Ranch have ATMs.

Emergencies For emergencies, dial © **911** or 307/739-3300.

Hospitals & Clinics **Grand Teton Medical Clinic** at Jackson Lake Lodge is open mid-May to mid-October (© **307/543-2514**). The nearest hospital is **St. John's Hospital** in Jackson (© **307/733-3636**).

Information For information, write Grand Teton National Park, P.O. Drawer 170, Moose, WY 83012; call © **307/739-3300;** or check the website www.nps.gov/grte.

Pharmacies You can find pharmacies in most major Jackson grocery and discount stores. Also look in **Stone Drug** at 830 W. Broadway, Jackson (© **307/733-6222**).

Post Office Branches are located at Moose, Moran, and Kelly, as well as in Jackson.

Time Zone The park is on **Mountain Standard Time.**

Weather Updates For weather updates, look on the Internet at www.crh. noaa.gov/riw.

13

Rocky Mountain National Park

The tops of the Rocky Mountains are an edge. At the top, you're at the tip of North America, above the whole continent. You're higher than almost all the people, plants, and animals, above everything but air and space. Rocky Mountain National Park contains a lot of special places, but none more memorable than these high edges of the earth. Even visitors who don't want to get far from their cars can experience the thin, cool air and pure light via Trail Ridge Road, which rises to an elevation of 12,183 feet above sea level. Hardier travelers can use the road as a trail head to get to places that might normally be out of reach for them.

The park rests like a saddle on the back of the Rockies' Front Range. On either side, the land rises through different life zones of plants and animals, each step of elevation providing just the right temperature and moisture for its own community of plants and animals. The park begins in big ponderosa pines, just above the level of the sagebrush range. Higher, Engelmann spruce and alpine fir grow, then shrivel into low, stunted Krumholtz formations as you rise and timberline approaches. At the top, the mountains' backs stretch away from the trees, granite barely clothed by the thin alpine tundra. Less than a dozen miles farther, you're over the spine and back down into the trees on the other side. Everywhere in the park the elevation is written all about you in the kinds of trees, animals, flowers, and ponds you see—if you know how to read nature's handwriting.

Parts of the park are quite crowded in the summer, but without much effort you can leave the most popular trails and venture off on your own. The park has some beautiful campgrounds and exceptional educational offerings, too.

BEST THINGS TO DO IN ROCKY MOUNTAIN NATIONAL PARK

- **Take a hike.** Trails range from easy walks on the shore of a mountain lake to a famous climb to the top of 14,255-foot Longs Peak.
- **Ride a horse or bicycle** through the park.
- **See elk, bighorn, and moose** in their natural habitats.
- **Backpack** in the high country, connecting campsites as close as a mile or two apart.
- **Join** one of the exceptional educational programs.

For more information, see "For the Active Family" (p. 358).

1 History: Estes, Mills & Muir

The crest of the Rockies was never a place where people lived. In the summer, Native Americans hunted on the alpine tundra, but they generally made their homes in warmer, lower lands. The same was true of white settlers. The Rockies were a barrier to overcome on the way west, not a place to build farms and ranches. Trappers, explorers,

Rocky Mountain Address Book

Rocky Mountain National Park   1000 Hwy. 36, Estes Park, CO 80517-8397. ℂ **970/586-1206.** TDD 970/586-1319. www.nps.gov/romo.

Rocky Mountain Nature Association   P.O. Box 3100, Estes Park, CO 80517. ℂ **800/816-7662** or 970/586-0108. www.rmna.org. For maps, books, and seminars.

Arapaho and Roosevelt National Forests   Forest Service Information Center, 2150 Centre Ave., Building E, Fort Collins, CO 80526. ℂ **970/295-6600.** TTY 970/295-6794. www.fs.fed.us/r2/arnf.

Estes Park Convention and Visitors Bureau   500 Big Thompson Ave., Estes Park, CO 80517. ℂ **800/443-7837** or 970/577-9900. www.estesparkcvb.com.

Grand Lake Area Chamber of Commerce   P.O. Box 429, Grand Lake, CO 80447. ℂ **800/531-1019** for recorded information, or 970/627-3402. www.grandlakechamber.com.

Estes Park Welcome Center   www.estes-park.com. Good website info.

and gold prospectors came through and named some of the mountains where the park is now, but the first people to settle in the area were the family of Joel Estes, who built a ranch in Estes Park in 1860. (Around here, a "park" is a warm, open valley.)

Estes didn't stay long—ranching, even in Estes Park (elev. 7,500 ft.), was too cold and wintry. But the valley the family had pioneered soon became a center of activity for people coming to see and climb the mountains and to hunt. Estes Park was special because you could reach it by following not-too-steep river valleys from the east, as you still do on U.S. Highways 34 and 36. It's like a staircase landing on steps into the mountains. The town of Estes Park has developed and spread since the earliest days, but it's still mainly a base for recreation in the surrounding Rockies.

Enos Mills arrived in the area in 1884 at the age of 14 and went to work as a guide on Longs Peak. Later he built an inn near the mountain, and over his life he climbed Longs Peak almost 300 times. But a trip he made to San Francisco in 1889 turned out to be more important for the history of the park. Mills was looking at a plant growing on sand dunes where Golden Gate Park is today when a gentleman in his 50s approached and struck up a conversation. It was the great nature writer John Muir, who helped protect Yosemite National Park and many other parks. Muir and Mills hit it off. They visited Muir's ranch and hiked on Mount Tamalpais together, and when Mills went back home to Colorado, they wrote to each other.

Mills decided to model his life on Muir's. In the summer, he guided visitors up Longs Peak and ran his inn. In the winter, he wrote and traveled to tell people about the beauty of the area and the need to protect it. He wanted to transform a huge area of the Rockies, from Longs Peak most of the way across Colorado to Pikes Peak, into a park. In 1913, when Muir lost his greatest battle—to stop the damming of the Hetch Hetchy River in Yosemite National Park—Mills wrote to encourage him with the news that the loss would make him work harder. "As you well know, it is the work you have done that has encouraged me . . . in the big work that I am planning to do,"

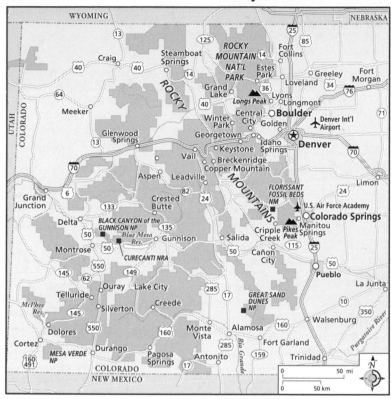

he wrote. In 1915, Congress created Rocky Mountain National Park. It's not the huge park Mills had originally wanted, but he still is deservedly called the father of the park.

The park has changed a lot since those days. Hunters had wiped out the elk by the time the park was set aside. The Park Service handled the problem by bringing in 49 elk from Yellowstone National Park and killing off the animals that prey on them—gray wolves and grizzly bears. Today the park needs the wolves and bears again, because there are too many elk for the area that's left for them. Hunters keep the numbers down by killing elk that wander outside the park.

Another change came with the construction of roads. In 1932, the Park Service built Trail Ridge Road to connect Estes Park and Grand Lake, on opposite sides of the park, and to provide access to the high country. Building a road at over 12,000 feet elevation was a difficult project, and the road is unique in giving car travelers the ability to see this kind of mountaintop terrain. But it's also safe to say that today the Park Service would never build such a road across such pristine scenery. The government also built a tunnel under the park, another project that would probably not be approved today. It brings water from Grand Lake and the man-made reservoirs nearby across the Continental Divide to the drier, east side of the Rockies.

Today, the park's biggest problem is too many people. It's a relatively small park, and roads and hiking trails can get crowded in the summer. More important, animals that use the park in the summer need winter habitats lower down the mountain, but those areas weren't all set aside for preservation. Development of roads and towns has slowly taken away land the animals need. Elk even wander the streets of Estes Park in the winter—it's their normal winter habitat.

2 Orientation

Rocky Mountain National Park is a rectangle roughly 16 miles wide (east-west) and 25 miles long (north-south). It's only 65 miles from Denver, making it a popular weekend destination for that metropolitan area. It's quieter during the week. The park has four main areas.

ARRIVING
BY CAR
Several interstate highways converge near Denver, which is only 65 miles from the park on **U.S. 36. Interstate 25** is 30 miles east of the park by way of U.S. 34. The west entrance is connected to **U.S. 40,** which goes due west or joins I-70.

BY AIR
Fly into **Denver International Airport** and rent a car there from any national rental agency. **United** (© **800/864-8331;** www.united.com) and **Frontier** (© **800/432-1359;** www.frontierairlines.com) both have hubs in Denver, and many major airlines have daily service.

VISITOR INFORMATION
NATIONAL PARK VISITOR CENTERS
Alpine Visitor Center   The location, not the building, draws throngs of people, giddy in the thin air at 12,000 feet, to this visitor center. It contains exhibits on alpine ecology and has a viewing area where you're likely to see elk. There are also a huge gift store and a snack bar. From the parking lot, a short path climbs to a knob where car passengers can get a sense of walking in the mountains.

Trail Ridge Rd., 23 miles from headquarters. No phone. Late May to mid-June and early Sept to early Oct daily 10:30am–4:30pm, mid-June to Labor Day daily 9am–5pm. Closed mid-Oct to Memorial Day.

Beaver Meadows Visitor Center   The small main visitor center, made of stone and steel, hums with activity. People collect information, make backcountry camping reservations, and watch a new orientation film, shown with the latest equipment, that includes lots of scenic shots.

U.S. 36, at the Beaver Meadows Entrance, Estes Park. © **970/586-1206.** Summer Thurs–Sun 8am–9pm, Mon–Wed 8am–8pm; off season daily 8am–5pm.

Fall River Visitor Center   This center looks like a mountain lodge. Inside are exhibits on park wildlife, including full-size bronzes of elk and other animals, an activity room for children, an information desk, and a bookstore. The attached **Rocky Mountain Gateway** (© **970/577-0043**) offers snacks and sandwiches from a cafeteria, as well as souvenirs and clothing.

On U.S. 34, just east of the Fall River entrance to Estes Park. No phone. May–Oct daily 9am–5pm; shorter winter hours.

Kawuneeche Visitor Center   This attractive building with a patio crossed by a creek has displays on what to do in the park on the western side of the Front Range,

Rocky Mountain National Park

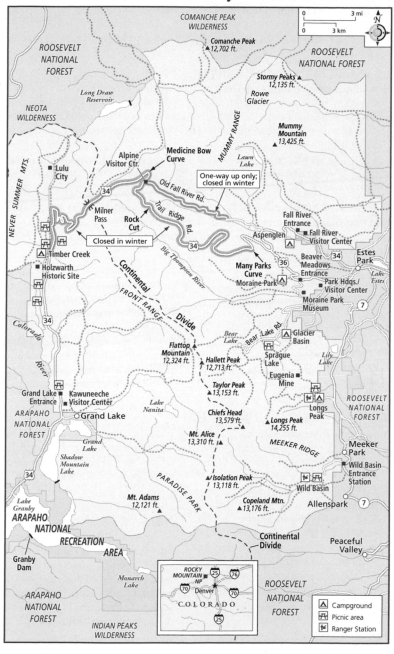

and how nature here differs from nature on the eastern side. You can get backcountry permits here, too.

Near Grand Lake Entrance Station, Trail Ridge Rd. (U.S. 34). © **970/586-1513.** Summer daily 8am–6pm; off season daily 8am–5pm.

COMMERCIAL VISITOR CENTERS

Estes Park Visitor Center   This spacious building offers the usual information racks with brochures on restaurants, lodgings, and activities. The center also features a national park exhibit and a kiosk where you can buy your park pass. Outside, a footpath leads to a small playground. Shuttles that lead both into the park and into town also stop here.

500 Big Thompson Ave. (Hwy. 34, just before split of bypass and business routes). © **800/443-7837** or 970/577-9900. www.estesparkcvb.com. Mid-May to early July and Sept to mid-Oct daily 9am–8pm; late July to Labor Day and weekends in Sept 8am–10pm; mid-Oct to May daily 9am–5pm.

Grand Lake Area Chamber of Commerce Visitor Center   Pick up business and recreation information for the west side here.

Rte. 34 (P.O. Box 429), Grand Lake, CO 80447. © **800/531-1019** or 970/627-3402. www.grandlakechamber.com. Summer daily 9am–5pm; reduced hours in winter.

READING UP

The best source for books on the park is the **Rocky Mountain Nature Association,** Rocky Mountain National Park, Estes Park, CO 80517 (© **800/816-7662** or 970/ 586-0108; www.rmna.org), which operates the visitor center bookstores and sells online or by mail order.

Hiking: *Hiking Rocky Mountain National Park,* by local experts Kent and Donna Dannen (Globe Pequot Press, $15), is exhaustive, clearly written, and easy to use.

Maps: National Geographic's Trails Illustrated topographic map ($10) covers the park in adequate detail and contains the backcountry campsite numbers.

THE NATIONAL PARK IN BRIEF

Estes Park & Moraine Park

Most of the campgrounds and visitor facilities and the most popular trails are on the park's east side, around Estes Park and on roads that punch part way into the park from there. Moraine Park, a valley just inside the national park, is the site of a museum, campground, trails, and stables. The main roads to Estes Park are U.S. Highways 34 and 36, which loop around and connect in the front part of the park. Estes Park is a thriving tourist town with every service you might need.

The High Country

The central, alpine area of the park is the famous highlight. It's reached by 48-mile Trail Ridge Road (U.S. 34),

which crosses the whole park, from Estes Park on the east to Grand Lake on the west. The road closes for the winter from mid-October to May.

The Western Side & Grand Lake

The western side of the park, near the little resort town of Grand Lake, is quite different from the east. The mountainsides here are thickly wooded with fir, spruce, and pine. Below are lakes and swampy moose habitat. The west side gets more snow, has colder winters, and is less used by people, in part because of its greater distance from Denver.

Longs Peak & Wild Basin

The southeast area of the park contains the path to Longs Peak and other mountain trails. This less-used area, including the secluded Wild Basin, is accessible from several points along Route 7, which runs along the national park boundary south of Estes Park.

3 Getting Around
BY CAR
The park is easy to navigate using the map rangers hand out at the gate. It's small enough that you can camp or stay in one place as a base and go to the opposite side for a day hike. Be judicious in arranging your day so you don't have to keep returning to your "base camp" to collect gear or clothing.

Pick up a free map of Estes Park at the town visitor center, 500 Big Thompson Ave. Walk whenever you can in town—traffic can be slow, and the streets are confusing at first.

BY SHUTTLE
The free shuttle system in the Moraine Park and Bear Lake road areas makes good sense. Leave the car behind to help relieve traffic congestion, save parking hassles, and enable yourself to hike trails with different start and end points, completing your loop on the shuttle. The system has two loops. The **Moraine Park loop** runs from the Fern Lake trail head, past the Moraine Park campground and museum, and up Bear Lake Road to Glacier Basin Campground. The **Bear Lake route** runs between that campground and Bear Lake. A large parking lot at Glacier Basin is the best place to leave your car if you are not camping somewhere along the shuttle route. The bus stops at all the trail heads along the way. Check the park newspaper for times of service, which are quite frequent in the busy summer period.

4 Planning Your Outings
WHEN TO GO
The summer months are all busy, but July and August are the prime tourist season. Daytime temperatures are comfortable to cool at the high elevations in the park. Thunderstorms routinely come in the afternoon through mid-September, so early starts are always necessary for outdoor activities. In June, snow lingers in the high country, although Trail Ridge Road usually opens in late May. September may be the best time to visit—crowds are smaller and the weather is still comfortable.

Lower-elevation trails on the east side of the park stay open to hikers most of the winter. Snow often closes the high country roads in October. January and February are the favored months for winter sports, when the thick snowpack hasn't yet gotten wet or mushy.

HOW MUCH TIME TO SPEND
Most visitors to Rocky Mountain National Park just drive through for the view. The park doesn't have a lot of varied activities or sightseeing destinations to keep you busy, although you could spend a day or two that way. It's mostly a park for relaxation and hiking. With the perfect summer temperatures, spectacular scenery, and choice of trails, you could easily spend a week exploring, getting in shape, and forgetting your problems.

HOW FAR TO PLAN AHEAD
Often a couple of weeks or a month of advance planning is enough for rooms in Estes Park, even in the summer. For the best selection, call 3 months ahead. For campground sites at Moraine and Glacier campgrounds, reserve as soon as possible, using

the national reservation system outlined in chapter 2, "Planning a Family Trip to a National Park."

Weather Chart: Estes Park & Grand Lake

	Avg. High (°F/°C)	Avg. Low (°F/°C)	Avg. Precip. (In.)	Avg. Snow Depth (In.)
January–February				
Estes Park	40/4	17/–8	.4	1
Grand Lake	33/1	3/–16	1.6	22
March–April				
Estes Park	49/9	24/–4	1.1	.5
Grand Lake	45/7	15/–9	1.7	19
May–June				
Estes Park	68/20	38/3	1.9	0
Grand Lake	65/18	30/–1	1.8	.5
July–August				
Estes Park	77/25	45/7	2.1	0
Grand Lake	75/24	37/3	2.2	0
September–October				
Estes Park	65/18	34/1	1	0
Grand Lake	62/17	26/–3	1.5	3.5
November–December				
Estes Park	43/6	20/–7	.5	.5
Grand Lake	36/2	8/–13	1.5	7

WHAT TO PACK
CLOTHING
Most of the park is above 8,000 feet, and it reaches to over 14,000 feet. Air temperature is 3° to 5° lower for each 1,000 feet you rise, so it's about 20° cooler at the Alpine Visitor Center than it is in Estes Park. It's also consistently windy up there. You'll need layers of clothing that allow you to strip down on a hot hike and then warm up and protect yourself from a chilly wind or rain squall. And, with the good odds of encountering wet weather, good rain gear is a necessity. You can even encounter snow in July at the top of the road! Winter visits require heavy winter clothing and breathable, synthetic clothing for skiing or snowshoeing. (See "When It's Cold & Wet," in chapter 2.)

GEAR
Be sure to bring sun hats, sunblock, and high-quality sunglasses for time spent at high elevations. At 10,000 feet you have one-third less atmosphere above you to protect you from the ultraviolet wavelengths of the sun than you do at sea level. Use only quality UV sunglasses; cheap children's sunglasses can cause eye damage by dilating the pupils but not screening out ultraviolet light. You'll also need good boots or hiking shoes—even for the kids—to keep your feet in shape over several days. If you have a toddler, bring a quality backpack carrier—strollers aren't practical here. Summertime camping doesn't require any special gear, as long as you have an extra layer for cold nights.

KEEPING SAFE & HEALTHY
Besides the specific advice here, see "Dealing with Hazards," in chapter 2, for information about bears and other dangerous wildlife, Giardia, hypothermia, and sunburn.

ELEVATION

Most people never go to elevations as high as those found along Trail Ridge Road except in airplanes (which are pressurized to the equivalent of about 5,000 ft.). The air up here is much thinner than you're used to, and it typically can take at least 2 days for your body to adjust, especially if you're exerting yourself. You may feel dizzy or lightheaded, or have headaches, a fast heartbeat, or nausea. If you push yourself too hard, it could be dangerous. Children are more susceptible to altitude sickness and may feel it first and become sluggish—check on kids being carried in backpacks to make sure they're alert.

To reduce the effects of elevation, start your vacation with hikes at lower elevations and work your way up to more strenuous expeditions higher in the mountains. Also, drink lots of water. The only cure for altitude sickness is to return to lower elevation. You should feel better in a day or two. (Although after a long plane ride, people can also suffer from dehydration, which does have "cures.") Also, make sure children and adults have protection from the sun at high altitudes, where ultraviolet radiation is much stronger than at lower elevations. See "What to Pack" (p. 346).

LIGHTNING

Lightning is a special concern at Rocky Mountain. Thunderstorms come almost every afternoon in the summer, and alpine terrain above the tree line is a dangerous place to be when they do. You may be the tallest thing around. Plan your hikes so that you're back in the trees by afternoon, and review "Dealing with Hazards," in chapter 2, so you know what to do if you're in an exposed area when lightning comes.

SERIOUS DISEASES

You should never let your children feed small rodents such as squirrels anywhere, but there is an added reason at Rocky Mountain National Park: They carry bubonic and pneumonic plague. Ticks in this area can cause Colorado tick fever and deadly Rocky Mountain spotted fever (but not Lyme disease). Hikers should tuck in their pant legs and use insect repellent on the outside of clothes to keep ticks off. Check everyone after a hike, and remove any ticks you find completely with a pair of tweezers. For more on these risks, including symptoms, and other hazards at the park, go to www. nps.gov/romo/visit/hazards.html. For information on removing ticks, check out www. kidshealth.org.

5 Family-Friendly Accommodations

CAMPGROUNDS

NATIONAL PARK CAMPGROUNDS

Rocky Mountain is a great park for camping. The campgrounds are beautiful and woodsy, and town is never more than half an hour away. There are five campgrounds in the park. Just two, Moraine and Glacier Basin, are reserved through the National Park Service's reservation system described in chapter 2. During popular summer weekends campsites can fill up almost as soon as reservations are accepted, although midweek dates and shoulder seasons fill much more slowly. In general, it's best to make your reservations as soon as you know when you'll be visiting to ensure that you get a site.

The three campgrounds that don't take reservations fill every night, and sites are especially difficult to get on weekends. Arrive early in the morning, when people are leaving, to have a good chance for a site.

Campgrounds in the Rocky Mountain Area

Campground	Elevation	Total Sites	RV Hookups	Dump Station	Toilets	Drinking Water
IN THE PARK						
Aspenglen	8,230	54	0	No	Yes	Yes
Glacier Basin	8,500	150	0	Yes	Yes	Yes
Longs Peak	9,405	26	0	No	Yes	Yes
Moraine Park	8,160	245	0	Yes	Yes	Yes
Timber Creek	8,900	98	0	Yes	Yes	Yes
NEAR PARK'S EAST SIDE						
Camp Dick	8,650	41	0	No	Yes	Yes
Mary's Lake	8,200	150	90	Yes	Yes	Yes
Meeker Park	8,600	29	0	No	Yes	No
National Park Retreats	8,200	100	88	Yes	Yes	Yes
Olive Ridge	8,350	56	0	No	Yes	Yes
Peaceful Valley	8,500	17	0	No	Yes	Yes
NEAR PARK'S WEST SIDE						
Arapaho Bay	8,320	84	0	No	Yes	Yes
Green Ridge	8,360	77	0	Yes	Yes	Yes
Stillwater	8,350	129	20	Yes	Yes	Yes
Winding River	8,672	148	98	Yes	Yes	Yes

* *These fees are for winter (when the water is turned off), followed by the summer rates.*

The maximum stay in summer is 7 days, except at Longs Peak, where the limit is 3 days. Winter camping is limited to 14 days. Ice and firewood are often for sale at the campgrounds, except at Timber Creek, which doesn't have ice. None of the campgrounds have hookups for RVs. For general campground information, call the park headquarters (© **970/586-1206**).

Aspenglen   The campground is in a steep river valley, with sites not as far apart as at Moraine, but pleasingly arranged on the slope. Tent platforms have gravel pads to help you keep dry.

On U.S. 34, just inside the Fall River entrance. © **970/586-1206**. 54 sites, tents or RVs. $20 site. Closed mid-Sept to mid-May. **Amenities:** Flush or vault toilets, picnic tables, fire pits and grates, running water.

Glacier Basin   This campground is about halfway up Bear Lake Road, across from the shuttle-bus stop that can take you down to Moraine Park or up to trail heads. The area is thickly wooded with pines.

Showers	Fire Pits/Grills	Laundry	Public Phones	Reservations	Fees	Open
No	Yes	No	Yes	No	$20	Mid-May to mid-Sept
No	Yes	No	Yes	Yes	$20	Late May to early Sept
No	Yes	No	No	No	$14/$20•	Year-round
No	Yes	No	Yes	Yes	$14/$20•	Year-round
No	Yes	No	Yes	No	$14/$20•	Year-round
No	Yes	No	No	Yes	$14	Mid-May to mid-Oct
Yes	Yes	Yes	Yes	Yes	$26–$40	May–Sept
No	Yes	No	No	No	$8	Memorial Day to Labor Day
Yes	Yes	No	Yes	Yes	$18–$38	Year-round
No	Yes	No	No	Yes	$16–$19	Mid-May to early Sept
No	Yes	No	No	Yes	$16–$19	Mid-May to mid-Oct
No	Yes	No	No	Yes	$16–$32	Memorial Day to Labor Day
No	Yes	No	Yes	Yes	$16–$48	May–Sept
Yes	Yes	No	Yes	Yes	$19–$36	Year-round
Yes	Yes	Yes	Yes	Yes	$28–$36	Mid-May to Sept

On Bear Lake Rd. ℂ **970/586-1206.** 150 sites, tents or RVs. $20 site. Reservations accepted. Closed mid-Sept to late May. **Amenities:** Flush or vault toilets, dump station, picnic tables, fire pits and grates, running water.

Longs Peak   This campground, at 9,400 feet elevation, is intended as a base for hikers planning to climb Longs Peak (p. 357). It's a low-key campground among thick, small pines, with gravel tent pads. Stays are limited to 3 days in summer.

1 mile off Rte. 7, south of Lily Lake. ℂ **970/586-1206.** 26 sites, tents only. Summer $20 site; late Sept to Memorial Day (when water is turned off) $14 site. **Amenities:** Flush or vault toilets.

Moraine Park   This campground sits among little hills, granite boulders, small pines, and meadow grass. It was ingeniously designed to tuck sites away from each other, so some feel like the backcountry. Elk wander around the edges at times. You can hike right from the campground, and the stables and museum are close by. A shuttle bus comes by regularly in the summer.

Tips **Park Camping Basics: Toilets, Showers & Laundry**

The park campgrounds have bathrooms with cold water. Public bathrooms are at the visitor centers, at Bear Lake and Sprague Lake, along Trail Ridge Road at the Alpine Visitor Center and Milner Pass, and at other points, all marked on the park map. **Dad's Maytag Laundry and Shower** (⊘ **970/586-2025**) is in Estes Park across Highway 34 from the visitor center. In Grand Lake, public showers are available at Winding River Resort (p. 352).

Near Estes Park off Hwy. 36. ⊘ **970/586-1206.** 245 sites, tents or RVs. Summer $20 site; mid-Oct to mid-May (when water is turned off) $14 site. Reservations accepted. **Amenities:** Flush or vault toilets, dump station, picnic tables, fire pits and grates, running water.

Timber Creek   Towering pines block the light but offer little privacy between the sites at this flat campground near the highway. Moose are common visitors. It fills later than others, but you should still be there by noon in summer.

Trail Ridge Rd., Kawuneeche Valley. ⊘ **970/586-1206.** 98 sites, tents or RVs. Summer $20 site; mid-Sept to mid-June (when water is turned off) $14 site. **Amenities:** Flush or vault toilets, dump station, picnic tables, fire pits and grates, running water.

BACKCOUNTRY CAMPING PERMITS

Rocky has more than 120 backcountry campsites, spaced closely along the hiking trails. Some are only a mile or two from the trail heads, making backpacking for families practical even if you can't cover much ground in a day. There are also off-trail camping zones in the backcountry, for more ambitious trips.

The first step to getting a permit for backcountry camping is to buy a map and trail guide (see "Reading Up," p. 344) and figure out where you want to go. The sites are also marked on the *Rocky Mountain Backcountry Camping Guide* distributed free by the Park Service and downloadable from the website (www.nps.gov/romo/visit/park/camp/info.html), which also has a lot of detailed information about sites and routes. Reservations open March 1 for the whole summer, by mail or in person at the Headquarters Backcountry Office or the Kawuneeche Visitor Center. You can reserve by phone (⊘ **970/586-1242;** TDD 970/586-1319) from March 1 to May 15 and again beginning October 1 for the remainder of that calendar year, but between those times you can reserve only by mail (Backcountry/Wilderness Permits, Rocky Mountain National Park, Estes Park, CO 80517) or in person. Besides the obvious, like your name and address, you'll need to specify the campsites you want and the exact dates, and pay a $20 fee when you receive your permit. The first sites to go are those in the areas of Glacier Gorge and Andrews Creek.

You often can get sites, especially out of the peak season, without reserving, just by showing up at the office or visitor center, but I wouldn't count on it. No sites are held back specifically for walk-ins, but the park reallocates canceled reservations as well as permits that are not picked up by 10am on the first day of the hike. See "Backpacking" (p. 358) for more details on setting up a trek.

FOREST SERVICE CAMPGROUNDS

Arapaho and **Roosevelt** national forests, which are managed jointly, surround the park with a larger area of backcountry, much of it wilderness, and many campgrounds. Forest Service campgrounds handy to the park's entrances are marked on the park map, and I've provided basic information here on each. All six can be reserved through the national system described in chapter 2, which carries an extra fee beyond the camping fee noted below. All have drinking water and vault toilets, unless otherwise noted.

East Side

These campgrounds are in the **Boulder Ranger District** (*C* **303/444-6600**). All are usually open from mid-May to mid- or late October, depending on the weather. Sites are in high demand in the summer, filling as early as Thursday nights for many weekends.

Camp Dick   A former Civilian Conservation Corps camp, Camp Dick lies a mile west of Peaceful Valley campground. There are four nice walk-in tent sites down along the Middle St. Vrain Creek that get you away from some of the RV traffic.

Just beyond Peaceful Valley campground on an unpaved road, southeast of the park. *C* **303/444-6600**. 41 sites, tents or RVs. $16–$19 site. **Amenities:** Vault toilets, picnic tables, fire pits, grills, running water.

Meeker Park   When everything else is full, this is a campground of last resort. You won't find any extras here, not even running water, but there are 29 sites that attract mostly a tent crowd and so it's a quieter spot. And the price is right.

13 miles south of Estes Park on Hwy. 7 at mile marker 11. *C* **303/444-6600**. 29 sites, tents or RVs. $8 site. **Amenities:** Portable toilets, fire pits.

Olive Ridge   This large campground along the Middle St. Vrain River is the closest to the east entrances of the park, but not as close to trails in the national forest.

Hwy. 7 near Wild Basin. *C* **303/444-6600**. 56 sites, tents or RVs. $16–$19 site. **Amenities:** Vault toilets, small playground w/climbing stairs, hanging rings, and a slide for young children, picnic tables, fire pits, grills, running water.

Peaceful Valley   This campground is in a glacial valley next to Middle St. Vrain Creek, but it's not as peaceful as the name sounds as campers heading to Camp Dick drive by.

On Hwy. 72 off Hwy. 7 southeast of the park. *C* **303/444-6600**. 17 sites, tents or RVs. $16–$19 site. **Amenities:** Vault toilets, picnic tables, fire pits, grills, running water.

West Side

These campgrounds are around the reservoirs southwest of the park, in the Arapaho National Recreation Area, which, in addition to camping fees, charges day-use fees per vehicle of $5 for 1 day, $10 for 3 days, and $15 for 7 days. They are oriented toward fishing and boating. For information, call the **Sulphur Ranger District** (*C* **970/887-4100**). These campgrounds also are on the national reservation system described in chapter 2.

Arapaho Bay   Southern end, Lake Granby, Arapaho Bay Road, off Highway 34. 84 sites, tents or RVs. $16 to $32 site. Closed Labor Day to Memorial Day. **Amenities:** Vault toilets, picnic tables, fire pits and grates, running water, boat ramp.

Green Ridge   Southern side, Shadow Mountain Lake, on U.S. 34. 77 sites, tents or RVs. $16 to $48 site. Closed Labor Day to Memorial Day. **Amenities:** Vault toilets, dump station, picnic tables, fire pits and grates, running water, boat ramp, phone.

Stillwater   Western side, Lake Granby, on Highway 34. 129 sites, tents or RVs. $19 to $36 site. Open year-round but with reduced services Labor Day to Memorial Day. **Amenities:** Flush toilets, showers, dump station, picnic tables, fire pits and grates, running water, boat ramps, hookups.

COMMERCIAL CAMPGROUNDS

There are plenty of good campgrounds in Estes Park and a few in Grand Lake. Making reservations is a good idea in the summer. Besides those listed below, I can recommend **Elk Meadow Lodge and RV Park** (© 800/582-5342 or 970/586-5342; www.elkmeadowsrv.com), just outside the Beaver Meadows entrance. The **Estes Park KOA Kampground** (© 800/562-1887 or 970/586-2888; www.estesparkkoa.com) is on U.S. Highway 34 as you enter town.

Mary's Lake Campground and RV Park   On 50 acres at the edge of a small lake just outside town, this campground has a real Rocky Mountain feel. While the RV area is drab and units are tightly parked, tents have more woodsy places to set up among pine trees and rock outcroppings, not much different from a national park campground.

2120 Mary's Lake Rd., 3 miles south of Estes Park (P.O. Box 2514), Estes Park, CO 80517. © 800/445-6279 or 970/586-4411. www.maryslakecampground.com. 150 sites, tents or RVs. $40 for full hookup for 2 people; $26 tent for 2 people. $3 extra person over age 5. Closed Sept–May. **Amenities:** Full hookups, laundry, playground, swimming pool, store, basketball, fishing, game room, ATM, TV hookup, dump station.

National Park Retreats   The campground, set on 13 acres, is right on the edge of the park in the steep valley of the Fall River among ponderosa pines. Many sites have views back onto the woods and the park. There are also some cabins available.

3501 Fall River Rd. (U.S. 34), Estes Park, CO 80517. © 970/586-4563. www.nationalparkretreats.com. 100 sites, tents or RVs. $25–$38 full hookup for 2 people; $18–$28 tent for 2 people. $3 extra person over age 12. Open year-round. **Amenities:** Full hookups, laundry, store, horseback riding, coffee shop, Wi-Fi

Winding River Resort   Back in the woods by itself a few miles from Grand Lake, this campground is abuzz with activities: hayrides, ice-cream socials, chuck-wagon breakfasts (a sort of Western picnic), and the like. The resort will even board your horse.

From Trail Ridge Rd. (U.S. 34), just north of Kawuneeche Visitor Center, turn on County Rd. 491 (P.O. Box 629), Grand Lake, CO 80447. © 970/627-3215 or 303/623-1121. www.windingriverresort.com. 148 sites, tents or RVs. $36 full hookup for 2 people; $28 tent for 2 people. $4 extra person over age 4. **Amenities:** Full hookups, laundry, playground, store, petting farm, horseback riding, snowmobile rentals.

HOTELS, MOTELS & CABINS

There are no lodgings inside the park, but you'll find lots of family-oriented motels and cabins in Estes Park and Grand Lake. A good room in the summer in Estes Park costs about $125 a night, and a nice cabin big enough for a family of four is about $150 a night. Lodging in Grand Lake costs a bit less. All rates below are for the high season, late June through August; rates drop around 25% in the off season.

ESTES PARK
The Baldpate Inn *(Finds)*   This is an extraordinary bed-and-breakfast in many ways. Built from native timber in 1917, it looks like a treehouse from the outside. The rooms are charming, with beds topped by handmade quilts. There are no phones or TVs, bathrooms are small, and the access road is rough. The place also is weathered and off-kilter, but that's part of the ambience. Rates include an elaborate breakfast from the restaurant downstairs, which is one of the area's most popular and renowned. It's so popular, in fact, that dinner reservations are essential, despite a menu that includes only soup (anything from beef or buffalo stew to pumpkin-curry), salad, bread, and muffins. Dinner is served from Memorial Day to mid-October. Hours are 11:30am to 8pm daily, and a meal is $12 for adults and $3.95 for children under 12.

All that leaves out the most extraordinary thing: a collection of 20,000 keys, started in 1923 at Clarence Darrow's suggestion. It contains many fascinating and historic keys in a room from a locksmith's fevered nightmare—that's worth the trip by itself.

4900 S. Colo. 7 (P.O. Box 700), Estes Park, CO 80517. ℂ 970/586-6151. www.baldpateinn.com. 12 units, 2 with private bathroom, 4 cabins. $110 double with shared bathroom; $115 double with private bathroom; $185 cabin. Rates include breakfast. $15 extra person. Crib $15. DISC, MC, V. Closed mid-Oct to Memorial Day. **Amenities:** Restaurant; Wi-Fi throughout lodge; TV in library w/video collection. *In room:* Hair dryer, iron/ironing board, safe available.

Glacier Lodge

This is a place where you can really stretch out and relax. Cabins sit on a 19-acre grassy compound across the Big Thompson River from the road. There are a swimming pool, playground, sport court, riding stable, and lots of other recreation facilities, including good fishing right on the property. Most cabins have cooking facilities and fireplaces, and the resort sometimes offers activities for children. Rooms do not have phones. There are many options here, more than we could list. So, if you have a big group, ask about the large cabins they have.

Along the same road, several other attractive cabin lodgings sit by the river. Many charge lower rates and don't have a 4-day minimum, but they don't offer Glacier Lodge's extras. **Rockmount Cottages** (ℂ **970/586-4168**), next door to Glacier Lodge, has trim log cabins and lots of flowers; two-bedroom cottages are $129 to $299 a night.

2166 Colo. 66, south of park entrance (P.O. Box 2656), Estes Park, CO 80517. ℂ 800/523-3920 or 970/586-4401. www.glacierlodge.com. 25 cabins, 4 lodges. $153–$220 cabin for 4. $25 extra person. Rollaway bed free, crib $5. 4-day minimum stay in summer. DISC, MC, V. Closed Nov to mid-May. **Amenities:** Pool; basketball; horseshoes; shuffleboard; table tennis; tetherball; Wi-Fi in lodge lobby; laundry. *In room:* TV, kitchen/kitchenette, fridge, coffeemaker, microwave, dishes, no phone.

Marys Lake Lodge *(Finds)*

Built in 1913, by the same family that built the Grand Lake Lodge on the other side of the park, this lodge at the foot of Rams Horn Mountain blends the new with the old, as a fire in 1978 led to substantial renovations. The 16 lodge rooms retain some of the flavor of the original building—they're smallish, but comfortable. Many of the original claw-foot tubs and wall-hung sinks remain in use, yet modern amenities such as cable TV and Internet access are available in all rooms. The condos are perfect for extended stays, as they offer multiple bedrooms, living rooms with fireplaces, and full-size kitchens. Per-night rates decline for multiday stays. You also have two restaurants to choose from at the lodge. The **Tavern,** open 11am to 11pm, offers pub fare such as burgers and sandwiches around $10 as well as steaks, poultry, and seafood entrees ranging up to $22 served along with live music. The **Chalet Room** is much more formal with lavish entrees such as baked stuffed shrimp, Colorado lamb chops, and chicken saltimbocca. Dinner entrees range from $19 to $30. Kids' menu for both lunch and dinner is $7.95.

2625 Marys Lake Rd., Estes Park, CO 80517. ℂ 877/442-6279 or 970/586-5958. Fax 970/586-5308. www.maryslakelodge.com. 62 units. $149–$229 lodge room; $209–$489 condo. No rollaway beds, Pack 'n Play. AE, DISC, MC, V. **Amenities:** Restaurants. *In room:* TV, Wi-Fi, condos have fireplaces and kitchens.

Stanley Hotel

This grand white clapboard hotel overlooking the town aims to maintain the style established in 1909 by its builder, F. O. Stanley (inventor of the Stanley Steamer car). It was the model for *The Shining:* Stephen King was staying here when he wrote it. With its formal feeling, the Stanley isn't for all families, but the history and scale make it fun, and it's even worth a walk-through if you are staying somewhere else (the hotel charges $3 per car for the privilege). There is a huge outdoor pool, plus two restaurants.

333 Wonderview Ave. (P.O. Box 1767), Estes Park, CO 80517. © 800/976-1377 or 970/586-3371. Fax 970/586-3673. www.stanleyhotel.com. 158 units. $161–$319 double; $249–$279 suite. $10 extra adult, children under 18 free in parent's room. Rollaway bed and cribs $10. AE, DC, DISC, MC, V. **Amenities:** Restaurant; outdoor pool open season-ally; exercise room; spa; business center w/printer, copier, and fax; salon; Wi-Fi and dataports in common areas. *In room:* Dataport, minifridge on request, coffeemaker on request, hair dryer, iron/ironing board, Wi-Fi.

GRAND LAKE

Besides the choices below, **Lemmon Lodge** (© **970/627-3314** in summer, or 970/725-3511 in winter; www.lemmonlodge.com) is an attractive, old-fashioned cabin resort on 5 acres at the edge of town, right on the lake. Open from late May through mid-September, the lodge offers cabins, which sleep 2 to 12 people, from $90 to $410 per night.

Western Riviera Motel and Lakeside Cabins   This property right next to Grand Lake, where there's a beach, playground, and boat rental, is the best motel in town, thanks to its waterfront feel. Plus, it's added 22 cabins, including some on the lake. The units vary in size—from ones that will accommodate solo travelers to others that are good for six people.

419 Garfield Ave. (P.O. Box 1286), Grand Lake, CO 80447. © **970/627-3580.** Fax 970/627-3320. www.western riv.com. 42 units. $75–$175 unit (1–6 people). 2-night minimum July–Aug, June and Sept weekends. No rollaway beds, crib free. MC, V. *In room:* TV, fridge, hair dryer, microwave, dial-up Internet, Wi-Fi in motel rooms.

6 Family-Friendly Dining

LOW-STRESS MEALS

FAST FOOD

Estes Park has plenty of franchise fast food. Some of the chains in town include **Dairy Queen, Kentucky Fried Chicken/Taco Bell, Subway,** and **McDonald's,** all of which you can easily see along the main highways as you pass through town.

DINERS

In Estes Park or Grand Lake, it's easy to find cafes serving burgers and fries where your coffee cup is never allowed to sit empty.

ESTES PARK

Big Horn Restaurant   This Estes Park restaurant, family owned and operated since 1972, is a justly popular Western cafe—nothing fancy, but hearty meals and fast serv-ice. Breakfasts center around biscuits and gravy, omelets, and griddle items; lunches are built upon burgers, quesadillas, and sandwiches; while dinners revolve around bar-becue chicken, ribs, fish and chips, and steaks.

401 W. Elkhorn Ave., Estes Park. © **970/586-2792.** www.estesparkbighorn.com. Kids' menu, highchairs, boosters. Breakfast $3.75–$8.85; lunch $4.50–$9.95; dinner $10–$17; kids' menu $2.95–$4.50. DISC, MC, V. Daily 6am–9pm; shorter in winter.

Bob and Tony's Pizza   This pizzeria has perfected an atmosphere that kids will enjoy. A brick wall in the dining room has graffiti on it, and a back room has a pool table, foosball, and video games. Order at a counter and eat in or carry out. It's open daily 11am to 10pm in summer, shorter hours the rest of the year. Pizzas range from a plain 10-inch cheese to a 15-inch "super special" that's smothered with nine toppings.

124 Elkhorn Ave., Estes Park. © **970/586-2044.** Lunch and dinner $9.25–$25. AE, DISC, MC, V. Summer daily 11am–10pm; shorter hours rest of year.

Grumpy Gringo With private booths, plants, and decoration, this eatery might strike you as too fancy, but in fact the service and atmosphere are casual and the prices low, with a children's menu. Choose from a good selection of burritos, enchiladas, fajitas, and other Mexican standards, plus burgers and sandwiches.

1560 Big Thompson Ave., Estes Park. ℭ 970/586-7705. www.grumpygringo.com. Kids' menu, highchairs, boosters. Lunch and dinner $6.70–$16. AE, DISC, MC, V. Summer daily 11am–9pm; closed Tues–Wed in winter.

Molly B This easily overlooked restaurant proves appearances can be deceiving. The thoughtful, varied, and well-priced dishes include a range of omelets for breakfast, sandwiches, burritos, stir fries, salads, and quesadillas (the seafood version is stuffed with crab) for lunch. The dinner menu reprises lunch, with the addition of three nightly specials. Salted throughout all the menus are many vegetarian options. There's also a basic kids' menu with chicken nuggets, grilled cheese, hamburgers, and fish and chips.

200 Moraine Ave., Estes Park. ℭ **970/586-2766.** www.estesparkmollyb.com. Kids' menu, highchairs, boosters. Breakfast $4.25–$8.50; lunch $6.25–$7.75; dinner $6.25–$19; kids' menu $3.95. AE, DISC, V. Thurs–Tues breakfast 6:30–11am; lunch 11am–3pm; dinner 4:30–9pm.

GRAND LAKE
Black Bear Bakery and Café Don't let the name fool you. This is a highly inventive eatery for its park-side setting. Inexpensively priced omelets, Belgian waffles, and breakfast burritos generate crowds in the morning, while the lunch menu that's built around tamales, tacos, lettuce wraps, and spring rolls draws into the early evening hours. Of course, there are also the pastries. Aside from a short period between late October and Thanksgiving, this cafe is open year-round.

928 Grand Ave., Grand Lake. ℭ **970/627-0304.** Kids' menu, highchairs, boosters, chalkboard for doodlers. Breakfast $5.25–$10; lunch and dinner $3.75–$10. MC, V. Daily 6am–9pm.

BEST-BEHAVIOR MEALS
For details on a couple of favorite restaurants in the area, at **The Baldpate Inn** and **Marys Lake Lodge,** see "Family-Friendly Accommodations" (p. 347). Here's another choice:

Dunraven Inn This is a place where parents can enjoy scampi, veal parmigiana, or a variety of steaks, ranging from the Lord Dunraven, a 10-ounce center-cut top sirloin, to an 8-ounce filet paired with a lobster tail. It will be a fairly elegant evening, but the restaurant also offers a kids' menu that features familiar items such as spaghetti and meatballs and cheeseburgers as well as fettuccine Alfredo, and fanciful decoration including various images of the *Mona Lisa,* one with a mustache. Reservations are highly recommended.

2470 Colo. 66, Estes Park. ℭ **970/586-6409.** www.dunraveninn.com. Kids' menu, highchairs, boosters. Main courses $10–$38; kids' menu $6–$9.75. AE, DISC, MC, V. Summer Mon–Sat 5–10pm, Sun 5–9pm; shorter hours in winter.

7 Exploring Rocky Mountain National Park with Your Kids

ENTRANCE FEES The entrance fee is $20 per vehicle per week, although you also can gain entrance with the America the Beautiful Pass. For details, see chapter 2.

NATURAL PLACES
TRAIL RIDGE & THE MUMMY RANGE
The road that crosses the park follows a natural ramp up into the mountains, Trail Ridge, which Native Americans used to cross the Rockies thousands of years ago. **Trail**

Tundra Etiquette

Trampled tundra plants can take 100 years to return. Close to the road, you must stay on trails; farther out on the mountainside, when trails give out, you can walk on the tundra, but avoid going in single file. If the weather is good, there's no reason not to wander out on a heathery mountainside. Venturing farther, as you climb, even the tundra gives out, and you can walk across broken granite that no plant has yet pioneered.

Ridge Road crosses alpine tundra above tree line for 11 miles, giving hikers and walkers unique access to a huge swath of mountaintops and high-elevation terrain. The Park Service gives away a brochure with commentary for each of the pullouts.

On the other side of a steep mountain valley, unpaved **Old Fall River Road** winds up into the mountains to the same point, near the Alpine Visitor Center. It opens alpine and wooded terrain in the Mummy Range to hikers.

On each side you can learn how plants survive in the wind and cold. It's almost always very windy up here, and the thin, cool air is dry. Any branches that stick out quickly dry out and die. The same drying-out process happens to you—a good reason to bring and drink lots of water and wear clothing that protects you from the wind. Trees that get a start in a protected spot behind a rock grow gnarled and short (they're often referred to as "Krumholtz") as the wind twists them back, in a manner similar to the way salt spray shapes trees and bushes at the seashore. Tundra plants survive by growing very slowly—so they don't need much food or energy—and staying low, out of the wind. Try lying down on the tundra to feel how the wind calms a few inches from the ground. Because the tundra grows so slowly, it's important not to harm it.

There are several trails to hike in the area. From Trail Ridge Road, the **Old Ute Trail** follows the original ridge route 6 miles down to Beaver Meadows, across each life zone. Unless you have a vehicle at either end, you'll want to hike partway and double back. From the top, you can go about 2 miles before the steep elevation loss begins that would be hard to climb back up. The **Tundra Communities Nature Trail** is near the road's high point and is accessible to strollers and wheelchairs. More trails start at **Milner Pass,** on the Continental Divide. From Old Fall River Road, you can reach trail-less alpine hiking and a series of easy, high-altitude mountains to climb at the **Chapin Pass Trailhead.** Be sure to take a topographic map and check the weather before hiking off trails above tree line. For more on hiking, maps, and guides, see "Hiking" (p. 359) and "Reading Up" (p. 344).

MORAINE PARK & HORSESHOE PARK

The park areas of the Front Range are valleys protected from extreme weather by the mountains. The meadows and gentle terrain make a safe home for wildlife in the winter. These two parks, just inside Rocky Mountain near Estes Park, were beds for glaciers. Looking at a topographic map, you can see where a glacier pushed down the path of the Big Thompson River, which now flows in Forest Canyon, and plowed out a flat area in Moraine Park. The rock that the glacier took from the mountains piled up around its sides and front in hills called moraines that still surround the valley. Horseshoe Park, site of Aspenglen Campground, lay under the front of a glacier that came down the valley where Fall River is now.

Besides having great campgrounds, these parks are places to hike on relatively level trails where you're likely to see a lot of birds and animals. You also can join trail rides on horseback at Moraine Park. In the summer a free shuttle bus runs to the Fern Lake trail head in Moraine Park, allowing different loop hikes that end with a ride back to the car and alleviating parking difficulties (see "By Shuttle," earlier).

BEAR LAKE ROAD AREA 🐾

Bear Lake Road runs from Moraine Park about 9 miles and 1,500 vertical feet upward into an area of steep, craggy mountainsides and small, round reflecting lakes. An extraordinary network of trails connects to the road at spots all along the route, including at a stable at Sprague Lake. There are flat, .5-mile interpretive loops suitable for toddlers, and more ambitious hikes that climb right up to the Continental Divide. At Glacier Basin a campground and a parking lot are on the route of a shuttle bus that drops off and picks up hikers along the road. Leave your car here to avoid parking problems and to have access to longer hikes, perhaps downhill all the way, that don't require you to double back (see "By Shuttle," earlier).

At the top, near the round mirror of Bear Lake, a ranger answers questions at a kiosk and helps hikers figure out which route is best for them. The Park Service's free trail map of the area shows the web of trails, with mileage and difficulty ratings. The biggest drawback of the area is that it is the park's most crowded, especially on weekends. For families, the short—1.2-mile round-trip—hike to Alberta Falls is a pleaser. The grade isn't significant, and the view of Glacier Creek turning into Alberta Falls is gorgeous.

LONGS PEAK

Thousands of hikers climb this—the highest mountain in the park—in summer. Most traverse an 8-mile-long trail that gains almost 5,000 feet. Sixteen miles with 10,000 feet in total elevation change is a hard day for the strongest hikers, so Longs Peak should come only after you (and your kids) have proven yourselves on other all-day hikes at high altitude. About half of the trail is above tree line, so to be out of areas exposed to lightning by afternoon, you have to start before dawn. The hike begins at a tents-only campground and ranger station on Route 7 on the southeast side of the park. It ends on the granite slab of the peak, at 14,255 feet, a significant and memorable accomplishment. The tallest mountain in the Lower 48 is Mount Whitney, in the Sierra Nevada, which is only 240 feet higher.

WILD BASIN

In the extreme southeast of the park, this area is reached by a dirt road, which holds down the number of people who use the trails. High peaks surround the basin, and trails trace among them to high-elevation lakes. It's a good area for a backpacking trip, with lots of backcountry campsites. Most of the hikes are fairly challenging for families, though. The trail to Ouzel Falls, though, is only moderate in difficulty, gaining 950 feet in elevation from its start at the Wild Basin Ranger Station. However, it's a 5.4-mile round-trip, too much for most youngsters. You could turn around at Calypso Cascades, where tiny pink calypso orchids bloom in July, which makes for a 3.6-mile trek.

THE WEST SIDE & THE COLORADO RIVER

Trail Ridge Road drops down into the Kawuneechee Valley, facing the Never Summer Mountains, about 5 miles south of the valley's head. It runs due south about a dozen miles to Grand Lake. During the last ice age, a glacier made this valley, its face molding the dip where the lake settled in. The Colorado River starts at the head of the valley, building from its wetland bottoms and coursing south among the towering trees. It flows freely for about 20 miles from the Continental Divide, then leaves the national park and almost immediately gets caught by a series of dams. The Colorado is waylaid many times more before an intermittent trickle makes it to the Gulf of California.

Here in the Rockies, the river is born wild from the clouds that hit the west side of the Front Range and drop their rain and snow. This moisture affects the valley's habitat in many ways. The forest of spruce and fir is darker than the pine woods on the drier, east side of the park. The willows and other swamp-loving brush make food for moose, which don't live on the east side. The deep snow attracts skiers and provides the water that fills lakes for boaters and waters the American West. Grand Lake is a natural lake next to the park, and two man-made lakes lie just south and west. The west side attracts far fewer visitors than the east, but has many miles of backpacking trails that climb the back side of the park and the Never Summer Mountains.

PLACES FOR LEARNING
Moraine Park Museum   This museum explains the creation of the landscape. It covers geology, glaciers, thunderstorms, and other forces in a creative, engaging way that will interest visitors at every level. In one of many interactive exhibits, a glacier really moves, showing how it works. Downstairs is a good little bookstore with a kids' section and gifts.

Bear Lake Rd. No phone. Free admission. Mid-Apr to mid-Oct daily 9am–4:30pm. Closed mid-Oct to mid-Apr.

Holzwarth Historic Site (Never Summer Ranch)   A half-mile off the road, the restored buildings of an old dude ranch remain open for inspection and hold original furniture and equipment. Guides lead tours, and a brochure describes self-guided walks.

Trail Ridge Rd., just south of Timber Creek Campground. No phone. (Call the main park number for more information: ℂ 970/586-1206.) Free admission. Mid-June to late Aug daily 10am–4pm. Closed late Aug to mid-June.

8 For the Active Family
BACKPACKING
Camping out in the backcountry allows you to get away from the busy day-hiking trail heads and into your own wild area where you can be alone. You don't have to be able to hike far in—backcountry campsites are plentiful and often less than a mile apart. Beginners can reserve sites near the trail head. You'll get used to hauling all your stuff out into the woods, and learn what it's like to lie down to sleep with your family with no other human being in earshot. A piece of empty countryside is an excellent playground. If your family can hike 5 miles a day with a pack, you can experience the park's more remote trails. Strong hikers can cover the park's longest trails in a few days.

Grizzly bears are gone from the park, but you do need to prepare for black bears and smaller mammals like porcupines, which can smell food that's left out and go after it in bags and packs. Learn how to avoid attracting animals by reading "Dangerous Wildlife," in chapter 2, and from the backcountry guidance the Park Service offers. Bring plenty of rope to hang food and garbage from a high tree branch. Campfires are not allowed in most of the backcountry, and then only in metal fire grates at a few sites. Trail guides and maps are covered in "Reading Up" (p. 344). Also see "Backcountry Camping Permits" (p. 350).

CLIMBING

These high granite peaks challenge with some famous climbs. Beginners and families can get started in the sport easily at the park, where at least two reputable schools cater to family travelers who want to climb. **Estes Park Mountain Shop,** 2050 Big Thompson Ave., Estes Park (© **866/303-6548** or 970/586-6548), offers lessons and indoor and outdoor climbing, even for children. The park concessionaire for guided climbing and instruction is Total Climbing, which is a partnership of three entities including the famous **Colorado Mountain School, the Boulder Rock Club,** and **ABC for Kidz,** which specializes in teaching youngsters how to climb (341 Moraine Ave., Estes Park, CO 80517; © **800/836-4008;** www.totalclimbing.com).

FISHING

Trout fishing is allowed with a Colorado fishing license in some of the park's lakes and streams. High-altitude lakes often can't support fish, and the Park Service no longer allows stocking of nonnative species. Lists of places where fish may be found are available with regulations from the Park Service. The rules differ from state regulations, so read them carefully. The many places to fish outside the park include Estes Lake and Grand Lake.

Scot's Sporting Goods, on Moraine Avenue (Hwy. 36) in Estes Park (© **970/586-2877;** www.scotssportinggoods.com), is run by a friendly couple that loves fly-fishing and offers lessons and guided trips. They also sell and rent fishing packages and other gear. A fishing license costs $9 for a day, $26 for 5 days; children under 16 don't need one.

Kids may also enjoy fishing in a commercial fishing pond on Moraine Avenue in Estes Park, where there's no chance of not catching a fish. **Trout Haven** (© **970/586-5525;** http://trouthaven.net) fills a little pond with rainbow trout, gives you the gear, helps you use it, and even cooks the fish for lunch, if you like. It charges 85¢ per inch of fish you catch.

HIKING

Rocky Mountain National Park is one of the nation's greatest places for day hiking. On any summer day, you can hike in mountain meadows, in marshy river bottoms, in forests of pine or fir, around alpine lakes, or above tree line among the rocks and tundra at the top of the Rockies. There are hikes for every level of age and fitness. The Park Service has built flat, paved nature trails around three lakes (Bear, Sprague, and Lily) that are accessible from the road. Most families will be able to handle the somewhat more challenging trails that loop in ever-greater distances from Bear Lake and Moraine Park, or short doubling-back nature walks and trail segments in every one of the park's ecosystems. When you work up to a tougher hike, there are plenty of those, too. They include the unique opportunity to walk self-directed across the alpine tundra, or to climb a high-altitude peak without special equipment or training.

I've covered specific trails above under "Natural Places" (p. 355). The park has many more than I can mention, and often the most important thing is to find a trail that isn't too crowded. One way to do this is to start from one of the main trail head areas and choose a route after you get the lay of the land, simply hiking as far as you wish and turning back. This is a reasonable approach for **Bear Lake Road, Moraine** or **Horseshoe Park, Wild Basin,** and the **Kawuneeche Valley.** Along **Trail Ridge Road** you can find open tundra to break out on your own; just be sure not to trample the tundra near the road.

You can find many other great hikes in the guides mentioned under "Reading Up" (p. 344). Without buying a book or map, you can get help choosing a trail from a list printed in the park newspaper. With the free park map to find the trail head, that list or the park's other hiking handouts are all you need for most hikes. Of course, another option is to join one of the ranger-led jaunts, which are listed in the park newspaper.

HORSEBACK RIDING

Unlike the standard 1-hour circles at many national parks, the trail-ride concession-aire at Rocky offers rides as long as all day, going a considerable distance within the park. You also can book pack trips. **Moraine Park Stables** offers rides from Moraine Park (℅ **970/586-2327;** www.sombrero.com) and at Glacier Creek (℅ **970/586-3244**), near Glacier Basin Campground on Bear Lake Road. Reservations are recommended. Rides leave beginning at 8am and at various times during the day, and last from 2 to 10 hours. A 2-hour ride costs $45, 3-hour ride $55, 4-hour ride $65, 5-hour ride $75, and all day is $100. There's even a 10-hour "Continental Divide Ride" that goes from Estes Park to Grand Lake for $170. Children as young as 6 can ride their own horse, and younger children can ride with a parent.

MOUNTAIN BIKING

Roads in the park are open to mountain biking, and on the national forest lands out-side the park you can ride on trails. **Colorado Bicycling Adventures,** 184 E. Elkhorn Ave., Estes Park (℅ **970/586-4241;** www.coloradobicycling.com), rents bikes and offers guided mountain-biking rides. It's the only agency permitted to do so in the park and in Roosevelt National Forest. A couple of these trips coast downhill much of the way from above tree-line down into forests and are geared to families. They cost about $72 per rider, 10 and above. The company will also give you a map and advice on where to ride if you rent.

WILDLIFE-WATCHING

You'll likely see animals if you spend much time hiking in the park. You can wildlife-watch from the car, too. If you do, stay in the car, because moving or approaching the animals will frighten them, ruin the viewing for everyone, and possibly endanger your family. Bring binoculars or a long camera lens.

The best places are open meadows and alpine areas where you can see a long way. In the spring and early summer, bighorn sheep go to **Horseshoe Park** to lick minerals that they can get from certain spots (the Park Service sometimes posts a crossing guard for them). Later, they spend time on **Specimen Mountain,** reachable on the **Crater Trail,** which starts at the Milner Pass pullout. (Before heading out, ask a ranger if the trail is open—it closes during the spring and early summer lambing season.) Moose like the swamps and ponds of the **Kawuneeche Valley,** on the west side. Elk and mule deer show up commonly in the meadows in places like **Moraine Park** in the fall, and you can pick out elk on the tundra on drives on **Trail Ridge Road.** In the fall, elk congregate for mating in the eastern parks, and even in the town of Estes Park. They are most active early and late in the day. Ask a ranger about the best places to go dur-ing the season you visit. For kids, it may be more fun to concentrate on the animals you can easily find in your campground and on your hikes. They can figure out what the animals are and watch their behavior, rather than spending a lot of time trying to see a specific species of big game.

Tips Places for Relaxed Play & Picnics

The meadows and tundra-covered mountainsides of Rocky Mountain National Park are wonderful playgrounds where kids can romp and experience a special freedom. A playground with equipment is near the visitor center in Estes Park, and there's a lot more to do at Estes Lake, described below in "Entertainment Outside the Park." Numerous picnic areas are marked on the park map.

WINTER SPORTS

On the east side of the park, where snow is scarce, people mostly use snowshoes for spring hiking to see wildlife and to explore higher-elevation trails while the snow lingers. There are no groomed ski trails, but you can rent backcountry skis and snowshoes and get advice at **Estes Park Mountain Shop,** 2050 Big Thompson Ave., Estes Park (© **866/303-6548** or 970/586-6548).

The west side of the park gets good, deep snow from late December through February. Here you can explore the spectacular hiking trails in white on cross-country skis and snowshoes. Rangers lead outings from the **Kawuneeche Visitor Center** (p. 342). Snowshoes and cross-country skis are available for rent in Grand Lake at **Never Summer Mountain Products,** 919 Grand Ave. (© **970/627-3642**), open daily 9am to 5pm. Rental cost is $12 to $20 for a 24-hour period for cross-country skis and snowshoes. Snowmobiling is not allowed within the park except for a short section of a trail from Grand Lake into Arapaho National Forest that skirts the boundary. Snowmobiling is popular in Grand Lake; contact the Grand Lake Area Chamber of Commerce (see "Rocky Mountain Address Book," p. 340).

9 Kid-Friendly Programs

CHILDREN'S PROGRAMS

The **Junior Ranger** program is one of the best in the park system. The kid-size 26-page Junior Ranger Log Book is free at the visitor centers. After finishing it, attending a ranger program, talking to people, handing out stickers about not feeding animals, and collecting 10 pieces of trash, children get a plastic badge that looks like the ones real rangers wear. Rangers make a big deal with the award, announcing it over the public-address system. The material is fun and well thought out and doesn't require parents to drive all over the park, as some programs do. There's even a field guide where kids can check off plants, animals, and birds they see. Children 6 to 11 or so should enjoy the activities; younger kids will need help reading the booklet.

The weekly schedule of ranger programs published in the park newspaper usually includes activities specifically for children ages 6 to 12 during the summer. Rangers teach about insects, birds, fire, and other natural-history topics with stories, puppets, games, and the like. Generally, parents have to chaperone their kids.

The **Rocky Mountain Nature Association** (© **970/586-3262;** www.rmna.org) offers more in-depth programs for children as young as 6 or as old as 16. Most are half-day outings and cost only $20. They do require prior reservations. Participants do arts and crafts or learn about nature or Native American ways. A few more demanding programs, for adults, last all day and do need advance registration. Get information and even sign up online on the website (www.rmna.org); other contact information is under "Rocky Mountain Address Book" (p. 340).

FAMILY & ADULT PROGRAMS

During the summer, the park offers a long list of ranger programs daily on a range of nature, history, and outdoor topics, including many guided hikes. Evening programs take place at the Beaver Meadows Visitor Center and all the campgrounds except Longs Peak. A schedule appears in the park newspaper.

In addition to its children's programs, mentioned in the previous section, the **Rocky Mountain Nature Association** offers an extensive program of seminars and outings aimed primarily at adults but also accessible, in some cases, to teens and families. They cover natural history, art, outdoor skills, and other topics, and last from a half-day to a week. On summer weekends, there are many choices, and even a few in later fall and early spring. Check the catalog and register online at www.rmna.org, or use the contact information in "Rocky Mountain Address Book" (p. 340).

SUMMER CAMPS

The **YMCA of the Rockies** owns a large conference center and family resort on the east side of the park. It offers a day camp for children from potty-trained 3-year-olds through high school, with an amazing variety of outdoor activities. One-day sessions, which might involve rock climbing or rafting, range from $24 to $55 depending on age and activity. Call ahead, because the sessions (especially overnights) book up. Check lodging availability online at www.ymcarockies.org, or contact **Estes Park Center,** YMCA of the Rockies, Estes Park, CO 80511-2550 (© **800/777-9622**).

10 Entertainment outside the Park

ESTES PARK

The town of Estes Park was born to serve tourists, and it takes that job seriously. **Elkhorn Avenue,** also known as U.S. Highway 34 Business, is home to a cute pedestrian-oriented row of businesses, just scruffy enough to avoid seeming like plastic tourist stuff. Besides the restaurants and shops, it has little museums, arcades, and other attractions that amuse children. Beyond this core, the town consists mostly of car-oriented strip development, where you'll find plenty of kid activities: minigolf and go-carts, the fishing pond described under "Fishing" (p. 359), and so on. They're empty calories compared to the national park, but you can't eat granola for every meal. The **Estes Park Ride-A-Kart Family Amusement Park and Cascade Creek Mini-Golf,** at U.S. 34 just west of Mall Road as you enter town (© **970/586-6495;** www.rideakart.com), is the ultimate in this kind of thing. It has bumper boats, a tiny train, 36 holes of minigolf, and more.

You can rent canoes, paddleboats, and fishing boats on Estes Lake from a little marina operated by the **Estes Valley Recreation and Park District** (© **970/586-2011;** www.estesvalleyrecreation.com). It also rents bikes and has a wading area, picnic area, and kids' play area. A **public swimming pool** is south of the lake at Brodie Avenue and Community Drive.

GRAND LAKE

People visit Grand Lake and the reservoirs nearby for boating, fishing, and recreation around the lakes. Boats are for rent in town, and there's a lake beach along the town, although the water is quite cold.

FAST FACTS: Rocky Mountain National Park

Area Code The area code is **970**.

ATMs There are ATMs all around Estes Park.

Emergencies For emergencies, dial 🕾 **911** or call 🕾 **970/586-1399** to reach the Park Service.

Hospitals & Clinics The **Estes Park Medical Center** is at 555 Prospect Ave. (🕾 **970/586-2200**).

Information For information, write Rocky Mountain National Park, 1000 Hwy. 36, Estes Park, CO 80517-8397; call 🕾 **970/586-1206**; or check the website www.nps.gov/romo.

Pharmacies The **Rocky Mountain Pharmacy of Estes Park** is at 453 E. Wonderview Ave. (🕾 **970/586-1930**).

Post Office A post office is at 215 W. Riverside Dr. in Estes Park.

Time Zone The park is on **Mountain Standard Time.**

Transit Info You can board both the Park Service shuttle system that serves the Bear Lake and Moraine Park areas and the Estes Park shuttle system at the Estes Park Convention and Visitors Bureau at 500 Big Thompson Avenue.

Weather Updates For weather updates, look on the Internet at http://weather. noaa.gov.

14

Yosemite National Park

You can't avoid being impressed by Yosemite Valley. On the valley floor, you might get caught up in the everyday world of buses and campgrounds, but then a patch of light will catch your eye, way up at the top of your field of vision where all you expect to see is blue sky. And it will suddenly impress you again: That's solid rock up there, catching the light straight above you. Just to see the granite cliffs, you have to tip your head back, so the wonder of it keeps surprising you whenever your attention settles back to the earth. This is one of the world's unique places, where you can stand at the foot of a waterfall that's nearly a half-mile high. Unfortunately, being unique, it's also terribly popular and fills with people in the summer. Sometimes seeing the cliffs up above is a special relief because it takes your eyes away from the uncomfortable crowd you're standing in.

What most people haven't discovered, or don't care to know, is that Yosemite Valley is only a very small part of Yosemite National Park. If you dislike crowds, as we do, spend just a day in the valley to see the sights, then head out to the other 1,169 square miles of the park. In the Wawona area, the Hetch Hetchy valley, or the high country of the Tuolumne Meadows, you can hike all day and see only a few other people. One memorable day we hiked a couple of miles to a mountain lake and found we had it to ourselves, surrounded by rock and water and sky. These were some of the most beautiful and spiritually refreshing places I'd ever visited. I had the feeling we'd left the city behind in Yosemite Valley, and now we were visiting the real national park. No one should miss Yosemite Valley, but the park is big enough to do much more, and to do it without being in a crowd.

BEST THINGS TO DO IN YOSEMITE NATIONAL PARK
- **Hike over the bedrock high country** to see unbelievable scenery.
- **Play in the streams** of Yosemite Valley or Wawona.
- **See the high waterfalls and cliffs** of Yosemite Valley and the giant Sequoias of the Merced Grove.
- **Backpack** in the cool, spectacular mountains.
- **Try cross-country skiing or snowshoeing** in the winter.

For more information, see "For the Active Family" (p. 398).

1 History: Fight for the Valley

The southern Miwok Indians called Yosemite Valley *Awahni*, which means "big mouth" in their language. The band that lived there in the summers was the *Awahnichi*, or "people of Awahni." In the winter some moved down the Merced River into the warmer foothills. They ate mainly acorns from the black oak, which they made into mush and bread, as well as deer, trout, mushrooms, and other wild foods. The

Yosemite Address Book

Park & Forest Information

Yosemite National Park   P.O. Box 577, Yosemite, CA 95389. ℭ **209/372-0200.** TDD 209/372-4726. www.nps.gov/yose.

The Yosemite Association   P.O. Box 230, El Portal, CA 95318. ℭ **209/379-2646.** Fax 209/379-2486. www.yosemite.org. For books, maps, and educational programs.

Delaware North Companies Parks & Resorts at Yosemite   6771 N. Palm Ave., Fresno, CA 93704. Lodging and general information: ℭ **559/253-5635.** Fax 559/456-0542. Tour desk: ℭ **209/372-1240.** www.yosemitepark.com.

Stanislaus National Forest   19777 Greenley Rd., Sonora, CA 95370. ℭ **209/532-3671.** www.fs.fed.us/r5/stanislaus.

Sierra National Forest   1600 Tollhouse Rd., Clovis, CA 93611-0532. ℭ **559/297-0706.** www.fs.fed.us/r5/sierra.

Inyo National Forest   Mono Basin Scenic Area. P.O. Box 429, Lee Vining, CA 93541. ℭ **760/647-3044.** www.fs.fed.us/r5/inyo.

Regional Traveler Information

Mariposa County Visitors Bureau   5158 Hwy. 140 (P.O. Box 967), Mariposa, CA 95338. ℭ **866/425-3366** (for recorded messages) or 209/966-7081. www.homeofyosemite.com.

Yosemite Sierra Visitors Bureau   41969 Hwy. 41, Oakhurst, CA 93644. ℭ **559/683-4636.** www.yosemitethisyear.com.

Tuolumne County Visitors Bureau   P.O. Box 4020, Sonora, CA 95370. ℭ **800/446-1333** or 209/533-4420. www.thegreatunfenced.com.

Spanish met the native people of the Sierra in the 1780s, and within a few decades many members of the Southern Miwok and other mountain tribes were dead from diseases brought by the newcomers. They lacked natural resistance. The surviving Awahnichi left Awahni and lived with other tribes. Years later, Tenaya, the son of an Awahnichi chief and a Mono woman, gathered some of the former Awahnichi and members of other tribes and returned to the valley.

Tenaya had the misfortune of leading his people when their tribe was defeated and broken up. Soon after the great gold rush of 1849, whites began taking over the area, killing natives and grazing cattle on their mountain land. The cattle ate the precious acorns. The Awahnichi reacted to the threat to their traditional food source by hunting the livestock and raiding the whites' stores, killing some ranchers and storekeepers. Whites in the area formed an army, the Mariposa battalion, to force the Indians out of Awahni, which they called Yosemite Valley, in 1851. They moved Tenaya and his people to a reservation near Fresno, but the Awahnichi kept returning to their valley. In 1852, they killed two gold prospectors who came into the valley, and the U.S. Army killed five Indians in return. Tenaya led his people out of Awahni for the last time, to live near Mono Lake, but the next year he was killed in an argument, and his band broke up.

The Southern Miwok and other tribes of the Sierra had to take on white ways to survive. They worked for ranchers, danced and made baskets for tourists, ate new foods, and lived in new houses. When John Muir arrived he wrote that the Indians were dirty people; in fact, the opposite was true. They bathed often, more than the white settlers who forced them from their land. But they wore dirt on their faces when they were in mourning, and they had a lot to mourn when Muir met them.

Some of the soldiers who invaded Yosemite Valley in 1851 recognized it as a special place. They were probably even more impressed by the cliffs and waterfalls than we are when we first visit, because they didn't know what to expect. The Native Americans had cleverly spread the word that their valley was a horrible place, so whites hadn't bothered to go there. After the Awahnichi were forced out, several artists and photographers came to Yosemite. Their works spread all over the United States, and Yosemite became famous for its beauty. John Muir was recovering from an injury in 1867 when he saw a folder of pictures of Yosemite and decided he would go there. Other visitors came, too, and hotels were built in the valley and on the horse and stagecoach trails along the way, including one at the historic site at Wawona. In 1864, the Congress and President Abraham Lincoln gave Yosemite Valley and the Mariposa Grove of Sequoias to the state of California, with the promise that it would be used only for the enjoyment of the public. It was the first time in the United States that nature was preserved.

But the original state park was badly run and too small. The forests and meadows around Yosemite Valley continued to be damaged by logging and too much livestock grazing, and the valley was turned over to tourism businesses that commercialized it and plowed up the wildflowers for crops and grazing. John Muir and other conservationists wanted a park that would include areas around Yosemite Valley as well. In 1889, Muir met the editor of an important national magazine, the *Century,* and showed him his concerns about the damage to the high country in Tuolumne Meadows. The editor published an article Muir wrote calling for a national park to protect the area around Yosemite Valley. In 1890, Congress quickly passed a law setting aside the park, before the sheep and lumber businesses had a chance to react and fight it. In 1906, Yosemite Valley and other areas the state owned were added to the national park.

The history of the park since then has been about the changing goals of the people running it. First there was an effort to get parkland under control, getting rid of the herds of sheep in the backcountry and stopping logging companies that still owned timber within the park boundaries. John D. Rockefeller, Jr., the wealthy giver to many national parks, contributed half of the funds to buy the trees back from the loggers before they were cut down. Next, the park had to find a way to deal with ever more visitors coming to see Yosemite. People have complained about crowding in Yosemite Valley since John Muir's day. At first the Park Service tried to solve the problem by building more roads, hotels, campgrounds, trails, and visitor centers to accommodate more people. As the number of visitors kept growing, however, it became clear that more facilities didn't solve the problem. No one could enjoy nature in such a crowd. At times Yosemite Valley became a busy and dangerous city.

Finally, the Park Service recognized that saving Yosemite meant protecting it from visitors, too. In 1997, a huge flood on the Merced River swept through Yosemite Valley, washing away some campgrounds and hotel buildings. It was an opportunity to begin restoring the valley to a condition closer to the way nature made it. After 3 years of planning and discussion, the Park Service decided not to rebuild the washed-out

National Parks of the Sierra Nevada & the West Coast

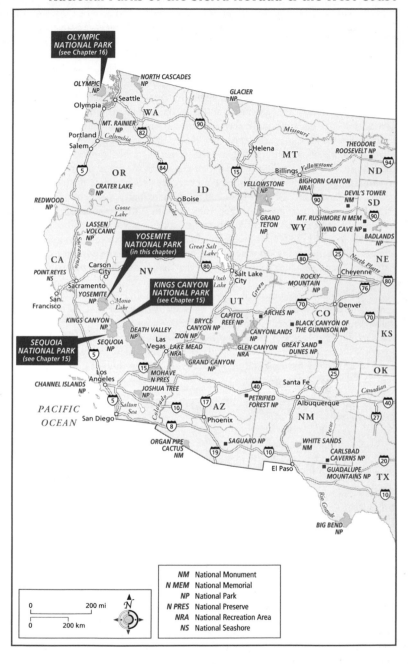

OLYMPIC
NATIONAL PARK
(see Chapter 16)

NORTH CASCADES
NP

OLYMPIC
NP
Olympia   Seattle

GLACIER
NP

WA

MT. RAINIER
NP

Portland   Columbia

Salem

Helena   MT

THEODORE
ROOSEVELT NP

5   84

Billings   Yellowstone   ND
94

CRATER LAKE
NP

ID   YELLOWSTONE
NP   BIGHORN CANYON
NRA

15   Boise   DEVIL'S TOWER
NM   SD
90

REDWOOD
NP   Goose
Lake   Snake

GRAND
TETON
NP   MT. RUSHMORE N MEM   90

LASSEN
VOLCANIC
NP   Sacramento   WIND CAVE NP

YOSEMITE
NATIONAL PARK
(in this chapter)   Great Salt
Lake   WY   BADLANDS
NP

CA   Carson
City   80   NE

POINT REYES
NS   NV   Salt Lake
City   Cheyenne
80

KINGS CANYON
NATIONAL PARK
(see Chapter 15)   Utah
Lake   ROCKY
MOUNTAIN
NP   76

Sacramento   YOSEMITE   Mono   UT   Green   Denver
San   NP   Lake   70
Francisco

KINGS CANYON
NP   BRYCE
CANYON NP   CAPITOL
REEF NP   ARCHES NP   CO   70

DEATH VALLEY
NP   ZION NP   BLACK CANYON OF
THE GUNNISON NP   KS

SEQUOIA
NATIONAL PARK
(see Chapter 15)   SEQUOIA
NP   Las
Vegas   LAKE MEAD
NRA   CANYONLANDS
NP   GREAT SAND
DUNES NP

5   GLEN CANYON
NRA

Los   15   GRAND CANYON
Angeles   MOHAVE   NP   OK
N PRES

CHANNEL ISLANDS
NP   JOSHUA TREE
NP   40   Santa Fe   Canadian

PACIFIC   5   Salton   AZ   PETRIFIED
Sea   17   FOREST NP   Albuquerque   40
OCEAN   San Diego   10

8   Phoenix   NM   27

ORGAN PIPE
CACTUS
NM   SAGUARO NP   WHITE SANDS
NM   CARLSBAD
CAVERNS NP   20
19   10

El Paso   GUADALUPE
MOUNTAINS NP   TX

10

BIG BEND
NP

NM	National Monument
N MEM	National Memorial
NP	National Park
N PRES	National Preserve
NRA	National Recreation Area
NS	National Seashore

0   200 mi
0   200 km

N

campgrounds and to rebuild hotel rooms in ways that would do a better job of fitting into the area. The biggest changes in this plan were along the river, where a bridge, camping, and hotel rooms would be removed and the land returned to its natural state. Trails, parking lots, and roads would be moved along with lots of other changes.

But at this writing, not much of the work had happened as litigation had effectively stopped the projects. The problem stems from the different visions of how the Yosemite Valley should be managed. Environmental and conservation groups that brought the lawsuits that halted the "Yosemite Valley Plan" from taking root are concerned that the valley is simply overrun with visitors and the Park Service needs to limit visitation. Park managers, however, believe they can adequately control visitation's impacts by how visitors are managed in the valley. Yet some lovers of the park thought the Park Service didn't go nearly far enough in the original version of the plan to save the valley from overcrowding. For example, while the new plan would reduce lodgings and campsites by more than 200 units, more than 1,400 units would remain. And the dream of getting rid of cars from the valley, written into the park plan in 1980, was forgotten. But the park is battling congestion with shuttle buses that have somewhat lessened the need for visitors to hop into their cars to get about, and it continues to work on a transportation management plan. How the current round of litigation ends, and what the results mean for the Yosemite Valley, remains to be seen.

My own feeling is that the valley simply is too small for all the people who want to see it. While removing some buildings and roads would help, the wilderness feeling I most value from the national parks can't be brought back that way. Yosemite Valley is still worth seeing as a great monument to nature's strength, but a visit also is a constant reminder of how people are changing the world with our growing numbers and wealth. Like a rising tide, we're filling places like this. Unless we start holding people out, the only hope for a natural experience is to climb to higher ground the crowds haven't found yet.

2 Orientation

Yosemite National Park is an oval roughly 45 miles long and 30 miles wide. The long part lies north-south, the direction of the 400-mile-long Sierra Nevada range. The mountains rise gradually on the wooded western side to over 13,000 feet before dropping abruptly to the desert on the east. Here are the main areas.

ARRIVING
BY CAR
From the west, the drive from the San Francisco Bay area is 5 hours on interstates 580 and 205 and Route 120. Beware of a sign that tries to send you through Modesto; instead, take I-205 toward Stockton and exit onto I-5 north, traveling north on I-5 for just 1 mile before exiting onto 120, which goes east all the way to the park.

From the south, take Highway 99, exiting either in Fresno to take Route 41 to the southern, Wawona entrance, or in Merced to take 140 to the Arch Rock entrance, near Yosemite Valley. It's about 7 hours from Los Angeles.

From the east, the most direct route to the park, open only in the summer and fall, is Tioga Road, Route 120. It connects to north-south U.S. 395 near Lee Vining, which eventually connects to the major east-west routes.

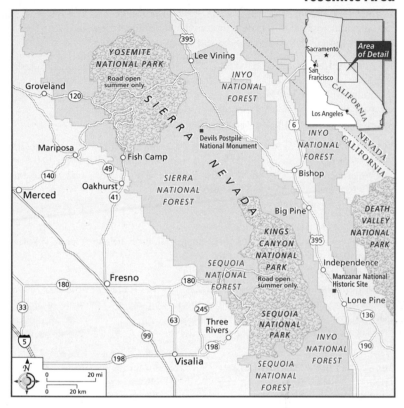

BY AIR

The closest city with a significant airport is **Fresno-Yosemite International** (www.fly fresno.org), 60 miles south of the park's south (Wawona) entrance. Fresno's airport is served by seven major and commuter carriers, including **United** (© 800/241-6522; www.united.com), **Delta** (© 800/221-1212; www.delta.com), and **Northwest** (© 800/ 225-2525; www.nwa.com). Most major car-rental agencies are represented there, including **Budget** (© 800/527-0700 or 559/253-4100; www.budget.com), **Avis** (© 800/331-1212 or 559/251-5001; www.avis.com), and **Hertz** (© 800/654-3131 or 559/251-5055).

To shop around for prices or spend time in a more interesting gateway, try the **San Francisco, San Jose,** or **Oakland** airports and visit the Bay Area before Yosemite.

VISITOR INFORMATION

NATIONAL PARK VISITOR CENTERS

Hours at the visitor centers change with annual budgets, and what I've listed may change. Read "Places for Learning" (p. 397) for information on the park's museums.

Big Oak Flat   Stop here, near the northern end of the park roads, for questions, maps, and backcountry permits.

At the park entrance on Hwy. 120. © **209/375-1899**. Apr to mid-Oct daily 8am–5pm. Closed mid-Oct to Mar.

Tuolumne Visitor Center   This visitor center has a modest set of displays on park history and nature, an information desk, and a bookstore.

East end of Tioga Rd. © 209/372-0263. June–Sept daily 9am–6pm. Closed Oct–May.

Wawona Information Station at Hill's Studio   The studio of 19th-century landscape painter Thomas Hill, off the Wawona Hotel parking lot, is a place to inquire about the shuttle to the Mariposa Grove, which leaves from near here, as well as pick up maps and get backcountry permits.

Wawona Hotel. © 209/375-9531. May–Sept daily 8:30am–5pm. Closed Oct–Apr.

Yosemite Valley Visitor Center   The park's main visitor center has a slide show, a busy information desk, a bookstore, and a room of exhibits. The Wilderness Center just down the street handles backcountry permits and might be a quieter place during the day to ask about hiking and the outdoors.

Yosemite Village. © 209/372-0200. Summer daily 9am–7pm; spring, fall, and winter daily 9am–5pm.

OTHER VISITOR CENTERS

Contact information for each of these organizations is below or under "Yosemite Address Book" (p. 365).

From the North or West, Highway 120

Groveland Ranger District   This office is on the route from the west, about 8 miles east of Groveland. It has information on camping and recreation in Stanislaus National Forest.

24525 Old Hwy. 120, Groveland. © 209/962-7825. Summer Mon–Fri 8am–4:30pm, Sat 8am–3:30pm; off season Mon–Fri 8am–4:30pm.

Tuolumne County Visitors Bureau   This route to the park is largely undeveloped. Sonora lies about 10 miles north of Route 120 on Route 49. The center offers hotel referrals and other advice.

542 W. Stockton Rd., Sonora. © 800/446-1333 or 209/533-4420. Summer daily 9am–7pm; mid-Oct to mid-May 9am–6pm.

From the West, Highway 140

Mariposa County Visitors Bureau   Mariposa is the last decent-size town on the route to the Arch Rock entrance. The staff will help you find lodgings that meet your specifications.

5158 Hwy. 140, Mariposa. © 866/425-3366. Summer Mon–Sat 7am–8pm, Sun 8am–5pm; mid-Oct to mid-May Mon–Sat 8am–5pm.

From the South, Highway 41

Yosemite Sierra Visitors Bureau   This nonprofit bureau is the last information stop outside the Wawona entrance. It offers hotel referrals.

41969 Hwy. 41, Oakhurst. © 559/683-4636. Mon–Sat 8:30am–5pm; Sun 9am–1pm.

From the East, Highways 395 & 120

Mono Basin National Forest Scenic Area Visitor Center   Plan to spend an hour at this center if you're in the neighborhood. It contains a fascinating museum on the weird desert lake, which has no natural outlet except evaporation, and its interesting ecology, geology, and human history. A desk and bookstore provide information on the surrounding campgrounds and wilderness.

Hwy. 395 just north of Lee Vining. © 760/647-3044. Daily 9am–4:30pm.

Mono Lake Committee Information Center   The committee is a unique organization. It helped save Mono Lake, which was shrinking, and continues to teach and advocate for it, but also offers visitor information, a bookstore, public Web access, and an interesting shop.

Hwy. 395, Lee Vining. (✆ **760/647-6595**. Mid-June to Labor Day daily 8am–9pm; spring and fall daily 9am–5pm.

READING UP

The **Yosemite Association** ((✆ **209/379-2648;** www.yosemite.org) carries a large selection of books and maps you can order online, by phone, or at visitor centers, including these.

Trail Guides and Maps: Day hikers need no more than the map and guide publications sold for $2.50 by the Yosemite Association. They're available for Yosemite Valley, Tuolumne Meadows and the Wawona areas, and their environs. Backpackers and hikers who want to know more and use more obscure trails should buy Jeffrey P. Schaffer's encyclopedic *Yosemite National Park: A Complete Hiker's Guide to Yosemite and Its Trails* (Wilderness Press, $20), which covers every route in detail and includes a plastic topographic map.

THE NATIONAL PARK IN BRIEF

Yosemite Valley

The center of activities and services is Yosemite Valley, a 3,000-foot-deep crack in the side of the Sierra in the southwest part of the park. This is the place with the high waterfalls that most people think of when they hear the word *Yosemite*—that's why it's crowded. Besides hiking, biking, rafting, and swimming, there are museums, shops, large hotels, and the tourist facilities of Yosemite Village and Curry Village.

The High Country

At Yosemite, outside of winter, you can drive to wonderful hiking trails and views of amazing bare granite peaks and canyons high on the back of the Sierra. On the east side of the park, on Tioga Road, **Tuolumne Meadows** is the park's developed visitor destination in the high country. On the west side, the road to **Glacier Point,** above Yosemite Valley, leads to trails and a high-country campground as well.

The West Side

Wawona, at the southern tip of the park near the Mariposa Grove of Sequoias, is a historic visitor area, with hotels and services. North from Yosemite Valley, forest campgrounds and trails are scattered throughout the west side of the park. At the north the primitive **Hetch Hetchy** area is beautiful and little used.

The Gateway Towns

There are no sizable towns near the park. Small gateway communities are at **El Portal,** beyond the Arch Rock entrance, close to Yosemite Valley; at **Fish Camp,** outside the Wawona entrance at the south end of the park; and at **Lee Vining,** on the east side near the Tioga Pass entrance. Farther afield, **Mariposa** is beyond El Portal, **Oakhurst** is beyond Fish Camp, and **Sonora** is beyond the north entrance.

3 Getting Around

IN YOSEMITE VALLEY
BY CAR OR RV

The park's roads have various names and segments, but the pattern is simple. A twisting north-south road, which has different names in different sections, runs along the western edge. It connects three entrances from Wawona, past Yosemite Valley and the entrance there (a section called Wawona Rd.), north to the Big Oak Flat entrance (Big Oak Flat Rd.), where Evergreen Road and then narrow Hetch Hetchy Road run farther north to the reservoir. The Glacier Point Road leads into the high country above Yosemite Valley from the Wawona Road.

The 39-mile **Tioga Road** (Hwy. 120) runs east-west across the park north of Yosemite Valley, from Crane Flat, on the western end, to the eastern park entrance, then down the steep mountainside to Lee Vining and the Mono Lake area. Open only in the summer and fall, the eastern half through the park's bare granite high country is one of the world's most spectacular drives.

Avoid driving in the Valley, because it's aggravating and too many cars degrade the experience for everyone. As you drive into the valley, stop at the pullouts for meadow walks and to see Bridalveil Falls; then park at the day-use parking area near Yosemite Village (arrive early to find a space), or park at your hotel or campsite and go from there by shuttle bus, foot, or bike.

BY BUS

The free **shuttle bus** comes every 10 minutes during peak times and every 20 minutes in the spring and fall. The system is simple and much easier than driving. The bus stops are numbered; buses run in a loop from lower to higher numbers. Maps are posted everywhere and are given away free in the *Yosemite Today* park newspaper when you enter the park. Windows are removed in summer, and the ride can be a fun time to meet other families. There's also a shuttle to the El Capitan picnic area that runs from the valley visitor center from mid-June through Labor Day on the hour and half-hour. The park also has experimented with a shuttle from Yosemite Valley to Wawona; check the park newspaper to see if it's still running.

Two-hour narrated **tours** of Yosemite Valley in open-topped vehicles leave every half-hour from Yosemite Village and the hotels. They cost $22 for adults, $12 for children 5 to 12.

Buses for tours or to shuttle hikers to Glacier Point and elsewhere are covered under "Outside the Valley," below.

BY BIKE

If your group is fit, the best transportation option in the valley is bicycles. Twelve miles of paved bike trails, separate from traffic, weave through the upper valley, and there are bike racks anywhere you might want to stop. Bring your own if you can. If not, bikes are for rent at **Yosemite Lodge** (© 209/372-1208) and **Curry Village** (© 209/372-8319). Rates are $7.50 an hour or $25 a day for one-speeds with pedal brakes; children's sizes cost the same. Six-speeds with trailers go for $14 an hour or $42 a day, and jogging strollers cost $7.50 an hour or $11 a day. Hours vary by the season and are as long as 8:30am to 7:30pm in the high season and as short as 10am to 4:30pm in the winter. Biking on hiking trails is forbidden. Mountain biking, and any family biking outside the valley, isn't a good option at the park.

OUTSIDE THE VALLEY

BY CAR

The practical way for families to get to and around most of the park is in a car. Allow at least double the time you normally would, not including stops. Even without traffic, you can't travel fast on these winding mountain roads, and there usually is lots of slow traffic. Also, be prepared for carsick kids, if that's a concern in your family, especially when driving north and south along the west side of the park.

In the winter you must carry chains, which can be required in slick conditions. For current road conditions, call © **209/372-0200.**

BY BUS

A **free shuttle bus** runs up and down Tioga Road in the summer, connecting Olmsted Point (west of Tenaya Lake) to Tuolumne Meadow and the points between. This is handy for hiking, because it allows you to hike between different trail heads and get a lift back to your car or the campground. Between 7am and 7pm the bus runs roughly every half-hour in the high season; check *Yosemite Today* or ask a ranger for current operating times. The shuttle from Wawona to Mariposa Grove is explained under "Sequoia Groves" (p. 395).

Paid shuttles and tours also serve much of the park. All are operated by the concessionaire, Delaware North, and can be reserved at hotel activity desks or by calling ahead (see "Yosemite Address Book," p. 365). Some buses offer one-way tickets so hikers can plan one-way day hikes or backpacking into or out of Yosemite Valley. The **Glacier Point Tour** travels 3,214 feet upward (see "Glacier Point," p. 395) to the fantastic views into the valley. You can hike 4.8 steep but glorious miles back down, or ride back on the bus if your knees won't take it. The bus runs three times a day from Yosemite Lodge at the Falls. Round-trip tour tickets cost $33 for adults, $26 children; one-way $20 and $12. To hike one-way between Tioga Road and Yosemite Valley, or for other hikes with starting and ending points along the road, the **Tuolumne Shuttle & Hiker's Bus** runs daily in July and August, leaving Curry Village at 8am for an 8-hour round-trip to Tuolumne Meadows. Get the timetable and fare schedule to plan your stops; the reasonable prices depend on how far you ride (go to www.yosemite park.com, click "Activities" and then "Guided Bus Tours"). The round-trip fare is $23 for adults, $12 for children. Reserve a day ahead. Finally, the **Grand Tour** goes from the valley to Glacier Point and Mariposa Grove, taking all day; it's way too much for most kids. It costs $62 adults ($70 with lunch), $33 ($41) children.

4 Planning Your Outings

WHEN TO GO

The 3 months of summer vacation from school are the busiest at Yosemite; but it gets busy in May, and crowds at popular spots can last well into September. The dry summer weather pattern brings clear skies and little rain, except occasional afternoon thunderstorms. In the foothills and lower on the mountains, including Yosemite Valley (4,000 ft.), it can be quite warm in midsummer (see the weather chart below). Temperatures are 10° to 15° cooler in Tuolumne Meadows, perfect weather for hiking. The high country is snowbound through May, and Tioga Road opens only around the end of the month or in early June, with dry hiking postponed until July. Avoid summer weekends if you can, especially around holidays. But expect crowds in Yosemite Valley at any time during the summer, and make your reservations way ahead.

Yosemite National Park

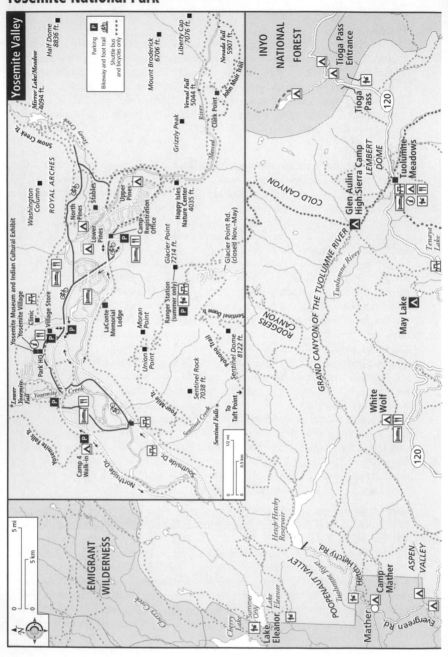

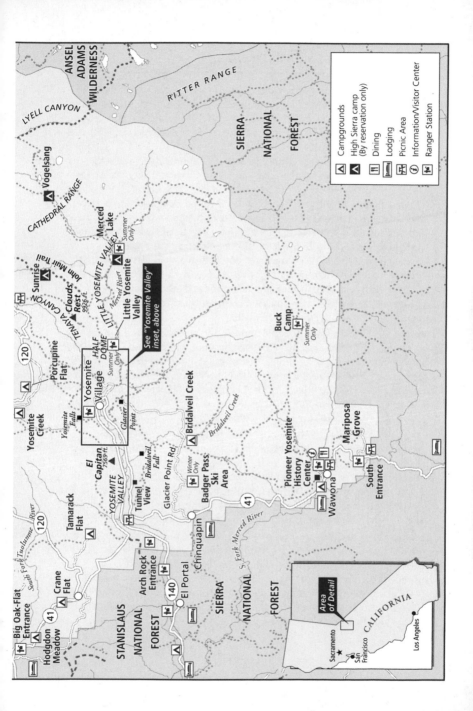

Campgrounds

High Sierra camp
(By reservation only)

Dining

Lodging

Picnic Area

Information/Visitor Center

Ranger Station

ANSEL ADAMS WILDERNESS

RITTER RANGE

SIERRA NATIONAL FOREST

LYELL CANYON

Vogelsang

CATHEDRAL RANGE

Merced Lake
LITTLE YOSEMITE VALLEY
Summer Only

John Muir Trail

Sunrise

TENAYA CANYON

Clouds Rest
9926 ft.

Little Yosemite Valley

Merced River

See "Yosemite Valley" inset, above

Buck Camp
Summer Only

Porcupine Flat

120

HALF DOME
Summer Only

Yosemite Village

Yosemite Creek

Yosemite Falls

Bridalveil Creek

Bridalveil Creek

Mariposa Grove

Glacier Point

El Capitan
7569 ft.

YOSEMITE VALLEY

Bridalveil Fall

Tunnel View

Glacier Point Rd

Badger Pass Ski Area
Winter Only

Pioneer Yosemite History Center

Wawona

South Entrance

41

Tamarack Flat

South Fork Tuolumne River

120

Chinquapin

S. Fork Merced River

Crane Flat

41

Arch Rock Entrance

140

El Portal

STANISLAUS NATIONAL FOREST

SIERRA NATIONAL FOREST

Big Oak Flat Entrance

Hodgdon Meadow

41

Area of Detail

CALIFORNIA

Sacramento

San Francisco

Los Angeles

Experiment: Finding Glacier Tracks

Yosemite's huge glaciers have been gone for more than 10,000 years, but their tracks remain. You can see the signs all over the hard granite of the Sierra if you know what to look for—the polish, scratches, and chatter marks; huge rocks moved far across the landscape; U-shaped valleys; and long, skinny piles of rubble.

You can see the evidence of glaciers at many national parks and seashores that are now far from large glaciers, including Yosemite, Sequoia, Yellowstone, Grand Teton, Rocky Mountain, Acadia, and Cape Cod.

In the 1830s, Louis Agassiz, a scientist, first had the idea that glaciers shaped the mountains in his country, Switzerland. He developed a theory, totally new and outrageous at the time, that the country had been covered with thousands of feet of moving ice. Then he carefully gathered the evidence to prove it, finding the same signs on the rocks and land that you can find yourself. Finally, others began to believe, too, but exactly where glaciers once were and what they did is something geologists still study and argue about.

Here are some of the signs you can look for on your hikes and drives—the same signs Agassiz first recognized.

Polish: On exposed granite bedrock, look for places where the normally rough rock is smooth and shiny. Often, the smoothness will be in patches, surrounded by rough dents in the rock where some of the granite has since worn away. Imagine moving ice thick and heavy enough to cut through this rock and leave this polished surface. Examples are all over Yosemite, especially on domes around Tuolumne Meadows.

Grooves & Chatter Marks: The same kind of rock outcropping where you might find glacial polish is a good place to look for grooves and chatter marks. When a stone gets stuck under a sliding glacier, it can cut a line in the bedrock below. Notice how these grooves all point the same way—that's the direction in which the glacier was going. Chatter marks happen where a rock moving with the glacier gouged out a line of small dips. Instead of scratching steadily, it built up pressure and then suddenly jerked forward. They're rarer than grooves, but quite obvious when you find them.

Erratics: Some of the best pieces of glacier evidence that Agassiz and his colleagues found were big boulders in places where they didn't belong. A glacial erratic might turn up in the middle of a field or on top of another piece of rock of a completely different type. By finding rock just like the out-of-place boulder (often miles away), you can figure out where it came from. How else could a huge boulder move so far except in a glacier? An erratic along Tioga Road is near Tenaya Lake.

Good weather usually lasts through September and part of October. From December to March, winter sports gear up, including cross-country and downhill skiing, snowshoeing, and ice-skating. Spring break isn't the best time for Yosemite because of the lingering snow and mud.

Domes, Nunataks & Cirques: Some dome-shaped mountains, like Lembert Dome in Tuolumne Meadows, got their rounded shape from glaciers moving over them. In many places in the Sierra, you can find spots where hard granite is in wavy forms left by a flowing glacier. Some domes, though, including Half Dome in Yosemite Valley, were made by a process called exfoliation, which has nothing to do with glaciers. Right near a dome, and a bit higher, another mountaintop might be pointy and jagged. Maybe it was sticking up from the top of glaciers that were flowing over the lower mountains, rounding them down. Mountain peaks sticking above glaciers are called nunataks. Another common glacier-made form is a cirque, a bowl-shaped valley or amphitheater on the side of a mountain. It's where a glacier started. With cirques on two or three sides, very pointy mountains stick up in the middle. Mount Conness, visible from the trail to Gaylor Lakes from the Tioga Pass entrance, is an example of a peak surrounded by cirques.

Moraines: The rock carried away by glaciers has to go somewhere. Like huge conveyor belts, glaciers carry the fine rock dust, pebbles, and boulders they scrape from the mountains down into the valleys, leaving the stuff in lines at the front and side edges of the ice. These line-shaped mounds are called moraines. They can be large hills or small berms. Often, they dam up a lake or river in front of the glacier, which later will become a flat meadow, as in Yosemite Valley. You can still see that moraine on the left as you drive out of the Valley, past El Capitan but before Valley View. Geologists use moraines to figure out the shape and order of the glaciers that moved through an area.

U-Shaped Valleys: When a river runs through a valley, it wears away rock in the riverbed and along the banks, carving deeper in a narrow line. The sides might fall in and be washed away, widening the top of the valley, but the bottom of the valley stays narrow. In a sandbox, you could copy the way a river works by digging with a narrow stick. A glacier carves rock, too, but it's much wider, filling the valley from rim to rim. Its scraping is like digging in a sandbox with a wide board. Valleys and canyons shaped like a V were probably made by rivers. Valleys with flat bottoms and steeper walls, shaped like a U, were probably made by glaciers. Yosemite is the most famous glacial valley. It was started by a river, then widened and deepened by glaciers. You can look at any valley and make an educated guess from its shape whether a river or glacier made it. Your educated guess is your hypothesis. If you can find other glacier tracks in the valley, your hypothesis might be confirmed.

HOW MUCH TIME TO SPEND

Yosemite is not a place to pass through quickly. Just getting to the park and around on its twisting roads takes a long time. No one should miss seeing Yosemite Valley, but I wouldn't want to spend my whole visit there, either, because of all the people.

A minimal trip would spend 1 or 2 days in the valley and 2 or 3 in one of the other areas, relaxing and hiking. A week would be ideal.

HOW FAR TO PLAN AHEAD

Reservations are tight from May through September, especially if you want to stay in Yosemite Valley. Campground reservations during the peak book up as soon as they become available, 5 months ahead (chapter 2, "Planning a Family Trip to a National Park," explains the national reservation system). Some campgrounds don't take reservations (p. 379), but you should arrive early to grab one of those sites. Reserving backcountry camping permits is covered on p. 387.

Rooms at Yosemite should be the first thing you plan, so you can take what's available and then work out the rest of your arrangements around those dates. Hotel reservations open 366 days before the stay, and to be assured of a room with a private bathroom, you need to call or reserve online the minute your date becomes available. You have a better chance of reserving tent cabins closer to your date, often just a few weeks out. You might be able to upgrade after you arrive. With a reservation system that books up so early, cancellations are frequent. You often can get a room by checking exactly 10 days before the stay—as cancellations can be made without penalty up to that point. You can also find rooms on the day of the stay when visitors check out early. To help with your budget, know that Mariposa County levies a 10% lodging tax.

Weather Chart: Yosemite Valley

	Avg. High (°F/°C)	Avg. Low (°F/°C)	Precip. (in.)
November–March	48–59/9–15	26–31/–3 to –1	5.6
April	65/18	35/2	3
May	73/23	42/6	1.3
June	82/28	48/9	.7
July–August	90/32	53/12	.3
September	87/31	47/8	.9
October	74/23	39/4	2.1

Elevation 4,000 feet.

WHAT TO PACK
CLOTHING

The dry summers at Yosemite can bring cool mornings in the high country and hot afternoons in the valley. On visits in July and September, we spent most of our time in shorts and wore sweatshirts and sweaters in the evening and the first hours after waking up. Waterproof clothing and layers of warm synthetic underwear and wool are safety precautions for backpacking or longer hikes in the high country, where snow could show up even in the summer. In mid-May 1904, John Muir and President Teddy Roosevelt slept under the stars at Glacier Point and woke to find 4 inches of snow on their sleeping bags! Cold, wet weather is common in the spring and fall. See "When It's Cold & Wet," in chapter 2.

Bring swimsuits for hotel pools, streams, and mountain lakes. If you stay at one of the historic hotels, you'll need nice shirts and pants to eat in the formal dining rooms; at The Ahwahnee, coats and ties are required for men in the dining room in the evening.

GEAR

Summer-weight gear is adequate on most nights, but in the high country you'll want an extra layer, such as an extra bag or synthetic long underwear, in case unusually cold weather hits. In the spring and fall, you might need heavier sleeping bags. Mosquito repellent and good tent screens are often a necessity. If you're driving from home, consider bringing your own bikes for the paved trails in Yosemite Valley, because the rentals are expensive and mostly of low quality.

KEEPING SAFE & HEALTHY

About 10 or 20 visitors die at Yosemite each year. The Park Service launches far more search-and-rescue operations here than at other mountain parks, even allowing for the larger number of visitors. Rangers blame the tendency of visitors used to the urban world to underrate the dangers of the vertical landscape, fast rivers, and high elevation. In the wilderness, only you control your safety. Besides the points below, read up on these safety topics covered under "Dealing with Hazards," in chapter 2: elevation, Giardia, hypothermia, lightning, Lyme disease, motion sickness, and snakebites.

BLACK BEARS

The bears of Yosemite are so used to humans that encounters are common. They've never killed anyone, but because the meeting can be scary, know what to do in advance. Backpackers should use bear-resistant canisters. Read the Park Service material or "Dangerous Wildlife," in chapter 2.

DROWNING

Keep a close eye on kids playing in or near streams and lakes. If in doubt, don't swim. Moving water is more powerful than it looks and can have dangerous vertical eddies. Swim only from sandy banks, not rocks, which can be slippery and difficult to climb. Also, due to the obvious danger, swimming is not permitted in Emerald Pool above Vernal Fall.

FALLS

There are many places where a careless person can fall to his or her death. Don't expect guardrails. Many fatalities are young males engaging in risky recreation. Young children are usually smart enough to hold hands and stay safe in high places, but keep an eye on your teenagers. If they want to scale rocks, sign them up for rock-climbing classes with a professional (see "Climbing," p. 399).

5 Family-Friendly Accommodations

CAMPGROUNDS

NATIONAL PARK CAMPGROUNDS

There are 13 campgrounds in the park, including one run by the park concessionaire with tents provided. Seven of the campgrounds are on the national reservation system (© 877/444-6777; www.recreation.gov). The car-camping areas in Yosemite Valley are the most popular; book your summer dates as soon as they become available on the national reservation system (see chapter 2). Sites are easier to come by outside the valley, and first-come, first-served campgrounds are available (as noted below), but you still must reserve well ahead or arrive early in the day to get a site. On weekends it might not be possible to get a site, but during the week there are a few campgrounds with better availability, which I've noted below. A couple of campgrounds, at Hetch

Campgrounds in the Yosemite Area

Campground	Elevation	Total Sites	RV Hookups	Dump Station	Toilets	Drinking Water
INSIDE YOSEMITE NATIONAL PARK						
Bridalveil Creek	7,200	110	No	No	Yes	Yes
Camp 4	4,000	35	No	No	Yes	Yes
Crane Flat*	6,191	166	No	No	Yes	Yes
Hodgdon Meadow*	4,872	105	No	No	Yes	Yes
Lower Pines*	4,000	60	No	Nearby	Yes	Yes
North Pines*	4,000	81	No	Nearby	Yes	Yes
Porcupine Flat	8,100	52	No	No	Yes	No
Tamarack Flat	6,315	52	No	No	Yes	No
Tuolumne Meadows	8,600	304	No	Nearby	Yes	Yes
Upper Pines*	4,000	238	No	Yes	Yes	Yes
Wawona*	4,000	93	No	Nearby	Yes	Yes
White Wolf	8,000	74	No	No	Yes	Yes
Yosemite Creek	7,659	75 (tent only)	No	No	Yes	No
OUTSIDE THE PARK						
Dimond O	4,400	36	No	No	Yes	Yes
Ellery Lake	9,500	12	No	No	Yes	Yes
Junction	9,600	13	No	No	Yes	No
Lost Claim	3,100	10	No	No	Yes	Yes
The Pines	3,200	11	No	No	Yes	Yes
Summerdale	5,000	30	No	No	Yes	Yes**
Sweetwater	3,000	12	No	No	Yes	Yes
Tioga Lake	9,700	13	No	No	Yes	Yes

* Reservations required (either part of the year or year-round).
** Not potable.

Hetchy Reservoir and along Tioga Road, are only for hikers with backcountry permits and aren't listed here.

We wouldn't have missed camping at Yosemite, but the campgrounds tend to be poorly maintained, presumably due to overuse. Many are badly laid out and barren of ground cover. Showers are hard to come by, and bathrooms are often below normal standards, many even lacking lighting. Under the proposed Yosemite Valley Plan the Park Service plans to redesign and rehabilitate the Yosemite Valley campgrounds. However, litigation has blocked implementation of that plan and, as of fall 2007, officials

Showers	Fire Pits/Grills	Laundry	Public Phones	Reservations	Fees	Open
No	Yes	No	Yes	No	$14	June–Oct
Nearby	Yes	Nearby	Yes	No	$5/person	Year-round
No	Yes	No	Yes	Yes	$20	June–Oct
No	Yes	No	Yes	Late Apr to early Oct	$20	Year-round
Nearby	Yes	Nearby	Yes	Yes	$20	Mar–Oct
Nearby	Yes	Nearby	Yes	Yes	$20	Apr–Sept
No	Yes	No	Yes	No	$10	July to early Sept
No	Yes	No	Yes	No	$10	Late May to mid-Oct.
Nearby	Yes	No	Yes	Yes/50%	$20	July–Sept
Nearby	Yes	Nearby	Yes	Yes	$20	Year-round
No	Yes	No	Yes	May–Sept	$20	Year-round
Nearby	Yes	No	Yes	No	$14	Late May to mid-Sept
No	Yes	No	Yes	No	$10	Early June to early Sept
No	Yes	No	No	No	$19	Mid-Apr to Oct
No	Yes	No	No	No	$21	June to mid-Oct
No	Yes	No	No	No	$12	June–Oct
No	Yes	No	No	No	$14	May to Labor Day
No	Yes	No	No	No	$14	Year-round
No	Yes	No	No	Yes	$19	June–Oct
No	Yes	No	No	No	$16	June–Sept
No	Yes	No	No	No	$17	June to mid-Oct

had no idea when the lawsuits would be resolved. It can't come soon enough. Most campgrounds are as crowded as RV parks and feel as natural as parking lots.

The park allows firewood gathering outside Yosemite Valley and below 9,600 feet elevation as long as you don't cut live or standing wood and don't use a chain saw. The result seems to be woods near campgrounds unnaturally denuded by people aggressively attacking with saws and hatchets. Buying firewood is a better bet, both environmentally and so that you can build a good fire. In Yosemite Valley, to improve air quality, campfires are limited to 5 to 10pm. Don't start the fire with pine needles or cones, which smoke; use newspaper or fire starter instead.

Human-dependent black bears are a major problem at Yosemite. Listen to the instructions you're given. All food and anything like soap that has an odor should be stored in the metal cabinets at the campsites when you're not actively using them. Latch the cabinet. On more than one night we have listened from our tent as a bear worked at the latches. All but the largest coolers will fit in the lockers; if in doubt, measure before you leave home. Locker dimensions (in.) are 33×45×18. Bears have ripped open many hundreds of cars to get food left in the trunk or passenger compartment. Don't even leave untidy papers in the car that a bear might mistake for food wrappers. For more on bears, see "Dangerous Wildlife," in chapter 2.

For campground questions, either visit the park's website (www.nps.gov/yose) or call park headquarters ℂ 209/372-0200.

Yosemite Valley

The Yosemite Valley Plan calls for the campgrounds to be rehabilitated and reconfigured, with new walk-in sites and more natural surroundings. The total number of campsites would actually go up by 25, while many sites near the Merced River would be removed. It's hard to imagine how all this will happen, because the campgrounds already are extremely tight in the land they've got, but the rehab work is badly needed.

All the valley campgrounds have flush toilets. A dump station is at Upper Pines. The three Pines drive-in campgrounds adjoin each other near Curry Village, where you can shower, do laundry, buy groceries, swim in the pool, and rent bikes and rafts. They're open to tents or RVs. The Housekeeping Camp is ½ mile west and has laundry facilities. The shuttle bus can take you to Yosemite Village.

Camp 4 Walk-In   Populated by young rock climbers with beards or ponytails, this crowded encampment offers an idea of what a Civil War bivouac would have looked like if the soldiers had just been on an REI shopping spree. Sites are simply rectangular patches of ground, and they are allocated like hostel dorms, with more tents added until each site contains six people. To get a place, you should be in line early in the morning.

North side of Yosemite Valley. 35 sites, tents only. $5 per person. No reservations. Open year-round. **Amenities:** Flush toilets, picnic table, fire pits, running water, bear boxes.

Housekeeping Camp   Don't stay here unless you're desperate. The grim units resemble cells, with bare cinder-block walls, and can be dirty and ill-maintained. The roof is canvas, and the beds are metal cots with plastic-covered mattresses. You rent linens separately at the office, where you can also get a camp stove to cook on the picnic table at your unit. Showers, toilets, and a huge coin-op laundry are in a central bathhouse, where soap and towels are provided. The location on the riverbank is good, and the units have a loyal following.

Yosemite Valley. ℂ 559/253-5635 for reservations. 266 units, tents provided. $76 site for up to 4 people. $5 extra person over age 12. Closed mid-Oct to mid-Apr. **Amenities:** Flush toilets, showers, laundry, picnic tables, running water, camp stoves available.

Lower Pines   Across the street from Upper Pines, this campground has the same poor design and other disadvantages, but it is smaller and has some river frontage, making it a more attractive choice.

Yosemite Valley. 60 sites, tents or RVs. $20 site. Reservations required. Closed Nov–Feb. **Amenities:** Flush toilets, picnic tables, fire pits, running water, bear boxes, close to Camp Curry.

North Pines   The Park Service plans to remove this riverside campground to reclaim the natural vegetation, but work has yet to be scheduled. The waterside sites provide more room and a more natural setting than nearby Upper Pines, but otherwise it is the same.

Yosemite Valley. 81 sites, tents or RVs. $20 site. Reservations required. Closed Oct–Mar. **Amenities:** Flush toilets, picnic tables, fire pits, running water, bear boxes, close to Camp Curry.

Upper Pines   This is the valley's big campground, covering a large, flat area under trees without lower branches. The Park Service plan adopted in 2000 would redo the campground; nothing has happened so far. As currently configured, the campground is unappealing, with small sites crammed in, no screening other than the thick smoke from your neighbors' campfires, and no ground cover other than pine needles. I've never felt claustrophobic while camping before. The huge size makes bikes handy and strollers essential for little ones, because you could have a significant walk just to get to the shuttle stop.

Yosemite Valley. 238 sites, tents or RVs. $20 site. Reservations required. Open year-round. **Amenities:** Flush toilets, dump station, picnic tables, fire pits, running water, bear boxes, close to Camp Curry.

The Western Side

These campgrounds are reached by the roads of the western side of the park, with its tall forests of ponderosa pines and firs. These sites are easier to get into than the Yosemite Valley campgrounds, but securing your spot should still be your priority. Make reservations where possible (noted in the listings below). Lines often form in the morning for first-come, first-served sites.

Bridalveil Creek   At 7,200 feet elevation, well off Glacier Point Road, the campground is cooler, quieter, and more natural than those in Yosemite Valley, which lies to the north. Trail heads for excellent hikes are here and elsewhere along the road; many have stupendous views into the valley. Small pines separate the sites, and there are ample unspoiled lands nearby for exploration and play. Arrive early to get a site.

Glacier Point Rd., 7½ miles from Hwy. 41. 110 sites, tents or RVs. $14 site. No reservations. Closed Sept–May. **Amenities:** Flush toilets, picnic table, fire pit, running water, bear boxes.

Crane Flat   Sites are on a gentle hillside among large, shady evergreens and massive rock outcroppings. There's a peaceful feeling. The location, near the Merced and Tuolumne Sequoia groves, is 17 miles from Yosemite Valley and near the store and gas station at the western end of Tioga Road. The elevation of 6,191 feet puts the weather in between that of the valley and the high country.

On Hwy. 120, north of Yosemite Valley. 166 sites, tents or RVs. $20 site. Reservations required. Closed Oct–May. **Amenities:** Flush toilets, picnic table, fire pit, running water, bear boxes.

Hodgdon Meadow   The sites are on a hillside among huge pine trees. They tend to be small, but you can wander into the woods, which are open and free of undergrowth. The elevation of 4,872 feet is relatively warm, like Yosemite Valley, which is 25 miles away. Since few popular attractions are near, reservations are relatively easy to get; in midweek, you can even get one with little planning.

On Hwy. 120, just south of the Big Oak Flat entrance. 105 sites, tents or RVs. $20 site during reservation period; $14 otherwise. Reservations required late Apr to early Oct. Open year-round. **Amenities:** Flush toilets, picnic tables, fire pit, running water, bear boxes.

Wawona   This low-elevation campground, at 4,000 feet, is among my favorites at Yosemite. Sites are strung on terraces along the bank of the south fork of the Merced

River among oak, pine, and cedar trees. Water conditions permitting, there are plenty of swimming holes near campsites, and a great family float ends here (see "Rafting," p. 400). The best sites are in loop B, sites 31 through 44; loop C (45–99) is also attractive, but more tightly spaced. The area's attractions include the Mariposa Grove, the Pioneer Yosemite History Center, and the steam railroad; a grocery store and restaurants are also on hand.

On Hwy. 41 near the south park entrance. 93 sites, tents or RVs. $20 site during reservation period; $14 otherwise. Reservations required May–Sept. Open year-round. **Amenities:** Flush toilets, picnic tables, fire pits, running water, swimming, bear boxes.

On Tioga Road

These five campgrounds are along Tioga Road (Hwy. 120 E.), which rises to almost 10,000 feet over the top of the Sierra. The road closes in the winter and doesn't reopen until late May or early June. Snow and mud might linger through June. Mosquito repellent is indispensable in July at all these campgrounds. These are the easiest campsites to get without a reservation, but they do fill up on summer weekends. Bring good lights, because the bathrooms generally lack electricity. I've arranged the campgrounds by distance from the western, Crane Flat end of the road.

Tamarack Flat   This place is for those who enjoy natural, primitive campgrounds where you can camp in a private site, well separated from your neighbors by thick trees and rock outcroppings, but where you also must gather and treat your own water and use a crude, aged outhouse. The campground is 3 miles from Tioga Road on a very slow and nearly disintegrated winding way—the remains of the old stagecoach route that continues as a hiking trail into Yosemite Valley—about halfway to being backcountry, far from electricity or road noise. Chances are better of finding a site here than at most other places. Boil or use filter treatment on water from Tamarack Creek before you drink it.

Take Tioga Rd. 3 miles from Crane Flat and turn right on the 3-mile access road. 52 sites, access road not passable for large RVs or trailers. $10 site. No reservations. Closed mid-Oct to late May. **Amenities:** Pit toilets, picnic tables, fire pits, bear boxes, no tap water, treat creek water.

White Wolf   This campground is at an elevation of 8,000 feet near White Wolf Lodge and trail heads for Harden or Lukens lakes, or longer backpacking trips into the Hetch Hetchy area and Grand Canyon of the Tuolumne River. The campsites sit among pines and rock outcroppings, which offer some screening missing with the lack of ground cover. By arriving early, you may be able to get an outer-loop site with plenty of space. Limited showers and meals are available at the lodge; see "High-Country Camps (Tent Cabins)," p. 387.

On Tioga Rd., 15 miles from Crane Flat. 74 sites, tents or RVs. $14 site. No reservations. Closed mid-Sept to late May. **Amenities:** Flush toilets, picnic tables, fire pits, running water, bear boxes.

Yosemite Creek   This is a very secluded, primitive campground. It puts you well away from the road and at the trail head for some great hiking and backpacking, including the 13-mile trail down into Yosemite Valley at the falls. Treat water you draw from the creek.

Take Tioga Rd. 15 miles east from Crane Flat, then turn right on Old Tioga Rd. and drive 5 miles. 75 sites, access road not suitable for large RVs or trailers. $10 site. No reservations. Closed early Sept to early June. **Amenities:** Pit toilets, picnic tables, fire pits, bear boxes, no tap water, treat creek water.

Porcupine Flat   Sites are broadly separated among pines in this primitive campground, just off Tioga Road at 8,100 feet. It meets some of the same trails as the

(Tips) Camping Basics: Toilets, Showers & Laundry

Bathrooms in the large, heavily used campgrounds can get grungy and lack hot water. Sometimes portable toilets are set up outside to deal with all the people. The park's primitive campgrounds don't have running water, and nearby streams can dry up late in the season. Bring as much water as you can. Water you gather from streams must be treated with a filter or by boiling before drinking. Learn how to do that under "Packing 101: Gear," in chapter 2.

In Yosemite Valley, the showers at the pool and elsewhere at Curry Village are open to the public 24 hours a day all year. You have to wait at popular times. Showers at the Housekeeping Camp also are open to the public, operating in season daily 7am to 10pm; the large coin laundry there operates all year daily 8am to 10pm. Showers, towels included, cost $5 per person at all the showers in the park (except for hotel guests). Pay an attendant or at the front desk.

Outside the valley, it might be easier to stay dirty and rinse off when you take a swim. There are no public showers at Wawona. Showers are available at White Wolf and Tuolumne Meadows lodges, on Tioga Road, but in each case they are available for campers only after the guests are done, in the midafternoon, so you waste the best part of the day. Also, at each site there are only a few stalls for many people, and the water is on a push-button arrangement that makes washing difficult, especially with kids. Consider camping several days and then spending a night in a real hotel (not a tent-cabin lodge) to clean up before returning to camping.

Yosemite Creek Campground, which is just a couple of miles away on foot. Treat water you gather.

Tioga Rd., 24 miles from Crane Flat. 52 sites, RVs not allowed in some sites. $10 site. No reservations. Closed early Sept to July. **Amenities:** Pit toilets, picnic tables, fire pits, bear boxes, no tap water, treat creek water.

Tuolumne Meadows   This huge campground with small hills is close to Tuolumne Meadows and many supremely lovely hikes. You can use the shuttle, attend campfire programs, shop for groceries, and join horseback riding nearby. Showers of sorts are at the lodge of the same name (see the box below). The thin mountain air, at 8,600 feet, is cool and dry. Make reservations or arrive early, especially on weekends.

Tioga Rd., 37 miles from Crane Flat. 304 sites, tents or RVs. $20 site. Half reservations, half same-day check-in. Closed Oct–June. **Amenities:** Flush toilets, picnic tables, fire pits, running water, bear boxes.

FOREST SERVICE CAMPGROUNDS

Yosemite is surrounded by Stanislaus, Sierra, and Inyo national forests (see "Yosemite Address Book," p. 365). Each park has campgrounds near the park entrance, some of them as attractive as the park campgrounds and almost as likely to fill on summer evenings. There are also places for dispersed camping or setting up your tent anywhere you choose; check at a ranger station.

Inyo National Forest

These campgrounds lie east of the park, where Tioga Road descends steeply from the Sierra to the strange Mono Lake basin, an amazing piece of topography. Despite the elevation of 9,500 feet or more, the mountains' rain shadow makes the area around the campgrounds an arid zone. All are closed from mid-October through May, and none take reservations. Many more campgrounds are a little farther afield, as are trails and a lot of interesting sites around Mono Lake. Get area information from the Mono Lake center (p. 371).

Ellery Lake Across the road from Junction, this lakeside campground is paved and trim, with brush effectively screening the sites.

Hwy. 120, 2 miles outside park. ℂ **760/647-3044.** 21 sites, tents or RVs. $17 site. Closed mid-Oct to May. **Amenities:** Pit toilets, picnic tables, fire pits, running water.

Junction About half of the campsites lie among protruding bedrock and shady evergreen trees, a very pleasant setting. The junction in the name is for a road that leads up to Saddlebag Lake and other campgrounds there. Treat water you get from the stream.

Hwy. 120, 2 miles outside park. ℂ **760/647-3044.** 13 sites, tents or RVs. $12 site. Closed mid-Oct to May. **Amenities:** Pit toilets, picnic tables, fire pits, bear boxes, no running water; water can be gathered at Tioga Lake campground.

Tioga Lake Some campsites sit by the lake, but none has much shade or privacy. The other two campgrounds are preferable.

Hwy. 120, 1 mile outside park. ℂ **760/647-3044.** 13 sites, tents and small trailers or small RVs only. $17 site. Closed mid-Oct to May. **Amenities:** Pit toilets, picnic tables, fire pits, running water.

Sierra National Forest

Summerdale Just outside the park near Mariposa Grove and the steam railroad, this is one of the area's loveliest campgrounds. Quietly nestled in a valley far below the highway, the broadly separated campsites sit under large deciduous shade trees around a meadow. Campers swim in the creek. The outhouses are lighted.

Hwy. 41, 1 mile south of the south entrance station, near Wawona. 30 sites, tents or RVs. $19 site. Reservations accepted. Closed Nov–May. **Amenities:** Vault toilets, picnic tables, fire pits and grills, running water (but boil), swimming.

Stanislaus National Forest

These campgrounds are near the park's north entrances, at Big Oak Flat and Hetch Hetchy. On the way east on Highway 120 to the Big Oak Flat entrance, Sweetwater, The Pines, and Lost Claim all sit at about 3,000 feet in the often-hot foothills.

Dimond O Below the narrow, winding road to Hetch Hetchy, the well-built campground occupies a shady hillside of pines. It's a place of peaceful beauty and repose. The Middle Fork of the Tuolumne River, a popular fishing spot, flows by. Some sites have good privacy, and the campground is accessible for travelers with disabilities. Elevation is 4,400 feet.

Evergreen Rd., 6 miles north of the Big Oak Flat entrance. 36 sites, tents or small RVs. $19 site. Reservations available. Closed Nov to mid-Apr. **Amenities:** Vault toilets, picnic tables, fire pits and grills, running water.

Lost Claim Choose Lost Claim only if you want to deal with pumping your own well water.

Hwy. 120, 13 miles from park entrance. 10 sites, tents or small RVs. $14 site. No reservations. Closed Labor Day to Apr. **Amenities:** Vault toilets, picnic tables, fire pits and grills, hand-pumped water.

The Pines Near the Groveland ranger station, the Pines sites are rather exposed in a dry, pine-oak plant community. But it does have running water and vault toilets.

Hwy. 120, 16 miles from park entrance. 11 sites, tents or small RVs. $14 site. No reservations. Open year-round. **Amenities:** Vault toilets, picnic tables, fire pits and grills.

Sweetwater   Of the three small campgrounds near the Big Oak Flat entrance, Sweetwater is the most appealing, with large sites on a single loop under big pine trees.

Hwy. 120, 10 miles from park entrance. 11 sites, tents or small RVs. $16 site. No reservations. Closed Oct–May. **Amenities:** Vault toilets, picnic tables, fire pits and grills, running water.

BACKCOUNTRY CAMPING PERMITS

Unlike other parks, Yosemite doesn't have camping zones or backcountry sites, but you need a free wilderness permit from the Park Service to camp in the backcountry. Permits are rationed according to the trail head where you'll enter the backcountry. Once in, you can camp anywhere you want in open areas, as long as it's at least 1 mile from the road or 4 miles from a developed area (Yosemite Valley, Tuolumne Meadows, Wawona, Hetch Hetchy, or Glacier Point). This is a good, flexible system.

Of 100 trails, most don't fill their quotas, but if you are planning a trip, it makes sense to reserve a permit anyway. The permits in highest demands, requiring early reservations, include Half Dome (which books up as soon as it becomes available), Cathedral Lakes, and the Tuolumne Meadows to Glen Aulin trail. Reservations open 24 weeks before the start of the trip and close 2 days before. You can find detailed information at www.nps.gov/archive/yose/wilderness. To reserve, go online (www.yosemitesecure.org/wildpermit), call © **209/372-0740,** or write to **Wilderness Permits,** P.O. Box 545, Yosemite, CA 95389. If you write, first call or go online to find out what information to send. The reservation fee is $5 per person on confirmed trips, payable by major credit card or by check to the Yosemite Association.

At least 40% of each trail's quota of permits are available for walk-ins beginning the day before the trip starts. These permits, along with the reserved permits, are given out at five offices: the **Wilderness Center** in Yosemite Valley, the **Tuolumne Meadows Wilderness Center,** the information centers at **Big Oak Flat** and **Wawona** (listed under "Visitor Information," p. 369), and the **Hetch Hetchy** entrance station. Hours vary by season and are on the Web and in the park's *Yosemite Today* publication. Lots of trail head permits will be available when you arrive, even without a reservation, but get there early the day before your hike to have a good choice. You'll have to listen to an orientation before going out to get important information about bears, safety, and protecting the wilderness. Be prepared to keep your food in bear-resistant canisters, which you can rent for $5 when you get to the park.

See "Backpacking" (p. 398) for more advice, including suggestions on where to go.

COMMERCIAL CAMPGROUNDS

If you're looking for an RV park with full hookups, the closest is the small, basic **Indian Flat RV Park** in El Portal (© **209/379-2339**), 6 miles outside the park on Route 140. Others are sprinkled around the area. Ask for referrals at the visitor centers listed above.

High-Country Camps (Tent Cabins)

The concessionaire, **Delaware North** (see "Yosemite Address Book," p. 365), operates two lodges of tent cabins along Tioga Road and five backcountry camps during the summer only. Contact Delaware North directly for reservations; the numbers listed below are for the front desks. Cribs are not available. Dining at each lodge is described under "Family-Friendly Dining" (p. 391).

High Sierra Camps   These five camps allow you to hike a 50-mile loop through the Sierra's most beautiful high country without carrying a tent, stove, or food. You might want to pack a sleeping bag, though. While the tents come with pillows and blankets, there are no linens. Be sure to pack flashlights and batteries, as there's no electricity here; candles provide the illumination in your tents. You can hike with a ranger, ride a mule, or go on your own. Each night hikers sleep in male and female dorms (although efforts are made to keep families and parties in the same tent), eat gourmet meals (filet mignon, chicken *cordon bleu,* and halibut frequent the dinner menus) in a tent dining room, and can take a hot shower. And the camps are well-tended. Sunrise Camp, for instance, has a solar-energy system and a shower building that put to shame those found at the lodges on the road. Unfortunately, an experience of such quality must be rationed. Reservations for the following summer are awarded by lottery from applications received from October 15 to November 30. Sometimes you can get late reservations at the Merced Lake Camp, and cancellations after May 1 are awarded to those who call the desk. It's also possible to reserve meals through the lottery for independent backpacking trips.

On the High Sierra Loop Trail. High Sierra Camp desk (information and applications) ℭ 559/253-5674. 204 cots in 5 camps. $136 adults; $91 children 7–12; rates are per person per night and include breakfast and dinner. No children under age 7. Closed mid-Sept to June. **Amenities:** Hot showers, dining room.

Tuolumne Meadows Lodge   I love this place. It's out of the hustle and bustle of Yosemite Valley, and while the tent cabins provide minimal shelter—just canvas over a concrete slab—with metal cots and a wood stove, they lend a rustic charm to stays, if that's what you're looking for. And the location can't be beat. The Dana Fork of the Tuolumne River roars over granite boulders out back, and some of the park's best trails leave from the grounds. About 20 tents are saved for guests starting a week's circuit of the High Sierra Camps, described above. As a bonus, the lodge's chefs create incredible meals. I ordered lamb chops one night only to have the waitress return to say they were out of chops and would I like lamb tenderloin. Tough decision.

Near the east park entrance on Tioga Rd. (Hwy. 120). ℭ 559/253-5635. 69 tents. $78 double. $10 extra person over age 12, $6 for child under 13. Closed mid-Sept to mid-June. **Amenities:** Bathhouse, dining room.

White Wolf Lodge   The lodge consists of a group of tents and cabins among the trees behind a small bathhouse and a permanent main building, which contains the dining room and the tiny store. The only attraction, certainly a good one, is the trails nearby, including the route to the High Sierra Camps (see above).

On Tioga Rd. (Hwy. 120), 15 miles from Crane Flat junction. ℭ 559/253-5635. 4 cabins with private bathroom, 24 tents. $96 double with bathroom; $73 tent double. $10 extra person over age 12, $6 child under 13. Closed mid-Sept to early June. **Amenities:** Bathhouse, camp store, dining room.

HOTELS
YOSEMITE VALLEY

The concessionaire, **Delaware North Companies Parks & Resorts at Yosemite** (see "Yosemite Address Book, p. 365), operates these lodgings in the valley and the Wawona Hotel (p. 390). All are open year-round, except Wawona, which closes a bit during the winter. The seasonal Housekeeping Camp is listed under "Campgrounds" (p. 382). Use the central Delaware North number for reservations; the phone numbers below are for the hotels' front desks. Delaware North accepts American Express, Discover, MasterCard, and Visa. See "How Far to Plan Ahead" (p. 378) for tips on reserving rooms. If the concessionaire doesn't have a room available when you call, the staff will try to book you into one of a few places the company represents outside the park. Keep in mind the 10% lodging tax.

Rates listed here are for the high season. Modest off-season discounts apply. Kids under 13 stay free with their parents except where noted, and cribs are available except in the tent cabins. Unless otherwise noted, none of the accommodations have TVs or phones. You can park at the hotel when you arrive; leave your car there and get around on the shuttle or a bicycle.

Look for reviews of hotel restaurants under "Family-Friendly Dining" (p. 391).

The Ahwahnee   Built in 1926 to serve wealthy park visitors and fully restored in 1997, the hotel has a grandeur approaching the absurd, like a Cecil B. DeMille stage set for an emperor's mountain lodge. Stop in to see the incredible common rooms, museums of past opulence full of fabulous Native American art, spectacular stained glass and ceilings, and fireplaces big enough to walk around in. Of course, the rooms are posh, too, decorated with mission furniture and lots of fabric, and supplied with TVs, DVD players, phones, refrigerators, bathrobes, and all you would expect from an upscale hotel. The hotel has its own pool, off-limits to the riffraff from the other lodgings.

Yosemite Village. ℂ 209/372-8333. 123 units. $426 double; $930–$990 suite. $21 extra person over age 12. AE, DISC, MC, V. Open year-round. **Amenities:** Restaurant; pool; shops. *In room:* TV, DVD player, fridge, coffeemaker, hair dryer, iron/ironing board.

Curry Village *Overrated*   This place is a city of tents and cabins, with kids running around happily and screaming in the pool. It reminds me of a summer camp, including the central bathhouses. The majority of the units are tent cabins, which consist of wood-framed canvas tents on wooden platforms with lights but without electric outlets; 65 have heat. About 140 of the tent cabins were to be removed under the now-stalled Valley plan because of the danger of falling rock from the cliffs above. The advantages of staying at Curry Village are the low rates, relatively easy availability, and ultracasual atmosphere. The disadvantages: a crowded, institutional feel with a constant rush of people and lines, noise, and spartan lodgings, like basic roadside motel rooms at best. Not a good location for youngsters who need their sleep.

South side of Yosemite Valley. ℂ 209/372-8333. 18 units, 100 cabins with private bathroom, 80 cabins without bathroom, 427 tent cabins. $147 double room, $13 extra person over age 12; $120 double cabin with bathroom, $14 extra person; $93 double cabin without bathroom, $12 extra person; $81–$85 double tent cabin, $10 extra person over age 12, $6 child 12 and under. AE, DISC, MC, V. Some units open year-round. **Amenities:** Restaurants; pool. *In room:* TV in some cabins.

Yosemite Lodge at the Falls   This is the park's one big hotel with standard American rooms (with phones, televisions, and Wi-Fi). It has been a focus of rehabilitation plans since some of the buildings disappeared in the 1997 flood. The plan calls for rebuilding the hotel with more economy lodgings in new buildings that fit in better with the park setting; construction, however, has been blocked by litigation over the Yosemite Valley Plan. In the meantime, you will find comfortable rooms in two classes, with a single double bed or with two beds and a patio. Rooms lack air-conditioning, bathrooms are quite small, and common areas are worn and unimpressive, but they're still the best choice for most people who want a normal hotel room in the valley. Besides the ice-cream stand, the complex contains a choice of restaurants (p. 392), the valley's main tour desk, a large outdoor pool, and an amphitheater where evening ranger programs are held.

North side of the valley, west of Yosemite Village. ℂ 209/372-1274. 245 units. $147–$176 double. $11–$13 extra person over age 12. Family room $173. AE, DISC, MC, V. Open year-round. **Amenities:** Restaurants; pool; shops; ranger programs. *In room:* TV, hair dryer, iron/ironing board, Wi-Fi.

WAWONA TO OAKHURST

Other than Yosemite Valley, only Wawona has real hotel rooms within the park. You'll find many more good choices just outside the south park entrance, in Fish Camp, and down the road in Oakhurst. The area has the Mariposa Grove of giant Sequoias, the Pioneer Yosemite History Center, and the steam railroad. Fish Camp is a wide place in Highway 41. Oakhurst, 15 miles downhill from there, is a highway community in the warm foothills. Establishments are listed here by distance from the park. Hotel restaurants are described under "Family-Friendly Dining" (p. 391).

Wawona Hotel   These big wooden buildings—the oldest date from 1879—preserve the feeling as well as the look of early vacation travel. They have wooden recliners on broad verandas and big lawns, inviting a slower pace. The rooms have antique or period furniture, such as marble-topped dressers, and the bathrooms have claw-foot tubs. Some of the discomforts have been preserved, too—the rooms tend to be small and lack air-conditioning or other modern features. Unusual for a national park, there's an outdoor pool, tennis courts, and a 9-hole golf course.

On Hwy. 41 in Wawona, near the south park entrance. Policies and reservations covered under "Yosemite Valley" (see above). ℭ **209/375-6556.** 104 units, 50 with bathroom. $192 double with bathroom, $21 extra person over 12; $126 double without bathroom, $13 extra person over age 12. AE, DISC, MC, V. Open Apr to Thanksgiving, mid-Dec to Jan, weekends Jan–Apr. **Amenities:** Pool; tennis courts; 9-hole golf course.

Tenaya Lodge   Set on 35 acres back in the trees just 2 miles outside the park, this luxurious resort is everything a family could want in park lodgings. A recent $3-million renovation brought new linens, down comforters, furniture, and carpeting into the rooms. Besides offering large, sumptuous rooms decorated in a Native American motif and containing every upscale amenity, the resort emphasizes its family activities, including horseback rides to the nearby Mariposa Grove and an all-day "adventure camp" for ages 5 to 12 that keeps youngsters busy with activities such as rock climbing, archery, and hikes. Large indoor and outdoor pools, a playground, and an arcade are on-site. Reserve 60 days ahead for stays between Memorial Day and Labor Day.

1122 Hwy. 41 (P.O. Box 159), Fish Camp, CA 93623. ℭ **877/322-5492** or 559/683-6555. Fax 559/683-6147. www. tenayalodge.com. 244 units. $185–$350 double. $15 extra adult, children under 18 stay free in parent's room. Rollaway beds and cribs free. Internet discounts and packages available. AE, DISC, MC, V. **Amenities:** Restaurant; pools; health club; spa; children's activities; shops; guided hikes; fishing. *In room:* TV w/video game console, dataport, coffeemaker, hair dryer, iron/ironing board, safe.

Best Western Yosemite Gateway   In a series of nine buildings on a meticulously landscaped hillside, behind a water wheel and mock Statue of Liberty, the comfortable rooms are an excellent value, with handy features such as microwaves, coffeemakers, and refrigerators on request. One building holds two-bedroom family suites, which accommodate up to six people. Some have kitchenettes, too. The children will enjoy the lawns, garden paths, good playground, and beautiful indoor and outdoor pools. By staying here you save money and get a better room than in the park; but you add a half-hour drive from the south entrance, which is 15 miles away, and the area is hot and not scenic.

40530 Hwy. 41, Oakhurst, CA 93644. ℭ **800/545-5462** or 559/683-2378. Fax 559/683-3813. www.yosemite gatewayinn.com. 122 units. $99–$112 double; $159 family suite. $8 extra person over age 12, children under 13 stay free in parent's room. Rollaway bed $8, crib $2. AE, DC, DISC, MC, V. Small to medium dogs accepted. **Amenities:** Restaurant; pools; health club; spa; Jacuzzi; sauna; playground; laundry; Wi-Fi in lobby. *In room:* A/C, TV, fridge on request, coffeemaker, iron/ironing board, free high-speed Internet access.

EL PORTAL

A few businesses stand along the road just outside the park downstream from Yosemite Valley on the Merced River, near the Arch Rock entrance. Two large hotels under one family's ownership offer good standard rooms and have pools. Each stands in the Merced's rocky canyon at a hot, treeless elevation of about 2,000 feet. The riverside **Yosemite View Lodge** (© **209/379-2681**) is the newer and better appointed of the two, with double rooms with kitchenettes starting at $159, and family suites priced from $219 all the way to $439 (all summer rates). **Cedar Lodge** (© **209/379-2612**) has many family suites and even one huge unit with a private swimming pool. Rooms start at $120 double in summer. Reserve either hotel at © **888/742-4371** or www. yosemite-motels.com.

The Yosemite Bug Rustic Mountain Resort   Located in the woods 23 miles west of El Portal and just 25 miles from Yosemite Valley, this once-upon-a-time dorm camp and lodge today offers good, inexpensive lodging and a great cafe that long has drawn honors thanks to its fresh foods and somewhat eclectic, family-style atmosphere. The setting, a quarter-mile off the main road, lends itself to relaxation and provides a woodsy setting where kids can run free. While hostel-like dorm rooms are available, so too are comfortable guesthouses, private cabins, private rooms, and tent cabins. Stay in a tent cabin and you have access to a central bathhouse with restrooms and showers. Befitting the wilderness setting, there are no phones or TVs in the rooms.

6969 Hwy. 140, Midpines, CA 95345. © 866/826-7108 or 209/966-6666. Fax 209/966-6667. www.yosemitebug. com. 3 guesthouses $205–$335; 14 private rooms with private bathroom $65–$125; 8 private rooms with shared bathroom $50–$85; 12 tent cabins $30–$55; 64 dorm beds $15. Rollaways $10. DISC, MC, V. **Amenities:** Restaurant; spa; guided hikes and backpacking trips; live music; Internet access in lodge.

EAST OF THE PARK

Route 120, Tioga Road, plunges within 10 miles from Tioga Pass, just below 10,000 feet, to the desert around Mono Lake and the little community of Lee Vining. A charming, historic lodge with well-kept cabins, the **Tioga Pass Resort** (no phone; www.tiogapassresort.com; $115–$228 double) sits just outside the park boundary at 9,641 feet. Rooms book up far in advance, but you can sometimes grab a last-minute cancellation. There are several nice-looking motels in Lee Vining; the Mono Lake Committee Information Center offers referrals (p. 371).

NEAR HETCH HETCHY

Well off the beaten track, **Evergreen Lodge** (© **800/935-6343** or 209/379-2606; www.evergreenlodge.com) offers nice, old-fashioned cabins under the shade of towering pines. A double cabin is $129 to $219, family cabins $119 to $259 a night. It's on the narrow, twisting Evergreen Road just outside the Hetch Hetchy entrance. Guests can join trail rides or use the pools and tennis courts across the road at Camp Mather, a facility owned by the city of San Francisco.

6 Family-Friendly Dining

IN YOSEMITE VALLEY

LOW-STRESS MEALS

The **Pavilion Buffet cafeteria at Curry Village** feeds families by the thousands, which helps explain the bland, institutional food. The interior is dark but was not too noisy when I visited. The setup of the place gets you in and out quickly: You pay by the person when you enter, then pick whatever food you want. Breakfast runs from 7 to 10am and costs $9.50 for diners 13 and older, $7.50 for children 6 to 12, and $5.75 for children under 6; dinner is 5:30 to 8pm and costs $12, $10, and $6.50, respectively. It is open daily April through October. The **Pizza Patio** next door, open daily noon to 9pm in the same season, is very popular but lacks indoor seating. A summer-only hamburger stand carries the usual fast-food choices.

Yosemite Lodge at the Falls has a year-round food court serving fish, chicken, ribs, steaks, pizza, pasta, burgers, and salads. High-season hours are daily 6:30am to 9pm. Breakfast prices run $3.75 to $7 while lunch and dinner range from $6 to $9.25. The outdoor mall of Yosemite Village has several quick food choices. **Degnan's Deli** is open year-round, selling sandwiches and fast food to eat on the picnic tables outside; the **Village Grill** sells fast-food fare mid-April through October; and **The Loft** offers pizza and pasta in summer only. At least one of the three is always open 7am to 5pm.

ON TIOGA ROAD

Tuolumne Meadows Grill, a snack bar in a tent, is at the store on Tioga Road, serving only lunch items—burgers, hot dogs—between 11am and 5pm. Items range from $2.50 to $8.75. Otherwise the only eateries are **White Wolf Lodge** and **Tuolumne Lodge.** Facilities in the high country are open daily mid-June through mid-September, weather permitting. Heavy snows during the winter of 2004–05 pushed the season back to mid-July.

Tuolumne Meadows Lodge   If I'm somewhere near the Tioga Road and I'm hungry, I'm going to try to land a table at this lodge's dining room. Its outward appearance is nothing special: a tent dining room with long tables and stacking metal chairs standing on a painted concrete floor. But the food—eggs, cereals, and grill items for breakfast, beef, fish, poultry, vegetarian, and occasionally lamb for dinner—is surprisingly good. There's little leeway, time-wise, for meals, so don't be late.

Tuolumne Meadows Lodge. (℃) **209/372-8413.** Kids' menu. Nonguests can reserve for the same day, guests can reserve farther out. Breakfast $5–$6.75; dinner $8.75–$24. AE, DC, DISC, MC, V. Mid-June to mid-Sept daily breakfast 7:30–8:30am; dinner 6–7pm, 7–8:15pm for walk-ins.

White Wolf Lodge   As with its companion lodging down the road in Tuolumne Meadows, this tent-cabin camp has its own dining room inside a cottage-style building to feed breakfast and dinner primarily to those who stay here, although if you just came out of the backcountry they'll let you reserve a seat. The decor isn't memorable: a tiny dining room with six or seven tables and chairs standing on a wooden floor, with another five or six tables outside on a covered patio. The menu here is fairly simple, revolving around beef, fish, poultry, salads, and vegetarian entrees for dinner, and the small dining room makes it hard to get a table on your time frame.

White Wolf Lodge. (℃) **209/372-8416.** Kids' menu. Nonguests can reserve for the same day, guests can reserve farther out. Breakfast $5.75–$9.50; dinner $7.75–$23. AE, DC, DISC, MC, V. Mid-June to mid-Sept daily breakfast 7:30–8:30am; dinner 6–7pm, 7–8:15pm for walk-ins.

AT WAWONA

Your best bet for a simple family meal is to drive 2 miles from the south park entrance to the **Tenaya Lodge** (p. 390), which has a deli, a grill serving burgers and pizza, and a casual fine-dining restaurant. The restaurant at the Wawona Hotel is described below.

BEST-BEHAVIOR MEALS

Each of the park's three hotels has a formal dining room. Delaware North seems to find good chefs, and the meals I've had have ranged from quite good to brilliant. Only well-behaved older children and teens (and not all adults) will have the patience required. The first two are open year-round; Wawona is open mid-March though November and some winter weekends.

Ahwahnee Dining Room   This grand palace is not for most park visitors, though you'd be remiss to not walk through it even if you don't plan to take a meal here. Outside of the dining room rises the Grand Lounge with its two spacious fireplaces, couches and arm chairs, the Under Lounge, the Mural Room, the Winter Club Room, and the Solarium. You even can sign up for a 50-minute tour of the grand hotel and its grounds at the concierge desk in the lobby. Perhaps the focal point of this grand luxury hotel, the dining room is certainly something to look at, with its high vaulted ceilings and tall windows, but many families would not be comfortable there. The evening dress code requires jackets and ties for men and dresses or pantsuits for women, and the atmosphere remains stiff and proper at other, casual-dress meals. Still, the meals are sumptuous, well-prepared, and expensive, and kids have their own menus to choose from.

The Ahwahnee Lodge. ℰ 209/372-1489. Kids' menu, highchairs, boosters, crayons. Dinner reservations required. Evening dress code (see above). Breakfast $9–$19; lunch $11–$19; dinner entrees $25–$40; kids' menu $6–$10; Sun brunch (7am–3pm) $33 adults, half price for kids 6–10, free for under 3. AE, DISC, MC, V. Mid-Mar to Nov Mon–Sat 7–10am, 11:30am–3pm, and 5:30–9:15pm; Sun 7am–3pm and 5:30–9:15pm.

Mountain Room   This restaurant at Yosemite Lodge is far more relaxed yet maintains a pleasingly opulent feel, with large windows looking out on the cliffs and falls above. My meal, after a daylong hike to the top of Half Dome and back, was impeccable: sesame ahi filet seared rare and accompanied by wasabi mashed potatoes and a cucumber-radish salad served with soy glaze. The children's menu offers chicken, grilled cheese, spaghetti, and other kid-friendly items for a fairly friendly $5.75 to $7.75 for those 12 and under.

Yosemite Lodge. ℰ 209/372-1274. Kids' menu, highchairs, boosters, crayons. Reservations suggested for parties of 8 or more. Dinner $15–$29; kids' menu $5.75–$7.75. AE, DISC, MC, V. Mid-Mar to Nov daily 5:30–8:30pm.

Wawona Hotel Dining Room   The dining room at the Wawona Hotel is a charming throwback with its old-fashioned wood floors, high ceilings, tall windows, and tablecloths. The food can be extraordinary, and while the setting suggests formality, the service is professional enough to put all at ease, even children. The fatal flaw is that the dining room doesn't accept reservations for dinner (except parties of eight or more), and no family can wait as long as may be necessary—over 90 minutes at times. There is a fun outdoor barbecue on Saturdays from 5 to 7pm. The items, which change frequently, might include a half chicken, southwestern steak, or a grilled fish, although there are always burgers and hot dogs; adults pay $21, children 7 to 12 $11, 4 to 6 $5.75.

Wawona Hotel. ℰ 209/375-1425. Kids' menu, highchairs, boosters, crayons. No reservations. Breakfast $8–$11; lunch $9.50–$17; dinner $9.50–$30; kids' menu $4.50–$9.75. AE, DISC, MC, V. Mid-Mar to Nov daily 7:30–10am, 11:30am–2pm, and 5:30–9pm.

7 Exploring Yosemite National Park with Your Kids

ENTRANCE FEES   The park entrance fee of $20 per vehicle is collected at each entrance and is good for 7 days. You also can gain entry with the America the Beautiful Pass (see "Entrance Fees" and "Passes," both in chapter 2). Entry stations don't take credit cards.

NATURAL PLACES
YOSEMITE VALLEY

As you enter Yosemite Valley, the mountains seem to open like a curtain onto one of the world's main attractions. It's not something you can be prepared for. The granite walls of the valley soar up to 3,000 feet, more than a half-mile, where the sun treats their bold shapes differently than the shadows in the ordinary world below. Waterfalls tumble from the top, disintegrating into showers of mist and spray during the long free fall. As you stand below in the sun, the water cools your cheek.

Yosemite Valley started as a crack in the granite that the Merced River slowly carved into a V-shaped canyon about 2,400 feet deep (measuring from the top of El Capitan). Then a series of glaciers plowed through. The big one was about 1 million years ago, when a glacier filled the valley with so much ice that only the tip of El Capitan stuck out. We know it went that high because it left boulders behind called glacial erratics, up on the rim (see "Experiment: Finding Glacier Tracks," p. 376). That glacier ground out the valley something like 2,000 feet deeper and about a mile wide, straightening out the crooked river canyon and making the sides smoother and steeper. Later, at least two more glaciers came through, but they didn't get nearly as high on the sidewalls. If they had, they would have worn away the huge spires and cracks on the valley sides that help make it so beautiful. Each glacier left behind broken rock in the bottom of the valley. The last glacier, at its largest about 20,000 years ago, went only as far as Bridalveil Meadow, and it built a line-shaped hill across the valley called a **moraine.** The moraine worked as a dam to hold back a lake that filled the valley. That lake slowly filled with dirt carried down from the mountains, leaving the flat meadow and forest now on the valley floor. This dirt layer is about 1,000 feet deep, lying above the true rock floor that the glacier carved out. Downstream, the Merced still runs through a V-shaped valley as it leaves the park, because the glaciers didn't make it down that far.

There's a lot for a family to do in Yosemite Valley, including fun stuff like floating down the Merced in a little raft, biking the paved trails to hiking trail heads and other sites, seeing the museums, and hiking to the spectacular waterfalls. But it's not a wilderness experience, or even, much of the time, a natural experience. The valley is a city, or at least a town. It has thousands of visitors and the workers to serve them, stores, health facilities, churches, and everything else a town has, all squeezed into the 7×1-mile valley floor. Yosemite Village is a busy pedestrian mall served by frequent and often-crowded buses. On the short trail to Lower Yosemite Falls one summer day, I was so surrounded by people I felt claustrophobic, unable to get far enough away not to smell others' perfume and cologne. While the trail has been rebuilt and the parking is being removed, the people will still be there. Steeper trails are less crowded once you get beyond a level that weeds out hikers in poor physical shape, including the wonderful Mist Trail and John Muir Trail to Nevada Falls from Happy Isles, with its unfolding series of waterfalls, and the Upper Yosemite Falls Trail, from Camp 4. But the steepness that weeds out couch potatoes also eliminates most kids younger than about age 10. (Consider instead the trails on Glacier Point Rd., in the next section.)

While the **Mist Trail** 𝆑𝆑 can be grueling for inexperienced youngsters if you try to drag them to the top of Nevada Fall (a steep, 7-mile round-trip), it's a great hike to let older kids test their endurance. They won't get bored, either, watching as the Merced River crashes out of the high country. On a hot summer day, the spray is especially cooling, and you can stop by the riverbank to splash along the way. A good turnaround point, and a noteworthy goal that will pump up a younger hiker's self-esteem, is the 3-mile round-trip to the top of Vernal Fall.

For many families, the solution is to take advantage of the fun here and accept all the other people. Just plan to find your solitude elsewhere. The families I saw floating and splashing in Merced River had the right idea. They were using Yosemite Valley as the world's most beautiful playground, knowing that playgrounds are crowded. (See "Places for Learning" and "For the Active Family," below, for what to do in the valley.)

The maps contained in the park newspaper, *Yosemite Today,* are handy for understanding the layout of the valley, the walking and bike paths, and the order of the bus stops. The paper also has schedules of activities and other changing information. Our valley map (p. 374) is useful, too, but it may not be as up-to-date. The inexpensive guide listed in "Reading Up" (p. 371) is all you'll need for hiking.

GLACIER POINT

This is a mind-blowing overlook directly above Yosemite Valley's Curry Village. Standing at the railing, you are at the top of a 3,200-foot vertical cliff, able to see almost straight down. It's a short, paved walk from the large parking lots to the overlooks. From different spots you can see in different directions across much of the park. Rangers wander through the crowd to answer questions and offer talks, which you can find out about in *Yosemite Today.* A snack stand is open 10am to 4pm during the summer, but go earlier than that to avoid the crowds.

After you get a load of the view, use Glacier Point Road to get off into high country, away from most other people, on some terrific family hikes. The road is 16 miles long, splitting from the Wawona Road south of Yosemite Valley, and is closed beyond the Badger Pass Ski Area (see "Winter Sports," p. 401) during the winter. From the point itself, two paths lead down to the valley. Hiking both ways would be well beyond most families' abilities, but you can take a shuttle bus one-way (see "By Bus," p. 372). The Four Mile Trail takes you right down into the valley, a walk that should take 3 hours or less. For a longer and even more interesting hike, with three incredible waterfalls, take the Panorama Trail and John Muir Trail via Nevada Falls, a downhill hike of 8.5 miles. These are busy trails. At mile 13.2 of the Glacier Point Road, some great short hikes may be less crowded (still, get there early) and offer little ones the chance to climb one of Yosemite's granite domes. Sentinel Dome is 1.1 miles from the trail head, an easy climb with incredible views. At 8,122 feet it is the highest viewpoint into the valley other than Half Dome. Taft Point, 1.1 miles the other way from the trail head, has weird and scary cracks as well as cliff-overhang views. The hike itself isn't threatening, but hold hands near the end. You can link both into a 4.5-mile loop by using a 2.3-mile section of the Pohono Trail from Sentinel Dome to the midpoint of the Taft Point Trail. (From the Sentinel Dome end, it is confusing: Follow the sign to Glacier Point, turning left or west at the T.)

SEQUOIA GROVES

About 500 giant Sequoias grow in **Mariposa Grove,** the park's largest, near the south entrance. These huge, ancient trees are among the world's greatest natural wonders. You can't help but be impressed by the 2,700-year-old Grizzly Giant, with its immense base, or the amazing length of the fallen monarch. The grove's most famous tree, the Wawona Tunnel Tree, with a 30-foot vehicle tunnel cut in 1881, died of the wound, falling in 1969, but there are other trees you can walk under, including the bizarre Clothespin Tree, with its natural tunnel.

The grove covers a large area, and the big trees are separated more widely than at the groves in Sequoia and Kings Canyon national parks (covered in the next chapter). This more sparse character, combined with the land's steepness, forces visitors to decide how to see the Mariposa Grove. The popular way is to ride an open-air tram pulled by a tractor over a road up to the Upper Grove area, site of the thickest stands of trees and the Wawona Tunnel Tree. There it stops for a look at the tiny, dark Galen Clark Museum and a chance to get out and hike back down, skipping the last half of the tour. The tram usually leaves every 20 minutes in the summer for a 1-hour ride (call © **209/375-1621** for departure times) and costs $16 for adults, $14 for seniors, $11 for children 5 to 12, free for children under 5. It's appealing to get a ride up the hill, but the forest seemed diminished by the corny narration and the crowded cart. A guy sitting next to me said, "That tree don't look so big," an impossible reaction for someone walking through this grove. Instead, I recommend picking up the 50¢ guide brochure and hiking up the hill as far as you can; a 2.5-mile round-trip, with little elevation gain, will take you to the Fallen Monarch, Grizzly Giant, California Tunnel Tree (still standing), and the Clothespin Tree. The museum is 2.1 miles from the trail head, one-way, and the top of the grove is 3 miles.

Parking is a problem at the grove. The lots at the trail head fill quickly (again, starting early helps). When they do, you have to take a shuttle, which stops at the park's south entrance, where the small lot fills fast, and at the Wawona Store. That's inconvenient, since Wawona is several slow miles away and you have to wait for the bus both ways. The solution is to plan plenty of time for your visit; half a day would be reasonable.

Two other, smaller groups of Sequoias, **Tuolumne** and **Merced groves,** are along Big Oak Flat Road, north of Yosemite Valley. Tuolumne has 25 trees and Merced even fewer. You have to walk into both groves, so they're more peaceful than Mariposa Grove. To get to Tuolumne Grove, you park near Crane Flat and walk 1 mile on an old road that meets a half-mile nature trail. Merced Grove, a little farther north, is 1½ miles off the road; if you make the hike, you might have it to yourself.

TUOLUMNE MEADOWS & TIOGA ROAD 𝕽𝕽𝕽

Tioga Road rises into the mountains and crosses the top of the Sierra. From the west, you come up through towering pines and then break out on solid granite highlands shaped like the billowing folds of a windswept flag. The biggest views start around Olmsted Point, where Tenaya Canyon falls away to Yosemite Valley. The road is chipped from granite. A lake fills a bowl of solid rock. A cliff juts up at random, without a tree to give a sense of how high it is—then you see rock climbers on it, the size of ants, and you know it's very big. At Tenaya Lake, canoeists and swimmers splash around. At Tuolumne, the meadows spread broad and green, decorated by bright points of wildflowers and surrounded by towering white mounds of granite domes. Then, after the pass, the mountains drop abruptly to a desert basin and Mono Lake.

The air is cool and fresh along Tioga Road, which crests at an elevation of 9,900 feet, and there's more room to spread out away from crowds than in Yosemite Valley. The area isn't rich in sightseeing, but it is a great place to camp, take easy or challenging day hikes or go backpacking, swim in cold water, and perhaps join a horseback ride. A free shuttle runs back and forth on Tioga Road to link trail heads, so you can plan a hike with different starting and ending points (see "By Bus," p. 372). The area doesn't open until snow clears from the road, around late May or early June. Mosquitoes are intense though July.

Soda Springs is a flat, 1-mile hike that anyone can manage; it starts near the Tuolumne Meadows campground. Naturally carbonated water bubbles up in the meadows in tiny ponds. Another great family day hike is the climb to **Dog Lake.** We had a picnic and a swim from the point that sticks out into the lake. The trail behind **Lembert Dome** is the less steep of two routes; the other trail head is near Tuolumne Meadows Lodge, and you can connect the two with the shuttle. Just the loop with the lake is 2.6 miles. If you climb to the top of the dome, the total is 4.2 miles—an easy half-day with two great destinations. From White Wolf Lodge, the Harden or Lukens lakes trails are good, easy day hikes, each around 5 miles, round-trip. Many of my favorite hikes in the area are more challenging, however, rising up into the bare, rounded granite mountains to strange, rock-rimmed lakes. Teens and strong 10-year-old hikers can manage the steep, 8-mile round-trip hikes to Lower Cathedral Lake, on the John Muir Trail from Tuolumne Meadow, or Sunrise Lakes, starting from the west end of Tenaya Lake. If you can spend a couple of nights, these and other trails link for spectacular backpacking trips. A string of five High Sierra Camps offers dormitory beds in tent cabins for hikers (see "Family-Friendly Accommodations," p. 379). Or, if you don't win the lottery for a bed, you can get a permit to camp nearby, use the outhouse and bear lockers, use piped water at some, and perhaps buy a meal in camp.

HETCH HETCHY

The Hetch Hetchy area at the north of the park is an easy and little-used way into the wilderness. This canyon on the Tuolumne River is most famous for the conservation fight over the O'Shaughnessy Dam, which was approved by Congress in 1913 over the objections of John Muir and still gathers drinking water for San Francisco. But even with the reservoir, the valley remains a grand area with good hiking and great views. As with Yosemite Valley, and on a similar scale, river erosion started digging Hetch Hetchy and glaciation followed to straighten out the valley, deepen it, and widen it. Unlike in Yosemite Valley, however, glaciers here continued to come right to the top of the canyon during each ice age, grinding the sides to the end of the last glacial period, 10,000 years ago. The result is that Hetch Hetchy's walls are relatively smooth, without the cracks and spires that give Yosemite some of its character. It's a good place to find glacier tracks such as polish and chatter marks.

The roads coming here are narrow, winding, and scenic. Exit the main part of the park at Big Oak Flats and drive 7½ miles north through a thick, dark forest on Evergreen Road, then reenter the Hetch Hetchy entrance and take Hetch Hetchy Road 9 miles to the dam. The views into Poopenaut Valley are dizzying, and remote trails climb and descend from the road. The best family hike leads across the dam, through a tunnel, and 2.5 miles to **Wapama Falls,** which tumbles 1,000 feet down the canyon walls. It's an easy, mostly level trail though rocky, arid terrain under 4,000 feet, and can be warm. Many other trails lead from here for steeper hikes or backpacking expeditions. The campground at the dam is for backpackers with permits only. Other than the bathroom and pay phone, there are no services.

PLACES FOR LEARNING
YOSEMITE VALLEY
Yosemite Museum and Indian Village of Ahwahnee *Finds*   Ongoing talks and native craft demonstrations are the great attractions of this little museum. Our son was fascinated. The small gallery displays a collection of southern Miwok and Paiute artifacts. Outside, a nature trail re-creates the tribes' buildings and shows their ways.

Families shouldn't miss it. Sometimes demonstrations take place there; other times, you can follow the self-guided path with a booklet. Another gallery, open daily 10am to noon and 1 to 4pm in the summer and sporadically the rest of the year, shows a collection of art on the valley or revolving exhibits.

Next to the visitor center, Yosemite Village. No phone. Museum: Year-round daily 9am–noon and 1–4:30pm. Indian Village: Open daylight hours.

Nature Center at Happy Isles   This one-room nature center has up-to-date exhibits on the park's plants and animals and on bear avoidance. Younger children may enjoy the animal dioramas, but it's not a hands-on place. The wooded streamside trails welcome a few minutes' ramble.

In the upper valley. June–Sept daily 10am–noon and 1–4pm.

LeConte Memorial   The Sierra Club runs a library, a children's corner, and education programs (listed in the park newspaper) from this former visitor center.

Yosemite Valley. ℂ 209/372-4542. May–Aug Wed–Sun 10am–4pm. Closed Sept–Apr.

Ansel Adams Gallery   Adams' black-and-white photographs of Yosemite helped to popularly define the area and made him one of our best-known photographers. The shop sells his prints and those of other photographers, as well as inexpensive gifts and cards.

Next to the main visitor center. ℂ 209/372-4413. www.anseladams.com. Year-round daily 9am–5pm.

WAWONA

Pioneer Yosemite History Center   Kids enjoy this little village of old cabins and other buildings brought from all over the park, the covered bridge, and the collection of antique carriages. In July and August, Wednesday through Sunday, volunteers often dress in costume and play the roles of historic park figures. (Check the park newspaper—this is a volunteer program, and plans can change.) We talked with a blacksmith hammering away at a horseshoe. You can take a short stagecoach ride at times, too ($3 adults, $2 children 3–12). At other times, pick up the guide booklet to find your way around.

On Hwy. 41, Wawona. No phone. Open-air displays always open. Check park newspaper for hours of demonstrations and coach rides.

8 For the Active Family

BACKPACKING

Yosemite has more than 800 miles of trails, including many that are mostly above tree line, crossing the granite bedrock of the high Sierra. Besides the beauty, I enjoy the way this alien terrain helps peel away the world of people on an overnight. Also, by spending the night out, you can explore longer trails and get away from the day hikers. You may start to meet others so rarely that you're eager to see them and compare your adventures. The high country is cool in the summer, and the weather is usually fine (of course, you must still prepare for bad weather). Other advantages of backpacking here include a simple backcountry permit system (see "Backcountry Camping Permits," p. 387) and ample support provided by the park and concessionaire, which ranges from equipment rental to facilities in the backcountry. The five High Sierra Camps have dorms and showers for hiker guests, and backpackers can eat there by prior arrangement and camp nearby to use outhouses, bear boxes, and, at some, running water (see "High Sierra Camps," p. 387).

The disadvantages of a backpacking trip at Yosemite depend on your group's abilities. These trails tend to be steep, and at high elevations that can be tough, especially if your pack is heavy. I've seen miserable backpackers huffing and puffing up the trails with huge loads (overpacking is the most common beginner's mistake). There are easier places to take your kids on a first backpacking expedition. The other big factors in planning are the season and elevation. The high country isn't free from snow until July, and mosquitoes last through the month. Lower-elevation trips, including some around Hetch Hetchy, are open earlier, but those areas get hot in midsummer. If you're up for a week or more on the trail, there are few better opportunities in the country than the **John Muir Trail,** running from Yosemite Valley through Tuolumne Meadows and 211 miles down the Sierra to Mount Whitney, in Sequoia National Park, or the **Pacific Crest Trail,** which runs from Mexico to Canada.

You'll need to start planning at home. Maps and trail guides are covered under "Reading Up" (p. 371). Although you can camp anywhere off the roads, you'll want to find out where good sites are. Also prepare by learning black bear avoidance techniques and planning to fit all your food, soap, or anything else with a strong odor in a bear-resistant canister, for rent at the park. The park provides copious advice (or see "Dangerous Wildlife," in chapter 2).

You can also backpack at Yosemite with a guided group, offered by **Yosemite Mountaineering School** (see "Climbing," below). Make a reservation, but the school will take drop-ins if there's room. Planned excursions range from a short-distance learning-to-backpack trip to 4-day excursions with mountain climbing on the way. With a group of three or more, you can set up a custom trip for a little more than the cost of joining one of the regular hikes. They cost about $133 per person per day for groups of four or more and include all meals and tents, stoves, and water filters. **Yosemite Field Seminars** include educational backpacking trips (see "Kid-Friendly Programs," below).

CLIMBING &&&

Yosemite's solid and spectacular granite cliffs are the most challenging and the most popular places to rock climb in the United States. **Yosemite Mountaineering School** has taught climbing here since 1969; it sells climbing equipment and sells and rents camping equipment. Daily beginning classes take students up 60 feet after they learn the necessary skills. Kids as young as 14 are accepted, and the fee is around $117 (more if fewer than three sign up). Advanced classes are available, too. The school is based in Tuolumne Meadows from June to September and year-round in Curry Village in Yosemite Valley (© **209/372-8344;** www.yosemitemountaineering.com).

HIKING

There are other things to do at Yosemite, but they're mainly garnish to the main meal, hiking. You have to walk in the high country and through the Sequoia groves to really get what the place is about—the textures of rocks and plants, the smell of the clean high country and the dusky forest, the way the sun feels on your cheek at the end of a long, tough climb. Just driving to overlooks doesn't do it. Bring your hiking shoes and try to do a trail every day.

I've covered some favorite trails in each of the sections under "Natural Places," which begins on p. 394. Of course, there are many other choices. Use a book such as the one I've recommended under "Reading Up" (p. 371), or buy the inexpensive map guides to the three main park areas published by the Yosemite Association, which include trail maps, descriptions, and lots of other interesting information.

RAFTING

River floating at Yosemite mostly is for fun and splashing around, not thrills. The easiest and busiest spot for a float is the Merced River as it flows through Yosemite Valley. The river can be ferocious during spring melt, and late in the summer water gets scarce; but in June and July it's generally gentle enough for family play with inflatables. You can use an air mattress or **inner-tube,** slowly floating under the branches of spreading trees and past swimming beaches. To save the riverbanks, try to get in and out at sandy or gravel spots. Floating is allowed from Stoneman Bridge to Sentinel Beach (the picnic and swimming area below Sentinel Dome). The concessionaire rents **six-passenger rafts** at Curry Village (© 209/372-8319) that you can paddle yourself 3 miles downstream. The per-person cost is $21 for adults, $6 for children under 13. Children under 50 pounds are not allowed. A shuttle picks up rafters and brings them back.

There's an even better place outside the valley, where you are more likely to have the river to yourself. In the Wawona area you can float 3 miles down the Merced's south fork from Swinging Bridge, above the history center on Forest Drive, down to the Wawona Campground, passing through the pines and under the covered bridge. Use whatever you like—raft, tube, air mattress, or canoe—but you'll have to bring it along, because there are no rentals or shuttle. Stop at the campground; below that, the water gets too rough.

In either case, floating is allowed only from 10am to 6pm, and you must have life jackets on or handy.

SADDLE RIDES

Stables operated by the park concessionaire in **Yosemite Valley** (© 209/372-8348), at **Tuolumne Meadows Lodge** (© 209/372-8427), and at **Wawona** (© 209/372-6502) offer guided trail rides on mules daily in the summer and private pack trips. Two-hour rides are $53 per person, 4-hour rides are $69, and all-day rides are $96. Besides more time in the saddle, the longer rides take on more challenging and potentially scarier trails. Children must be at least 7 years old and 44 inches tall, and riders can weigh no more than 225 pounds. Call the stables for details and advice, or check Delaware North's website (www.yosemitepark.com; click "Activities," then "Recreation," then "Sports").

SWIMMING

The cold, pure water flowing from the Sierra is irresistible on a hot hike. A plunge into a mountain lake is a shock to the system that brings me back to life when I'm tired. After you strip down and dive in once, you want to do it again every time you see inviting water, but that happens far too often. Hikers can swim all over the park wherever they find safe and inviting water. Avoid swift or powerfully moving water, test cautiously before your kids jump in, and don't swim if you're unsure. And, as the Park Service warns, don't dive and don't swim above waterfalls—obvious advice, but people have died that way. Also, Hetch Hetchy Reservoir and Lake Eleanor are off-limits for swimming. The most popular stream for swimming is the **Merced River** as it passes through Yosemite Valley. There are plenty of spots to get in; just find a sandy place where you won't slip on rocks or damage the bank.

In the valley, large outdoor pools at **Yosemite Lodge** at the Falls and **Curry Village** are open to the public daily in the summer. Hours vary. The fee for nonguests is $5 for adults, $4 for children.

WINTER SPORTS

The high country is inaccessible to vehicles in the winter; but you can get there on skis, and roads are plowed in the western areas and up Glacier Point Road as high as the Badger Pass ski area. The landscape is more beautiful in the snow, when the coating of white puts colors in stark contrast. You can still tour the Sequoia groves and many trails on skis or snowshoes, and you have an improved chance of seeing mule deer and other animals that remain active in the winter. The skiing season is December through March, if snow allows. There's downhill skiing and snowboarding at the **Badger Pass ski area** (7,000 ft.), and cross-country trails go higher from there, up Glacier Point Road, which is groomed for classic or skate techniques all the way to Glacier Point, more than 10 miles away. That's where to go: Snow is unpredictable in Yosemite Valley, Wawona is at the same elevation, and Mariposa Grove is only a little higher. There are plenty of rooms available in Yosemite Valley in the winter, with discount skiing packages offered, and a free shuttle from there to Badger Pass. For current snow conditions, call © **209/372-1000.**

CROSS-COUNTRY SKIING & SNOWSHOEING

Yosemite's cross-country and backcountry skiing is truly exceptional: plenty of snow, lots of groomed trail, varied terrain, and fabulous views. Some 25 miles of groomed tracks start at Badger Pass, including an 11-mile skating or diagonal-stride track that leads up to Glacier Point and the incredible views there. There are no trail fees.

Ninety miles of marked trails from Badger Pass aren't groomed by machines, and the backcountry is open to exploration without limit. Backcountry camping permits are issued at the Badger Pass Ranger Station.

The Nordic Ski School (© **209/372-8444**), operated by the concessionaire, teaches all techniques and ability levels, as well as telemark skiing, and rents touring, skate, and telemark skis. Backcountry trips include introductory overnights to the ski hut at Glacier Point, cross-park camping expeditions, and custom trips.

DOWNHILL SKIING

Partway up Glacier Point Road, the **Badger Pass ski area** has been in operation since 1935. Most experienced skiers will find the area less than challenging, on the level of a community ski slope rather than a destination resort, but for beginners it's great. There are four lifts and a cable tow, with 85% of the hill rated beginner or intermediate. The vertical drop is 800 feet. The area offers skiing and snowboarding instruction, rentals, festivals, and activities. Weekend all-day lift tickets are $38 for adults, $32 for children 13 to 17, $15 for 12 and under, free for children under 7 with a parent. Ski packages rent for $24 for adults and $19 for kids, and snowboard packages are $35 and $30. Lessons are offered daily, with programs for children as young as 4.

SKATING

An outdoor rink at Curry Village in Yosemite Valley (© **209/372-8319**) is open all winter. Admission is $8 for adults, $6 for children under 13 for each session, of which there are two to four daily (check the park newspaper). You can rent skates for $3.

(Tips) Places for Relaxed Play & Picnics

There are limitless places for relaxed play at Yosemite, but no public playground equipment in or near the park. There are a couple of picnic areas at swimming spots along the Merced River in Yosemite Valley and one near the Ahwahnee hotel. In Wawona, picnic grounds are at the Pioneer Yosemite History Center, near the campground, and in Mariposa Grove. Several picnic areas are along Tioga Road, with especially appealing spots near Tenaya Lake.

SNOWSHOEING

The ski school at Badger Pass rents snowshoes for $20 a day. Modern snowshoes are easy to use even for beginners and give you great freedom in the backcountry, where you can hike all alone on trails that are jammed with people in the summer. Two-hour ranger-led snowshoe outings go daily from Badger Pass in the season. There's a $5 fee, and snowshoes are provided.

9 Kid-Friendly Programs

CHILDREN'S PROGRAMS

The Park Service, Sierra Club, Yosemite Institute, and Delaware North concession all offer programs for kids, which are listed with other family and adult programs in the *Yosemite Today* park newspaper and start from many different sites.

The park's **Junior Ranger program** takes two forms. In the summer, children can join a 2-hour ranger-led session for ages 7 to 13. At the end, participants receive a badge. Generally, parents have to go along. The other way for your children to earn a badge is by completing a booklet of activities, attending a ranger program such as a campfire, picking up trash, and handing in the work at a visitor center. The booklets, published by the Yosemite Association, are the *Little Cub Handbook* ($3), for ages 3 to 6, and the *Junior Ranger Handbook* ($5), for ages 7 to 13. These are excellent educational materials, spiral bound, printed on stiff paper, and amusingly illustrated, with activities that help children use their own senses to deepen their appreciation of the park, not the typical busywork you would want to do only on a rainy day. Pick up a copy for your children even if you don't intend to work toward a badge.

FAMILY & ADULT PROGRAMS

NATIONAL PARK PROGRAMS

Check *Yosemite Today* for the schedule of programs at each park area offered by a variety of organizations. Park rangers lead activities at Yosemite Valley, Wawona, Mariposa Grove, Crane Flat, Big Oak Flat, White Wolf, and Tuolumne Meadows. Campfire programs take place nightly at many campgrounds. Many of the offerings are guided hikes that take much of the day and include casual natural history commentary. In Yosemite Valley, painting and photography classes for adults, families, and kids take place many summer days. Because some programs have size limits, check the park newspaper when you arrive to decide what you might want to do, and sign up at the visitor center.

YOSEMITE THEATER

Live dramatic performances take place several nights a week in the summer at the visitor center auditoriums. They're staged by professionals and sponsored by the park concessionaire. Tickets cost less than a night at the movies. Shows last 60 to 90 minutes. Past performances have included music about the park and the environment—great for kids—and one-man shows on the life and thoughts of John Muir. The park newspaper lists times.

YOSEMITE FIELD SEMINARS

The **Yosemite Association,** listed under "Yosemite Address Book (p. 365), offers dozens of hikes, natural history lessons, art and writing workshops, and backpacking trips that use the park as a classroom. The sessions, which typically last a few days, are offered from March through October. Only a few sessions are intended for families, but teens can join others with their parents when appropriate—call and ask. A typical 3-day session is about $250.

10 Entertainment outside the Park

Yosemite Mountain Sugar Pine Railroad (℄ 559/683-7273; www.ymsprr.com) runs a steam-powered excursion train around a 4-mile loop south of the park from April to October. A self-propelled Jenny Car—an enclosed, gas-powered vehicle historically used by railroad and logging workers—takes tours when the steam engine isn't fired up. The noise, steam, and fire of the locomotive are a thrill, even if the route of the narrow-gauge line through the pines isn't spectacular. The operation re-creates a logging train that operated here from 1908 to 1924. The station is at 56001 Hwy. 41 in Fish Camp, just outside the park's south entrance near Wawona, and has a little museum, shops, and places to picnic. Tickets are $15 for adults, $7.50 for children 3 to 12 for the 1-hour steam-train ride, and $11 and $5.50 for the 30-minute Jenny Car tour. Children under 3 ride free. Train seating is not covered, so wait for a sunny day.

FAST FACTS: Yosemite National Park

Area Code The area codes are **209** and **559.**

ATMs ATMs are available at Yosemite Village (just south of and inside of the Village Store), Yosemite Lodge, the gift shop at Curry Village, and the Wawona store.

Emergencies For emergencies, dial ℄ **911.**

Hospitals & Clinics Healthcare is available at the **Yosemite Medical Clinic** on Ahwahnee Drive (℄ **209/372-4637**). If you require dental services, you can find them adjacent to the medical clinic (℄ **209/372-4200** or 209/372-4637).

Information For information, write Yosemite National Park, P.O. Box 577, Yosemite, CA 95389; call ℄ **209/372-0200;** or look on the Internet at www.nps.gov/yose.

Pharmacies The Yosemite Medical Clinic on Ahwahnee Drive has a limited pharmacy (℄ **209/372-4637**).

Post Office You'll find post offices in Yosemite Village, Yosemite Lodge, Curry Village, Wawona, and Tuolumne Meadows.

Time Zone The park is on **Pacific Standard Time.**

Weather Updates For weather updates, look on the Internet at www.crh.noaa.gov/riw

15

Sequoia & Kings Canyon National Parks

These two parks, knit together like Siamese twins, create memories at every turn. The silent reverence you feel walking among the giant Sequoias. The sight of families splashing about in the granite pools of the Marble Fork of the Kaweah River at the Lodgepole campground. The sense of achievement you get from climbing from the Mineral King area to upper Monarch Lake, 10,700 feet high, cooling in the frigid water, and then drying in the sun on the warm bedrock. And, for a park focused on tall trees, going underground into the cool, damp darkness of Crystal Cave. The feeling that this is the way a national park is meant to be. National parks were never intended as places to worry about crowds, reservations, regulations, and how to find a leftover piece of wilderness no one else has taken. At Sequoia and Kings Canyon, crowds are few, and no one seems to be worrying about anything or in a hurry to get anywhere.

Sequoia and Kings Canyon are officially two national parks; but they're connected and managed together, so there's no real reason for them to be separate. Sequoia contains most of the world's largest giant Sequoias, including huge groves where you can hike and camp without seeing another person. With a little effort, you can also explore the park's vast backcountry of granite mountains. Kings Canyon National Park contains more Sequoias, and one of the nation's deepest and most impressive canyons. Roads reach only the tiniest sliver of the park, leaving immense backcountry for long hiking or horse-packing trips. Neither park has many hotel rooms, and RVs have trouble on many of the narrow, twisting roads; mostly, families tent in the many superb campgrounds, where finding a site is never much of a problem. Surrounding and between the parks, Sierra and Inyo national forests take in many more miles of wild land with roads to get to remote places and recreation facilities that offer some unique ways to have fun together.

BEST THINGS TO DO IN SEQUOIA & KINGS CANYON NATIONAL PARKS

- **See the world's biggest tree;** walk in the Giant Forest to see this and many other giants.
- **Hike along the Kings River** in a canyon meadow or up into the granite high country.
- **Tour Crystal or Boyden Cave** to see weird rock formations and branching passages and to experience total darkness.

Sequoia–Kings Canyon Address Book

Sequoia and Kings Canyon National Parks   47050 Generals Hwy., Three Rivers, CA 93271-9700. ℂ **559/565-3341**. www.nps.gov/seki.

Sequoia Natural History Association   47050 Generals Hwy., #10, Three Rivers, CA 93271. ℂ **559/565-3759**. www.sequoiahistory.org. For books, maps, and seminars.

Kings Canyon Park Services   P.O. Box 907, Kings Canyon National Park, CA 93633. ℂ **866/KCANYON** or 559/335-5500. www.sequoia-kingscanyon.com. Park concessionaire.

Delaware North Companies Parks & Resorts at Sequoia   P.O. Box 89, Sequoia National Park, CA 93262. ℂ **866/807-3598** or 559/253-2199. www.visitsequoia.com. Park concessionaire.

Sequoia National Forest   900 W. Grand Ave., Porterville, CA 93265. ℂ **559/784-1500**. www.fs.fed.us/r5/sequoia.

Inyo National Forest   351 Pacu Lane, Suite 200, Bishop, CA 93514. ℂ **760/873-2400**. www.fs.fed.us/r5/inyo.

- **Swim in river pools** where Native Americans bathed in the foothills near the Ash Mountain entrance.
- **Backpack or take a horse-packing trip** into true mountain wilderness.

For more information, see "For the Active Family" (p. 430).

1 History: A Messy Democracy

It has been said that only God can make a national park, and it's true that no one knows how to create natural wonders like the giant Sequoias and the cliffs of Kings Canyon— only how to destroy them. But it takes a law passed by the U.S. Congress and signed by the president to draw boundaries on a map around those places and call them a "national park," protecting the land forever. And even doing that isn't easy. Most parks had at least some people against them, and for some parks, it took many years to get Congress to agree—84 years in the case of Kings Canyon. Long after the job is done, when visitors love a park, it can be hard to imagine why anyone would want it any other way. Few people remember the fierce disagreements. But the truth is that the real reasons some parks were created didn't have much to do with the reasons we love them.

The story of Sequoia and Kings Canyon shows the weird way we make national parks. Sequoia National Park was born in the mind of a young newspaper editor, George Stewart of the *Visalia Delta*. He saw the giant Sequoias being logged in the mountains east of town in the 1870s and thought they should be saved. He wrote in his newspaper about the waste of the ancient trees and persuaded his neighbors, farmers in the San Joaquin Valley, to tell their representatives in Congress about it, too. The farmers thought the loggers up in the mountains should be stopped, but their main reason was not the beauty of the trees. They believed logging and grazing sheep in the Sierra made the water run off faster during the spring snowmelt, so that none was left for their farms in the late summer.

Under the laws of that time, the government gave away land or sold it for next to nothing for people to cut down the trees and make lumber for building or paper manufacturing. While Stewart tried to convince people there should be a park, loggers cut down large areas of the forest. One group, the Kaweah Colony, received the Giant Forest area and started to build a road to the Sequoias so that it would have a way to remove the downed trees. By the time a representative introduced a bill to set aside the park (the first step to making a law), all that was left available was a small area in the south. Everything else had been given away for logging. The bill made it through Congress very quickly, in only 2 months. President Benjamin Harrison signed it on September 25, 1890.

At the same time that Stewart was lobbying, unbeknown to him, Congress had been working on a bill to create Yosemite National Park. Just before it came up for a vote in the House of Representatives, a congressman presented a different version of the bill, with a changed list of the lands to be included in the park. The members of the House didn't know what they were voting on, because they had no written copy of the new bill. It passed anyway. When people sorted it out later, they realized that Congress had made Yosemite five times larger than they had originally planned. Sequoia National Park, which had been created less than a month earlier, was also expanded by more than five times and now included Giant Forest. Grant Grove was protected in brand-new General Grant National Park.

To this day, no one knows exactly what happened. There's no record of who came up with the new boundaries, and even the original papers disappeared. Someone made a secret agreement to create these huge parks, but who did it and why? Historians studying the story believe that the most likely explanation is that the Southern Pacific Railroad was responsible. It owned large logging businesses in other parts of California. If customers bought wood from the Sequoia groves instead, it might hurt the railroad's wood business. The new park boundaries stopped that from happening. When Congress made Sequoia National Park so much bigger, it took most of the large Sequoia trees, including the Kaweah Colony, away from the loggers. It's likely that one of the railroad's people slipped a friendly congressman the boundaries for the larger parks just before the vote.

However it happened, we can be glad Giant Forest was saved, but George Stewart was unhappy about the sneaky way the park grew. He thought the Kaweah Colony was treated unfairly. The group had followed the government's rules to get Giant Forest, and the new road was almost done, but the company men were forced off the land and arrested for cutting trees in the new national park.

Kings Canyon National Park took much, much longer, but its story also is strange. John Muir got it started. After helping make Yosemite National Park (see "History: Fight for the Valley," in chapter 14), in 1891 he wrote an article about Kings Canyon. He called the canyon "a grander valley of the same kind" as Yosemite and included a map of the area he thought should be set aside. His important friends in Washington, D.C., got to work, and within 2 years, President Harrison placed Kings Canyon and almost all the rest of southern and central Sierra Nevada in new forest reserves, which we now call national forests.

When this was happening, most people thought a national forest was the same as a national park, but it turned out the two were quite different. The U.S. Forest Service protected the national forests from being sold, but allowed people to use them for logging, grazing, hunting, or building dams. The National Park Service, on the other

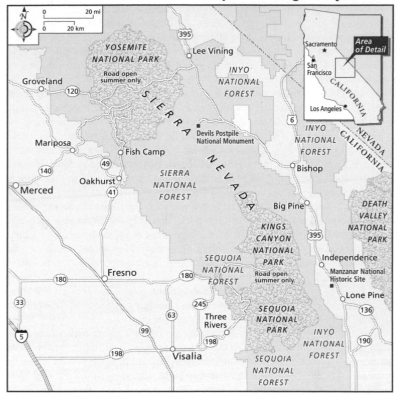

hand, has only two uses for the national parks. It preserves the land naturally for future generations, and it allows visitors to come and enjoy the land. For many years, the Park Service asked to take more of the Sierra Nevada into Sequoia National Park, but the Forest Service didn't want to give up its land. Even though the agencies were part of the same government, they spent a lot of time fighting and spreading nasty rumors about each other. In 1926, the Park Service won some national forest land when Congress expanded Sequoia National Park to take in the mountain area in the east of the park, but that land that wasn't very useful for the national forests anyway, because it was remote and didn't have many trees.

The fight for Kings Canyon was much harder. The Park Service wanted to protect the canyon John Muir had said was even better than Yosemite Valley (I think he was exaggerating, but it is very beautiful). Many other people wanted to build a dam there to hold back the Kings River in a big lake, something they could do only in a national forest, not in a national park. The city of Los Angeles wanted the dam for drinking water, the electric power companies wanted it for power, and the farmers of the San Joaquin Valley wanted it so they could water their crops. Like children fighting over a toy, they battled back and forth. And, as often happens with children who can't share, no one got any of it. The dam wasn't built as their disagreement went on, year after year and then decade after decade.

In 1939, Congress discussed creating Kings Canyon National Park, including the whole area of the park today except the canyon itself. Representative Alfred Elliot, who was against the park, tried to stop it by making people believe that the main supporter of the new park was dishonest. Elliot wrote a fake letter to park supporter Representative Bud Gearhart and put $100 in the envelope. Then Elliot started privately passing around copies of the forged letter. But Gearhart heard about what Elliot was doing, and he did something very clever. Instead of complaining about what Elliot was doing, he secretly investigated what had really happened but said nothing. Then, as Congress got ready to vote on the park, Gearhart stood up on the floor of the House of Representatives and laid out all the evidence, uncovering Elliot's nasty doings. The other congressmen and the crowd watching from the gallery roared with applause for Gearhart. Then Elliot got up to speak, but he couldn't think of anything sensible to say back, and he was jeered and laughed at. When the vote came up, the park bill passed, creating Kings Canyon National Park.

But the new park left out the most important part, the Cedar Grove area of Kings Canyon itself. It was added only in 1965, long after the people who originally asked for it had died. For most of that time, the supporters of building the dam had done the park supporters' job for them by fighting over who would get to use the water from the dam they hadn't built yet. By the 1960s, most people no longer believed in putting such a unique and beautiful place underwater, regardless of who would use the water. So Congress finally added the canyon to the park. The farmers were able to build other dams lower down the river, which took care of their need for water. L.A. got its water from other projects. And we all get the park.

In 2000, President Clinton set aside more land with a proclamation that created Giant Sequoia National Monument from part of Sequoia National Forest. It's an area not that much smaller than Sequoia National Park itself, taking in the entire gap between Sequoia and Kings Canyon national parks, including the recreational area at Hume Lake, a lot of land around Grant Grove, and a huge area south of Sequoia National Park. The new monument is like a park but is managed by the Forest Service. Its main use is preservation. Adding the two parks and the monument together, the idea started by that one Visalia newspaper editor has preserved a stretch of the Sierra about 100 miles long.

To learn more about this area, read *Challenge of the Big Trees*, by Lary M. Dilsaver and William C. Tweed (see "Reading Up," p. 410).

2 Orientation

Sequoia and Kings Canyon national parks take in much of the southern Sierra Nevada. The rest is in Sequoia, Sierra, and Inyo national forests, which surround the parks. The two national parks are connected and operate as one. Roads reach only a small part of each park, on the west side.

Sequoia National Park is the southern park. Its main visitor facilities are near and just north of the Lodgepole visitor center, midway along Generals Highway through the park. Giant Forest, Crystal Cave, and the warm, dry foothills area are to the south on the highway.

Kings Canyon National Park is the northern park. Most visitor facilities are in Grant Grove Village, a pocket to the west of the main part of the park on Highway 180, which continues east through part of Sequoia National Forest and into 3,000-foot-deep Kings Canyon. The small developed area here is called Cedar Grove.

No road crosses the Sierra Nevada in these parks, or anywhere close by. The east side of the parks is all remote backcountry (see "Arriving," below, for how to get there).

ARRIVING
BY CAR
The parks are 300 miles from San Francisco and 240 miles from L.A. From either city, use north-south I-5, Highway 99, or both. Head to Visalia for Sequoia National Park, or to Fresno for Kings Canyon National Park. From Fresno, **Highway 180** leads to the north (Big Stump) entrance, at Grant Grove. Use this route if you have a large RV or trailer. From Visalia, **Highway 198** leads to Three Rivers and the Ash Mountain entrance, near the Foothills visitor center. Large RVs should avoid that route unless they park outside and bring along a car for going on, because Generals Highway leading into the park isn't suitable for vehicles over 22 feet.

You also have the option, for $10 per person, of leaving your car in Visalia and taking a shuttle to the Giant Forest Museum. This shuttle also connects with the park's shuttle system.

There's no route to the east side of the Sierra for many hours' drive north or south. No road even touches the parks on the east, but you can get close on routes into Inyo National Forest from **Highway 395,** the north-south route that runs on the east side of the Sierra. See "Getting Around" (p. 412) for more on that area.

BY AIR
Fresno is the major airport in the region. See p. 369 for information on carriers and car rentals there.

VISITOR INFORMATION
NATIONAL PARK VISITOR CENTERS
Cedar Grove   This is essentially a station to make a quick stop to ask questions and to buy maps and guidebooks.

Near the end of Hwy. 180, in Kings Canyon. Visitor center 📞 559/565-3793. Late June to early Sept daily 9am–5pm. Closed mid-Sept to mid-May.

Foothills   Stop here as you enter the park or on the way out of the park to Mineral King to ask questions, buy maps and Crystal Cave tickets, and look at a modest collection of exhibits.

South end of Generals Hwy., just inside the Ash Mountain entrance. 📞 559/565-3135. Summer daily 8am–5pm; off season daily 8am–4:30pm.

Kings Canyon Visitor Center   This visitor center, informally known simply as the Grant Grove Visitor Center, recently had a makeover of its exhibits. The latest collection focuses on the geology and topography of Kings Canyon National Park, the High Sierra, and the giant Sequoias. One exhibit is a cross-section model of the park's topography that points out that Kings Canyon is actually deeper than the Grand Canyon. Video programs lead you off into different areas the park, a great addition if you don't have time to trek down to Cedar Grove.

Hwy. 180, near the Big Stump entrance in Grant Grove Village. 📞 559/565-4307. Summer daily 8am–6pm; spring and fall daily 8am–5pm; winter daily 9am–4:40pm.

Lodgepole   You could spend more than an hour in this visitor center's excellent museum on park nature. A wall mural explaining the food web fascinates kids. There's also a slide program on natural history and an extensive bookstore. Buy tickets for Crystal Cave here. The Lodgepole store, showers, and other facilities are nearby.

Off Generals Hwy., just north of Giant Forest. © 559/565-4436. Summer daily 8am–6pm; spring and fall daily 9am–5pm; winter Fri–Mon 9am–4:30pm.

FOREST SERVICE VISITOR CENTERS

Hume Lake Ranger District   Approaching the north end of the park on Highway 180, you can pick up National Forest Service information at Sequoia National Forest's center here.

35860 E. Kings Canyon Rd., near Dunlap. © 559/338-2251. Year-round Mon–Fri 8am–4:30pm.

READING UP

Sequoia Natural History Association (© 559/565-3759; www.sequoiahistory.org) carries a large selection of books and maps in visitor centers and a mail-order catalog. The books are for sale online, too.

   Hiking: The association publishes a Map & Guide for each park area, including trail descriptions and fine-scale topographic maps. They cost $3.50 each and are all most visitors will need for day hikes or short overnights. Coverage includes Grants Grove, Cedar Grove, Lodgepole, Giant Forest, and Mineral King. For more detailed descriptions, get Steve Sorensen's *Day Hiking Sequoia* (Sequoia Natural History Association, $13), which covers 50 hikes, including suggestions on where to fish, swim, and explore history. Sorensen has children, and his book gives special attention to hikes that kids will enjoy. Sadly, a companion volume on Kings Canyon National Park is out of print.

   Maps: If you want to go beyond the maps mentioned above, several topographic trail maps covering the whole park are printed on plastic. I think the best is from **Tom Harrison Cartography** (© 800/265-9090 or 415/456-7940; www.tomharrisonmaps. com); it costs $8.95. Contact the publisher directly for its more detailed maps of areas within the park. You can order finer-scale USGS topographic maps from SNHA, too.

   History: *Challenge of the Big Trees,* by Lary M. Dilsaver and William C. Tweed (Sequoia Natural History Association, $11), is an authoritative, readable account for adults.

THE NATIONAL PARKS IN BRIEF

Generals Highway

The main thoroughfare in **Sequoia National Park,** 46-mile Generals Highway, is among the nation's most scenic and memorable drives. It leads from **Grant Grove** south through part of **Sequoia National Forest** and then along the park's western side. South of **Lodgepole,** the road weaves among the huge trees of **Giant Forest**—sometimes even splitting in half to go around them—then descends steeply, with fabulous views, to the south and the Ash Mountain entrance in the foothills. This part of the road is as wiggly as a wet strand of spaghetti and perpetually

under construction. A vehicle over 19 feet long is physically unable to stay in its own lane on some of the curves, and it's unwise to take trailers or RVs over 22 feet. Those who are susceptible can count on carsickness.

Kings Canyon Highway

This road, an extension of **Highway 180,** passes over steep, dry terrain that will take your breath away. It's quite different from the luxurious forest of the roads in Sequoia. Entering the canyon, the highway runs along the bank of the **Kings River** until it reaches the tiny lodge and store and

Sequoia & Kings Canyon National Parks

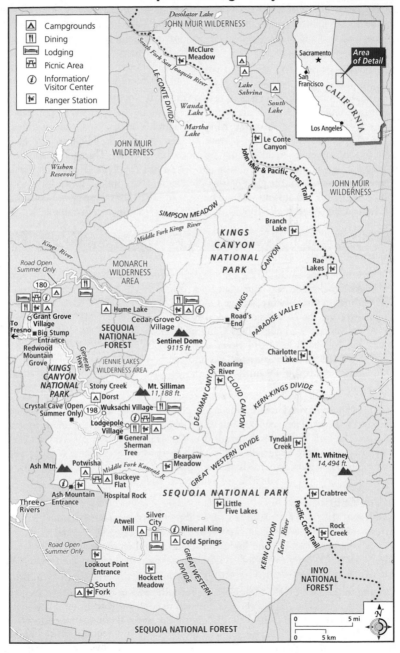

the large campgrounds at **Cedar Grove,** 28 miles from Grant Grove. The road is closed in the winter.

Backcountry Roads

Various dirt roads or narrow paved roads pierce a little way into the parks or approach their edges in places. These difficult routes are tough or impossible for RVs to navigate. **Mineral King Road** is an incredibly twisty, narrow, and partly unpaved road leading up into the mountains in the southwest of the park; you pay for the great destination with an exhausting ride. The **Hume Lake Road** (C.R. 13S09) runs

from Kings Highway 6 miles east of Grant Grove to Generals Highway, 5 miles south of Grant Grove, with many winding curves through the trees. Several other minor back roads are covered in the sections about their destinations.

Gateway Towns

The only town right at the park is **Three Rivers,** a small tourist-oriented settlement along Highway 198 at the south entrance. The nearest major centers are the flatland cities of **Visalia,** about 30 miles from the south entrance, and **Fresno,** more than 50 miles from the north entrance.

3 Getting Around

BY CAR

The twisting roads, especially the south half of **Generals Highway,** cause carsickness and make for slow driving. Allow an hour from the south entrance to Lodgepole, another hour to Grant Grove, and an hour from Grant Grove to Cedar Grove. Allow 2 hours to cover the 24 miles of **Mineral King Road.** Several roads close in the winter. After November snows, **Kings Canyon Highway** (Hwy. 180) closes until late April, and Mineral King Road closes until late May. Generals Highway north of Lodgepole closes in heavy winter snows and can be blocked for days or even weeks. Other, minor roads also remain closed in the winter.

BY RV

This is not a great park for RVs. Only a few places allow you to hook up your rig near the park, and several key roads are not recommended or are just plain unsafe for large vehicles. The Park Service recommends that RVs over 22 feet stay off Generals Highway (Hwy. 198) from Lodgepole to the south entrance, and very large RVs or trailers are prohibited on most park roads; they simply won't fit. Narrow roads closed entirely to RVs large or small include Mineral King Road and the road to Crystal Cave.

IN ANY VEHICLE

Gasoline   No gas is for sale in the park proper, but there are gas stations at Three Rivers, at Hume Lake Christian Camps, at Silver City Lodge on Mineral King Road (p. 424), and at Kings Canyon Lodge on Highway 180 on the way to Cedar Grove. Silver City and Kings Canyon lodges both use old-fashioned pumps that measure the fuel in a glass cylinder—museum pieces in action.

Driving to the East Side   You can't drive from the west to the east side of the parks directly, and unless you have a very good reason to go, the trip probably isn't worth it. Without delays, the trip from the midpoint on the west side to the midpoint on the east side takes 6 hours. The year-round route takes you south to Bakersfield, east on Highway 178, then north on Highway 395. The other way is to go north and cross the mountains on Yosemite's Tioga Road (open in the summer only), and then go south on 395. Or you could hike it. That takes about a week.

4 Planning Your Outings

WHEN TO GO

While below the parks the San Joaquin Valley burns in a furnace of summer heat, Giant Forest and Grant Grove, at elevations of 6,500 feet and above, are almost 20° cooler. Cedar Grove, on the floor of Kings Canyon, is between those levels in elevation and can be desertlike.

Crowding isn't a big problem even in the summer, but weekends are the busiest times. Fall is fine, too, and the park is largely deserted.

When snow comes, Kings Canyon Highway and Mineral King Road close, and Generals Highway between Grant Grove and Lodgepole can be closed for days or even weeks after a storm. Trails are marked for cross-country skiing and snowshoeing among the Sequoias. For spring break, most of the park remains snowed in, although campgrounds and trails in the foothills area are open. In heavy snow years, snow remains at the elevation of the Sequoias and main campgrounds through Memorial Day.

HOW MUCH TIME TO SPEND

Most people just drive on Generals Highway, look at the Sequoia trees, and drive out the same day. That's like bicycling through a museum. If you enjoy the outdoors, you can spend your whole vacation at these parks. A week would be well spent hiking and relaxing in the area. In the front country of Sequoia National Park, a short visit would take 2 or 3 days and include the Sequoias, Crystal Cave, hiking, and maybe river swimming. Spend at least a full day at Kings Canyon; several days would be better. The Mineral King area demands a couple of days to justify the arduous drive.

Weather Chart: Sequoia National Park

Lodgepole, elevation 6,750 feet

	Avg. High (°F/°C)	Avg. Low (°F/°C)	Precip. (total in.)
December–February	39/4	16/–9	25.6
March	44/7	21/–6	7.5
April	49/9	25/–4	3.1
May	57/14	32/0	1.3
June	67/19	38/3	.7
July	75/24	44/7	.5
August	75/24	43/6	.3
September	68/20	38/3	1.5
October	58/14	30/–1	1.8
November	46/8	22/–6	4.6

Ash Mountain, elevation 1,690 feet

	Avg. High (°F/°C)	Avg. Low (°F/°C)	Precip (total in.)
December–February	57/14	37/3	13.2
March	64/18	42/6	4.3
April	71/22	46/8	2.5
May	79/26	53/12	1
June	90/32	61/16	.4
July	98/37	68/20	.1
August	97/36	67/19	.1

	Avg. High (°F/°C)	Avg. Low (°F/°C)	Precip (total in.)
September	91/33	61/16	.5
October	81/27	53/12	1
November	67/19	43/6	2.9

HOW FAR TO PLAN AHEAD

Most people visit these parks on the weekends, with far fewer visiting during the week. If you plan your visit for Sunday through Thursday, you'll find it easier to get reservations and avoid crowds at popular sites such as the caves. Hotel rooms and cabins should be reserved at least 2 or 3 months ahead for the summer. If you don't book space until later, you still have a good chance of getting a room.

Only two campgrounds, Lodgepole and Dorst, have sites on the national reservation system (see chapter 2, "Planning a Family Trip to a National Park"); call as soon as you make your plans, even though sites don't all book up right away. Those campgrounds are full all summer. Many other campgrounds in the park and in the nearby national forests don't take reservations. Sites are abundant on weekdays, and you can get a site on weekends by arriving early in the day. Cedar Grove and the national forest campgrounds are the last to fill up.

WHAT TO PACK
CLOTHING

In the summer you'll spend most of your time in shorts and T-shirts. Summer rains come mostly in afternoon thunderstorms. Be prepared for cool mornings, but generally the climate is perfect. Bring your swimsuits for playing in streams. Bring a layer of warm wool or synthetic clothing for backpacking in the high country. There's little need for clothes more formal than those you wear camping. In the cold months, be ready for heavy snow and temperatures around freezing at the elevation of the Sequoias (see "When It's Cold & Wet," in chapter 2).

Temperatures depend on elevation. In summer the foothills area, at around 2,000 feet, is scorching. Grant Grove, Giant Forest, and other main visitor sites along Generals Highway are at around 6,500 feet, and about 20° cooler, just about perfect in the summer. Cedar Grove in Kings Canyon is at 4,600 feet, and Mineral King, in Sequoia, is at about 8,000, with corresponding temperature differences.

GEAR

Lightweight gear will handle all but exceptionally cold nights at the elevation of Lodgepole campground during the normal camping months of the summer and fall; for cold nights, prepare with an extra layer. Backpackers heading for the high country could encounter freezing temperatures at night even in the summer. Strollers can navigate some Sequoia grove trails, but using a backpack to carry your baby or toddler gives you far more freedom.

KEEPING SAFE & HEALTHY

Besides the special warnings below, Sequoia and Kings Canyon have risks associated with black bears, dehydration, elevation, Giardia, lightning, poison oak, and snakebites. Check chapter 2, p. 38, for specifics.

CARSICKNESS

The twisting Generals Highway and Mineral King Road could upset the strongest stomach. Leave plenty of time so that you can stop and get some air. Make sure those who are susceptible can see outside and get fresh air. Avoid greasy foods. For more information, see "Seasickness & Motion Sickness," in chapter 2.

DROWNING

This is the most common cause of death in the park. Swimming in the rivers is fun, but it's easy to misjudge the power of moving water, which can appear still on the surface. Once you're in, getting out on slippery rocks can be difficult. Children playing near streams can fall in and disappear. Accidents happen quickly. Your good judgment is your safeguard. If in doubt, swim only where others are swimming, or talk to a ranger. Never, ever dive in.

5 Family-Friendly Accommodations

CAMPGROUNDS

These parks are heaven for tent campers, who have far more choices and flexibility than do those who stay in hotels or come in an RV (RVs can't go everywhere; see "By RV," p. 412). The campgrounds here are some of the best designed and maintained in the national park system.

Two Park Service and several Forest Service campgrounds take reservations through the national system described under "Camping & Hotel Reservations," on p. 29. Even without a reservation, sites are easy to come by at many first-come, first-served park and national forest campgrounds. Some Forest Service campgrounds are equivalent to the park campgrounds even in location, because they lie in gaps between sections of the parks, while others lie along the remote eastern edge of the park. I've listed the two agencies' campgrounds together, grouping the campgrounds by location.

Black bears invade campgrounds every night, often tearing cars open looking for food. Use the steel cabinet at your campsite to store food you're not eating, and latch it, because bears do try the latches. Also, don't bring a huge cooler unless you have verified that it will fit in the cabinet. I've listed the sizes of these bear boxes below where I have the information; the dimensions are for the largest if sites have more than one, and are in inches, length then depth then height. Firewood gathering is permitted, but buying your wood is easier and more environmentally sound. Gather only wood that's both dead and down. RV generators are allowed from 9am to 9pm only.

Questions for Park Service campgrounds can be answered at © **559/565-3341.** For those in the Inyo National Forest, call © **760/873-2400,** while questions for campgrounds in the Sequoia National Forest can be answered at © **559/784-1500.**

GENERALS HIGHWAY

These five campgrounds are on Generals Highway between the Ash Mountain and Grant Grove entrances, arranged by their distance from the south, Ash Mountain entrance.

Potwisha   At 2,100 feet, the low elevation makes it hot in the summer and comfortable in the winter. The ground cover is desertlike, and there's not much shade or screening to sites. Sites are large; many have a pull-through arrangement for RVs. The Kaweah River runs along the campground, with spots for river play down an embankment. The Potwisha Indians used this area for its year-round warmth and rivers. The Potwisha Pictograph Loop goes from near the campground dump station to the pictographs and one of the swimming holes in the Kaweah where the Potwisha bathed every morning.

Campgrounds in the Sequoia/Kings Canyon Area

Campground	Elevation	Total Sites	RV Hookups	Dump Station	Toilets	Drinking Water
INSIDE SEQUOIA NATIONAL PARK						
Atwell Mill	6,650	21	No	No	Yes	Yes
Buckeye Flat	2,800	28	No	No	Yes	Yes
Cold Springs	7,500	40	No	No	Yes	Yes
Dorst	6,700	204	No	Yes	Yes	Yes
Lodgepole	6,700	214	No	Yes	Yes	Yes
Potwisha	2,100	42	No	Yes	Yes	Yes
South Fork	3,600	10	No	No	Yes	No
INSIDE KINGS CANYON NATIONAL PARK						
Azalea	6,500	110	No	No	Yes	Yes
Crystal Springs	6,500	36	No	No	Yes	Yes
Canyon View	4,600	23	No	No	Yes	Yes
Moraine	4,600	120	No	No	Yes	Yes
Sentinel	4,600	82	No	No	Yes	Yes
Sheep Creek	4,600	111	No	No	Yes	Yes
Sunset	6,500	157	No	No	Yes	Yes
OUTSIDE THE PARKS						
Hume Lake	5,200	74	No	No	Yes	Yes
Landslide	5,800	9	No	No	Yes	No
Princess	5,900	90	No	Yes	Yes	Yes
Stony Creek	6,400	49	No	No	Yes	Yes
Tenmile	5,800	13	No	No	Yes	No

Generals Hwy., 4 miles from the Ash Mountain entrance, Sequoia National Park. ✆ **559/565-3341**. 42 sites, tents or RVs. $18 site. No reservations. Open year-round. **Amenities:** Flush toilets, dump station, picnic tables, fire pits, running water, pay phone. Bear boxes: 47¼×34×22.

Buckeye Flat   I love this campground! Accessible only to tenters because of the narrow half-mile access road, it is on a peaceful and shady hillside among a variety of deciduous trees. Sites are large and have great privacy among boulders and rock outcroppings. Best of all, a lovely swimming hole in Paradise Creek is a short walk, down the bank between sites 17 and 18. A trail leads up the creek to more swimming spots. At an elevation of 2,800 feet, this campground is hot in the summer.

Showers	Fire Pits/Grills	Laundry	Public Phones	Reservations	Fees	Open
Yes	Yes	No	Yes	No	$12	May–Oct
No	Yes	No	Yes	No	$18	May to Labor Day
No	Yes	No	Yes	No	$12	Late May to early Oct
No	Yes	No	Yes	Yes	$20	June to Labor Day
Yes	Yes	Yes	Yes	Yes	$18–$20	Year-round
No	Yes	No	Yes	No	$18	Year-round
No	Yes	No	No	No	$12	Year-round
Yes	Yes	No	Yes	No	$18	Year-round
Yes	Yes	No	Yes	No	$18	Mid-May to mid-Sept
Yes	Yes	Yes	Yes	No	$18	Late May to early Oct
Yes	Yes	Yes	Yes	No	$18	May–Oct
Yes	Yes	Yes	Yes	No	$18	Late May to early Oct
Yes	Yes	Yes	Yes	No	$18	Late Apr to early Oct
Yes	Yes	Yes	No	No	$18	Late June to early Oct
No	Yes	No	Yes	Yes	$19	Memorial Day to Oct
No	Yes	No	No	No	$15	May–Oct
No	Yes	No	No	Yes	$17	Memorial Day to Labor Day
No	Yes	No	Yes	Yes	$15–$19	June–Oct
No	Yes	No	No	No	$15	Memorial Day to Labor Day

Half-mile off Generals Hwy., about 4 miles from the Ash Mountain entrance, Sequoia National Park. © 559/565-3341. 28 sites, tents only. $18 site. No reservations. Closed Labor Day to late spring. **Amenities:** Flush toilets, swimming, picnic tables, fire pits, running water. Bear boxes: 47½×34×22.

Lodgepole   Strung along the banks of the Marble Fork of the Kaweah River at an elevation of 6,750 feet, Lodgepole is the kind of campground that could be the center of your whole vacation. It combines a beautiful place to camp with proximity to family-oriented facilities at Lodgepole Village, including a good visitor center, showers, laundry, store, snack bar, and shuttle stop for rides to Giant Forest. The children's Walter Fry Nature Center, in the middle of the campground, offers excellent ranger programs. Getting the right site is important. Sites 1 to 22, nearest the visitor center, are small and lack ground cover, and are reserved for RVs; sites 36 to 60 and 151 to 214, for tents or RVs, lie on each side of the river; and sites 69 to 150, in upper Lodgepole, are for tents only, near where the river tumbles over granite shelves and boulders. Campers play in the river, horseback riding and Sequoias are just down the road, and several hiking trails leave from here (see "Lodgepole & Wolverton," p. 428).

Generals Hwy., just north of Giant Forest, Sequoia National Park. ② 559/565-3341. 214 sites, tents or RVs. $20 site during reservation period; $18 site off season. Reservations accepted May–Sept. Open year-round. **Amenities:** Flush toilets, showers, dump station, laundry, store, picnic tables, fire pits, pay phone, running water, ranger programs in summer. Bear boxes: 47×17×17¾.

Dorst   This is a nicely developed campground, nestled among pine and fir trees that screen the many sites. A meadow borders the campground, and a branch of Dorst Creek flows by at 6,800 feet elevation. Three excellent day hikes start from the campground. It's 2 miles (one-way) to the remote Sequoias of Muir Grove, 2.5 miles to Lost Grove, and 3.8 miles to the spectacular views from the top of Little Baldy (cut off 1½ miles by starting from Generals Hwy.). There's a place to play .5 mile up the Cabin Creek Trail in Dorst Creek, when the water isn't too high.

Generals Hwy., 8 miles northwest of Lodgepole, Sequoia National Park. ② 559/565-3341. 204 sites, tents or RVs. $20 site. Reservations accepted. Closed Labor Day to late May. **Amenities:** Flush toilets, dump station, picnic tables, laundry and showers nearby, fire pits, running water, pay phone. Bear boxes: 47×17×17¾.

Stony Creek (Upper and Lower) *Finds*   Conveniently located just outside Sequoia between the two parks, these U.S. Forest Service campgrounds are on either side of the highway. The lower campground is attractive and well wooded, with sites far apart, the creek running by, and rock outcroppings shaping the land. The upper part is dusty and undeveloped. Elevation is 6,400 feet. The Lost Grove of Sequoias is just inside the park, about 1 mile away.

Generals Hwy., 10 miles southeast of Grant Grove, Sequoia National Forest. ② 559/784-1500. 68 sites, tents or RVs. $19 site lower campground; $15 site upper campground. Reservations accepted for lower campground. Closed Oct to Memorial Day. **Amenities:** Flush toilets at lower campground, vault toilets at upper, picnic tables, fire pits, running water.

GRANT GROVE

Azalea   This sprawling campground is open year-round and offers nice sites under broken stands of tall pine, fir, and cedar on a boulder-strewn hill. Sites inside the loops are barren and exposed, but some sites on the outer edge of loops are large and more interesting. A quarter-mile away is a Sequoia grove, while a half-mile away is the Grant Grove visitor center, grocery, restaurants, and shower facilities.

Along Hwy. 180 3 miles from Big Stump Entrance, Kings Canyon National Park. ② 559/565-3341. 110 sites, tents or RVs. $18 site. Open year-round. **Amenities:** Flush toilets, picnic tables, fire pits, running water, pay phones, summer ranger programs. Bear boxes: 47×34×22.

Crystal Springs   This site is similar to Azalea, although only a third as big, which translates to a quieter, more appealing environment. The ground cover has not been trampled as much as at Azalea and Sunset, and the setting on a rocky hill makes for many good campsites.

Along Hwy. 180, 3 miles from Big Stump Entrance, Kings Canyon National Park. ② 559/565-3341. 36 sites, tents or RVs. $18 site. Closed mid-Sept to late May. **Amenities:** Flush toilets, picnic tables, fire pits, running water, ranger programs in summer, close to Grant Grove village with its showers, store, restaurant, pay phones, visitor center, and horseback riding. Bear boxes: 47×17×17¾.

Sunset   This is the biggest of the Grant Grove sites, and so the noisiest. Like the other two, it sits at an elevation of about 6,500 feet in a shadowy, needle-carpeted forest.

Along Hwy. 180, 3 miles from Big Stump Entrance, Kings Canyon National Park. ℂ 559/565-3341. 157 sites, tents or RVs. $18 site. Closed mid-Sept to late May. **Amenities:** Flush toilets, picnic tables, fire pits, running water, pay phone, summer ranger programs, close to Grant Grove village with its showers, store, restaurant, visitor center, and horseback riding. Bear boxes: 47×17×17¾.

HUME LAKE

In the woods east of Grant Grove, Sequoia National Forest contains a rich recreation area around Hume Lake. Campgrounds are scattered along narrow and twisting County Road 13S01, which runs 15 miles from Kings Highway at Princess Campground, 6 miles northeast of Grant Grove, to Generals Highway, a few miles south of Grant Grove. I've described campgrounds in north-to-south order on that road. All are between 5,000 and 6,000 feet elevation. Princess and Hume Lake campgrounds accept reservations. Several other primitive Forest Service campgrounds are in the national forest. Get information from Sequoia National Forest's **Hume Lake Ranger District** (ℂ 559/338-2251) on Highway 180 near Dunlap.

Princess   The meadow campground occupies space among large boulders and the huge stumps of giant Sequoias, which were logged a century ago when they were as much as 2,500 years old. The sites are large and well separated, along three paved loops.

Hwy. 180 and Rd. 13S01, 6 miles from Grant Grove, Sequoia National Forest. ℂ 559/338-2251. 90 sites, tents or RVs. $17 site. Reservations accepted. Closed Labor Day to Memorial Day. **Amenities:** Pit toilets, dump station, picnic tables, fire pits, running water.

Hume Lake   This is a well-developed campground on the hillside over the north side of the fishing lake. Sites are broadly separated among pine and cedar trees, but dusty due to the trampling of long use. A nearby road leads down to the water for swimming or boating.

On Hume Lake, 3 miles from Hwy. 180, Sequoia National Forest. ℂ 559/338-2251. 74 sites, tents or RVs. $19 site. Reservations accepted. Closed Oct to Memorial Day. **Amenities:** Flush toilets, picnic tables, fire pits, swimming, pay phone.

Landslide   The campground is small, rough, and remote, but lovely, with just a few huge sites on a hill among pines and cedars.

South of Hume Lake, 6 miles from Hwy. 180, Sequoia National Forest. ℂ 559/338-2251. 9 sites, tents or RVs. $15 site. Closed Labor Day to Memorial Day. **Amenities:** Pit toilets, picnic tables, fire pits, running water.

Tenmile   This primitive campground, along Tenmile Creek, shady and dusty, is like the backcountry. Just be sure to bring your own water, as there's none here.

South of Hume Lake, 8 miles from Hwy. 180, Sequoia National Forest. ℂ 559/338-2251. 13 sites, tents or RVs. $15 site. Closed Labor Day to Memorial Day. **Amenities:** Pit toilets, picnic tables, fire pits.

AT CEDAR GROVE

Canyon View   This small campground, which also fronts the Kings River, is open only when needed. Since RVs can't use this campground, it tends to be a bit quieter.

Cedar Grove area, Kings Canyon National Park. ℂ 559/565-3341. 23 sites, tents only. $18 site. Open May–Oct when needed. **Amenities:** Flush toilets, picnic tables, fire pits, running water, village with grocery, showers, laundry, phone, and restaurant is ¼ mile away. Bear boxes: 48×34×28.

Moraine   This is the largest of the four Cedar Grove campgrounds, but it often isn't open because there's no need for the sites. As a result, the vegetation gets a chance to recover from use.

Cedar Grove area, Kings Canyon National Park. ℂ 559/565-3341. 120 sites, tents or RVs. $18 site. Open May–Oct when needed. **Amenities:** Flush toilets, picnic tables, fire pits, running water, village w/grocery, showers, laundry, phone, and restaurant nearby. Bear boxes: 48×34×28.

Sentinel   This nice area along the south side of the Kings River features sites scattered among an evergreen forest.

Cedar Grove area, Kings Canyon National Park. 𝄢 559/565-3341. 82 sites, tents or RVs. $18 site. Closed mid-Nov to late Apr. **Amenities:** Flush toilets, picnic tables, fire pits, running water, ranger programs in summer, village nearby w/grocery, phone, restaurant, and showers. Bear boxes: 47¾x34x22.

Sheep Creek   This sprawling site, like the other three, also can claim proximity to the Kings River. At 4,600 feet, the area is warm and dry in the summer. As with Moraine, it's only open when needed.

Cedar Grove area, Kings Canyon National Park. 𝄢 559/565-3341. 111 sites, tents or RVs. $18 site. Open May–Oct when needed. **Amenities:** Flush toilets, picnic tables, fire pits, running water, village w/grocery, showers, laundry, phone, and restaurant nearby. Bear boxes: 48x34x28.

MINERAL KING & SOUTH FORK

These three primitive Park Service campgrounds are in the remote southwestern area of Sequoia National Park, where toilsome roads hold down the number of visitors. RVs and trailers should not attempt Mineral King Road or South Fork Drive. The Mineral King area and road are covered on p. 420. None of these campgrounds take reservations.

Atwell Mill   If you're used to busy, trampled campgrounds, the lush grass and ferns among large pine, fir, and cedar are refreshing. Sites are large and screened by a small hill. One-hundred-year-old Sequoia stumps are scattered around, the remains of the mill of the campground's name. At the nearby Silver City Lodge (p. 424), you can shower and get a meal. The campground is rough and primitive, however, with pit toilets. Two lightly used trails reach secluded Sequoia groves.

Mineral King Rd., 19 miles from Hwy. 198. 𝄢 559/565-3341. 21 sites, tents only. $12 site. Closed Nov to Memorial Day, water off mid-Oct. **Amenities:** Pit toilets, picnic tables, fire pits, running water, pay phone, showers nearby. Bear boxes: 47x17x17¾.

Cold Springs   The highest campground in the park sits by the East Fork of the Kaweah River under huge, shady conifers. Sites are far from each other on rugged ground. At 7,500 feet, the rocky high country above Mineral King Valley is near at hand. It's a great starting point for spectacular high Sierra backpacking or rides with the pack-station operator (see "Horseback Riding & Stock Packing," p. 431).

Mineral King Rd., 23 miles from Hwy. 198. 𝄢 559/565-3341. 40 sites, tents only. $12 site. Closed Nov to Memorial Day, water off mid-Oct. **Amenities:** Pit toilets, picnic tables, fire pits, running water, pay phone, ranger programs July–Aug. Bear boxes: 47x17x17¾.

South Fork   The campground is at the edge of the park at 3,600 feet, at the end of a partly unpaved road that branches from the highway outside the park. The Park Service does not charge an entrance fee on this route. The main feature is the Ladybug Trail, good in the spring while the high country is still under snow. Boil or treat water from the South Fork of the Kaweah River for drinking or cooking.

On South Fork Dr., 13 miles from the Hwy. 198 intersection in Three Rivers. 𝄢 559/565-3341. 10 sites, tents or RVs, but road not recommended for RVs. May–Oct $12 site; free in winter. Open year-round. **Amenities:** Pit toilets, picnic tables, fire pits, no drinking water. Bear boxes: 47x17x17¾.

EAST SIDE OF THE PARKS

These campgrounds are off Highway 395, the north-south route along the east side of the Sierra. For backpackers heading to wilderness trips in the remote eastern area of the parks, this information on the campgrounds in **Inyo National Forest** might be useful (see contact information in "Sequoia–Kings Canyon Address Book," p. 405). *Tip:* Families visiting the parks' main areas should not consider these campgrounds, which are many hours from where you want to be.

At **Whitney Portal,** 13 miles west of Highway 395 at Lone Pine, a substantial campground sits at the starting point to climb Mount Whitney. See "Mount Whitney," p. 430, for information about permits for hiking here. Farther north, the 9,200-foot-high **Onion Valley Campground** is 13 miles west of Independence near the trail head over **Kearsarge Pass,** a backpacking route that runs due west into Kings Canyon. On the same road 6 miles west of Independence, **Gray's Meadow Campground** is on a stocked trout stream. Sites at all three campgrounds can be reserved through the national system (see "Camping & Hotel Reservations," in chapter 2; you may need to reserve 5 days or more ahead) or obtained on arrival.

Continuing north on 395, Big Pine is the turn for campgrounds in the high, narrow canyons up Big Pine Canyon Road, just outside the John Muir Wilderness. **Upper Sage Flat** and **Big Pine Creek** take reservations. Several other campgrounds near the wilderness are reached from Bishop, on Route 168.

BACKCOUNTRY CAMPING PERMITS

To sleep outside a campground in the backcountry (more than 84% of the parks), you need a $15 permit from the Park Service or Forest Service. The nearest ranger station issues a certain number of permits for each trail head, ranging from 15 to 30 people per trail head in the park to more than 70 for some Forest Service trail heads. The Park Service takes reservations by mail or fax (© **559/565-4239**) from March 1 until 14 days before the start of your hike. It holds back about a quarter of the permits for people who ask for them on arrival, starting at 1pm the day before the hike at the ranger station for the trail head you want to use. After 9am on the day of the hike, rangers give away permits that haven't been picked up by people with reservations. Most trails don't fill the quota most days, but the popular trails do. Long weekends are the busiest. At quiet times, when some ranger stations close, you just fill out a permit form and leave it in a box.

To start, get a good topographic map, a trail guide (see "Reading Up," p. 410), and the Park Service's *Backcountry Basics* newspaper, which you can download from the park's website. If you have specific questions, including those on the availability of particular trail heads, or need to have *Backcountry Basics* mailed to you, call the **backcountry office** (© **559/565-3766**). You can reserve only in writing. After selecting your route and an alternate, send in your request, which requires a complete itinerary and other information explained in *Backcountry Basics* or on the park's website (www.nps.gov/seki/planyourvisit/wilderness_permits.htm). Include the $15 reservation fee, payable by Visa or MasterCard if by fax; if using the mail, you can also pay by check or money order (**Wilderness Permit Reservations,** 47050 Generals Hwy., #60, Three Rivers, CA 93271). There's no fee if you don't make a reservation.

Many trails cross Park Service and Forest Service land; you need only one permit, from the agency where your hike begins. The Forest Service system differs from the Park Service system in some respects, but its list of trail heads and ranger station addresses is included in *Backcountry Basics.* See "Sequoia–Kings Canyon Address Book" (p. 405) for national forest contact information. For more on backpacking and wilderness travel with pack and saddle animals, see "Backpacking" (p. 430).

RV CAMPGROUNDS

If you need full RV hookups, try **Lemon Cove/Sequoia Campground,** in Lemon Cove, 13 miles west of Three Rivers on Highway 198 (© **559/597-2346;** www.lemon covesequoiacamp.com), which has a pool and laundry. Rates are $25 to $32.

HOTELS, LODGES & CABINS

The main lodgings at Sequoia and Kings Canyon have been rebuilt from the ground up in recent years. You have a choice of a nice hotel or a run-down but oddly quaint old cabin. Each park has lodgings run by a concessionaire, but private and national forest land intermix with parkland and have lodging options just as good or better. I've addressed the choices geographically. All rates are for the high season; off-season rates drop as much as 40%.

ON GENERALS HIGHWAY

These lodgings are along the main road that connects the two parks and runs through a section of Sequoia National Forest. They are arranged north to south.

Grant Grove Village and John Muir Lodge   The wood-sided Muir lodge fits in well on a hill above the village facilities. It has comfortable rooms with rustic-style furniture. The rooms have telephones and coffeemakers, but bathrooms are small. Some rooms stay open year-round. Some of the cabins and their shared bathhouse are worn and overdue for replacement. The slow pace of renovation is a complicated story of the relationship of the Park Service to its hotel operators. However, if you're looking for a rough outdoors experience, they do have some charm, with primitive dwellings not much different from those pioneers would have lived in. About half of the units are tents; the other half consist of shedlike cabins of bare boards with flashlights for light. Some of these have been remodeled, but even they are poor in quality.

3 miles inside north park entrance (5755 E. Kings Canyon Rd., #101, Fresno, CA 93727). © 866/KCANYON (866/ 522-6966) or 559/335-5500. www.sequoia-kingscanyon.com. 35 lodge units, 53 cabins, 9 with bathroom. $170–$180 lodge double; $129–$140 cabin double with bathroom; $62–$91 cabin double without bathroom. $12 extra person over age 12, children under 13 stay free in parent's room. Rollaway bed $12 (can't be put in cabins), crib $12. AE, DISC, MC, V. **Amenities:** Restaurant; grocery; camp store; visitor center; village w/ATM. In room: Coffeemaker.

Montecito-Lake Resort   Wonderfully located inside the Sequoia National Forest in between the two parks, this resort offers a great base camp, especially so for families. Long known as the Montecito-Sequoia Lodge, the property changed hands recently but the philosophy didn't. In the summer it is a combination children's summer camp and adult resort. Families visit together for weeklong sessions, but the children go off during the day to structured, supervised activities—including archery, art, crafts, canoeing, fencing, naturalist walks, horse and pony rides, riflery, sailing, swimming, tennis, water-skiing, and more. A single day's choices fill a page. Meanwhile, the parents do whatever they want outdoors in the park, joining in resort activities or just sitting around the pool. At mealtimes and in the evening, the families come together. In the winter the resort grooms 85 miles of cross-country ski trails for skate or diagonal stride, rated beginner to expert, and rising to the top of an 8,500-foot mountain. There is a rope tow with a 350-foot drop for sledding and skiing. Instructors teach all skiing styles, including telemark for getting into the backcountry, and you can leave your kids in activities while you ski. At this elevation, 20 feet of snow falls each year.

There's a philosophy behind all this—bringing families together in the great outdoors—and profit is not the top motivation: The rates are very reasonable for an all-included vacation. The lodge is old and not fancy, but enjoys a lovely setting in woods with its own large pond. Meals are buffet style (and there's a full bar). Accommodations are in rustic cabins using a shared bathhouse or in strictly utilitarian but well-kept rooms in various buildings without phones or TVs. A typical unit has a private bathroom, a kids' room with four bunks, and a master bedroom. Mattresses are good. You're not expected to spend much time there, but you'll be perfectly comfortable. Reserve well in advance for camp.

South of Grant Grove, Sequoia National Forest (63410 Generals Hwy., Kings Canyon National Park, CA, 93633). ℭ 800/227-9900 or 650/967-8612; 559/565-3388 at the lodge. www.mslodge.com. 36 units with bathroom, 13 cabins with shared bathhouses. Summer $975–$1,215 per person for weeklong family camp; $179–$189 double; spring and fall $119–$189 double, $20–$30 extra person; winter $99–$159 double, $61–$123 extra person; holidays higher. Rates include meals and most activities. Rollaway beds and cribs free. AE, DISC, MC, V. **Amenities:** Tennis; swimming; boating; fencing; naturalist walks; horse rides. *In room:* No phone.

Stony Creek Lodge   Located along the General's Highway between Grant Grove and Giant Forest, I like this river-rock and timber lodge for it's a perfect middle ground from which to base your explorations. With just 11 rooms, the lodge operates much like a bed-and-breakfast. The spacious lobby has a stone fireplace to relax in front of after a day in the parks. Rooms come with televisions and dataport phones; some have three beds.

Just south of Montecito Resort along the General's Hwy. in the Giant Sequoia National Monument (P.O. Box 907, Kings Canyon National Park, CA, 93633). ℭ 866/K-CANYON or 559/565-3909. www.sequoia-kingscanyon.com. 11 units. $130–$160 double. 12 and under stay free in parent's room, $12 additional person. Cribs $12. AE, DISC, MC, V. Closed Nov to mid-May. **Amenities:** Restaurant; ATM; grocery; gas station. *In room:* TV, dataport, coffeemaker.

Wuksachi Lodge   This lodge shows how classic rustic park architecture can be updated into a modern hotel. The hillside buildings are solid as rock, with cedar and granite exteriors, and the rooms were built with top-quality materials and craftsmanship—doors are solid wood, and the large bathrooms have the finest countertops. The large rooms have high ceilings and are decorated with mission-style furniture. They have sleeper sofas, telephones, and coffeemakers. There are downsides. The lodge building, with the lobby and restaurant, is separate from the three buildings of rooms, and it's a long walk (the staff uses golf carts). The two-story structures have no elevators. You'll drive to most activities, because the lodge stands off on its own. In the winter, a network of 28 miles of diagonal stride ski trails meets the hotel, and the inexpensive winter rates include equipment use. The restaurant offers stunning views of 11,188-foot Mount Silliman and serves dinners that can become quite elaborate, and expensive; it's listed under "Family-Friendly Dining" (p. 426).

Just north of Lodgepole, P.O. Box 89, Sequoia National Park, CA 93262. ℭ 888/252-5757 or 559/565-4070. www. visitsequoia.com. 102 units. $119–$219 double. $10 extra person over age 16, children under 16 stay free in parent's room. Crib or extra bed $10. AE, DC, DISC, MC, V. **Amenities:** Restaurant; gift shop; Wi-Fi in the main lodge. *In room:* TV, dataport, fridge, coffeemaker, hair dryer, iron/ironing board.

OFF THE BEATEN TRACK
Cedar Grove Lodge   The location on the floor of Kings Canyon is what makes these rooms precious—they're the only ones. The accommodations consist of dated but comfortable standard rooms with two queen-size beds, off a central hallway above the grocery store and snack bar, in a somewhat rumbly plywood structure. On one end, the hallway ends in a pleasant upper deck where guests sit and look out over the Kings River. The small bathrooms have shower stalls, not tubs. Rooms are air-conditioned but lack telephones or TVs. Unless you book one of the three kitchenette units,

which rent for the same price, you will have to eat at the restaurant (p. 425) with its modest menu. Also, don't stay here if you have trouble with stairs.

Hwy. 180, 32 miles from Grant Grove (5755 E. Kings Canyon Rd., #101, Fresno, CA 93727). © **559/565-4040.** www. sequoia-kingscanyon.com. 21 units. $119–$135 double. $12 extra person over age 12, children under 13 stay free in parent's room. Cribs $12. AE, DC, MC, V. Closed Oct–Apr. **Amenities:** Restaurant; camp store. *In room:* A/C, some have kitchenette, no phone.

Silver City Lodge   On the road to the remote Mineral King Valley, the same family has offered lodgings, meals, and famous pie since the 1930s. It's a place to come for a while and decompress in the cool mountain air, far from traffic or travel but near great high-country trails; getting here is too hard to justify less than a couple of nights at least. There's a playground, too. The eight cabins are cute and cozy, ranging from a rustic unit with kerosene light and bare wood walls and floor to one with a full kitchen, two bedrooms, and a big wood stove. They share a central bathhouse. Five larger chalets are modern three-bedroom houses with cedar siding, stone foundations, and full bathrooms. They have electricity and limited Internet access, but no phones. Book the chalets at least 3 months ahead; the cabins are easier to reserve. Some of the higher-end chalets have hide-a-beds and portable cribs.

Mineral King Rd. (P.O. Box 56), Three Rivers, CA 93271. © **559/561-3223** summer, or 805/461-3223 winter. www. silvercityresort.com. 13 units, some with shared bathhouse. $75–$195 cabin; $225–$395 chalet. MC, V. Closed Oct–May. **Amenities:** Restaurant; playground. *In room:* Some have kitchen, some have electricity and Internet access, no phone.

IN THE BACKCOUNTRY
Bearpaw Meadow High Sierra Camp   Twelve miles east of the Giant Forest via the High Sierra Trail, this camp operated by Delaware North (see "Sequoia–Kings Canyon Address Book," p. 405) gives those lucky enough to get reservations the chance to hike into the mountainous backcountry without having to carry gear—a bed and an excellent hot meal are waiting. The camp is at the intersection of several trails at 7,500 feet elevation. Tents are set up for two, but a third person can sleep on the floor with his or her own sleeping bag. Reservations become available January 2 for the whole summer and fill quickly; however, there is a 60-day cancellation policy, so if you call exactly 60 days before the date you want, you have a chance of getting it.

12 miles east of Giant Forest. © **866/807-3598.** 6 2-bed tents. $350 for 2; $75 for 3rd person in tent (without bed). Rates include 2 meals. Closed mid-Sept to mid-June. **Amenities:** Dining room.

Pear Lake Ski Hut   A cabin where everyone packs in together after skiing to the site at 9,200 feet elevation. It's a steep, 6-mile route for experienced skiers, and you must be prepared for winter backcountry travel; the SNHA website has a checklist, and a form to enter the lottery for reservations.

6 miles from Wolverton Meadow. Contact Sequoia Natural History Association (SNHA). © **559/565-3759.** www.sequoiahistory.org. $24 per person. AE, DC, MC, V.

IN THREE RIVERS
The small town of Three Rivers, along Highway 198 outside the parks' south (Ash Mountain) entrance, has groceries, family restaurants, and hotels. The highway is known as Sierra Drive in town. This is a hot, arid area, below the Sierra forests. Besides the place I've described below, here are two other family hotels with swimming pools and in-room refrigerators: Comfort Inn & Suites Sequoia Kings Canyon National Park, 40820 Sierra Dr. (© **800/331-2140** or 559/561-9000; www.sequoiahotel.com), and **Buckeye Tree Lodge,** 46000 Sierra Dr. (© **559/561-5900;** www.buckeyetree.com).

Tips Park Camping Basics: Toilets, Showers & Laundry

The campground bathrooms at Sequoia and Kings Canyon are typical of national parks and forests. We found that some were better kept up than those at other parks, perhaps because of lighter use. They have only cold water. Public showers are more plentiful here than at other parks.

The showers at **Lodgepole,** open early May to late October, operate with quarters and cost $3.50 for the first 10 minutes. They're open 8am to 7:45pm during the summer months, shorter hours during shoulder seasons. There aren't enough, though, so you might have to wait at popular times. The year-round coin-op laundry is large and stays open daily 8am to 8pm during the high season. The showers might be closed for cleaning at midday. The **Grant Grove** showers, which are used by guests staying in the cabins and tent cabins at Grant Grove, are open in summer for campers and hikers from 11am to 4pm. After Labor Day, hours are 9am to 4:30pm. A shower cost $4 in 2007, but new facilities in 2008 could result in a price increase.

Showers at **Cedar Grove** are dedicated to the campers. A $3 token gets you 10 minutes of water. The showers are open 8am to 6pm, except between 1 and 3pm when they're cleaned. The laundry also is open round-the-clock.

Best Western Holiday Lodge   This nicely landscaped motel with a shady picnic area beckons kids with a swing set, basketball hoop, outdoor pool, and path to the nearby Kaweah River. It's worth spending a little extra for one of the larger rooms with patios and fireplaces, big TVs, microwaves, and other amenities. The older rooms also are comfortable. A small guest laundry is on-site, and the rate includes continental breakfast. The Foothills Entrance to Sequoia is just 8 miles.

40105 Sierra Dr., Three Rivers, CA 93271. (© **888/523-9909** or 559/561-4119. Fax 559/561-3427. www.bestwestern california.com. 54 units. $109–$199 double. $10 extra person over age 12, children under 12 stay free in parent's room. Rollaway $15, cribs $10. Rates include continental breakfast. AE, DISC, MC, V. **Amenities:** Pool; spa; playground; fishing; laundry. *In room:* A/C, TV, dataport, fridge available, tea/coffeemaker, hair dryer, microwave available, fireplace available, iron/ironing board.

6 Family-Friendly Dining
LOW-STRESS MEALS

A snack bar and deli at **Lodgepole** have patio seating and are open daily 8am to 8pm in summer.

Cedar Grove Cafe   Cedar Grove's only restaurant is a snack bar that's been beefed up with a menu to serve lodge guests items such as New York steak, trout, and pasta. There also are nightly specials that vary based on who's cooking. You order at the counter and sit at picnic tables either out on the deck or down by the river.

Cedar Grove Lodge, Kings Canyon National Park. (© **559/565-0100.** Kids' menu, highchairs, boosters, crayons. Breakfast $1.50–$6.25; lunch $2.50–$6.95; dinner $8–$15; kids' menu $3–$6. AE, DISC, MC, V. June–Sept daily breakfast 7–10:30am, lunch 11am–2pm, dinner 5–9pm. Closed mid-Oct to mid-May.

Grant Grove Restaurant   This good, old-fashioned family restaurant looks as if it hasn't changed in 30 years. As with many other national park restaurants, this one has turned to a breakfast buffet built around grill items, fresh fruit, and cereals, which is the best deal for families. The cost for adults is $9.95, and kids $4.95. There is a lunch counter, a buffet, and big platters heaped with food. Service is friendly and familiar, like that at a truck stop. The servers know how to treat children, although the portions are too large for little ones.

Grant Grove Village, Kings Canyon National Park. ℂ **559/335-5500.** Breakfast $2–$9.95; lunch $3.25–$15; dinner $5.95–$35. AE, DISC, MC, V. Summer daily 7–10:30am, 11am–2pm, and 5–9pm. Winter hours shorter.

Wolverton BBQ *Finds*   A great evening meal for kids and adults is the "Dinner with a Ranger" barbecue staged at Wolverton Meadow just down the road from Lodgepole. This all-you-can-eat feast of well-prepared ribs, chicken, and burgers runs from June to September and is followed by an interpretive program given by a ranger. This might involve a campfire singalong or a meadow nature walk.

Wolverton Meadow. No phone. No reservations; first-come, first-served. Adults $20; kids 12 and under $9.95. Tickets may be purchased at either Wuksachi Lodge or the Lodgepole Market.

BEST-BEHAVIOR MEALS
Wuksachi Lodge   With its big windows framing the High Sierra, vaulted ceilings, and large fireplace, the lodge's dining room is an inviting place for meals. Although somewhat new, it looks historic. While you need reservations for dinner, which has an inventive menu built around beef, fish, poultry, and vegetarian offerings, you don't need to spend a lot, because the lunch menu is served in the evening, too. For breakfast, hit the buffet table with its pastries, fresh fruit, eggs, grill items, and hot and cold cereals and forget about the menu. For lunch and dinner, kids can fill up on PB&Js, grilled cheese, hot dogs, and fish sticks.

Wuksachi Lodge. ℂ **559/565-4070.** www.visitsequoia.com. Kids' menu, highchairs. Reservations recommended for dinner. Breakfast $6.50–$10; lunch $8–$13; dinner $8.75–$32; kids' menu $3.45–$5.60. AE, DISC, MC, V. Year-round daily 7:30–9:30am, 11:30am–2:30pm, and 5–9pm.

---

7 Exploring Sequoia & Kings Canyon National Parks with Your Kids

ENTRANCE FEES   Sequoia and Kings Canyon national parks are one park in all but name. The entrance fee for these two parks was scheduled to jump to $25 in 2008 per vehicle, good for 7 days in either park. The America the Beautiful Pass also covers the fee (see "Entrance Fees" and "Passes," both in chapter 2, for details).

NATURAL PLACES
GRANT GROVE
A mile from the visitor center, compact Grant Grove is a good place to see your first Sequoias on entering the park. A paved loop trail less than a half-mile in length has stops keyed to an inexpensive guide brochure available at the visitor center.

The **General Grant** tree, the third largest in the world, is the national Christmas tree and a national shrine. It's 40 feet across at the base but relatively young among the biggest Sequoias, at 1,800 to 2,000 years old. This and many other Sequoias got their names from Civil War heroes, because that war was still fresh in the memories of explorers who came here in the 1870s. In more than a century since, the trees haven't changed much, but the names have come to seem strange—not big enough for these big trees.

Another highlight of Grant Grove is a hollow fallen tree you can walk through. It was once used as a stable, a cabin, and even a hotel, although not one I think I would recommend. The north loop, in a less visited area of the grove, adds an unpaved mile to the walk.

NEAR GRANT GROVE

The park and national forest around Grant Grove contain some incredible and rarely visited places, open secrets that most visitors fly right by.

My favorite area here is peaceful, awesome **Redwood Canyon,** the largest surviving Sequoia grove. It's a little tricky to find. Drive 5 miles south from Grant Grove on Generals Highway to a sign pointing left that reads HUME LAKE/QUAIL FLAT; turn right instead of left, on the unmarked dirt road, descending among immense trees 2 miles to the Redwood Canyon Trailhead. Here a network of trails descends into the grove, with loops of up to 10 miles (pick up a map at the Grant Grove visitor center). Gigantic trees fill the land, and there are few other people; you get the opportunity to feel an ant-size part of the forest, not just a tourist. With a backcountry permit (p. 421), you can spend the night among the big trees.

A great family hike is on the **Park Ridge Trail,** a mountaintop with great views that you can hike without much elevation gain because your car does the climbing to the trail head. Take the road marked Panoramic Point behind Grant Grove Village and drive 2⅓ steep, twisty miles to the parking lot. The trail follows the ridge, with views on both sides (smog permitting), 2.5 miles to a fire lookout.

Hume Lake, part of Giant Sequoia National Monument, lies in national forest land behind Grant Grove. It is a woodsy recreation area, with lake swimming, boating, and fishing, and many miles of dirt forest roads for biking. Climbing those roads to the east leads to the top of the mountains above Kings Canyon, beautiful high country with trails leading down into the park. Explore! To get there, take the roads to Hume Lake and Quail Flat 5 miles south of Grant Grove on Generals Highway; or take the Kings Highway 6 miles to the Princess Highway and turn toward the lake there.

GIANT FOREST &

The biggest Sequoias grow in Giant Forest, including **General Sherman,** the world's largest tree. But it's not just the size of the biggest tree that makes the grove special. The place feels like a towering cathedral of trees. Even the air feels ancient.

The 2-mile **Congress Trail** weaves through the forest. It's the most inspiring paved nature trail we've ever walked. Buy the inexpensive guide booklet first. Strollers do fine. A web of other, unpaved trails weaves deeper through the forest. Handy, inexpensive trail guides are for sale at the visitor center, so you can connect loops for a hike of any length.

On the south side of the forest, a narrow paved road leads 3 miles through the trees past several curious sites on the way to **Moro Rock** and **Crescent Meadow.** A climb up the rock is not to be missed. It's a barren granite dome with a quarter-mile staircase tracing dizzying drops on each side. If the weather is clear, the view from the top is mind-blowing. Drive to the end of the road for the trail head at Crescent Meadow. Sequoia walks are different here because the meadows contribute light, flowers, and wildlife. At least do the 1.6-mile **Crescent Meadow/Log Meadow Loop,** with the goal of seeing Tharp's Log, a home in a fallen tree made by the area's first white settler. Kids love it.

The Crescent Meadow trail head also is the starting point for the High Sierra Trail, a backpacking route all the way across the range, or a good day-hiking route that rises gently into the mountains with good views.

LODGEPOLE & WOLVERTON

The Lodgepole campground and visitor center lie in the glacier-carved Tokopah Valley, along the Marble Fork of the Kaweah River. The lodgepole pines in the valley are the last before the tree line and the open granite of the High Sierra. An easy 1.7-mile trail along the river leads to that terrain before coming to a dead end at the head of the valley and **Tokopah Falls.** Along the way, water pours over round granite shelves and boulders, making inviting pools for a swim on a hot day; check at the visitor center to find out whether water levels are safe for swimming.

Many other trails, horseback riding, and skiing start from **Wolverton Road,** which branches a bit over 1 mile south on Generals Highway. The **Alta** and **Lakes trails** lead from Wolverton into the spectacular high country.

CRYSTAL CAVE & BOYDEN CAVE

Crystal Cave was carved from marble by Cascade Creek, part of which still flows through a smooth stone trough on the floor of the passages. Millions of years of dripping water formed thin strands of rock that look like sticky melted cheese stretched apart from a sandwich. In other places the rock makes daggers, fins, narrow holes that lead into darkness, and a big gallery where the floor drops away into a chasm. A ranger-led 45-minute tour travels .5 mile of the 3-mile cave from mid-May through October. Hours vary by the season; at the peak, they're every half-hour from 10:30am to 4:30pm daily; complex off-season schedules are posted at www.sequoiahistory.org/cave/cave.htm, or call the park. You have to buy tickets in advance at the Lodgepole or Foothills visitor center; they're not available at the cave, because the ticket system meters the number of cars at the small lot. Buy your tickets early on weekends. They're $11 for adults, $6 for kids 6 to 12, free for children under 6. You can't buy a ticket within 90 minutes of your tour's start. With tickets in hand, drive Generals Highway to a dirt road about 14 miles from the Foothills visitor center, and then go 7 miles on that narrow, winding route. RVs and vehicles over 22 feet are not allowed. After parking, present your ticket at a booth and descend a steep .25-mile trail past the lovely Cascade Falls. Going from Lodgepole to the cave's mouth takes 45 minutes of driving and 15 minutes of walking. By the time you get to the cave mouth, you're hot, and the cool dampness inside the mountain feels good—but bring a sweater to avoid a chill in the 48°F (7°C) underground cave.

Boyden Cave also has a neat tour. The rock formations aren't as many or as bizarre as Crystal Cave and the tour is shorter; but Boyden is a lot easier to get to and is plenty long and impressive enough to give you that spooky cave feeling. You also have a good chance of seeing bats. The 45-minute tour covers 750 feet of a 1,000-foot cave in the wall of Kings Canyon in Sequoia National Forest on the way to Cedar Grove. There's a short but steep climb to the mouth from the parking lot and ticket booth by the Kings River. Privately operated tours take place summer daily 10am to 5pm. In April and May and in September until snow closes the road, hours are shorter: Call or check the website (℡ **866/762-2837;** www.caverntours.com). Admission is $11 for adults, $6 for children 3 to 12, free for children under 3.

KINGS CANYON & CEDAR GROVE

In 1891, John Muir wrote that Kings Canyon was similar to Yosemite Valley but grander. I'm not sure if that's true, but I do think Kings Canyon is a better place to visit. The similarity comes from the way the canyons were made. In each, a river cut a narrow valley; then a glacier followed, steepened the walls, and flattened the bottom.

In each, you can stand in a green meadow by a river and look straight up at cliffs of granite 3,000 feet high. But Kings Canyon is wilder. Partly that's because the rock is cracked instead of rounded, the river faster, and the journey into the canyon more of an adventure, passing through a narrow gorge of marble. But mostly, Kings Canyon is wilder because it is not clogged with people. There are only 21 hotel rooms here, and day-trippers usually don't bother with a drive of about an hour one-way from Grant Grove. There are plenty of campsites, plus river fishing and swimming, and wonderful hikes where you see few other people.

The **Zumwalt Meadow Trail,** near the end of the road beyond Cedar Grove, is a flat 1-mile loop that crosses the river and then circles the meadow, where you can see the contrast of the powerful cliffs above and delicate ferns and flowers below. The meadow was a glacial lake that has slowly filled. It's a lovely hike, easy enough for anyone in the family. There's a sandy spot just over the footbridge where people swim, but check with a ranger on the safety of the river level.

For a more challenging outing, the **Paradise Valley Trail** is a gorgeous, mostly shady hike to scenic Mist Falls, at 4 miles, or 6 miles to Paradise Valley itself, a beautifully pastoral mountain valley. The trail begins at the end of the road and is flat or rises only gradually until you approach the falls, when it gets quite steep the rest of the way to Paradise Valley. After the 2-mile mark, you branch to the left to follow the South Fork of the Kings River as it tumbles over rounded granite down the canyon. There are several appealing spots to play in the water, conditions permitting. Beware of slippery rocks, however, especially when walking near the falls, where there are some dangerous spots. On the way back, hike on the south side of the Kings River on the Sentinel Trail.

From near Cedar Grove Village, the **Hotel Creek Trail** climbs steeply through arid terrain to pine forest on the north side of the canyon, looking back down into the canyon with impressive views. Once you make that stiff climb, you can return on the Lewis Creek Trail to make a 7-mile loop. Start early, because it's hot. The **Don Cecil Trail** takes you up the canyon side on the south, with a spur to the top of 8,500-foot Lookout Peak; only strong hikers should try to go all the way. Or have a horse do the work. Trail rides and backcountry trips are available from a stable listed under "Horseback Riding & Stock Packing" (p. 431).

MINERAL KING VALLEY

By starting at this rocky, 7,500-foot-elevation valley, you can quickly hike into the Sierra's open high country on an extraordinary network of lightly used trails. The routes tend to be steep, but they lead to amazing places, with grand views every time you turn around. I'll never forget an overnight to the Monarch Lakes, a steep 4.5 miles to a pair of lakes sitting above 10,000 feet in the lap of sheer, rocky peaks. It seemed primeval. Short of the road's end, there are several good forest hikes, too, including hikes to remote Sequoia groves from the Atwell Mill area. But don't zip up here for a day hike. Unless you are camping at Atwell Mill or Cold Springs campground (p. 420) or have a cabin at Silver City Lodge (p. 424), reserve this area for backpacking or horse trips (there's a pack station at the end of the road; see p. 431). The drive and the hikes are too long and the elevation is too high to try to do much in 1 day.

The remoteness and quiet that make the area so appealing owe to the difficulty of getting there. The ludicrously windy Mineral King Road leads 24 miles from Three Rivers, about 1 mile outside the park. Over much of its length it snakes back and forth so sharply that you can do less than 10 mph, and it is wide enough only for one car.

RVs can't use the road. Cars have to creep along, and even then you will need to stop to prevent motion sickness. The road is closed due to snow from early November to Memorial Day.

MOUNT WHITNEY

At 14,494 feet, Mount Whitney is the highest peak in the United States outside Alaska. It's on the east side of the park, and you can't see it from the west side where visitors normally go. To get from the west to the east takes more than 5 hours of driving (see "Getting Around," p. 412). From mid-July to early October, climbing Mount Whitney requires no technical skills, but the elevation and 7,000-foot gain over an 11-mile trail, one-way, are beyond the ability of all but the strongest hikers, especially those who aren't used to the elevation. Also, due to crowding, you need a permit even for a day hike on the Main Mount Whitney Trail, which starts in Inyo National Forest; permits are given by lottery, and applications are accepted only in February. Details are online at www.fs.fed.us/r5/inyo/recreation/wild/mtwhitney.shtml, or call the Inyo **Wilderness Permit Office** (© **760/873-2485**). There are many other beautiful climbs in the park without red tape or travel hassles; check at the visitor centers.

PLACES FOR LEARNING

The visitor centers are described on p. 409.

Giant Forest Museum ⟨★⟩   This great little museum in the heart of the Sequoia groves contains exhibits about the giant trees that surround it, their natural history, and how they are being protected. The museum occupies an old market in a park village that used to stand here among the Sequoias (the Park Service wisely decided to demolish the other buildings to bring back the trees' natural setting). Out front on the asphalt the Park Service has painted lines indicating the size of a Sequoia, which makes it easy for youngsters to truly appreciate how big these trees are.

On Generals Hwy. in Giant Forest. © 559/565-4480. Free admission. Daily 9am–4:30pm year-round.

Walter Fry Nature Center   Located within the Lodgepole campground (no phone), the center houses a simple but engaging children's natural history museum, with hands-on displays that could keep a curious kid's attention for more than an hour. The center is the base for a children's program that's as good as any we encountered at the parks we visited; check there to find out what your kids can get involved in.

In Lodgepole Campground. No phone. Free admission. July to Labor Day weekends 10am–5pm. Closed rest of year.

8 For the Active Family

BACKPACKING

No road crosses the Sierra Nevada from Yosemite to Bakersfield. That's one measure of how remote this country is. Including the wilderness areas in the national forests, a 150-mile-long section of the Sierra is largely without human mark, one of the biggest such areas in the U.S. outside Alaska. Ninety percent of the national parkland is accessible only by foot—yours or a horse's. There are 800 miles of trails in the parks, more in the surrounding national forests, and significant areas without trails to be explored on side hikes or orienteering treks.

But to get into the wilderness, you don't have to attempt a weeklong journey across the mountains or climb the highest peaks. You also can enjoy the parks, and really get to know your family, by hiking 4 or 5 miles to a mountain lake and camping there for a couple of days, exploring the area on day hikes or just playing in the mountains. With areas like Redwood Canyon (p. 427) to explore, you don't need to choose a very tough route, so there's no need for beginners to shy away from giving it a try. Books and maps for planning a trek are listed under "Reading Up" (p. 410).

Backpackers need to learn about avoiding black bears, especially how to store food. Some backcountry campsites have bear-proof metal cabinets; otherwise, you need to use a bear-resistant canister. Read "Dangerous Wildlife," in chapter 2, and ask for details when you get your backcountry permit.

Another option is to join a guided hike (see "Field Seminars," p. 433), or to travel guided on horseback or with pack animals to carry your gear (see "Horseback Riding & Stock Packing," below).

FISHING

Lots of people fish for trout with spinning or fly-fishing gear all over the parks; almost everywhere is open. However, complicated state fishing regulations apply in the park and should be studied. You can get regulation information, limited tackle, and licenses at the Lodgepole, Grant Grove, and Cedar Grove stores. Anyone over age 15 needs a California license. Fishing gear is not available for rent anywhere in the parks, so bring your own. Steve Sorensen's *Day Hiking Sequoia* (see "Reading Up," p. 410) contains advice on where to fish, and rangers will give you ideas, too. Some popular areas suitable for kids are the **Kings River** in Cedar Grove, the **Kaweah River** along the Tokopah Falls Trail near Lodgepole, and **Dorst Creek.** Harder-to-reach spots will have bigger and more numerous fish.

HIKING

These parks have as many great day hikes as anywhere we have visited, with wonderful destinations and not too many other people. On many routes, welcoming stream pools beckon for a cooling splash. Even many of the Sequoia grove trails are lightly used, although highlights in Grant Grove and Giant Forest are liable to be crowded on weekends. There are two main kinds of hikes at the parks. The easier routes explore the forests, meadows, river valleys, and Sequoia groves of the western Sierra's wooded, midlevel elevations or follow creeks in the hot foothills. More challenging routes climb up into the high Sierra terrain of granite bedrock and long views.

Almost anywhere you find yourself, good hikes are nearby. I've listed some favorites with each area covered under "Natural Places" (p. 426), and with the descriptions of the Atwell Mill, Buckeye Flat, Dorst, Lodgepole, and Potwisha campgrounds. Get maps and trail details from the publications listed under "Reading Up" (p. 410); for most visitors, the $3.50 *Map & Trail Guide* for each park area is sufficient but essential.

HORSEBACK RIDING & STOCK PACKING

Pack stations are located at several places in the parks. Each is a little different; I've described them below. You can take a short beginner's ride or a long trip into the wilderness. Day trips range from 1 hour to all day and travel through level terrain or climb to high overlooks. Overnight trips penetrate the backcountry. The outfitters provide the food and gear and cook for you, or you can bring your own and get a discount. They'll even pack you out to a backcountry location and leave you, then come back and get you at a prearranged time. Few parks are better suited to seeing wilderness this way. Reserve backcountry trips as far ahead as possible—some dates book up 1 year in advance. Day trips might not require reservations, but call ahead anyway. The following two outfitters are in Kings Canyon.

At **Grant Grove Stables** (© 559/335-9292; www.sierragatewaymap.com/grant_ grove_stables.html), rides leave from a stables about a quarter-mile from the lodge and go through the forest. A 1-hour ride is $30; the longest ride, 2 hours, costs $50. Beginners and kids as young as 7 are okay on those rides. A "Little Buckaroo" ride for kids under 7 costs $10 for a half-hour.

Cedar Grove Pack Station (© 559/565-3464) is where you head if you're looking for a backcountry horse trip or for one of the packers to haul your gear into the backcountry, drop it off, and return at a prearranged date to collect it. Overnight pack trips into the backcountry cost around $210 per person per day, with food and gear included.

SWIMMING

On a hot hike, a dip in a chilly mountain stream is a dose of paradise. Children don't seem to worry so much about how cold the water is. Grown-ups may not stay in for long, but they still get a clean, rejuvenated feeling from a quick splash. Mountain lakes tend to be extremely cold, suitable only for in-and-out shock therapy for hot, sweaty bodies. Beware of hypothermia if the weather is anything but warm and still. Other safety information is covered under "Drowning" (p. 415); take it seriously, because these waters take lives every summer.

The best river swimming holes are in the foothills, near the south end of Generals Highway. Just inside the park, before the Ash Mountain entrance, the **Indian Head Swimming Hole** is a quarter-mile off the road. A .1-mile trail leads to **Hospital Rock Swimming Hole** from the picnic area of the same name on Generals Highway. Other good spots are at the Potwisha and Buckeye Flat campgrounds (p. 415 and 416). Some of these spots, with clear, glassy water overhung by tree branches, are lovely and wonderfully peaceful, a small slice of the Eden the Potwisha Indians must have enjoyed in these mountains. Fewer pool-size swimming holes occur at the higher elevations, but there are spots to splash in the water in the Kaweah River near Lodgepole and on hikes from Kings Canyon. Hume Lake has good swimming, covered above under "Natural Places" (p. 426). Other possibilities show up on hikes, but be careful.

WINTER SPORTS

With many roads and facilities closed by snow, the parks receive far fewer visitors in the winter than in the summer. But those who do come have the chance to see the giant trees on a sharply contrasting background of white, and there are some superb cross-country ski trails and snowshoeing opportunities. Experienced backcountry skiers will find few better places for adventures. There's even a hut for overnight stays at Pear Lake (p. 424). Snow conditions at the elevation of Grant Grove and Giant Forest usually allow for cross-country skiing and snowshoeing from January to March. Some excellent trails can be found at Lodgepole, Wolverton, and Wuksachi Lodge. Both groomed and ungroomed trails exist. In the foothills snow doesn't stick, and hiking continues all year. There are several places to rent snowshoes and skis for touring on trails made by other skiers and for backcountry trekking. The best ski trails are in Sequoia National Forest, at Montecito-Lake Resort, which has an extensive network professionally groomed for diagonal stride and skating, a small rope tow, rentals, and lessons for all levels and styles, including backcountry skiing (p. 422). Sledding areas are at Wolverton, Big Stump (near the north entrance), and Azalea Campground, near Grant Grove.

9 Kid-Friendly Programs

CHILDREN'S PROGRAMS

The rangers at the **Walter Fry Nature Center,** in the Lodgepole campground, run summer sessions that children enjoy and learn from. Programs change annually, but often a ranger leads a daily kids' activity for children ages 5 to 8, such as the Critters of the Sierra program. Programs also are offered at the Beetle Rock Education Center near the Giant Forest Museum. The park newspaper, *The Guide,* lists times. Outside the Walter Fry Nature Center, a **campfire program** just for kids takes place on summer afternoons.

The **Junior Ranger program** at Sequoia is simple and nicely pitched at the right age levels. The Jay Award is for children 5 to 8; it uses a booklet with activities that don't require much reading. The Raven Award, for ages 9 to 12, gets into more complex natural-history topics and involves more writing. In addition to the workbooks, kids collect trash and attend at least two programs or go on a nature walk; it's not difficult to do in a day. The best part is getting the award, a badge. Go to a campfire program 20 minutes before it starts so that the ranger can check the child's work. When the program begins, each badge winner is called in front of the audience to receive the badge and get a round of applause. There also are patches available for kids who complete the program, but they're sold for a small fee. You can pick up the program's activity booklet at the visitor center or nature center.

FAMILY & ADULT PROGRAMS & CAMPS

Besides these options, Montecito-Lake Resort (p. 422) and Hume Lake Christian Camps offer some great family choices with structured activities and camps.

PARK SERVICE PROGRAMS

The schedule of ranger walks and talks changes often. Current offerings are listed on bulletin boards at campgrounds and visitor centers. Generally, they're casual—you just show up at the time and place.

Campfire programs happen most summer nights at Lodgepole, Dorst, Sunset (at Grant Grove), and Sentinel (at Cedar Grove) campgrounds, and less frequently at Potwisha Campground, Mineral King, and Silver City Lodge. The programs usually involve an outdoor slide show and lecture and, depending on the ranger, some singing or other fun.

FIELD SEMINARS

Sequoia Natural History Association offers Field Institute sessions with qualified leaders teaching natural history and outdoor skills. Most sessions are 1 to 3 days long,

---

Tips Places for Relaxed Play & Picnics

A campsite or a patch of the woods is the perfect playground, but adults should check for poison oak. Most picnic areas are marked on the park map you'll receive when you arrive. The picnic areas that aren't shown are at the **Foothills and Lodgepole visitor centers, Big Stump,** and **Mineral King.** In Sequoia National Forest, picnic at **Stony Creek,** which is on Generals Highway between Lodgepole and Grant Grove, or **Grizzly Falls,** just outside the park near Cedar Grove.

and many include group camping. Generally, they're aimed at adults, although teens would enjoy some of the offerings; call and ask before signing up. The Kids and River Critters program is perfect for youngsters 5 and older. This 4-hour-long program focuses on water and the critters in it. Time is spent dipping out water bugs and other critters, splashing, and swimming. Some other sessions are especially for families, but the lineup changes annually. Prices range from $40 to $70 for most daylong sessions, up to $565 for a weeklong trek. For program information, contact the association (see "Sequoia–Kings Canyon Address Book," p. 405).

FAST FACTS: Sequoia & Kings Canyon National Parks

Area Code The area code is **559.**

ATMs You can find **ATMs** at Grant Grove, Lodgepole Village, and Stony Creek Lodge.

Emergencies For emergencies, dial ✆ **911.** The main park number (✆ **559/565-3341**) connects to park dispatch 24 hours a day. First aid is available at the visitor centers.

Hospitals & Clinics The hospital is the **Kaweah Delta Hospital** located at 400 W. Mineral in Visalia (✆ **559/624-2000**). Another is the **Community Regional Medical Center,** located at 2823 Fresno St. in Fresno (✆ **559/459-6000**).

Information For information, write **Sequoia & Kings Canyon National Parks,** 47050 Generals Hwy., Three Rivers, CA 93271-9651; call ✆ **559/565-3341;** or look on the Internet at www.nps.gov/seki.

Pharmacies One local pharmacy is **Three Rivers Drug Store** at 40907 Sierra Dr. in Three Rivers (✆ **559/561-4217**).

Post Office Branches are located at the Lodgepole Market Center (✆ **559/565-3468**) in Sequoia National Park and in Grant Grove (✆ **559/335-2499**) in Kings Canyon National Park.

Time Zone The park is on **Pacific Standard Time.**

Weather Updates For weather updates, go to the park's website, www.nps.gov.seki, and follow the link to weather.

16

Olympic National Park

The hook of land anchoring the northwest corner of the state of Washington in the Pacific Ocean is a rich, wondrous kingdom of sea, forest, and snow. On the outer coast, waves roar in from the vast sea, seething against rocks and sea stacks that stand away from the shore like the teeth of the continent. The sea's moisture blows ashore in ragged mists and overstuffed clouds that soon spill out clattering drops of rain. The hypnotic dampness clings to tall, dark evergreens, with branches and trunks that drip with moss and sprout ferns.

The rainforest is like a place under a spell that makes everything grow, life piling upon life in deep, pillowy layers. Your hair feels damp, as if ferns could sprout from between its roots at any moment. Rivers rush through Olympic National Park, carrying water that fell as snow on the alpine tundra back to the sea. Salmon use watery passages into the forest to swim up from the ocean. They pass over clean gravel in clear creeks and into silver-surfaced lakes, drawing the forest's animals to feed on their rich flesh, fattened at sea. Only a few people are there to see; mostly, the forest is silent and unbroken by voices.

The people of the Northwest have these places largely to themselves. Visitors come out to the peninsula from Seattle when the weekend forecast promises sun, but the great masses of people who fill many parks in the summer haven't found their way to Olympic. A single two-lane highway loops around this large rural maritime and logging region. The little towns are only partway through the switch from muscular logging communities to softer-edged tourism towns. Campgrounds are everywhere, on park, national forest, state, and county lands. Old wooden lodges are tucked up in the rainforest valleys, along lakes edged with timber, and standing out on the coastal bluffs above raging, misty seawater.

The park is huge, and the other public lands around it make it seem much bigger. Rather than a single, simple highway through the park, roads wind up valleys and out to points on the coast in many branches—a good match for the infinite, branching variety of nature here. The deep heart of the park can be reached only on long backpacking trails. There's no way to take it all in. Instead, relax and enjoy being part of a living system much larger than you are.

BEST THINGS TO DO IN OLYMPIC NATIONAL PARK

- **Hike a rainforest trail,** seeing the moss and ferns and feeling the enveloping dampness, or an alpine path with sweeping views.
- **Play on the rocky outer beaches,** searching at low tide for weird little sea animals.
- **Swim at Sol Duc Hot Springs** or one of the lakes.
- **Plan a backpacking trip** to get deep into the park away from other people.

For more information, see "For the Active Family" (p. 460).

Olympic Address Book

Olympic National Park   600 E. Park Ave., Port Angeles, WA 98362-6798.
℗ **360/565-3130.** www.nps.gov/olym.

Northwest Interpretive Association   164 S. Jackson St., Seattle, WA 98104.
℗ **877/874-6775** or www.nwpubliclands.org. For maps and books.

Olympic National Forest   1835 Black Lake Blvd. SW, Olympia, WA
98512-5623. ℗ **360/956-2402.** TDD 360/956-2401. www.fs.fed.us/r6/olympic.

Washington's Olympic Peninsula   P.O. Box 670, Port Angeles, WA 98362.
℗ **800/942-4042.** www.olympicpeninsula.org.

Port Angeles Chamber of Commerce   121 E. Railroad Ave., Port Angeles,
WA 98362. ℗ **360/452-2363.** www.portangeles.org.

Forks Chamber of Commerce   P.O. Box 1249, Forks, WA 98331. ℗ **800/443-
6757** or 360/374-2531. Fax 360/374-9253. www.forkswa.com.

Washington State Ferries   Seattle Ferry Terminal, 801 Alaskan Way/Pier 52,
Seattle, WA 98104-1487. ℗ **888/808-7977** in Washington only, 800/843-3779
(automated information line), or 206/464-6400. www.wsdot.wa.gov/ferries.

1 History: Logs or Trees?

Driving along Highway 101 between the park's coastal strip and its main mass of
mountains, you pass through forests in varying stages of growth. A hill that's stripped
bare of trees follows a dense forest of medium-size trees growing close together. Next
comes land clear-cut 15 years ago and replanted with Douglas firs, which have grown
as large as Christmas trees. The logging companies often post signs giving the years
the trees were harvested, replanted, thinned, and harvested again (usually in cycles of
60–90 years). Even a child can see the differences between these tree farms and the
old-growth forests in the national park. In the natural setting of the park, huge and
small trees grow together in patches of shadow and light, and the forest seems always
to change, but the changes are slow—it takes many human lifetimes for the trees there
to grow old and die.

These patches of ancient forest and replanted trees tell the story of the Olympic
Peninsula. When you drive from a patch of little trees to a stand of huge ones, you're
seeing the results of a century of disagreement over how to use this land—whether to
save the big trees or make them into products for people to use. So far, the results have
come out about half and half.

The first people of the Olympic Peninsula used wood, as all the Native Americans
of the Pacific Northwest did. They chopped down western red cedar to split into
planks for clan houses and to carve into art and useful items. They carved huge logs
of red cedar into long oceangoing canoes. They used other kinds of wood for bows,
spears, harpoons, or bowls; they knew what kind of tree was best for each. But the
natives didn't clear-cut old forests (which means cutting down all the trees). There
weren't that many people, and they were using the trees only for their own needs. The
loggers who came later were selling wood to the whole world.

White Americans started settling on the peninsula in the 1850s. Like the indigenous people, they settled around the coast. The middle, where the mountains hold glaciers and thick rainforests, was left blank on maps long after most of the connected part of the United States was explored and settled. The area was too rugged to cross; even today, no roads traverse the middle of the peninsula, only around the edges. In 1889 and 1890, a group sponsored by the *Seattle Press* took 6 months to make the trip from Port Angeles, on the north, to Aberdeen, on the southwest side. A group of scientific explorers crossed going the other way in 1890. They found the big trees of the rainforest and knew right away that loggers would want them.

When they returned, the leaders of the trip set to work to protect the land they had explored. Judge James Wickersham, a member of the expedition, wrote to Major John Wesley Powell, the head of the U.S. Geological Survey, asking that this land be set aside before the entire West was stripped of old trees. Powell had explored the Grand Canyon and much of the Southwest; Wickersham later went to Alaska, where he explored and helped set aside Denali National Park. In 1897, President Grover Cleveland made 2.25 million acres on the peninsula a forest reserve, including all the land from the mountains to the western coast.

From that day until the present, logging companies and conservationists have fought over how much of that forest reserve should be saved in old growth and how much used for timber harvest. Soon after the forest reserve was set aside, logging interests tried to get land out of it. They complained to the government in Washington, D.C., that the western lowlands in the reserve should be used for farming, not forests. They weren't telling the truth—the area had forests of huge trees, and the forest soil and constant rain made it useless for farming. But they won, and within 3 years of the reserve's being made, one-third of the land was taken out of the reserve and put into private ownership by farmers. People did apply for farm homesteads, but many quickly sold the land to the lumber companies. The companies cut down the old-growth trees and started the tree farms we see in the western area of the peninsula today.

The first land set aside for preservation was protected to save the Roosevelt elk. The largest wild herd lives on the peninsula. These are the largest elk, and members of Elks clubs across the country wanted their teeth for souvenirs; to get the teeth, commercial hunters slaughtered thousands of elk, leaving the meat to rot. In 1909, President Theodore Roosevelt—after whom the elk were named—set aside a national monument on the Olympic Peninsula to help save the elk from extinction. The monument took in rainforest valleys in the mountains, including about two-thirds of the land that's now in the national park. But those lines didn't last long, either. People in favor of more logging persuaded President Woodrow Wilson to take away about a third of the national monument just 6 years later.

In the 1930s, conservationists mounted their strongest push to protect the trees, and Congress began discussing a new national park on the peninsula. The fight continued for some time, until President Franklin Roosevelt took the problem into his own hands. He went to the Olympic Peninsula in 1937 and met the local people in Port Angeles who wanted the park. He told the two sides that he agreed there should be a park, and that the park should be larger than many logging supporters wanted. In 1938, Congress passed the law that set aside the park, which was a little bit larger than the original national monument.

Battles over the park's boundaries continued for decades. Today Olympic National Park totals 922,651 acres. It is a bit less than half of President Cleveland's forest reserve, but almost twice the size of President Wilson's national monument.

The park we visit today, and the sharp lines between areas of ancient forest and areas of young, all-the-same trees, are like a recording of the decisions made over the past 100 years. Today disagreements are settled about the land in the national park, but they go on in many other places here in the Pacific Northwest and around the world. Conservationists think more land needs to be protected to provide areas of habitat large enough for some kinds of wildlife. Loggers and businesspeople, on the other hand, say that they should be able to continue using the forests to produce wood and paper that people need and to make jobs for people in their towns. In recent years the conservationists have been winning in the Northwest, and fewer old trees than ever are available for cutting.

On the Olympic Peninsula, towns are changing with the changes in how the land is used. Port Angeles still has mills that devour trees from the peninsula, but the townspeople also have spruced up their downtown area to make it more attractive to national park visitors. More and more people get their jobs from businesses for visitors. Those visitors come to see the old trees still standing. In the long run, the ancient forests may be worth more alive than dead.

2 Orientation

The park has three main parts. Roads lead around the rim of the park to connect them. Except for the lodges and towns, the area is rural, with many miles of undeveloped forest highways and occasional country stores.

ARRIVING
BY CAR OR FERRY

To **Port Angeles** from Seattle's Sea-Tac Airport or other mainland points north or east, you can choose the fun way or the fast way. The fast way is to take **Interstate 5** to Tacoma, crossing the Tacoma Narrows Bridge, and then take Route 16 north through Bremerton to Route 3. Then cross the Hood Canal Bridge on Route 104, and meet Highway 101 about 40 miles east of Port Angeles.

For added fun, take a **ferry** across Puget Sound, from Seattle's Pier 52, at 801 Alaskan Way, to Bainbridge Island. From there, drive north to the Hood Canal Bridge. The ferry is slower because of the wait to get onboard, but you can spend that time exploring the touristy waterfront. The ferry itself is large and comfortable, and the views of the city and boats are great. Without boarding delays (which can be a couple of hours) the trip from Sea-Tac to Port Angeles takes 2½ to 3 hours by road or ferry. For more ferry information, contact **Washington State Ferries** (see "Olympic Address Book," p. 436). A Washington State Ferry also connects Victoria Island, British Columbia, to Seattle. (**Note:** Sometimes the delays can be a bonus, if a farmer's/crafts market is set up for travelers.)

If you're going to the **southwest part of the park,** including Lake Quinault or Kalaloch Lodge, from either north or south, or going anywhere in the park from the south, take I-5 to Olympia. To go north, join U.S. 101 there and follow it to Port Angeles. To go west, take four-lane highways 8 and 12 to Aberdeen, and join the other end of the 101 loop north from there. From Olympia, either Quinault or Port Angeles is 2 hours away. If you're already on coastal 101 going north, you just keep going north.

A **Black Ball Transport ferry** (© 360/457-4491; www.ferrytovictoria.com) carries passengers and vehicles most of the year from Victoria, British Columbia, to Port Angeles, making it possible to loop across Victoria Island and return by the Washington ferry mentioned above to Seattle.

BY AIR

Seattle-Tacoma Airport, known as Sea-Tac, is served by all major airlines and car-rental firms. From King County International Airport, known as Boeing Field, you can save a 3-hour drive by flying to Fairchild International Airport, in Port Angeles, on **Kenmore Air** (© 866/435-9524; www.kenmoreair.com) for around $165 round-trip. **Budget** (© 800/527-0700 or 360/452-4774; www.budget.com) rents cars in Port Angeles at the airport and at 111 E. Front St.

VISITOR INFORMATION
NATIONAL PARK & FOREST SERVICE VISITOR CENTERS

Besides the visitor centers listed below, there are ranger stations, many open in the summer only, all over the park. Locations are marked on the map on p. 440 and on the fold-out park map, and phone numbers for each are on the website (www.nps.gov/olym/tourmap.htm).

Olympic National Park

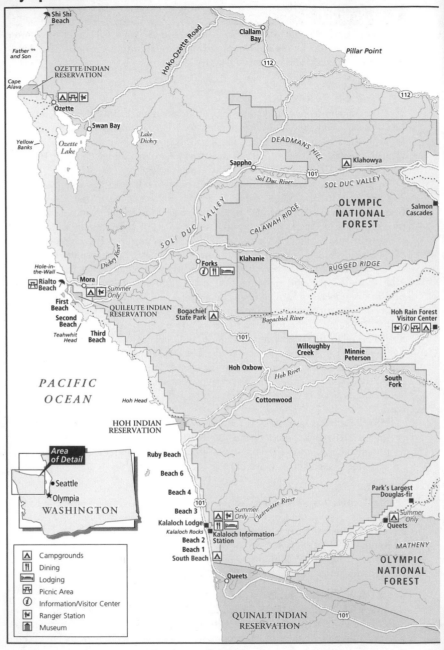

PACIFIC OCEAN

WASHINGTON

- Seattle
- Olympia

Area of Detail

	Campgrounds
	Dining
	Lodging
	Picnic Area
	Information/Visitor Center
	Ranger Station
	Museum

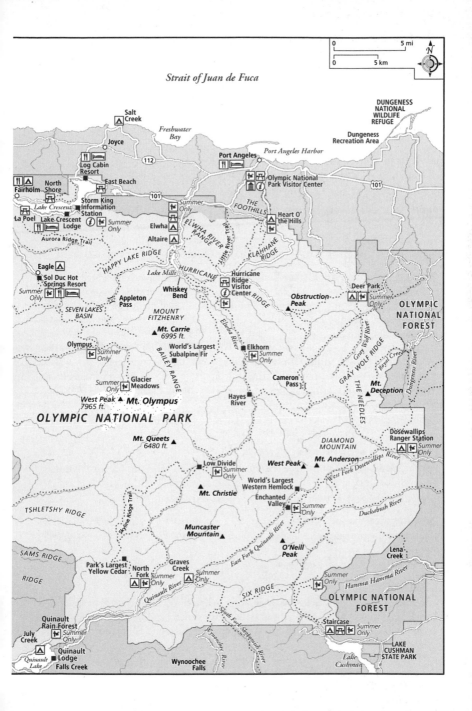

Hoh Rain Forest Visitor Center The good little museum, though somewhat aged, explains the rainforest and identifies trees and plants. The area's amazing rain records are posted. Ranger programs start here, and the rangers post trail conditions for longer hikes.

Upper Hoh Rd., Hoh Rain Forest, east of Forks. © 360/374-6925. Summer daily 9am–4pm; spring and fall Fri–Sun 10am–4pm; winter hours irregular.

Hurricane Ridge Lodge Rangers and exhibits share the skiing warm-up building, which also has a snack bar and ski rental. In summer rangers lead hikes from this center, while in winter they offer snowshoe tours of the ridge.

Hurricane Ridge, south of Port Angeles. © 360/565-3131. Hours vary (generally open 10am–6pm daily in summer, Fri–Sun winter).

Forks Park and Forest Information Office This center in Forks houses rangers offering advice, handouts, and Forest Service permits. You also can pick up wilderness use permits here as well as animal-resistant food containers.

Hwy. 101, Forks. © 360/374-7566. Summer daily 9am–4pm; off season Mon–Fri vary.

Olympic National Park Visitor Center ⟨ This is the main center, where you can buy books and maps, get backcountry permits, and learn about the park's natural history. Pick up copies of exceptionally interesting natural trail guides for areas you will visit; they cost only 50¢ each. A small museum explains the biology of different park areas, and a terrific little discovery room for kids has bones, hides, puzzles, and the like. Two trails start here: the short, wheelchair-accessible **Living Forest Trail,** and the lovely **Peabody Creek Trail.** Families should not miss the Peabody Creek Trail of less than a mile, which descends steeply from the west side of the parking area among huge trees to a pair of bridges on the creek. It's a perfect introduction to the kind of beauty you come to the park for.

3002 Mount Angeles Rd., Port Angeles (1½ miles up from town, on the way to Hurricane Ridge). © 360/565-3130. Summer daily 9am–5:30pm; winter daily 10am–4pm.

COMMERCIAL VISITOR CENTERS
Forks Chamber of Commerce Visitor Center The center is next to the town's Timber Museum.

Hwy. 101, at the south end of Forks. © 800/443-6757 or 360/374-2531. Daily 10am–4pm.

Port Angeles Visitors Center Near the ferry dock in Port Angeles, this center offers brochures on businesses all over the area and is staffed by volunteers who answer questions.

121 E. Railroad Ave. © 360/452-2363. Summer daily 9:30am–5pm; off season daily 10am–3pm.

READING UP
The **Northwest Interpretive Association** (see "Olympic Address Book," p. 436) sells a good selection of books and maps in park visitor centers and by mail order.

    Maps: The plastic Trails Illustrated topographic trail map ($10) covers the park in adequate detail.

    Hiking: Robert L. Wood's *Olympic Mountains Trail Guide: National Park and Forest* (The Mountaineers Books, $19) covers every trail in the region.

    Nature: Tim McNulty's *Olympic National Park: A Natural History Guide* (Houghton Mifflin, $19) is engaging, well researched, and comprehensive.

THE NATIONAL PARK IN BRIEF

The Eastern Mountains

Starting from park headquarters in Port Angeles at the park's northeast corner, a road leads up into the alpine section of the park at **Hurricane Ridge**. It's popular for skiing and sledding in the winter and for views and mountain walks in the summer. Just west of town a road following the Elwha River leads up to trails that rise from big trees into the mountains. From the southeast, dirt roads lead through the national forest to remote backpacking trails.

The Western Forests

Along the west side of the Olympic Mountains, roads lead up a series of lushly forested river valleys. I'll describe them from north to south. The **Sol Duc Valley** has a lodge and hot springs; the **Hoh Rain Forest** is in the next valley, of the same name, and has a visitor center and campground; the **Queets Rainforest** is a less visited area reached by a long unpaved road; and the **Quinault** is at the park's southeast corner, where a historic lodge sits by a large lake. **Lake Crescent,** which also has a lodge, lies on lowlands on the north side of the park, surrounded by big trees, between the Elwha and Sol Duc rivers.

The Coastal Strip

The park protects a long, narrow coastal strip on the western edge of the Olympic Peninsula facing the open Pacific Ocean. This is a land of enormous surf, rocks, and sand, tide pools, and long backpacking beach walks. It's separated from the rest of the park by a strip of Olympic National Forest and state and private timberlands 12 to 25 miles wide. **Kalaloch Lodge** is at the south end of the coastal strip.

Port Angeles

Port Angeles is the commercial center for the region. It's a typical northwestern town, with a few streets of businesses in old downtown buildings and a larger highway area of fast-food outlets and parking lots. It's a good place to start your visit, seeing a few sites and stocking up before heading into the park. The main park visitor center and the road to Hurricane Ridge are just above the town.

Forks

On the western side of the peninsula, in the logging district between the mountain and seashore areas of the park, Forks is a rural logging community along Highway 101. The only sizable town in that part of the park, it has a few motels.

---

3 Getting Around

BY CAR

Any visit will require a car. The park is large, and the roads rarely go in a straight line between two points. From Sol Duc Hot Springs to the Hoh Rain Forest, for example, is about 8 miles as the crow flies, 23 miles on foot, and 72 miles by car. From Port Angeles to Quinault is 128 miles of often-slow driving on two-lane Highway 101. It's difficult to use a single base to see the whole park. If you have time, stay in two or three places; if your visit is short, concentrate on one part of the park and see more areas the next time you come.

The main road is **U.S. Highway 101,** a two-lane loop that circles the entire peninsula, from Aberdeen to Olympia. All other roads into the park branch from U.S. 101 at one point or another.

4 Planning Your Outings

WHEN TO GO

Anytime you visit the Olympic rainforests, you have a good chance of getting wet. The driest (and most popular) months are July and August, when there's a 20% to 30% chance of rain on an average day. June is next driest, followed by May and September, then April, when the chance of rain is more than fifty-fifty on an average day. From October to March, as much rain falls here in a month as many other places get in a year. December and January are the wettest months—a typical day has a 70% chance of rain.

Olympic is never crowded the way some other national parks are, but there are some shortages on weekends in the July and August high season. Sometimes the parking lots in the Hoh Rain Forest fill and cars are held back until someone leaves; the same can happen at Hurricane Ridge in the winter. Lodge reservations for the high months must be made many months ahead. Many facilities close in the winter, but the weather remains mild. If you can stand the rain, you can have the park to yourself.

HOW MUCH TIME TO SPEND

The quick, drive-through approach to visiting national parks won't work well at Olympic. It's too big and varied, and to see much you have to take long spur roads and hike. For a long vacation, however, there are few better places. The park has many interesting destinations that reward time and exploration, with lots of campgrounds and lodges you can link together in a slow tour from point to point. Many people come for a weekend from Seattle to visit just one area of the park. To see each of the park's ecosystems, the coast, rainforest, and mountains, you need 4 to 7 days; 2 weeks will give time to relax and really explore.

Weather Chart: Quinault & Port Angeles

	Avg. High (°F/°C)	Avg. Low (°F/°C)	Precip. (in. in total period)
November–February			
Quinault	46/8	35/2	78
Port Angeles	47/8	35/2	15
March–April			
Quinault	55/13	37/3	24
Port Angeles	53/12	38/3	3
May–June			
Quinault	67/19	46/8	15
Port Angeles	63/17	46/8	2
July–August			
Quinault	74/23	52/11	6
Port Angeles	68/20	51/11	1
September–October			
Quinault	65/18	47/8	20
Port Angeles	62/17	47/8	4

HOW FAR TO PLAN AHEAD

If you intend to camp, no advance planning is needed. Park Service campgrounds, except for Kalaloch, don't take reservations, and usually they all fill only on sunny summer weekends. At busy times, you need to arrive early in the day, but if you miss out on your first choice, there are many public campgrounds near the park.

Motel rooms in the towns should be reserved ahead for the summer high season. The lodges in the park fill much earlier. July and August can book up by March, with less lead time required for other times. Reservation rules vary at each, but it's wise to call as soon as you know your plans.

WHAT TO PACK

The weather in the Olympic Peninsula varies from dry to soggy within a few miles. The temperature stays pretty much the same wherever you are at the same elevation; it's mild year-round near sea level and cool or snowy up above. As you can see from "Weather Chart: Quinault & Port Angeles," above, Quinault Ranger Station, in the rainforest on the west side of the park, gets almost six times the rainfall of Port Angeles, on the east side. The moisture coming off the ocean causes the difference in rainfall. Clouds drop about 80 inches of rain a year on the coast, 140 on the rainforest valleys on the west side of the mountains, more than 200 inches (that's more than 16 ft.) of water in rain and snow on the mountaintops, and as little as 10 inches a year on the eastern side of the mountains, in Sequim. It's all because of the way the mountains force air rising across their western slopes to cool, condensing the moisture into rain. On the far side, the air drops down again, warms up, and can hold much more water without producing rain.

CLOTHING

Bring rain gear that will keep you dry so you can keep hiking and seeing the park when rain is falling. You'll also need warm sweaters for the damp chill. Don't forget warm-weather clothes and swimsuits, too—it won't rain all the time, especially in the summer. Trails can be muddy, so you may need extra socks and pants. Pack two pairs of shoes, one to keep clean and one you can get dirty on the trail. You won't need formal clothing in the best restaurant in the area, but you may need something better than camping clothes. In the winter or spring, bring winter clothes for skiing or sledding at Hurricane Ridge. Remember, wool, fleece, and polyester are better conductors of warmth when they get wet; don't wear jeans or cotton, if you can help it.

GEAR

Make sure your tent is waterproof. Bring plastic tarps and cord, or buy them when you arrive, to shelter your picnic table and keep your tent dry. Unless you hike to high elevations, you won't encounter severe cold. A camp stove is a necessity, because any wood you find will be wet and difficult to burn. For watching whales and other wildlife on the coast, bring good binoculars.

KEEPING SAFE & HEALTHY

Dampness brings a risk of **hypothermia** at any time of year; see "Dealing with Hazards," in chapter 2.

SURF & LOGS

The waves on the ocean beaches of the Olympic Peninsula can be incredibly powerful, picking up huge tree trunks that have washed down the rivers and smashing them repeatedly against the rocks and sand. Logs have crushed people on the shore. Be careful climbing among the driftwood logs that pile up on the beach; they can shift easily and trap a child's ankle or do other damage.

TIDES

At low tide in many places on the coast, you can walk around rocky headlands that are partly underwater when the tide comes in. Don't get trapped by the incoming tide. Hike these routes only when the tide is going out, and make a mental note of paths over the top that you can use if you get cut off. Tide tables are available from the visitor centers and at many stores.

5 Family-Friendly Accommodations

CAMPGROUNDS

The northern Olympic Peninsula has an extraordinary number of campgrounds, run by the Park Service, the Forest Service, the state of Washington, and the counties. Most of them are memorable places to camp—in mossy forests, on riverbanks, on lakeshores, and by the sea. The map on p. 440 or the fold-out park map shows each, and is a better guide to finding them than written directions I can give. I've listed campgrounds by area, with the name of the agency that runs each after the name. Kalaloch Campground accepts reservations through the national system during the summer (p. 29), but otherwise campsites in the area cannot be reserved. They are plentiful during the week, although some campgrounds fill in the morning on weekends in July and August.

Olympic National Park has 16 campgrounds, though the Queets Campground is closed indefinitely due to storm damage. The Park Service advises that they're not appropriate for trailers longer than 21 feet, and some have shorter limits. The Park Service doesn't establish precise seasons of operation, although I've given the general rule for each below. All open in May, but even those that remain open all winter may not have water turned on. If you're visiting outside the summer months, call to find out which campgrounds are open and have water. If the water is off, there's usually no fee. Five campgrounds have RV dump stations, as noted below.

Firewood collection is permitted in most places where it isn't for sale, but the wood you find in this wet climate is difficult to burn.

Campfire **ranger programs** take place in the summer at the larger campgrounds. Check the *Bugler* park newspaper for locations, days, and times; topics are posted on campground bulletin boards. Questions about the park campgrounds can be directed to © **360/565-3130.**

NORTH SIDE

Altaire   This wooded campground, similar to Elwha, is near the dam and ranger station and has some nice sites down along the Elwha River. Many trails start near here.

Olympic National Park. Up Elwha River Rd., about 1 mile beyond the Elwha Campground, west of Port Angeles. © 360/565-3130. 30 sites, tents or RVs. $12 site. Closed winter. **Amenities:** Flush toilets, picnic tables, fire pits and grates, running water.

Elwha   This is a pretty spot, on the floor of the narrow Elwha Valley. Moss-covered trees that branch high above the ground provide shade, but there's no screen between the sites. A picnic shelter has a stone fireplace. Many trails start near here.

Olympic National Park. About 3 miles up Elwha River Rd., just west of Port Angeles. © 360/565-3130. 40 sites, tents or RVs. $12 site. Open year-round. **Amenities:** Flush toilets, picnic tables, fire pits and grates, no water in winter.

Fairholm   On a ferny slope above the west end of the lake, this pleasant campground is a center of activities. The lake has a boat ramp and swimming area, and up on the road there are a restaurant and store. A nature trail circles through the woods.

Olympic National Park. Hwy. 101, west end of Lake Crescent. ℂ 360/565-3130. 88 sites, tents or RVs. $12 site. Closed winter. **Amenities:** Flush toilets, dump station, general store, picnic tables, fire pits and grates, running water, restaurant.

Heart O' the Hills   Just inside the pay station on the way to Hurricane Ridge, this campground is the most convenient to Port Angeles, but it has a deep-forest feeling, among tall red cedars, hemlocks, and big boulders on hilly ground. Our site, like many on the outside of the loops, faded into the mossy woods and massive trees in the back and was visually blocked almost completely on the other sides, so we felt as though we were camping alone in the deep woods. The lovely Heart O' the Hills Trail extends 2 miles from the east side of the campground among ferns and immense trees. It's an easy family hike.

Olympic National Park. About 5 miles up Hurricane Ridge Rd. ℂ **360/565-3130.** 105 sites, tents or RVs. $12 site. Open year-round. **Amenities:** Flush toilets, picnic tables, fire pits and grates, running water.

Salt Creek   This wonderful 196-acre park, around a World War II defensive site on the Strait of Juan de Fuca, includes a prime tide-pooling shore, fishing, trails, a playground, and lots of open lawn for play. Many sites nestle in the trees along the bluff over the water.

Clallam County Parks Dept. Off Rte. 112 west of Port Angeles (3506 Camp Hayden Rd.). ℂ **360/928-3441.** www. clallam.net/countyparks. 90 sites, tents or RVs. $16 site. 39 sites have water and electric service (30- and 50-amp). Gates close at dusk. Open year-round. **Amenities:** Flush toilets, showers, dump station, picnic tables, fire pits and grates, running water.

WEST-SIDE FORESTS

Bogachiel   This attractive little state park campground runs along 123 acres on the Bogachiel River at the west end of the Hoh Rain Forest. It seems well maintained and comfortable and has coin-op showers. Six sites have water and electric hookups.

Washington State Park. Hwy. 101, south of Forks. ℂ **360/374-6356.** www.parks.wa.gov/parks. 36 sites, 6 with power and water, tents or RVs. $17 site; $24 site with water and electricity. No reservations. Open year-round. **Amenities:** Flush toilets, showers, dump station, picnic tables, fire pits and grates, running water, hookups.

Graves Creek   This isolated campground is deep in the rainforest along a dirt road. It's not a good place to haul a trailer or drive an RV. There is a mile-long nature trail among the trees and a trail head to backpack up to the Enchanted Valley, one of the park's most beautiful trips.

Olympic National Park. Up South Shore Rd. in the Quinault Rain Forest. ℂ **360/565-3130.** 30 sites, tents or RVs. $12 site. May close in winter. **Amenities:** Pit toilets, picnic tables, fire pits and grates, no water in winter.

Hoh   Although the big, mossy trees of the rainforest are nearby, this campground is on open ground among smaller trees near the Hoh River, which rushes right by some sites. It's pleasant but doesn't have the deep-forest feel of some others.

If you can't get in here, a series of primitive Washington State campgrounds lies along the road on the way in, where you'll also find some handy little stores.

Olympic National Park. Near the Hoh Rain Forest Visitor Center. ℂ **360/565-3130.** 88 sites, tents or RVs. $12 site. Open year-round. **Amenities:** Flush toilets, dump station, picnic tables, fire pits and grates, running water.

Klahowya   This is a lovely, shady U.S. Forest Service campground by the highway. Some sites are private, in dense forest, and others front the Sol Duc River. There's a nature trail, too.

Olympic National Forest. On Hwy. 101, west of Lake Crescent. ℂ **360/374-6522.** 55 sites, tents or RVs up to 30 ft. $12 site. Closed winter. **Amenities:** Flush toilets, vault toilets, picnic tables, fire pits and grates, running water.

Campgrounds in the Olympic Area

Campground	Elevation	Total Sites	RV Hookups	Dump Station	Toilets	Drinking Water
Altaire	450	30	No	No	Yes	Yes
Bogachiel	N/A	46	Yes	Yes	Yes	Yes
Deer Park*	5,400	14	No	No	Yes	No
Dosewallips*	1,540	30	No	No	Yes	No
Elwha	390	40	No	No	Yes	Yes
Elwha Dam RV Park	N/A	39	Yes	Yes	Yes	Yes
Fairholm	580	88	No	Yes	Yes	Yes
Graves Creek	540	30	No	No	Yes	Yes
Heart O' the Hills	1,807	105	No	No	Yes	Yes
Hoh	578	88	No	Yes	Yes	Yes
Kalaloch	50	170	No	Yes	Yes	Yes
Klahowya	800	55	No	No	Yes	Yes
Log Cabin Resort	580	40	Yes	Yes	Yes	Yes
Mora**	35	94	No	Yes	Yes	Yes
North Fork	520	9	No	No	Yes	No
Ozette	N/A	15	No	No	Yes	Yes
Queets	290	20	No	No	No	No
Port Angeles KOA	N/A	87	Yes	Yes	Yes	Yes
Salt Creek	N/A	90	No	Yes	Yes	Yes
Sol Duc	1,680	82	No	Yes	Yes	Yes
South Beach	50	50	No	No	Yes	No
Staircase	765	56	No	No	Yes	Yes
Willaby and Falls Creek	N/A	21 and 30	No	No	Yes	Yes

* *Trailers/RVs prohibited.*
** *Group reservations only (must be made directly through the ranger station).*

North Fork This primitive campground lies in mossy trees. It's close to the start of backpacking trails and near the end of a long dirt road. It's not recommended for RVs or trailers.

Olympic National Park. Up North Shore Rd. in the Quinault Rain Forest. ℂ **360/565-3130.** 9 sites, tents only. $10. May close in winter. **Amenities:** Picnic tables, fire pits and grates, no running water.

Showers	Fire Pits/Grills	Laundry	Public Phones	Reservations	Fees	Open
No	Yes	No	No	No	$12	Year-round
Yes	Yes	No	Yes	No	$17–$24	Year-round
No	Yes	No	No	No	$10	Seasonal
No	Yes	No	No	No	Free	Seasonal
No	Yes	No	No	No	$12	Year-round
Yes	Yes	Yes	Yes	Yes	$19–$27	Year-round
No	Yes	No	No	No	$12	May–Oct
No	Yes	No	No	No	$12	Seasonal
No	Yes	No	No	No	$12	Year-round
No	Yes	No	No	No	$12	Year-round
No	Yes	No	Yes	Yes	$14–$18	Year-round
No	Yes	No	No	No	$12	May–Oct
Yes	Yes	Yes	Yes	No	$37	Seasonal
No	Yes	No	Yes	No	$12	Year-round
No	No	No	No	No	$10	Seasonal
No	Yes	No	No	No	$12	Seasonal
No	Yes	No	No	No	$8	Closed indefinitely
Yes	Yes	Yes	Yes	Yes	$26–$149	Mar–Nov
Yes	Yes	No	No	Yes	$16	Year-round
No	Yes	No	No	No	$14	Year-round
No	Yes	No	No	No	$10	Memorial Day to Labor Day
No	Yes	No	No	No	$12	Year-round
No	Yes	No	No	No	$13–$15	Seasonal

Queets   A primitive campground, more than 10 miles up a bumpy dirt road from Highway 101, is at the start of trails up the Queets River. Roosevelt elk are often seen here. However, the campground was closed indefinitely following severe storms in November 2006.

Olympic National Park. More than 10 miles off Hwy. 101 in the Queets Rain Forest. ☏ **360/565-3130**. 20 sites, tents only. **$8** site. May close in winter. **Amenities:** Picnic tables, fire pits and grates, no running water.

Sol Duc   This may be the park's best vacation campground. It lies near the end of the spur road into the valley, just below a short trail to the misty Sol Duc Falls and the steep but beautiful Deer Lake Trail to the high-country lake. Just down the road in the downstream direction are the warm and hot pools, restaurant, RV park, and store at Sol Duc Hot Springs Resort. Pool fees and facilities are covered on p. 453. The campground itself is long and narrow, giving many sites their own place in the woods above the river.

Olympic National Park. Sol Duc Hot Springs Rd. (C) 360/565-3130. 82 sites, tents or RVs. $14 site. Year-round. Amenities: Flush toilets, dump station, picnic tables, fire pits and grates, running water.

Willaby and Falls Creek   These two campgrounds, about a mile apart on the south side of the lake, perch among large trees where you can swim right from the campground. Anglers get trout and Dolly Varden char. The beautiful lodge, a network of trails, and a store are nearby.

Olympic National Forest. South Shore Rd., Quinault Lake. (C) 360/565-3130. 21 and 30 sites, tents or RVs up to 16 ft. $15 site drive-in; $13 site walk-in at Falls Creek. Closed winter. Amenities: Flush toilets, boat launch, picnic tables, fire pits and grates, running water.

WESTERN COAST

Kalaloch   Two lines of sites sit on a strip of windblown grass and small twisted trees between the highway and the steep bluff overlooking the beach. Sites are well screened, and many have dramatic views. The store and restaurants at Kalaloch Lodge are nearby.

Olympic National Park. Hwy. 101, north of Kalaloch Lodge. (C) 360/565-3130. 170 sites, tents or RVs. Summer $18 site; off season $14 site. Reservations accepted through national system summer only. Open year-round. Amenities: Flush toilets, dump station, picnic tables, fire pits and grates, running water.

Mora   More than a mile from Rialto Beach on a quiet, paved road, this campground is among tall, shady trees near the Quillayute River.

Olympic National Park. Mora Rd., west of Forks. (C) 360/565-3130. 94 sites, tents or RVs. $12 site. Open year-round. Amenities: Flush toilets, dump station, picnic tables, fire pits and grates, running water.

Ozette   The area on the north shore of large Ozette Lake is a long drive from the rest of the park but has a lot to offer, including a remote beach that's a 3-mile walk along a board trail through the woods.

Olympic National Park. Hoko-Ozette Rd., Ozette. (C) 360/565-3130. 15 sites, tents or RVs. $12 site. May close in winter. Amenities: Flush toilets, picnic tables, fire pits and grates, running water.

South Beach   This campground, which resembles a parking lot in an open field, is unappealing for tenting, but it may be the thing if you are traveling in an RV. There are good views from atop the open coastal bluff at the south end of the park's shoreline strip.

Olympic National Park. Hwy. 101 at south end of park. (C) 360/565-3130. 50 sites, tents or RVs. $10 site. Closed Labor Day to Memorial Day. Amenities: Flush toilets, picnic tables, fire pits and grates, no drinking water.

EAST SIDE

This less-visited area of the park is reached by roads through the Olympic National Forest and doesn't connect easily to the rest of the park. Besides various national forest and state park campgrounds, there are three national park campgrounds: **Staircase,** $10 per site, 56 sites, RV accessible, with flush toilets; **Deer Park,** $8 per site, 14 sites, tents only, with pit toilets; and **Dosewallips,** which at this writing could not be

> **Tips   Park Camping Basics: Toilets, Showers & Laundry**
>
> In Port Angeles, there are public restrooms on the city pier near the end of Lincoln Street, in The Landing Mall behind the Chamber of Commerce Visitor Center, and at the park visitor center. In the park, campgrounds, visitor centers, and lodges have the closest bathrooms.
>
> In Port Angeles you can shower at the William Shore Memorial Pool on 5th Street (© 360/417-4595), where admission for open swimming is less than $5.25 adults, $3.40 for children under 18. Access to the showers alone is $2.25. Spic & Span Laundromat is at 1105 E. Front St.
>
> At Quinault Lake, coin-operated showers and laundry machines are in a building next to the post office, on South Shore Road across from the Rain Forest Resort east of the lodge.
>
> In Forks, public hot showers are at Bagby's Town Motel, on Forks Avenue at the south end of town.
>
> Away from towns, public hot showers are at Salt Creek and Bogachiel campgrounds, listed above. At Sol Duc Hot Springs Resort, you can take a hot shower at certain hours even without paying to use the hot springs (p. 453).

reached by vehicles due to a road washout. Walk-in camping with pit toilets and no water was still permitted.

RV PARKS

Within the park, RV parks are at **Sol Duc Hot Springs Resort** (p. 453) and **Log Cabin Resort** (p. 453). Many more RV parks are in and around Port Angeles. They include the following:

Elwha Dam RV Park   This wooded park comes with 39 RV sites plus 2½ acres for tenters.

Off Hwy. 112 west near the Elwha River at 47 Lower Dam Rd. © 877/435-9421 or 360/452-7054. www.elwhadam rvpark.com. 39 full-hookup sites with 30- and 50-amp service. $27 full hookup; $19 tent. MC, V. Open year-round. **Amenities:** Full hookups, coin-operated showers, laundry, Wi-Fi, store, play area, duck pond, horseshoe pit.

Port Angeles KOA   This brand-name campground has nearly 100 sites to choose from—some with views of the Olympic Range, some without—RV pads and fully equipped cabins, as well as all the usual KOA amenities, from cable TV to bike rentals. During the high season, the campground offers hayrides.

7 miles east of town on Hwy. 101 at 80 O'Brien Rd. © 800/562-7558 or 360/457-5916. www.portangeleskoa.com. 90 RV sites. $37–$65 full hookup including cable TV; $50–$149 cabin; $26–$30 tent. MC, V. **Amenities:** Full hookups, pool, cable TV, sauna and hot tub, minigolf course, bike rentals.

BACKCOUNTRY CAMPING PERMITS

You need a backcountry permit to camp overnight on trails and beaches outside the campgrounds. They're easy to get, and permits are limited only on seven routes from May through September. Other than those seven, you can be certain of getting a permit at a ranger station or the **Wilderness Information Center** (© 360/565-3100; www.nps.gov/olym/planyourvisit/wic), near the visitor center in Port Angeles. The highly informative website gives pointers. Some trails have self-registration where you fill out a form at the trail head and mail in the money. Permits cost $5 each for groups up to 12 people, plus $2 per person per night.

The reservation system is for the eight areas with limits on the number of permits between May 1 and September 30. At this writing, permits for four routes (Hoh River Trail, Ozette Loop, Royal Basin/Royal Lake, and Lake Constance) were given by reservation only; on the other four routes with reservations, half the permits were held back for walk-ins 24 hours before the hike. For Ozette and Royal Basin, you had to have the permit in hand before going to the area of the hike. Check the website or call for the current list of hikes on the reservation system. To make a reservation, call the Wilderness Information Center beginning 30 days before the starting date of the hike, then pick up your permit and pay for it when you arrive.

Proper food storage is important because of black bears and, on the coast, raccoons. Bear-resistant canisters are for loan at the Wilderness Information Center; it requests a $3 donation (see "Dangerous Wildlife," in chapter 2). At many sites, you can hang your food from wires put there for the purpose (bring plenty of rope), but rope hanging from branches is no longer effective.

You don't need a backcountry permit in the national forest, but you do need a Northwest Forest Pass to park at the Forest Service trail heads, which costs $5 per vehicle per day. They're sold at all Forest Service offices and some businesses.

HOTELS, MOTELS & LODGES
IN THE PARK

A different park concessionaire runs each of these places. Except for special suites and the like, they generally do not have telephones, TVs, or air-conditioning. Taxes as high as 13% apply to the rates listed.

Kalaloch Lodge   The lodge, sided with weathered shingles, and its cabins stand along a bluff overlooking the beach, where frothy surf constantly pounds. Erosion has threatened the lodge, but life goes on. Motel rooms are nearby in a wooded area, but the cabins are the best place to be. From atop the grassy, bluff-top grounds, it's a short walk down to the beach; you even receive a tide table when you check in. The cabins are great for families. Many have kitchenettes and wood stoves or fireplaces to chase the evening chill and dampness, with wood supplied daily. Many have incredible views. The cabins book as much as a year ahead, and by 6 months out you should have your place at this most attractive place to stay in the park. Motel and lodge rooms are available later; they're nice, too, but notable mostly for the fantastic location. A convenience store is in the parking lot.

The lodge's **dining room** (p. 456), with a great view of the Pacific, serves three meals a day from a surprisingly diverse menu.

157151 Hwy. 101, Forks, WA 98331. © 866/525-2562 or 360/962-2271. www.visitkalaloch.com. 20 units, 44 cabins. $113–$289 double. $13 extra person over age 6. Rollaway beds and cribs $10. AE, DISC, MC, V. Pets accepted. **Amenities:** Restaurant; convenience store; beach. *In room:* CD player, kitchenette, fridge, coffeemaker, hair dryer, 2 hiking sticks, microwave, toaster, wood stove.

Lake Crescent Lodge   Here Franklin Roosevelt laid down the law to his staff and said there would be an Olympic National Park; looking out on the lake under big trees, you can see why. The best cabins were built for his 1937 visit. Stone fireplaces, warm wood floors, plank paneling, and Adirondack chairs by the lake add to their historic atmosphere; worn 1970s-style furniture undercuts it. The lodge building is a grand three-story gray-shingle structure with dormers and a relaxing veranda. Most of the inexpensive, shared-bathroom accommodations in this building are too small for families. Other rooms occupy simpler cottages or motel buildings that seem transported from the 1950s. We found all of them out-of-date in style, but exceptionally clean and well kept. Cabins book up 6 months to a year or two out. Rowboats rent for $9 an hour, $25 a half-day, or $40 for all day, and good trails are nearby.

The **dining room** (p. 456) is airy, echoes with a wood floor, and provides sweeping views of the lake.

416 Lake Crescent Rd., Port Angeles, WA 98363-8672. ℂ 360/928-3211. www.lakecrescentlodge.com. 36 units, some with shared bathroom, 20 cottages. $99–$158 double; $180–$231 cottage for 2. $15 extra person (adult or child). Rollaway bed and crib $15. AE, DISC, MC, V. Closed late Oct to late Apr. Pets accepted. **Amenities:** Rowboat rentals; fishing; hiking. *In room:* Free Wi-Fi.

Log Cabin Resort   This is the budget version of the Lake Crescent Lodge, facing the lake from the northeast corner. Families have fun on the grass and lake beach without worrying about bothering anyone. Barbecues are all over the place. There are five categories of accommodations. At the top are the lodge rooms and six-person chalets, which have lakefront patios and everything you would expect from an old-fashioned lake resort. You'll need your own utensils, though. The rustic cabins, on the other hand, are little changed from the 1920s, and the camping log cabins are like frontier shelter. A boathouse rents rowboats, canoes, pedal boats, and kayaks. There's also a store on-site.

The **restaurant** (p. 456) also is a down-market alternative to the Lake Crescent Lodge. There is also a small snack bar in the store.

3183 E. Beach Rd., Port Angeles, WA 98363. ℂ 360/928-3325. www.logcabinresort.net. 4 units, 24 cabins, some with shared bathroom. $114 double; $55–$145 cabin for 2. $12 extra person over age 4. $35 full-hookup RV sites. Limited number of rollaway beds free, no cribs. DISC, MC, V. Closed Nov–Feb. **Amenities:** Lakefront; boating; grills. *In room:* Some have kitchenette, some have fridge, microwave.

Sol Duc Hot Springs Resort   The hot-springs pools are the centerpiece of this resort at the head of a long valley. It has a big pool for swimming under the branches of big trees, two hot pools for soaking, and a toddler pool. Every member of our diverse family easily found hours of amusement one long afternoon. The modern cabins are serviceable, but surprisingly spare and unadorned. The more expensive duplex units have cooking facilities. Outside, there's plenty of grass for play, and the river. If you're not staying over, you can use the pools for $11 adults, $8 children 4 to 12, $3 children 1 to 3. Nonguest campers can use the locker rooms and showers just to wash up for $3, 9 to 10am and the last hour of the day (8–9pm in high season). The RV park has only electric and water hookups, but there's a dump station. A gatehouse at the entrance to the valley collects the park fee (see "Entrance Fees," below); present your receipt if you have already paid.

The **dining room** caters primarily to resort guests, serving breakfast and dinner. There's also a pool-side deli where you can order lunch.

Sol Duc Rd., off Hwy. 101 south of Lake Crescent (P.O. Box 2169), Port Angeles, WA 98363-0283. ℂ 866/4-SOL-DUC or 360/327-3583. Fax 360/327-3593. www.visitsolduc.com. 32 cabins. $92–$171 cabin for 2. $22 extra person over age 4. Cabin rates include pool pass. $23 RV sites. Rollaway bed $22, cribs free. AE, DISC, MC, V. Closed mid-Oct to mid-Mar. **Amenities:** Hot springs–fed pools; massage; hiking trails. *In room:* 6 cabins have full kitchen w/microwave, coffeemaker, fridge, and stove; the rest have coffeemaker.

QUINAULT LAKE

Lake Quinault Lodge *(Finds*   If you were making a movie, you'd choose this place for the historic Northwest resort. Old evergreens and the lake surround the big, graceful central building, roofed and sided with cedar and trimmed in white. The rooms, in various buildings, are uneven in quality, but some are quite large and welcoming. Fortunately, an ongoing renovation program is trying to even out the quality by upgrading bedding, furniture, and carpeting in the rooms. When you make your reservation, be sure to request one of the renovated rooms. There is a game room and a swimming pool in a rather dark chamber. An excellent set of easy hikes through the national forest begins just across the road.

The lobby and **Roosevelt Room** restaurant (p. 455) are grand and comfortable.

South Shore Rd. (P.O. Box 7), Quinault, WA 98575-0007. © **800/562-6672** or 360/288-2900. Fax 360/288-2901. www.visitlakequinault.com. 87 units. $104–$219 double. $12 extra person over age 6. Rollaway beds and cribs $15. AE, MC, V. Pets accepted in some rooms. **Amenities:** Pool; sauna; game room; hiking trails; softball; puzzles; badminton; croquet; horseshoes; arcade games; table tennis; boating. *In room:* Some rooms have TV/VCR, 2 hiking sticks, some rooms have fireplace, no phone.

Lake Quinault Resort   A couple turned a run-down lakefront motel into a showplace with a broad lawn that stretches to the water from a covered deck with planters and wooden lawn chairs. It feels more like a bed-and-breakfast than a resort, however, and you may not be able to relax with children for fear they'll mess up the Martha Stewart decoration. In fact, the owners ask that only "quiet, well-supervised children" stay here. Several large rooms and suites with limited cooking facilities are suitable for families. There even are two good-size cabins that could handle a family of four. All rooms have satellite TV but no telephones.

314 North Shore Rd., Amanda Park, WA 98526. © **800/650-2362** or 360/288-2362. Fax 360/288-2218. www.lakequinault.com. 9 units. $138–$179 double; $220 cabin. $20 extra person. Free for infants under 1. AE, DISC, MC, V. **Amenities:** Lakeside campfires; gas barbecue. *In room:* TV, some units have kitchenette, fridge, coffee/tea maker, hair dryer, some units have microwave, no phone.

PORT ANGELES

Portside Inn   On the east edge of town, with other familiar highway businesses on a commercial strip, this three-story stucco building contains excellent budget motel rooms. All have queen-size beds, refrigerators, microwave ovens, coffeemakers, and hair dryers. Suites are large and well suited for families. All rates include continental breakfast. There are a laundromat and a small pool.

1510 E. Front St., Port Angeles, WA 98362. © **877/438-8588** or 360/452-4015. www.portsideinn.com. 109 units. $90–$110 double; $140–$170 suite. Children under 18 stay free in parent's room. Rates include continental breakfast. No rollaway beds, cribs free. AE, DISC, MC, V. **Amenities:** Pool; laundry. *In room:* Fridge, coffeemaker, hair dryer, microwave, Wi-Fi.

Red Lion Hotel Port Angeles   For a family on a park tour, this is the place to stay in Port Angeles. Besides offering big rooms with upscale amenities right on the water, it makes a point of enhancing park visits, with ranger-led evening campfires on the beach outside, bike and sea-kayak rentals, and other activities. The location is prime, near the ferry dock, waterfront park, tide-pool aquarium (p. 460), and cool little playground, and within walking distance of downtown restaurants. The waterfront bike trail passes right by. A swimming pool and hot tub are next to the parking lot. Everything was perfect on our visit, and we hated to leave.

The **Crab House** restaurant offers a setting suitable for a family dinner and provides room service in the hotel. It is open Monday through Friday 5:30 to 9pm, until 11pm on weekends.

221 N. Lincoln St., Port Angeles, WA 98362. © **800/RED-LION** (reservations) or 360/452-9215. Fax 360/452-4734. www.redlionportangeles.com. 187 units. $179–$199 double; $259–$299 suite. $10 extra person. Children under 18 stay free in parent's room. Rollaway bed $15, cribs free. AE, DISC, MC, V. **Amenities:** Restaurant; lounge; pool; health

club; hot tub; business center; waterfront; bike trail. *In room:* Satellite TV, dataport, fridge, coffeemaker and microwave available, free Wi-Fi.

FORKS

The Forks Motel   The attractive rooms at this family-operated motel offer good value but vary widely in size and amenities. All were very clean and well maintained when I visited, with up-to-date bathrooms even in the economy units. Each of the eight kitchen suites holds three queen-size beds. A smallish pool surrounded by a fence sits in a landscaped parking-lot courtyard. There's also a good coin-op laundry.

351 S. Forks Ave., Hwy. 101 (P.O. Box 510), Forks, WA 98331. (C) 800/544-3416 or 360/374-6243. Fax 360/374-6760. www.forksmotel.com. 73 units. $65–$85 double; $98–$143 suite. $5 extra person over age 12. Rollaway bed $5, cribs free. AE, DC, DISC, MC, V. **Amenities:** Pool; laundry. *In room:* TV, some have kitchen, fridge, microwave, Wi-Fi.

6 Family-Friendly Dining

PORT ANGELES

LOW-STRESS MEALS

Port Angeles has many fast-food franchises, mostly on the east side of town along Highway 101. Some healthier and more memorable places are downtown.

BEST-BEHAVIOR MEALS

Besides these choices, the Red Lion Port Angeles hotel has a restaurant, mentioned on p. 454. Each of these accepts credit cards.

Bella Italia *(Finds)*   This wonderfully sophisticated southern Italian restaurant on historic 1st Street is charming and intimate, and the service highly professional. The cuisine shows signs of successful experimentation using fresh local seafood in traditional themes—Dungeness crab or smoked salmon ravioli, for example. The proprietor, Neil Conklin, emerges from the kitchen periodically to strike up conversations with guests. The "bambini" menu is exceptional, too, with everything from chicken strips to steamed clams.

118 E. 1st St., Port Angeles. (C) 360/457-5442. www.bellaitaliapa.com. Kids' menu, highchairs, boosters, crayons. Dinner $11–$28; kids' menu $3–$7. AE, DISC, MC, V. Daily 4–10pm.

Chestnut Cottage Restaurant   Great for breakfast, where the menu revolves around egg dishes and grill items, this place makes a point of serving families well. Lunches are based on sandwiches, wraps, soups, and pizza. It's as far from the typical diner as can be, with elaborate country and Victorian decor in a brick building with high ceilings. Considering the fancy surroundings, prices are reasonable for the rich meals. Kids' menu items are cute, fun, and inexpensive.

929 E. Front St., Port Angeles. (C) 360/452-8344. Kids' menu, highchairs, boosters, crayons. Breakfast and lunch $5–$12; kids' menu $3–$4. MC, V. Daily 7am–3pm.

QUINAULT LAKE

Roosevelt Room   Tucked inside the Lake Quinault Lodge, this dining room offers a dinner menu inspired by the sea. When I visited I faced the prospect of starting my meal with a bowl of homemade clam chowder followed by a seafood pasta dish with halibut, salmon, Chilean shrimp, and clams sautéed with mushrooms and red onions. There also were seared honey-glazed sea scallops and the usual steaks. Breakfasts include the typical grill items and cereals, while lunches offer a variety of sandwiches and burgers. The kids' menu is a little pricey at dinner (up to $15).

Lake Quinault Lodge, South Shore Rd., Quinault. ℂ 800/562-6672 or 360/288-2900. www.visitlakequinault.com. Kids' menu, highchairs, boosters. Breakfast $6–$11; lunch $9–$17; dinner $18–$25; kids' menu $4–$8. AE, MC, V. Daily 8am–9pm.

IN THE PARK

Kalaloch Lodge   You can get the usual diner food for breakfast or lunch, and in the evening choose that sort of inexpensive meal or order from a fairly diverse and tasty fine-dining menu that revolves, naturally, around seafood such as salmon, crab, and scallops, but also features chicken, steaks, pasta, and vegetarian dishes. Most tables have a view of the Pacific. Near the front of the lodge is a coffee shop where you can order breakfast or a sandwich for lunch.

157151 Hwy. 101, Forks. ℂ 866/525-2562 or 360/962-2271. www.visitkalaloch.com. Kids' menu, highchairs, boosters, crayons. Dinner reservations recommended. Breakfast $5–$13; lunch $9–$12; dinner $16–$24; kids' menu $3–$5. AE, DISC, MC, V. Sun–Thurs breakfast 7–11:30am, lunch 11:30am–5pm, and dinner 5–8pm; Fri–Sat 7am–8:30pm.

Lake Crescent Lodge   There's been an emphasis on the lodge's menu in recent years, and it now arguably offers the best meals in the park. The dinner menu blends expected seafood dishes such as Northwest cioppino and wild-caught salmon with smoked quail, lamb chops, and chicken Marsala. My youngest son discovered the joy of crab cakes here. Seafood omelets, traditional egg dishes, fresh fruit crepes, and "Candy Apply French Toast" hold down the breakfast menu. There's a decent children's menu with the usual suspects: grilled cheese, spaghetti, burgers, hot dogs, chicken fingers.

416 Lake Crescent Rd., Port Angeles. ℂ 360/928-3211, ext. 17. www.lakecrescentlodge.com. Kids' menu, highchairs, boosters. Dinner reservations required. Breakfast $6.25–$12; lunch $6.95–$15; dinner $11–$29; kids' menu $4.95–$16. AE, DISC, MC, V. Late Apr to late Oct daily 7:30–10am, noon–2:30pm, and 6–9pm. Closed late Oct to late Apr.

Log Cabin Resort   Not surprisingly, considering the location, the dinner menu here is built around seafood caught locally, but you can get steak, chicken, and vegetarian dishes, too. Try the Neah Bay halibut, which is either grilled with green onions, garlic, and white wine, or deep-fried. Don't like fish? There's always chicken, top sirloin steak, or pot roast.

3183 E. Beach Rd., Port Angeles. ℂ 360/928-3325. www.logcabinresort.net. Kids' menu, highchairs, boosters, crayons. Dinner reservations required. Breakfast $1.95–$7.95; dinner $8.95–$25; kids' menu $5.95. DISC, MC, V. Memorial Day to Labor Day daily 8am–8pm. Closed early Sept to late May.

Sol Duc Lodge   If you just stopped in for a dip at the hot springs, you might consider dinner at The Springs Restaurant here before heading back to your campsite or room. The dining room is somewhat small and rather unimpressive compared with those at Kalaloch, Lake Quinalt, and Lake Crescent. It is nicely situated, though, in the main lodge, and an entire side of the dining room has windows that look out on the pools. Dinners are built around chicken, pasta, beef and seafood, such as the ahi tuna steak rubbed in a sashimi spice mix or the grilled Pacific salmon that is seasoned with citrus and topped with a caper béarnaise sauce. There's a breakfast buffet with the usual grill items, cereals, and fruit, while lunches from the Poolside Deli involve wraps, salads, and sandwiches.

Sol Duc Rd., off Hwy. 101 south of Lake Crescent. ℂ 866/4-SOL-DUC or 360/327-3583. www.visitsolduc.com. Kids' menu, highchairs, boosters, crayons. Breakfast buffet $7.95 for noncabin guests, $4.95 5 and under; lunch $5.95–$7.25; dinner $8.50–$21; kids' menu $5.25–$5.75. AE, DISC, MC, V. Daily 7:30am–10am, 11am–4pm, and 5:30–9pm. Closed mid-Oct to mid-Mar.

7 Exploring Olympic National Park with Your Kids

ENTRANCE FEES   The park entrance fee of $15 per vehicle is good for a week. It isn't collected on every road into the park, and in the winter it's hardly collected at all, although you always have to pay to enter Hurricane Ridge or the Hoh Rain Forest. In the summer fee stations also operate at Elwha, Sol Duc, and Staircase. Fees are not collected along the coast, at the Quinault Rain Forest, or in other areas on small roads. America the Beautiful passes cover the fees (see "Entrance Fees" and "Passes," both in chapter 2). A self-service $1 parking fee applies at Ozette, on the west coast. The Forest Service charges a $5 trail-head parking fee, covered in a previous section.

NATURAL PLACES
THE WESTERN COAST

You can smell the salt spray before you get to the ocean. When you break through the last line of trees, you can see why. From the beach to the horizon, the white froth of surf is tearing the water's streaked gray surface to pieces, flinging salt water into a powerful wind. On their way to shore waves crash against tiny, rocky islets rising from the water, called sea stacks. On the beach, the last gasp of each wave spends itself rattling pebbles and throwing seaweed, logs, floats, shells, and puffy froth onto the beach. It's not a stormy day, but you can imagine what storms must be like here from looking at the sand, pebbles, and huge trees that storm waves have left above the beach, and even back in an eroding forest.

The violence of the sea here makes life in the tide pools and the summer visits of marine mammals along the shore even more impressive. When the tide is out, the brutal surf pulls back and leaves shelves of rock where tiny animals carry on in temporary ponds of clear, cool seawater. Ranger walks explore the tide pools in the summer at **Rialto Beach** *★★★* and **Beach 4,** north of Kalaloch (times are listed in the park newspaper, the *Bugler*) but you don't need an expert to study the strange and sturdy plants and animals that have adapted to live here (see "Tide Pooling," p. 462, and "Whale- & Wildlife-Watching," p. 462).

There are four parts to the park's more than 60 miles of coastline. The Park Service gives out a handy map and guide. The easiest section of beach to get to, and the least isolated, is the southern portion where Highway 101 runs along the bluff. Access trails descend steeply to the beach from small parking lots every few miles. Even on a crowded day at a spot like Ruby Beach, a short walk puts you on your own; we spent a memorable afternoon there building sand castles, running from waves, and looking at little creatures. The only campgrounds and lodgings right on the sea are in this section, at Kalaloch and South Beach (see "Family-Friendly Accommodations," p. 446), but overnight beach hiking isn't allowed here. Roads go all the way to the beach only at Rialto Beach and La Push, west of Forks on Route 110.

The rest of this coastline may be the most remote in the nation outside Alaska. The access points at Ozette, the Makah Indian Reservation, and the mouth of the Hoh River, near Oil City Road, require visitors to hike at least part of the way to the shoreline. The **Ozette Loop** leaves from the ranger station, follows a boardwalk trail to the beach at Cape Alava, runs along the beach to Sand Point, and returns on a trail to the ranger station. It's the most popular overnight route on the beach, and you must reserve your permit before going to the ranger station (see "Backcountry Camping Permits," p. 451). The 23-mile section from Ozette to Rialto Beach is a good, challenging backpack route.

The easiest approach for families is to backpack north from **Rialto Beach,** where you can park, camp when you get tired at least a mile up the beach, and hike back the same way. Good tide pools are at the Hole-in-the-Wall Rock, a little over a mile from the parking lot. Camping in the trees above the beach, you can hear the waves' constant roar and, at night, see the vague shapes of towering sea stacks against dark, swirling mists. Except for occasional scrambles on the steep, muddy trails that go over points you can't walk around, the hike is easy. These headland trails are marked with orange and black targets. The other remote coast sections, north of Ozette and from the Hoh to La Push, have more rugged beaches, trickier stream crossings, and longer and more challenging headland trails. Time your movements to avoid high tide. Tide tables are posted at trail heads, and you can get them from the visitor centers.

THE NORTHERN COAST

The national park doesn't include shoreline along the Strait of Juan de Fuca, but I would be remiss not to mention the pretty places to get down to the sea on that coast. Since it isn't exposed to waves from across the Pacific, the northern side of the peninsula is better for marine recreation; sea-kayaking tours go there. **Freshwater Bay County Park,** at the end of Freshwater Bay Road off Route 112, is a gentle shore, the site of kayaking tours, and a great place to find crabs, seabirds, and other creatures that prefer a muddy, low-energy environment. It has a boat ramp, a picnic area, and toilets. **Salt Creek County Park,** site of a terrific campground (p. 447), has rougher, rockier shores appealing for exploration at low tide.

THE RAINFORESTS &&

The western region of the Olympic Peninsula gets enough rain to be called rainforest, but it's in the valleys between the paws of the mountains that the moisture gets thick enough to grow strange, enchanted groves of giant trees. The .75-mile **Hall of Mosses Nature Trail** in the Hoh Rain Forest is an exquisite and dramatic example accessible even to young children. The hike is well worth the effort even when the trail is crowded; you see and learn from vivid examples of rainforest life that you will see again on longer, more secluded hikes. This area averages 150 inches of rain a year. Pointy sword ferns grow from the trunks of big, healthy trees. Big-leaf maples stand like skeletons for communities of moss, with leaves breaking free from just the tips of their branches. The club moss hangs down from these trees in big green globs. It's an epiphyte, a kind of plant that doesn't need to touch the ground because it takes nutrients and water straight from the air. Even on sunny days, the air here is full of tiny drops of water holding even tinier dots of dirt—that's why each breath you take tastes so rich.

On the forest floor, you can see how the rainforest recycles life. When a big tree falls and its trunk begins to rot, new trees sprout there. The raised log—called a nurse log—gives the seedlings minerals they need and, by being off the ground, warmth and protection from competing plants. As the new trees grow, their roots eventually reach around the nurse tree down into the soil. In 100 years, the dead tree will rot away completely while the new trees continue to grow, seeming to stand on legs over the opening where the old log used to be. You can see nurse logs at each stage of decay in the Hoh and learn to recognize them anywhere you see them in the forest. Wherever trees are in a line, a nurse tree probably lay long ago.

The mile-long **Spruce Trail** shows a younger rainforest, closer to the Hoh River, where floods and storms have cleared out the trees from time to time. An 18-mile trail goes up the valley to the Blue Glacier, with long connecting trails to other areas of the park.

The other west-side rainforest valleys you can reach by road are the **Queets** and **Quinault valleys.** Each has its own character. A long gravel road leads up the Queets River to a quiet campground and trail head. You'll have it much to yourself. The Quinault Rain Forest is easier for visitors, but still less crowded than the Hoh. Long Quinault Lake has the park on the north side with a ranger station and nature trails through huge trees, and national forest on the south side, with a historic lodge and a network of trails. Farther up the valley, longer park trails branch off into the forests and mountains. Roosevelt elk are common in the Hoh, Queets, and Quinault valleys, especially in places with low trees and brush to nibble on.

SOL DUC VALLEY

Facing north instead of west, the Sol Duc valley doesn't catch enough moisture to be called a rainforest, but it's among the park's best places for a family to visit. A road leads south into the valley from U.S. 101 just west of Lake Crescent, tracing the salmon-rich Sol Duc River. At Salmon Cascades you can see silver (or coho) salmon leap upstream to their spawning grounds in August and later in the fall; at other times, the Cascades are a pleasant stop on an easy walk. At the head of the valley, the river pours over a misty waterfall, and the 3.5-mile **Deer Lake Trail** leads up to the high country, one of the park's shortest routes above tree line. The Sol Duc Hot Springs are a great family swimming place; the lodge and campground there are covered on p. 450 and p. 453, respectively.

LAKE CRESCENT

This placid lake, surrounded by big evergreens, is on the north side of the park, west of Port Angeles on Highway 101. It makes a good center for a park visit because you can swim, fish, and paddle in the lake, and some inviting family hikes or bike rides are nearby. (Fishing at this writing was catch-and-release only.)

There are three main visitor areas on the lake. The best developed is on a point on the south side, site of the Lake Crescent Lodge (p. 452), where you can rent rowboats by the hour; of the Olympic Park Institute (p. 463); and of a picnic ground, boat ramp, and ranger station. From the station, the mile-long **Marymere Falls Trail** crosses under the highway and then passes through huge trees in green, mossy light, over a pair of log bridges, and up a few stairs and switchbacks to where Falls Creek pours on rock through a grove of tall trees. It's an easy family hike; if you want more of a challenge, a steep hike up Mount Storm King branches off. The second area is the Log Cabin Resort (p. 453), on the northeast edge of the lake, which has a swimming beach and a more extensive boat-rental operation. The third area is at the west end of the lake, site of the Fairholm Campground (p. 446), which has a swimming beach and a nearby store and restaurant. Down a quiet road from here, the **Spruce Railroad Trail** runs around the north side of the lake to near the Log Cabin Resort. Made from the abandoned roadbed of a rail line built during World War I to haul out strong, light Sitka spruce for airplanes, it's a broad, level trail bordered by ferns, thickly shaded, with glimpses of the lake flashing through. Rare in the parks, mountain biking is permitted on this trail.

THE ELWHA RIVER

The Elwha River runs through a narrow valley above the highway, just west of Port Angeles, into deep forest. The **Geyser Valley Loop Hike** is a mostly flat 5-mile route that starts at the end of the narrow, unpaved road that forks left from the pavement just beyond the ranger station. It's a good family day hike past abandoned cabins of early settlers, with views of the river canyon.

HURRICANE RIDGE 𝕽𝕽

A steep, spectacular drive 15 miles from Port Angeles leads to this area at the tree line, where subalpine forest bounds broad meadows. In the summer, the trails lead past wildflowers and sweeping views over the mountains of the peninsula, offering a good chance to see alpine wildlife. Paved nature trails show off some of the best views near the visitor center, but summer crowds can be thick enough to spoil the experience. The paved 1.5-mile Hurricane Hill Trail, from the picnic area at the very end of the road, gets somewhat lighter use. More rugged trails lead to other, less crowded heights, but you may not feel comfortable with younger children on the steep drop-offs. Perhaps the best alternatives for longer hikes are to descend by trails to a lower point on the road or into the Elwha Valley, but for such one-way hikes, you need transportation at the other end. In the winter, Hurricane Ridge is a small skiing area with a rope tow, and good for sledding (p. 462); it is open and the road plowed of snow only Friday through Sunday. There are a visitor center and a snack bar.

PLACES FOR LEARNING

Arthur D. Feiro Marine Biology Laboratory *Finds*   We love tide pooling, so we loved this lab on the waterfront at the north end of Lincoln Street. It's just one room, but it has several touch tanks containing tide-pool specimens of prodigious size and a few aquariums of local marine life. Volunteers engage kids, letting them touch creatures they may not be lucky enough to find in the wild.

Railroad and Lincoln St., on the waterfront. © 360/417-6254. www.olypen.com/feirolab. Admission $3 adults, $2 seniors, $1 children 3–17, free for children under 3. Memorial Day to Labor Day Tues–Sun 10am–5pm. Call for off-season hours.

8 For the Active Family

BACKPACKING

Trails cross the Olympics from each of the valleys around the mountains' edges, offering an extraordinary choice of long-haul backpacking trips. You can rise from rainforest to alpine terrain and big blue glaciers, and descend on the other side back to the forest. I put on my pack and hiked on the coast. When I woke up in the night, I could hear the roar of the waves smashing against sea stacks; outside, the driftwood logs glowed like bones in the dim mist.

The challenges of backpacking here are the dampness and the long, rugged routes. Rain and fog can test your gear and patience, and fires are just about impossible to light. Most trails cover large distances, and it's easy to overestimate what your family can manage. On the other hand, you don't have to go far to find a campsite. You will need a permit and gear to store your food against black bears and, on the coast, raccoons; see "Backcountry Camping Permits" (p. 451). Trail maps and guidebooks are covered under "Reading Up" (p. 442).

FISHING

Salmon and trout fishing are a major draw. Knowing when and where the fish are running is critical to success. Moreover, the regulations are complex, and state and park regulations overlap on the same lands. You can get all the regulations from the park or its website (www.nps.gov/olym/regs/fishregs.htm). There are lots of guides and places to get gear in the area; ask for referrals at the town visitor centers (see "Olympic Address Book," p. 436).

HIKING

The trails and beaches of Olympic National Park offer solitude and stirring beauty, and you can't really appreciate the park without walking some of them. I've mentioned some favorites in the Hoh Rain Forest, in the Sol Duc and Elwha valleys, at Lake Crescent and Hurricane Ridge, and along the western and northern shores, under "Natural Places" above, and in the descriptions of the Heart O' the Hills and Graves Creek campgrounds (both on p. 447), and the Olympic National Park Visitor Center in Port Angeles (p. 442). But I've only scratched the surface. Great hikes lead from every park area; many start at the ends of remote dirt roads and other out-of-the-way places on the way to real wilderness.

The Park Service hands out informative lists and descriptions of dozens of trails all over the park. See "Reading Up" (p. 442) for resources with more detail. One drawback to consider in planning your route is that there are few day-hike loops except the easy nature trails. Most trails are long, requiring you to hike a few miles and then double back. Set a realistic goal. Trails in the rainforest can be muddy, so prepare with extra shoes, socks, and pants, as well as rain gear.

MOUNTAIN BIKING

In the park, Spruce Railroad Trail around the north side of Lake Crescent (see "Lake Crescent," p. 459) is open to biking. Olympic National Forest has more mountain-bike trails. Bikes are for rent at **Sound Bikes & Kayaks,** 120 E. Front St., Port Angeles (© **360/457-1240;** www.soundbikeskayaks.com).

RAFTING

Concessionaires offer rafting on the Elwha and Hoh rivers, both fairly gentle floats with mild white water and forest scenery. Children can go along. **Olympic Raft and Kayak,** 123 Lake Aldwell Rd., Port Angeles (© **888/452-1443** or 360/452-1443; www.raftandkayak.com), has daily summer trips on each river for $54 per person, $44 for children under 12.

SEA KAYAKING

The park's coastal waters are too rough for sea kayaking, but guided outings do go to lakes in the park and the more protected ocean waters of estuaries and the Strait of Juan de Fuca, where you have a good chance of seeing seabirds, sea lions, and other marine mammals. **Rainforest Paddlers,** 4883 Upper Hoh Rd. (© **866/457-8398** or 360/374-5254; www.rainforestpaddlers.com), offers kayak and raft trips and kayak rentals; **Sound Bikes & Kayaks,** 120 Front St. (© **360/457-1240;** www.soundbikes kayaks.com), also rents sea kayaks. **Olympic Raft and Kayak** (see "Rafting," above) offers several daily trips in the summer to Freshwater Bay (see "The Northern Coast," p. 458), just west of Port Angeles, and on Lake Crescent and the dam-filled Lake Aldwell, on the Elwha River. The trips last 2 to 4 hours, and cost $42 to $99 per person. The company also rents kayaks and canoes.

SWIMMING

We enjoyed splashing around in Lake Crescent at the Log Cabin Resort, and you can also swim at Lake Crescent Lodge, East Beach Picnic Area, and Fairholm Campground. There are no lifeguards. The water wasn't warm in mid-July, but it was refreshing and fun. Swimming in **Ozette Lake** 🌟 and **Quinault Lake** is informal, from docks or a place you choose on the shore.

TIDE POOLING

The western coastal strip has shores of sand, pebbles, cobbles, boulders, and bedrock. For tide pooling, the easiest places are bedrock shelves that extend out flat near the low-tide line, where water collects in little ponds. These shelves can occur on any kind of shoreline, but they're most frequent near rock headlands. Also good are muddy shores without much wave energy, such as Freshwater Bay (see "The Northern Coast," p. 458). Generally, you can find good tide pooling at **Beach Four,** north of Kalaloch on Highway 101, and at **Rialto Beach,** west of Forks, and many other places are also promising; the fun of tide pooling is relaxed exploration and discovery. Ask at a visitor center for directions and consult a tide chart—the lower the tide, the more you'll see. Go out at least an hour before low tide and see what you find. A hand lens and field guide add another level of fascination. Inexpensive tide-pool identification booklets are available at visitor centers.

Turn over rocks to see what's under them, pick up mobile creatures with shells, and catch tiny fish in a bucket, but put them all back exactly where they were. Be gentle. Don't step on plants or animals if you can help it, don't pry or force anything, and try to preserve every life. Protect your own life, too: Know what time the tide will change, and keep an eye on your watch so that it doesn't sneak up on you. Don't walk on slippery rocks over water, and keep your children nearby.

WHALE- & WILDLIFE-WATCHING

High places along the coast are the best spots to watch migrating whales and to see sea lions, seals, and sea otters that come to the ocean shore in the summer to feed. The visitor centers can provide information on the Olympic Coast National Marine Sanctuary, an ocean area that protects the waters off the park's coastline and a bit north and south. Gray whales pass by the peninsula on their way north from Mexico to Alaska starting in March and April, and go back in the winter. With binoculars and patience (perhaps more patience than many children possess), you can see them from high places all along the coast, including **Kalaloch,** the parking lots on Highway 101 above **Beach 4** and **Beach 6,** and **Cape Flattery,** at the tip of the peninsula in the Makah Indian Reservation.

Other marine mammals use the shore in the spring, summer, and fall. Seeing them is never a sure thing, and you may need a spotting scope to get a good look. Harbor seals show up all along the shore. Seeing sea lions and sea otters may require a hike that's beyond the range of young children, and if your goal is to see them and you don't—a significant possibility—disappointment will follow. It's better to just take the hike and count the sightings as a bonus. **Cape Alava** 🌟🌟, a 3.3-mile hike from the Ozette Ranger Station, looks out on islands where sea lions haul out and where sea otters show up in the floating kelp beds. Both also may be seen off **Cape Flattery.** The beach south from **Third Beach,** off La Push Road, may have sea lions and seals. Sea otters could also be in the kelp off **Cape Johnson,** about 3.7 miles north of Rialto Beach, which is accessible by beach at low tide.

WINTER SPORTS: SKIING, SNOWSHOEING & SLEDDING

Most places you can get to by road in Olympic National Park receive little snow, but **Hurricane Ridge** typically gets more than 30 feet a year (the drought winter of

2004–05 was an aberration). Ski season lasts from late December to March. A non-profit organization operates a couple of rope tows and a Poma lift on a small ski area (only about 70 acres) with a vertical rise of 665 feet. A full-day pass is $25; call ℭ **360/457-4519** or visit www.hurricaneridge.net for information. There are also more than 20 miles of ungroomed cross-country ski routes, most of them hilly, and some good for telemark skiing. Rangers lead snowshoe walks in the winter, and there's an area for sledding. A desk on the bottom floor of the lodge rents gear at reasonable prices. Snowstorms and other factors permitting, the area is open on weekends in the winter, Friday through Sunday 9am to 4pm; on weekdays, a gate generally blocks the road well below the area of heavy snow. Call ℭ **360/565-3131** for a recorded message about snow conditions.

9 Kid-Friendly Programs

CHILDREN'S PROGRAMS

The Northwest Interpretive Association produces a meaningful workbook of nature activities for kids. Children who finish the workbook, attend a ranger-led program, and go for a hike earn a **Junior Ranger** badge. The booklet costs $1 at the visitor centers, and children as young as 5 will be able to do it, with help. Don't get into it unless you have time to devote. If children are going to learn the answers to the questions in the booklet on their own, a visit of at least a couple days is required.

FAMILY & ADULT PROGRAMS

Ranger programs take place at many sites all over the park. Times and topics appear in the park newspaper, the *Bugler*. Occasionally, programs target families with children; more often, the walks and talks are for adults, but are open and enjoyable to children. Also check the *Bugler* for schedules of evening campfire programs, which take place at the larger campgrounds in the summer.

You might consider spending a Saturday with naturalists exploring Lake Crescent and its surrounding forest. The **Olympic Park Institute (OPI)**, 111 Barnes Point Rd., Port Angeles, WA 98363 (ℭ **360/928-3720;** www.yni.org/opi), offers free "Lake Crescent Adventures" on Saturdays in late June, July, and early September. These first-come, first-served trips involve guided canoeing on the lake followed by a hike through old-growth forest. The program begins at OPI's Lake Crescent campus at 10am; you can sign-up beginning at 9:30am. The day usually ends around 3pm. Bring your own lunch and drinks.

FAST FACTS: Olympic National Park

Area Code The area code is **360**.

ATMs There are banks with ATMs in Port Angeles and Forks.

Emergencies For emergencies, dial ℭ **911**.

Hospitals & Clinics **Olympic Memorial Hospital** is in Port Angeles at 939 Caroline St. (ℭ **360/417-7000**), and **Forks Community Hospital** is in Forks at 530 Bogachiel Way (ℭ **360/374-6271**).

Information For information, write Olympic National Park, Visitor Center, 600 E. Park Ave., Port Angeles, WA 98362; call (© **360/565-3130**); or look on the Web at www.nps.gov/olym.

Pharmacies There is a Rite Aid Pharmacy in Port Angeles, located at 110 Plaza St. (© **360/457-3456**), and a Safeway at 110 E. 3rd St. (© **360/457-0788**).

Post Office There are post offices in Port Angeles at 424 E. 1st St. and in Forks on E. Division Street.

Time Zone The park is on **Pacific Standard Time.**

Transit Info The park does not have a public transportation system.

Weather Updates For weather updates, call for recorded information (© **360/565-3131**) or the visitor center (© **360/565-3132**).

17

A Little Field Guide

1 Eastern Seaboard

MAMMALS & MARINE LIFE

In addition to the creatures here, you might also want to refer to some in other sections: white-tailed deer (p. 469), gray fox (p. 469), common murre (p. 481), limpet (p. 479), sea anemone (p. 479), and sea urchin (p. 480).

BARNACLE

Barnacles live all along the world's shorelines wherever there's something solid to hold on to, and even on the bottom of ships. The northern rock barnacle shows up as far south as Delaware, and many other similar barnacles are found at Cape Hatteras, too. On the West Coast, the acorn barnacle is common. When the tide is out, barnacles close the doors of their little white houses to avoid drying out. When moving water returns, they stick out a fanlike filter that catches plankton from the passing seawater. If you swish water past a closed barnacle with your finger, you often can see it open and wave its fan.

BLUE CRAB

Found all along the East Coast, but most commonly from Cape Cod south, these tasty crabs grow up to 9 inches across. They live in calm, shallow estuaries where they can find dead animals to eat, but they also can swim fast enough to catch small fish and shrimp. You can catch a blue crab with a piece of smelly meat hung on a string, but look out for the scary claws, which can really hurt you when they pinch (see "Crabbing," in chapter 5).

HARBOR SEAL

Harbor seals are among the most common seals. You can see them lazing on sandbars and rocks all along the East Coast as far south as South Carolina, and on the West Coast from Southern California to Arctic Alaska. Harbor seals grow 4 to 6 feet long, and their short-haired coats are gray or tan. Unlike sea lions, they have no visible ears. Seals are mammals, so they have to hold their breath when they swim underwater. They eat fish.

Barnacle

Harbor Seal

Hermit Crab

Horseshoe Crab

HERMIT CRAB

The hermit crab is the most interesting common animal you'll see during tide-pool explorations on Maine's rocky shores; they can also be found on tidal flats at Cape Cod and Cape Hatteras and all along the West Coast. A dozen kinds of hermit crabs live in different habitats, but all are the same in that they don't have their own shells. They live in old snail shells they find empty. When a hermit crab gets too big for its home, it has to find a larger, unused shell somewhere in the intertidal zone. They're easy to catch for observation in a watery sand bucket before you let them go. The wonderfully illustrated book *Pagoo,* by Holling C. Holling (Houghton Mifflin, $12), tells the story of a hermit crab and the whole tide-pool world; it's best for ages 8 and older.

HORSESHOE CRAB

This weirdest of crabs is not really a crab but an arachnid, like spiders and scorpions, which makes it seem even creepier. But horseshoe crabs are harmless, crawling along the sand to find food that they can grind up. They're the only animals I know that have four eyes on their backs. Horseshoes often are called "living dinosaurs" because the fossil record shows that they look the same now as they did millions of years ago.

HUMPBACK WHALE

An estimated 10,000 humpbacks migrate through the North Atlantic annually. Many pass by and feed off Cape Cod or off Acadia's Mount Desert Island, where shallow waters and upwelling currents bring food to the surface. Whales spend the winter mating and having babies in tropical waters but don't eat there. In the summer they come to northern waters, where there's more food, and bulk up with a year's worth of nourishment. The same pattern holds off the West Coast. Humpbacks can grow to 56 feet in length and eat small fish. They appear on the surface in four postures: just cruising along and resting, when you can see the humped back arching slowly from the water; sounding, which is diving straight down into the water for several minutes, when you can see the huge tail sticking straight up into the air; lunge feeding, when they encircle a school of fish with a ring of bubbles and then surge up from beneath to gobble them up; and, if you're really lucky, breaching, when the whale leaps entirely clear of the water's surface.

Humpback Whale

NORTHERN MOON SNAIL

Found from Maine to North Carolina, this snail spends its time in intertidal sand flats digging for clams. When it finds one, it drills though the shell and sucks out the meat inside. (This may explain clamshells you find with holes in them.) The northern moon snail can grow to the size of a grapefruit, but more commonly the shell is around 2 inches. Smaller species of moon snails also show up at different places all along the East Coast; on the West Coast, the giant moon snail is much the same.

QUAHOG (HARD CLAM)

The gray shells that make good fences on the tops of sand castles often come from this tasty clam, which lives just below the surface of the sand in the intertidal zone or just offshore all along the East Coast. Clams reach to the surface of the sand with siphons—tubes they use to pull in and push out water and to catch particles of food and get oxygen. Quahogs grow up to 4 inches, but you usually find them smaller. People catch them from shore with rakes and shovels, and the whole thing—except the siphon tube—is good to eat. Surf clams are similar but larger, more symmetrical, and yellowish white. Oysters are more oblong than quahogs, with wavy, bumpy shells. Scallops have shells that look like fans.

SAND FIDDLER CRAB

Found at Cape Cod and Cape Hatteras, this is one of the amphibious crabs (meaning it lives in water and on land). It lives in a burrow in the beach sand, and at low tide it runs along the water to find little nuggets of food in the grains of sand where the foam licks the shore. Another is the ghost crab, which lives only south of Delaware and seems to appear at night from nowhere, like a ghost. You can have fun on the beach, watching the ghost crabs by the light of the moon or chasing them with a flashlight and putting them in a bucket (set them free when it is time to go). We did this one night on Ocracoke Island with a screaming mob of children; it was great fun. Both species are less than 2 inches in size.

Sea Stars (Starfish)

SEA STARS (STARFISH)

There are many varieties of sea stars. The best place to find them is a rocky shore at low tide, but they show up on sand and mud, too. All sea stars are predators. If you have an hour or two to watch, you can put one on a mussel or clam and watch how the sea star slowly grabs the outside of the shell with the suction cups on its arms (called rays), pulls the shell open, then inserts its stomach into the shell to digest its prey in place. Sea stars also have the amazing ability to grow back parts that are cut off. One that's cut apart can even grow into two or three sea stars.

BIRDS

In addition to the birds here, you might also want to refer to the barred owl (p. 470), common loon (p. 480), golden eagle (p. 476), hairy woodpecker (p. 476), and great horned owl (p. 481).

Great Blue Heron

GREAT BLUE HERON

With their long legs and necks, these large birds like to stand on the edge of the marsh scanning for fish or frogs to eat. They spend the summer in the north and winter in the south. The heron looks similar to the egrets that you may see around Cape Hatteras.

HERRING GULL

This is the classic seagull. It can be quite a pest: Never feed a seagull, because you'll soon be surrounded by them. Herring gulls are scavengers, and they can be aggressive and pesky. You can always find them at a garbage dump, but they also eat seashore animals. To open clams, they drop them from great heights on rocks and parking lots to smash the shell.

OSPREY (SEA HAWK)

Although it may look like a gull from a distance, up close you can see that the osprey is a member of the hawk family, with a sharp hooked beak for tearing apart prey. If you're lucky, especially at Acadia, you may see an osprey hunting. Using its sharp vision, it picks out fish in the water, then dives from the air down into the ocean and snatches fish in its sharp talons.

Osprey (Sea Hawk)

Sanderling

SANDERLING

These little shorebirds run in groups in front of incoming waves on sandy beaches, then run back toward the receding water to catch little shrimp and other food. They're small and have sticklike beaks and white bellies.

2 Eastern Forests

MAMMALS & MARINE LIFE

In addition to the creatures discussed here, you might want to check out the black bear (p. 477).

Gray Fox/Red Fox

GRAY FOX/RED FOX

The gray fox's back is gray, and the sides of its neck are red. The red fox is similar but larger and red on the back. The red fox is more common in the Smokies, but it's shy and likes to lurk in the underbrush. Be patient and make quiet squeaking sounds to help lure the curious animal out. Cades Cove and Cataloochee are good places to look.

WHITE-TAILED DEER

White-tailed deer are the common deer of the eastern United States. Once rare from hunting, they now are so numerous that they're a nuisance in some places. To keep the population down, hunters outside Great Smoky are allowed to take great numbers. You're almost sure to see white-tailed deer in Cades Cove grazing on the grass in the fields, especially at dusk.

WOODCHUCK (OR GROUNDHOG)

Woodchucks are about 2 feet tall when they stand and, especially when getting ready for winter, can be hilariously fat. They like open areas near roads or clearings. You can find them by locating the piles of dirt they leave near their burrows.

BIRDS

Besides the birds listed here, you will see some described in other sections, such as the raven (p. 472), and the great horned owl (p. 481).

BARRED OWL

If you hear an owl hooting while you're in your tent at night or while hiking during the day in the thick lowland forest, it's probably one of these big guys. One writer describes the cry as "who cooks for you, who cooks for you all." Barred owls are gray-brown with round heads and pronounced spectacles around the eyes. They come out at night, so to see one you have to explore the deep woods, following the hooting.

RUFFED GROUSE

This gray-brown bird, which looks something like a chicken, hides on the ground in underbrush, then bursts up into the air when people pass. That makes it a popular game bird. But the regrowth of big trees on logged land has made grouse rarer, because they like thick undergrowth and bushy clearings. The forests of big trees are the wild turkey's favorite habitat, so they are taking over where grouse lived.

WILD TURKEY

The male looks just like the cartoon turkey you see at Thanksgiving. The female lacks all the fancy feathers. Turkeys were hunted almost to extinction. Now, with protection and the return of their favorite habitat—mature forest without much undergrowth—they're becoming more common. You might run across them while you're hiking or at Cades Cove in the evening.

Ruffed Grouse   *Wild Turkey*

3 Canyon Country

MAMMALS & OTHER DESERT CRITTERS

Besides the plants and animals pictured here, you might also see North American elk (p. 475), mountain lion (p. 474), and bobcat (p. 477).

COYOTE

These wild dogs are midway in size between wolves and foxes. Their natural habitat is in the deserts and grasslands of the West, but when bounty hunting killed all the wolves in the Lower 48 states, coyotes spread out over most of the country and changed their behavior. They now act more like wolves, hunting in packs and going for bigger game, like deer. In the Southwest they're more solitary, eating reptiles, rodents, insects, and fruit.

JACK RABBIT

You can tell a jack rabbit by its long ears and strong back legs. This rabbit is tan and white and about 2 feet tall. Jack rabbits are active at night, and you often see them in your headlights when driving. If you're camping, keep an eye out for their eyes reflecting the light of your fire or lantern from the woods.

Coyote

Jack Rabbit

MULE DEER

You might see elk, which are larger, but mule deer are much more common in this region. They are 4 to 6 feet long, have big ears like a mule, and have brown coats in the summer. Generally, mule deer in groups are females with offspring, while bucks travel alone.

Rattlesnake

Mule Deer

RATTLESNAKE

Watch out for these guys, and if you find one, just back off. Most people who get bitten step on one accidentally or are messing with the snake; it attacks an animal as large as a person only in self-defense. (See "Dealing with Hazards," in chapter 2, for what to do if someone gets bitten.) Rattlesnakes are dormant in the winter and come out only at night in the hot summer months. There are many kinds, including one that lives only in the Grand Canyon, but I wouldn't recommend getting close enough to check which one you're seeing.

SIDE-BLOTCHED LIZARD

There are 3,000 kinds of lizards in the world, many of which look alike, and you often don't see them for long—be happy just to say it was a lizard. This one is 4 to 6 inches long and is brown with spots. Like snakes and other reptiles, lizards are coldblooded. They use the environment around them to set their body temperature, hiding in the shade or basking on warm rocks to get it right. (We're called warmblooded animals because our bodies burn fuel to stay the same temperature.)

Albert's Squirrel   *Kaibab Squirrel*

SQUIRRELS

You might see many kinds of squirrels, but the relatively rare Abert's squirrel is noticeable because it has tall tufts of hair that stick up behind its ears. The back is gray, with white running on the underside from the belly to the tip of the tail. It's found only in pine and juniper forests, especially on the South Rim of the Grand Canyon.

The rare Kaibab squirrel, on the North Rim, evolved separately after the canyon formed, and has an all-black body and a white tail.

BIRDS

In addition to the birds below, you might also spot a golden eagle (p. 476) or a hairy woodpecker (p. 476).

CALIFORNIA CONDORS

These birds with wingspans that can reach 9 feet across are making a comeback in canyon country thanks to efforts by federal agencies and nonprofit groups. When not soaring on air currents, they like to perch on canyon walls.

RAVEN

You can see the raven, a black bird like a larger version of a crow, and hear its throaty caw all over the West into Alaska. The raven is common in the stories of many Native American cultures as a wily trickster and powerful creator. Ravens are extremely intelligent birds, able to solve problems. They eat many kinds of food, but a favorite seems to be garbage.

Raven

WESTERN BLUEBIRD

This is a striking bird, with a bright blue back and a red breast. Males compete for nest holes, using a red breast like the robin's to show other males that they're willing to fight for their place. Look for them in open areas where there are trees for nesting.

4 The Rockies

MAMMALS

In addition to the creatures here, you might also want to check out the black bear (p. 477), bobcat (p. 477), white-tailed deer (p. 469), mule deer (p. 471), and rattlesnake (p. 471).

BIGHORN SHEEP

The strong bodies and huge curling horns of bighorns are unmistakable. In the fall the males fight for the right to mate by bashing their horns together. You can hear it a mile away. At Rocky Mountain, you can often see bighorn in the late spring and early summer on Highway 34 at Sheep Lakes in Horseshoe Park, where they come to eat minerals they don't get enough of in their winter diet. They come to the area so predictably that the Park Service posts crossing guards on the highway. Later in the year, you can see them in alpine areas, sometimes along Trail Ridge Road or on the Crater Trail.

Bighorn Sheep

Bison (Buffalo)

BISON (OR BUFFALO)

When settlers first came to the West, 60 million bison roamed in huge herds across the plains. By 1890, excessive hunting had left fewer than 1,000 alive. Now there are more than 200,000 in North America, mostly on farms. The wild herds at Yellowstone and

Grand Teton national parks are unique, and number a few thousand animals. Bison eat grass, often near roads where you can see them. In Yellowstone the Hayden Valley and Lamar Valley are good spots to see them; in Grand Teton, look in the Antelope Flat area and along the Snake River. Amazingly, we saw people walking right up to bison. These animals are the size of a small truck, can run fast, and have horns that can inflict great damage. People get hurt every year.

GRIZZLY BEAR

Grizzly bears once lived in much of the United States, but they need large areas of undisturbed land. Now some biologists fear they don't have enough room left even in their last Lower 48 habitat, in the northern Rockies. Only about 500 to 600 live in the greater Yellowstone ecosystem, which includes Yellowstone and Grand Teton national parks, and more live in Glacier National Park. About 30,000 live in Alaska. The best way to tell a grizzly from the smaller and more common black bear is by the hump on the grizzly's back and the black bear's straighter face profile. A grizzly's brown or blond color isn't a good guide, because blacks can be brown and grizzlies can be black. Grizzlies mostly eat roots, berries, and the like, but they are predators. Adult males weigh more than 500 pounds in this area. (For bear safety tips, see "Dealing with Hazards," in chapter 2.)

Grizzly Bear

Moose

MOOSE

Moose are the largest member of the deer family, with large males growing to 1,600 pounds. They like brushy areas, willows, and swamps or shallow ponds, where they stand deep in the water and eat weeds from the bottom. They're excellent swimmers. Look for moose along the Snake River and near Jackson Lake Lodge at Grand Teton, and in the Kawuneechee Valley at Rocky Mountain. Only the males have antlers.

MOUNTAIN LION

Your chances of seeing a mountain lion are extremely slim because they're rare and appear only when they want to—and if a mountain lion wants you to see it, then you could be in danger. They are big cats and feed on large mammals like deer. Attacks on humans are rare but have happened, and are another good reason to keep your children near when you are hiking, especially in brush.

Mountain Lion

North American Elk (Wapiti)

NORTH AMERICAN ELK (OR WAPITI)

These large, noble-looking deer show up all over the Rockies, spending the summer in alpine meadows and moving down for the winter. They show up at many places in all four parks; at Yellowstone you commonly see them along the road. In the winter, elk are fed at a refuge between Grand Teton National Park and the town of Jackson. At Glacier, a good place to find elk is in the roadside meadows near Saint Mary Lake. Only the males have antlers.

Pika

PIKA

The pika is a cute little animal that lives in rocky areas high in the mountains. Pikas grow to 8 inches long and are related to rabbits but don't have long ears. Their coat blends in with the rocks, so look around carefully to see them. There is a good children's picture book called *A Pika's Tail*, by Sally Plumb (Grand Teton Natural History Association, $10).

WOLVES

Wolves once roamed throughout the United States, but as settlers colonized parts of the country they drove out these predators. With wolves no longer part of the ecosystem, populations of their prey, such as elk and deer, ballooned unusually high and overgrazed the landscape. In 1995, in an effort to make Yellowstone's animal kingdom complete, federal agencies began a wolf recovery program. Today about 400 wolves lope through the greater Yellowstone ecosystem, preying predominantly on elk. The result is a smaller, but healthier, elk herd and a healthier landscape. The best place to spot Yellowstone's wolves is in the Lamar Valley in late spring and early summer. Some wolves can be found in Grand Teton National Park, although they're not as visible to park visitors. Glacier National Park also has a wolf population.

BIRDS

Besides the birds listed here, you may see some that are described in other sections, such as the raven (p. 472), western bluebird (p. 473), and Steller's jay (p. 478).

BALD & GOLDEN EAGLES

These majestic birds can have wingspans of over 7 feet; they glide in the air before swooping down and grabbing their prey. While golden eagles will grab a rabbit or other rodent in its ferocious talons, bald eagles might also pluck a fat trout from a river or lake. While the bald eagle is known for its white head and tail feathers, the golden eagle is all brown, with a lighter brown neck.

Golden Eagle

HAIRY WOODPECKER

The hairy woodpecker is roughly the size of a robin, with black and white feathers; the male has a red spot on his head. It lives in deciduous forests (where trees have leaves). Male woodpeckers have long, hard beaks that they hammer against tree trunks to make holes. Females have shorter beaks that are better for prying. Together, they dig insects out of the wood.

MOUNTAIN CHICKADEE

This little bird looks a lot like the common black-capped chickadee but has an extra white stripe on its head, and gray sides. It is easy to find high in the mountains, hunting insects and flitting around the alpine forests.

Mountain Chickadee

Trumpeter Swan

TRUMPETER SWAN

These huge, graceful white swans are among the largest birds in North America. They are somewhat easy to find on the lakes of Yellowstone and Grand Teton national parks, but are found nowhere else except Canada and Alaska. They nearly disappeared, but conservation brought them back. *The Trumpet of the Swan,* by E. B. White (HarperTrophy, $6.50), is a funny and beautifully written novel to read aloud. It tells the story of Louis the swan, who has no voice and so learns to play the trumpet.

5 The Sierra Nevada

MAMMALS & REPTILES

Besides the creatures listed here, see the jack rabbit (p. 471), pika (p. 475), bighorn sheep (p. 473), mule deer (p. 471), coyote (p. 470), and rattlesnake (p. 471).

BLACK BEAR

Growing to 5 or 6 feet tall, black bears are common in the Sierra. Major problems have resulted from humans living in black bear country. Careless campers and picnickers have allowed bears to get their food and garbage, and now many bears are so used to thinking of humans as sources of food that they walk right through busy campgrounds and rip open cars. Blackies normally eat berries, nuts, and plants, with an occasional squirrel thrown in. You might be able to tell a black bear from the larger brown or grizzly bear (no longer found in California) by size or color. The sure signs are that the grizzly has a raised hump over the shoulders and its nose sticks out from its face, while a black bear's back and neck slope fairly evenly, and its nose and face form a smooth profile.

Bobcat

Black Bear

BOBCAT

Bobcats are common in the foothills and lower Sierra, but you're very lucky if you see one. They hunt rabbits, squirrels, and other animals, often at night, hiding under logs in rocky areas to sleep. If you hear a bloodcurdling howl at night, it could be a bobcat. They're about as large as a middle-size dog, growing to 2½ feet long.

SIERRA NEVADA GOLDEN-MANTLED GROUND SQUIRREL

These brave little guys will come right into campsites to raid picnic baskets. They have small tails and black-and-white stripes on the sides of their bodies. They look like chipmunks but are larger (the body is about 6 in. long) and don't have stripes on their heads as chipmunks do.

BIRDS

In addition to the birds listed here, you might see some described in other sections, such as the raven (p. 472), western bluebird (p. 473), mountain chickadee (p. 476), golden eagle (p. 476), and hairy woodpecker (p. 476).

Steller's Jay

STELLER'S JAY

This striking blue-and-black bird has a large black crest—it's the only Western jay with a crest. Steller's jays live in Sierra pine forests and often visit campgrounds to pick up crumbs. They also live in the Rockies, the Pacific Northwest, and coastal Alaska. They bear the name of the naturalist Georg Steller, who helped discover Alaska in 1741.

WHITE-HEADED WOODPECKER

Common in the Yosemite Valley, these 9-inch-long birds are black except for white heads and wing patches; they're the only woodpeckers in the Sierra with white heads. They can blend in and be hard to spot until they take flight. They feed by peeling scales of bark off trees, not by hammering them like other woodpeckers.

6 Olympic & Sequoia National Parks

MAMMALS & MARINE LIFE

Besides those discussed below, the following can also show up in this region: barnacle (p. 465), bobcat (p. 477), coyote (p. 470), gray fox (p. 469), harbor seal (p. 465), hermit crab (p. 466), humpback whale (p. 466), jack rabbit (p. 471), northern moon snail (p. 467), mountain lion (p. 474), mule deer (p. 471), sea star or starfish (p. 467), and white-tailed deer (p. 469).

Gray Whale

GRAY WHALE

In the spring, these animals, which weigh up to 80,000 pounds, pass close to shore on their migration from winter calving grounds off western Mexico to summer feeding grounds off western Alaska. They return in late fall and winter. They don't have fins on their backs. To feed, they dive down and sift food out of the gunk from the bottom through the comb-shaped baleen in their mouths. Watching from shore is popular at the Olympic Peninsula (see "Whale- & Wildlife-Watching," in chapter 16, "Olympic National Park").

Killer Whale (Orca)

KILLER WHALE (OR ORCA)

These whales either travel in organized family groups called pods, feeding mostly on salmon and other fish, or are loners, prowling for prey that could include sea lions or even humpback or gray whales. On the water you'll usually see only the whales' shiny black backs and long dorsal fins. When the whale sounds (dives), the flukes of the tail appear. Like people swimming, orcas turn head down when they want to go deeper. Orcas grow up to 30 feet long.

LIMPET

Limpets are common in West Coast tide pools. Their shells are shaped like small, shallow cones. There are many varieties, some large enough to be used as human food or decorations for Native American costumes. Most limpets eat algae, but they also can consume tiny mussels and barnacles that have just attached to rocks.

SEA ANEMONE

These are among the most fun and bizarre animals to find in a tide pool. They look like huge flowers with thick stalks, but the flower petals really are sticky tentacles that grab and poison fish or other small animals that come too close. Any gentle contact will make an anemone quickly close up, leaving it looking like a rock. Sea anemones come in many varieties, in different sizes and colors.

SEA LION

Groups of sea lions have certain rocks called haul-outs, where they rest together, and rookeries, where they mate and give birth. Like whales, otters, and seals, they're mammals and have to hold their breath to dive deep for the fish they catch. They are larger than seals and feed on salmon and other fish that people also eat, so commercial fishing can reduce their food supply and lower the number that can live in an area.

Sea Anemone

Sea Lion

SEA OTTER

Shiny otters float on their backs in groups called rafts, tying kelp around their legs to stay in place. Otters use their tummies as tables for food or to carry their babies. Unlike other marine mammals, they don't have a layer of fat to keep them warm. Instead, otters rely on their fur, which is the finest and most thickly spaced fur of any animal, and on their bodies' ability to produce heat from the huge amounts of food they eat. Otters like clams, crabs, and sea urchins, which they pick off the bottom of the ocean during long dives when they hold their breath.

SEA URCHIN

These animals have spines that stick out like pins from a pincushion. The spines protect the urchin and allow it to move, like a centipede's legs. They fall off when the urchin dies, leaving a delicate, beautifully etched shell. Kelp is a favorite food, although they eat almost anything, and sea otters are an important predator. Many kinds of urchins are common and interesting to find in tide pools; some have eggs that are eaten as sushi.

Sea Otter

Sea Urchin

TULE ELK & ROOSEVELT ELK

Tule elk like the open, grassy lands on Point Reyes National Seashore north of San Francisco. Commercial hunts killed them off during the gold rush in the 1850s, but they were brought back in the 1970s and now are easy to find in a reserve on Tomales Point, at the north end of Point Reyes. Roosevelt elk, also rare, are the largest elk. They prefer the forests of Olympic National Park, where I've seen them in the Hoh and Quinault rainforests. Both kinds of elk make a big difference in their ecosystems. Tule elk helped keep Point Reyes's grasslands from turning into bushes and forest. Roosevelt elk, which like to eat hemlock sprouts but not Sitka spruce, may help keep hemlocks from taking over the rainforest.

BIRDS

Besides the birds listed here, you may see some described in other sections, such as the osprey (p. 468), herring gull (p. 468), sanderling (p. 469), great blue heron (p. 468), raven (p. 472), ruffed grouse (p. 470), hairy woodpecker (p. 476), and Steller's jay (p. 478).

COMMON LOON

These large, striking birds with sharply contrasting black-and-white coloring have an unforgettable, mournful cry that is symbolic of America's outdoors. In the summer, they nest on northern lakes. They spend the winter fishing in coastal waters all over the United States.

COMMON MURRE

The size and shape of a football, these birds don't look as if they'd be able to fly, but they do. Their little wings flap like crazy as they skim over the waves. Murres live in huge colonies on rocky islands, making them very vulnerable to oil spills and El Niño weather changes. Each female has only one egg a year. They depend on having a lot of birds together on the rocks for protection, so recovery from die-offs is slow.

GREAT HORNED OWL

This big owl, found all over North America south of the Arctic, is a fierce hunter at the top of the food chain. It preys on rabbits, ducks, and even other owls, including the endangered spotted owl of the old-growth forest in the Pacific Northwest. The owl's powerful flight, hypnotic eyes, and "hoo-hoo-hoo hooooo" call even give shivers to some people.

Great Horned Owl

Index

Fun destinations for all ages!

Let Frommer's take you across town or around the globe to some of the kid-friendliest places in the world. From the best hotels, restaurants, and attractions to exact prices, detailed maps, and more, Frommer's makes the going easy—and enjoyable—for the whole family.

Don't miss these other kid-friendly guides:
Frommer's Hawaii with Kids
Frommer's London with Kids
Frommer's National Parks with Kids
Frommer's San Francisco with Kids
Frommer's Washington, D.C. with Kids

The best trips start here. **Frommer's®**

A Branded Imprint of ⊕WILEY
Now you know.

Available wherever books are sold.

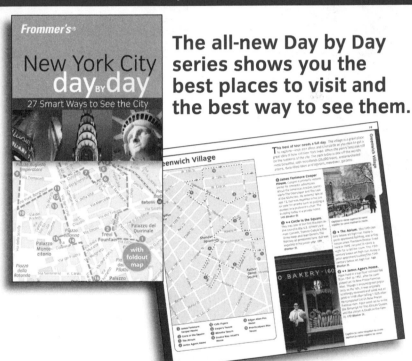

A Guide for Every Type of Traveler

Frommer's Complete Guides

For those who value complete coverage, candid advice, and lots of choices in all price ranges.

Pauline Frommer's Guides

For those who want to experience a culture, meet locals, and save money along the way.

MTV Guides

For hip, youthful travelers who want a fresh perspective on today's hottest cities and destinations.

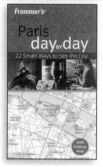

Day by Day Guides

For leisure or business travelers who want to organize their time to get the most out of a trip.

Frommer's With Kids Guides

For families traveling with children ages 2 to 14 seeking kid-friendly hotels, restaurants, and activities.

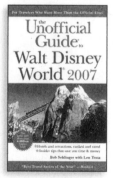

Unofficial Guides

For honeymooners, families, business travelers, and others who value no-nonsense, Consumer Reports–style advice.

For Dummies Travel Guides

For curious, independent travelers looking for a fun and easy way to plan a trip.

Visit Frommers.com

FROMMER'S® COMPLETE TRAVEL GUIDES

Alaska
Amalfi Coast
American Southwest
Amsterdam
Argentina
Arizona
Atlanta
Australia
Austria
Bahamas
Barcelona
Beijing
Belgium, Holland & Luxembourg
Belize
Bermuda
Boston
Brazil
British Columbia & the Canadian
  Rockies
Brussels & Bruges
Budapest & the Best of Hungary
Buenos Aires
Calgary
California
Canada
Cancún, Cozumel & the Yucatán
Cape Cod, Nantucket & Martha's
  Vineyard
Caribbean
Caribbean Ports of Call
Carolinas & Georgia
Chicago
Chile & Easter Island
China
Colorado
Costa Rica
Croatia
Cuba
Denmark
Denver, Boulder & Colorado Springs
Eastern Europe
Ecuador & the Galapagos Islands
Edinburgh & Glasgow
England
Europe
Europe by Rail

Florence, Tuscany & Umbria
Florida
France
Germany
Greece
Greek Islands
Guatemala
Hawaii
Hong Kong
Honolulu, Waikiki & Oahu
India
Ireland
Israel
Italy
Jamaica
Japan
Kauai
Las Vegas
London
Los Angeles
Los Cabos & Baja
Madrid
Maine Coast
Maryland & Delaware
Maui
Mexico
Montana & Wyoming
Montréal & Québec City
Morocco
Moscow & St. Petersburg
Munich & the Bavarian Alps
Nashville & Memphis
New England
Newfoundland & Labrador
New Mexico
New Orleans
New York City
New York State
New Zealand
Northern Italy
Norway
Nova Scotia, New Brunswick &
  Prince Edward Island
Oregon
Paris
Peru

Philadelphia & the Amish Country
Portugal
Prague & the Best of the Czech
  Republic
Provence & the Riviera
Puerto Rico
Rome
San Antonio & Austin
San Diego
San Francisco
Santa Fe, Taos & Albuquerque
Scandinavia
Scotland
Seattle
Seville, Granada & the Best of
  Andalusia
Shanghai
Sicily
Singapore & Malaysia
South Africa
South America
South Florida
South Korea
South Pacific
Southeast Asia
Spain
Sweden
Switzerland
Tahiti & French Polynesia
Texas
Thailand
Tokyo
Toronto
Turkey
USA
Utah
Vancouver & Victoria
Vermont, New Hampshire & Maine
Vienna & the Danube Valley
Vietnam
Virgin Islands
Virginia
Walt Disney World® & Orlando
Washington, D.C.
Washington State

FROMMER'S® DAY BY DAY GUIDES

Amsterdam
Barcelona
Beijing
Boston
Cancun & the Yucatan
Chicago
Florence & Tuscany

Hong Kong
Honolulu & Oahu
London
Maui
Montréal
Napa & Sonoma
New York City

Paris
Provence & the Riviera
Rome
San Francisco
Venice
Washington D.C.

PAULINE FROMMER'S GUIDES: SEE MORE. SPEND LESS.

Alaska
Hawaii
Italy

Las Vegas
London
New York City

Paris
Walt Disney World®
Washington D.C.

FROMMER'S® PORTABLE GUIDES

Acapulco, Ixtapa & Zihuatanejo
Amsterdam
Aruba, Bonaire & Curacao
Australia's Great Barrier Reef
Bahamas
Big Island of Hawaii
Boston
California Wine Country
Cancún
Cayman Islands
Charleston
Chicago
Dominican Republic

Florence
Las Vegas
Las Vegas for Non-Gamblers
London
Maui
Nantucket & Martha's Vineyard
New Orleans
New York City
Paris
Portland
Puerto Rico
Puerto Vallarta, Manzanillo &
   Guadalajara

Rio de Janeiro
San Diego
San Francisco
Savannah
St. Martin, Sint Maarten, Anguila &
   St. Bart's
Turks & Caicos
Vancouver
Venice
Virgin Islands
Washington, D.C.
Whistler

FROMMER'S® CRUISE GUIDES

Alaska Cruises & Ports of Call

Cruises & Ports of Call

European Cruises & Ports of Call

FROMMER'S® NATIONAL PARK GUIDES

Algonquin Provincial Park
Banff & Jasper
Grand Canyon

National Parks of the American West
Rocky Mountain
Yellowstone & Grand Teton

Yosemite and Sequoia & Kings
   Canyon
Zion & Bryce Canyon

FROMMER'S® WITH KIDS GUIDES

Chicago
Hawaii
Las Vegas
London

National Parks
New York City
San Francisco

Toronto
Walt Disney World® & Orlando
Washington, D.C.

FROMMER'S® PHRASEFINDER DICTIONARY GUIDES

Chinese
French

German
Italian

Japanese
Spanish

SUZY GERSHMAN'S BORN TO SHOP GUIDES

France
Hong Kong, Shanghai & Beijing
Italy

London
New York
Paris

San Francisco
Where to Buy the Best of Everything.

FROMMER'S® BEST-LOVED DRIVING TOURS

Britain
California
France
Germany

Ireland
Italy
New England
Northern Italy

Scotland
Spain
Tuscany & Umbria

THE UNOFFICIAL GUIDES®

Adventure Travel in Alaska
Beyond Disney
California with Kids
Central Italy
Chicago
Cruises
Disneyland®
England
Hawaii

Ireland
Las Vegas
London
Maui
Mexico's Best Beach Resorts
Mini Mickey
New Orleans
New York City
Paris

San Francisco
South Florida including Miami &
   the Keys
Walt Disney World®
Walt Disney World® for
   Grown-ups
Walt Disney World® with Kids
Washington, D.C.

SPECIAL-INTEREST TITLES

Athens Past & Present
Best Places to Raise Your Family
Cities Ranked & Rated
500 Places to Take Your Kids Before They Grow Up
Frommer's Best Day Trips from London
Frommer's Best RV & Tent Campgrounds in the U.S.A.

Frommer's Exploring America by RV
Frommer's NYC Free & Dirt Cheap
Frommer's Road Atlas Europe
Frommer's Road Atlas Ireland
Retirement Places Rated